MW01060314

BREAD WINNER

EMMA GRIFFIN

BREAD

WINNER

AN INTIMATE HISTORY OF
THE VICTORIAN ECONOMY

YALE UNIVERSITY PRESS
NEW HAVEN AND LONDON

For information about this and other Yale University Press publications, please contact:
U.S. Office: sales.press@yale.edu   yalebooks.com
Europe Office: sales@yaleup.co.uk   yalebooks.co.uk

Set in Adobe Garamond Pro by IDSUK (DataConnection) Ltd
Printed in Great Britain by TJ International Ltd, Padstow, Cornwall

Library of Congress Control Number: 2020931824

ISBN 978-0-300-23006-2

A catalogue record for this book is available from the British Library.

10 9 8 7 6 5 4 3 2 1

CONTENTS

ILLUSTRATIONS

NOTE ON THE TEXT AND ACKNOWLEDGEMENTS

This project has grown out of my earlier work on life during the Industrial Revolution as seen through the prism of working-class autobiography. My original plan was to take advantage of the wider source base available for the nineteenth century (the popular press, trade union records, material culture, workhouse records), but in the event I could not wean myself off life writing as a historical source. The generations born after 1830 not only continued to write autobiographies, they also did so in ways that illuminate the interior workings of family life in new and fascinating ways. As the century progressed, more female writers began to pen their life story and all writers offered up far more detail about intimate areas of family life that earlier autobiographers had taken some care to conceal. And in so doing, they revealed a fact of the historical world that is easy to miss: the private world of the family is not separate from the public sphere of politics and economics. In this book we will look at the little details our writers thought to mention – a father who vanished from the household overnight; a daughter who packed in her job to care for her younger siblings; a household that fell apart when mother was put in the asylum. These domestic details of obscure lives may seem small, but the domain they speak to is large. At heart here is nothing less than the distribution of power, wealth and well-being in Britain as it transitioned to a modern nation.

As will be seen, I make some attempt to quantify some of my statements and arguments about men and women's work, earnings and behaviours. But I have resisted appeals to provide graphs and tables to support these statements. This is not an attempt at subterfuge, but stems from a more fundamental belief that transforming stories into histograms risks concealing as much as it reveals. Life stories are messy, and it can be difficult to pin down standard historical categories within them. Even apparently simple factors such as the location of the writers or their family size prove tricky to categorise. Poor people move around, a lot, so which home do we count as their residence? Is family size the number of siblings born, or the number who did not die? I can do no better than to repeat Carolyn Steedman, whose editorial introduction to one working-class autobiography (that of Kathleen Woodward) observes that all 'is not what it seems . . . Details of time, place and politics are used by Kathleen Woodward to construct a psychological narrative rather than a historical one.' As we move away from apparently simple questions about geography and family size to more complex questions about the quality of a man's breadwinning or about how writers felt about their intimate relationships, the difficulties of fixing meaning become yet more acute. To borrow from Steedman once again, in life writing 'the *meaning* of events is of a different order from that of the very same events when written about elsewhere'.[1] Tables may look transparent and objective, but filling tables requires a flattening, a forcing of narrative into one box or another, an imposition of meaning that may be at odds with that intended by the writer. My method involves a careful reading and rereading of every autobiography, and it is the reading, not the final boxes into which we can sort the writers, that is significant. To make transparent the conclusions I have reached, however, I provide a full list of names to support any quantitative statements. For convenience, I have also provided an online appendix which lists all the autobiographers and provides an outline of the characteristics of their family. It can be found at www.yalebooks.co.uk/page/griffin_bread_winner_appendix

I am indebted to many individuals for creating the archive that forms the spine of this book. Historians, both professional and amateur, librarians and family members coaxed older family and neighbours to share their life stories and assisted them in writing, and sometimes publishing, their work. Librarians and archivists have kept the records safe and assisted me in my quest to track them down. My especial thanks go to Katie Flannagan at the Burnett Archive based at Brunel University. Research funding from the British Academy and funding and support from the University of East Anglia allowed me to visit numerous archives and, more importantly, provided me with the time to consider what I found there. My agent James Pullen and editor Heather McCallum played a vital role in helping me turn the idea for this book into an actual book.

Kind friends and colleagues have helped me to reach this point in numerous ways. They have read draft chapters, shared unpublished work, references and ideas, loaned books and sometimes just cheered me on from the sidelines. Their invites to speak at seminars and symposia have also helped me to clarify the limits of my arguments in hugely helpful ways. I would particularly like to thank Robert Colls, Jennie Davey, Lucy Delap, Lyndsey Jenkins, Ben Jones, Victoria Kelley, Sarah Knott, Claire Langhamer, Jon Lawrence, Rohan McWilliam, Peter Mandler, Chris Minns, Sue Morgan, Lydia Murdoch, Sarah Pearsall, Helen Rogers, Camilla Schofield, Alex Shepard, Julie-Marie Strange, Penny Summerfield, Becky Taylor, Nicola Verdon and Tony Wrigley.

Finally, as I observe of the female autobiographers who became involved in the suffragettes and other political causes, women often required the support of other adults in their lives if they were to escape domestic grind and enter the public sphere. More than a century on, the same has been true for me. My parents nurtured my interests from my earliest days and have never failed to support me since. My sisters, aunts, cousins and friends have continued to take an interest in my various projects, and I have enjoyed many conversations with them about the timeless themes of work, pay and the burdens of motherhood that underpin this work. I would like to thank my children, but given all that I shall say in the following pages about the burdens of domestic responsibility, that would just be silly. It is not silly though to thank David Milne. For his unfailing support and love in matters both intellectual and mundane, I owe more than I can ever put into words.

INTRODUCTION
'THE GREAT ENIGMA OF OUR TIMES'

In 1894, at the relatively late age of thirty, Mary Molloy got married. She had met her new husband, James O'Meara, in the local pub and he was by all accounts a most plausible bachelor. Thirty-seven years old, he had worked as a merchant sailor, in the army, as a coachman, and had recently arrived in Liverpool to work in the docks. Better still, he was reputed to come from a family of some means and was telling tales of the good fortune that would come his way should he decide to marry.[1]

But even without the prospect of a family inheritance, marriage to James O'Meara promised Mary a better life than she could ever achieve on her own. She had been at work for nearly twenty years but was still sharing a couple of rooms with her parents in the slum quarters of Liverpool. She had little hope of moving out into a home of her own on her pay of twelve shillings a week. As a docker, Jimmy could earn almost three times that amount – thirty shillings a week. In this marriage Mary saw an opportunity to 'wrench herself free from poverty'.[2] She had waited a long time for this day to come and embarked upon the union with high hopes.

And the time for a union such as James and Mary's could hardly have been more propitious. Victorian Britain has long been recognised as a place of unrivalled progress and prosperity. A series of extraordinary inventions – trains, railways, bicycles, trams, tarmac, sewing machines, gas lighting, lightbulbs, flushing toilets, typewriters, photography, telegraphs, telephones – were helping to transform the very fabric of life.[3] All the standard economic measures – Gross Domestic Product (GDP), Gross National Product (GNP), real wages – indicate steady rises throughout the nineteenth century.[4] This combination of economic growth and new technologies was to usher in levels of wealth and comfort of which earlier generations could only dream.

Yet as the century drew to a close, it became ever more apparent that not everyone was sharing in the nation's newfound riches. Large cities with their trams, railways and modern civic buildings might have signified the march of progress, but they also housed large slum populations living in appalling squalor. And the newly created sensationalist newspaper press of the late nineteenth century lost little time in sharing lurid tales about the poverty and vice in the urban slums with its readers.[5] Scandals such as the Jack the Ripper murders brought salacious stories of crime, drunkenness and prostitution in the East End to the sitting rooms of the well-to-do.[6] Evidently, the world's most prosperous nation was home to some very old problems.

Perhaps the greatest surprise, however, was that more sober attempts to quantify the extent of urban poverty painted the same grim picture. In the 1880s, the wealthy businessman Charles Booth set out to use his statistical skills to put some reliable figures to the prevalence of urban poverty.[7] He was surprised to discover that around one-third of the population of London were living without adequate means for a decent subsistence. Attempts to recruit for the Second Boer War at the end of the 1890s provided further evidence of the wretched living conditions in the slums, with large numbers of volunteer recruits failing the medical examination. This, then, was not just the scaremongering and make-believe of socialists and newspaper hacks. By the end of the century, the British public and their politicians were forced to face an unpalatable truth: a century of prosperity had failed to lift many families out of poverty.[8] It was as if, the American radical Henry George wrote, 'material progress does not merely fail to reduce poverty – it actually produces it'.[9] And this, he declared, was the 'great enigma of our times'.

From a twenty-first century perspective, the problem that Henry George identified does not, perhaps, seems so enigmatic. Certainly, Britain's national wealth grew throughout the nineteenth century, but as political economists since Karl Marx have pointed out, it is possible for newly created wealth to become concentrated in the hands of the few, leaving the masses as impoverished as ever. Few today would accept the breezy optimism associated with the mid-twentieth-century economist Simon Kuznets that 'growth is a rising tide that lifts all boats'. Since the publication of Thomas Piketty's *Capital in the Twenty-First Century*, it has become commonplace to argue that no less important than the *amount* of economic growth is the matter of how those gains are shared.[10]

In fact, we do not need to turn to the discipline of economics to find evidence that national wealth and working-class gains may follow different trends. Recent research on Victorian and Edwardian Britain reveals much the same thing. There is, for instance, a burgeoning literature on human heights, which indicates that heights made little improvement over the nineteenth century.[11] The evidence on body mass is equally bleak, with the most recent research suggesting that body mass among some segments of the population actually declined down to 1900.[12] Work on infant and child mortality and nutrition tells a similar story.[13] And research into family budgets testifies to the existence of that large subset of the population first described by Booth who were not simply failing to prosper, but scarcely managing to get by at all.[14] Non-wage evidence of this kind has been used as powerful ammunition against optimistic interpretations of the Industrial Revolution, but analogous evidence for the later period is never quite sufficient to prompt a wholescale rethink. Part of the reason for this, no doubt, is that the non-wage evidence runs counter to all that we know about real wages. Real wages are still used today as a key indicator of the extent to which wealth is evenly distributed (or not) across the social classes, and the nineteenth-century wage data is relatively unambiguous: steady rises across all sectors. There is, then, a fundamental tension between the wage data and other forms of evidence, and this leaves us with an uncertainty about the true nature and meaning of prosperity in Victorian Britain.[15]

Certainly, very little of the nation's rising GDP ever found its way into the hands of Mary O'Meara. Pressing poverty had forced Mary and her family from Dublin to Liverpool when she was a small child. In Liverpool, the family found itself in a room in a tenement building on St James Street in the heart of the city's slums. There the family continued to grow: five children had been born in Ireland and a further four were born in Liverpool. But the family's finances did not grow: there was 'no schooling or shoes or regular meals for any of them as children'.[16] Nor did marriage offer Mary the escape she had hoped. The O'Meara estate of course quickly proved to be a mirage. Worse still, James O'Meara turned out to be far more interested in drinking than he was in working at the docks. He had realised that he could earn ten shillings for a couple of days – enough for 'the rent and enough to get the barest necessities of living' – leaving him free for the rest of the week to pursue interests closer to his heart – drinking and carousing. And so Mary's two children (she had given birth to seven) were raised in just the same slums and abject poverty that she had ever known, living in one or two rooms in the worst courts of the city, often 'very hungry' and 'shoeless and in rags'.[17]

At the heart of Mary's inability to find a better life for herself was her marginalisation in the labour market. Mary could never hope to earn the thirty shillings a week that was in James's grasp: she had long ago reached her earning potential as an unskilled female worker – a paltry twelve shillings weekly – and it was not enough for her to move out of her parents' slum dwelling. There were, of course, no state-sponsored mechanisms for redistributing wealth or sustaining low-income families in Victorian Britain; wages were the sole mechanism by which wealth flowed into the working classes.

But the workforce – and therefore those able to earn wages – looked very different to today. At the start of Victoria's reign children as young as five or six could be put to paid employment, and although successive legislation restricted the employment of young children, in the 1890s children could still legally start work from the age of ten. Furthermore, though children joined the workforce in large numbers, their mothers generally did not. This was the logic of the so-called 'breadwinner wage' – a bargaining concept that was successfully deployed by several campaigners and trade unions throughout the century.[18] The breadwinner wage was one that was substantial enough for a man to keep his wife and young children out of the labour market altogether. This inevitably was an aspiration rather than a reality for many working-class families. Nonetheless, it was a powerful ideology, and one that effectively closed many avenues for women to earn a living wage for themselves.[19] At the age of thirty, Mary had been at work for well over half her life, yet she still could not earn a wage that enabled her to live apart from her family. She took the only option available to her: marriage to a male wage earner. And she learned the inadequacy of the breadwinner-family model in the cruellest way possible. Unable to earn herself, she and her two children were heavily dependent on James O'Meara's wage, and when that failed they were plunged into a desperate poverty from which there was no escape.

The highly gendered nature of the pre-1914 labour market has often been acknowledged, but its full implications have not. As highly marginalised members of the workforce, adult women did not take a direct share in the wealth created by industrialisation. Instead, their share reached them through the hands of their husbands and older children, for whom they, in return, performed the unpaid work of the house.[20] Real wages, so often held up as the gold standard measure of living standards, are useful for telling us what men were able to earn, but they allow us to do no more than scratch the surface of the experiences of everyone else. For women (and children), economic security was determined by a host of smaller, personal matters that cannot be captured by such a smooth measure as the real wage. Matters such as finding a suitable husband, persuading him to spend his wages on his family, and agreeing how best to allocate food at the dinner table – should eggs be a treat for the hard-working male breadwinner, for example, or put into a pudding the whole family could enjoy? Economics always has the veneer of neutrality, of objectivity. But its analyses stop at the threshold of individual homes. Opening the door and peering inside reveals a deeply human story, and it is only by unpacking this story that the true meaning of shifts in aggregate totals such as GDP and real wages may be properly understood.[21]

In order to make sense of the rapidly changing social world of Victorian and Edwardian Britain we need to put women and families into the centre of our analyses. Path-breaking work by the first generation of historians of women's history, mostly writing within the tradition of second-wave feminism, have demonstrated the possibilities. In diverse ways, Anna Clark, Jane Lewis, Elizabeth Roberts, Ellen Ross, Melanie Tebbutt, Pat Thane and others shed light on the previously neglected experiences of women in Victorian and Edwardian Britain and taught us that women's experiences cannot be subsumed within conventional narratives centred upon men.[22] This first generation of women's historians showed us the divided and conflicted nature of the home and the gulf between male and female experiences. They provided a template for the study of family life, which has now broadened to include men, masculinity and fatherhood. Whilst recent studies of masculinity are for the most part more sympathetic to the adversities faced by working-class men than the feminist histories that preceded them, they too underscore the difference between male and female lives, and remind us that men's experiences are distinct, not universal.[23]

Collectively, historians of women and masculinity have succeeded in establishing domestic life as a subject to be taken seriously. Where they have been less successful, though, has been in inserting the domestic into the mainstream. Although we know more than ever before about the lived experiences of the working classes of Victorian and Edwardian Britain, these ordinary lives remain notably absent from survey texts of the period, which remain focused upon their traditional concerns of politics, empire and prosperity. Our challenge, therefore, is to find ways of bringing together subjects that we have become accustomed to considering separately. After all, working men and women did not live apart from each other, each gender in its own separate silo. Nor did their lives bifurcate along that other division that tends to structure the way that historians look at the past: the 'social' and the 'economic'.[24] Working-class men, women and children were packed together into small, cramped houses, their lives deeply and messily entwined. And as families played such a key role in the earning and allocation of resources, the tendency of historians to situate the family as a subject of 'social' rather than 'economic' history must be recognised as an analytical device rather than historical reality.

Amongst the great mass of the population we designate the 'working class', wages were earned by men and shared at the level of the family. But the family is not an egalitarian institution.[25] Even in the small, simple nuclear family of nineteenth-century Britain, divisions of gender and age structured the family unit and laid down expectations for the division of work and resources amongst its members. Father, mother, son, daughter: these are not simple descriptors delineating biological relationships. They are social categories used to determine who gets what. And those raised in a Victorian family understood these prescriptions only too well. Growing up in Preston, Elizabeth Twist lived just thirty miles away from the family of Mary O'Meara, yet she inhabited a social world that could hardly have been more different. Her father had risen through the ranks of the elementary school system to become a schoolteacher himself, and thanks to that Elizabeth knew that 'the pattern of [her] childhood was a comfortable one compared with other babies in the neighbourhood'.[26] But whilst Elizabeth and her family enjoyed a life of affluent, working-class respectability, it was still structured by prevailing norms of family life. She recalled how as a child she used 'to observe my mother beat up an egg in a glass of milk and watch enviously as [her father] drank it. Nobody else was so indulged. Consequently, from my earliest years I, too, got the impression that there was something very special about my father.'[27] Economic historians may be correct in their calculations that the British economy increased threefold over the nineteenth century, whilst real wages roughly doubled.[28] But it is salutary to remember that for all this growth, the humble egg – price less than one penny – remained a luxury good, quite beyond the reach of women and children in even the most respectable working-class households.

This book seeks to rethink Victorian and Edwardian Britain by looking through the lens of the family. It starts from the observation that before the

First World War, the British state played a minimal role in ensuring that its citizens were provided for. The twentieth-century response to those unable to provide for themselves and their dependent children was the welfare state. But there was no welfare state during this period. Although socialist and redistributive ideas were well established and widely discussed by the late nineteenth century, they made little headway in British politics. Successive governments remained firmly wedded to an individualist ideology in which families looked after themselves.

By any measure, British society was changing dramatically. During the nineteenth century, it clocked up the fastest rate of population growth ever previously recorded, as well as very high levels of urbanisation.[29] Yet despite these demographic developments, the nation remained organised around a much older set of beliefs that placed the family at the centre of social and economic life. Individuals were responsible for meeting their own needs, as well as those of their dependants, for housing, food and healthcare. Free schooling came only in 1880, and beyond that the state made virtually no provision for any aspect of the welfare or well-being of its citizens. For the truly destitute, the Poor Law – an institution dating back to the sixteenth century – remained in operation. Under its provisions, workhouses offered food and lodging to those too ill, too old, too young or too encumbered with children to go out to work. But the Poor Law was essentially punitive in intent, or at least became so following reforms at the start of the Victorian period aimed at cutting costs. It served as a last resort rather than a safety net.[30] At the very tail end of our period, Lloyd George's Liberal government introduced a series of modest welfare reforms, with old pensions for those over seventy, a compulsory health insurance scheme for low earners, sick pay, and trade boards to set minimum wages in certain industries.[31] These arguably marked a sea change in the responsibility of the government for its citizens, but were simply not substantial enough to make more than a small dent on the crushing poverty experienced by some of the families in need. Certainly, taking the period as a whole, there was no legislative response to match the phenomenal social, economic, demographic and technological changes that had occurred. The family, not the state, emphatically remained the institution responsible for the distribution of wealth. And recognising this means thinking more carefully about the story of Victorian Britain that historians generally accept – one of growing prosperity that was shared by all. We need to investigate what really happens when wages rise, and this requires looking more closely at the family. As we shall see, families are not simply fascinating in their own right. They also contain the key to understanding how wealth travelled through society.

As such, I take up the themes of my last book, *Liberty's Dawn. Liberty's Dawn* drew on over three hundred working-class autobiographies to explore how life changed for working people during the world's first Industrial Revolution, concluding that industrialisation, so long perceived as deleterious to working-class living standards, in fact brought significant gains to men in the form of higher wages, more varied work and – no less importantly – a measure of personal autonomy. This book continues the story down to the eve of the First World War. It extends the narrative chronologically, but it also aims to widen the aperture and think more deeply about how – or indeed, whether – the gains that men made were translated into gains for their wives and children.

In common with *Liberty's Dawn*, this book draws upon an exhaustive study of working-class life stories. My starting point has been a comprehensive survey of the available records as listed in the bibliography of working-class autobiography compiled by John Burnett and his team in the 1980s. This indicates the existence of almost seven hundred autobiographies written by individuals born into impoverished, working-class families in Britain between 1830 and 1903, and therefore describing childhoods from the start of Queen Victoria's reign in 1836 down to the outbreak of the First World War.[32] Although any definition of the 'working class' is necessarily imprecise, I use it here to refer to families who lived off their own earnings rather than capital and whose earnings were insufficient to employ servants to assist with domestic labour. A small proportion of these have proved unsuitable, usually because the author did not provide any detail about their family of origin, and thus cannot be used to probe the relationship between family, wealth and well-being in any meaningful way. In addition, some of the listed authors were not working class or were not based in Britain during the period of interest here. A few others have become lost or proved unobtainable. This, along with other autobiographies that have come to light, provides a total of 662 autobiographies. A close and careful reading of these life histories forms the basis of the stories and arguments that follow.[33]

But whilst I have sought to obtain and consult all the surviving autobiographies from the period, the writers inevitably constitute no more than a very small subset of those who were alive and potentially able to write.

It goes without saying that most individuals did not write an autobiography, so there is an obvious problem that we need to consider at the outset: do these 662 writers roughly resemble the working-class society from which they were drawn? Do those who penned an autobiography capture the spread of working-class families, not just the most well-to-do and literate families with the best access to education, but also those from the most impoverished and marginal quarters? It is well known that autobiographers tended to have achieved something of note by the time they penned their autobiographies, so it is necessary to consider whether these future achievements correlated with a set of family characteristics that all had shared earlier in life, or in some other way distorted the origin stories they told.

The extent to which the working-class autobiographers were 'typical' of their class can only be sketched in outline and in a few specific ways. Household earnings were not systematically provided by the writers, so we cannot establish where our writers sit on the income spectrum. Even apparently straightforward characteristics, such as geographical origins, family size and family structure can be difficult to pin down precisely, as families moved, siblings died and households broke down and reformed in multiple ways. Two reference points, however, can be pinned down with some degree of certainty – geographical location and family structure. Neither departs significantly from the evidence corralled from more conventional demographic sources. Throughout the period, the proportion of writers raised in urban areas was slightly lower than that measured by census, but only very modestly so.[34] The prevalence of one-parent families amongst the autobiographers was also typical of the period. A range of different demographic estimates indicate that somewhere between 20 and 30 per cent of children had lost either their father or their mother before the age of sixteen and the experiences of the autobiographers fit comfortably within this range.[35]

Where the profile of the writers departs most dramatically from that of Victorian and Edwardian Britain is in the matter of gender. It comes as no great surprise to discover that there is a gender imbalance amongst the writers of the autobiographies. Of our 662 autobiographies, the majority – 443, or just over two-thirds – were written by men; the remaining one-third was written by women. There is also a chronological dimension to this imbalance. The asymmetry between male and female writers is most acute amongst those born in the early nineteenth century and starts to even out as we move towards

0.1 and 0.2 These autobiographical writers came from families enjoying vastly different levels of wealth and comfort. Harry Pollitt came from a small family and both his parents worked – his father was a blacksmith striker and his mother worked in a cotton mill. Maggie Newbery's father gave up farming and moved his family to Bradford when Maggie was a child. His low earnings (Mr Newbery was a carter for a woollen mill and his wife did not work outside the home) and large family (twelve children) provided the family with considerably less to live on.

the end of the century. Amongst those born after 1890, men and women wrote autobiographies in roughly equal numbers: almost half of all writers after that date – 45 per cent – were female. The flip side of this, of course, is that the autobiographers born in the pre-1890 period were overwhelmingly male.

Not only did the gender composition of the authors change over the nineteenth century, but so too did the art form itself. As a literary genre, the working-class autobiography had developed in the eighteenth century. At this time, working-class writers were almost exclusively male, and most were moved to write because they had achieved something notable in their life – one thinks of such examples as the historian and antiquarian William Hutton, the bookseller James Lackington or the well-known radical Francis Place. As public

10

achievements formed the primary motivation for writing, these men tended to be reluctant to digress from the 'important' aspects of their life – their religion, politics, union activity, business success, artistic achievement or whatever it was they had done to justify the writing of an autobiography.

These values are still visible in some of the earliest autobiographers of this study, but become far less evident as time moved on. There was inevitably a lag – typically of some fifty years or more – between the time of an author's birth and the time of his or her writing. Authors born before around 1850 usually wrote their autobiography at some point during the Victorian period, and as ideas about how to write a life story did not change significantly over the century their stories followed the traditional autobiographical format. The rapidly changing nature of British society in the twentieth century, and particularly after the Second World War, however, had far-reaching consequences for the ways in which later autobiographers wrote their stories. For those born in the 1860s and later, ideas about who could write an autobiography, and what they should write about, had all been all radically renegotiated by the time they came to write, and this created a substantial break in the nature of the records they produced.

In fact, even in the heyday of the 'great man' autobiography, there had always been some whose life story had not been inspired by achievement. John Hemmingway, for example, had been born in the 1790s and had spent his life cycling through various unskilled, working-class occupations: he worked variously as a factory worker, weaver, soldier, cart driver and shopkeeper. He wrote his memoirs, 'The Character or Worldly experience of the writer', in the 1860s, indicating on his opening page that he was not 'a learned man' and was not writing for 'profitt' or 'for the public at large'. His goal, he explained, was far more modest: 'to make known to one or more of my children a few incidents with which they at present are unacquainted'.[36] Throughout the Victorian period, a small core of male writers carried on this tradition, writing their life story primarily for their own family. They did not claim their life was of especial interest or importance, but did believe that times were changing and that it was valuable to keep a record of those earlier times. So in a similar vein to John Hemmingway, William Webb (born in the 1830s and writing in the 1880s) recognised that his biography would not be 'of interest to the world generally'. Nevertheless, he thought that his story 'may be of value to my own family', to 'my children, and after them their children also, will feel an interest in knowing from whence they sprung'.[37] It was a perspective that became increasingly common throughout the period under review.

In addition, however, more fundamental shifts in ideas about the value of life writing from the late 1960s helped to create new authors and audiences for working-class autobiography. The expansion of the universities and concurrent development of social history, women's history and oral history in that decade all helped to change assumptions about whose history was important, and whose voices deserved to be heard. Academic historians and local and community history groups collaborated to collect the memories of elderly residents, which at that point comfortably went back to the late Victorian and Edwardian periods.[38] Some projects sought to encourage elderly neighbours to write down their memories; others made cassette recordings or provided amanuenses to capture the recollections of those who were unable or unwilling to put pen to paper.[39] In Islington in the 1980s, for example, a project to collect local people's memories grew out of the library's 'Under-Fives Fortnights'. For local projects such as these it was precisely the point that the contributors were ordinary people rather than extraordinary individuals who had achieved something of great note. As the pamphlet created by the Islington project explained, the contributors were 'not known outside their own circles'. But as it quickly added, the contributors' lack of fame did not render their stories unimportant: 'there has been as much interest and drama in many of their lives as in those of more famous people.'[40]

Rising literacy and new ideas about whose history was worth telling cracked open a new form of working-class life writing that departed from the traditional model of male achievement. It established a genre of life writing by ordinary people, by men and women who had not only been born into the working class, but who still belonged to that class when they recorded their life story. Men like Charles Hansford, who spent his life as a bricklayer in Hampshire. His father was a policeman-turned-publican, but when he developed an appetite for consuming the drinks he was supposed to be selling, Charles's mother left him to start a new life in Southampton with a bricklayer named Tom. Tom and Mrs Hansford lived as husband and wife until Mr Hansford's ill health conveniently finished him off and his wife was able to remarry; and it was Tom, of course, who launched Charles's career in the bricklaying trade. As Charles observed in old age, bricklayers, 'unlike actors, politicians or eminent military men . . . have not made it their practice to leave memoirs'. He wrote down his life story precisely in order to help 'fill the gap'.[41] Herbert Harris was also keen to emphasise that he did not fit the rags-to-riches model of achievement. Following the sudden and catastrophic breakdown of his family when his mother was exposed for adultery, Herbert spent a childhood in an orphanage and an adult life that alternated between various unskilled and semi-skilled jobs and lengthy stints in different 'mental hospitals' for incapacitating psychiatric illness. He warned his reader that 'there would be no happy ending' to his story and 'things did not work out right in the end, as so many stories of adversity do'.[42] He eventually married a woman whom he met through an advert in a shop window – she had written that she hoped 'to meet a gent with a view to friendship'. When his new friend, then spouse, turned out to be pregnant, Herbert raised the child that he knew was not his own. Hansford and Harris did not *do* anything that would qualify them for entry to the history books, and they both knew it. But they both wrote an autobiography – or, in Herbert's case, fragments of one – and their writing allows us to penetrate British history in new and illuminating ways.

Some life stories needed to be teased out, and local history groups and professional historians played an active role in encouraging individuals who had always presumed that their stories had no value to share their experiences. Authors could be remarkably hesitant to do so. For example, Clayton Edward Joel was persuaded to write down his life history in the 1980s by the oral historian Paul Thompson, yet he displayed a great diffidence about the task. Joel feared his reminiscences might be 'of no interest or relevance', in which case he advised Dr Thompson to 'just scrap it'.[43] If the second version did not meet 'expectations', Dr Thompson could 'just throw it in the wastepaper basket'.[44] Female writers were particularly given to such doubts. Of her life history, Hilda Fowler thought, 'Perhaps it will make interesting reading for my family,' but she did not think it would go much further: 'I doubt if it will prove good enough to go into print.'[45]

Even with encouragement, writing a life history could be a difficult task, particularly if it contained painful memories. On receipt of Clayton Joel's manuscript autobiography, Paul Thompson encouraged him to provide a little more detail about his family, about how he 'felt about them at different stages in your childhood and youth'. Joel had by this point climbed from his humble origins in Southwark to become a university lecturer in anthropology, and Thompson suggested he might assess his family history from that perspective.

But whilst Joel was clearly eager to please the esteemed historian, he struggled with the instruction: 'the difficulty' was that his memories were 'too vague and fragmentary'; in fact he had 'no memory of my childhood', just 'long blanks' and occasional episodes. For the same reason, he felt unable to write about the 'break-up (or breakdown) of the family': his 'anthropological professionalism' could not help him out; he just could not 'get [my] bearings' on the subject.[46] And yet some details did slip out. Joel did not want to write about how it felt when his mother 'parked' himself and his elder sister on her mother, but within a full page of ramblings about his inability to write about his feelings towards his mother, he did comment that she had taken a 'descent into bare literacy' over her adult life, and also alluded to her (unspecified) 'personal inadequacies'.[47]

These new, twentieth-century attitudes about whose history mattered helped to shape the content of the records, and they also played a powerful role in correcting the gender imbalance that had characterised the earlier autobiographies. Oral history and community history projects in the second half of the twentieth century were just as interested, indeed sometimes particularly interested, in learning about the lives of women. The endeavour was undoubtedly assisted by the rise of second-wave feminism and the creation of a new academic discipline – women's studies – in the universities. The importance of gathering women's memories as well as men's was underscored in an observation of one of the great pioneers of social history, Margaret Spufford, when she became involved in a local oral history project that three brothers had established in the 1970s. She noticed that 'there was a skew in the records that were being collected'. The men's endeavours had focused on their fathers' work and hobbies, rather than the cooking, cleaning and care provided by their mother. As Spufford observed: 'They didn't ask questions about this. It just WAS, like the sun coming up every day, one doesn't remark on it.'[48] By this decade, feminists were making it part of their political agenda to record women's history, and it is thanks to their efforts that so many female-authored life stories survive for the period from the 1890s onwards.

In the past two decades, historians have started to make use of female autobiography and they have revealed the different ways in which women have approached the autobiographical form.[49] But there is still a long way to go. Whilst researching this book, I discovered more than two hundred female autobiographies, and none but a handful has ever been studied at all. It must be acknowledged that most of the female autobiographies do not fit the template with which we are familiar. Many female writers were timid and unconfident writers, and their stories were very short. The Burnett Archive of Working-Class Autobiography, collected by John Burnett, David Vincent and David Mayall during the 1970s and 1980s, contains 116 unpublished items. The gender split between the authors was roughly equal, but the length of their works was not. The average length of the female-authored autobiographies was 26,000 words, and more than half contained fewer than 7,000 words. None contained more than 60,000 words. The average length of the autobiographies written by men was more than three times that written by women – 81,000 words. Seventeen of the male autobiographies wrote life stories that exceeded the length of the longest autobiography written by a woman. Although women born in the late Victorian period began writing accounts of their lives in the twentieth century, much of their work was short and sketchy and it has simply been overlooked by historians.

Not only did women write fewer and shorter autobiographies, they also produced their work in more ephemeral formats, which has made the survival of their writing less secure and further contributed to its neglect. Most of the autobiographies written by women were never published, and work in unpublished form is far less likely to survive than published work. Well over half of the autobiographies written by men were published by national presses during the author's lifetime, and so they are relatively easy to obtain from libraries and second-hand booksellers. By contrast, fewer than 20 per cent of the women's autobiographies were published by commercial presses. Even where female autobiographies were published, they were often printed by a small, local history society, often as a stapled pamphlet rather than a bound book, and although such records are more likely to survive than handwritten documents, they are still difficult to locate. 'Amateur' histories of this nature do not generally end up in academic libraries or bibliographies, and although many have been deposited at the British Library, they have never been catalogued or recorded as female autobiography, and can therefore be virtually impossible to find.

Yet when female voices are included, a different kind of history starts to emerge. Tabitha John's 'Story' appears never to have been cited by any historian.[50] It was dismissed by Burnett and his team in their bibliography of working-class autobiography as being 'rather desultory', 'anecdotal' and 'concerned with personal affairs'.[51] I disagree. Her account contains a very rare first-person account of child loss, unwanted conjugal sex and pregnancies, and marital discord. This is not 'desultory'; it is fascinating and important in equal measure. These are the things that mattered for that half of the population who were never going to lead a strike, represent their class in Parliament or go to university. The autobiography of the best-selling author Catherine Cookson has escaped such obscurity, but even here scholars struggle to understand why Cookson did not write about the important things of her time.[52] She was 'not really a regional writer', laments one; and her books contain 'little sense of history' adds another.[53] Why did women repeatedly and so spectacularly fail to write about the things that mattered? The answer, of course, is that they did not. They wrote about the things that mattered to them, but these things were very different to those that look important through the male gaze. James Brady perceptively observed that his mother's horizons were confined to the immediate neighbourhood in which they all lived and from which she rarely escaped: 'The cobble-stoned cul-de-sac, with its squalid row of shared privies in the middle, was her world from Monday to Sunday.'[54] Too often women's lives were hemmed in both physically and intellectually. We need to explore why women were so restricted and how this affected their mental horizons, not to label their writing as 'narrow' and condemn it accordingly.

As the authorship of working-class autobiographers changed, so inexorably did the nature of their writing. New writers brought with them new ideas about what they considered appropriate to write about and what they considered taboo. The most striking manifestation of these developments was the way in which family moved to the foreground. The traditional autobiography had always opened with a brief account of family and childhood, but before the twentieth century writers tended to provide only the barest outline of their family history. Authors typically wrote little more than a page or so about their childhood and the information they provided often did not extend beyond the genealogical. The author's siblings went unnamed, and even parents were discussed in clipped, formulaic ways. Writers usually provided their mother's maiden name, some information about her birth family, and perhaps some detail regarding where she had lived and what she had been doing before her marriage. Her personality, if addressed at all, was covered by a few standard epithets such as she was 'industrious, tidy, and very careful',[55] or 'of a pious inclination'.[56] Autobiographers usually wrote more about their fathers, but most of the discussion turned upon their occupation (and perhaps their religious disposition) rather than anything of a personal nature. Once again, a broadly similar set of terms was used to described fathers in a variety of different contexts: 'a humble man of God',[57] 'a most industrious and hard-working man'[58] and so forth. These early autobiographers paid very little attention to the functioning of their family unit or how it might have differed from that of their neighbours. Indeed, a few writers were even unsure about such simple matters as the size of their family. Thomas Sanderson (born in 1808) was the eldest of a family which contained (he thought) 'eight or nine children'.[59] Sukey Harley (born around 1810) knew her mother had had 'sixteen of us altogether', but she was not sure how many of these had died in infancy – 'two or three', she decided.[60] The lack of detail that early autobiographers provided about their upbringing makes it very difficult to probe the inner workings of the working-class family or to explore the interplay of emotions and resources within the family unit.

Twentieth-century writers, describing childhoods from the last quarter of the nineteenth century onwards, were generally far more forthcoming about all aspects of their early home life and so the records start to illuminate the interior of family life in new ways. In stark contrast to the Victorian writers, twentieth-century authors were likely to provide intimate and personal details about childhood and family, about unfulfilled hopes as well as actual achievements. The structure of an autobiography remained beguilingly simple – a run through the author's childhood, school, work, marriage, adulthood; but their pages are increasingly filled with detail of the kind historians very rarely handle. The writers shared good memories, but also turned over events that continued to rankle – 'kind of incident . . . best forgotten in a biography'.[61] Albert Jasper described how his father, a confirmed drunkard, once failed to make it back from the pub in time to use the privy, and 'shit himself' in the scullery.[62] Kathleen Dayus recalled the only time she saw her mother undressed – she caught a glimpse of her 'flabby flesh' flopping out of her nightdress.[63] The loneliness of being left locked in an empty house at night;[64] the dawning realisation that you are much poorer than your schoolfriends;[65] the terror of seeing one's own, unexplained, menstrual blood for the first time;[66] the childish confusion of loving one's mother yet seeking to escape both her and her strange, depressive moods[67] – these and countless other incidents are described by the autobiographers as they sought to retrace their developing understanding of the world, and of their own place within it. They provide a raft of intimate details that historians can usually only dream of.

Yet if these later autobiographical sources are rich and illuminating, they are not simple windows onto the way life was. All autobiographers needed to confront the problems of memory, as mature writers reflected upon events that had occurred many decades earlier. Occasionally writers feared that the long passage of time might render some memories unreliable. James Crawford confessed to his reader that his greatest problem 'in writing this is the fact that I have never kept a diary and it is therefore a possibility that I might err occasionally in exactitude on dates, or whether one thing was mentioned before or after another'.[68] But perhaps more problematic than chronological accuracy for the historian is the matter of interpretation. Autobiographical accounts involve the re-evaluation of earlier lived events at many years' remove, the rendering of complex lived experiences into simple, intelligible narratives, acceptable both to surviving family members and to the book-buying public, or to other audiences.[69] They can be slippery sources and difficult to work with. Inevitably, finished works contain silences, absences and contradictions, as the author picked out some themes to discuss yet left other things unsaid. Edward Balne described himself as an orphan who had been given up at birth and explained how when he obtained his birth certificate later in life he discovered that the parents who had abandoned him had not named him before doing so. The forename column on his certificate was left empty and he was registered simply as 'male Balne'. (He did not mention, and indeed does not appear to have known, that he was not an orphan. He was the third of his parents' five children and the only one who they had placed in an institution. Why they gave up the middle of their five children is anyone's guess.) Balne discussed his fear that his incomplete birth certificate might disqualify him from claiming his old age pension, but he never reflected upon how it had felt to learn he had been given up as a tiny infant by parents who had not even found him a name.

Yet in many respects, the way in which he wrote about his abandonment was typical of this generation of writers. Balne wrote his autobiography in 1972 – so considerably earlier than the late-twentieth-century phenomenon of the 'misery-memoir', spawned by Frank McCourt's best-selling *Angela's Ashes*, published in the mid-1990s. Balne did not seek to conceal unflattering details of family life, but he did not dwell upon them either. In common with many writers from his generation, he included unconventional elements of his life, yet sought to contain complex, unfathomable personal experiences in his writing, rather than to unravel them.[70]

Our writers had a range of different motivations for putting pen to paper – to tell of success in the arts or in business; to describe a life devoted to service to politics or the church; or simply to share the details of an 'ordinary' life with family members or a community history project. But they were emphatically not salacious or sensationalist. No matter what the author's motivation, recollections of early family life usually formed just one element of a narrative constructed for a different purpose. Most writers told the story of their family and childhood in a few opening pages, or perhaps an opening chapter or two. Some despatched their early years in a matter of lines, and (as ever) some wrote nothing at all. With all these records created before, sometimes long before, the rise of the misery lit, family origins for most writers were an interesting, yet ultimately incidental, detail and there was an unmistakable desire to downplay, rather than to exaggerate, the sordid.

For example, Mary Luty, in her published autobiography, avoided the fact of her parents' marital breakdown altogether. Her early memories, as she told them, were of living with her mother on her grandparents' farm. Her father's absence from the scene was never stated, nor explained; it would be natural to assume he had died. But her unpublished life story indicated that her father had not died: her parents' marriage (she wrote there) 'broke up' when she was eighteen months old and her brother a mere infant of three weeks. Mary did not indicate what lay behind the separation, but the register for Wakefield Prison records her father serving two brief sentences for being drunk and disorderly over the next few years, which hints at a possible cause.[71] Mary was very young when her parents separated, so she may not have known about her father's drinking. But she did know about the separation and had opted to silently edit it out of her book.[72] Published autobiographies were clearly not perceived as the right place to air one's dirty laundry.

The writer Flora Thompson, in her lengthy, three-volume trilogy of semi-autobiographical writings about her life in rural Oxfordshire, similarly skirted around the darker aspects of her childhood. Thompson wrote her autobiography in the third person and changed all her family's names, yet despite these precautions she still hesitated to describe 'Laura's' father, his drinking, and the impact that had had on her family, relegating it to a brief note in the second volume of her trilogy.[73] And although she had more to *write*, she clearly struggled to *publish* those thoughts. A draft version of a chapter of the first time she lived away from the family home spelled out how far matters at home had deteriorated since her departure, as her father's 'weakness for drink had grown upon him'. The paragraph was cut before publication. It was only in private correspondence discovered by her biographer, Margaret Lane, that Flora revealed that her father was not only drinking heavily, but he was reserving a large chunk of his wages for himself, sometimes failing to bring home any wages at all, other times handing over the wage and then 'extort[ing] the greater part back in the way of pocket money'.[74]

Together Mary Luty and Flora Thompson suggest that writers were more willing to discuss events that they considered to lie outside the bounds of normal family life in work that would remain unpublished, and so it is encouraging that so many unpublished autobiographies have survived. Unpublished records constitute around a third of all the sources consulted here, the majority concentrated towards the tail end of our period. Yet it is worth pointing out that even those who had no intention to publish their life story sometimes kept their secrets close. Rose May Downer, for example, wrote a thirty-page life story in the 1970s, most of it focusing upon her work as a dressmaker. She did mention her marriage and the birth of her only son, but she was vague on all the dates and details. From the official record, however, it is apparent that she was heavily pregnant at the time of her wedding. Her son, Eric (unnamed in her account) was born within a month or so of the wedding.[75] Thomas James was a lifelong supporter of the Communist Party, so he did not shy away from mentioning a birth in the workhouse – he presented it as an example of the state's inhumanity towards the poor. He described how his parents had brought him back into their home a few years later when their circumstances had improved. But there were certain details about his birth and parentage that he left out of his narrative. His mother was sixteen and unmarried at the time of his birth. She did not marry William James until about six months after Thomas's birth.[76]

The chance survival of two versions of Arthur Harding's autobiography provides further evidence that the desire to airbrush unsavoury elements of family life from the record could extend to unpublished life stories. Arthur Harding wrote his autobiography – 'My Apprenticeship to Crime' – in the late 1960s. In 1970, he sent a copy to his MP, Stan Newens, who two years later passed it on to the historian Raphael Samuel. It was eventually deposited at the Bishopsgate Institute in 1998, where it still remains.[77] Samuel was so fascinated by Harding's extraordinary account of life in the East End of London at the turn of the century that he made contact with Harding and spent several years interviewing him, publishing his interviews in 1981 as *East End Underworld: Chapters in the Life of Arthur Harding*. As a result, we have two versions of Arthur Harding's life: 'My Apprenticeship', the written story which Harding conceived and created himself; and *East End Underworld*, the oral account, which emerged thorough his dialogue with Samuel.

As was often the case, Harding could not talk about his childhood without referencing certain domestic difficulties, and unfortunately for the young Arthur there was quite a lot to say under this heading: he spent three years in a Dr Barnado's orphanage, owing to his parents' drinking and inability to care for him. But whilst the life story recounted in both versions is recognisably the same, there are important differences in style and emphasis between the two. Harding's unpublished autobiography did not conceal that his mother had been an alcoholic, but it depicted her as victim rather than villain – she was a 'poor crippled mother'. Her drinking was a forgivable consequence of the difficult life she had: she 'had to drink' in order to 'drown the pain' from a road accident earlier in life.[78] The same pattern is evident in Harding's account of his father. In the autobiography, Harding's father was a pitiful victim suffering from bad eyesight, and it was only 'through failing sight [that he] could not keep us'.[79] When he failed to provide for his family it was either because he was 'unemployed'[80] or because of his 'failing sight'.[81] In Harding's original life story the poverty and problems of his childhood are not omitted. These aspects were clearly sketched out, but the reasons given for them were a number of external circumstances beyond his parents' control, rather than any personal failings to be placed at their door.

In discussion with Samuel, however, Harding took a very different stance towards both his parents. A more rounded, and less flattering, picture of his mother quickly emerges. Despite her disability, Mrs Harding, he told Samuel, was no victim. He described her as resourceful and shrewd – pinching, foraging and telling half-true 'hard-luck' stories to the ladies at the Mission so as to inveigle money (which she would spend on drink) from them. As for his father, the gloves were now off. Harding told Samuel that like most men of his class he was 'ignorant and brutal' towards his wife. He 'used to knock my mother about' and was 'a bully'. At times he neither provided for, nor lived with, his family, and this was not because of the unemployment or bad eyesight mentioned in the original autobiography, but because he was a selfish man who 'only lived for himself'. His failure to provide for his family began long

0.3 Arthur Harding was born in 1886 to a troubled family living in the East End of London. By the age of nine, his home life had deteriorated to the point that he had 'drifted away from home' and was living on the streets. He was admitted to a Dr Barnardo's Home 'as in need of care and protection' and this photo of him was taken at the time of his admission in 1896.

before his sight began to fail, and was rooted in his unwillingness to work and heavy drinking. He was 'a loafer', 'too lazy to earn a living', 'just an encumbrance really'.[82] In fact, on reflection Harding declared that 'he wasn't really an invalid' at all. Clearly, although Harding was willing to voice his criticisms of his father to Raphael Samuel in the 1970s, he had not viewed his autobiography as a place to air such thoughts a decade earlier. At that time, he had glossed his parents' failings and left the truly unredeemable details out.

This desire to downplay negative experiences is evident even amongst those with a more exceptional story of neglect or abuse to tell. There are miserable childhoods in the autobiographical literature to rival the most dismal misery lit, yet they were retold and packaged in very different ways. Jack Martin, for instance, had a tale of horrific violence and abuse that he and his family had suffered at the hands of his drunken father, but that was not where his story began, and it in no way formed the core of his story, either. Before writing about his childhood, he filled the first thirty pages of his book with the reminiscences of a local doctor. His section on childhood – 'My fight for existence in a family of 19 children' – was just one of nineteen chapters. The other eighteen made virtually no reference to his desperate childhood or its legacy for the rest of his life.[83]

It is important to emphasise this point. As we will see in the pages of this book, domestic difficulties shaped the lives of many of these working-class writers, so it is necessary to recognise at the outset that this body of sources was not written with the intention to shock. Autobiographers did not want to dwell upon the difficulties of their home life or to analyse their meaning in detail. They wrote about their families, warts and all, because they had to. A child's home life was so significant for his or her welfare that most writers simply could not write their story without some reference to their family. Family was the means of understanding and explaining childhood experience, and it was this, not the pursuit of entertainment or sensation, that motivated their inclusion.

Individual stories of family life can be humorous or heartbreaking, but collectively we can also use them to deepen our understanding of the world we live in. Nestling deep in these stories is a more fundamental story about the relationship between wealth and welfare that needs to be told. Through autobiographies we see the family as the motor by which wages and well-being were moved through society, but we are also able to grasp what a deeply inegalitarian and inefficient motor the family was, riven with divisions of gender and age which determined who got what. We will use individual stories to enter the hitherto closed box of the working-class family, to explore the territory between families and material living standards. We will bring together spheres that are usually kept separate: the 'male' world of the economy, work and wages; and the 'female' world of family, sex and marriage. Not only does uniting these male and female spheres provide us with a much truer understanding of life in Victorian Britain, it also reveals the deeply human character of economic life.

PART ONE

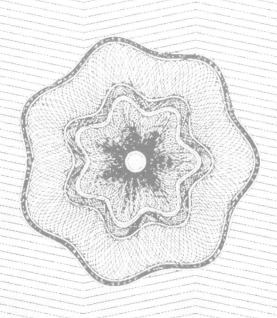

WORK

⤙ 1 ⤚

'I WORKED ALRIGHT, BUT I NEVER GOT PAID FOR MY LABOUR'
WOMEN AND WORK[1]

In the 1970s, in response to a call from a social historian based at Brunel University, Bronwen Morris sent an untitled, handwritten text describing her childhood and married life in the Welsh valleys. She had been born in Aberdare in 1896 and started work at the age of twelve and a half. Bronwen was eighty when she wrote her autobiography, yet she drew a clear continuity between herself as a twelve-year-old child-worker and the life she still lived. Like many women from the lower classes, Bronwen's entire life had been devoted to housework. She had started working as a house servant in the 1900s and in the 1970s continued to fill her days with much the same tasks: that is what '[I] still do – washing, ironing, cleaning'. The only thing that had changed was the matter of pay: 'In those days I performed these tasks in other people's homes . . . for the princely sum of one shilling and sixpence a day.'[2] Since marriage she had carried on with the same round of washing, ironing and cleaning, but in her own home and, of course, without payment. Bronwen's life did not have sharp edges between things that we tend to assume as distinct: childhood and adulthood, paid work and unpaid work, work and home. For Bronwen, each of these categories blurred into the next. It was the defining characteristic of women's lives.[3]

For many of the female writers, the normal divisions between childhood, adolescence and adulthood that structure the traditional (male) autobiography are difficult to delineate. Looking back on their schooldays, for examples, female writers did not necessarily perceive them to have been free from 'work'. Schooling was made compulsory in 1880, and as the majority of the female autobiographers were born after that date, recollections of the writer's schooldays were a common feature of their narratives. Yet whilst education was a distinctive and relatively brief moment in a working-class childhood, many of the female writers revealed that their life had already become filled with a raft of domestic duties long before leaving school. Lily Purvis, for instance, considered that she had become a 'little maid of all work' by around the age of seven. At ten she 'could bake, wash, iron, sew' and even repair a pair of stockings.[4] The assumption of domestic duties was particularly common for the older daughters in a family, who were put to looking after younger brothers and sisters some years prior to the end of their own schooldays. Some of the writers dated the end of their childhood to the birth of a younger sibling – an event that could happen while they were still just children themselves. Doris Hunt mused that at the age of six she 'was the eldest of four sisters, and looking back, that seemed to be the end of my care-free childhood'.[5] When Amy Langley's mother gave birth to her final child, she 'became, from her birth, [Amy's] responsibility'. Amy was just eight years old at the time.[6]

Similarly, it was sometimes the birth of a younger child that triggered the end of a girl's education. Isabella Cooke's schooldays ended with the arrival of her younger brother Tommy: 'I didn't go to school anymore after that, I had to stay at home and help.'[7] Isabella was thirteen when Tommy was born, so her parents were legally permitted to withdraw her from school and put her to childminding, but when Isabel Templeton's mother did the same thing she was only eleven and her mother's actions therefore broke the law. Years after the event, Isabel recalled with bitterness how her mother had illegally taken her from school so that she could be 'put in charge of Mama's seventh child' and 'become a skivvy' for the family.[8] From that moment, 'My childhood had gone.'[9] (Her mother's defence was that she believed 'a girl's place was in the home, learning how to be a good housewife and mother, and that this was far more important than learning things that were of no practical use in after years'.)[10] The unpaid domestic work that would characterise the lives of most working-class women started early for many girls, and often several years before the time of leaving school.

Just as some girls had begun to assume domestic responsibilities before the end of their schooldays, so did others find that leaving school marked an increase in such responsibilities, rather than their first forays into the world of paid work. Certainly, a girl's school-leaving did not necessarily coincide with the moment when she took up employment outside the home. Instead, it might mark the beginning of a transitional period of unpaid labour, usually in the first instance for her own family. As Alice Chase explained, at the age of fourteen she had left school, but not yet started work: 'I mean paid work. I worked alright, but I never got paid for my labour . . . [Mother] never gave me

1.1 A local newspaper photographer, Fred Halliday, captured this young girl in the streets of inner-city Newcastle minding her much younger sibling in her shawl in the early 1900s. Though young girls caring for babies was a very common sight in this period, it was rarely captured on film.

any money at any time, and nearly ran my feet off doing errands.'[11] Indeed, some parents were deeply ambivalent about sending daughters out to work at all. As Isabel Templeton's mother defiantly informed the school inspector when he came round to investigate the cause of Isabel's absence, 'A girl's place was in the home.'[12] As an elderly woman, Amy Gomm ruminated upon how out of character it had been of her parents to allow her older sister to take a job at the factory: 'This was a thing with our parents. Home was the place for girls.'[13] At the age of eighteen, Amy Andrews was still living with her parents and helping her mother with the two children that she had taken in to nurse, but when the youngest of these started school Amy decided it was 'time to start earning my own living'. Yet even at this relatively advanced age, her mother disputed her need to leave home at all, asking: 'why couldn't I be satisfied as I was'.[14] These girls' experiences were not unusual. Amongst the 140 female autobiographers who provided a detailed account of what they had done on leaving school, more than a third, 38 per cent, indicated that they had spent a period of time doing unpaid domestic work, usually for their immediate family, though occasionally for members of their extended family instead. For these girls, leaving school had not heralded the start of a paid job, but the intensification of unpaid work for their families.[15]

The connection between school-leaving and domestic work may help to explain why so few girls had thought the end of their schooldays heralded an exciting or significant turning point in their lives. A girl of twelve or thereabouts knew enough about the world to know there was little but housework awaiting her outside the school gates and a sizeable minority of the female authors had viewed further schooling as their one and only hope for a more interesting life. A recurring motif amongst the female autobiographers is the disappointment of reaching school-leaving age and the regret felt about the end of their education.[16] Others wrote wistfully about scholarships to the grammar school that they had never been able to take up. Joan Bellan was one of nearly a dozen female writers who had won a scholarship for the grammar school but had not been able to go. Although the school did not charge fees, her parents decided they could not afford all the attendant expenses of sending her there, so they found her a position in service instead.[17] It was an outcome that was only too common for working-class girls.

This loss of education was interpreted in different ways. Looking back on their experiences, some adult writers were sympathetic to the hardships their families had faced, and accepted the end of their schooldays as part of the natural order of things. May Jones, for example, knew that staying on at school had been 'an utter impossibility' and left it at that.[18] Alice Collis believed that her great disappointment at abandoning her attempts to enter high school were shared by 'Dad', as he had suffered the same fate as a boy when his father was blinded at work.[19] Edith Pratt was sorry not to take up her place at the grammar school with her two friends, but she had a wise head on her young shoulders and even at that age she had understood why her friends' lives were diverging from her own. One was 'the farmer's daughter' and the other 'the draper's daughter', so unlike her (the farm labourer's daughter), their families 'had plenty of money'.[20] Others harboured resentments that were slow to dissipate. Martha Heaton was less forgiving about the lack of support she had had from her parents whilst preparing for the entrance exam for the high school: 'Mother was one of those who thought the education of girls was wasted.' In fact, it was not only her mother who failed to back her. When the forms for the county scholarships arrived at home, her father refused to fill them in. But in Martha's narrative it is her mother who gets the blame for her lost opportunities. Despite all her hard work and excellent exam results, it 'made no difference . . . Mother had her wish: **I did not get to the Grammar School**'.[21] Despite their promising starts at elementary school, these grammar school hopefuls joined the bulk of their peers and followed the traditional pathway mapped out for a working-class girl: they left school and either stayed at home as a full-time mother's helper or they took up a job with very limited prospects.

Of these two alternatives, unpaid work inside the home was undoubtedly the least favoured. Alice Chase recounted the list of duties she had during the fifteen months she spent running around as her mother's unpaid helper, including chopping wood, carrying coal, clearing grates, dusting, cleaning, sewing and washing. She concluded it had been a 'hard life' and that she had been 'most unhappy' during this period.[22] At the age of fourteen, Agnes Cowper would 'have liked, very much, to do what most girls of my acquaintance seemed to do': start work. But she was told by her parents that her 'place was in the home helping mother with the children and with household duties'.[23] Kay Pearson also grew to hate her position as her family's 'house-keeper, washer-woman, errand girl and cook'. After a while in this role, she had a 'great desire' to go out to work, and regretted that her mother would not let her go: 'my services', she glumly noted, 'were required at home'.[24] Housework for the family was perceived as hard and thankless work and was rarely a young girl's first choice.

Part of the problem was that working with mother at home did not come with payment, or any of the other rewards enjoyed by those who worked outside the home, so these girls found themselves enduring the loss of freedom that went with work with none of the advantages. The lack of any money was particularly irksome as girls became older and increasingly desired some autonomy in their lives. Amy Gomm recalled how her elder brother's weekly earnings of five shillings had enabled him to devote some attention to his appearance – collars, ties and socks were bought from his allowance and 'were an expression of his personality'.[25] No such expression was permitted for the girls in the family, who worked within the home rather than outside it. Amy and her sisters' clothing was made by their mother until their early twenties: 'the recipient had no say in the choice of colour or style'. Mother chose 'the material, the style. There was really no "choice" about style.'[26] Nellie Barter found herself in the same position. As the daughter helping at home, she had 'no money at all, just my food and clothes', and a few coppers from her father if she ever asked for them – 'but I very rarely did'.[27] Grace Foakes resented the difference between herself and her older sister. Grace stayed at home to care for her sick mother and run the home and was dependent upon her father for a small amount of pocket money, whilst her sister was out at work and earned enough to buy herself 'nice clothes' and go on the day trips run by the Girls Guild.[28] Very few of the female autobiographers indicated that work inside the home was easier than work outside it, but several commented on the distinct disadvantage it entailed. Domestic work was not paid, and the lost opportunities for self-individuation that even a small amount of pocket money provided were keenly felt.

Even when girls did eventually start work outside their own home, they sometimes found themselves working without payment. Some parents were simply relieved if they were able to find another family better placed to feed their growing daughter and did not consider whether the position came with payment, let alone training or long-term potential. Writing about how she had been sent to her aunt's to work as a servant, Bessie Wallis recalled in disgust, 'I received the magnificent wage of absolutely nothing!'[29] When Ada Hutchinson turned thirteen, her elder, married sister decided the time had come for her to start work and sent for her. Ada had to 'earn her food' and become her sister's unpaid drudge: 'milking, digging, churning, washing, cleaning and looking after [her sister's] eight children'.[30] Occasionally, even more formal arrangements with non-family members went unremunerated. Dot Starn remembered turning up for her first day at work – a job in a florist shop that had been advertised in the newspaper – only to be told by her new employer: 'I don't pay wages, you know. Many people would pay me to teach them the trade.' She did not even let Dot keep the occasional tips she was given.[31]

Not only did girls tend to enter the labour market later than boys, they also frequently found that their employment, once it started, was interrupted according to the situation at home. Several of the female autobiographers spent their teens moving in and out of paid work according to their parents' needs and wishes, and it was not unusual for them to be recalled by parents who felt their services would be better employed under their own roof. As a result, daughters remained at the beck and call of their family well into their twenties, and sometimes beyond. Amy Andrews had been delighted to leave her domineering mother and work as a nursery nurse for a family in Lowestoft, but it wasn't long before she found herself back home again. After a few short months at Lowestoft, her mother sent a letter indicating that she was ill and that Amy needed to return to look after her. She packed up, leaving all her 'happiness behind me', only to discover on her arrival that her mother had made a miraculous recovery.[32] Some parents did not even bother to confect a reason for their daughter's return. Mrs Stringer simply told her daughter's employer that she would leave after serving her month's notice as she was 'wanted at home', and then wrote a letter to Maggie informing her of what she had done.[33]

Mothers with several daughters divided the responsibility for wage-earning and domestic work between them, and very often made their decisions without so much as consulting the individuals concerned. Hannah Mitchell's mother rotated her three daughters between living-out dressmaking apprenticeships, schooling and domestic work at home. Hannah enjoyed her stint as a dressmaking apprentice with Mrs Brown: looking back, she realised 'this was the first time in my life when I was really happy'. But when the situations of her two sisters changed, her mother 'decided that I must return home . . . to be the domestic drudge'.[34] The same thing happened to Gertie Slack. She left school a little before her thirteenth birthday and spent the next two and a half years at home helping her mother, after which her parents decided to send her out to service: 'They never asked me if I wanted to go – it was just fixed up and that was it.' After a while her mother decided it was time for her younger sister, Winnie 'to go out and get some money for herself'. So Gertie was recalled back to the family home, where she stayed until she married.[35]

And there was another consideration in many families. By the time she reached her mid to late teens, a girl was capable of running the family home, freeing a mother for paid employment or substituting for her if she was unable to perform the housework. There has been much debate amongst historians about the impact of marriage on women's employment, but the autobiographies remind us that many girls had family responsibilities long before they married.[36] Amy Gomm's mother set up a home laundry in Oxford, to capitalise on the city's large population of single men needing laundry services. Her small business was only viable because she established Amy and her sister as 'the home-makers, more or less' – purchasing and preparing the family's food and taking care of their younger brother.[37]

In other households, daughters were retained at home in order to help ailing mothers who were starting to struggle with the housework. Vera Wright's fledging career as a teacher came to an early end when her mother fell ill, and she had to return home 'to look after the family'.[38] Mildred Curtis gave up her teaching dreams in similar circumstances. She had to pass up the opportunity to stay on at school and train to be a teacher because 'my mother's health was failing, so it was housework for me, cooking, cleaning, washing, mending and so on'.[39] Nellie Barter did not have such an illustrious career as teaching within her sights: she was a domestic servant. Yet her life was disrupted in much the same way when her mother became bedridden. Nellie was nineteen and realised that as she was 'the last girl not married, it was my duty to give up my work to take care of her', and this she duly did.[40] This consideration was of course even more acute for those who had lost their mothers. Indeed, it was almost inevitable that motherless daughters would spend some part of their adolescence helping to run the family home.[41] Hilda Barnard had initially escaped the role of family housekeeper following her mother's death, as an elder sister had stepped in to take over the running of the home. Hilda had moved over thirty miles away and was working as 'a sewing maid and that'. But the reprieve was only temporary. When her elder sister died, it was Hilda's turn to return home and 'look after Father and my brothers'.[42]

Just occasionally female writers indicated that they had preferred working for their families to paid employment outside the home. Rosa Bell, for example, had enjoyed helping her mother with the housework and was sickened when her sister returned home from a broken marriage, forcing her to find work away from home, rising at five in the mornings and generally 'slaving away'.[43] Sarah Churchman also enjoyed the time she spent at home before going out to work. Her mother had kept each of her daughters at home for a year or so after they left school, and they were 'taught to cook, mend, and make beds and the general run of housework'. Sarah thought that she and her sisters had 'appreciated [this training] when we got older' and had their own families to look after.[44] But within a large collection of autobiographies, such sentiments were expressed extremely rarely. In general, the female writers only indicated a preference for working inside the home when they were already shouldering a double burden of paid work outside the home and unpaid housework within it. Ellen Calvert, for example, had eight younger brothers, and when she was informed by her father that she should give up her job 'as Mother would need me at home', she was more than happy to do so. But as she went on to point out, whilst working she had had 'a good lot of housework to do as well as my job', so paid employment had not in fact provided an escape from domestic work.[45] Aside from the opinions expressed by Bell, Churchman and Calvert, the attitude shared by the autobiographers was remarkably consistent: housework was drudgery and a paid position outside the home was distinctly preferable.

Given the low regard that girls had for doing the family's housework, it is yet more remarkable just how many girls were occupied doing precisely that. No matter how a girl felt about the relative merits of paid employment outside the home and unpaid domestic work for their family, the decision was largely out of her hands. There is virtually no evidence in the autobiographical record of daughters objecting to doing the family's housework, even when the prospect clashed with their own inclinations or ambitions. There is just one writer who revealed she had refused to comply with her family's wishes. This was the forthright Mrs Marrin, who was told by her father that she should stay at home and help with the housework when her schooling came to an end. Whilst she appears to have done as she was told initially, she 'soon got tired' of it and found herself a dressmaking apprenticeship. When that finished, she went to work in the West End, despite this being 'much against my parents' wishes'.[46] But apart from Mrs Marrin, the autobiographers uniformly report dutifully, if reluctantly, falling into line with their parents' requests. When Alice Chadwick was told to leave a job that she enjoyed and return home because her mother was pregnant and she wanted help when the baby arrived, she 'wasn't all that pleased about' it. But 'there it was'. Return she did.[47] Elizabeth Holder described herself as 'very happy' in her position as a live-in nanny, and was devastated when her father called her home to be his housekeeper. He had decided to move to the country to take a smallholding and as her mother did not want to accompany him and 'he would not have dreamed of looking after himself, he decided that [Elizabeth] would have to give up [her] post with the Armstrongs and go to keep house for him'. Elizabeth was appalled at the idea, but 'His word was law. I had no alternative but to give in my notice.'[48] Of course we might suspect that Mrs Marrin was not the only writer to have rejected her parents' authority, that there was a little more daughterly defiance that never got reported in the autobiographies. Yet, even if this is the case, it is surely significant that the authors, writing many years after the death of their parents, did not betray this in their narratives. It seems that parents and daughters were largely agreed about the primacy of family life for daughters, and that writers continued to hold these values through to old age.

The youthful experiences of working-class girls also had long-term significance for their prospects. Whilst their brothers left school and swiftly entered the workplace, accruing skills and experience throughout their adolescence, many girls spent much of their teens engaged in unpaid domestic work, both under the parental roof and elsewhere. As a result, they did not enter paid employment until their mid to late teens. In effect, the girls spent their adolescence in preparation for their adult life: learning (as Isabel Templeton bitterly noted) to be 'a good housewife and mother'. And this delayed entry to the labour market also betokens something more significant. It meant that many girls reached adulthood without having acquired the skills to earn their own living. The absence of training opportunities for adolescent girls set the stage for low female wages and a life of adult dependency on male earnings.

In large part, of course, the decision of parents to keep their daughters under their own roof was a reflection of the poor employment opportunities available to women and girls rather than a deliberate attempt to stifle their opportunities. The range of female employments was extremely restricted, and most girls were shoehorned into a small number of low-paying occupations. We can use the female autobiographies to track their employment destinations, though as the majority of female authors were born after 1880, the exercise sheds light primarily on the years 1890–1914 rather than earlier. If we list the first jobs of the women who wrote an autobiography, the limited nature of their options is readily apparent. Amongst those girls whose education had not progressed beyond elementary school, almost 80 per cent were employed in just four areas: domestic service (fifty-two girls); manufacturing in factories (twenty-eight) and workshops (seventeen); shopwork (seventeen); and needlework (seventeen). A further twelve girls who took up positions outside these sectors generally worked in trades that were closely related to them: four girls found work in commercial laundries,[49] two in commercial kitchens,[50] one found work as a nurse,[51] and another did sweated labour inside the home.[52] The remaining four found work in agriculture, which had once been a significant employer of women but had ceased to provide full-time, paid positions for young girls in the late Victorian period. In most cases, agriculture was a brief interlude before moving into service.[53] There was, of course, considerable variety within these broad occupational groupings. Domestic service included the classic domestic servant who boarded with her employers, but also encompassed a wide range of daily service jobs in private homes. Industrial occupations ranged from the relatively skilled and well-paid machine operators of Lancashire to the lowest-paid sweated labourers in London workshops. And, of course, these were first jobs. There was inevitably some subsequent movement across occupations, particularly amongst women who were still working (rather than married) by their early twenties. Yet the general contours of unmarried women's employment is clear and the narrow range of opportunities is unmistakable.[54]

With more than a third of all writers with known destinations taking up jobs in service, this sector was the single most significant employer of unmarried women from working-class families.[55] Service positions, whether living in or living out, were valued by parents on a number of levels. One of the most basic of considerations was that domestic work was nearly always remunerated in part by meals, so it not only provided wages, it also solved the problem of feeding a growing adolescent. Nellie Barter recalled how pleased her mother had been when she found a post for Nellie as a daily maid for two and six a week and her lunch: 'It all helped Mother if we could have a job where we could have some meals out.'[56] In addition, service offered girls training in a useful set of skills that they could put to use throughout their lives both in the labour market and in their own homes. The difficulty for many families in late Victorian and Edwardian Britain was finding a household willing to hire a teenage girl, particularly if she had never had a live-in position before.

This marked a decisive shift from the early nineteenth century, where the custom of employing very young children as domestic servants was considerably more widespread. Although the autobiographical evidence for the early Victorian period is relatively scarce, it seems that live-in situations were regularly found for children as young as eight. It is likely that the employment of such young girls was part and parcel of an older pattern of social relations, whereby richer households provided food and housing for the children of their poorer neighbours in return for whatever work they could provide – an act that was often perceived as charitable rather than exploitative, at least on the part of employers. Hannah Cullwick was born in 1833 and in her memoirs she described living away from home as a servant when just eight years old.[57] And in the 1850s, Polly King's mother sent all three of her daughters away from home as soon as they reached the age of ten. As her youngest daughter recalled: 'It was Mother's rule that at ten years we should go out to service.'[58] Even so late as the 1860s, some girls as young as eight were working away from home in exchange for food and lodging rather than wages.[59]

But with the establishment of compulsory schooling until the age of ten in 1880, and a steadily rising school-leaving age from that point onwards, the culture changed. The employment of children aged eight or ten was outlawed, and households became more hard-nosed about the kind of workers they hired. Employers did not generally want very young girls, for although they might be cheap, they also needed considerable supervision and were, in reality, of only limited use to a busy household. Even at the ages of twelve of thirteen, many of the girls in late Victorian and Edwardian Britain discovered that they were unable to enter straight into domestic service, as they lacked the skills or stamina that would make them attractive to employers.[60]

Instead they had to gain experience by doing daily work before they could graduate to a live-in position. Indeed, the practice of retaining girls at home after their schooling may in some instances have been a strategy to improve their prospects on the job market. Bess Passiful described the pathway that had become typical in the late nineteenth century. She left school shortly before her thirteenth birthday, and after a very brief period at home helping her mother, she started work at around the age of thirteen. The only position her mother could find was mornings only. It was for the local dentist, and involved cleaning the front step, the boots, and helping the maid with 'various other household jobs'. After leaving that post, she did 'various other jobs of housework' for two years, at which point, aged seventeen, she took up a live-in position. In Bess's eyes, this was not simply another job, but an opportunity – her chance (as she wrote) 'to train as house parlourmaid'.[61] The pride that young women felt in taking up a live-in position in a large house was palpable. Elizabeth Holder's first paid work at the age of thirteen was 'cleaning and washing dishes' for a family who lived a half-hour walk away from her home. She worked around fifty hours a week, but nonetheless described this as a 'little job'. It was not until she was fifteen that she needed cotton dresses, caps and aprons for her 'first real job', as a live-in second maid for a household a fifteen-mile train ride away from home.[62]

It was not just lack of skills that prevented young girls from taking up a live-in position. Domestic service could be hard, physical work, and young girls were likely to be rejected as lacking the necessary maturity or strength. Rosa Bell wanted to become a nanny, but at her first interview for such a post was rejected by the existing nurse as 'much too young for the responsibility'. She started instead as a 'nurse housemaid', and worked her way up from there.[63] For some, deprivation during childhood and adolescence had left them ill equipped to undertake the demanding physical labour. At the age of seventeen, Lillian Mara gave up a position in 'High Society' after three months because she found the work too hard: 'The work needed the stamina of an ox, and years of semi-starvation meant I hadn't this sort of strength.'[64]

Whilst live-in positions were warmly anticipated and highly prized, the reality of life as a domestic servant was, of course, more complex. Some girls relished their escape from the overcrowding and complex relationships of their homes; others, particularly younger girls, missed their families. But as the homesickness passed, most girls began to feel some pride in their new status as an independent worker. A place in service offered excitement, wages and friendships, as well as the prospect of better food than they had enjoyed at home. Despite the long passage of time between a girl's first job and the time of writing an autobiography much later in life, food was one of the aspects of service most reliably reported. Edith Pratt's overriding memory of her first position as a live-in servant for a farming household was the meals: steak and kidney pudding, pigs fry with potatoes, even roast chicken – 'which I never had at home'.[65] (The situation came to an end when her mistress informed her family that she would cut Edith's wages because she 'eats so much'. Her family brought her home rather than accept such a transgression on the part of an employer.[66]) Bessie Harvey fondly recalled the meals she had enjoyed as a kitchen maid in her teens: they had 'good food in the kitchen, a joint to ourselves when we wanted it'.[67] Good food was not universal, but if it was not up to scratch, girls at least had some autonomy as to whether or not to stay.[68] Unlike working inside the home, if a place did not suit, girls simply left.

Alongside the expectation of good food, most girls viewed domestic service, particularly living-in positions, as an opportunity for advancement. In the right house, domestic service offered training as well as wages, and unusually for women's work it offered some prospect of progression. Minnie Jones jumped at the opportunity to take her friend's place in service to a wealthy

1.2 After leaving the Essex countryside, Edith Pratt moved to Cambridge and worked in a variety of households as a domestic servant. It was at this stage in her life that she had this professional studio photograph taken.

gentleman farmer, and clearly considered that getting away from home and into service was the gateway to something better. Her new mistress, Mrs Tapp, was a 'real lady and said she would train me to be a house-maid and she did'. Minnie learned to turn a room out, make beds, lay the table, wait at table, 'and also the proper way to answer the door and announce visitors'.[69] Though only there for seven months, Minnie believed she had learned as much as she 'might have learnt in years at some places', as well as growing 'very big and strong' from the good diet she enjoyed there.[70]

Along with the acquisition of experience and new skills, so did the girls' wages rise. When Rose Gibbs took her first position in service, she received just ten shillings a month and her keep. By the time she left her second position, her wages had doubled to a pound a month. Yet she concluded that 'for what I'm doing [that] isn't enough', and handed in her notice, informing her employer that she was 'going to better myself'. She found herself a job as third-laundry maid in a large house with twenty-two servants. The food was 'wonderful', and her wages doubled once more, to just under two pounds a month – 'that was a fortune to me'.[71] Alice Chadwick also enjoyed her work as a domestic servant. She had started work as a 'tweeny – helping cook and house parlourmaid, as they needed me', for the equivalent of £13 a year plus her bed and meals.[72] This later rose to £18 a year, and once she was able to take a cook's job 'on her own account', they 'soared to £24 yearly'.[73] Like Rose, she approvingly noted the satisfactory combination of increasing responsibility, more interesting work and a steadily rising wage.

Yet there were, of course, problems with domestic service as well. Living-in positions were certainly the most favourable form of domestic work in terms of pay and career development. And yet living with an employer could be irksome, and required girls to give up control over large aspects of their private lives. 'In those days you just seemed to belong to the people you worked for and you did whatever they wanted,' one former servant glumly noted.[74] Furthermore, employers had control not only over how long their servants worked, but also over what they did when they were not at work. One writer recalled how her first mistress had called her in to her room shortly after her arrival to tell her how she was to wear her hair at church – scraped back in a bun rather than loose. She listened in disbelief at her mistress's demands and 'wondered if for thirteen and sixpence per calendar month she had bought me entirely'. And although she won the battle over how to wear her hair at church, she could not evade other aspects of her mistress's control, such as her morning prayers – or indeed, the obligatory trip itself to church each Sunday.[75] One girl ran the risk of visiting her sister instead of the church some Sundays, although she knew that she would get the sack if ever found out.[76] As a young girl of sixteen, Gertrude Cottrell's great love was dancing, but her mistress would not allow it: 'the only thing she would not allow was for us maids to go to dancing'. When Gertrude received an invitation to a ball, her mistress 'would not hear of it'.[77] Time off for domestic servants was always scarce – often no more than a half-Sunday a week – and some employers also sought to dictate how and where that time off could be enjoyed. In her late teens, Mrs Wrigley's employer had allowed her one Sunday afternoon every week and one Sunday evening a month, and she spent her free time at a Sunday school where she met her husband. When her mistress found out about the relationship 'she stopped me going out altogether'.[78]

More seriously, the safety of women and girls was not always assured whilst living under other people's roofs.[79] In one of her service positions, Lilian Mara was 'worried' by her mistress's nineteen-year old son, who 'thought me fair game and kept trying to corner me in the bedroom'. She handed in her notice in order to get away from him.[80] On taking up her first job, Joan Bellan discovered that the husband of her mistress was a 'lecherous old man'. He chased the parlourmaid around and then started on Joan, touching her and cornering her when alone: 'He frightened me to death.' Joan's problem was only resolved when she decided to tell her parents. They took her away, though, as Joan realised, whilst this solved her particular problem, it did not address the more general one of women's vulnerability in service: 'That's what used to happen in some of those houses.'[81] Emma Sproson had to leave a place abruptly when her mistress's brother took to making frequent visits to the home. On one occasion he entered her bedroom, locked the door and attempted to sexually assault her. She saw him off by brandishing the poker, but in the fallout that ensued, Emma was 'ordered off without a character'.[82] Whilst working for an aristocratic household, Rosa Lewis suffered similar problems. In this particular house she felt 'frightened of every man, thinking that they were going to get me', and slept with her furniture pushed up against her door. She knew that if any man made it into her room, she would lose her job, just as she had seen happen 'to many of my fellow workers'. Her fears were not unfounded, as she returned one night to find a visitor in 'tight pyjamas' in her room. She too had to use her wits to see him off.[83] As both Emma and Rosa indicated, if such incidents came to the attention of their employers it would be them, the victims, rather than the perpetrators, who would be expected to leave.

The difficulties that some women found with respect to the men in the household is symptomatic of the dependency that went hand in hand with domestic service. Live-in service did not provide the kind of independent living that most adults ultimately desire. The drawback was captured by Christian Watt who, despite quite enjoying her years as a lady's maid in London and conceding that she had probably enjoyed a greater degree of affluence than she could ever attain in her Highland fishing village, had 'no intention of accepting this life at everybody's beck and call . . . in much the same way as a caged wild bird. It was preferable to be a poor fisher compared to being a well-fed lady's-maid.'[84] And although domestic service offered some professional progression, it did not offer the kind of progression that enabled a woman to live independently in a home of her own. For this reason, service was widely understood as part of a stage in life, rather than as a long-term proposition, and one that would of course come to an end should a woman choose to marry.

The incompatibility of service with marriage is widely recognised, but the autobiographies reveal that it was not simply marriage that stood in the way of girls working in service. Unmarried girls also had family commitments, and all daughters, married or not, were at risk of being summoned home to families who needed them. We met Rose Gibbs a moment ago enjoying earning her 'fortune' of two pounds a month. Rose was unmarried, but with an invalided father and an ageing mother she was far from free of family obligations. After just three months work at the Hall, Rose returned home weighed down by the worry of matters there. 'That was the finish really of my being "in service" . . . I never had a really big job again'.[85] Minnie Jones's education with Mrs Tapp also came to a swift end for reasons beyond her control. After seven short months, Minnie's elder sister was widowed with a baby-in-arms, so Minnie 'was taken away to go and live with her'.[86] It was always difficult for a woman to combine domestic service with her own domestic responsibilities, and although we tend to imagine that unmarried women were unencumbered by such responsibilities, the autobiographies make plain that this was not the case. All households required considerable domestic labour, and although this burden fell primarily to wives and mothers, it also, for all manner of different reasons, fell to daughters as well.

Second in importance as an employer of the female autobiographers was manufacturing. At the pinnacle of Britain's manufacturing sector were the textile districts of Lancashire, Cheshire and Yorkshire, which offered female employment opportunities superior to those available anywhere else. In addition, however, there was widespread employment of women in sweated trades – manufacturing goods either in small workshops or in the home. The umbrella term manufacturing therefore covers a diverse range of experiences, from the relatively well-paid textiles machines operators of Lancashire and Cheshire at one end to the poorly paid sweated labourers of London at the other – a considerable difference which calls for further investigation.

In order to understand the creation of well-paid women's work in the factory districts we need to understand the distinctive set of historical forces that had occurred during the Industrial Revolution. Before industrialisation, women had been employed widely throughout the textile industry, in both spinning and weaving, and the many intermediary stages. The work was performed on simple machines and inside the home. When industrialisation established factory production on more complex machines around the end of the eighteenth century, the new methods had been grafted on the existing workforce of women and children. From the new factory employers' perspective, young and female workers offered important advantages. Most obviously, they were cheap: women could be paid less than men, and children less again. In addition, women and children were believed to be a docile and obedient workforce, with nimble fingers and a particular capacity for attention to detail.[87] As each of the constituent steps for processing raw cotton into woven textiles was mechanised during the nineteenth century and moved from workshops and cottages into factories, much of the work was taken over by the existing, and largely female, workforce. As a result, women had assumed a role as skilled machines operators in one of the most technologically sophisticated (and most highly paid) sectors of the economy. By the late nineteenth century, when the autobiographical evidence for women's employment comes on stream, they were still there.[88]

Yet whilst female employment was widespread in the textile districts, we should not imagine that the factories offered equal opportunities to men and women. Just as the various stages of textile production had been segregated by gender in the pre-industrial period, so they were in the factories. The new industrial factories comprised a complex hierarchy of machines and processes, and each was coded either male or female. With the exception of weaving, where men and women worked on power-looms alongside each other for the same rate of pay, most machines were operated exclusively by men or exclusively by women, with higher pay for male workers. In addition, the supervisory roles within factories with the best rates of pay were always allocated to men rather than women. So whilst the tradition of female labour was carried into the modern factory environment, so too were entrenched beliefs about the superiority of male workers and the custom of rewarding them with higher pay.[89] Nonetheless, cotton mills clearly did offer a wide range of different employments to women at relatively good wages, and it is unsurprising, therefore, to find that women's work was common throughout the region.

The existence of factory employment ensured a very different kind of childhood for the girls in the community. In contrast to the faltering entry into the workplace of most girls, those living in the factory districts usually

1.3 Female mill workers with their male overseers from Cox Green Mill, *c.* 1901.

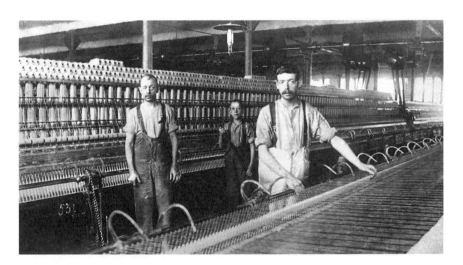

1.4. Although spinning was traditionally a female occupation, once it had been mechanised it was regarded as skilled work suitable for men. This photo shows three male spinners standing by their machines at Times Mill, Grimshaw Lane, Middleton in *c.* 1912.

made a swift start at the mill as soon as the law allowed.[90] Until the 1870s, the age for starting half-time at the mill was eight years; it then rose to ten years of age, then eleven and subsequently to twelve. Children were legally permitted to progress to full-time work from the age of fourteen, though many started younger on production of an easily obtainable school certificate indicating they had reached the requisite educational standard.[91] A few of the girls from better-off families bypassed the half-timer stage, and spent an extra year or so at school before starting full-time work at the mill, but the direction of travel was the same: full-time mill work which continued throughout a girl's teens.[92]

Whatever the precise age at which a girl started work, the transition from school to work was swift and certain. Nor were the girls who started work in the mill arbitrarily called back home in order to help with the housework – though they might, of course, be expected to undertake some domestic duties in evenings and at weekends if the family situation demanded. Amongst the autobiographers, it appears that just one of the twenty-eight girls who started work in a textile mill were reassigned by their families to domestic work. This

1.5 Three young mill girls in Wigan holding their baskets and billy cans containing their day's provisions, 1891.

1.6 Two early twentieth-century weavers standing by their machines in Cox Green Mill, Egerton.

was Ellen Calvert, who had no fewer than eight younger brothers, and whose family, therefore, had a particularly pressing need for domestic assistance.[93] In general, however, from the family perspective, a daughter's earning capacity was more valuable than her household labour, and families organised their allocation of waged and domestic work accordingly.

A girl's first job at the mill was an exciting event, and several writers recalled their delight at joining sisters and friends at work. The camaraderie of work could be fun, and the feeling of importance that went with wage-earning was satisfying. Elsie Dutton contrasted her time at a Salford sugar mill with the oppressive atmosphere of school: 'It was wonderful to mix with young people who were laughing, singing and cracking jokes with one another . . . They were such a happy crowd at the factory and there were quite a few comedians amongst them . . . They were a grand lot to work with.'[94] Mary Sutton spent ten years in a hosiery mill after leaving school and later recalled that she had '<u>really</u> <u>liked</u> my work'.[95] Martha Heaton had wanted to go to the grammar school, not the mill, but even she conceded that 'we did not have too bad a time on the whole' and recalled how there used to 'be much fun and laughter at meal times'.[96]

It was not usually long, however, before the excitement of wage-earning gave way to fatigue. Mill work was hard. Though the hours were shorter than service, they were still long, particularly once girls had transitioned from half-time to full-time. In addition, the machines were very noisy, and the work physically demanding. At the very least it required standing on one's feet all day long, though in addition several of the machines were also onerous to operate. The women who had worked in textile mills frequently recalled being stunned by how hard they had found the work and at how quickly (as one writer put it) 'the glamour of wage earning began to fade'.[97] 'I never liked the job but had to "stick it" ', recalled Anita Hughes.[98] Ellen Calvert also reported that she had 'never liked working at the mill'. She only 'stuck it so long' because jobs for girls 'in those days . . . were not so plentiful'.[99] Some of the writers indicated that factory work had been more than they could cope with, and described their efforts to quit the mill and find some other line of work.[100] And whilst it is important to recognise that *all* nineteenth-century employers demanded far more time and physical effort from their workers than we are accustomed to today, the autobiographers, both male and female, consistently described factory work as a particularly demanding way to earn a living.

The incentive, of course, was the pay. The process of transforming raw cotton into woven textiles is complex, with the fibres passing through more than a dozen different stages. The mills therefore contained a wide variety of rooms and machines, which in turn provided workers with a range of different employments at different rates of pay. As a young mill girl, Hilda Snape had initially been attracted by the high wages of the weavers so started in the weaving room. But she soon discovered that 'a lot of things are involved in weaving' and decided to look for an alternative. She opted to join her sister in the card room, starting on

48

the carding machines and then moving onto another unnamed machine in the carding room: 'I liked this much better as it wasn't so involved.'[101] She was then promoted to work on the drawing frames.[102] As girls moved through different roles, their wages would rise. Hilda's promotion to the drawing frame, for instance, came with a doubling of her wages – from fifteen shillings a week to thirty.[103] To put this wage in context, the highest the domestic servants were able to earn was about £24 a year, which equates to around nine shillings a week.

The higher than average wages made mill work an attractive option for families to whom it was available and explains why they so consistently prioritised paid work for their daughters over housework. Half-timers aged twelve years or less usually started on two shillings and sixpence. By the age of thirteen, full-time girls could expect to earn five shillings a week.[104] As girls spent their teens progressing through the different machines, they found, like Hilda, that their wage tended upwards. Anita Hughes may not have enjoyed factory work much, but she did think 'it was grand to see a shining half sovereign [ten shillings] in my pocket'.[105] Doris Hunt 'hated the mill-work', but after four years as a full-timer she was earning a hefty three pounds (sixty shillings) a week.[106] As the girls who earned them recognised, these were good wages and considerably higher than anything they could earn anywhere else.

Equally, the girls understood that whilst the work was hard, the fact of wage-earning had some compensations. Annie Kenney was one of several women who had not particularly liked her work at the mill, but there was 'one redeeming feature': the fact that it allowed her to enjoy a weekly girls' paper.[107] Martha Heaton recalled that after a hard week's work, the weekends brought rail trips to the nearby town and a tea out at the Co-op café.[108] Other girls described the pleasure they had taken in spending their pocket money on accessorising their wardrobe – a sharp contrast to the many girls who remained dependent upon their mother's housekeeping money for their clothes, and therefore at the mercy of her dress tastes as well. Elizabeth Blackburn enjoyed the fact that working gave her access to women's magazines 'from which we learned quite a lot about how to dress and groom ourselves'.[109] When Maggie Newbery worked at the mill, she liked to 'treat myself to a quarter of sweets to eat in the mill; it was surprising how they helped the time along', but she also enjoyed spending her money on buying 'my own hair ribbons and sometimes a pair of stockings'. She was also able to ignore her father when he scoffed at her for wanting a pair of shoes rather than workaday boots: 'I still wanted shoes so I would save for them myself.'[110] It took a long time, but she did it, and she managed to save for a holiday as well.

For individual girls, the most tangible advantage of their mill work was the spending money it brought. But as we read across the autobiographical sample as a whole, it becomes clear that the ability to earn good wages had other, less immediately obvious, advantages. As revealed by Maggie Newbery's determination to go ahead and buy herself a pair of shoes despite her father's criticism, wage-earning signified a change in a girl's place within her family. It allowed a girl to redefine her relationship with her family on her own terms and provided her with some power within her family circle. Deborah Smith did not specify exactly how much she had earned as a mill girl; instead she gave meaning to her earnings by describing what they meant for her family. Her first wages bought a new dolly tub for her mother, then came 'a chest of drawers in the same way'. Her parents looked at her as a 'gold mine'; her weekly wage packet 'was more than father had ever earned in his life'.[111] In some families, wage-earning was even sufficient to free a girl from helping with the housework. When a former Lancashire mill worker was interviewed for Granada Television in 1963 she was asked: 'What kind of household jobs did you have to do . . . to help in the home?' She explained that she had not really had to worry about that. When she returned from the mill she 'was really worn out. And I didn't do much in that way. I'd wash up you know. Clear the table and wash up but I didn't do any heavy work.'[112] Others indicated that whilst they had had to undertake some chores at home in addition to working, so too had their brothers.[113]

The change in status that came with wage-earning was captured by Alice Foley, when looking back on her elder sister, Cissy, who worked on the jack-frame, a kind of spinning machine, in one of Bolton's many cotton factories. Alice noted that by her mid-teens, her sister 'earned enough to "keep herself"'. She gave 'a portion' of her wages to her mother for housekeeping, and used the rest to buy her own clothes and accessories. But in return for this 'portion', Cissy claimed a right to institute a number of modernisations in the family's domestic management – a new linoleum floor, cups and saucers, an egg-timer and a gas-jet light. She also claimed the family's best room on Sunday afternoons so that she could entertain her friends, forcing 'father and the lads' to remain in the 'back regions' of the house.[114] (It is interesting that Cissy chose to exercise her rights in the sphere of domestic management, speaking volumes about the limited horizons of women's lives.[115]) Jane Walsh also started exerting her rights within the family once she was 'grown-up, a wage-earner' at the cotton mill at the age of thirteen. For years she had been 'the member of the family dispatched to the pub and the pawnshop', a role she disliked 'heartily'. When she started earning for the family, her trips to the pub and the pawnshop came to an end: ' "From now on Mum," I said, clutching my first week's pay, "you can send our Bernard to the pub and the pawnshop, because I'm not going any more, say what you like." ' Her mother certainly did have plenty to say about this act of mutiny, but Jane did stop running errands for the family. It was, she noted in reflection, her great 'triumph'.[116]

There were also significant long-term gains for the girls in the factory districts. In addition to pocket money for girls' papers and sweets, and to an improvement in their position in the family, factory work provided girls with several years of training and equipped them with the skill needed to earn a proper livelihood throughout (or later in) their lives. As Doris Hunt noted, her starting pay as a half-timer in the mill was a derisory two shillings and sixpence, but she 'was learning the craft of weaving which was the most skilled of the textile processes'.[117] Four years later she was earning three pounds a week. Alice Foley joined her sister Cissy working in one of Bolton's many cotton factories when she was thirteen years of age. Over the next seven years, she worked in the knotting room, in the weaving shed, as a cloth fettler, and in the preparation department, before migrating from the mill to the union's offices. Over that period, her wages rose from five shillings a week to twenty-five shillings a week. The contrast between her situation and that of her exact contemporary – Kate Taylor – is clear. Kate started working at the same age as a live-in servant for a local farmer. Her first six months were unpaid and she then advanced to the measly sum of one shilling a week.[118]

The difficulty, of course, was that well-paid mill work was simply not available to most women. The textile industry was located in the north-western corner of England and Scotland's Central Belt, and although women were involved in manufacturing elsewhere in Britain, they were not generally employed as operators of complex machines. Elsewhere women were employed in box-making, packing and sorting, tanning yards, and factories producing foodstuffs such as chocolates, sweets and pickles – all low-skilled and low-paid work.[119] Lily Astell lived in London, and when her parents sought employment for her at the age of fourteen they ruled out domestic service as they did not want her to live away from home. Instead, they found a two-year apprenticeship with a bookbinding firm looking to hire six new apprentices. Like many apprentices, she found the work 'very boring and monotonous' and felt 'very unhappy and tired'. But this was not an apprenticeship as commonly understood, providing a pathway into skilled and well-paid employment. At the end of the girls' two-year term they were all sacked and six new school leavers were taken on. 'Looking back,' mused Lily, 'I realise it was sweated labour.'[120]

Beyond domestic work and manufacturing, the only remaining employment destinations of any significance for young women were needlework[121] and shopwork.[122] Both were clearly regarded as somewhat more genteel than the alternatives of service and manufacturing and they tended to be the destinations of the girls from better-off families. Learning to sew was a part of most girls' lives: they were taught by their mothers, often from a very young age, and not necessarily with a view to paid employment. Alice Green, for example, reported having learned a wide range of needlecraft – sewing, simple embroidery, crocheting, rug-making and how to make patchwork quilts and cushion covers – whilst still at elementary school.[123] These were all skills that were highly useful to the functioning of the home. Yet although most girls acquired a basic grasp of needlework during childhood as part of their upbringing, it was widely understood that additional training was required in order to earn a living from dressmaking. Some parents were even willing to pay a premium for a dressmaking apprenticeship so their daughters could learn the more skilled branches of the dressmaking trade. Louise Withers's father paid his daughter's employer no fewer than three guineas for an apprenticeship to learn skilled dressmaking.[124] Most parents managed to apprentice their daughters without paying a premium, but they still had to support their daughters as they received a reduced, or even no, wage. When she was fifteen, Alice Chase was released from her position as her mother's unpaid helper and apprenticed to a dressmaker. For a working week of nearly sixty hours, she was paid 'the princely sum of one shilling'.[125] At the same age, Isabella Piper earned just two shillings and sixpence a week as an apprentice for a London dressmaker.[126] But Alice and Isabella were both better off than the girls who worked with Margaret Penn, who joined a workshop in Manchester that described itself as 'Court Dressmakers', and which 'apprenticed' its girls for three years, paying them no wages during that period.[127]

For those girls whose parents lacked either the resources or the inclination to invest in training their daughters in dressmaking, shopwork was an acceptable alternative. This too was considered a step above service and regarded as a desirable line of work for working-class girls. Although jobs in shops were not formally framed as apprenticeships, many employers nonetheless paid artificially low wages on the pretext that they were teaching the girl the trade. As we have already noted, Dot Starn's first job at a florist's shop was unpaid for this reason. Mrs A. C. Davis started her working life in a dyers and cleaning shop. She was fourteen at the time and her employers too claimed she was 'learning a trade' and so paid her only two shillings and sixpence a week. Mrs Davis was not too impressed with the training she received, though, when she discovered that her role in fact involved little more than 'taking the owners' children to school and taking special orders'.[128]

Despite the low wages and promises of training, none of these jobs offered any real prospect of progression. In reality, they were dead-end jobs with no hope of advancement. Even those who had entered the ostensibly skilled work of dressmaking grumbled that the work was dull, monotonous, tedious and largely unchanging. After a lengthy eight years of training, Alice Chase recalled being 'shut up in one room for almost twelve hours a day – one long dreary round of tacking, stitching, pressing, oversewing, boning and trimming, over and over again ... I sometimes wonder how I stood eight years of it.'[129] Mobility between employers was relatively low. Many girls spent long periods with one employer, and they were as likely to move back to their families to help with the housework as they were to move on to new positions. Emily Lea reluctantly left school at the age of eleven to work in Hordan's Toy shop, but she didn't like the way she was treated there and didn't think much of her wage either: one and six a week hardly 'weighed [her] down'. After six months she was 'bored and fed up and decided to seek something else'.[130] She decided to try dressmaking, reasoning that at least she should learn something useful. But she only gained sixpence on her weekly wage and spent as much time running errands as she did learning to sew – she thought she had paid 'most of [her] pittance out in shoe leather' running those errands. Many young women found that all they could really do was, like Emily, circulate around different forms of low-paid female work, and this removed much of the incentive for moving from one employer to another. After her two-year bookbinding 'apprenticeship', Lily Astell was fortunate to be kept on by the firm: she stayed with the same firm for fourteen years. It was the only job she ever had before marriage.[131] Sarah Churchman started working with a clothes wholesaler and she too spent the next fourteen years with the firm.[132] Women did not tend to move quickly from one job to the next as there was little prospect of earning high wages or promotions, no matter where they worked.

Indeed, the most problematic aspect of all these jobs was the pay. Even after probationary or training periods were over, these jobs paid considerably less than either live-in domestic service or mill work and rarely offered wages that were good enough for independent living. In workshops, for example, girls usually started out on the customary low wage of one or two shillings a week, and whilst this wage would rise with age and experience, it did so neither fast nor far. Alice Collis had started working for a London printing firm at the age of fifteen, operating a machine that folded envelopes. It was 1909 and she was paid a mere four shillings a week. This rose by a shilling a year, so by the age of seventeen her pay had risen to a paltry six shillings per week. With her co-workers she went on strike, demanding a 50 per cent increase in her wages, and as this was successful her pay rose to nine shillings a week. It was an

1.7 Most manufactured goods needed packing or boxing before dispatch and this was poorly paid work done by women. This photo from 1909 shows women packing boxes for the tinplate industry and was taken as part of an investigation into low pay in the sector.

improvement but, as she noted, 'Our wages were still miserably low.'[133] Few of the women who worked in factories outside the textile industry recalled earning more than ten or twelve shillings a week.[134] The customary hallmarks of women's work – low status and low pay – were apparent in almost all manufacturing outside the modernised textile sector.

And pay was no better for girls working in the more coveted spheres of dressmaking and shopwork either. As we have seen, the training wages paid to girls learning dressmaking were so low that they effectively required a subsidy from the girl's parents. It did not take long for Isabella Piper's parents to realise that her work in their sweetshop was worth more than the two shillings and sixpence she earned a week learning skilled embroidery work. Her position was duly terminated, along with her dreams of becoming a court dressmaker and earning 'big money'.[135] Winifred Rutley despaired of her options as a young woman seeking work. She was interested in learning dressmaking but realised that 'as a learner in any job I could not hope to be self-supporting', so if she lived with her parents they would effectively be 'subsidising' her. Given the limited options available in the area, 'from their point of view it was better for me to live at home' and help with the housework.[136] Low pay was disempowering and increased parental power over a daughter's decision making throughout her adolescence.

Nor did these problems afflict girls only during their training. Even once training had been completed, most girls struggled to earn enough to live independently of their families. Needlework was supposed to be skilled work. In practice, however, a fully trained seamstress earned so little that it was scarcely enough to live on. Tabitha John had no interest in following in her mother's footsteps and learning dressmaking because the pay was so poor – her mother thought her sewing had just been 'a thank you job'.[137] This was indeed the experience of several of the autobiographers. Just two of the many autobiographers who had learned dressmaking succeeded in making a decent living from it. One was Rosa May Downer, who in the early twentieth century was earning fifteen shillings a week, plus her food and travelling expenses, making luxury evening gowns and dresses for well-to-do-families.[138] The other was her contemporary, Elizabeth Andrews, who managed to earn almost a pound a week, in addition to food and lodging. But Elizabeth had not only completed an apprenticeship, she had also gone on to become the boss: she was in charge of 'a large workrooms and a number of apprentices'.[139] Clearly the

1.8 Despite long years of training, dressmakers rarely earned enough to live independently. This rare photograph of a dressmakers' workroom was taken by Sheffield's Medical Officer of Health in the early twentieth century as part of an investigation into their poor working conditions.

average seamstress was far more likely to be one of the many hands in the workroom rather than the supervisor, each earning very much less than Elizabeth's pound a week.

Hannah Mitchell was one of a small number of particularly determined women amongst the autobiographers – a pioneering suffragette, feminist and socialist with a powerful desire for a life that transcended the domestic sphere to which she had been assigned. But even her drive and determination could not be translated into a living wage. As a young woman, she had followed the only path open to her: domestic service. Time quickly proved how unsuited she was to domestic service: not only did she hate housework, she also objected to the submission required from a live-in servant. After a couple of years she sought to find another way of earning her living, surmising – not incorrectly – that her brief dressmaking apprenticeship with Mrs Brown qualified her to earn a living as a seamstress. Her weekly pay – ten shillings, as against the four shillings she had earned in service – was certainly better, but it did not include food and lodging, and Hannah was soon to learn the true value of these on the market place. With her family living in a remote corner of the peak district she could not economise by living at home; she needed to maintain herself in lodgings closer to her place of work. But her weekly wage simply did not cover both rent and shop-bought meals. Her long hours of work made it impossible for her to buy ingredients and cook her own meals, and in any case she did not have access to the kitchen. It was only because her landlady kindly left a plate of food out for her in the evenings and asked for no payment in return that her situation was sustainable.[140]

Hannah's experience was not unusual. Several of the girls who had served a dressmaking apprenticeship went on to discover that they were unable to earn a living from their skill once they had completed their training. As a learner dressmaker, it took Alice Chase eight years for her wages to rise to eight shillings a week, and this was still less than a living wage.[141] Alice Green was a skilled dressmaker, but after completing her apprenticeship she found she earned 'only enough to pay my board and lodging' with nothing left over. She had to get another post, as she realised 'the needlework did not pay'.[142] Emily Lea encountered the same problem, despite enjoying the advantage of living with her parents. Her dressmaking wages were 'almost impossible to live on [even] at home'.[143] After a two-year apprenticeship, Louise Withers became an 'improver' in her dressmaking shop for wages of three shillings weekly. When she reported this to her parents 'the storm broke', as after a two-year apprenticeship they thought their daughter was worth 'at least a shilling a day'. Louise's employer explained to her irate parents that this was the normal wage for girls in her shop, as 'her class of work was mostly taken up by girls who only needed the money to supply dress expenses etc. while living at home'.[144] Even after she managed to get a pay rise from her mistress, she was unable to ignore her parents' displeasure at her low earnings and was eventually 'worried into giving my notice'.[145] The girls working in shops faced the very same problem: their wages were too low, even once training had been completed, for them to set up a household of their own. Aged nineteen, Agnes Cowper earned only eight shillings a week as an assistant in a department store, though this did include 'dinner and tea'.[146] It was only a viable wage because she lived at home. It is also clear that the 'apprenticeships' that some girls had served in order to learn dressmaking or shopwork did not really qualify for the term. As properly conceived, an apprenticeship involves reduced earnings during the training period, which is compensated by the premium that skilled workers can command after having learned their skill. Yet, clearly, these women did not enjoy enhanced wages once they had completed their training. Most remained dependent upon their families for food and lodging, and those who were unable to live at home were scarcely able to survive.

Low wages were of course inconvenient for the women who earned them, but there is a wider social significance to low female pay that we need to consider. Low pay was also a form of control. After all, the inability of most women outside the factory districts to earn a living wage effectively forced them to remain dependent upon their families well into adulthood, and upon their husbands after marriage. We have seen just how common it was for young women to be put to unpaid domestic work by their families, and how rarely they resisted these demands, even when they ran counter to their own wishes. Yet this dynamic was inescapable when the girls in question were unable to earn a living wage. How could any worker who earned less than her keep insist on her right to work outside the home rather than inside it? Low female pay transformed the question of whether a woman would work or not into a matter for the household, rather than the woman in question, to decide. Low female wages were thus an important structural element of society, playing a vital role in ensuring that all families had access to the unpaid domestic work that they required in order to function.

We have been looking at women whose education had terminated after primary school. But what happens if we include those who made it to secondary school? The exercise is depressing. Even if we extend our list to include the fortunate few who managed to progress beyond elementary school, the range of destinations remains extremely narrow. Several of the girls with a post-elementary education ended up in one of the sectors already mentioned – shopwork and needlework were particularly favoured amongst the later school-leavers. And just two more occupations can be added to our original list: teaching (sixteen) and clerical work (fifteen).[147] The actual number of autobiographers who made it into these two professions is possibly exaggerated in the source base by the fact that teachers and clerks were more likely to have the skills and confidence to write their life stories. Nonetheless, it is clear that a few extra years of schooling had a tangible benefit and provided a doorway into employment that was less physically demanding and that offered better pay and greater autonomy.

But we must not exaggerate the opportunities available, as these sectors were very difficult for girls who had not attended secondary school to enter, and as we know working-class girls struggled to access that secondary education. Most of the clerical workers had received schooling until the age of fifteen, though a handful had left earlier and managed to learn enough typing and shorthand through night classes to qualify them for a clerical job. As a mill worker, Doris Hunt took evening classes where she learned (amongst other things) office skills. This allowed her to leave the mill and take an office job (along with a sizeable cut in her wages from £3 a week to £1 a week) at the age of seventeen.[148] Isabel Templeton, whose mother had illegally removed her from school when she was eleven, also subsequently found work in an office. She managed to persuade her mother to pay for her to learn typing and shorthand when she was fifteen, thanks to which she was able to find an office job in an accountancy firm. But like Doris Hunt, she found the pay less rewarding than she might have hoped. Despite the additional skills she had acquired she earned a very low wage: just eight shillings a week – less than a living wage and one she could only survive on because she continued to live at home.[149] Indeed, it is sobering to realise that even these women, with the skills and education to qualify them for office work, struggled to earn enough to live independently of their families. When the motherless Marjory Todd's stint of housekeeping for her father came to an end, she scoured the local paper for a job and hoped her few years at the grammar school might qualify her to work in an office. She knew there would be other more qualified applicants, but the real problem was the pay: 'Wages were based on the assumption that one lived at home and so had no rent to pay.' Marjory's strained relationship with her father meant that she was unable to remain at home, so clerical work was not an option as 'even had I been successful I would not have been self-supporting'.[150] This, as we have seen, was a familiar predicament for women. Even those fortunate girls who had managed to obtain a few extra years of education were not shielded from the problem of chronically low pay for female workers and the way in which this forced them into dependency on male wage earners.

Teaching alone offered working-class girls a living wage and the prospect of independence. The autobiographers who had completed teacher-training and went on to obtain work as a teacher reported advantages and experiences that have no parallel elsewhere amongst the female writers. Although there was a large gender pay gap in the teaching profession, with female teachers earning on average around half as much as their male counterparts, a female teacher's salary was nonetheless sufficient for independence from a male breadwinner.

As an uncertified teacher, Maud Clarke could earn eighteen shillings a week and when (following a further two years' study at night school) she became a certified teacher, her weekly earnings doubled.[151] Alice Bond's earnings as a newly qualified teacher were sufficient for her to pay eighteen shillings a week for her food and lodgings – bedroom, private sitting room, full board and laundry. The landlady provided 'better food than [she] had been used to' and even brought her breakfast in bed on Sundays.[152] This was a far more comfortable standard of living than most working-class women could dare to dream of. Newly qualified teachers were expected to go where they were needed, and they were paid a salary that permitted them to do this. The work was undoubtedly hard, but the reward was clear.

The long-term advantages that came with a teaching career help to explain why so many of the female autobiographers had regretted leaving school. Most of the girls who had longed to attend secondary school had had a future as a teacher in their mind's eye. For girls outside the factory districts, this was their one chance of an independent life, and secondary school was the only way to get there. In reality, though, this requirement for an extended schooling also made a career in teaching unobtainable for most. Amongst the autobiographers, all of the teachers had remained at school until the age of sixteen – many years after the statutory leaving age – and most had done some additional training at a teacher-training college as well. A teaching career was thus only accessible to girls whose families had both the means and the desire to maintain them for several years in pursuit of this goal. It was precisely this kind of familial support that most working-class girls lacked.

Not only were teaching and clerical work difficult for working-class girls to access, they also represented, with the exception of a handful of writers who progressed from secondary school to university, the furthest that most of our female autobiographers were able to go.[153] This is not to suggest that there was no female achievement of any kind. As we might expect amongst those who decided to write an autobiography, a small number of writers had achieved something of note in the fields of politics, social activism or the arts.[154] We will consider some of these exceptional women who managed to forge an adult life outside the usual bounds of working-class culture in this book's final chapter. Here it is important to note that even these women, who managed to achieve something unusual in their lives, had generally done so without enjoying any especial advantages in the workplace. Their achievements occurred *outside* the sphere of paid employment, rather than within it. Just two of the female autobiographers achieved some form of financial success through their own employment. One was Madge Barnetson, who obtained a job as a pharmacist's assistant at the age of fifteen and was then trained up by her employer to become a pharmacist herself.[155] She later married a pharmacist and they jointly ran their own business and raised their family of two sons. The other was Rosa Lewis, who started life as a general servant for a shilling a week and rose to become a highly sought after private cook to aristocratic households and a hotelier.[156] But for most working-class women, the world of professional work was completely inaccessible, no matter what combination of talent, drive, ambition and luck fell their way. Working-class girls joined the workplace in a limited number of roles in service, manufacturing, dressmaking, shops and offices, or just possibly teaching, and no matter how well they performed, they remained forever stuck in largely the same set of jobs at the same dismal rates of pay.

It is unsurprising, then, that so many women opted to marry. In most parts of the country, all that was available for women was a small range of poorly renumerated jobs with no prospect of progression. It was virtually impossible for most women to achieve a life of independence through their own labour, and this forced them to look elsewhere for economic security. It was not through work that women would take their share of Victorian Britain's economic boom for themselves; it was through marriage. Pat O'Mara observed that before her marriage in her late twenties, his mother was working in the clothing industry, 'a hard job, holding out little economic hope'. No wonder, he thought, she had taken the fateful decision to 'throw in her lot with my father'.[157] Marriage presented women with their best chance of a home of their own, a family and some kind of economic security.

Low female wages were not merely a passive reflection of a society that devalued women and their work. They also played an active role in keeping women subordinate, by forcing them into a position of dependency on men, first with respect to their fathers, then with respect to their husbands. Making sense of women's lives therefore requires us to move into an unfamiliar terrain. Women's experiences were not captured by male wage rates, yet they were deeply bound up with male earnings and male patterns of behaviour. As such, we need to bring the economic histories of men and women together. It is time to think afresh about women's lives by looking at the intimate, personal and sexual relationships in which money was generated and shared.

⤙ 2 ⤚

'A MAN'S WORK WAS A MAN'S LIFE'
MEN AT WORK[1]

'Work boy, work and be contented.'[2]

Looking back over more than sixty years, Jack Lawson observed that a man's life 'brings him memories so thick that they crowd each other out until only the few more vivid than the rest remain'. And he, like most men, had a few particularly vivid early memories seared on his mind. They were of his father – or, more specifically, of his father as the breadwinner of the family. Living in Whitehaven, Cumbria, Jack's father worked as both a sailor and a miner, a combination that was not uncommon in the town at that time. Thinking back to his father he remembered his early rising, his work clothes ('corduroy trousers and rough jacket'), his trade unionism, his 'long day of killing work in the mine', his climbing the steep road home from the pit, and his washing away of the grime of the pit when his day's work was done. In Jack's eyes, it was impossible to separate a man from his work. His father was 'an experienced pitman of the first rank'. And for precisely this reason, he was also 'a great man'.[3]

Work defined his father, and when Jack joined his father and elder brothers at the pit he quickly discovered that it now defined him too. He only earned tenpence for a ten-hour day, but 'still I was a man and I knew it'. And so did his family. No more minding younger children, washing dishes or cleaning boots. 'No more drudgery at home.' Now he could eat as much meat as he liked at mealtimes and wear shop-bought clothes rather than his brothers' hand-me-downs and cast-offs. He sat at the table with his elder brothers and father, talked about life at the pit 'and generally tried to live up to my newly acquired status'. It was a strange thing, he mused: 'ten hours a day in the dark prison below really meant freedom for me.'[4] Jack's observation captured the contradiction that lay at the heart of men's working lives. Male workers experienced low pay, long hours and dangerous, unregulated workplaces. Yet work also provided men with status and identity, and even a small wage assumed large significance in the midst of a poor and needy family.

It would be hard to exaggerate the significance of work for male identity, and though not all men provided such a clear account of the relationship between work and status in working-class communities as Jack Lawson, the centrality of work shines through the male autobiographies. Work was the key feature of a man's life and it was very often the motif by which male writers structured the story of their life. The titles of men's autobiographies underscore the point: *Autobiography of a Handloom Weaver*; *Autobiography of a Steel-Maker*; *Reminiscences of a Stonemason*; *Autobiography of a Cornish Miner*; *Memoirs of Gaius Carley, A Sussex Blacksmith*; *Autobiography of a Hackney Shoemaker*; *An Inspector's Testament*; *Garden Glory: From Garden Boy to Head Gardener at Aynhoe Park*, and so on. These are not isolated examples: the titles of around a third of all the male autobiographers contain information about the writer's employment or trade. It is a feature of the male autobiographies that forms a very stark contrast with those written by women. The number of female autobiographies that provides evidence of the author's employment in the title can be counted on the fingers of one hand, and in most of these cases it is not even clear if the title was provided by the writer or subsequently imposed by the editor.[5] For male writers, however, work was central to a life story, stamped on the title page and woven through the text as well.

As Jack Lawson's account of starting at the mine indicates, work was equated with manhood – 'I was a man and I knew it.' But Jack was not 'a man' when he began work. He was a boy of only twelve years old. Indeed, many Victorian children commenced their working lives considerably younger than that, particularly early in the reign when the place of children in the labour market was much more loosely regulated.

To a far greater extent than girls, boys' experiences of work were shaped by the legislative framework. In 1819, the Cotton Mills and Factory Act had prohibited the employment of children in cotton factories under the age of nine, and paved the way for subsequent amendments that protected older child workers and extended the provisions to children working in other textile industries, though enforcement remained lax until the establishment of the Factory Inspectorate in 1833. The Mines and Colleries Act of 1842 prohibited the employment of boys under the age of ten underground and of girls of all ages. As factories and mines had been the most voracious employers of child labour in the early years of the Industrial Revolution, these acts went a considerable way towards restricting the employment of the very young.[6]

This changing legal framework for child labour is clearly visible in the male autobiographies. Amongst the boys born before the 1870s, several entered the workforce before the age of ten, though generally only in those sectors permitted by law. We find a few writers who turned out for work at the very young age of five – they had undertaken simple employments such as bird scaring, bobbin-winding for parents and working at the mine surface.[7] Several more boys started work at the ages of six,[8] seven[9] and eight[10] – generally performing basic agricultural tasks such as crow-scaring and herding, or assisting parents who worked as weavers. Others worked in non-regulated industrial sectors, such as brick-making, metalworking, and at mine surfaces.

New legislation in the final quarter of the nineteenth century eliminated these remaining young workers from the workforce. The Factory Act of 1878 prohibited work before the age of ten and applied to all trades, and it was bolstered by the Education Act of 1880, which introduced compulsory schooling up to the age of ten. Subsequent amendments raised the school-leaving age first to eleven (1893), then to twelve (1899), with dispensations to leave before this age if pupils reached the required standards in reading, writing and arithmetic.[11] Unlike girls, there was no delay between leaving school and starting work for boys: they typically finished their schooling on one day and started at work the next. Harry Gosling, for example, spotted a bill in the window of some offices on his way home from school one Friday, and went into enquire. He got the job, and went home and told his father that he would be 'going to work next Monday', which he duly did.[12] As a result, the age of leaving school was very strongly correlated with the age of starting full-time work amongst the male autobiographers: in fact, in all but a few rare instances, they were identical to within a matter of days.

The 1878 Factory Act curtailed the full-time employment of children under ten virtually overnight. Very young child workers swiftly disappeared from the autobiographical record, and only a handful of parents managed to find employment for their underage sons. Seven years after the advent of compulsory schooling to the age of ten, Alfred Coppard's mother obtained a doctor's note for Alfred, at this point nine years old, declaring him unfit for school. As the adult Coppard continued, since affairs at home were 'in bad shape', his unfitness for education did not in the event 'preclude my going out to work' as a street-seller's assistant.[13] Rather later in the century, Sam Shaw's parents, similarly with 'family affairs . . . in a very bad way', withdrew him from school at the age of eight so he could sell matches instead. But their actions broke the law and were not free from legal consequence. In 1894, at the age of ten, he was still out of school and match-selling, but as the school leaving age had been raised to eleven a year previously he was still working whilst underage. He was arrested and sent to an industrial school.[14] The only other boys to leave school and start work in defiance of the law were Harry Fletcher and Henry Kelly. Harry's parents operated and lived on a barge and they put Harry to work with them when he was six. With no settled abode, it was easy for his parents to evade the attention of the school authorities: the family were effectively beyond the reach of the law.[15] Meanwhile Henry Kelly had no parents, nor even any memory of them. He spent his early years as a street urchin and received no formal schooling of any kind. Predictably, he was at work at an early age, though with no knowledge of his date of birth it is not possible to establish the age at which he entered the workforce.[16] Clearly, however, these were rather exceptional examples. Most families lived a more settled existence and could not circumvent the requirement to send their children to school.

The progressive raising of the legal age for starting work was highly effective in removing young boys from the workplace and can be traced in the average ages for starting work of the male autobiographers. Most of the boys in the pre-1878 period started work somewhere between the ages of six and fourteen, the average age being just over ten years old. After the legislation, the lower floor for starting work became ten years, and the average age shifted sharply upwards to thirteen. The new legislation was also accompanied by a cultural shift about the desirability of boys in the workplace, so rather than finding clustering around the new legal minimums of ten, eleven and twelve years of age, we continue to find a wide spread in the ages at which boys started work. In effect, the poorest families removed their boys from school as soon as the law permitted, just as they had ever done, whilst the more aspirational families continued to keep their children at school a year or two longer than their poorer neighbours. As a result, the average age at which the boys left school always hovered a few years above the rising legal minimum.

But whilst the age of leaving school and starting work captures a key aspect of the working lives of boys, there is one other aspect that it misses: the paid jobs that many boys did whilst still at school. Several of the male autobiographers indicated that they had obtained their first employment before ever having left school. The kind of work they did varied according to the locally available opportunities, but was always low-skilled work that could be fitted around the school day. In rural areas, most of the boys' work consisted in helping with the harvest during the summer holidays and other agricultural tasks, often on a seasonal basis.[17] Those in towns found work out of school hours as milk sellers,[18] newspaper sellers[19] and as errand boys and assistants for a wide variety of shops and businesses.[20]

Part-time jobs for school-age boys were common, but they were not spread evenly amongst the autobiographical writers. As might be expected, they were heavily clustered among the poorest families. The boys from the better-off families, who generally remained in education the longest, almost never started working whilst still at school. There appears to be just one example. Herbert Bennett's father had disapproved of him staying at the Higher Grade school after the age of thirteen. He eventually relented but insisted that Herbert got a Saturday job by way of a compromise.[21] This, however, was unusual. More commonly, work that bookended the school day was done by the boys from impoverished families, most of whom also left school as early as was legally possible.

For the most part, these writers' early entry into the workforce was prompted by the state of the family finances. Where fathers were low earners, or were ill, absent or failing in some way to provide for their families, their sons were invariably hustled into the workplace at the earliest opportunity in an attempt to make up the deficit. Jim Garnett's father, for example, had died in the Boer War when Jim was six. In order to help the domestic situation, Jim started working outside school hours for a 'Hairdressers Business' at the age of ten.[22] Allan Taylor's father was absent and he and his mother lived in her parents' two-bedroom house: there were twenty-one people living in the home. Unsurprisingly, Allan was involved in a variety of income-generating activities – selling newspapers, delivering milk and cleaning out herring boats – from a very young age.[23] A similar set of forces propelled John Edwin into the workplace before leaving school. His father was an alcoholic, 'unreliable and erratic . . . [and] frequently losing his means of livelihood', so there were 'hard times at home'.[24] It is little surprise, then, to find that whilst still a schoolboy, Edwin 'resorted to selling newspapers on the streets' on Saturday mornings. With little doubt, part-time work by schoolboys was a response to their family's poverty.

And the numbers involved were significant. In total, 30 per cent of the male writers indicated that they had begun paid work before leaving school. At the same time, the experiences of these boys illustrate how gendered all notions of work were, even in young children below the age of puberty. As we saw in the previous chapter, many of the girls had also indicated that they had begun 'working' whilst still at school, but for girls, this work meant childcare and housework, not paid jobs outside the home. Almost none of the girls had earned any income for their families before leaving school and, as we saw, many of them (a third) did not start earning when they left school either. For boys, the meaning of 'work' is much more familiar to us. It meant going out and earning a wage. Almost one-third of the male writers had started doing this whilst still at school, and the rest started wage-earning at the moment of leaving.

The part-time wages that boys were able to earn were of course small, yet it is still illuminating to probe the value of boys' earnings within the context of the family. The first wage that a part-time errand boy or milk boy could earn was often low – one shilling and sixpence – yet this was still on a par with the wage that some of the female learner dressmakers, domestic helps and shopworkers reported earning for a working week of up to sixty hours.[25] With a little more experience, this wage would rise and schoolboys were often able to earn as much from their part-time endeavours as girls in their mid to late teens could earn from full-time employment. Several of the Saturday boys and milk boys reported earning two shillings and sixpence per week, which was the customary starting wage for girls doing full-time work in many trades. This was the wage that James Clunie earned as an errand boy for a butcher's shop, though he also took home tips.[26] Jim Garnett's job at the hairdresser's involved only two nights after school and all day Saturday, yet he still earned more than the customary girl's wage: three shillings a week.[27] At the age of twelve, Walter Citrine had two part-time jobs before leaving school: a newsround before and after school, and a position as an errand boy for a butcher's on Friday evenings and all day Saturday. They each paid two shillings and sixpence, which put his total part-time earnings comfortably ahead of the full-time wage of a girl of his age.[28] One former newspaper boy calculated that if the news was 'hot' he could earn up to ten shillings a week from his after-school selling.[29] These sums also help to make sense of why so many families chose to keep their daughters at home rather than sending them out to work. It was not simply that girls' earnings were low, but rather that the inequality between the earnings of girls and boys was so great. Families split their sons and daughters between wage-earning and housework in order to pool the household labour in the most advantageous way.

Despite the prevalence of part-time work, school-leaving still maintained its significance as a turning point in a boy's life. After the age of around eleven or so, many boys began to perceive themselves as ready for work and were eager to leave the confines of the classroom. Their anticipation of full-time work is evident in their writing. A boy's first job was his gateway from childhood to adulthood, an event much anticipated and an important rite of passage reliably recorded in autobiographies written many decades later. For Bernard Taylor, starting work at the colliery as a half-timer 'was an occasion, a red-letter day, an important mile-stone in life's journey, a new venture'.[30] The milestone was even marked by a change of clothes. Out went the 'baggy knickerbockers' and in came 'long, smelly corduroy trousers held up by braces' – a new outfit which 'transformed you in a day from boyhood to manhood'.[31] Whilst still at school, Harry Dorrell was wearing an outfit that had been remodelled from clothes once worn by an older sister. As his fourteenth birthday approached his mother provided him with 'newly bought long trousers' – a change of wardrobe that was 'full of meaning'.[32] Jack Lanigan's mother spent no less than four shillings and sixpence on 'coat, trousers, shirt, stockings and shoes', but it proved a good investment because within a week she had secured him a job as a grocer's errand boy earning six shillings a week.[33] For boys, the break between childhood and work was clearly defined. Boys remained at school for as long as the law required and their parents' means allowed, and then directly entered the workplace and a new era in their lives. It forms a stark contrast to the experiences of girls, both in the clarity of the break between schooldays and work and the high hopes that surrounded it.

Connected with this enthusiasm for paid work was a radically different set of perceptions between girls and boys of the value of schooling and education. As we have seen, schooling was highly valued by the girls, and widely regarded as the ticket to something better. Few of the male writers shared this view. There were, of course, a handful of autobiographers with a desire for education and who expressed gratitude to parents who allowed their education to continue beyond the legal minimum.[34] Equally, a very small number of the male writers resented either their parents or hostile educational authorities for

2.1 A photograph of young male workers in their long trousers and waistcoats with their supervisors at Crowley's Ironworks in Sheffield. The back of the photograph reads: 'My colleagues at John Crowley Ltd most of these boys aged 13 years 6 months.'

thwarting their ambitions.[35] Yet in a collection of more than four hundred male-authored autobiographies, such sentiments were only rarely expressed and a great many more writers recalled their haste to get away. In the eyes of most male writers, extended schooling was not an opportunity, but an inconvenience that stood in the way of what a boy ought really be doing. For example, when Sam Smith was the runner-up for the scholarship to the grammar school, it 'caused [him] little worry'. Sam knew that the expense would have been a strain on the family income, and anyway, he 'wanted to earn wages'.[36] Several writers indicated that staying at school after others had started work was considered infra dig. Most of the boys at James Griffiths's school left after turning thirteen, which left him, as one of the youngest boys in the year, 'very lonely' at school. But worse still were the evenings, and his realisation that his 'old mates now belonged to a different world to me. They wore long trousers and flashy cravats.' They had money to spend on Saturdays and 'would keep chattering about their new world'.[37] James's thirteenth birthday could not come fast enough so that he too could leave school and join them. John Paton's mother had harboured a dream for her youngest son to stay on at school, but he had a different ambition: 'to cut clear from the prison that was school at the earliest possible moment, and go out and get a job'. This, he thought, was the ambition 'of nearly every boy of my time'.[38]

And whereas for girls the decisions about whether they would be occupied by school, paid work or housework were made by parents, in the case of boys, it was they, rather than their parents, who usually ended up calling the tune. For example, Wilfrid Beswick's parents were eager that he should have a secondary education so sent him to the Higher Grade School in Manchester after his elementary schooldays had ended. But he soon became 'restless and impatient to find a job' and left to start work as an errand boy after two years. After this failed, his parents, still keen for him to acquire an education, returned him to the school. But Wilfrid 'was tired of school', and so found himself a position as an office boy. This time he did not return to school.[39] Albert Pugh's mother had hopes that he might train as a teacher as he had always been a quick learner, but Albert had other ideas: 'no . . . I was determined to go to work'. He went ahead and got himself a job in a stone-breaking gang.[40] Just as girls had very little agency over their own destiny, parents had little agency over the destiny of their sons.

One of the most enduring themes of the male autobiographies, a tale told over and over again, was the great excitement they had felt at entering upon this new stage of life. The transition from schoolroom to workplace was a thrilling proposition in the eyes of most. Joseph Toole recalled his delight at the prospect of leaving school: 'Work! Independence! Wages and all they meant were on the horizon.'[41] Repeatedly, writers equated entering the workplace with freedom. Edward Stonelake, along with all the other boys in his class, were 'looking forward to our day of emancipation'. Quitting school meant 'freedom, freedom from the boredom and imprisonment' of the schoolroom.[42] For Edward Humphries, the prospect of leaving school to join the marines gave him 'the glorious feeling of freedom . . . freedom from school, from household chores, and doing jobs for other people; freedom to do the job I know I should like, and what is more be paid for it and never more be without food, bed, or clothing'.[43]

The reality of work for some of these young enthusiasts was inevitably sometimes rather different from the expectation. Like many a determined young lad, Ted Humphris had ignored his schoolmaster's suggestion that he continue at school after reaching the leaving age: 'I was adamant and disregarded his advice.' Instead he started work in the village as a farmer's boy. But he quickly realised he 'was not happy working on the farm, and was beginning to regret [his] hasty decision'.[44] These glum reports were also emphatically shared by those who started at the mill, and who, like the girls, soon discovered that the early rising, hard work and monotony of factory life were much more challenging than they had anticipated. Thomas Thompson realised in less than a week of starting at the mill that he had been 'led into a trap'.[45] In similar vein, when Harry Pollitt left school to start work as a half-timer in Benson's factory, it was at first 'a great thrill'. But rising at five-thirty in order to be at the mill by six was simply exhausting and 'the romance soon wore thin'.[46]

Yet if first jobs sometimes proved disappointing, they were just that: a first job. And for boys, first jobs were, by definition, temporary. Boys were expected to move through a range of employments throughout their adolescence, some of which might suit whilst others would not. Parents usually played a role in finding a boy's first employment, but from the age of around twelve boys could exercise some agency over how and where they wanted to be employed. If they were dissatisfied at work, they simply traded in their position for something more suited to their tastes. As we saw above, Edward Humphries had high hopes of joining the Royal Marines, but when those hopes were dashed he found himself employed instead as a sort of 'handy lad for odd jobs' at the vicarage – a position far from the one he had dreamt of. Nonetheless, he soon found there was 'much pleasure to be derived from doing my many jobs at the Vicarage well'.[47] But perhaps most importantly, it was, like most boys' first job, short term. Over the next few years, he moved through more than half a dozen posts, including as butcher's boy, page boy, kitchen boy, still-room boy, servant boy and pantry man. He finally realised his ambition of joining the military at the age of sixteen. Meanwhile, Ted Humphris may have regretted his hasty decision to start working as a farmer's boy but he did not have to live with those regrets for long. Within a month he had an interview with the head gardener at Aynhoe Park lined up and was soon off to start his training as a gardener.[48]

And although a boy's first job might be relatively menial, it was still an important part of growing up and it gave him higher status in the eyes of his peers. Even the lowliest part-time employment fitted around school hours was something to be proud of. As an adult, James Crawford could recognise that his first job – he worked on Saturdays as an errand boy for a grocery store – was 'not of earth-shaking dimensions'. But at the time, the position had given him a wonderful 'sense of achievement'. Best of all was being spotted by classmates around the town whilst touting deliveries in a heavy laden basket on his head:

'When I saw the envious and admiring looks of my school chums, I wouldn't have changed places with the winner of the Powderhall Sprint.'[49] Herbert Hodge's job as a baker's errand boy gave him 'the delight of doing real work just like a man'.[50] 'I now wanted to tell the world that I was now a man,' declared Jack Lanigan when he first started work.[51] And as boys moved onto full-time and higher wages, these feelings of pride intensified.

Along with the pride came an important process of acquiring skills. Adolescence was an extended period of work experience, and by his late teens a boy would have passed through this experience and be on his way to earning a man's wage. Wal Hannington's father was a bricklayer who suffered from the seasonal unemployment of the trade, and he wanted his son to enter a trade with better prospects. He gave his son 'free rein' for eighteen months to 'choose any available job in any industry', in order to establish for himself what line of work he would like. The young Hannington took 'full advantage' of the scope this afforded him, and had no fewer than ten jobs 'with a variety of experience' during the first eighteen months of his working life.[52] Work for boys during the teenage years was all about on-the-job learning and gaining experience. Hence the male autobiographies are peppered with phrases such as 'I spent about 2 years there and learnt a good deal';[53] 'I made good progress at the trade';[54] 'I thought it best to go to a place like that because you got wide experience';[55] 'I was learning and this meant a lot to me. And the more I learned the more satisfied I became'.[56] Indeed, learning was one of the most recurring themes of the men's recollections of their adolescent work and surely helps us to make sense of the rather negative attitudes that working-class boys had towards school. For a lad in Victorian or Edwardian Britain, the end of school did not mean the end of learning; instead it marked the beginning of a new period of learning, one that came with the considerable advantage of a weekly wage. As Ernest Adsetts summed up his leaving school and starting at the steelworks, 'and now my real education was about to begin!'[57]

For the first few years of a boy's working life, parents often played some role in determining how and where he was employed, but from the age of around fifteen or so, boys expected a greater say in the matter and parents ceased to exercise much control over their sons' choices. Rowland Kenney had started work as a half-timer in a cotton mill at the age of eleven and had 'loathed it' from the get go. After four and a half years an opportunity to work in a local stable opened up. Rowland was now fifteen years old, and he knew that leaving the factory would be met with 'opposition at home', but he still managed to get his way. He listened to his father's arguments against the proposal, but 'nothing he could say or do would prevent me from giving a week's notice, which I did, on the next pay-day'.[58] Bonar Thompson endured his job at a cardboard-box maker's for a year but 'a day came when I could stick it no longer', so he handed in his notice, much to his mother's displeasure. He too was fifteen at the time. This first act of independence marked the beginning of his adult life as he worked through a succession of jobs in search of employment that would suit him for the longer term. He found work as a van boy, but the work was too 'hard'. Then as a grocer's boy, but a month was as much as he 'could stand'. Next up was a position in a wine shop: the work was 'far too grievous to be borne'. He finally found work on the railways as an 'oiler and greaser', a position that he found far more congenial, and continued in for the next four years.[59]

Some boys had started to exercise autonomy over their work at an even younger age, particularly if relatively high waged work for boys was available. That was certainly the case for Frank Bellamy, living on the Durham coalfield. Frank was only thirteen when he contrasted the long hours that he was working as an errand boy with the shorter hours of the colliers and decided it was time for a change.[60] He soon had a job at the pit instead. Conversely, in the low-wage rural areas, parents could hold onto their control for a little longer, though even here such control could not be maintained into adulthood. In rural Herefordshire, Bert Coombes had lived out his parents' expectations throughout most of his teens but by the age of eighteen he had had enough of working on his family's farm for 'little pay'. As he later reflected, farm work did not 'suit my ideas of life. I wanted good clothes, money to spend, to see fresh places and faces, and – well, many things.'[61] Against his parents' wishes, he left the farm and migrated to south Wales to take up work as a miner's helper, then collier, and to explore the life that he felt he was missing.

Teenage boys were capable of finding their own jobs and were soon making their employment decisions independently of their family. The only critical thing was to remain in work. When Thomas Westwater lost his first job, he found that he 'got little sympathy at home'. 'I had brought it on myself and was told to get another job as quickly as possible.' He appeared to have done so on the second day of looking.[62] Other writers indicated the care they had taken to conceal any gaps in employment from their parents. When Leonard Ellisdon got into trouble at work, he was given a week's notice. He spent the week finding himself a new position so that he could 'evade telling them [his parents] I had got the sack'.[63] Neville Cardus lost his job at the printing works, and fortunately had no trouble finding another: selling chocolates in a comedy theatre. The difficulty, however, was that he was too ashamed to tell his family he had lost his job, so 'found myself obliged to continue getting up every morning in the freezing dawn and pretend I was still going to the printers'.[64] Very few boys spent much of their teens out of work. As Thomas Westwater concluded, his period of unemployment was anxious, but brief.

And as boys gained greater experience and skills in the workplace, they also began to derive greater satisfaction from their labours there. Work provided men with their male identity, and several of the working men recalled what Stanley Rice described as the 'sense of satisfaction' that came from work.[65] As an elderly man, William Watson could still recall 'the feeling of elation I experienced' when he was promoted from sweeping the floor and having to 'generally fetch and carry for everybody' in the workshop to using a handheld machine to make tiny iron rivets: 'it was the awakening of the creative instinct'.[66] When Harry Pollitt completed his boilermaking apprenticeship he had a 'great feeling of pride and craftsmanship'.[67] And attachment to work was not simply the preserve of the skilled workers. Satisfaction from a job well done could be felt by workers from all walks of life. James Brady's father was a humble clog-iron maker, but he was 'damn good at it' and 'proud of it'. His son remembered how he had enjoyed 'nothing more than working hard during the week', and spending his Saturday night with workmates in the pub.[68]

Along with the acquisition of skills and experience, a boy's wages started to rise. Thomas Bell started work for a local farmer at around the age of 'eight or nine' – delivering his milk in the hours before school for one shilling and sixpence a week. On leaving school at eleven he started working full time for a dairyman for three shillings and sixpence a week – a shilling more than the customary two and six that girls were able to earn. And he did not spend too long on this wage either. His next position as a van boy for a fizzy drinks manufacturer paid him seven shillings a week; then nine shillings a week for a job washing the bottles inside a drinks factory, graduating from the washing room to the 'syrup and labelling' for twelve shillings a week which rose in time to sixteen shillings a week – a decent wage for a boy of fifteen. Furthermore, this was still far from the end of his climb through the ranks of the labour market. At this point, his parents found him work in the iron foundry and a new cycle of progress began.[69]

The steady rise in a boy's wages was particularly pronounced in the high-wage industrial sectors. As a boy starting at the mine, Mr Roberts first earned seven shillings and sixpence a week, though he soon left this for a job paying half a crown a day – or twelve shillings and sixpence a week. By the age of nineteen he was working in the most skilled branch of mining, and by that age was able to earn more in a day that he had a few years earlier earned in a week: when working on a particularly favourable seam he could take home as much as twelve shillings a day.[70] There were many other forms of industrial employments, such as factories, foundries, engineering, quarries and docks, offering good daily rates of pay. William Collison threw in his work for a tea merchant once he realised that he could reduce his hours and still earn more by working as a casual worker in the docks. His new job paid nearly twenty shillings a week, and although the work was hard, 'the money was sweet and the freedom sweeter still'.[71] When he moved from there to warehouse work, his wage increased once more, earning 'as much as ten shillings a day'.[72]

These rising wages were also very much a male privilege, as all elements of production processes were divided by gender and remunerated accordingly. Looking back at his early work experiences as a 'machiner' in a sewing factory, one male autobiographer was keen to draw a distinction between the work that he did and the (somewhat similar) needlework that many women did. 'Let me explain,' he wrote. He was 'not a machinist. A machinist sounds somehow like a girl. A machiner was a man, a machinist was a girl. At first I worked on the linings and then sleeves. Eventually I could make a whole suit by myself.' It is hard to argue that making the lining and sleeves requires more skill than making any other part of a man's suit, or that making the constituent parts of a suit require skills that are unique to one sex. Yet dividing the work in this way was the foundation for setting unequal pay. As Burnett continued, 'I was paid £2 a week, good money in those days.'[73] It certainly was – comfortably higher than the wages that women could earn from needlework, even when they were operating sewing machines rather than working in workshops. Machiner, machinist: it made a very big difference.[74]

And of course, these wages were – and in stark contrast to those paid to girls – sufficient for independent living. George Barber's mother had died whilst he was very young and he did not have a family home to live in. At the age of fifteen, he was earning seventeen shillings a week. His board and lodging with Mrs Snow cost twelve shillings a week, leaving him five for his pocket.[75] By his late teens, Paul Evett had completed a printer's apprenticeship and was 'disgruntled with my pay, and anxious to leave home'. He admitted he did not have a clear motivation for wanting to leave, he just 'wanted to be independent', and on a wage of a pound a week he could have his wish. He found himself a new job and lodgings in Clacton-on-Sea.[76] Or Bert Edwards who, at the age of seventeen and a half, decided he wanted 'to leave home for the first time and stand on my own feet'. When he spotted an advert for a harness-maker in London that paid '25 shillings per week' he made the decision to move. With 'lodgings at 12 shillings per week' he had both independence as well as a quantity of spending money that was simply unimaginable for any woman of that age.[77]

Of course, not all male workers were on track to earn a pound a week by their late teens. As we would expect, there was a spectrum of earnings, and many men had to content themselves with far less. But even in low-wage sectors of the economy, the same trajectory towards wages that were sufficient for independent living was evident. Elijah Wells lived in the Suffolk fens, a region which could not provide wages to rival those of a miner, mill worker or docker. Yet he too retold a familiar tale about wages that rose steadily to the point of independence. Until he was fifteen years old, Elijah had spent his working life 'doing all kinds of farm work' and 'any work that came along', earning about six shillings a week, which he turned over to his mother for his upkeep. At fifteen years of age, he moved on to better-paid work for the Mildenhall Drainage Commissioners. In addition, he extended his earnings by doing carpentry in the evenings and harvest work – for 'double pay'. 'From now,' he reported, he 'was independent and self supporting'.[78] Male wages could be, and often were, low, but they were still enough for independent living. A boy's early wages were pocket money – often hardly enough to keep him in food and clothing. But they rapidly grew to a level that was sufficient to cover his family's expense maintaining him, and then rose beyond that, to provide him with enough to live independently of his family should he so desire.

The relatively good wages that were available to working-class boys and the ease with which they were able to move up the employment ladder, help to explain why they and their families did not tend to prioritise schooling above work. Instead, there was considerable concordance between parents and sons that entry to the workforce at some point between the ages of around twelve and fourteen was desirable. Work was not a second-rate choice to an extended education: it was an alternative and equally acceptable route to getting on in the world. Of course, when boys went to work they earned some income for the family and this was certainly a motivating factor in some families. Walter Southgate, for example, complained that his father had 'put a cold blanket' on his hopes of an expensive apprenticeship to a sculptor: 'The main consideration,' he explained, 'was that I had to bring a little cash into the home each week and to feed myself.'[79] Yet it is equally clear that work for boys was generally regarded as more than a short-term gain for the family coffers. All parties concerned realised that a job offered a boy the vital grounding he needed for the life he would spend in the labour market.

By the same token, it was quite possible for a family to take rather little interest in their son's schooling and yet still have ambitions for him. Bob Stewart, for example, grew up in a factory town, and his parents, like most others in the factory districts, took him out of school as soon as he was of legal age. At the age of ten he became a half-timer in one of Dundee's many jute mills, and at the age of thirteen he graduated to full-time employment. By the time he was sixteen he had worked in several of Dundee's mills in numerous different roles.[80] But his family had never believed him to be destined for a life in the jute mills. His mother's plan was to make an artisan of her son and after his six years in various mills she embarked on this endeavour. She found him an apprenticeship with a firm of joiners. The transition from the mill to apprenticeship was accompanied by a drop in wages, but Mrs Stewart had her eye on the long game. As a newly qualified journeyman shipbuilder, Bob was able to earn thirty-eight shillings a week.[81] For working-class boys in Victorian Britain, schooling, education and examinations were not perceived as central to getting on in life. Work was understood as the way to get ahead.

Even outside the confines of a formal apprenticeship, which was generally the preserve of the sons of better-off families, the right job offered the possibility of training. The autobiographers described a number of alternative, and more accessible, routes to the ranks of skilled workman for those who could not afford an apprenticeship. William Watson, for example, observed that his parents 'were far too poor to afford the £40 premium necessary for indentures' to become an engineer. In any case, they were not particularly interested in exactly what he did; they just wanted him out of the house and earning. Through a piece of good fortune, he found himself a job as a 'boy' in an engineer's workshop, and although he started by sweeping, running errands and being the shop's general dogsbody, he was soon given a simple task making rivets. He was good at it and so was moved on to other machines and processes. In this way began a long and successful career as an engineer.[82] George Healey turned his hand to over a dozen different occupations – including working in a silk mill, in domestic service, as a hotel porter, a travelling salesman, a butler, a hotel valet, a hatmaker, a dyer, a street seller, a waiter and a milkman – before setting up in business in one of these lines of work: hatmaking.[83] Even navvying, often depicted as requiring nothing more than brute strength, in fact embodied a host of specialised knowledge and skills. Albert Pugh described how he had rapidly moved across eight different roles after entering the trade – stone breaking, fatting and dodging the waggons, point turning, tool carrying, operating a steam crane, engine cleaning and firing a locomotive engine – before realising his ambition: driving the engine. And although Pugh spent the remainder of his working life building the railways, engine driving was of course a highly valuable skill in the context of the nineteenth-century economy.[84]

It is inevitably the case that those sons from more prosperous families enjoyed several advantages when they entered the workplace, enjoying better access to apprenticeships, to well-paid work and to jobs with training opportunities. Yet the workplace was extremely fluid, and it is evident that the higher echelons of skilled male labour were still accessible to those who started out with very few advantages. Robert Smillie had an upbringing as impoverished as they come. He and an elder brother had been raised in Belfast by their grandmother following the death of both parents. Although unable to start full-time work in one of the towns mills until he was twelve, poverty dictated that he turned out to work at a much younger age: by nine he was working as an errand boy. He had worked in 'several jobs' before he was eleven, at which point he started working in a cotton mill, first as a half-timer and then as a full-timer. At fifteen he crossed to Glasgow, where some experience he had already picked up with 'hammer, chisel, and file' found him a job in a brass foundry. The better pay – fourteen shillings as against the five he had been earning in the mill – was a definite attraction. From there he moved fourteen miles to Larkhall to join his brother working at a colliery. His new job – operating the pump – was 'dreary', but it came with a further pay rise: he knew he was earning ' "good money" for a lad of seventeen just commencing his mining career'.[85] In similar vein, George Mallard had experienced a miserable childhood, and was at work as a farm-boy by the age of nine. Yet he too subsequently managed to enter the ranks of the skilled working class. George was still working as a farmhand when the railway building for the Northampton to Market Harborough line passed through his village, so, fed up with farm work, George left his employer to become a railway navvy. He was not minded to return to the low pay and long hours he was used to when the railway around his village had been laid. Fancying to 'see something different or better', George took a train down to London on the new railway line he had helped to build in search of new opportunities. He soon found himself more work navvying on the London Underground, and from there he graduated to a position as a guard on the trains of the Great Western Railway that ran out of Paddington.[86] This was working-class respectability and provided George with an adulthood that was substantially more comfortable than his desperately impoverished childhood in the Northamptonshire countryside.

Regardless of when and where a man entered the world of work, it was often possible to move up within any given professions with relative ease. The tradition of on-the-job training offered men wide scope for finding employment that suited their interests, and progression was not governed by examinations and qualifications gained prior to starting work, but by the experience of work itself. It was thus possible for men who had left school many years earlier with no more than an elementary education to use opportunities in the workplace to progress into the more skilled branches of their chosen trade. And when on-the-job training petered out, there were night classes and technical colleges that provided a route upwards. When George Hodgkinson decided that his work at the Beeston Boiler Company was 'regimented, repetitive, and boring', he took a night class in order to improve his skills and find work with 'a greater challenge'.[87] Like many an ambitious young man, Jack Lanigan soon tired of his work as an errand boy and was pleased when his elder brother found him a new job for the corporation as a drain examiner. It was paid at a 'man's wage' – a handsome twenty-eight shillings a week, which marked an eight-shilling advance on what he had earned in the grocery shop. But the new role not only paid more, it also led him to 'take more notice of the structure of the department' he worked in and introduced him to the possibility of taking up a yet more senior position as a sanitary inspector. He started to take night classes in preparation for the exam. It was not easy. Lanigan's childhood had been extremely deprived and his schooling had been meagre. He lacked the literacy to have a successful go at the exams, and it was only thanks to some schooling from his wife (and after numerous attempts) that he eventually passed them.[88] Of course, the use of night schools and other forms of adult instruction suggest that education was in fact valuable as a means of progression within the workplace, yet this contradiction was not picked up by the male autobiographers themselves. Despite the reality it was very rare for male writers to interpret childhood schooling as the basis of success later in life. Instead a man's progress in the workplace was rooted in the experience of work itself.

Examples like these are not given to suggest that social mobility was the norm and that all men progressed easily and inexorably from their menial teen employments to well-paid, working-class jobs. Of course, a great many men stayed within the lower echelons of the labour market throughout a long working life – performing work that was hard, dirty, demanding and not especially well paid. It is also quite possible that such men were less likely to write an autobiography, and so the sources over-sample those who moved upwards compared to those who stayed put. But if autobiographies cannot be used to quantify social mobility, they can shed light upon its mechanisms. They reveal that although schooling for working-class children was limited, it was also largely tangential to a working man's job prospects. Aptitude and on-the-job experience counted for far more than qualifications in directing a man's working life. Indeed, Thomas Hunt recalled working in a paper mill in the 1870s, where boys of eight or nine started on the low wage of two shillings and sixpence a week. He observed the firm employed men who could neither read nor write, yet who could earn thirty shillings a week 'if they were good workmen'.[89] As Hunt indicated, men made progress in the workplace through the skills and effort they demonstrated there, not through advantages they had acquired before entering it.

Gender played an important role in allowing men to advance in this way as the large number of autobiographies written by women allows us to demonstrate. The employment opportunities that male autobiographers described cannot simply be explained away by suggesting that it was precisely owing to their successes in the workplace that they had written an autobiography. After all, women wrote autobiographies too, and they most emphatically did not describe analogous stories of upward progression through their paid labour. The explanation for this lies not in who got to write an autobiography, but is rooted in a more fundamental, social difference that existed between the sexes which restricted the ability of women to control the direction of their lives. The labour market offered men a variety of mechanisms by which they could find work that interested them and that paid well, even if they had had no more than a few years of primary schooling. These mechanisms simply did not exist for women.

The opportunities and mobility available to working men should not, of course, be allowed to conceal the disadvantages under which many men laboured. Much of the unskilled labour market was highly casualised, so earnings tended to be irregular. As the miner Emanuel Shinwell explained, mine owners could cut overheads by employing 'the largest possible labour force for three or four days, and then closing the mine for the rest of the week'.[90] So although the miner's day rate was good, weekly earnings were less predictable. Outside the casual labour market, very long hours rather than short-time working tended to pose the greater problem. Harry Hemmens's father was a journeyman baker and was regularly at work by six in the morning, continuing until eight or nine at night.[91] Harry Grossek's father was a tailor. He worked a twelve-hour day, with meals 'hastily snatched' and holidays 'at his own expense'.[92] Those in service worked particularly long hours. At the very end of the century, Ernest King worked seven days a week, starting at six-thirty and continuing until eight-thirty at night. 'Time off?' he asked. 'Every other Sunday after lunch and two afternoons a week – for a couple of hours.'[93]

As well as low pay and long hours, men also frequently had to work in environments which were unregulated and sometimes highly dangerous. Employers were under no legal obligation to ensure they provided a safe place to work. Nor did they need to offer their employees any kind of compensation for injuries sustained at work. The onus was upon the workers to assess the risks they were willing to take, which could leave them with some unpalatable choices. For example, William Armstrong's work in a smelting mill took a serious toll on his health. His son observed that those working with one newly introduced compound began suffering from a 'new disease . . . known as cholic', and nobody had ever survived three bouts of cholic. After suffering two debilitating attacks himself, William realised he had no alternative but to leave the mill and seek employment elsewhere. Not only was his health now permanently damaged, but the cost and responsibility for relocating and starting over was his alone.[94] When John Fraser slipped and fell off a wagon he was loading for the North Eastern Railway Company, he was not only confined to his bed for several weeks without pay, he was also dismissed. The superintendent refused to have him back, pompously declaring that he had been 'careless' and was a danger to himself and other workers.[95]

Nor was it simply in the modern industries that dangerous workplaces were to be found. Almost all the manual jobs of Victorian and Edwardian Britain carried some risks for their workers. John Hemmingway, for instance, worked driving a horse and cart and suffered two serious accidents that incapacitated him for several weeks at a time, one when he was loading the cart and another when his horse took fright and bolted.[96] He received neither sick pay nor help with his medical bills. And the outdoor nature of farm work carried a host of risks. Something as innocuous as pricking his finger on a thorn during the harvest caused Joseph Mayett to lose several weeks' pay.[97] It made no difference that John and Joseph had fallen ill whilst in paid employment. The minute they stopped working, the pay stopped coming in. In reality, male workers were forced to endure some serious disadvantages. All workers were but a hair's breadth away from injury, and entirely without protection should the worst happen. Although the final decades of the century saw some major victories for workers' rights, with the legal recognition of unions, a number of high-profile and successful strikes, and the passage of the Compensation Acts, these were as yet small steps and we must not underestimate the highly unequal balance of power between workers and employers.

Yet even if we acknowledge the very real difficulties and disadvantages that men faced in the workplace, it remains undeniable that their pay, conditions and opportunities were vastly superior to those available to women. For many writers, both male and female, the gendered nature of work was too obvious and too natural to warrant much discussion, but the situation was explained with great clarity by one woman who felt disgruntled at the gulf between her and her brothers. Bessie Wallis recalled how much she had dreaded the thought of leaving school. 'I didn't mind going out to work. It was just that girls were so very inferior to boys. They were the breadwinners and they came first. They could always get work in one of the mines, starting off as a pony boy then working themselves up to rope-runners and trammers for the actual coal-hewers. Girls were nobodies. They could only go into domestic service.'[98] When girls left school, they faced the prospect of unskilled, often heavy work for low wages and long hours, with very little prospect of advancement. And this was why marriage was so vital. Young women needed to forge a relationship with a male wage earner if they were ever to leave their family home, whereas men could achieve this through their own labour.

But perhaps the most important point to make about men and their work is also the most obvious: they got paid for it. Wages were paid to males, who carried them back to the family – and that act of bringing money into the home changed the bearer's relationship to those with whom the money was ultimately shared. With paid work came an enhanced position within the family. As one former miner perceptively noticed, when they started work, 'sons earned status as well as wages'.[99] The feeling of importance that came with handing over a wage, no matter how meagre, was frequently captured by the autobiographers. James Sexton's early employment in the local glass works earned him two shillings a week and paid the rent of the family's slum dwelling. As he later observed, his mother's appreciation of the money gave him 'an exaggerated idea of my importance in the scheme of things'.[100] Wilfred Pickles shared that 'feeling of importance' when he started work as an errand boy and made a much needed contribution to his family's income.[101] Even very small sums were sufficient to stir a boy's pride. David Davies earned a weekly shilling for a hard day's work as a butcher's Saturday boy: 'I was conscious of being somebody when I handed the shilling over to my mother . . . I glowed with pride. I was a wage-earner . . . I was a somebody for I was earning a shilling a week.'[102]

More than one writer recalled how the cachet that came with wage-earning more than compensated for the actual work itself. John Patterson's first thought at being put to work as a gardener's assistant for a penny a day was resentment over the loss of liberty, but he soon came to appreciate the benefits that came with his new role. After all, the job itself was not too bad: 'I did not mind work; I liked digging, weeding, sowing, attending to the cattle and what not.' Furthermore, there was something more intangible about his new place in the social order as a wage earner: 'Such things gave life an air of responsibility and made me somebody.'[103] As the autobiographers repeated many times over, male labour had a value which was universally respected within their families. Wage earners made a vital financial contribution to the household, which freed them of the obligation to help out with the housework. Michael Conway did not much enjoy working as a half-timer in a Stockport mill but, as he noted, as each child started in the mill 'they were relieved of most of the home jobs'.[104] Harold Brown observed that although his work as a miner was 'a strain', it came with the distinct advantage of freeing him from 'chores at home. These were now performed by my younger brothers.'[105]

Not only did male workers enjoy the status that went with wage-earning, they also got to enjoy some of the actual money itself. From the earliest age, boys were taught that, however meagre their earnings, some small portion was theirs and for their own exclusive use. Whether in the form of a hot dinner whilst at work, a few coppers returned to their own hands, or (as Jack Lawson remembered) shop-bought clothes and a bigger share of the food at the family table, boys soon learned about the privilege that came with being a wage earner.[106] Indeed, this no doubt formed some part of their enthusiasm for joining the workforce in the first place. At age eight and a half Ben Turner started helping his aunt with her handloom weaving for a minuscule threepence halfpenny, yet even these small earnings contained some reward for himself: threepence went to his mother, whilst Ben got 'a halfpenny for myself, and a new-baked, currant tea-cake to eat on my way home'.[107] And this lay at the heart of the breadwinner model. Men were supposed to use their earnings to support their family, but as wage earners they were also given to understand that a worker was entitled to enjoy some of the fruits of his labour. The point may seem small, but it was not for the millions of women and children outside or on the margins of the labour market and dependent upon a male wage.

The conflicting demands that earning and sharing a wage made on men who suffered from the usual frailties and vices that come with the human condition were captured by the autobiographer William Arnold, who glimpsed the possibility of escape from his miserably impoverished rural childhood when he found work as riveter in Northampton's thriving shoe industry. His family was large and his father, a rural shoemaker, earned little more than twelve shillings a week. William was at work in the fields from the age of six and had progressed to working in a boot-making shop by the age of ten. He used to 'bring home every copper I possibly could to my mother' to help feed his younger brothers and sisters: 'My money was a wonderful help to mother, I knew.' On finding better paid-work at the age of fourteen, he was able to earn more than twenty shillings – 'more than my father had ever earned . . . his whole life'. He thought himself 'a man now, taking man's wages'. And what could be more natural than spending some of his hard-earned wages on some little treat? After receiving his pay packet: 'Elated, I went and bought a little pork pie, which I enjoyed very much, and a pint of beer at the Rifleman public house, which suited also . . . and then gave my mother the rest.'[108] On moving to another employer, his earnings rose again, to twenty-seven shillings a week

– 'remarkably good money'. But as William's earnings grew, so did his sense of entitlement. His parents had only ever known poverty, he reasoned; they would not know what to do with his newfound wealth. Soon he was giving only 'part of my money to my mother', and keeping the rest back for himself. He developed a taste for beer, skittles and card playing, and by that means 'used to fool away a lot'.[109] It was almost inevitable that, as wages increased, so too did the amount that wage earners wanted to keep for themselves, particularly once workers were earning more than they owed for their keep. With even the most superficial understanding of human nature, it is possible to see the potential for conflict between male workers on the one hand and dependants on the other.

Many of the differences between men and women were not new. Men had always earned higher wages than women and women had always been marginalised in the workplace, only ever able to earn the most miserable of wages. This situation received a more formal intellectual justification in the nineteenth century as male unionists started to campaign for a 'breadwinner wage', but the phenomenon of unequal pay was not new.[110] What had changed, however, and remarkably so, were the opportunities open to working men. Prior to the Industrial Revolution, all workers – both male and female – had had limited options in the labour market. Of course, men had enjoyed access to a wider range of employment than women, and of course their wages had been higher. But they were still shoehorned into relatively few sectors, many of them providing very little in the way of opportunity. And this was what changed over the nineteenth century. Industrialisation helped to produce a dramatic expansion in employment opportunities for men and most of them could be grasped with nothing more than a few years of elementary schooling.[111] Low pay for women was nothing new; but the divergence in men and women's earning potential was. The significant improvement in real wages that men gained over the nineteenth century have been widely recognised and rightly celebrated. The purpose of this chapter has been to suggest that something less positive was hiding in its the slipstream: a sharp uptick in inequality between the sexes.

⤙ 3 ⤚
'REAL DRUDGERY'
HOUSE WORK[1]

'Housekeeping was no joke.'[2]

When Maud Clarke looked back over her life, she had very little to say about her husband or their adult lives together. Most of her recollections centred upon her childhood, schooling and the early home life she had shared with her parents and younger brothers and sisters in West Bromwich. Her husband was unnamed, though other records indicate that he was Nehemiah Clarke and that he worked (as his father had done) as a plater and foreman in the West Midlands metal industry. Maud wrote simply that she had given up work to 'marry my dear husband, whose life I shared for 52 years'. And although she did not provide any detail about their life together, she did make the following general observation about married life: 'Marriage is not just spiritual communion and passionate embraces. It is also 3 meals a day and work both inside and outside the home.'[3] Maud made it clear that she disapproved of mothers working outside the home, and she, like her mother before her, spent her married life engaged in what one later census-taker described as 'unpaid domestic duties'.[4]

Maud's assessment of marriage would have been recognisable to many of the autobiographers. No doubt some young men and women married because they had met and fallen in love and a few of the autobiographers enthusiastically retold the story of their courtship and wedding. But no matter what had brought a couple to the church porch, the nature of the relationship thereafter went far beyond the romantic. A bargain lay at the heart of the working-class marriage.[5] Marriage was a legal contract with economic implications: husbands brought home the wages; wives transformed them into care and comfort for the family. As Isabel Templeton explained, the young people in her days had been 'realistic' about the matter of marriage: 'Marriage was a contract of a

86

kind, an arrangement between two parties for their mutual benefit.'[6] It was a principle universally understood, and, of course, the roles were sharply defined by gender. John Blake pointed out that when his father returned from work on a Saturday and handed his 'quota to Mum . . . he considered his duty had been carried out', but her work 'just started from then'. The money Mr Blake handed over was not food and it could not be eaten. Considerable labour was required in order to turn that 'quota' into the material elements that ensured the family's well-being – 'faggot stews, with onions, turnips, and carrots and stewing meat', 'constant renewals of footwear and clothing', and much else besides.[7] After marriage, women were not expected to be wage earners, or at least not if there were children who needed looking after. But this did not mean that marriage heralded the end of their labour. It meant instead a fundamental change in the nature of the work that women performed. It is the task of this chapter to look more closely at the neglected history of housework and at why the need for unpaid domestic labour in Victorian and Edwardian households was so great.

The meaning of 'housework' has altered so significantly over the past two centuries that it can be difficult for modern readers to grasp exactly how labour intensive that work once was. The work of the house – the 'housework' – was not simply about cleaning, enhancing and generally improving the domestic environment. Before 1914, it involved the performance of more fundamental tasks necessary to sustain life. The home called for a daily round of collecting water, purchasing and preparing food, lighting and clearing fires, cleaning and repairing clothes and looking after children. In rural areas, firewood needed to be collected as well. The home could not function without water, fuel and food, and obtaining these things involved hard, physical work and took many hours daily.[8] Marriage and housekeeping might be an exciting prospect, but the reality of running a house was not. As one of the female autobiographers wrote: 'Without a doubt much of the work in the house was tiring or dreary.'[9]

Few working-class homes had an indoor water tap before the late nineteenth century, so running a home required a significant investment of energy in water collection. The experiences of Lewis Watson's family, living in rural Lincolnshire in the 1870s, were typical. His mother drew the household water from the village well and drinking water from the nearby river; she carried it back using a yoke and buckets.[10] In Robert Kerr Murdie's Northumberland village, the water spring was situated a quarter of a mile from the house – fetching water was one of the many jobs that fell to him to do after school.[11] Occasionally, families living in remote areas needed to travel longer distances in their pursuit of water. One writer recalled having lived in a house where the well that supplied the water was situated nearly a mile away.[12] Those living in towns generally enjoyed better access to water, and by 1900 some working-class families enjoyed their own indoor tap, though this yet remained firmly an urban phenomenon and largely the preserve of better-off families.[13] In the first decade of the twentieth century, Leily Broomhill shared a couple of rooms with her family 'at the top' of a large house on the Kingsland Road, Hackney, and they had to go 'right down to the bottom for every drip of water we wanted'. The toilet was even further away – 'right down, in the back garden'.[14]

Access to water was best in the Lancashire cotton districts. By the early twentieth century, a few families here even knew the luxury of hot water on tap fired by a coal- or gas-driven boiler. Elsie Dutton was living in a small terrace in Salford at the turn of the century and enjoyed hot water thanks to a coal-heated iron boiler 'bricked into the back kitchen', but she also noted that her neighbours had 'few facilities such as hot water' and that it was 'easy to be dirty'.[15] Hot water was working-class respectability, as those who had it understood only too well. Mrs Dickenson moved into a house in Manchester with a water boiler in 1907, yet it is clear that the hot water was quite a novelty. She mentioned it no fewer than four times in an autobiography that only ran to two pages. She also indicated that the family's possession of a hot-water tap was the cause of jealousies with the extended family who lived without any such comfort in the neighbouring streets.[16]

The relatively early uptake of heated water in the Lancashire cotton towns was no doubt related to the fact that hot running water was something especially valued by women and that women's work and wage-earning in the factory district empowered them to invest in this area. None of the autobiographers outside the cotton districts mentioned hot-water taps and many, even in towns, were still collecting their water from a shared standpipe in the street. Interior cold-water taps were particularly rare in the mining districts, and heated water was unheard of.[17] Progress was also uniformly slow in the countryside, with many rural families continuing to collect their drinking water from rivers and wells down to the First World War and beyond, and heated water an unimaginable luxury.[18] Despite some improvements in urban areas, particularly the cotton districts, at the very tail end of our period, water fetching was the norm for the great majority of Victorian families and for many Edwardian ones

3.1 Water collection in Guestling, East Sussex, in the early 1890s.

as well. This constituted a considerable labour requirement for all homes and helps to explain the ongoing importance of unpaid female labour in the working-class household.

The same was true of fuel for both cooking and heating. Throughout the nineteenth century, most working-class families used solid fuel – coal, usually, in urban areas and wood in rural areas – for all their cooking and heating needs. Both required constant cleaning of grates, ranges and flues, and for those families who burned wood rather than coal the wood had to be collected and chopped before use, which (as one writer noted) 'meant a lot of hard work'.[19] Gas cookers and gas ranges became available as an alternative to solid-fuel ranges in the homes of working families in the 1890s, but at this point it was very much the preserve of better-off, urban workers. Reader Bullard's father had once worked as a casual dock labourer, but by the time his son was born he had regular employment as a foreman on the British and Foreign Wharf and earned a very good wage of thirty-five shillings a week. When the gas main was

3.2 Collecting firewood in East Sussex, *c.* 1890.

laid, his was 'the first house to be connected up'.[20] As with the laying of water pipes, there was some further improvement after 1900, but large parts of the country remained untouched by the new technology. Maud Clarke and her family moved into a new house in 1903 which she described as 'large' and 'modern', but she also noted that all cooking was still done on coal fires.[21] The use of gas for cooking and heating remained unknown in most working-class homes, particularly those in the countryside, where families remained dependent upon solid fuel up to and well beyond the First World War.[22]

In the absence of gas or electricity, even such a simple requirement as lighting for the long winter evenings involved labour. Lewis Watson recalled that in the early years of his childhood, the home was lit by tallow candle, but after his father got a better job and 'our conditions had improved', the family decided to invest in 'a fine large paraffin lamp with glass chimney and globe and a small benzolene hand-lamp to carry about'. The paraffin lamp emitted much better light than a candle, but what stood out most in Lewis's memory was the work that went into maintaining it: 'In looking back at all these things, one sees the drudgery the mothers of those days had to perform. These lamps had to be "trimmed" and cleaned three or four times a week, and if the wick had not been properly attended to, we had a smoky lamp chimney and a bad light.'[23] Vera Wright concurred. The daily trimming of the oil-lamp wicks was 'quite a chore', she recalled.[24] Gas lighting very slowly started to enter working-class homes, but only in the last decade of the century, only in urban areas, and of course only in the most affluent households.[25] Gas lighting was hardly a new technology at this point. It had started to enter middle-class homes in the 1850s, yet it was far from unusual for our working-class writers to recall first witnessing the innovation in the twentieth century.[26]

Added to the work surrounding the collection of water and fuel was an unending cycle of meals to prepare, and although the labour surrounding water and fuel was starting to diminish in some urban households by the end of the century, cooking remained an unremitting and inescapable element of housekeeping. Solid fuel ranges made even the simplest of culinary tasks time-consuming and arduous, as the substitute housewife, Benjamin North, could testify. Benjamin had lost his mother at the age of four and his only sister lived out in service, so by the age of seven 'most of the domestic work fell on me'. As an adult he could vividly recall his struggle to boil the water for his father's tea: if 'my fire was too big, [the] kettle would boil over and put my fire out', forcing him to start a second time with a new fire and causing a considerable delay in preparing his father's tea.[27] There was no refrigeration, and for most of the nineteenth century there was very little in the way of processed foods to buy outside London and other major cities. In small towns, there were few opportunities to cut back on meal preparation beyond buying a loaf of bread from the bakers rather than baking it at home, and in rural areas not even that was available. In many homes, bread was made by hand, and almost all other elements of the family meals were bought on a near-daily basis and made from scratch. The provision of three meals punctuated a woman's working day, starting with an early rising to light the fire for breakfast and continuing until evening.[28]

On top of this was the washing and cleaning. Without electricity and modern appliances, this too was hard and heavy work. Over and again the autobiographers, both male and female, recalled the early morning lighting of

3.3 Wash day in a Manchester court in 1908. On the left of the frame, two dolly tubs are situated beside the stand pipe, and another two sit in front of the woman and child in the centre. A line of washed linen is hanging on the right.

the fire, their mothers' heavy dolly tubs, the carrying of water from tap, to fire, to washtub, and the mangle for wringing the clothes.[29] Some writers devoted pages to describing the now-forgotten equipment and processes that had formerly consumed their mothers on the weekly washday.[30] Frank Rayment considered that his mother's weekly washing day 'was really hard labour'.[31] Yet more energy was devoted to trying to get the clothes dry, outside weather permitting or inside in small, cramped homes.[32] And along with the clothes, the interior of houses had to be kept clean. The amount of physical effort that had gone into the scrubbing of floors and polishing of ranges was recalled by several of the autobiographers.[33]

In addition to the cleaning of clothes was the making of them, that 'constant [renewal] of footwear and clothing' to which John Blake referred. This, like the collection of water, fuel and food, was necessary work for the functioning of the household. Throughout the nineteenth century, working families spent little on readymade clothing. Underwear, hosiery and children's clothes were usually made in the home, and most mothers undertook an extensive programme of repairs and alterations in order to extend the life of all clothing.[34] George Ratcliffe recalled that his mother had 'made everything that was worn by the family except boots and my father's hats'.[35] In all households, when repairs were no longer feasible, the fabric was cut up and remade into clothes for a smaller child in the household. Francis Crittall noted how the 'discarded garments' of parents, relatives and elder siblings were 'restored, remodelled and reduced' by his nimble-fingered mother until they fitted the 'various shapes' of the younger children.[36] George Gregory's mother was a skilled seamstress whose programme of alterations resized clothes from one child to the next 'until the point of non utility was reached'.[37]

The work involved in keeping clothing in decent repair was particularly important in the mining communities, where sturdy moleskin clothing provided a vital protection for its wearer. Elizabeth Andrews recalled being put to this task from a very young age: it 'was hard work. The needle and thread had to be waxed for nearly every stitch before I could get it into the moleskin. This job often kept us at it until the early hours of the morning because of the long hours the miners worked.'[38] Some writers noted their mothers occupied with knitting or sewing in the evening or observed how their mothers had never sat down with their hands empty. Alice Bond's mother, for example, 'was never without knitting in her hands unless doing other work'.[39] This was not crafting as a form of leisure. It was an important contribution to the household's resources. Mrs Bond had a family of thirteen and she knitted the socks and stockings for every member. Disposable income was scarce in a rural family like the Bonds and the provision of clothing was a contribution no less valuable than the cash earnings of other members of the household.

A layer of labour surrounded many aspects of household life in ways that have now been long forgotten: salt that came in a solid block and had to be crushed with a rolling pin before it could be used;[40] ovens with flues that needed weekly cleaning if they were to function properly;[41] toilet paper that had to be fashioned from old newspaper and threaded onto a piece of string;[42] beds that 'got very lumpy if not pummelled regularly every morning';[43] laundry soap that had to be made from rendered fat and wood ashes and grated before it could be used;[44] fires that needed to be 'banked' with household waste and cinders last thing at night in order to provide some warmth for a five-thirty start the following morning.[45] The unpaid, domestic work performed by mothers was central to any child's welfare. As one writer observed, 'I learnt at a very early age that a child's health and happiness depended so much on a mother's care and good management.'[46] Little wonder, then, that physical aspects of maternal work formed such a staple element of working-class reminiscences. Nor were a mother's domestic labours necessarily considered easier than paid work outside the home. As Henry Hemmens noted, 'If a man's hours were long in those days, those of a woman were longer still.'[47]

Of course, some corners could be cut, particularly when it came to washing and cleaning as opposed to the more unnegotiable requirements of water and fuel collection, food preparation and clothing repair. The wash might be left for another week, the floors left unscrubbed, the blackleading of the grate or the stoning of the front doorstep left for another week. But scrimping on the cleaning was a perilous route, because cleanliness formed the dividing line between decency and poverty. Mothers had various ways of explaining the principle to their girls. Mrs Green told her daughter in the 1880s that 'it was no disgrace to be poor but it was to be dirty or ragged'. Unmended clothes 'betokened poor housekeeping and low standards'.[48] Nellie Carbis's mother 'had a saying: "Being poor and seeming poor is the Devil all over." ' Despite the family's lack of funds, she considered it important to 'put a good face on things'.[49] Looking back on her childhood in Salford, Elsie Dutton noted that 'poverty, dirt, and squalor were everywhere' and she recorded in some detail the battle that her mother and two foster mothers had waged against dirt. It was necessary work: keeping the home, children and clothes clean was a vital way of differentiating the family from those who had 'let themselves go to the dogs and [given] up trying', those who had lost 'all self respect'.[50] As an adult, Richard Hillyer realised just how heavily the fear of dirt had fallen on his mother's shoulders: 'For anyone to have found her house dirty, or her children's clothes unmended . . . was torture.' Her simple wish was that no one should look down on her.[51]

The significance of dirt and squalor was also understood by those who were raised on the other side of the poor but respectable dividing line. Jane Walsh recalled the dawning realisation during her childhood that as well as being poor, her family was (to borrow Mrs Green's terminology) in the 'dirty or ragged' category. She was a 'dirty slum kid'. Her home was 'mucky'. Washing herself and her clothes was a novelty, and one that she learned about outside her home rather than within it.[52] As a young adult, Jane took on the responsibility of doing a weekly clothes wash for the family, despite now being at work herself and despite the considerable labour it involved. From her perspective it was worth the effort – her act of resistance to her poverty-stricken surroundings, a weekly reminder that an alternative life was possible.

A few of the autobiographers believed that their mother's cleanliness had served as a public statement of respectability rather than a task that was strictly necessary in its own right. Harry Pollitt, for instance, thought that all the cleaning, scrubbing and polishing that went on in his working-class community was driven by appearances – a subterfuge so that 'people thought you were better off than you ever dared hope to be'.[53] But subterfuge or not, cleanliness could also be important for a woman's own well-being and sanity. Married women spent most of their lives in the domestic sphere and generally lacked any other outlets for self-expression, creativity or autonomy. Alice Foley considered her mother had led a difficult life, yoked to a 'feckless husband whom she neither loved nor understood' and drained by his frequent 'drunken binges'. Yet she kept her home 'beautifully clean'. The grate was thoroughly raked each day, the floor freshly sanded, irons scoured, the house was 'really spic and span'.[54] It is likely that cleaning provided Mrs Foley with a way of creating some peace in a life that was often anything but peaceful.[55]

3.4 This unnamed woman was photographed cleaning the exterior of her home in Wigan by the local photographer, William Wickham, in 1891.

The amount of domestic work required by any given household depended on a number of factors, such as the local availability of water and fuel and the size of the household. But the division of responsibility was always the same. Running the household was women's work, and although some chores, such as wood-chopping or boot-cleaning, were often undertaken by the men of the household, the overall responsibility lay always with their wives. Marriage thus marked a discernible shift in a woman's life, and one that female writers frequently commented upon. The change was obviously most dramatic for those who were working in service. They had to hand in their notice. Sarah Jones noted with some regret that once she and her fiancé decided to marry, she had to leave her position. Her employers were 'real Christian' and treated her with respect: she was 'sorry to give up such a good home'.[56] (She had been hurried into marriage by a suitor who 'wanted to get married for he had no mother' to keep house for him.[57]) But even those who had not been working in service usually needed to make some fairly major adjustments to their working arrangements. Hannah Mitchell was a dressmaker living in lodgings, but she realised that she would not be able to combine the long hours expected by her employer with her housekeeping duties as a married woman. She too gave up her position when she married.

By the early twentieth century, and if the husband's earnings were sufficient, some women gave up all form of work at the point of marriage. Jack Lanigan recalled the conversation that he and his wife had had when they returned from their honeymoon. 'Should I go back to work Jack?' she asked. No, he told her: 'The doctor advised you to obtain a lighter occupation and so you shall, you shall stay at home, besides . . . it is infra dig for a newly married woman to turn into work.'[58] But this was 1912. Jack was a respectable council employee earning twenty-eight shillings a week, and the couple, unusually, were economising on the cost of housekeeping by house-sharing with her parents. Maud Clarke, whose very brief account of her married life was discussed at the start of the chapter, also permanently gave up work when she married. But once again, her situation was unusual for a working-class woman. She was working as a teacher, a professional occupation where a marriage bar operated requiring her to give up her position. And she was also, like Jack Lanigan, marrying in the Edwardian period, by which point ideas about the incompatibility of marriage and paid work were becoming more widespread.

The majority of the female autobiographers who married before 1900 had not only continued to work after marriage, they do not even appear to have expected otherwise. Of course, marriage meant giving up their current position of full-time employment, but it did not mean giving up *all* paid work. After marriage, work had to fit around the housekeeping, and most women found something better suited to their new status rather than stop working altogether. Sarah Jones may have given up her place in service when she became Mrs Wrigley, but she soon discovered that her husband's wages of eighteen shillings a week did not go far: two shillings and eight pence went on the rent and an almost equal sum went on his tobacco and 'pocket money', leaving, after other expenses, too little for comfortable living. She took in plain sewing and washing – 'anything to save a shilling or two' – before her first child arrived.[59] And though Hannah Mitchell gave up her position in the dressmaking shop, she too continued to earn money after marriage. Also finding it difficult to make ends meet on her husband's wage, she began to take in dressmaking. This, she recalled, 'eased the financial strain', but it was bought at a price: 'sewing, cooking, washing, clear starching, and baking bread, pies and cakes . . . I found myself caught in a sort of domestic treadmill'.[60] But this was marriage. In every household, the cooking and cleaning needed to be done, and on getting married these duties became the wife's responsibility.

The assumption of a raft of domestic duties was, for women at least, the most frequently discussed aspect of marriage, but there was of course another change. Along with marriage and housekeeping came sex. What sexual pleasures, or otherwise, that the autobiographers found in marriage is difficult to discover, as they were far more reticent about sex than about most other aspects of married life. It is likely, though, that for many, sex was a new experience. Some form of sexual activity prior to marriage was of course not unknown, but the rates of both illegitimacy and bridal pregnancy were low and declining up to the outbreak of the First World War. In contrast to the early nineteenth century and earlier, when sexual experimentation before marriage was widespread and pregnancy was often the spur for marriage, couples in the second half of the nineteenth century and the early twentieth century were more risk averse and, judging by the bridal pregnancy rate, less likely to engage in penetrative sex before having tied the knot.[61]

The autobiographies make plain that both men and women were often woefully ignorant of sex before their wedding. In fact, women's ignorance of sexual matters extended beyond birth control and encompassed all matters of female sexuality and fertility. When Amy Taylor began to menstruate, her mother dispensed her one and only piece of advice about 'anatomy': 'You'll have this every month until you're fifty and keep away from the boys . . . that was every bit of information I was given.'[62] Edna Wheway was one of several female writers who had not understood what was happening to her when she began to menstruate. She had seen the girls in her orphanage making 'white dusters' and been given six herself when she left, with the instruction, 'You will know what they are for when your time comes.' Edna was sixteen and working as a domestic servant when her 'time came', but she did not know what was going on: 'What a shock I had then. I thought I must have done something wicked and was being punished.'[63] A fellow housemaid filled her in, and she at last realised what the white dusters were for. Edna's ignorance was not due to the fact that she was raised in an orphanage: it was entirely typical of girls of her generation. For a host of reasons, generally rooted in poverty, women did not typically reach the age of menarche until their late teens. Many had left home by this age without having received any guidance from their family or schools. As Margaret Bondfield wrote, when she first began to menstruate (or, as she more discreetly wrote, 'began the usual phenomena connected with maturity'), she was 'terribly frightened'. She thought she must have 'burst a blood vessel and was doomed to death'. She put her ignorance down to the fact that her mother, though a radical in politics, 'was not advanced on the subject of sex'.[64]

Given this reticence about basic bodily functions, it is hardly surprising that most grew up without any knowledge of sex. Patrick McGeown was raised in a one-roomed tenement 'without the least hint or training about sex'. The subject was taboo amongst his peers, for they had all 'inherited the vast reticence of our parents'.[65] For simply asking his mother where he had come from (on the encouragement of some 'bigger boys playing on the road outside'), one child immediately received 'a terrific smack on the side of the head which sent me reeling away'.[66] Despite the lack of space in most working-class homes, the sexes were kept separate and bodies were firmly covered up. When Lennox Kerr was asked to strip naked for a medical examination at the age of sixteen, it occurred to him that the sensation was highly unfamiliar: 'I could not remember ever having the whole of my body naked at the one time.' It was the same for everybody in his household, as he realised that he had 'slept with my brothers for many years, but I had never seen their bodies'.[67] Some did not know that underneath all the clothing lay anatomically different bodies. At the age of thirteen, one male writer caught an unintended glimpse of a female cousin's 'nakedness' whilst she was changing her clothes in the kitchen. This was his first realisation that 'they are built differently from me', and it gave him 'a lot of food for thought'.[68] Innocence about sex was shared by all. Looking back, Herbert Hodge concluded that 'I don't think my ignorance was exceptional. None of my friends seemed to know much about it.' Just one of Herbert's friends claimed any knowledge – though it transpired, in fact, that 'all he knew was how to masturbate'.[69]

Pregnancies were unnoticed and unremarked in many households, their significance not understood by the children. Several of the autobiographers reported that their mothers, though repeatedly pregnant, had never intimated as much and that as children they had been wholly unaware of impending births.[70] 'Nobody discussed the coming of babies' in James Drawbell's household, so the arrival of new babies occasioned some surprise.[71] Even the word 'pregnant' was too much to handle for some. When Jennie Lee's mother was expecting she described herself as 'heavy footed'. In fact Jennie herself, writing in the 1930s, also avoided the world pregnant: 'Heavy footed', she noted, was 'her reticent way of saying she was with child.'[72] The mere sight of a pregnant woman made Margaret Bondfield feel 'hot all over', for, as she explained, 'one was not supposed to know anything about a baby until or unless it appeared'.[73] Many girls believed in storks and doctors' bags well into their teens. Going on fifteen, Kay O'Loughlin had thought the nurse had brought her sister-in-law's 'baby in her black bag'. She was puzzled though: 'How could baby fit into such a small bag?'[74] Maud Clarke noted the large black bag that her mother's birth assistant brought and thought 'she must be bringing us a new baby in that black bag'. She also wondered, however, 'why mother should scream, when Mrs Knowles had been kind enough to bring us a new baby'.[75] Mary Flood was told by her mother that 'she had ordered a baby' and given to believe that it would arrive (from Heaven) when they had got enough money together to pay for it.[76] The lie had to be fleshed out further when Mrs Flood had a stillbirth. Mary was informed that the baby had caught cold 'on its way from Heaven . . . it's a long journey'.[77] Elizabeth Harrison summed up the situation for all: 'Sex education was completely absent from my upbringing both at home and at school.'[78]

Inevitably, then, some women entered marriage with very little understanding of the sexual side of their new status. Sex was, quite simply, a closed subject. Kay Pearson recalled the sick fear she had felt on her wedding night. When she was young, she explained, 'girls could not converse with their Mothers as to-day, so knowledge of intimacy and matrimonial matters were also zero'.[79] Jessie Gear had been raised 'not knowing where babies came from, or how they got there'. She was twenty-one before she learned the 'facts of life'.[80] Marjorie Graham's mother had explained to her about the 'bleeding', but 'told me nothing about boys' – indeed, she only learned about the anatomical difference between men and women when she became sexually active.[81] Others despaired: 'My Mum told me nothing.'[82] 'I was very naïve and knew nothing about sex,' recalled Vera Ward. Her mother had warned her that 'you had to be married before you let a man touch you' – advice that she took quite literally: 'I thought she meant kissing.'[83] Growing up in the slums, Jane Walsh had witnessed many 'drunken scufflings in back alleys' and considered she knew about the facts of life – 'you could hardly help that . . . in our neighbourhood'. But she did not understand the 'emotional implications' of sex or how the scufflings in the back alleys related to the 'physical side' of her own impending marriage. She would have liked to talk about it with someone, but 'it wasn't any good asking poor mother. She just got terribly embarrassed and changed the subject.'[84] One of the autobiographers managed to get pregnant with no idea as to what had happened or why. After a few months of marriage, Amy Rose noticed she did not want her breakfast and 'felt rather queer . . . my tummy seemed all wrong and felt rather funny'. After a week with no improvement, she confided in her sister who replied 'well you're married', but even this explanation was lost on Amy: 'I could not think what ever she could mean.' Amy was 'simply done' when she at last realised that she was pregnant.[85]

Childbirth also remained shrouded in mystery. Once again, the female writers indicated that knowledge about birth was not passed from mother to daughter. One woman went into labour without knowing 'where she [the baby] was coming from'. She had thought 'they cut you up the front'. And this was despite the fact that her mother had seven children and also worked as the local midwife. She had never mentioned 'anything like that' to her daughter.[86] Nor was she alone in her ignorance. Another entered her first labour assuming her baby would 'come out from the navel'. Like other female writers, she had been ignorant about her first period and 'was frightened to death' by it. For many years she did not realise her periods and pregnancies 'were connected'.[87]

Maybe marriage brought sexual pleasure to some – we cannot know, as the autobiographers do not tell us. But what it certainly brought was a cycle of pregnancy and childbirth. And Victorian and Edwardian families were relatively large. Demographers have estimated that the average family size was around six live births in the Victorian period, declining in middle-class families around the 1870s and falling in other sections of society in a piecemeal process thereafter.[88] The size of the autobiographers' families closely matches those of the general population. The average size of the writers' sibling group was six children, though as infant death and child mortality were high, this suggests a higher than average birth rate amongst the autobiographical mothers. There is also some evidence of a modest decline in family size over the period, though the effect was slight. Amongst the writers born before 1860, the average family size was six children. From 1890, the average family size was 5.5 children.

Inevitably, a more diverse pattern underlay these averages. After 1890, the most common family size of the writers was in fact just three children, yet this was counterbalanced by a sizeable cohort of much larger families. For some of the autobiographical mothers, marriage had brought on a decade or more of largely uninterrupted childbearing. James Bullock was one of twelve children and reported that 'never since her firstborn arrived could [his mother] remember when she was not either suckling a baby or expecting one'.[89] Bert Edwards's mother had a family of thirteen children, with about sixteen months between each, thanks to which (he wrote) she 'was always ill'.[90] Remarking on the large family of her husband – he was one of fourteen children – Annie Howell observed that people at that time (the 1890s) 'didn't know nothing about birth control. Or not much about it anyway.'[91] Maggy Fryett was equally fatalistic: 'I had nine. No way of stopping them. If there had been, I would have done. We never took nothing, nothing at all.'[92] Indeed, despite the preponderance of families of three children, there were still as many autobiographers raised in families of seven or more after 1890 as there were raised in families of three or fewer.[93]

Maggy Fryett was quite correct that there was 'nothing to take' to prevent her conceptions, but there were of course ways of reducing the probability of pregnancy even without anything 'to take'. Indeed, it likely that some form of family limitation was being practised even in some of the larger families. A family of six children may seem large to modern eyes, but the age of marriage in the nineteenth century was relatively young, and we would expect a woman marrying in her early twenties and not practising any form of fertility control to have more than six children. Certainly, many of those women who married in their late teens or early twenties yet went on to have just three or four children must have been practising family limitation. Yet there are few clues in the autobiographies as to quite what couples were doing, as not only did writers tend to know nothing about their parents' birth control, it was also very rare for them to write openly about their own solutions.

In the absence of proper information about contraception, most married women soon figured out that abstinence and withdrawal offered the best chance of limiting their family. The trouble was that these methods called for co-operation from their husbands, and with the home so sharply demarcated as a female rather than male sphere this kind of co-operation could be hard to obtain. Aida Hayhoe had three children and 'didn't want no more'. Her solution was to 'stay up mending [so] my husband would be asleep when I come to bed'.[94] It is likely that Aida's husband tacitly agreed to practise family limitation with her, though interestingly she does not describe this as a shared decision they had reached together. And inevitably, not all women were so lucky. With seven children and an unemployed husband, Tabitha John thought it was 'senseless' to have more children and she knew perfectly well what needed to be done. But she could not get her husband to agree. He, she continued, would 'not prevent them in anyway, he was a proper nature boy, always said, "You can't go against nature." ' Tabitha ended up with nine children, rather than the 'two or three at the most' that she would have had if she had had the choice.[95] At any rate some combination of abstinence and withdrawal explains how so many working-class children were raised in relatively small families.[96]

Occasionally the autobiographies provide a glimpse of the measures to which women turned in their desperation to limit their families. Faith Osgerby's mother told her daughter about her unsuccessful efforts to abort her – she took gunpowder, 'mixing it to a paste in a soapdish on her washstand every night'.[97] John Langley did not really know the cause of his mother's death, which had occurred when he was only five. The aunt who took him in a few years later was frank about most things, but 'would never tell me real things in an outspoken manner'. She told John that his mother had died from a perforated bowel, but from what he remembered of the terrible poverty of his early years and his mother's neglect of his twin sister, John later wondered if his mother had not perhaps passed away in the process of trying to procure an abortion.[98] But abortion was illegal, so it was, unsurprisingly, not something that the autobiographers routinely discussed. So far as we can tell, abortion was the very last resort for pregnant women, and married women were more likely to try to prevent a pregnancy than to terminate it.

So marriage meant sex and that meant children. And the raising of children emphatically fitted into the wife's sphere. Fathers were never present for the births of their children, and there is virtually no evidence of any of the fathers in the autobiographies being involved in the day-to-day work of caring for small children. Indeed, in many households, almost everything pertaining to the home, both large and small, was a mother's domain. As more than one writer explained, mothers were the pin that held the family together. 'Family life was closely knit, attached to mother, who was the linchpin of the family wheel,' wrote Walter Southgate. 'Nothing was done without mother being consulted.'[99] Fathers, by contrast, were often peripheral to the running of the domestic sphere. Catherine Cookson considered that in her Tyneside neighbourhood at the turn of the century, 'the house and all in it was the woman's task, and it lowered a man's prestige if he as much as lifted a cup'.[100] She believed that 'the lower down the working class scale you were the more this rule applied', and it may well be that in the very masculine world of Tyneside shipbuilding, men's disdain for the domestic sphere was particularly acute. Yet if disdain for domestic work was not universal, the belief that responsibility for it lay with women was. Herbert Wells's father was a respectable shopkeeper in Kent, but he too came from a family where 'the women folk saw to all the indoor business. A man just didn't bother about it.'[101]

Along with the housework and the children, there was the budgeting and general management of domestic affairs that fell within a woman's domain. Women did not necessarily earn money for the household, but they played a major role in determining how it was spent. As John Blake said, his father's duty was complete once he handed over the wages; but his mother's work just started from there. Women's financial contribution to the running of the home came in the form of spending money rather than earning it. The skill with which their mothers had transformed a small wage packet into a week's wholesome meals was fondly retold by many. David Kirkwood recalled his mother turning over her husband's pay in her hands: each week, 'she counted and took care of the scanty wages'. From that meagre sum, she 'planned out the week's need'.[102] The ingenuity and resourcefulness that lay behind their mothers' housekeeping was a regular source of pride for the autobiographers. The miracle of the 'loaves and the fishes is not in it', wrote one writer, recalling how his mother had provided for a family of eleven on a weekly wage packet of nineteen shillings.[103] Fred Kitchen thought that his mother's life had been 'a constant endeavour to make ends meet – ends that were too wide apart ever to make a straight and lasting joint'. How she had done it was just 'one of those mysteries'.[104] For families living close to the margins of a decent existence, the wise spending of the breadwinner's wage was hardly less important than its actual amount.

Although men provided the money, the gendered nature of domestic work meant they often played very little role in how it was spent. One of the female autobiographers, Nellie Scott, had thought it was laughable when her local co-op store informed her she needed her father's permission to take over the family's co-op book after her mother had passed away. She 'stood and looked at them, and then said: "My father takes no interest in this or in anything concerning us, and if I am not made the member not one penny will be spent here." ' They were clearly convinced by her argument as 'they made [her] the member right away'.[105] Isabel Templeton remembered how her father had 'left everything to do with the house' to her mother, 'even things like buying a chair or a bed. He would tell her, "you know best about these things" and he'd go off to his game of bowls, or he'd disappear outside to the garden.'[106] Len Wincott recalled the menacing interest that his father had taken in all his children's boots: after playing at football in the street 'we were obliged to remove our boots and hand them over to the ogre for inspection. Woe betide the unfortunate who had kicked out one of the heavy hob nails he had covered the soles with.' But as he also noted, it was his mother who solved the problem of replacing boots that had worn out or become too small. It was she who found 'the shoe factory which was selling rejects cheap – and found the money too, for that matter'.[107]

Gendered assumptions about budgeting and shopping accorded women considerable control over the allocation of resources within the household, but we should also be aware of the limitations of that control. Underneath the stories of female domestic authority is a more depressing reality: the endless worry that went with assuming control of a family budget the size of which lay outside your control. Hannah Mitchell described her attempts to get her husband 'to reckon up the cost-of-living with me and keep a sort of weekly budget' in the early days of her marriage. 'But he refused, just handing his wages over and leaving all the worry to me.'[108] Mrs Layton's father left 'the responsibility of the whole family to my mother'. As the family eventually comprised fourteen children in all, that responsibility was considerable. It rendered her (in her daughter's estimation) a 'perfect slave'.[109] 'What troubles, what stresses,' Arthur Newton observed, the family's perennial 'shortage of money caused her.'[110]

As the autobiographers repeatedly made clear, marriage was a partnership with different roles and expectations for husbands and wives. Fathers brought home the wages, and mothers converted those wages into care. For most writers, both male and female, marriage was keenly anticipated and warmly welcomed, but the transition to marriage and housekeeping was a much more transformative event in a woman's life than it was for her husband. For women, the start of housekeeping meant the immediate assumption of responsibility for running the home and although that might initially be combined with some form of paid employment, most women had to abandon their paid work once children started to arrive, as motherhood greatly increased both her work and responsibility, causing an ever deeper retreat into the home.

It should go without saying that some husbands and wives relished and enjoyed their gender-specific roles, to the benefit of the children who lived with them. Bertha Whittle's father had started work in a mill as a half-timer at the age of ten, rising to become 'a fully trained Loom Overlooker' by his late teens, and eventually an 'Inside Manager' – a position 'as high as he could [achieve] in his employment'. His efforts permitted his family to live in a comfortable, three-bedroom house. Theirs was regularly the first household in the neighbourhood to install the latest home improvements – an upstairs bathroom, a gas cooker, a modern, easily cleaned kitchen floor, heaters for the bedrooms. Meanwhile, his wife played out her part as the homemaker: she was 'the perfect helpmate and supporter for this very busy man'. Mrs Whittle was a 'marvellous cook' and 'very good self-taught dressmaker' – a 'real homemaker' who created a 'peaceful haven for her family'.[111] Together, Bertha makes clear, they created a very happy home for their three children.

But the rigidly divided gender roles could also be problematic. Mr Whittle's wages formed the foundation for all the family's security. The household functioned smoothly not only because Mr Whittle worked hard and earned a decent wage, but also because he invested his income in the family home. And this points us towards another possibility that we need to consider. How reliably did the wages paid to men reach their wife's purse? How many men lived up to the fine ideal of Mr Whittle? And what happened to families when they did not?

PART TWO

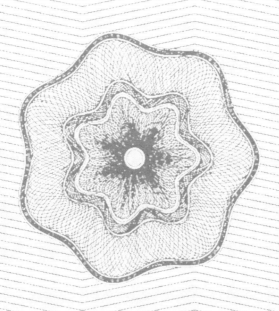

MONEY

4

'THE MEAL-TICKET'
FATHERS AND BREADWINNING

Daisy Cowper's father was a skilled mariner, but he was not the best worker. He was a heavy drinker and 'quarrelsome with crew and owners alike'. And although his family knew nothing about seafaring, they knew that his drinking and quarrelling was causing a problem. Frequently he would fall out with his crew and 'throw up the job', with the result that his intervals between jobs steadily increased whilst the jobs themselves became smaller, 'leaving mother struggling with little money and an ever growing family'.[1] Yet although Mr Cowper's contribution to his wife steadily diminished over the years, his claims upon her did not. His youngest daughter considered him 'selfish'. Whilst at home, he made heavy demands on both the family's resources and his wife's labour. He liked to receive the same food at home as he got at sea: 'So mother, with several boys to get off to school, and with a baby in arms, would have to manage to have a coal fire burning by his breakfast time to serve him with boiled potatoes, boiled fish, eggs and coffee . . . Yet he lay aloft in comfort.' And, of course, he never failed to claim his conjugal rights. He generally returned to sea leaving her 'as usual with another infant coming'. He fathered nine children in all.

At some point during twenty-five years of marriage, Matthew Cowper slipped from being a provider to being a burden, and when that happened his family's estimation of him slipped as well. When his ship was wrecked and Matthew was killed, the event was not the devastating blow to his family that he might have imagined. In fact, his daughter Daisy felt 'happy'. She wept when she saw her mother's grief, but that, she hastened to explain, 'was sympathy for mother's tears, not grief for a lost parent'. Admittedly, there was the loss of his income, but as he had long since ceased to make a regular provision for his family that was 'no new thing for mother'. His children did not miss a father who was 'always strict, and latterly, of uncertain temper', and his wife (Daisy later surmised) was 'relieved to know that her child-bearing was over'.[2]

As Daisy's account of her childhood makes clear, family life involved a complex web of rights and responsibilities. Her father's place in this matrix was simple: he was responsible for providing for his wife and children and his execution of this duty outside the home earned him special rights – with respect to food, service and sex – within it. Provision lay at the heart of working-class conceptions of fatherhood, and time and again, writers used this as the benchmark with which to evaluate their fathers.[3] We will use this benchmark as well. Let us ask simply: how well did the autobiographers' fathers provide for their families? The question should not be understood as asking how *much* they provided. Working men possessed very different levels of skill and so commanded widely differing rates of pay. Inevitably, those situated at the lower end of the scale handed over a far smaller pay packet than those at the upper end. The question, instead, is: given an individual man's skills and capacity for earning, how well did he actually provide for his family? The answer to this turned upon two related factors: how regularly a father worked, and – crucially – how much of his earnings he actually shared with his family.

In order to answer these questions, we need to work systematically through our collection of 662 autobiographies. Some need to be discarded at the outset. When a father had exited a child's life, either through death or desertion, the adult writer was often unable to comment reliably on his provision, particularly if the separation had occurred early in his or her life. For this reason, we will remove those writers who became separated from their fathers during childhood – their experiences are discussed more fully in the following chapter. This reduces our sample by just over 170 autobiographies, leaving us with a collection of 491 to work with. All of these writers were raised by their fathers and most, though not all, wrote something about them. And because of the huge importance of a father's wage-earning to the well-being of a working-class family, the quality of the father's breadwinning is relatively straightforward to establish in the majority of these cases.

The foundation of the working-class family was the male wage, and a recurring memory in the autobiographies was the weekly tradition of father handing his earnings over to mother. Billy Cotton recalled that his father was 'dead straight about money'. In old age, he could still see his father 'taking his leather purse, lifting up the flap, and putting the money down on the table.

"Here you are Sukey", he used to say, and mother would take it and reach high up to the mantelpiece and put it there.'[4] Edward Robinson's father was not a high earner, but he was a good provider for his family. Although his income as a cab driver was uncertain and sometimes small, he handed every penny he earned over to his wife on a daily basis, who set about transforming it into food. On a bad day, Edward's meal might consist of nothing more than a half-penny bloater with bread and butter, but anything more provided the family with 'a good dinner'. It helped that his father did not drink or smoke – his life 'was just work and sleep'.[5] Mr Robinson's behaviour did not provide his family with fine living; his earnings were simply too low for that. But it did ensure that young Edward enjoyed a degree of comfort and security throughout his early years.

Mr Robinson was certainly not alone in performing his breadwinning to the best of his ability and with good grace. Gratitude to hard-working fathers – to men like John Blake's father for their years of 'self-denial, devotion and constant effort' – runs throughout the autobiographical literature. Those writers who spoke positively of their fathers frequently framed their discussion around all that they had done for their family rather than their personal qualities. Harry Gosling, for instance, considered that his father had been 'a model father', who had done 'everything in his power for all of us'.[6] Bernard Taylor's father was always 'doing the best for his family'.[7] Arthur Horner's father had a responsible job on the railways and a number of interests outside the home, but above all, he 'always had a very high sense of responsibility and of devotion to his family'.[8]

A steady wage formed the bedrock of a family's welfare, and the father who had laboured hard to earn it was usually fondly remembered. John Clynes's father was a 'fine worker'. He took no holidays and used his earnings to ensure his children got the schooling that he had missed.[9] Some of the autobiographers were fortunate that their fathers took on additional work as well. Chester Armstrong's father had a demanding job in a smelting mill, but he always signed up for any overtime that was going spare.[10] Rosina Harrison's father added grave-digging, seasonal farm work and a post as the church caretaker to his regular job as a stonemason.[11] John Brady's father worked a series of second jobs around his main occupation as a clog-iron maker and spent what he earned on holidays for his family.[12] Phyliss Buss's father took on extra work for the fire department so as to be able to buy nice extras for his family.[13] Others kept gardens or allotments in order to make life more comfortable for their loved ones.[14]

4.1 Mary Bentley's father earned an above-average wage of twenty-eight shillings a week as a foreman at a firm of coopers and worked a second job as a collector for a local doctor. He took pride in providing for his family and pleasure in spending time with them, as illustrated by this studio portrait of a well-turned-out and contented family. Mary is the second from the left.

Along with regular work, overtime and additional jobs, good fathers made their earnings go further by depriving themselves of some of life's little pleasures. Henry Turner's father had regular work as a lamplighter and earned a little extra by spending his spare time cleaning windows, but it also helped that he spent very little on himself: he hardly drank, and his one indulgence was the occasional smoke – roll ups as thin as a matchstick.[15] Fred Bower's father was an 'exceptionally able, conscientious, and hardworking man', and the family coffers were further enhanced by the fact that he had 'no hobbies'.[16] Some fathers aspired to save money so that they could invest in a comfortable home that all the family could enjoy. Mr Howitt had a house built with a bathroom and 'modern washing facilities' and was delighted that his four older sons came and re-joined the rest of the family in it.[17] Thanks to the commitment of Frank Sturgess's father to the home, the family moved from candles to paraffin lamps, and then to electric lighting: 'we thought this was the height of luxury, you just press a switch and a light comes on'. Theirs was the first house in the village to install electric lighting and it was the 'talking point in the village for some time'.[18] Carpets, chairs and a piano adorned Dorothy Fudge's home, thanks to her father's efforts.[19]

Without a doubt, the breadwinner model worked well in some families, but it is still important to ask: how often did it do so? To answer this, we need to return to our collection of autobiographies. Of our 491 autobiographers, 213, or 43 per cent, provided evidence that their father had been a reliable wage earner who dutifully shared his earnings with his family. Good breadwinners were not necessarily those who earned the most: actual earnings could be, and often were, small. Instead, good providers were those who worked steadily and shared their earnings generously with their families. No matter the size of the pay packet, most of the autobiographers believed that a steady-working, family-oriented father had provided a reasonably comfortable and stable start in life. Yet these writers constitute less than half of all the autobiographers, so we clearly cannot close our account of fatherhood on the comforting image of men working second jobs to purchase little luxuries for their families. Although some fathers both worked hard and shared their earnings, a great many others, apparently, did not.

Breadwinning and provision were highly valued amongst working-class writers, yet time and time again the writers, like Daisy Cowper, make clear that this was not something that their own fathers had been able to achieve. To start with there was the perennial problem of unemployment. Margaret Powell's father was a painter and decorator – a 'sort of general odd-job man'. But, as his daughter explained, most people did not want the bother of home improvements during the coldest months, so every winter he struggled to find work.[20] In his daughter's eyes, his struggle to provide for his family did not diminish his worth as a father. He delighted in buying the children a comic and a bag of sweets on Sundays and his family knew 'he did the best he could'.[21] But it did, of course, have a very significant effect on his family's quality of life. Amongst Margaret's earliest recollections was the realisation that 'other children seemed to be better off than we were'.[22] That poverty of her upbringing, might, she later concluded, be sociologically interesting, but experiencing it 'was just plain foul'.[23]

More occasionally, men were afflicted with such bad health that they were unable to work at all. Arthur Collinson's father, for example, had worked as a coach-builder until Arthur was five. At that point he lost his sight and his family lost its position amongst the 'great mass of poor' and joined the 'under privileged'.[24] Cases such as these exposed the weakness of the breadwinner model. With virtually nothing in the way of state support for families that fell on hard times, breadwinners who were out of work, whether through unemployment or ill health, were left with nothing beyond what little insurance they may have been able to take out against such calamities. Inevitably, insurance was the preserve of the more skilled workers: the great mass of the workforce were never in a position to insure themselves against unemployment. And even for these privileged few, insurance was quickly exhausted, leaving not just them, but their entire families, facing destitution.[25]

Yet gesturing to unemployment and ill health scarcely scratches the surface of the weaknesses of the breadwinner model. Alongside the relatively small number of men who were unable to earn a living for their families was a much larger number of men who were able to provide, yet made choices that left their families with less than they might have had. Although fathers were supposed to be breadwinners, not all undertook this role with much relish. Joseph Wright's father simply did not enjoy hard, manual labour. He could earn a decent rate in the iron mines, but he much preferred leisure to work. If he worked steadily 'for perhaps a fortnight he would take a holiday and spend what he had earned'.[26] Jean Rennie also lamented that her father 'although a good workman, was not a steady one'.[27] Henry Coward's mother married a man who 'did not take to persistent regular work, but liked a job or post . . . that he could do when and how he liked'.[28] Arthur Harding thought that the presence of his father had done very little to add to the well-being of his family. According to Arthur, he was 'a loafer' and 'too lazy to earn a living'.[29] As such examples demonstrate, a small number of men did not work consistently. And when they did so, the consequences for their families were serious. As Harry Cast observed, when his father 'was not doing much in the earnings bracket . . . our standard of living deteriorated accordingly'.[30] Mr Wright's 'happy-go-lucky temperament' in the matter of work ultimately reduced his family to destitution. With four young children and a husband who refused to hold down a job, Joseph's mother eventually sought refuge in the workhouse as the only available source of support for herself and her children.

Unemployment, ill health or a simple disinclination to work could all leave families without access to a male wage. Yet amongst the autobiographers the number of fathers who did not bring home a weekly pay packet was relatively small. The autobiographers were far more likely to recall a father who earned a steady wage but failed to share it with their families than a father who did not earn at all. It was of course customary for men to keep a part of their wages as 'pocket money', or to expect special privileges in the form of a greater share of the family's food. It is difficult to get a sense of exactly what amount of pocket money was deemed reasonable, and it is worth pointing out that when earnings were low, even a small sum creamed off by the male head of household was to the detriment of everybody else's nutrition.[31] But let us accept that a small amount of pocket money and/or dietary privilege was a widely accepted perquisite for a male wage earner. The problem nonetheless remained that wages were paid into the hands of the male worker, not his wife. This is why memories about the passing of the wage packet between husband and wife on a Saturday after work were so significant. The manner in which this small, personal transaction took place was fundamental to the well-being of the entire household. Clearly, though, the allocation of wages between male pocket money and female housekeeping money was a matter that could be decided by the male wage earner alone, and the outcome of this imbalance for family finances is as predictable as it is obvious.

In the eyes of some autobiographers, their fathers had reserved for themselves more 'pocket money' than seemed acceptable from the family perspective. Muriel Box's father earned a respectable two pounds a week, but refused to hand it over to his wife for housekeeping, declaring, 'You can't draw blood out of a stone!'[32] The result was 'daily bickerings over money which erupted into savage rows and, on very rare occasions, blows'.[33] Various versions of this story were told many times over.[34] George Williams's father, for instance, had just the same attitude towards the money he earned. According to his son, he 'cherished one fixed idea about wages ... he would never disclose the amount of his weekly pay-packet, not under duress or caress, not by wheedle or needle. Every week a certain sum was handed over, the rest a private matter.'[35] There was a ritual in Leily Broomhill's household whenever her mother's housekeeping money ran low: 'she used to say to us children, "I'm going in the other room. Don't come in. I'm going to ask him if he'll let me have any money." ' The outcome of these attempts was always the same. She would return to the children and 'shake her head. He never hit her, and they never quarrelled, but he never gave her any money.'[36] Albert Jasper's father was so desperate to keep a chunk of his income for himself that he always slipped 'his money bag under his side of the mattress' before falling asleep. In order to make quite certain that his wife could not take his money for the housekeeping, he even occasionally slept with it in his sock.[37]

Men had a variety of motives for withholding part of their wages for themselves. A few were involved in worthy social or political enterprises. Robert Oakley, for example, fell in with the Methodists. He was not wasting his earnings in the pub, but he was still diverting money away from his family, and what was good for Robert's spiritual needs was much less beneficial for his children's nutrition. His wife lamented that he was 'going so much to chapel and taking the money away to give there that my children and I so badly wanted at home'.[38] John Allaway's father was a respectable supervisor for a metalworking business, and involved in a number of mutual societies – Grand Master for the Order of Buffaloes and 'chairman of this club and that'. In his son's opinion, his personal spending on these causes forced his mother to 'pinch and scrape more than she need have done'.[39] Kate Taylor's father's hobbyhorse was the village Salvation Army band. Despite the family's 'poverty-stricken condition', he used to invite his fellow bandsmen to dine on the Sunday meal his wife had prepared, leaving his hungry children to 'scavenge for any crumbs they may have left'.[40] Some men's desire to keep their earnings to themselves was simply inexplicable. As a child, Grace Foakes had never liked her father. He was 'unsociable', 'unfriendly' and 'grumpy'. In her teens, when her mother fell ill and Grace took over the family housekeeping, she realised that he was also a miser. Although he was earning 'quite good money' at this point, he gave her just £1 10s a week and told her she 'must learn to be thrifty'. When her father inadvertently left behind the key to a drawer in his bedroom that he always kept locked, Grace learned the huge chasm between her housekeeping money and his true means. The drawer was stuffed full of '£1 notes, all neatly tied in packets'.[41] For reasons that Grace was unable to fathom, Mr Foakes was hoarding his wages whilst his family went without.

In reality, though, most of the men who diverted their earnings away from their families were not inexplicably squirrelling it away in locked drawers or putting it towards religious, political interests or other worthy interests. They just liked to spend it on themselves. John Paton's father, for instance, was wrapped up in the pursuit of 'old glories as an athlete'; Frederick Gould's by a 'passion for the operatic stage'.[42] Vere Garratt could only marvel at his father's abiding passion for gambling on the horses. The sums he wasted on the horses were 'incredible' for a man 'with a large family and slender resources'.[43]

Mr Gawthorpe had no end of things he liked to spend his earnings on – he kept a mistress and fathered a child with her, he liked a drink at the pub, gambling on the races and placing 'adventurous sixpences and even shillings . . . [on] the pay-as you-enter competitions' advertised in the newspaper.[44] Joseph Sharpe's father was a 'connoisseur of whippets and greyhounds'. He had income sufficient to buy meat for his dogs, but not, unfortunately, for his children – his son recalled a scanty, vegetarian diet of 'tea sops, oatmeal porridge and flour porridge'.[45] He ran 'barefooted and barelegged' too. In other families, financial problems were caused by 'another lady',[46] a 'Lady friend',[47] 'another woman',[48] 'that woman',[49] 'a mistress, whom he referred to as his "partner" ',[50] and a 'glaring indiscretion' that resulted in the birth of a child.[51] Nellie Hoare's father believed in 'sharing' his wages with his wife. This meant keeping half of his earnings to himself and giving her the other half: 'He used to spend his fifteen shillings on beer and tobacco and I remember he used to smoke a clay pipe.' Mother's fifteen shillings went on rent, food and clothing for a family of ten.[52]

Most commonly of all, male wages were being used to fund drinking habits that had run out of control. Running like a thread through accounts of working-class family life is the father who earned a good wage, but drank away most of what he earned. Alfred Coppard summed up the situation for many. His father, he wrote, was 'something of a drinker, and so we were always shockingly poor'.[53] Drinking was the reason that Albert Jasper's father stuffed his money under the mattress or into his sock whilst he slept. Although he 'always had money', his son complained, his mother never had a full week's wages off him because 'his main object in life was to be continually drunk'.[54] Drink was also the reason that Jane Walsh's 'whole childhood was enveloped in the vicious circle of little money, more beer, and then even less money in consequence'.[55] In Bolton, Alice Foley's father only worked in 'fits and starts', as his life was punctuated with bouts of heavy drinking which incapacitated him for work. Occasionally, 'he disappeared for weeks, leaving his whereabouts unknown, then just as suddenly he turned up penniless and unkempt'. During such interludes, his wife took on the role of breadwinner, though her meagre earnings from the washtub were obviously no substitute for her husband's wage. And the loss of earnings was not the least of it. Sid Foley's drinking sprees not only impoverished his family; they also put it at risk of unpredictable eruptions of violence. When recovering from a boozing bout, 'his temper was most vicious and unpredictable' and Alice had a large stock of memories about the outbursts she had witnessed as a child.[56] Nearly ninety of the autobiographers described their father drinking to an extent that was at the least detrimental to the family finances, and very often detrimental to the family's peace and the father's health as well.[57]

We have encountered here men who were unable to find steady work or too ill to perform it, as well as a large cast of characters who chose leisure over labour, who spent their earnings on their own private pleasures and who drank away their wages. But it is not simply because the stories are colourful that they belong to our accounts. It is also because they are so numerous. Indeed, ineffective fathers were only a little less numerous amongst the autobiographers than the hard-working and steadfast ones. We opened this discussion by observing that 213 of the autobiographical writers provided evidence that their father had been a good breadwinner. We must now set this against the many others who indicated that their father had not been a good breadwinner, whether through ill health, unemployment, laziness, drunkenness or any other cause – a further 125 in all, or 25 per cent of the total. Clearly, the failings of the Mr Jaspers or Mr Gawthorpes of this world are not simply a colourful historical curiosity. The myriad different ways in which individual fathers failed as effective breadwinners had a tangible social effect as well.[58]

Dividing fathers into 'good' and 'bad' providers of course imposes a degree of simplification over family lives that were often anything but simple and we should be aware that providing could intersect with other aspects of fathering in complex and unexpected ways. A web of emotions overlay all questions of provision and family relationships. Poor providers could be companionate, kind and loving. Following an accident, Amy Rose's father was unable to earn much, but he was the only one in a large family who treated her with kindness.[59] It counted for a lot. On the other hand, fathers who worked hard for their families could be arrogant, overbearing or abusive. Albert Goodwin's father was a skilled pottery worker on a good wage and took on two additional part-time jobs to improve the family's living standards, but he was (according to his son) 'obnoxious' and 'boastful', and never tired of reminding his children of all that he did for them.[60] Questions of provision might be simple, but the emotions that went with them are not. Septimus O'Reilly's father was as drunken and violent as they come. His last attack on his wife was so brutal that when the children crept downstairs to investigate they feared she was dead. She was not dead, but in the family break-up that followed the assault Septimus departed with his father, later claiming that he could not comment on the 'rights and wrongs of the case' as his mother had been a 'whiner and a nagger' and declaring he had 'a real love for my father'.[61] Family relationships are complex and unstable and defy simple caricature. We will look more deeply at the messy web of emotions that overlaid provision in a later chapter, but for the present it is important to underscore the legitimacy of breadwinning as a historical problem in its own right. Breadwinning mattered because it mediated a child's experience of the world in such profound ways. Diet, schooling, housing, health and life opportunities were all powerfully influenced by family income, and for this reason the extent to which men provided for their families merits investigation.

One of the great advantages of the autobiographies is not only that they permit us to do this, but that they allow us to do so with considerable nuance. After all, the writers sketch out many different routes by which a father's breadwinning might fail. There was a large gulf between a kindly man like Mary Bertenshaw's father, who worked hard for his family but whose leg injury had seriously compromised his ability to do so, and a menacing bully like Jack Martin's who kept his wages to himself to spend at the pub – a 'hush would fall over the house' whenever he entered and the weekends were 'utter misery', filled as they were with 'rows, beatings of my mother and the clashes with the police'.[62] Bertenshaw and Martin highlight two very different contexts for non-providing fathers: those unable to work through unemployment or ill health; and those who could, and usually did, work, but who made decisions which nonetheless deprived children of the resources they needed. It is important to distinguish between them, not least as this often had a significant bearing on the severity of the problem it posed. Mr Bertenshaw's earnings were lowered by his disability, but he still made a regular contribution which guaranteed the family a certain level of comfort and security. In other households, illness or unemployment could be temporary or periodic, which helped to lessen its overall impact. By contrast, the consequences of Mr Martin's drinking and aggression were relentless and never ending, affecting every aspect of the life of each of his nineteen children until either their premature death or the moment when they managed to escape the misery that was home.

The evidence here is bleak. The autobiographies illustrate that neither ill health nor unavoidable unemployment was a major cause of families lacking a breadwinner wage. Of the fathers who did not for one reason or another provide for their families, only 30 per cent were unable to find work or physically incapable of undertaking it. Personal failings emerge as a more significant factor: drunkenness, irregular working patterns and a refusal to share earnings explain 63 per cent. The remaining authors did not provide enough detail about their family situation to enable us to comment on the causes of their lack of money.[63]

It is striking how clearly the contours of male breadwinning emerge in the autobiographies once the question has been asked. The manner in which a man provided for his family was of critical importance to a writer's early experiences and it was difficult to be both a good provider and a bad provider at the same time, and so the majority of writers slip easily into one category or the other. Nonetheless, 153 writers (31 per cent) cannot be categorised. Most of these autobiographers either did not write about their fathers or skirted around the issue of how effective his provision had been; the remaining few wrote about their fathers in inconsistent or contradictory terms, making simple categorisations impossible. Even if we were to conclude that all of these writers in fact had fathers who had been good breadwinners – and there are no real grounds for this assumption given that autobiographers had a very clear and accessible vocabulary with which to write about fathers who were good providers – we are still left with a very substantial proportion, some 25 per cent, of all writers raised in a home without the benefit of a full breadwinner's income. Alternatively, if we remove all these writers from our sample on the grounds that we simply do not know anything about how their fathers provided for them, then we are left with a closer split between the two types of father. On this assumption, 63 per cent of men were described as being good providers whereas 37 per cent were not. No matter what assumptions we use, it is clear that the question of wage-sharing at the family level is far more significant than scholars have realised. Indeed, the figures are so high that we need to consider the possibility that there is something about the autobiographies as a historical source that causes them to exaggerate the feckless father figure. Is it possible that writers were prone to exaggerating fatherly failings for dramatic effect, or even driven to write an autobiography precisely because they had a colourful tale of a good-for-nothing father to share?

There is of course no definitive way of establishing whether this is the case. We simply cannot know how the behaviour of the fathers described in the autobiographies corresponds to that of the fathers of the wider population. Yet there are no obvious grounds for thinking that these sources contain an unduly negative bias. They are not 'misery memoirs' – autobiographical accounts of childhood trauma made popular by Frank McCourt's *Angela's Ashes* in the 1990s. Our writers had a range of different motivations for telling their stories, but sensationalism was not one of them. We have no reason to think that autobiographers systematically lied about their fathers, exaggerated their flaws or made up stories that were not true. Quite the opposite, in fact: many writers did not want to dwell upon their fathers' failings and made efforts to couch their criticisms in soft tones. So, for example, Jane Walsh insisted, 'We missed him of course', when her father enlisted as a soldier in 1914, even though she could not get to the end of her sentence before adding that 'to be honest, there was much more peace and quiet in our household when he was away'. She also went on to point out that with her father gone there was more money too, as his military pay 'came in regularly', unlike his wage had done.[64] 'I don't want to blacken his character,' wrote John Bennett, after sharing the details of his father's heavy drinking and 'poor treatment' of his mother.[65] 'I hope I haven't given too biased an account,' apologised Daisy Cowper after her frank account of her father's failings and her confession that she had felt glad when she learned of his death.[66] 'It's a wrong thing for me to be telling you stories like this about my father . . . he had his kind moments I suppose,' admitted Evan Rogers, before going on to say that those moments had been 'very few, very few', and in fact he couldn't remember any.[67] When writers aired the unsavoury details of their fathers' bad behaviour, they were not doing so in order to regale their reader with sensationalist and sordid tales of life in the slums. Walsh, Bennett, Cowper, Rogers, and the many others we have looked at here, wrote about their fathers because there was no way of providing an account of their early years without reference to this vital family member. Time and again, commentary on a father's breadwinning crept into our writers' narratives, even though it led them to share details with which they were not entirely comfortable. They could not do otherwise, as the consequences of any failings had been so severe.

Learning that many, many children in Victorian and Edwardian Britain went without hot food and warm clothes owing to the actions of their fathers makes for uncomfortable reading. Yet this message is clearly communicated in one autobiography after another, and when we consider the autobiographies collectively, it is clear that these are not isolated examples.[68] This was part of the fabric of family life, part of the fabric of society, so, uncomfortable or not, it is a phenomenon that we need to explain. Neither good breadwinning nor erratic male wage-earning were universal. Instead, the autobiographies indicate that the breadwinning family took many different forms: it functioned well in some households but very badly in others. Why were experiences so diverse? Why did the young Henry Turner get to enjoy an annual summer holiday in Norfolk thanks to his father's commitment to his family, whilst Jack Martin's only nights away from home were spent cowering in the privy when his father locked the whole family out of the house in a drunken rage?[69] It is time to consider whether there are more general patterns underlying these highly unique stories, whether diverse patterns of experience can be linked to particular contexts, occupations or regions.

The choices that men made with regards to the spending of their income were, of course, to some degree contingent upon factors such as individual temperament and circumstances. But there was one environment in which the breadwinning family model worked consistently well: the countryside. Across this large collection of autobiographies, there were noticeably fewer cases of fathers in small, rural villages failing to provide for their families. Amongst our 491 writers, there were 142 individuals raised in families living in agricultural villages, and of these, just fourteen fathers were unreliable providers. As we saw above, 25 per cent of writers reported a father who failed to provide effectively, but clearly the figure for those raised in the countryside was lower – just 10 per cent. (The corollary of this, of course, was that the breadwinner model also functioned less successfully amongst urban communities than the average figure suggests: 32 per cent of the writers raised in towns and cities provided clear evidence that their father had not provided effectively for the family.)

Furthermore, even within the rural context there were occupational differences in the reliability with which male workers provided for their family. Agricultural labourers emerge as the most reliable fathers, whilst men pursuing a skilled, non-agricultural occupation were the least. Ten of the rural men who did not provide adequately for their families were agricultural labourers, but when we consider these cases it becomes clear that most of the men were in this position through reasons beyond their control. Three were invalids and this compromised their ability to work.[70] A further three, all raising their families in the early part of the Victorian period, were suffering from adverse economic forces beyond their control – chronically low wages, short stints of unemployment or high food prices.[71] This leaves just four farm workers who were able to provide for their family but did not do so reliably; three were spending money on drink and the fourth was withholding money from his wife as a form of control.[72] The other four fathers who did not provide for their families were not in fact involved in agricultural labour. One was a stonemason,[73] one was a higgler,[74] one ran a basket-weaving business[75] and the other was a journeyman bricklayer.[76] All four were effectively self-employed tradesmen or skilled craftsmen who happened to live in a village rather than a town.

This evidence offers a tantalising possibility. Nineteenth-century Britain was a rapidly changing society, undergoing urbanisation, industrialisation and significant population growth and movement. In the communities most isolated from these developments, the traditional family model of a male breadwinner worked moderately well, whereas proximity to these developments went hand in hand with an elevated risk that the male head of household would fail to provide for his family. Is it a simple coincidence that male breadwinning was less secure in the urban context? Or was economic growth and restructuring actually causing a change in the way in which resources were shared within families?

We can consider this question by looking at autobiographies written by an earlier cohort of writers. In addition to the 491 autobiographies that cover the period from 1830 down to 1914, there are also more than 250 written by authors born between 1750 and 1830. This makes it possible to probe the behaviour of fathers back to the middle of the eighteenth century. Although this earlier cohort of writers tended to be more reticent about family life, we can nonetheless identify some fundamentally similar patterns. Sixty-one of the autobiographers born before 1830 were raised in agricultural communities and of these thirty-five had living fathers employed in agriculture. The number of agricultural workers failing to provide for their families was small – just three. This amounts, once again, to around one tenth of the total. Furthermore (and once again), the causes of this failure to provide lay in factors beyond the men's control. One was an elderly father unable to work owing to ill health.[77] The other two were affected by low wages and unemployment.[78] None of the autobiographers from this period whose father worked as an agricultural labourer reported that he had diverted his wages to causes outside his family. There were a further five rural households that lacked a reliable breadwinner, but in each of these cases the father worked in a trade rather than agriculture.[79] The continuities in the behaviour of fathers in rural Britain throughout the long period from 1750 to 1914 are really quite remarkable.

It is important to underscore the significance of this finding. Agricultural wages were low, so many of the families in rural areas were, in absolute terms, poor. But throughout the eighteenth century and right down to the eve of 1914, so long as a father who worked in agriculture remained in good health he was highly likely to both work regularly and hand over the great majority of his earnings to his wife. Time and again the autobiographies reveal that the equilibrium in their families was destroyed by fathers who failed to provide adequately for them, yet one occupational group appears to be almost wholly unaffected by this problem.

Not only is there continuity in the way that men working in agriculture behaved throughout the period 1750–1830, there is also a longer history of those who failed to provide for their families. Male wages were generally lower before 1830 but there were nonetheless sizeable pockets of high-wage labour. And it was in precisely these pockets that the non-providing fathers were to be found. Emanuel Lovekin's terse description of his childhood (he was born in 1820) captures a number of features that must by now be familiar. His father was a furnace man and got 'a very good wage'. Unfortunately, he spent 'a great part of it in drink' and took 'very little interest in home matters'.[80] In Glasgow, James McCurrey's household was afflicted by the same combination of relative prosperity and heavy drinking: 'work was plentiful, and wages high. All these things were incentives to whisky drinking . . .'[81] In Somerset, George Mitchell's father worked at the stone quarry where he earned 'nearly double the wages of a farm labourer at that time'. Mitchell noted, however, that he had in fact been raised in just the same poverty as the ploughmen's families, owing to his father's 'love of cider'.[82] Indeed, these patterns pre-dated our customary periodisation of the Industrial Revolution. In the mid-eighteenth century, David Love's father was a coal miner, 'but very unsteady . . . never easy but amongst his bottle companions, hating his own home, was not willing to work'. In the 1750s, he entered himself and his seven children into a seven-year mining contract, took the money and deserted the family.[83] Nor was there anything special about industrial employment in mines, factories and quarries in new settlements. Just the same pattern could be seen amongst skilled workers in market towns. James Lackington's father was a shoemaker in the small

Shropshire town of Wellington when his father gave him some money so that he might open a shop. But the gift did nothing for the family's living standards, for 'as soon as he found he was more at ease in his circumstances, he contracted a fatal habit of drinking'.[84]

The autobiographical record does not reveal a clear historical turning point, with the breadwinning model working well up to a particular point in time, and starting to deteriorate thereafter. Instead, it reveals an enduring connection between high wages and poor breadwinning. The breadwinning model had long been vulnerable. It worked best where male wages were low and some kind of equivalence between men's paid labour and women's unpaid labour existed; but high male wages, however and wherever they were earned, always had the power to disrupt that equivalence. It is therefore important to ask what was distinctive about rural life that served to funnel male earnings so much more effectively into the common family fund.

There is no simple answer to this question as there were manifold differences between a small agricultural community and larger urban settlements which worked together to influence the ways that men behaved, but a number of factors were significant. In the first instance, a less buoyant labour market meant that men did not have the opportunity to trade labour for leisure. Most agricultural labourers were tied into year-long contracts and work was in any case far too scarce to risk losing a job for failing to turn up when expected, and this encouraged men to toil dutifully for their employers. But farm workers did not simply work regularly; they shared their wages with their wives, and, whilst it may appear counterintuitive, part of the reason they did so was precisely because wages were low. Several of the rural autobiographers noted how their family's limited means had deprived fathers of the freedom to spend any money on themselves. As one autobiographer raised in a poor agricultural family in rural Scotland explained, his father 'could not afford to be other than an abstainer'. A few pennies' worth of snuff was his only occasional luxury.[85] William Arnold's father, a poor village shoemaker, hardly drank at all: he was 'too poor' to do so.[86] Waged work might earn a farm worker an entitlement to a bigger share of the household's resources, but where wages were low there was very little left over for personal spending outside the home. Low wages also meant that men had no real choice but to hand their wages to their wives for housekeeping. Agricultural wages were never high enough to permit a man to purchase the kind of services that his wife provided – the provision of meals and clothing – on the open market. A man's basic human needs for food, clothing and warmth could only be fulfilled through the services of unpaid family members. There was thus some equivalence in the value of waged work and unpaid domestic work and this created a high degree of co-dependency between husband and wife.

In addition, there was a host of forces outside the home that reduced the scope for men to spend their earnings on themselves rather than their families. Rural communities often lacked anywhere to buy alcohol and they also exerted informal pressures on male heads of households to provide for their family. Rosina Harrison's father liked a glass of ale, but as there was no pub in the village, getting it meant a three-mile walk.[87] Arthur Rowse's father went to market every Friday night and that was the only time he was able to buy himself a drink – a 'pint of bitter and two-pennorth of rum'. There were no pubs in the village and 'no liquor was allowed inside our home by my mother'. Life was more controlled in small, rural villages. In Arthur Rowse's village, 'the farm gave employment to half the village in one capacity or another – hinds, labourers, stable-boys, maidservants'.[88] And a family that spent large sums on male wages did not also expect to see the money it paid into the rates being used to support the wives and children of men in its employ. Bert Coombes recalled how the local farmer had the villagers 'under his control. He could, and often did make them homeless and wageless for the least opposition to his wishes.' Bert recalled the example of a married man who had been dismissed for going to a public house one night after work.[89]

But it was not simply the external force of employers; there were forces internal to the family as well. The hundreds of autobiographers raised in rural homes vividly conjured a distinctive culture in which all family members pulled together in order that the household could function. In most rural homes, the labour involved in running the home remained high. Running water, gas and electricity were making slow inroads in urban areas by the end of the nineteenth century, and even in the absence of these luxuries, women living in towns still had the advantage of coal delivered to the house and conveniently located standpipes, and it all helped to reduce the physical effort needed to run the home. Very few of these advances had reached the countryside, however, so housekeeping required additional labour for water fetching and wood cutting. With few exceptions, the autobiographers raised in the countryside, both male and female, recalled being drawn into this work from a very young age.[90] As Lucy Linnett noted, 'we all had our jobs to do': fetching water, cleaning boots, chopping sticks for firewood, running errands, minding children, taking father his dinner, and (for the girls) mending stockings.[91] In her rural corner of north Staffordshire, Gertie Mellor recalled the joint effort required to keep the family clothed. Everything they wore, she recalled, was 'manufactured in the house', and this called for a contribution from everyone. Donated clothing had to be unpicked and made into something new: 'those as couldn't sew had to unpick and those as could sew could sew'. Even the shoes were produced in the home. The children 'always had clogs. My Dad made them.'[92] Fred Boughton described the various roles of each member of his rural household. In the evening: 'Mother would be sitting in her wicker armchair, knitting. Father would be mending boots, and each of us kids had a job, some knitting, some making rag mats, some cooking. Mother taught us to do every job in the house . . . from a young boy I was always working at some job.'[93] Life was hard in the countryside – a 'fierce and unbroken struggle for food and shelter', recalled one.[94] There could be no slacking from anyone; everyone had their role to play. In remembering his childhood in his corner of rural Herefordshire, Henry Jones described his father, mother, two brothers and himself as 'all partners on one family enterprise, and all things ran smoothly in their course'.[95]

Domestic life in larger urban or industrial settlements differed from rural life in multiple ways, but the foundation upon which so much rested was the higher male wage, which placed hitherto unknown levels of choice and power within the hands of the men who earned them. As male wages moved away from subsistence levels, it broke down the absolute necessity for all individuals in the family to pool their resources and labour for the common good, and created a new situation in which men could maintain a reasonable living standard by depositing only a part of their resources with their family, or even living away from them altogether. As male wages increased, the balance between a man's waged work and his wife's unpaid domestic work was disrupted and the co-dependency between marriage partners was lost.

The precise effects of higher male wages on family dynamics were played out in a number of different ways. Some men took advantage of higher earnings in order to trade work for leisure. Pat O'Mara's father was an alcoholic and a domestic abuser – one of a select group of the most deeply unpleasant fathers described within the autobiographical literature. He was imprisoned on a number of occasions for his brutal attacks on O'Mara's mother – no mean achievement, given that the policemen who were repeatedly called to the scene were entirely 'unappreciative of my mother's dilemma [and] had contempt for her'.[96] He was also a Liverpool dock labourer where the day rate – five shillings – was considerably higher than the wages in agriculture. Of course, this did not translate into a higher standard of living for his family. As O'Mara explained, his father lived 'the usual life of a dock labourer, seeking work when he liked and chucking it in when he liked'.[97] As a rule, he never worked more than a couple of days a week, as this 'would ensure the rent and enough to get the barest necessities of living'.[98] He liked to spend the rest of the week in the pub. The men who did not work regularly for their families were either concentrated in a small number of trades – mining, quarrying and dock work – or working as general labourers in the nation's largest cities – London, Liverpool and Birmingham.[99] In all of these contexts, men were hired and paid by the day and the ease of obtaining employment and the high wages they could earn permitted them to live a lifestyle of irregular labour that was not available to those working in most other sectors of the labour market. It is also noticeable that most of these men worked just enough to keep their families at subsistence level and out of the workhouse – as O'Mara observed, his father provided 'the barest necessities of living'. In some respects, Mr O'Mara adhered to an older ideal of maintaining a family at the lowest acceptable level, which was all agricultural workers had traditionally been able to manage owing to their low wages. His additional earnings were used to free him from the drudgery of working a seventy-hour week at back-breaking work rather than to raise his family's living standards.

Most men did not make the same choice as Mr O'Mara. As we have already seen, men were more likely to take advantage of better pay to increase their earnings rather than to reduce their hours of work. Yet even when men followed the path of steady labour, it is clear that not all believed that earnings above the family's subsistence needs belonged to the common family fund rather than to the wage earner himself. This lay at the root of a pattern of behaviour that we have repeatedly seen, where a man deposited a part of his earnings with his wife for his and his family's upkeep and kept a part for his own private use. As with the fathers who worked irregularly, these fathers provided for their family's basic needs – it was the ownership of the additional income that was contested. For the most part, all decisions regarding how male wages were shared lay with the man who earned them, but just occasionally wives were able to reach out and capture their husband's money for the household. Bessie Wallis's father had a nice baritone voice and could earn extra money from his singing engagements at the weekend. But he also used the engagements as an excuse to get 'blind-drunk' and would come home and tumble into bed. Bessie continued: 'As soon as he was fast asleep Mother would sneak out of bed, upend his trousers and help herself to exactly half of his money . . . no one ever gave her away! We children benefited enormously because that sly nest of money gave us many a day out at Cleethorpes!'[100] We have already met Mr Jasper – it was he who stuffed his earnings under his mattress and into his sock whilst he slept in order to prevent his wife from taking his drinking money and spending it on the family. For the most part his strategy worked, but when he got out of bed one night to watch a scuffle on the street his money fell into the wrong hands. Decades later, Albert could not conceal his glee at the unexpected turn of events. Feeling something against her leg, his mother 'immediately tumbled what it was' and hid the money in her nightdress. She taunted him the next day when she saw him 'looking all over the bed' for his lost loot: 'What a time Mum gave us the next day! I had new boots, Molly new shoes and Jo wasn't forgotten either.'[101] For Bessie and Albert, the story of what happened when Mum got hold of Dad's money was a humorous anecdote, but the humour derived precisely from the act of subversion that lay at its heart. Underneath the stories was a much more depressing reality about who really owned the money.

Occasionally the autobiographers provided a very distinct account of the ways in which money could destabilise, rather than enrich, the household. Kay Garrett's father, for example, had been invalided out of the army and received a quarterly pension of £9.00, but in Kay's memory his pension day was one of 'fearful anticipation'. It began with a nice breakfast and the purchase of some much-needed new clothes, 'but night was awful. They'd stay out till midnight – drinking.' In fact, Kay continued, 'home was happiest when Dad had no job and times were hard . . . When times were bad and Mum and Dad couldn't go out to the pub, we had lovely evenings playing cards . . .'[102] In a similar vein, John Murphy noted that the 'nineties were busy years for British industry' and so his father often worked overtime for extra pay. But as he continued, the overtime:

did not bring many blessings to our house. On the contrary, they meant an increase in the worries associated with dad's heavier drinking at the week-ends. It certainly brought a little more money into the house; but the joy of the 'extras' was somewhat short-lived. Usually they were used to clear off the debts incurred by some spell of recklessness on my father's part.[103]

There were also a handful of writers who observed that the absence of their fathers during the First World War actually raised their living standards rather than lowered them, owing to the fact that their father's military pay was paid directly to their mother.[104]

Indeed, male writers themselves sometimes made essentially the same observation about how high wages had derailed their decision-making. John Phillips was one of a small number amongst the autobiographers who had struggled with alcohol addiction during adulthood, and he linked his problems with alcohol to the ease with which he could access it. Drink had not been a problem in the early part of his life as he had grown up in rural Shropshire with 'no public-house in the village'. During his first post as a live-in farm servant he was given a daily allowance of one pint of beer and developed the habit of pub-drinking as his master liked to take him to the Fox for company, but there was no public house in the village of his next post so his drinking was brought to a swift end. When he ended up working in a hotel in Shrewsbury, however, he was 'doomed to get in the way of the drink'. His tips proved 'a great temptation to me' and he was soon gambling and drinking them away. He moved to Wales, married and found work in the Welsh coal mines, and of course quickly fell in with men who were 'very fond of their beer'. Two years into his marriage, and he was beginning to 'choose the public-house and its company, to neglect my own home, and grew more and more fond of the drink'.[105] We noted earlier that William Arnold's father had not been a drinker – he was 'too poor' for that. Reflecting on how his own heavy drinking had led him to the brink of ruin, Arnold traced the problem to the high wages he had been able to earn in the factory: 'My large earnings became a source of temptation.'[106] James Turner found just the same thing. His new job in a cotton-printing shed eventually paid him a pound a week, which he considered 'very good wages'. But the hefty pay packet 'cultivated some very bad habits', such as keeping his pay and 'going away from home for 3 or 4 days at a time'. His spending reached such a point that he would 'have been better had I never gone to work there'.[107]

Towns and cities not only provided higher male earnings, they were also far more complex societies which enabled men to find substitutes for the things that families had traditionally provided inside the home. Foremost amongst these was hot, cooked food. Where this could once only be obtained within the home, it was now for sale in the city and even a humble workman had the means to purchase it. Arthur Harding and his family lived in the East End of London in the 1880s and 1890s, and his autobiography captures the dizzying array of different foodstuffs for sale: fish and chip shops; coffee shops selling tea and bread or a meal of meat, two veg and a piece of jam tart; fish shops selling bloaters, smoked haddocks, kippers, herrings, mackerel and eels; the pork butchers where you could buy 'very good cooked food at very cheap prices'; the cake shops that sold large bags of broken biscuits for a halfpenny; the pudding shop, selling hot pies, jam roly-poly and beef soup; and the German pork butchers selling faggots which could be eaten hot or cold.[108] Mr Harding had access to a range of hot, pre-prepared food, which in turn weakened his dependency upon the home and his wife's cooking.

It did not help, of course, that one of the most attractive and accessible ways to spend income was on alcohol – a product with mind-altering and addictive qualities.[109] Irregular working, the non-sharing of wages and heavy drinking all played some part in the patterns of fatherhood we have described here, and these three factors were not, of course, mutually exclusive. Very often some combination of them worked together. But the one force that emerges over and over again was drinking. This was the single greatest cause of money haemorrhaging from family budgets. It was mentioned by eighty-eight writers, or 15 per cent of the writers with a memory of a living father and almost one half of all the households in which a father was failing to provide adequately for his family. In each of these cases, the father was drinking so heavily that their child had considered it to be a drain on the family finances, but in some the problem was so bad it was also affecting the man's ability to hold down a job and earn a steady wage.[110] It would indeed be hard to overemphasise the role that alcohol played in allowing resources to seep away from working-class homes.

This culture of heavy drinking in the urban working classes was something that Victorian commentators frequently criticised, and historians have rightly been circumspect about repeating or endorsing their censorious attitudes. Yet much as we might want to distance ourselves from middle-class prejudices about working-class lives, it is difficult to escape the conclusion that drinking was, indeed, a problem. It was also overwhelmingly an urban phenomenon. Just 5 per cent of the rural autobiographers described a father who was drinking to excess, whereas more than a quarter of the urban autobiographers did.[111] If we add to this all those who recalled excessive drinking by mothers, step-parents and other carers, around one-third of all the urban writers had first-hand experience of problem drinking.[112] Rather than denying this reality, the question we have to ask is: why?

From the autobiographers' perspective, drinking was a personal failing, and collectively the writers heaped considerable derision upon fathers who had spent their earnings on drink rather than their families. But looking over hundreds of autobiographies and seeing so many fathers failing in just the same ways again and again, we are forced to question whether this was a structural problem with roots outside the family rather than a personal failing. Albert Jasper was characteristically contemptuous of his father for drinking away his earnings and leaving the family trapped in poverty. He didn't neglect to mention the time when his father came home drunk and passed out in a

4.2 The Golden Lion Inn in Bigg Market, Newcastle, with a few male patrons standing outside in 1889.

pool of his own shit in the scullery.[113] But it is also hard to imagine that Mr Jasper, in the grip of a serious alcohol addiction and reviled by his own family, was living a good life. In truth, alcohol is a harmful substance, and at some point a drinking addiction caused considerable suffering not only for his family, but also for the drinker himself.

Of course, to some degree, the rising level of drinking was a straightforward result of the upward trend in male wages: higher earnings allowed men to purchase greater quantities of alcohol than ever before. But higher incomes do not always and inevitably lead to more drinking. Drinking can also be a response to a specific situation, and it is possible that changes in the conditions of men's working and home lives also played their part. The elevation of male labour as a marker of masculinity severed men from the comforts of home and thrust them into the masculine, alcohol-drenched world of the pub. We can see men turning away from the home as the source of human company and personal identity, and searching for these things in the public world of pubs and clubs instead. Joseph Stamper observed that each of the many pubs he used to visit with his father catered to its own clientele. Some were small, cosy and inward looking. Others looked outwards, providing rooms and facilities for their drinkers – debating clubs, literary societies, libraries, 'hot-pot suppers', sing-songs and 'mass merriment'.[114] A little spare change was the ticket to pursuing such things as male friendships, leisure and political engagement – all centred on the pub. John Allaway noticed that his father had attempted to buy 'personal popularity' by spending on beer and cigarettes for men at the public house.[115] Alehouses promised warmth and friendship to men who might struggle to find this anywhere else. One wrote that he fell into drinking because he enjoyed the alehouse as much as the drink – he just 'loved the company'.[116] Some of the autobiographers noted how willing their fathers had been to 'treat' their friends in the pub – a willingness that was frequently contrasted with their unwillingness to share with their wives and children.[117]

It is also noticeable that some of the male writers indicated that their drinking had become more problematic during times of crisis. The death of a cherished son,[118] the untimely death of a child in a house-fire,[119] the loss of a baby[120] – men gave these and other losses as the moment when once regulated drinking had begun to spiral out of control. Added to this is the fact that many forms of male labour were extremely demanding physically. One writer recalled how as an apprentice mason he had attempted to 'escape from [his] sense of depression and fatigue' by drinking whisky. It 'gave lightness and energy to both body and mind' and substituted for his usual state of 'dullness and gloom, one of exhilaration and enjoyment'. Whisky, he concluded, was 'simply happiness doled out by the glass'.[121] Even in the absence of loss and trauma, men's daily lives could be exhausting and draining and alcohol provided immediate relief from the day-to-day struggles of life.

We all like to believe that economic growth is a good thing, particularly when it is accompanied by wage growth. Real wages are still routinely employed as a benchmark by which to assess who gains from economic growth: when they rise, we assume that everyone is sharing in the gains. But the family perspective indicates that the reality was far more complex. Higher male wages did not simply raise the wage earner's income; they also changed his relationship to both his family and the world outside. They altered an individual's access to the fundamentals of human existence – food, clothing, warmth, companionship and contentment – in unexpected and highly gender-specific ways. This is not to suggest that money was always bad, or that working-class families would have been better off if male earnings had remained at the miserably low level that agricultural labourers had traditionally commanded. As we have seen, a majority of fathers (albeit not a very large one) did share their earnings with their family, and wherever they did so significant gains for their wives and children followed. The point rather is that we need to think more critically about the ownership of money within households and recognise the gap that could, and did, exist between real wages and family living standards.

This was an era not simply of newfound prosperity, but also of profound social change. And we should not discount social change as peripheral to the main business of economics, for when families began to change, wealth began to scatter through society in unpredictable ways. Families are not generally accorded a central place in economic history. But if we seek to understand how money, wealth and well-being travelled through society, it is here that we need to look.

5

'FATHER DISAPPEARED AND LEFT MOTHER TO BRAVE THE STORM'
FAMILY BREAKDOWN[1]

Charlie Chaplin brought laughter to millions and is now remembered and revered as one of the great comic creators of the twentieth century. But his childhood in the East End of London during the closing years of Victoria's reign contained little to laugh about.

His early years were blighted by domestic crises, poverty and neglect owing to his father's absence and his mother's recurring bouts of mental illness. In his sixth year, as his mother sank further into hopelessness, poverty and depression, she took the decision to enter herself and her two boys into the workhouse. Thus began a decade of regular moves in and out of different Victorian institutions – workhouses, asylums, orphanages – for all three. There were periodic reunions as his mother's health improved, followed by fresh separations as she entered a new downward spiral. The cycle continued until Charlie was in his late teens. Once more, Hannah Chaplin was found wandering the streets and once more, this time permanently, she was confined to the asylum. For her sons: 'There was nothing we could do but accept poor mother's fate.'[2]

At one point in this decade of intermittent institutionalisation, however, the parish officials, perhaps weary of the cost of maintaining the hapless family, noticed that the two boys had a legal – and solvent – guardian: Charlie's father, Charles Chaplin Snr. Charlie's parents had separated within two years of his birth, but never divorced. And although Charles Snr was not the father of Charlie's elder brother, he had taken custody of his new wife's illegitimate son at the time of their marriage. In the years following his separation, he had found a new partner and together they had had a child; all three were living in a couple of rooms in a house on Kennington Road. Despite a deepening alcohol dependency, Charles Chaplin was managing to earn a good living as a successful music-hall singer, and in the eyes of the cash-strapped authorities, he appeared to be the ideal solution to the problem of the motherless boys.[3]

It is worth taking stock of the family the parish authorities created when they returned Charlie to his father. The household consisted of Charles Snr and his unmarried partner, Louise; their illegitimate child; Charles Snr's legitimate child, Charlie; and Sydney, the illegitimate child of his estranged wife. It might come as no surprise that Charles's new partner took a dim view of the new arrangement and expressed her discontent by mistreating the two interlopers. This escalated to the point that it attracted the attention of the newly formed National Society for the Prevention of Cruelty to Children, though before matters deteriorated further, the boys' mother was fortunately discharged from the asylum and took back custody of her sons. Yet even this fails to do justice to the complexity of Charlie's family, for his mother not only had an illegitimate child before Charlie, she also had another after him – a son with the music-hall entertainer Leo Dryden born around a year after her separation from Charles. The child was taken by Dryden as an infant and raised without any contact with his mother and half-brothers – Charlie only learned of his existence in adulthood. Though the legitimate child of married parents, Charlie had no recollection of living with his birth family. He was one of a family of four brothers – none of them sharing the same set of parents.

The complexity of Chaplin's family hints at the unpicking of traditional social values, but it is important to emphasise that this story of infidelity and illegitimacy is not simply a colourful byway of social history. It also belongs to the domain of economics. After all, the separation of Charlie from his father caused his separation from both his father and his earnings, and this had significant financial ramifications for all concerned. As Charlie Chaplin explained in his autobiography, Mr Chaplin was a successful music-hall singer and could command a high weekly income – up to forty pounds a week during his heyday. But he never gave more than a tiny fraction of that sum to Charlie's mother for their upkeep. The initial agreement was a weekly payment of ten shillings, little more than 1 per cent of his maximum earnings.[4] Moreover, although Mr Chaplin did on occasion bring in very high earnings, he did not sustain these high earnings for long. The trouble, as his son recalled, 'was that he drank too much'.[5] As he descended into alcoholism, not only did his earnings dwindle, but his personal claim on them also increased. His paltry child maintenance dried up altogether, and the only time that he subsequently provided for his first family was during his sons' brief stay when Hannah was in the asylum. This lack of money had serious implications for every aspect of young Charlie's childhood. His earliest memories were of living with his mother and brother in 'wretched circumstances'. Later the trio 'sank further into poverty'. Then, later again, they were still living in 'a quagmire of miserable circumstances'.[6] Moreover, what was true for Chaplin on a personal level was also true on a much broader level for society at large. In Victorian and Edwardian Britain, nuclear families were the mechanism for distributing wage-earnings throughout society, so any developments that rendered families more fragile or less stable had an economic, as well as social, significance.

Chaplin's story also reminds us that families needed fathers. This should not be interpreted as a moral point about the emotional or social importance of a male role model for a child's development. It is simply a statement of fact. Men and women filled different roles within the family, and they could not easily substitute for each other. Men were breadwinners and commanded much higher rates of pay than women could ever earn. Women did the work of the home, and although this did not entirely preclude their going out to work as well, these domestic responsibilities limited the number of hours they could work, which, coupled with low female pay, restricted their wage-earning power. Families needed fathers because fathers were the source – largely the only source – of income.[7] Of course, as we have just seen, not all fathers were good breadwinners, so the presence of a father was hardly a cast-iron guarantee of economic security. Nonetheless, fathers provided the economic foundation of any family unit and their absence was therefore a serious matter. This, then, forms the focus of this chapter. Having investigated how well fathers provided for their families, we now need to consider what happened when fathers were not present at all.

For many centuries, the typical family form in Britain had been nuclear. Custom dictated that men and women delayed marriage until they were in a position to set up a household of their own: at that point they married, moved in together and started a family. And that step was permanent – it was, quite literally, 'until death us do part'. Inevitably, a few individuals had always fallen outside these social norms, but across the population levels of conformity were high. Most women did not have children outside wedlock and couples did not usually separate, no matter how unsatisfactory married life together proved to be. These, no doubt, were restrictive social regulations under which to live one's life, but they did have one important consequence: the tying together of fathers, mothers and children into legally binding, largely indissoluble unions, ensured that a man's wages were diverted towards his wife and his legitimate offspring so long as he lived. And this is why family is so critical to understanding who was able to share in the great prosperity of nineteenth-century Britain – as well, of course, as explaining why so many remained on the fringes of that prosperity.

The autobiographies provide a uniquely valuable source for the piecing together of family history. Family provided the context for one's earliest engagement with the world, an anchor to an individual's understanding of his or her lived experience, an element of a life story that could not easily be dispensed with. Most writers reliably reported the basic outline of their family, and so we can use our collection of 662 autobiographies to provide a relatively complete and robust account of family structure, as well as to probe a range of questions about families that are not directly measurable from other kinds of demographic data. For example, conventional demographic data puts male life expectancy at birth at around forty-five years, but does not enable us to translate this figure into a number for the proportion of fatherless families.[8] The autobiographies, by contrast, provide information about the size and structure of the households that our writers lived in. They not only permit us to estimate the proportion of families that lacked fathers, but also to untangle the different causes of fatherlessness and to investigate its consequences for the families concerned.

Given that divorce was not freely available before 1914, the proportion of autobiographers who had been raised without the presence of their father was surprisingly high. No fewer than 171 writers had spent at least part of their childhood in a fatherless household – 26 per cent or one quarter of the total.[9] There were a number of different means by which children became separated from their fathers and we shall consider them all, but our starting point should be mortality. Amongst the autobiographers, eighty-one had lost their father through death. The risk of paternal death was 2 per cent in the first year of life and then dropped – after that age, fewer than 1 per cent of writers lost their fathers through death in any given year. An elevated risk of paternal death in the first year of life and the cumulative effect of a lower risk over the subsequent years of a writer's childhood combined to deprive 12 per cent of all writers of their father by the age of sixteen.

Some families suffered catastrophic breakdown. Alice Pidgeon recalled the awful events of her seventh year. First her new sister died at ten days old; a week later her mother died; and seven weeks later her father died as well.

'Three deaths in eight weeks.' Alice and her sister were packed off to an orphanage in Clerkenwell, struggling to comprehend their trauma: 'There was the longing to see them again and I could not take in the fact that they were gone forever, I fretted over this for a long time, I used to dream that they were not dead after all and that I had only dreamt they were, then I would see mother die again and would waken up to reality.'[10]

But even in the absence of such catastrophe, the death rate was high, and chipped away relentlessly at the nuclear family leaving many fatherless families in its wake. Some children had lost their fathers so early in life that they were unable to remember them. John Carter Ley's father returned home from work complaining of pains in the head and passed away within a matter of weeks.[11] Mick Burke's mother was left on her own with two sons when her husband was found dead on the floor on Christmas Day following a Christmas Eve drinking binge.[12] Both marriages had lasted around two years and produced two children; none had any memory of their father. A steady process of attrition left many more children losing their father at some point during their childhood. Those who lost their father at an older age were usually able to reflect on the significance of that event, and the theme that they returned to over and again was the terrible impact their father's death had had on the family's living standards.

Of course, not all fathers were reliable breadwinners, so in some cases their earnings had dropped below anything of value to the family before the time of their death. Alice Foley observed that when her father died in front of his family on the day of his fifty-sixth birthday, the overwhelming emotion was one of relief. He had been recovering from a 'bad drinking bout'. In recent years his earnings had dwindled but his temper was as bad and unpredictable as ever. Watching their father die before them caused the family 'shock and profound pity', but did not give them 'a sense of personal grief'.[13] Alice was not unique. She belonged to a small group of writers whose father's contribution had deteriorated to such an extent that his death was recalled with a sense of relief rather than sorrow. In Len Wincott's memory, he believed that when his mother had called him in from his game in the streets to inform him that his father had just died, he replied, 'Oh!' and 'walked out to continue my game. I can't remember whether I told any of my chums but it seems to me that I did not. The game interested me more.' What with his father's heavy drinking and the well-oiled strap he kept hanging from a nail by the fireplace, his children had little to lament: 'We were tearless when we went [to his burial] and tearless when we returned.'[14] In a handful of families, a father's death was the lifting of a burden.

But where fathers had been providing for their families, their demise was much more serious. Quite apart from the emotional distress implied by the passing of a loved family member, a father's death involved a loss of income, and women needed to act quickly to find a new source of financial support. Very quickly, everything within the family changed. Winifred Relph could divide her childhood 'into two parts, before my father's death and after'. Her father died when she was eight and 'almost overnight our life changed from a happy secure family . . . to a fatherless family with a worried, irritable mother, struggling to "Make ends meet", with the few shillings she now had to live on . . . quite different to the steady regular wage which my father had earned all through their married life, giving us security and a good standard of living'.[15] It is, indeed, remarkable how many writers referred to the economic significance of their father's death: 'we had come down somewhat in life style from our circumstances before my father's death', recalled Clayton Joel.[16] According to Agnes Cowper, after her father's death, the family faced 'only indigence and bitter anxiety'.[17] In John Williamson's experience, the 'family's economic circumstances became very bad' following his father's accident, hospitalisation and subsequent death.[18] Such comments were not callous; they were simply a reflection of how large the fact of providing a wage loomed within the family circle.

A single mother's first tactic was to replace the missing spouse with a family member. A few women were fortunate enough to have an older son living at home who was able to step into the breadwinning role. Wil Edwards had never known his father – he had died in a mining accident before he was born. But his two elder brothers were 'big chaps' at the time of this catastrophe – young men in their twenties already at work in the mines. Their wages enabled Mrs Edwards to keep the home together until Wil himself was old enough to start making a small contribution to the family fund.[19] James Royce was also supported by the earnings of an elder brother. Following the departure of their errant father, his eldest son, Arthur, had taken his place: 'It was Arthur who ran the home.' Arthur even assumed a father's authority over his mother and siblings. As James continued: 'No one could do anything without getting his permission . . . we were all very much afraid of him.'[20] Ruth Slate noticed a very similar dynamic in the home of her boyfriend, Ewart Johnson, who began supporting his mother and siblings following the departure of his father.[21] In addition to providing for his mother and five younger siblings, Ewart – though aged only sixteen – became the head of the family: 'Ewart's opinion always seemed needed,' Ruth wrote, 'and the children obeyed him, just as they would a father.'[22]

Inevitably, though, most women did not have elder sons who were able or willing to step in as a surrogate breadwinner and so needed to look beyond their immediate family. Where women had small families and young children, they sometimes returned to their parents' home, and their own father took on the role of breadwinner for the fatherless family, though this solution was of course only available to those with living parents willing and able to shelter their daughter and grandchildren. Martha Luty took herself and her two children back to her father's smallholding when her marriage broke down and settled with her two children there.[23] Guy Aldred's mother did the same thing when it became apparent that her husband was not going to support her and their son.[24] Where parents were dead or unable to help, occasionally another family member was prepared to step in. James Carter Ley's mother was unable to remain on her in-laws' farm following her husband's death, but an uncle on her mother's side took her and her two young sons under his roof: 'He proved to us as a father, probably better than many.'[25] But although these kinds of arrangements were generally satisfactory so long as they lasted, they often proved to be relatively short lived. Martha Luty's father died within a few years of her arrival, forcing her to find a new home and source of support and Mrs Aldred's arrangement came to an end when she married her parents' lodger and the pair moved out into a home of their own.

It is little wonder, then, that many widowed mothers looked to a second marriage as the best way of plugging the hole in their family. Because of the sharply divided gender roles, both men and women needed a partner if they were to keep their household afloat.[26] Remarriage was thus a powerful mechanism by which broken families could be repaired, providing children with either a breadwinner or a housewife, as the need might be. Following the death of Mick Burke's father after his Christmas drinking binge, his mother 'soon married one of my father's mates . . . and [they had] my half-brother John'.[27] Alice Chase's mother married a widower more than twice her age with a family of seven children, so her own children were raised in a home shared with their half-brothers and -sisters. Mr Burke brought his wage to his new family, whilst Mrs Chase brought cleanliness and order to the 'dirty and neglected children' that now comprised hers.[28] Unlike sons, fathers and other male kin, who were often able to maintain another man's family for only a limited period of time, marriage offered the promise of long-term stability for both mothers and children.

But marriage was always a risky decision for women. As we have already seen, a sizeable minority of men did not provide adequately for their families, and women in search of a husband could hardly have failed to be aware of this problem. Henrietta Burkin's mother was widowed with a three-year-old child when she met a 'batchelor of about forty' who asked her to marry him, but she agreed only after 'very careful thought, and a lot of persuasion from her sister'.[29] There were good reasons for caution, as there was the very real risk that a new stepfather would be hostile to maintaining another man's children. Yet taking the autobiographical sample as a whole, relatively few writers suggested that their stepfathers had been unwilling providers for this reason.[30] The real problem was simply that many men were unreliable breadwinners and this unreliability was shared by biological and non-biological fathers alike. Indeed, it was this that had given Henrietta's mother such pause for thought prior to agreeing to marriage. Her hesitation turned on the fact that her suitor 'led a very gay life, drinking and gambling'. She only talked herself into the arrangement by reasoning that his desire for drink might make of him a reliable worker: 'The man who drinks will always work to provide the money for his drink, but nothing will make a man work if he's lazy.'[31] (Her perspective had no doubt been coloured by the privations of her own childhood with a father who had often been out of work and 'not too eager to get back' to it.) In the event, the new husband, Harry Hart, did indeed turn out to be something of a drinker, but he confined his drinking to Saturday afternoons. The rest of the week he worked steadily as the foreman at the Charing Cross electricity station, earning a good, and steadily rising, weekly wage. As the marriage did not produce any further children, his earnings provided a very comfortable living for a family of three, and Harry proved to be a reliable provider and a loving father to Henrietta.

Needless to say, many women were less fortunate. After a number of years struggling by with her mangle, Mrs Holloway made a convenient remarriage to a man 'with a family of children'. She soon realised the mistake she had made when her new husband proved to be 'a very drunken man'.[32] But she was hardly alone in finding her new husband a disappointment. We saw in the previous chapter that 25 per cent of the autobiographers who commented upon their father's aptitude as a breadwinner indicated that he had been a poor provider, so experiences such as Mrs Holloway's were regrettably common. The same sorry tale was repeated over and over again by the autobiographers. Doris Hunt's mother was left widowed with three children. 'Situated as she was', it was hardly surprising that she accepted a proposal of marriage from her new lodger – 'a tall, dark and plausible Irishman'.[33] Unfortunately, time soon proved that he was 'very fond of strong drink', so her mother's life 'was no easier than before'.[34] Will Thorne's father had been a heavy drinker and was killed in an accident at work when Will was a small child. He could only despair at his mother's poor choice the second time around: 'I thought that my mother would have been more careful in her selection of a second husband, after her first experience, but she made a worse choice.' George Thompson had a violent temper and was 'even a heavier drinker' than Will's father had been.[35]

Paternal death was a hugely significant event for any given family, with profound consequences both emotional and economic. Yet taking the autobiographical sample as a whole, mortality was just one element in the matrix of family breakdown. Although the proportion of writers who had lost their father through death stood at 12 per cent, the actual proportion of fatherless families was more than double this – 26 per cent. It is necessary to ask, then, why the rate of fatherless families was so much higher than the male death rate. What other forces were at work to leave so many children separated from their father?

We can investigate fatherlessness further by returning to Charlie Chaplin's family story. Death certainly played some role in the difficulties this family faced. Two years after Charles and Sydney's short stay with Charles's father and stepmother, Charles senior died of cirrhosis of the liver and Louise died a few years later, also of alcoholism. Their deaths removed a line of defence for Charlie and Sydney during their mother's subsequent health crises and also made an orphan of their own son – he ended up in the same workhouse and orphanages that had provided shelter to his elder half-brother a few years earlier.

But although death ultimately contributed to the undoing of Charlie's family, it was just one element of a more complex process of family breakdown. Long before their deaths and mental illness, Charles, Hannah and Louise had created a family that lay outside the social norm. Between them, Hannah and

Louise bore three illegitimate children; and Charles deserted his legitimate wife and son and raised instead an illegitimate son outside the confines of his marriage. Mr Chaplin (and his income) had become separated from his son many years before he died. And when these new forms of behaviour rippled through society more widely, more and more individuals found themselves living outside the nuclear ideal. In other words, what we find in Victorian Britain is that new patterns of decision-making by parents added another layer to the age-old problem of mortality.

One of the most constant and predictable triggers for separation of fathers and children was illegitimacy.[36] All of the autobiographical writers who mentioned their illegitimacy had been separated from their fathers at birth and were raised without any kind of paternal involvement or financial support. Indeed, many of the illegitimate children had become separated from their mothers as well. More than half of the children born outside marriage had been placed with grandparents, foster parents or institutions shortly after their birth, and although mothers sometimes returned for their children for the most part they did not.[37] Meanwhile, those who remained with their mothers were raised without any contact with, or financial support from, their fathers.[38] In most cases, the child concerned had virtually no knowledge of his or her father. Neville Cardus, for example, knew that he was illegitimate. No father was listed on his birth certificate, but Cardus believed his father to be 'one of the first violins in an orchestra'.[39] A more plausible, though rather less glamorous, candidate would be John Frederick Newsham – a 'smith' that his mother married three months after registering her son's birth. Whatever the truth, Cardus knew neither of the two men and neither played any role in his upbringing. There is also scant evidence of mothers subsequently marrying their children's fathers, though this may be because those children who had ended up being raised by their birth parents glossed over their illegitimate origins in their written accounts. At any rate, amongst the autobiographers, illegitimacy was strongly correlated with fatherlessness. The writers born outside wedlock had no contact with their fathers, and none even raised the possibility that their father might have provided for them. This fact of paternal absence appears to have been internalised and accepted by the writers themselves.

Other traces of illegitimate children in the autobiographical record confirm this suggestion. For instance, William Bowyer noted that at the time of his parents' marriage, his father had 'passed as a widower'. In reality, however, he already had a family with a woman 'he had picked up in a music hall'. Quite what the truth of the matter was, none of his second family ever knew, but it seems certain that Mr Bowyer was not providing for this first family.[40] More than one of the autobiographers' fathers managed to father an illegitimate child whilst married to the author's mother. Such indiscretions were not common, or at least they were not commonly talked about, and were little short of catastrophic. Mary Gawthorpe's father's 'glaring indiscretion' occurred when Mary was about seven, and at that age she was understandably unclear about exactly what had happened and what it signified. Nonetheless, she understood enough to recognise that the birth of his illegitimate child was a 'black cloud', a 'big crisis', a 'dreadful ordeal', a transgression which her mother was never to forget, forgive or discuss.[41] Children born outside wedlock were to be concealed and forgotten.

And yet, whilst illegitimate children were scattered through the autobiographical sample and although illegitimacy was strongly correlated with paternal absence, the overall numbers were fairly low and they remained stable during the nineteenth century. The taboo on illegitimacy was high, and this ensured that relatively few women took this route to motherhood. Most women regarded illegitimacy as a horrifying prospect, and one to be avoided at all costs. Margaret Penn's mother was unmarried and living in an agricultural village in Lancashire when she revealed her pregnancy to her family. It was more than they could bear. The prospect of illegitimacy within the family filled Margaret's grandmother with horror: she had never thought 'a child of mine would bring such shame on us'. In a small village, there was the matter of what the neighbours would think. How would the family ever 'hold up [their] heads again'?[42] Margaret's grandmother knew that a solution needed to be found. Marriage to the child's father was not an option (he was the squire's son), so she planned to marry her daughter off to a farm labourer in the village and sank her small savings into a plan to help the pair get away to Canada to start a new life.[43] (Unfortunately, the plan went awry when Margaret's mother died five months after the marriage had taken place. The new husband went ahead with the plan to migrate to Canada, leaving the grandmother holding the baby and the neighbours busy speculating as to why a newly wed father would behave in such a heartless way.)

It comes as little surprise that illegitimacy was frowned upon in the more socially conservative rural areas, but it is striking that much the same attitude was prevalent in towns and cities too. Although urban areas were certainly more likely to shelter any number of hybrid family forms, there was still a high degree of shame surrounding an illegitimate birth. Catherine Cookson was born into a desperately poor family on the South Shields docks, but the family nonetheless considered themselves respectable enough to conceal the fact that those Catherine called Ma, Da and her sister Kate were in fact her grandparents and mother. At the age of seven, the 'relationship was straightened out for [her] very forcibly' by some children in the street. (To spare her the shame of illegitimacy, her mother had even gone so far as providing a fictitious father with a fictitious occupation for her birth certificate, although the subterfuge had required her to lie about the date of Catherine's birth as well.)[44] Of course, despite the social disapproval, some women continued to give birth outside wedlock, but the social pressure – what Cookson called the 'cruelty of the bigoted poor' – to confine parenthood to marriage remained high throughout the period and this helped to supress the incidence of illegitimacy.

The taboo on illegitimacy makes it difficult to be certain of numbers. Taking the autobiographical sample as a whole, just 3 per cent of writers indicated that

5.1 Catherine Cookson aged about four at home with her grandmother (who at that age she believed to be her mother) in Tyne Dock, South Shields.

146

they were illegitimate. Because of the shame surrounding unmarried parents it is of course possible that some writers opted not to share this information about their origins, which would in turn have the effect of underestimating the true extent of illegitimacy.[45] Indeed, this shame may also help to explain the unusually large number of writers who reported having lost their father during infancy. As we noted before, almost 2 per cent of the writers reported their father dying in the first year of life, but in every other year group fewer than 1 per cent of the fathers had died. One possible explanation for this discrepancy is that some writers described fathers who had in fact been absent since before birth as dead.[46] Yet even if we were to accept that some of the writers who reported their father as missing were in fact illegitimate, we are still some way from explaining why so many children were raised in homes without fathers. Recall that 26 per cent of all the writers spent part of their childhood in a fatherless household. Twelve per cent lost their fathers to death, and a further 3 per cent were illegitimate, which together account for 15 per cent of all writers, and leave the final 11 per cent unaccounted for. What was going on with this 11 per cent?

Once again, Charlie Chaplin's story sheds light on our problem. Charlie had three illegitimate brothers, but he himself was the legitimate child of married parents. Yet this did not in the event shield him from the experience of fatherlessness, or the poverty that went with it. The root of his problems was more mundane. A few short years into his parents' marriage, their relationship broke down and his father left. It had all occurred when Charlie was too young to remember, but his mother later told him that his father 'drank too much . . . [and] had a violent temper when drinking', and that this had been the cause of their separation.[47] At any rate, his father had left, taking his weekly pay packet with him. As a successful stage performer herself, his mother had initially been able to provide a 'moderately comfortable home' for her two boys, but when her voice and health began to fail, the absence of her husband was calamitous: 'from three comfortable rooms we moved into two, then into one, our belongings dwindling and the neighbourhoods into which we moved growing progressively drabber . . . one back-room to another; it was like a game of draughts – the last move was back to the workhouse'.[48] And this – desertion – provides the key to understanding why so many of the autobiographers had ended up separated from their fathers. Three per cent of the autobiographers admitted to illegitimacy (though the true figure may be higher) and a further

11 per cent indicated that they had become separated from their living father before the end of their childhood.[49] Indeed, it is sobering to realise that the combined forces of illegitimacy and desertion surpassed mortality as a cause of fatherless for our writers.

A few of the writers had no more than a hazy recollection of fathers who had drifted away in the early years of their life. For example, Guy Aldred's father had never 'discharged his family responsibilities' and 'took no interest, either in her [his mother's] welfare or in mine'. His mother had only just managed to legitimise his birth – his parents tied the knot seven and a half weeks before he was born. But marriage had not led to housekeeping, and the newly weds had never set up home together. Mr Aldred had wandered completely out of Guy's life before he was six.[50] Edward Brown's parents had separated so early in his life that he had no real recollection of his father, nor any understanding of the cause of their separation. His family continued to refuse to discuss his father's departure throughout his adult life. His mother 'never referred to the subject on one single occasion', and carried the story to her grave: 'No secret was ever more closely kept.'[51] James Royce's father was 'just a shadow sort of father'. James could remember two brief interludes where his father had lived with them, one when he was about seven and another when he was about twelve. On the second occasion, Mr Royce stole a pair of second-hand boots for his son and spent a few days wandering around north London with him in an attempt to raise some money selling watercress before he took off again, never to return. Looking back, the adult James dismissed the man's significance: 'He didn't count.'[52]

Other men left their families much later in life, long after marriage and after the birth of several children. Some men disappeared, quite literally, overnight. A few years after moving from Norwich to Manchester, John Hemmingway's father slipped away whilst his family were sleeping, leaving his wife 'in the care of six children and all other concerns pertaining to the welfare of the family'. It was a devastating blow to those who remained. The family 'became hungry' and John's mother had to break up the family – the four older children were placed with far-flung relatives and just the youngest two remained with her. And quite apart from the material ramifications of his father's desertion, there was the emotional distress, although John struggled to find a vocabulary with which to talk about this. His father's departure, he declared, had undone 'all the ties of affection'. The whole affair was 'bad in the extreme'.[53]

Although some departures were swift and dramatic, in many other families desertion came at the tail end of several years of problems. Kay Pearson's father was a sailor and at some point during her adolescence he simply stopped returning to the family home. The fact of his desertion was never mentioned within the family, and as an adult Kay recalled the slow process of realisation that her father had abandoned them and was never coming back.[54] She was fifteen at this point, but the desertion had clearly happened some years beforehand. For Leonard Fagg, the absence of his father was equally difficult to fathom. His father was a construction worker who travelled the country for navvying jobs, but as the years passed the time he spent away increased and his trips home became more infrequent. Leonard did not understand his father's absence, he just knew his family 'did not live a normal happy life together' and felt a sense of loss for 'something most of my friends seemed to have'.[55] Women may have sought to avoid the prospect of illegitimacy by exercising caution when it came to sex outside marriage, but it was much more difficult for them to control desertion. In the fluid and anonymous society of the Victorian city, it was extremely easy for a man to slip away from his family, and there was very little that women could do to prevent this outcome.

In a few households, male desertion followed years of more serious problems, such as drunkenness, violence and cruelty. Thomas Luby's father, for example, was an 'absolute drunkard'.[56] Lucy Marshall's was a 'drunkard and a brute'.[57] James Drawbell's father was 'a drunken and unco-operative husband . . . morose [and] vindictive'.[58] Arthur Harding's father 'used to knock my mother about' and was 'ignorant and brutal'.[59] Needless to say, none of them were much missed by their children when they eventually skipped out altogether. Yet the opportunity to exit an unhappy marriage was highly unequal, and although these husbands had been far from ideal for many years, their wives had not been able to leave them. For women living with abusive partners, leaving the children behind in their care was hardly a satisfactory solution, whilst leaving the household with the children in tow was virtually impossible given that abuse generally included limiting access to the money needed to fund a departure. As a result, even where women were desperate to escape, the practical obstacles preventing them from doing so usually proved insurmountable.[60]

Just a handful of women managed to leave their husbands, usually when their children were older and able to substitute for the father's wage. Indeed, these separations were sometimes actually orchestrated by the older children. As James Drawbell observed of his father's banishment from the home after a brutal end to a family party: 'My brothers and sisters had reached an age when they could close their ranks . . . The future was to be no longer in my father's hands, but in theirs.'[61] As the eldest son, William Bowyer also took the responsibility for getting his mother away from an abusive father. Mr Bowyer subjected his wife to a regime of extreme cruelty and deprivation, which included keeping her locked in a damp scullery when he was out of the house during the day.[62] Yet even in the face of such abuse it proved extremely difficult to persuade her to leave. Indeed, as her son observed, one consequence of the abuse was to incapacitate her entirely from understanding or resolving her situation: 'Her will-power seemed paralysed as long as she remained in that house.'[63] For most women, leaving without the intervention of adult children was simply not a viable option. There are only a handful of women amongst the autobiographers who lived apart from their husbands, and these women either worked in the mill districts where they could earn relatively good wages or had grown children.[64] And as if the practical obstacles were not enough, there was one other disadvantage under which women laboured: stigma. Lennox Kerr thought that the 'whole business' of his parents' separation was 'a shameful affair I wanted to ignore'. For reasons that Lennox did not give, his parents were living apart and his mother 'was fighting desperately to build a new home and earn our forgiveness'. But she was facing an uphill battle. Lennox's feelings of shame about the break-up were so strong that a year on he still harboured a 'hatred for her'.[65]

Most of the autobiographers who had become severed from their fathers did so as a consequence of their father's unilateral decision to leave the family, though there were also some instances where children and fathers lived apart owing to a wider process of family breakdown. Some of these children were in fact separated from both parents, owing to a joint decision taken by the adults to offload one or two children to their own parents or some other caregiver in an attempt to provide them with a better life, to ease overcrowding at home, or for some other reason unknown to the writer.[66] Men also struggled to keep their children with them in the event of their wife dying or leaving the family home, so a further set of separations was rooted in the problems caused by a maternal absence rather than a father's decision to leave.[67] Yet whatever the precise reason that children lived apart from their fathers, there was a commonality to their experiences thereafter. Fathers and their children became separated for a host of different reasons, but in almost all cases the separation signalled the end of the father's financial responsibility for his child.

There can be no doubt that 'broken' families were frowned upon throughout this period, and that the loss of a father had an emotional significance that children needed to digest. But there was also a more prosaic consideration. Desertion always signalled the end of a father's breadwinning for the family, so it carried a heavy economic burden for children as well. The loss of income that accompanied a father's disappearance was signalled over and again. Jack Jones's father was hardly a model father, running up debts and drinking heavily, yet his departure still precipitated a significant drop in their living standards: 'The good days were over, the hard ones were beginning.'[68] With an absent father, Leonard Fagg noted, 'we were always poor'.[69] John Paton's father had also not made a particularly good breadwinner – he neglected his bakery shop in order to pursue his passion for athletics – but his erratic breadwinning was certainly better than what came next. When the bakery shop burnt down under suspicious circumstances Jamie Paton fled from Aberdeen to England to avoid the consequences. Although initially in contact with the family, he then 'contrived to make a completely successful disappearance', leaving John's mother 'with three children to begin a bitter struggle'.[70] When James Rennie's father set off for a trip one May morning, his family had expected him to return in a few days' time. They never saw him again. It is hardly surprising that the family looked out anxiously for his return, for he had left a wife and 'eight children to seek their way in this dark world alone'.[71] Mr Rennie's earnings were the sole source of his family's materials needs, and his departure was nothing less than a calamity for those he had left behind.

Part of the reason that desertion, as opposed to death, was so serious for families was that it closed down the possibility of remarriage. Working-class wives had no prospect of obtaining a divorce, so unlike widows, they were unable to patch their families back together again by having another go at marriage. Guy Aldred's mother circumvented the difficulties posed by her absent husband by remarrying bigamously, but intentional bigamy was not mentioned by any other autobiographer. Just one other bigamous marriage was recorded in our large collection of autobiographies – that of John Paton's mother, whose husband, Jamie, had disappeared when John was just two. Efforts to trace him drew a blank and after twelve years of silence, he 'was universally held to be dead'. She decided to remarry, only for him to return after an absence of nearly thirty years, raising the fearful prospect of a prosecution for bigamy. In the event she need not have worried. Jamie Paton was travelling with 'a lady he claimed as his wife' and was only back to find out whether he was a beneficiary of his recently deceased father's will. He was not, and when he realised that he quickly departed 'into the silence from which he'd come. My mother's fears of a prosecution for bigamy faded as the years passed and nothing more was heard from him.'[72] As Mrs Paton realised too well, bigamy carried heavy penalties, and it is highly unlikely to have been a common strategy.

It was equally rare for deserted women to live with another man outside wedlock. There seems to be just one example. After the unexplained breakdown of his parents' marriage, Charles Hansford's mother had set up home with another man, and they subsequently remarried after her first husband's death.[73] But her decision to live with a man outside marriage was unusual and not mentioned as a strategy by any other writers. Of course, cohabiting fits into the category of subjects that autobiographers might not want to mention, so the actual rate might be a little higher than these sources imply. Yet a bigamous remarriage was risky and cohabiting outside marriage was socially frowned upon; neither presented a straightforward, workable solution to a deserted mother's situation. Women were more likely to make doomed trips across the country with their children in tow in an attempt to re-establish a household with their absent husband than to pursue such high-risk strategies as starting over with another man, whether bigamously or otherwise.[74]

The rate of fatherlessness was high, affecting one in four of our working-class writers. But, as we know, this was not the only force that worked against family finances. As we saw in the previous chapter, a sizeable minority of fathers (125), though present, were not able to make a proper provision for their family, whether owing to unemployment, ill health or other reasons. If we add these families to the 171 with no breadwinner at all, it becomes clear that the 296 members of this group comfortably outnumber those families headed by a good provider – 213 writers provided evidence that their father was providing for his family.[75] To put this another way, amongst the entire sample, 45 per cent indicated they had no breadwinner or an ineffective one; 32 per cent that they had a good breadwinner, with the remaining 23 per cent not providing enough information to make a determination either way. Of course, the two groups are not strictly comparable. The 32 per cent of writers with a good breadwinner were well provided for throughout their childhood. By contrast, for the 45 per cent whose father had died, was absent, or was failing to provide effectively, the problem was sometimes transient and affected only a part of a writer's childhood, rather than its entirety. During the early years of Annie Jaeger's childhood, her father was drinking the family to destitution, but whilst she was still young he attended a temperance meeting and decided to sign the pledge. Overnight 'he became a changed man', and the family's fortunes improved dramatically.[76] This kind of character reformation was highly unusual, but there were other more common ways to restore a breadwinner to a family: widows could remarry, sick husbands could get better, poor providers could pass away and be replaced by somebody else. Yet if problems of breadwinning were sometimes short-term, it is still clear that they were not negligible either. Almost half of all the autobiographical writers spent at least some part of their childhood in a family without an effective breadwinner, and suffered all the stress, anxiety and poverty that inevitably followed.

In addition to using the autobiographies to provide aggregate totals for mortality, illegitimacy and desertion, we can use them to explore how factors such as region or occupation influenced the general trends. After all, our writers were drawn from all across a Britain that was becoming ever more complex, diverse and urbanised, and, as we saw in the previous chapter, fathers made far more reliable breadwinners in some contexts than in others. Male breadwinning functioned best in rural, and particularly agricultural, families and was far less dependable in towns and cities, especially when fathers had access to high-wage employment. It is time to consider how fatherlessness fits into this picture. Were the rates of mortality, illegitimacy and desertion also responsive to wider socio-economic shifts that were occurring throughout this period?

It is not possible to break down the illegitimacy figures by region. Not only are the numbers too small to allow for robust analysis, but many of the writers born illegitimate ended up living with grandparents or other carers, which did not necessarily reflect the situation in which their mothers had come to find themselves pregnant and unmarried. The proportion of illegitimate children was slightly higher in rural areas than it was in urban areas – 4 per cent as against 2 per cent – but most of these children had been deposited with their grandparents by mothers who lived elsewhere.[77] For this reason, it is safer to use the headline figure of 3 per cent, rather than attempt to break it down further.

For both mortality and desertion, however, it is possible to identify different patterns between urban and rural families. Just as fathers tended to be more reliable providers for their families in the countryside than in the towns, so were mortality and desertion both lower in rural areas – in the case of desertion rates, very considerably so. As a result, the profile of family breakdown was very much more varied than the headline figures imply.

Let us start by looking more closely at the 12 per cent of writers whose fathers had died. This aggregate figure for paternal loss in fact comprises two distinct rates: among the rural children, the figure was 9 per cent, whilst for those living in urban and industrial areas the figure was 14 per cent. (The national figure is closest to that for urban areas because the proportion of the population living in urban areas was greater than those living on the land.) There were two reasons for this divergence in the mortality rate. In part, it stemmed from the fact that men in towns and cities tended to lead unhealthier lifestyles. At least a dozen writers indicated that their father's heavy drinking may have played a role in their death, all of whom were living in large towns or cities – Liverpool, London, Birmingham, Salford, Sheffield and so forth.[78] The incidence of very heavy drinking was much lower in rural areas and was not given as a cause of mortality by any of the writers. Second, urban areas were home to some of the most dangerous industrial employments. Amongst the fatherless were the children of miners,[79] mariners,[80] a marine engineer,[81] a London dock worker,[82] a Durham shipyard plater,[83] a brick-maker,[84] a navvy,[85] as well as others who had contracted fatal injuries or illnesses at work.[86] Working in agriculture was of course not risk-free, but the rate of accidents was lower. Unhealthy lifestyles and more dangerous workplaces combined to provide the higher mortality male rate in urban areas.

Nor was it just the mortality rate that varied between different regions. The rate of desertion was also contingent on where the family was living. Across the autobiographical sample (and excluding the illegitimates), 11 per cent of children became separated from living fathers, but the actual rate of loss was higher in the towns and much lower in the countryside. Of the 167 writers raised in rural areas, just five reported living away from their fathers – 3 per cent of the total.[87] By contrast, 14 per cent of those raised in urban or industrial areas reported living away from their fathers. (Once again, the national figure is closer to the urban figure because the urban population was larger.) Furthermore, not only was the risk of paternal separation much higher in urban areas, the mechanisms were different. In the countryside, although a handful of children became separated from their fathers, in only one of these cases had the father left his family and given up his responsibility towards them.[88] In two cases of rural paternal separation, the parents in fact remained together: it appears that these families had shipped one of their children off to relatives as a response to poverty or overcrowding, or perhaps in order to help their ageing parents keep their household running.[89] In the other case, the mother had died and the child had ended up with his extended family rather than remaining with his single father.[90] Finally, there is the previously mentioned case of Charles Hansford, whose mother had separated from his father when Charles was about ten. Hansford's autobiography provides no detail about his parents' relationship, or the timing or the cause of its breakdown, but it is possible to use the census to learn more about the family. This reveals that although the Hansfords lived in the countryside, they were not an agricultural family: they were running a pub. It may be that an alcohol addiction was at the root of the discord between Hansford's parents and that this was why his mother decamped with the children to the nearest town. In the countryside, married men simply did not up stumps and desert their families – or, if they did, this action was so transgressive that it was not something that adult writers cared to write about. In the rare, reported instances where fathers and children became separated, they did so through a more complex set of circumstances.

In the towns and cities, by contrast, men most certainly did abandon their families. In the urban context, 14 per cent of the autobiographers had lived in households with a living, but absent, father. As with the rural families, a handful of children had been sent away from both parents to ease pressure on the household,[91] and a few had been entrusted to others following the mother's death.[92] But in the majority of cases, the mother was present and providing care for the children and the father had simply walked out and chucked in all responsibility for those he left behind. As the title for this chapter put it, 'Father disappeared and left mother to brave the storm.'[93] So it happened, many times over. What these children had lost was not simply their father, but also his wages. Indeed, it was this loss of the father's earnings that was the defining feature of paternal separation in these writers' childhoods.

Undoubtedly, the size and anonymity of towns and cities made it relatively easy for men to leave their families, yet there were also more fundamental social changes that were integral to this shift. Throughout history, soldiers and sailors had always had more opportunity to slip away than most,[94] but in the nineteenth century these men were joined by a raft of others. Most of the men who skipped town worked in high-wage sectors of the economy, and though most had not been particularly reliable breadwinners before their departure, they were nonetheless able to access higher than average earnings. Amongst the men who left their families were navvies,[95] a docker,[96] a plasterer,[97] a warehouseman,[98] a cotton weaver,[99] a skilled factory worker,[100] a quarryman[101] and a riveter in the shipbuilding industry,[102] as well as several other skilled workers and small business owners.[103] In economic terms, these workers earned considerably more than agricultural workers, which suggests a much more complex and ambiguous relationship between male wages and familial well-being than we might imagine.

The different patterns for male mortality and paternal desertion between rural and urban areas combined to create distinct regional patterns of fatherlessness. The higher rate of mortality (14 per cent) and desertion (14 per cent) in urban areas, when added to the 3 per cent illegitimacy rate, combined to deprive 31 per cent of children in urban areas of their fathers. The corresponding figure for the children raised on the land was less than half – 15 per cent – made up of mortality (9 per cent), absence (3 per cent) and illegitimacy (3 per cent). And if we add all the children raised in the fatherless households to those with unreliable fathers whom we considered in the previous chapter, an even more dramatic picture emerges. In the urban environment where death, desertion and unreliable breadwinning were all widespread, households without a steady breadwinner were in fact more numerous than those with. There were problems surrounding the male wage in almost 50 per cent of the urban households, whereas just 23 per cent indicated that their father had been present and providing for the family throughout their childhood (the remaining writers did not indicate either way). The situation was reversed in rural areas, where the majority of writers (56 per cent) indicated that their father had been a good breadwinner, whilst 18 per cent of households had lacked a reliable breadwinner – usually through ill health, unemployment or low wages rather than an absent father or one who failed to share his wages (the remaining quarter did not indicate either way).

We are brought again to the conclusion that for some households high male wages had the unexpected effect of destabilising, rather than enriching, the family. Cities offered men abundant work at good wages, but they were also places where the family was more fragile and the links between fathers and children were less certain. Nor were these patterns unique to the Victorian and Edwardian period. Once more, the earlier set of 250 autobiographers born between 1750 and 1830 permits us to sketch out the pre-history of the patterns we have uncovered, and show that these trends were bound up with broader socio-economic processes that had been occurring in Britain during the eighteenth century.

The records reveal that the overall total for fatherlessness was broadly the same over the entire period. It was (as we have just seen) 26 per cent between 1830 and 1914; it was 28 per cent between 1750 and 1830. The causes, however, were very different. After 1830, fatherlessness was split between mortality and separation from living fathers roughly evenly. Amongst the earlier autobiographies, by contrast, mortality was considerably higher – it explains the absence of 22 per cent of fathers – whereas separation from living fathers was much lower: illegitimacy and desertion together made up the final 6 per cent of missing fathers. As ever we should be wary of placing too much weight on the statistics, as the shame of illegitimacy and family breakdown may have prompted some writers to edit such information from their life story. Nonetheless, the evidence suggests that despite a marked improvement in male mortality over the period there was no corresponding decline in single-parent families. In effect, at the same time as mortality improved after 1830, marriages became less stable and more prone to dissolution by other means, thereby offsetting the decline in the death rate.

This suggestion is further reinforced if we look more closely at the small group of children – just fifteen in all – who were separated from living fathers in the period before 1830. Recall that for the later period, most separations were caused by desertion and illegitimacy played only a minor role. For this earlier period, by contrast, separations were evenly split between illegitimacy and abandonment. The illegitimacy rate was unchanged: seven of the autobiographical writers were illegitimate, 3 per cent of the total, and as was usual in cases of illegitimacy these fathers had played no role in their children's upbringing.[104] The remaining eight were legitimate and had begun life within their nuclear family, only to see this subsequently collapse – usually early in their childhood. In three of the cases, the father's absence appears to have been related to the death or absence of the mother: following this maternal loss the child's household had been broken up and children farmed out to extended family.[105] In the other five, the mother was present and running the home, but the father was no longer residing there.[106] It is also possible to identify a trace outline of the regional and occupational differences that are so clearly apparent for the later period. Before 1830, desertion tended to be located in high-wage families in urban and industrial areas, rather than in low-wage agricultural ones. Just one of the autobiographers living in a rural community reported that a living father had played no role in his upbringing. This was John Shipp, who described his father as 'a soldier in a foreign land'. When his mother died, both John and his brother ended up in the village workhouse.[107] Otherwise, the absent fathers and their families were all located in urban areas. One was a miner,[108] and the other three were living in large towns – Edinburgh, Chester, Manchester.[109]

Humans, as we all know, are fallible, so it should not occasion too much surprise to find that there had always been some men who walked out on their paternal responsibilities, whether before their child's birth or after. Yet it is historically significant that the number who did so in the poorer and more rural society of the eighteenth century and earlier was much lower. Before 1830, the majority of the population lived in villages, in smaller, face-to-face societies where men had few opportunities to evade their obligations and where communities were able to exert pressure on men to maintain their children. The Poor Law was used to extract payment from men for children they had fathered outside wedlock and local officials sometimes sought to facilitate marriages between pregnant women and their unwilling partners in an attempt to shift financial responsibility for the child from the parish to the father. Even so late as the 1820s, rural parishes could be found orchestrating marriages between pregnant women and their unwilling partners. For example, when James Holloway made his partner Celia pregnant, local bigwigs bought rings for the pair and escorted them to the parish church where they were forced to wed.[110] By the later nineteenth century, this kind of interference in the lives of a young couple was unthinkable and local officials had lost their authority to bring pregnant women into legal unions with the reputed father. The large cities simply lacked the mechanisms of control that had traditionally shepherded unmarried parents towards the altar. Britain's towns and cities were too large to exert the kind of social pressure that for generations had channelled men and women's desires into lifelong, legally binding unions.

But the outcome of these trends was highly unbalanced between the sexes. High waged employment in towns and cities enabled men to exit an unsatisfactory marriage but it offered no such freedom to women. Women could, and did, attempt to insure themselves against single-motherhood by delaying sex until marriage, but they could not prevent an unwilling breadwinner from leaving. From their perspective, the freedoms that came with the high-wage economy were not freedoms at all, but a serious threat to their economic security.

The distinctive features of urban and industrial areas are stark: a higher death rate, a much higher desertion rate and a significantly higher risk of being raised in a fatherless household. It is also clear that there was something within the shift from rural to urban areas that destabilised the traditional nuclear family and triggered a breakdown in the social mechanisms that had traditionally upheld the nuclear family of married parents and their children. In the new world of the city, when men found the pressures of marriage and parenthood more than they could bear, they were able to walk away. And the consequences of these changes for families and living standards were profound. In the gender-divided world of nineteenth-century Britain, fathers (and their wages) were vital for family well-being. Male earnings formed the bedrock of family life. Without a male wage earner, mothers had to step in and attempt to earn some income themselves. The ways in which they did so forms the focus of our next chapter.

6

'TOIL IN THE FACTORY, TOIL IN THE HOME'
WORKING MOTHERS

Like many of the mothers described in the autobiographies, Sarah Geary did not lead an easy life. She had been born in Bedfordshire in the 1850s into a family of at least nine children, and she had never been to school. Work began at the age of seven (like many women in the county she was employed in the local lace industry) and family life ended at thirteen: at that age, she was sent away to service, no doubt to help relieve the pressure at home.[1]

By her twenties, Sarah, for reasons unknown, had moved to Sheffield, and there she married an iron worker named Samuel Pratt. But (as her son later observed) 'marriage was no escape from hard work'. Samuel died a few years into the marriage, leaving her a single mother with a small child, 'so she had struggled along for some time "taking in lodgers", as working people do' and earning a little extra by baking and selling bread and cakes. Nor did her second marriage to John Murphy a few years later 'make things easier'. Murphy's weekly wage of twenty-four shillings was adequate, but the hefty weekly deduction that had to be made for 'his beer money' left 'not much' for a family of four. His regular overtime seemed to impoverish the family rather than enrich it, as it just encouraged even heavier drinking at the weekends. His periodic absences, or 'sprees', did not help either. He would disappear for weeks and return broke – 'it often took the best part of the year to clear up the wreckage'. So throughout this second marriage, Sarah found that she was unable to depend upon a man's wage and needed to turn out for work herself. She 'renewed the baking and selling of bread and cakes' and from a young age her son was pressed into service hawking her goods from door to door between school hours.[2] When her second husband met an accident and early death, she once again needed to find a more substantial source of income. This time Sarah established a small grocery and sweet shop, but her health broke down and the business failed, leaving her dependent upon her son for support.[3]

Sarah Geary's experiences remind us how powerfully a woman's life was controlled by the presence (or not) of a male breadwinner, and of the decisions and choices he made. Throughout much of her life, Sarah's maintenance depended upon her personal relationships to men – first her father, then her two husbands and finally her son – but there were frequently times when they had been unable to provide enough for a decent subsistence, so she too had worked, at least so far as her domestic responsibilities permitted. Of course, it should not occasion much surprise that many married women worked. We have seen enough about male breadwinning and family breakdown to know that a great many women could not rely on the men in their lives for their maintenance. But it is now time to address their experiences more directly. What kind of options were available to married women without a reliable breadwinner for support, and how did women navigate their way through these options?

Let us begin with the numbers. If we gather together all the information that the autobiographies contain about mothers working prior to 1914, just under half – 44 per cent – indicated their mother had undertaken paid employment during their childhood. As ever, we must be aware of the limits of our data. The autobiographies reveal that 44 per cent of mothers had worked, not that 56 per cent did not. Only 16 per cent of the autobiographers clearly indicated that their mothers had not worked outside the home. Henry Turner, for example, was one of ten children and he helpfully stated that his mother had not gone to work outside the home as she had 'enough to do with looking after us kids'.[4] But in the remaining 40 per cent of cases, the writers simply did not provide enough evidence about their mothers to enable us to determine whether they worked for wages or not.[5] The most we can say, then, is that at least 44 per cent of the autobiographers' mothers had undertaken some paid work, though some under-reporting in the sources means that the true number may be a little higher. At any rate, the evidence suggests that a very sizeable proportion of women worked after marriage, and their experiences merit further investigation.

Not only was the mothers' participation rate quite high, it was also quite stable, both over the century and across diverse geographical regions. Between 1830 and 1914, just over 40 per cent of autobiographers recalled that their mother had worked, and although the figures fluctuate slightly from one decade to the next, there is no clear trend in either direction. Likewise, participation rates did not vary sizeably between different regions, despite very significant variations in opportunities for female employment across the country. Industrial settlements, large cities, market towns and rural areas all reported roughly similar rates of employment: in each case, somewhere between 40 and 45 per cent of all writers indicated that their mother had worked.[6]

The remarkably stable nature of the married women's participation in the workplace deserves emphasis, particularly given what we already know about economic growth throughout this period. A wide range of economic measures have indicated that the economy underwent unprecedented growth and restructuring after 1830, yet none of these changes appear to have made much of an impact on the likelihood of married women participating in the labour market.[7] Equally, the nineteenth century witnessed the emergence of the breadwinning family model – the ideological justification for higher male wages, a wage sufficient to support the male breadwinner and his dependent wife and children at home.[8] Yet this too had very little impact on women's experiences, failing to raise male wages to a level at which paid work for married women became unnecessary in most families. Indeed, when we look more closely at the autobiographies, it becomes evident that married women's working patterns do not fit into our usual ways of conceiving work at all.

Although the participation rate of women in the workforce provides a useful starting point for our discussion of women's working lives, the autobiographies, unlike other sources documenting women's work, also contain a wealth of ancillary detail concerning the triggers that prompted women to undertake paid work outside the home (or indeed to give it up) and they thus permit us to extend our investigation considerably further. And when we ask why some mothers worked whilst others did not, it becomes evident that the apparent similarity between diverse regions conceals some very real differences. Above all, it is necessary to distinguish between the urban and rural families, for although the headline participation rate of the two groups was almost identical, the kind of work that women did and the motivating factors behind it were very different indeed. As we have previously seen, for those children raised in towns and cities, family life was often substantially different from that of children raised in the countryside. The paternal death rate was higher, families were less stable and male breadwinning was less reliable. For these reasons, families were more likely to lack a male wage, and this was a key driver for women's entry to the workforce. Indeed, for women living in urban areas, participation in paid employment was determined primarily by their relationship with a breadwinner. Like Sarah Geary, whose story opened this chapter, women in towns and cities weaved in and out of the labour market according to what was going on in their homes rather than the opportunities that were available outside it. In rural areas, by contrast, women's working patterns were far less sensitive to domestic affairs and were largely driven by custom and tradition. Let us begin to explore these differences by looking at the experiences of women in the urban context.

The average participation rate for the urban women was almost identical to the nationwide average – 43 per cent. But if we divide our mothers into two groups, those who had a reliable male income and those who did not, then it becomes clear that beneath the average figure lie two different groups, each behaving in its own distinct way. The women who were married to a good provider were less likely to work; those married to a poor provider were more likely to do so. In fact, the autobiographies allow us to quantify this effect. Amongst the urban women who were living with a reliable breadwinner, the proportion who added paid work to their housework drops from the average of 43 per cent to 25 per cent (thirty-seven mothers in all). In the other 75 per cent of cases, women took advantage of their situation to retreat from the labour market altogether. Amongst those women living in towns who did not have a dependable breadwinner the situation was largely reversed: almost 70 per cent of these wives went out to work, whilst just 30 per cent did not. For women living in urban areas, work outside the home was motivated primarily by the need to patch a hole in the family finances, and if this was not necessary, most opted to stay at home.

Not only did the urban women largely choose housework rather than paid work so long as their domestic situation permitted, but the minority who did work almost always did so in a part-time, and often short-term, capacity, and they usually worked within the home rather than outside it. Of the thirty-seven working mothers, just a handful worked full time and long term. John Griffin was raised in one of these rare families where both parents worked outside the home on a long-term basis. As a weaver, his mother was able to earn the same wage as his father – over thirty shillings a week – so there was a clear incentive for the family to operate with two breadwinners rather than one.[9] From John's account, it appears that she worked throughout John's childhood. The two other mothers who continued to work outside the home throughout their married life despite being married to a reliable provider each had an unusual and marketable skill: one worked as a singer,[10] the other as a schoolteacher.[11] In both these cases, the mother worked in addition to the father. Clearly, however, these women were exceptional in that they had a skill that gave them value in the labour market. It is also striking how rare this was. Indeed, amongst our entire collection of several hundred autobiographies, these three mothers appear to have been the only ones who kept working outside the home continuously throughout their marriage even though they were married to a reliable breadwinner. Dual-income families with both parents working outside the home scarcely existed within working-class communities.

This pattern of women withdrawing from paid employment after marriage and motherhood was even replicated in the mill districts, where – unusually – women had the capacity to earn relatively good wages. As we saw in Chapter 1, most of the girls raised in the mill towns started work in the mill once they had left school and by their late teens were earning a wage considerably in excess of the average wage of a male agricultural labourer. Yet despite the wage premium they could command, they too abandoned work once they had married. Unlike Mrs Griffin, who capitalised on the factory districts' high wages to increase the family's income, most mothers in the autobiographies took advantage of the relatively high male wage to take precisely the opposite course of action and withdraw from the workplace altogether. After all, mill work was demanding. The work was often physically arduous and the hours were always long. Whilst married mill workers with no or few children sometimes combined both roles for a limited period of time, most tended to give up this endeavour once their families had begun to expand.

The experiences of Mrs Yates's mother were typical. In the early years of her marriage, she managed to combine motherhood with paid employment. After the birth of her first child she returned to her work in the mill and left the care of her child to her mother. But as her family began to grow – she was pregnant multiple times though it is not clear how many survived infancy – her work at the mill had to go and she began to devote herself full-time to the running of the home.[12] In a few families, mothers remained at home throughout their children's early years, but traded domesticity for paid work once the pressures of a young family had eased. Philip Snowden's mother, for example, returned to the mill when her eldest daughter 'was old enough to look after the house'.[13] There were also a few mothers who managed to work through their children's early years, returning to work after each pregnancy, but who gave up their mill work once their eldest children were able to earn in their place.[14] Either way, though it was clearly not unknown for mothers to combine work with marriage, they generally did so on a short-term rather than long-term basis.

And, in fact, most of the mill-town mothers took neither of these courses of action if they were married to a man who was able to support them. Instead, they gave up their job as soon as their first child arrived, if not before, and did not return. Mrs Yates, like her mother before her, started work at the mill as soon as she was able – at ten years old. But unlike her mother she did not plan to continue there after marriage. Indeed, she made giving up her mill work a condition of getting married. As she recalled whilst retelling her life story: 'I said I wouldn't have anybody as couldn't keep me at home' – though she quickly hastened to add that she did 'love my husband you know' and 'didn't just marry him because he could keep me at home'.[15] For Mrs Yates, as well as for many others, factory work was just too hard to combine with running a home. After spending her early adolescence in the mill, Mary Gawthorpe's mother thought that 'home was heaven' and she had no wish to undertake any form of paid work after marriage. As her daughter explained:

Mother thought Father should support the family. That was the long and short of it. Never at any time did I hear a word to indicate that she felt called upon to do more than run the home and work in it. She would sew to the bone for that family in the home, but, as for going out to work, I doubt that [she could] . . . bear to think the words.[16]

Deborah Smith was forced by circumstances to return to the mill when she had two children under the age of three. Here is what she thought of it: 'It is a slave's life when you come home after a hard day's toil, to do the housework at night. Life is nothing but work, and sometimes you feel as tired in the morning as you did at night when you went to rest. Hurry all day long with meals, and home is worse than uncomfortable.'[17] The high wages that women could earn in the factories were simply not enough to compensate for the double burden of very long hours at the mill and the housekeeping. Although some women did combine mill work and motherhood at some point in their marriage, very few women actively made this choice over a sustained period.

The difficulties that women faced in returning to the mill after childbirth were compounded by the absence of childcare in the factory districts. Despite the prevalence of female employment, childcare for working mothers was difficult to find. A fortunate few had their own mothers in the neighbourhood willing to take over their domestic responsibilities – this, recall, was the solution that had allowed Mrs Yates's mother to return to the mill after the birth of her first child. But those without a family support network needed to find an alternative solution, and with very little commercial provision the barriers to working mothers were formidable. Most mothers had to fashion their own ad hoc solutions. As Joseph Barlow Brooks explained, when his mother returned to work, it 'meant leaving her baby to be nursed at a neighbour's house where it remained until night. The neighbour collected a few children and earned a weekly income in this way. It was a common practice.' But the consequences of herding large numbers of babies and toddlers in a small working-class home can be easily imagined. After a few months at his minders, Joseph's baby brother broke out in sores. His mother left her place at work, but despite her best efforts to nurse him back to health, he passed away from the infection he had picked up at the neighbour's home.[18] Sam Smith had also been put out to nurse by a mother who worked full-time in a factory. His mother suspected his nurse was dosing him with gin 'to keep [him] quiet'.[19] Occasionally, desperate mothers just dispensed with any form of childcare at all even from a very young age. One of Allan Taylor's earliest memories was of spending his days alone in his family's room in a Glasgow tenement with his mother returning twice in the day to check on him. During her long absences, she tied a rope around his waist and fixed it to the bed leg, so as to prevent him from reaching the fire. Allan estimated that he was just four years old at the time.[20]

Not only did working mothers struggle to find adequate care for their children, the responsibility for such arrangements always lay with the mother. Childcare was emphatically women's work and it did not cease to become so simply because a mother was out at work. When mothers needed to work, the responsibility for children could be passed on to other female family members, but there is no evidence anywhere within the autobiographical literature of fathers taking on this role, even when women were working because their husband was unemployed and was, therefore, presumably at home. As a result, these working mothers found that a very long working day was also bookended by the need to ferry children to and from their minders before and after work. When Hannah Burgess's husband found himself out of work, Hannah returned to her old occupation of power-loom weaver, leaving her young toddler at 'Sally Schofield's to be nursed', while her sister became 'a second mother' to the older children who remained at home. It was even her responsibility to take her daughter to her nurse's house, leaving the house at half-past five in the morning and collecting her on her way home in the evening.[21] What the unemployed Mr Burgess was doing at these times was unexplained.[22] It did not need to be explained: there was simply no expectation in the working-class family that fathers would ever look after small children. The sole responsibility that women bore for children no doubt helps to explain why working outside the home was such an unpopular choice for mothers.[23]

The mill workers were not alone in abandoning paid work once they had a house and children to look after. All forms of outside work available to women living in towns were extremely difficult to combine with motherhood, and there are very few examples of mothers attempting to do so if there was a male wage regularly coming in. Some women managed to continue with employment in the early years of their marriage, but they tended to give up when they had children to care for. Harry Gosling's mother had trained as a teacher at the Borough Road Training College and so long as she had just one child she had managed to hold onto her job, taking her 'baby to school with her to be able to look after it between whiles'.[24] But the strategy proved unsustainable once her family began to grow and she soon retreated to full-time motherhood. It was very difficult for women to work outside the home, particularly once they had children to care for: society simply lacked the support structures that would have enabled women to reconcile the demands of a full-time job with the needs of their household.

As a result, most mothers, if they chose to work, did so inside the home rather than outside. Almost all the women who worked whilst married to a reliable breadwinner were engaged in some form of income-generating activity based within the home, an arrangement that enabled them to meet their domestic duties at the same time as earning some income. In some of these, mothers were working alongside their husbands in a variety of small businesses typical of urban Britain. The grocery shops that were run by Mr Lipton, Mr Haddow, Mr Turner and Mr Hodge, for example, all benefited from the assistance of their wives, as did the pub that Mr Davis ran in an industrial village just outside Chesterfield.[25] As Martin Haddow recalled of his parents' grocery shop, 'my mother was the hard-working managing partner'.[26] In south-east London, Lily Astell's parents ran a café together.[27] A fruit-shop,[28] a tobacconist,[29] a coal business,[30] a bakery,[31] a couple of hotels,[32] two tailoring businesses and a hat-repair business were also mentioned as enterprises that were run jointly by both parents.[33]

Alongside these were a range of small businesses that women managed independently of their husbands. A small grocery shop operated from the family's front room was clearly perceived as being compatible with marriage and motherhood, and a few of the autobiographical writers indicated that their mother managed a shop whilst their fathers worked outside the home.[34] Grocery shops, sweet shops and tobacconists were those most commonly managed by women, but occasionally women traded on a larger scale. In Southwark, the enormously enterprising and energetic mother of Margaret Wheeler ran a succession of small businesses from the family's home, including curing and selling bloaters, running a small grocer shop in the front room, money lending, coal-selling, ice-cream selling and a chip shop. As Mrs Wheeler's daughter wearily recalled, as one business waned a new venture began, eventually terminating in the venture to fry and sell chips. As she told her family, 'there isn't any chip shop near we should do alright' – though, as her daughter observed, in the end 'the chip lark died a natural death the same as everything else'.[35]

In addition to the shopkeepers and traders, there was a small group of mothers who made some extra income for their families through skills they had acquired before marriage, but the range of their businesses is telling and clearly betrays the limited opportunities that had been available to these women when they first entered the labour market as young girls. For the most part, these endeavours were based upon domestic skills – needlework, cookery and laundry. Enterprises of this kind could be something as small-scale as taking in a lodger or two.[36] Those who had had the fortune to learn dressmaking had the possibility of making a little extra income by this means. Occasionally, married women succeeded in earning a significant income from their dressmaking. Mrs Downer, for example, had been a successful dressmaker before marriage and she kept many of her customers after marriage as well, specialising in expensive and fashionable evening dresses for wealthy ladies and

6.1 This photograph is of S. F. Leaver's General Confectioner's, although Stephen Leaver was recorded variously in the census as a 'paper finisher' or 'paper maker' and there is no evidence he knew the art of confectionery. The shop appears to have been established by his wife Kate at some point between 1901 and 1911. She is pictured here with her husband and two daughters, both living at home and likely assisting in the shop at the time of the 1911 census.

travelling widely to service her customers.[37] For the most part, however, women undertook needlework on a much smaller scale and with far less in the way of pecuniary reward. The experiences of David Martin's mother, who collected a small package of shirts from a local warehouse to sew together once a week, were more typical.[38]

Others made some extra money through their ability to cook. Mick Burke's mother, for example, 'opened a shop in the front of the house' and sold ribs, cabbage and roast potatoes 'for coppers' to customers who brought their own plates and basins. She also cooked a hot meal twice a day for two of her son's workmates.[39] Otherwise, the only skill that most women had available to trade was laundry. This might be a very small enterprise, taking in a few of the neighbours' washing or doing their mangling,[40] though once again there were occasionally more substantial ventures. Amy Gomm's mother set up a 'hand laundry' in Oxford to cater to the needs of male undergraduates who 'were used to having things done for them'. As she emphasised: 'It wasn't just a question of "taking in washing", and doing it in the kitchen between cooking the meals. These were purpose-built premises, with separate buildings equipped for washing, for drying, for hand ironing.'[41] Mrs Gomm employed six workers in her laundry, and the family believed theirs to be the second-largest hand laundry in the city.

Most of these writers also made clear that their mothers were fitting the running of these small businesses around managing the house and raising the children. Indeed, the timing and the scale of women's involvement in these various income-generating activities were often closely related to the needs of their families. Those trading on a very small scale usually did so because they were still in the midst of raising young children, and the larger undertakings were generally the preserve of women who had small families, who no longer had small children to care for, or who had older daughters capable of doing the family's childcare and housework in their place. For instance, Mrs Piper took on her sweet shop and tobacconist's with one pre-school child and an older daughter who had left school and started work – she, needless to say, was soon recalled from her employment and put to work in the home and family shop instead.[42] Alice Moody's mother 'kept up her tailoring' whilst Alice was small, but she too had older daughters to help with the running of the home.[43] Mrs Gomm set up her laundry when most of her eight children had grown up and she had two daughters of an age to act as 'the home-makers, more or less' and to keep an eye on her youngest child.[44] Only Mrs Wheeler's succession of business ventures bore little connection to the needs of her large family, but that was because she flatly disregarded the legal requirement to send her children to school. From a young age, all her children were drawn into working for her ever-changing portfolio of businesses. As her eldest daughter told her readers: 'I must tell you, Katie or I never hardly went to school. Mum would let us get ready and then say no school for you two today. I have a nice little errand for you . . .'[45] Mrs Wheeler aside, however, most of these women's ventures were fitted around the changing needs of their family and were consequently of limited duration.

Furthermore, as the writers consistently stressed, these kinds of home-based enterprises ran alongside a woman's ordinary domestic work; they did not replace them. Arthur Horner's mother may have 'looked after the shop' but this, he stressed, was in addition to '[looking after] the family'.[46] Lily Astell's mother 'didn't approve' that her sister-in-law went to work and left her children in the doorway waiting for her to come home, so one must assume that she believed it possible to fulfil her domestic responsibilities at the same time as running the café with her husband.[47] Wilfrid Middlebrook described how when his parents had set up their bakeshop, his mother had been 'deep in the running [of] both the household and the business'. Doing the baking as well as the housework clearly proved too much, for after a while they employed a professional baker, which gave her 'more time to look after the home'.[48] On the other hand, Dora Kerby's mother combined managing a tobacconist and raising a family of eight children by having 'a young woman to help in the house by the name of Polly Cannaway'.[49] Indeed, in many of these families, mothers managed the double burden of housework and running the business by buying in some extra help for the house – at the least, they hired a woman to help with the weekly wash, though sometimes they engaged more substantial domestic assistance as well.[50]

It is hard to be certain what motivated these women to add income-earning activities to their domestic labour as their ventures are recalled through the eyes of their children, who did not usually discuss why their mother had made this choice – who, indeed, may very often not have known what lay behind their mother's reasoning. As Mrs Gomm admitted when looking back over the six years when her mother ran a domestic laundry, 'There'd be a lot of "Don't Knows" if we had to fill in a questionnaire on the happenings at that time,' including whose idea the whole enterprise had been.[51] Yet so far as we can establish, most of these writers believed that their mother's work had not been strictly necessary from a financial point of view and stemmed from a desire to raise the family's living standards, as well, perhaps, as the desire to do something new. For these families with the security of a regular male wage, a mother's work seems to have been somewhat analogous to fathers taking on overtime so as to pay for treats for the family. David Martin, for example, made clear that his mother did her dressmaking to buy little extras for the children – she used the money that she made to pay for family holidays. When her children earned enough to pay for holidays, she gave up the work.[52] Most of the families where mothers took on some form of trading were stable and relatively prosperous, and the mother's work appears as a strategy to improve the family's financial position further. Indeed, none of these autobiographers indicated that their father's low earnings had been at the root of their mother's decision to work, whilst several emphasised in various ways that their mother's work had been a choice rather than a necessity. For example, when Wilfrid Middlebrook's parents started their bakeshop, his father was holding down two good jobs, one at the cotton mill and one as a musician in the evenings. In fact, he was 'earning more money than ever he had done before'.[53] When Alice Moody's father changed jobs, her mother 'found herself much better off', but she still kept up her tailoring: she 'steadily put her earnings in the Post Office Savings Bank for a rainy day'.[54] Similarly, Elizabeth Harrison's family was not in great need when her mother set up her tobacconist's. Her father was a schoolteacher and the family was 'comfortable' compared to the neighbours; her mother was 'not obliged to go out to work to make ends meet'.[55] Getting the shop was 'a step up the social ladder'.[56] Other writers indicated that 'we weren't that poor'[57] and that 'we were one of the luckier families'.[58] Mrs Wheeler's husband was also a steady worker and the family 'were considered very well off' by their neighbours.[59] As these women were married to good wage earners, their paid work was not needed in order to make good a deficiency in the male wage. Instead, it served to raise the family's living standards.

By the same token, however, taking on additional paid work was not universally understood by urban families as an effective means of raising living standards. Amongst the autobiographical writers living in towns, around 150 mothers were married to reliable breadwinners, yet fewer than forty had taken on paid work, and in almost every instance their work had been inside the home, and usually as an interlude that wrapped around the changing needs of their family rather than as a long-term undertaking. A comfortable majority of the women married to good providers – over 70 per cent – did not at any time undertake income-generating work in addition to their housework. We must conclude that they and their families perceived that unpaid domestic work made a greater contribution to the family's living standards than the limited financial contribution they were able to make through the various income-generating strategies available to women.[60]

But, of course, these women were married to reliable breadwinners and one thing we know about married life, and in particular for those who lived in towns, was that many households did not have a reliable breadwinner. Indeed, it is worth repeating that these were a minority of all urban households. As we saw in the previous chapter, just 23 per cent of the autobiographers raised in urban areas indicated that their father had been present and providing for the family throughout their childhood. By contrast, almost 50 per cent indicated that there had at some point been problems surrounding the male wage. We have seen that there were various ways by which this occurred: death, desertion and unreliable wage-earning or wage-sharing. All were common in the urban context and all reappear as forces prompting married women to re-enter the labour market. In these families, women did not take on paid work in order to supplement the male wage, or to raise the family's living standards. They did so in a desperate attempt to substitute for a male wage earner, though as must already be clear, the prospects for women to earn anything equivalent to a male wage were extremely slender.

At worst, death deprived a family of its much-needed breadwinner. As 14 per cent of the fathers of writers raised in urban communities had passed away during the writer's childhood, this constitutes a fairly sizeable group. The death of a father involved a substantial adjustment for any family and one very common outcome was for the mother to return to work. Of the sixty-two urban mothers who were widowed before their child reached the age of fourteen, forty-eight, or nearly 80 per cent, re-entered the workforce after their husband's death.[61]

But even in the absence of such a catastrophe as death, there were many other events that could disrupt the entry of a male wage into the family. For some families, a bout of ill health or unemployment provided the trigger for mothers to re-enter the labour market. These problems could be short term and temporary, and where this was the case, women accordingly returned to the job market on a temporary basis. Joseph Stamper's father was a well-paid moulder in an iron foundry, for example, and in normal times earned enough to keep the family well. But during occasional bouts of unemployment, his mother took in a little dressmaking – 'of a make-do-and-mend type' – to help tide the family over.[62] When Charles Humphreys's father was out of work for 'one long stretch' of thirteen weeks, his mother went out charring.[63] For these women, paid work was a very short-term measure to help the family through a difficult patch. In some households, though, health problems proved to be more intractable, with the consequence that the mother's involvement in the labour market was more sustained. When Rose Gibbs's father returned wounded from the Boer War he was out of work for eight long years. Inevitably, her mother had to find some paid work: she returned to the old employer for whom she had been a maid and did daily domestic work for them.[64] Mary Bertenshaw's mother also worked outside the home for several years. Her father, she explained, had been disabled by a bicycle accident and struggled to earn a regular wage, so her mother worked full-time as a 'fancy ironer' at a laundry in Manchester in order to help keep the family afloat.[65]

In addition, there was a significant core of fathers within the autobiographies who were irregular workers or who failed to share their wages, and as men tended to engage in such behaviours over the long term, these accordingly loom large as triggers for married women to return to work. The autobiographies contain several sorry stories about the shifts that mothers needed to make when their husbands failed either to work steadily or to share their wages with their families. Indeed, there were almost as many mothers amongst the autobiographers who returned to work because their husbands, though present, were unreliable providers as there were whose husbands had died: against the forty-eight working widows, there were forty-three writers who indicated that their father's irregular provision was the reason their mother had worked.[66]

Finally, there were those writers whose fathers had been alive but absent during their childhood, and because paternal absence was so widespread in urban areas, this too constitutes a significant group of families. In towns, 14 per cent of the autobiographers had an absent father, a figure equal to the 14 per cent whose fathers had died. And the proportion of mothers who returned to the workplace was once again high. In fact, the deserted wives had a slightly higher likelihood of entering the labour market than the widows. Of the forty deserted wives, all but seven, or 83 per cent of the total, were at work.[67]

There were a number of ways in which these women's strategies differed from those married to reliable breadwinners. First, when women did not, for whatever reason, have a husband providing a steady wage, they also did not have the luxury of fitting their income earning around the ages and needs of their children. These women started work when they needed to and kept going for as long as necessary. As a result, their employment tended to be much more sustained, with several writers indicating that their mother had worked throughout their childhood – some indeed only stopping when their sons were of an age to join the labour market in their place.[68] Second, these mothers were far more likely to be employed outside the home. This forms a stark contrast to the women married to good providers who very rarely worked outside the home and almost always made extra money for the family from activities based within the household. Whilst the women with either no or an unreliable husband also tried this strategy, they were far more likely to find that it was inadequate for their situation, with the result that many more of them took up work outside the home.

Only a small minority of women were able to make a going concern of a home-based business without the presence of a male wage earner to help sustain them. A few of the widows appear to have managed this, though in each case they drew upon their dead husband's assets before starting out. For example, Laura Walker's father had kept a watchmaking business. When he died, her mother converted the premises into a shop where she sold sweets, bread, teacakes and ice-cream.[69] But Mrs Walker was fortunate that her husband had been a good provider for the family and left a profitable business: it left her something from which to carve out a new livelihood. Most widows were left with far less, and those whose husbands were ill, unemployed, absent or failing to share their wages had no real hope of launching such an undertaking. Instead, they faced the very pressing problem of how to earn a living whilst also running a home and raising children.

More typical were the experiences of Hilda Snowman's mother. When she was widowed with two girls – one of seven years and one of just five weeks – she was left with nothing. All that was available to the family was a pittance from the parish, 'so mother had to find some way of earning a living whereby she could look after her children at the same time'.[70] She settled upon the same solution as Sarah Geary, whose story opened this chapter: 'baking bread and cakes' in her home.[71] Dressmaking was also suitable for women with little or no capital who wanted, or needed, to work from home. Following the death of her husband, Henry Tomlinson's mother got out her sewing machine and worked in the evenings once her children were in bed.[72] Taking in needlework was exploited by several of the women who needed to top up their family's income whilst also taking care of children.[73] The options for those who could not sew were more limited. They usually had few options other than taking in either lodgers or laundry – though the rewards from both were scant.[74] When James Whittaker's mother started doing her neighbours' laundry it was, he noted, 'the only way in which she could really earn money'.[75] Jack Martin's mother also resorted to taking in washing when his father was carted off to prison for an assault, though, as he indicated, her efforts did no more than help 'eke out some money for food'.[76]

6.2 Washerwomen in Wigan in the 1890s. The large wicker basket of washing suggests these women were running a small commercial operation – one of very few employment opportunities open to women with childcare responsibilities but no capital.

And undertaking these kinds of enterprises was considerably more challenging in households without a breadwinner. As we have seen, mothers' income-generating work within the home did not liberate them from the domestic work, it was simply added to it. More prosperous families could, and did, use their resources to buy in extra help for working mothers, whether in the home or in the business, but households that lacked a male wage were never sufficiently prosperous to take this course of action, and the only available source of assistance was that of the children. In order to keep her household afloat, Wil Edwards's single mother brewed ginger beer, baked buns, made toffee and cooked faggots – all of which had to be delivered to customers as well as made. Her various enterprises created considerable extra work inside the home which both Wil and his sister had to assist with as soon as they were able.[77] The women who took on such additional labour through necessity rather than choice almost always traded on a very small scale and none appears to have been sufficiently profitable to allow them to buy in domestic help. Instead, they were trapped in a vicious circle, as the absence of domestic help distracted them from their business and limited the possibility of expansion. Mrs Snowman's baking of bread and cakes proved so successful that her flour supplier suggested setting her up in a shop to trade her wares, but the success of her small business did not in reality offer a viable solution to her predicament. With sole responsibility for her young family, she 'felt it would be too much to cope with', so she reluctantly turned the offer down.[78] Other writers commented upon the strain caused by the double shift of paid work and housework as their mothers worked all hours to keep things afloat. Herbert Wells, for example, remembered his mother as 'continually vexed . . . constantly tired and worried' by the burden of caring for both a family and a small crockery shop.[79]

It was far from easy to combine a small business with the sole responsibility for running a home and raising children. But this was not the only problem. Like all women's work, these kinds of ventures paid poorly, so the women behind them struggled to earn enough to maintain their household.[80] For this reason, the majority of women who lacked a male wage had to find paid work outside the home. As ever, the range of options was extremely limited. Those women living in the factory districts had the possibility of mill work, and owing to the relatively good wages they could earn this was the obvious choice for any woman who had the necessary experience.[81] In other large towns and cities, female employment options were more limited, though a variety of workshops, factories and commercial laundries offered some opportunities.[82] And everywhere, female domestic work was available: most of the urban mothers who worked outside the home found daily work 'charring', that is cleaning other people's houses,[83] though occasionally they were employed in kitchens instead.[84] It was not unusual for women to take on a number of different daily jobs, according to what work they could find and the number of hours they were able to work. For example, Philip Inman's widowed mother took in laundry whilst her children were at school, cleaned a school on Saturday mornings and scrubbed the parish gravestones in the evenings.[85] Elsie Osman's mother had to return to work when her father was knocked over by a lorry and badly injured. He was out of work for three years, and during that time the family income had to be 'supplemented by Mother'. Mrs Osman found no fewer than four different jobs that fitted around her family commitments: she spent Mondays cleaning a house in Brookland Street, Tuesdays and Wednesdays taking in washing, Thursdays cleaning empty houses in Prestwich, and Fridays and Saturdays at a job at Eccles Market.[86]

Paid employment outside the home was clearly not the first choice for women who had a household to run, and a woman's ability to avoid it was closely linked to the severity of the financial problems she faced. Those most likely to work inside the home rather than outside it were those whose husbands were unemployed. As unemployment was often short-lived, many women in this situation managed to ride the difficult times without finding work outside the home. Where the cause was an unreliable earner, the situation was much more finely balanced – just under 50 per cent took up some employment outside the home, whilst just over 50 per cent managed to balance the family budget through paid work that they did from within it. A woman like Mrs O'Mara, whose husband worked very irregularly, who drank heavily and who refused to share what little wages he did earn, of course had no option but to work long hours away from home in order to keep a roof over her and her two children. The situation of Mrs Davies was rather different. Her husband was also a heavy drinker who did not believe in sharing all his earnings, but he was a skilled worker (a shipyard foreman), he worked regularly and he handed something over every week. It was not enough to spare his wife from paid employment, but it provided a firmer foundation for the family's housekeeping than Mr O'Mara's contribution.[87] Unreliable breadwinning was always a matter of degree, and mothers calibrated their wage-earning endeavours against what they received from their husbands, keeping their household solvent through some combination of taking in lodgers, laundry work and dressmaking and, where necessary, also adding paid work outside the home. The financial situation for single women was always more difficult. Jack Martin, whose father was eventually carted off to prison for a violent assault on his wife, captured the difference between a father who was a bad provider and one who was not there at all: 'Things had not been too good from the financial side when my father was with us, but they were much worse when he had gone.'[88] This distinction was evident across the autobiographies and single women were considerably more likely to work outside the home than women with husbands.

But women who needed to work soon hit against the problem of childcare. No matter what the precise trigger for a married woman to re-join the labour market, they all faced much the same set of problems. Even in the mill towns, with their tradition of well-paid women's work, finding adequate childcare was a problem. That problem was much more acute elsewhere. Here the provision of childcare was even more haphazard and the low wages that women earned handicapped their ability to pay for it. Indeed, the concept of childcare scarcely existed, so those who had been left in the care of others lacked a readymade vocabulary with which to relate their experiences. James Sexton's mother had left him with a neighbour as a young child when she left the house to sell the woollen caps her husband made. Looking back on this solution, James decided that his mother had left him in the care of the 'communal charwoman' – though, as he went on to add, he thought it unlikely that the term 'had been invented in those days' and certainly would not have been understood by his parents had they heard it.[89]

Pre-school children could sometimes be taken to a place of work. One child recalled being sat on a seat that moved round in a circle as his mother walked a horse around in circles to drive a grinding machine.[90] Another was taken by his mother to the kitchens where she worked and left 'tied in my pram' in the grounds so that she could attend to her work.[91] Others kept their children close by and did their best to keep an eye on them whilst they worked. As a

6.3 Nottingham was the home of a thriving domestic lace-making industry, made up largely of female workers. The eight women in this photo (taken in the early 1890s) were menders working from their own homes, and are managing to supervise four pre-school children while they work.

very small child, Elsie Oman's mother took her with her to her part-time job at a workshop making envelopes and paper bags and sat her 'on the bench' for the morning to amuse herself.[92] Aubrey Darby's mother had a job in the hat trade and as a single mother had little choice but to take her young son along with her, 'sitting me beside her not daring to move, for fear the boss take umbrage and booted us out'. As Aubrey could testify some seventy years later, at that age 'nine hours was a long time to sit inactive'.[93] Where this was not possible, working mothers relied on family or neighbours to mind their children, though their inability to pay much towards childcare inevitably limited the amount and the quality of the care they could purchase.[94]

Childcare was generally dispensed with once children had started school at the age of four or five and it was normal for children from this age to be left unattended in the hours before and after school. After the breakdown of her parents' marriage, Mary Luty's mother became 'the breadwinner'. She had to leave the home at half past five in the morning and did not return until the evening, so her two children were kept under the eye of the neighbours, who awakened them at eight so they could get to school and unlocked the house when they returned in the afternoon. At the age of ten, Mary, as the eldest daughter, acquired the duty of lighting the fire and preparing the evening meal.[95]

The responsibility for children coupled with the absence of childcare reduced the total hours that mothers could work, which in turn pushed them into the lowest-paid sectors of the economy. Dorothy Ash's mother's original response to widowhood was to go out to work as a midwife, but she soon found this impossible to sustain as night calls had a habit of extending into the morning and she had her own four children, aged ten, seven, five and three, to take care of. She had to swap her role as midwife with that of ' "char" (a "daily woman")' who went to clean for different employers on each day of the week.[96] Mrs Ash could see the older children off to school in the morning before leaving for work and left the three-year-old with a neighbour for the day. Her eldest daughter, aged ten, minded the two younger children after school until Mrs Ash returned home at six. Mrs Ash, like many other women, was in the proverbial catch-22: she could only work in the lowest-paid occupations, requiring her to work longer hours overall.

As a result, working mothers frequently found their lives consisted in a round of compromises – working full time to the detriment of their children's care; or part-time to the detriment of the family finances. Walter Greenwood's mother had started to work full time as a café waitress before the death of her husband. The child Walter linked her decision to a strike in the cotton mills, but as his father was by this time descending into serious alcoholism this was likely not her only motivation. At any rate, the absence of his mother when he returned from school at lunchtime and at the end of the day was keenly felt. When a burst varicose vein forced her to take to her bed for a while, Walter thought the development was 'Marvellous! Mother at home all day. Actually in the house when we returned from school at noon and when lessons were finished for the day; a fire burning and a meal ready!' But even young Walter knew enough about the world to recognise there was a 'fly in the ointment': his mother's forced unemployment meant no wages, no tips and no more food scraps brought back from the restaurant.[97] Needless to say, she was back at work no sooner than her leg had healed.

Nor should we underestimate the toll that paid employment took on the women themselves. Dorothy Ash noted what a long day her mother had had after her father's death, returning at six o'clock in the evening 'from her day of "doing" for other folk' to her 'own work in the house, cleaning, washing, cooking'.[98] Walter Hannington described how, when his father was out of work, his mother had to do the 'work of two women, carrying the heavy burden of her household duties for a large family and also becoming a direct breadwinner'.[99] The struggle of working mothers' lives was a frequent refrain amongst the autobiographical writers.[100] Long hours away from home also made it very difficult to care for children adequately. Alfred Coppard's mother worked a twelve-hour day at a laundry following the death of his father, which explained, Alfred noted, 'the inevitable neglect we, her four youngsters, and the domesticity suffered'.[101] Betty May also recognised that the circumstances of her mother's life meant that she could not care adequately for her four children. Having been abandoned by her husband, she worked twelve hours a day at the chocolate factory to keep her household running. 'It would have been excusable if she had neglected us,' Betty ruefully noted.[102] Or, as Albert Jasper glumly noted of his mother working on her sewing machine until midnight, 'It wasn't much of a life for us.'[103]

And the endless domestic grind did rather little for a woman's humour. As Alice Mullen remembered, her mother 'was so often tried and her patience gave out. She was very quick tempered and there was the stick very quickly or anything else handy.'[104] Long hours away from home not only made it impossible to provide adequate care to young children, it was also exhausting and left mothers without the resources to enjoy family life. Following the death of Jack Lanigan's father, his mother's life became one long grind of laundry work and domestic drudgery, and she 'didn't smile for years'. Her son noted her mood improved when he and his brother earned enough for her to reduce her hours at the laundry.[105]

But perhaps the most depressing feature of these women's experiences is the scant reward they got for their labour. The wages paid to women were invariably low and always much lower than those available to men, so despite the long hours of physically demanding work, these women and their families remained mired in a poverty from which there was no escape. Charles Humphreys indicated that whereas his father's work as a cowman had brought in around one pound a week, his mother's charring earned less than half of this – just nine shillings a week.[106] Betty May's mother earned the meagre sum of ten shillings a week for her sixty hours of factory work. John Paton noted that, although his single mother put in 'laborious hours every day scrubbing office floors', her efforts 'produced only a few shillings a week'.[107] In the Edwardian period, a day's charring or laundry work paid around two shillings a day – perhaps a little more in London.[108] Bertha Thornton's mother earned a paltry one shilling and sixpence a day for her childminding.[109] Of course, most of the writers did not know, or did not recall, precisely how much their mothers had earned. Instead, their memories turned upon how difficult their home life had been, the strain their mothers had been under and the absence of luxuries of any kind. Those raised on the earnings of their mother, rather than their father, sometimes held vivid memories of realising how much poorer they were than their friends. David Davies's father spent ten years out of work following a mining accident, so his mother took his place as the breadwinner. But as David recalled, 'no amount of camouflage and desperate managing could hide' his family's poverty or 'the difference between the clothes [he] wore and those of [his] playmates'.[110] Given the unequal pay for men and women, it could hardly be otherwise.

Our discussion so far has focused upon families in urban areas, where the inter-connected forces of higher male wages and more fragile families created new patterns of female engagement in the labour market. But around one-third of the autobiographers had been raised in rural families, and our final task is to consider what happened in these communities. As we know, rural families were distinctive from their urban counterparts in a number of ways. The male death rate was lower in the countryside, marriages were more stable and husbands tended to be much better providers, which all meant that women were likely to have a dependable, regular male wage. So it is something of a surprise to learn that female paid work was widespread – 43 per cent of the autobiographers indicated that their mother had undertaken some form of paid employment, hardly any different from the 44 per cent of urban women who had worked.

Yet when we look more closely at the information that writers provided about their mothers' work, it becomes clear that there were some important differences underpinning this superficial similarity. Most significantly, women's participation in paid employment in rural areas was far less responsive to the quality of their husbands' breadwinning. Women certainly did return to work when they had no breadwinner at all, which in rural areas invariably meant widowhood rather than desertion. In fact, widows returned to the labour market in roughly equal numbers regardless of whether they lived in towns or villages. The death rate was higher in the urban and industrial areas than in rural areas (14 per cent as against 8 per cent), so the likelihood of being widowed was also slightly higher, but the response of widows everywhere was exactly the same: in both urban and rural areas, widowed mothers quickly took up some form of employment. In all regions, around 75 per cent of widowed mothers worked.

But with the exception of single mothers, there is no clear evidence of a correlation between the state of the family finances and a mother's participation in the labour market. Instead, women's working patterns appear to be far more tightly bound to local custom and tradition. In the countryside, women performed specific, allocated tasks in the agricultural cycle, and they did so because the local women had always done these things at these times, rather than owing to forces internal and specific to their family unit.

The power of tradition in shaping rural women's working lives is particularly apparent amongst those families who farmed a smallholding of their own. In such families there was a very fine line between a woman's housework and other work she did to generate income for the household. It was simply taken for granted that wives would participate in running the smallholding in certain gender-specific ways: looking after poultry, pigs or cows;[111] managing dairies;[112] making and selling cheese;[113] selling produce at market;[114] or, if the farm was large enough, providing meals and lodgings for workers on the farm.[115] All those from farming families described the farm or smallholding as a shared enterprise, in which fathers, mothers and children were active participants.[116] These writers also evoke a different way of life, in which the boundary between paid and unpaid work, between 'work' and 'housework', was far less tightly drawn and in which women helped to generate income for the household without going to a job outside the home.

By the nineteenth century, the traditional rural family, farming its own land, was on the decline. Since the seventeenth century, the nation's farmland had been steadily reorganised into larger farms which employed hired labour, and in consequence most men who worked in agriculture did so as day labourers rather than by farming their own land. This shift away from the family farm did not radically alter rural perceptions of the household as a shared enterprise in which wives as well as husbands worked hard to keep things afloat, though it did modify the way in which women made their contribution. In larger commercial farms most tasks were performed by men, but a number of particular tasks, usually associated with the planting and harvesting of crops, were reserved for women. In Alice Bond's Yorkshire village there was a range of seasonal agricultural work available to women: 'setting potatoes, weeding or "singling" carrots by hand, or picking potatoes after a man digging them up [and] pea picking'.[117] Henry Snell's parents worked together in the fields at harvest time: he mowed and she gathered – she bound the sheaves of corn cut by her husband.[118] More unusually, William Arnold's mother worked alongside his father with a sickle to cut the corn.[119] Mary Coe's mother helped out with picking roots and weeding in her Cambridgeshire village;[120] Susan Silvester's with the haymaking and summer potato picking;[121] and so on. Larger, commercial farms had variable labour requirements over the agricultural calendar, and a limited amount of work for women was available at the busiest moments in the cycle.

Large farms also had large houses attached to them, and these too offered gender-specific work for women. In Sherborne, Dorset, for example, Dorothy Park's mother occasionally 'used to help at the Castle' – but just 'when they were extra busy', her daughter explained.[122] Others went to work in the dairies or kitchens. In Somerset, Maud Dark's mother used to go to 'the Big Houses to Cook', but again this was only necessary 'if they had company'.[123] It was not unusual for both marriage partners to work for the same large landowner – father on the land, mother in the house. Mary King's father was a labourer on Mr Brown's farm, and her mother also worked at 'Farmer Brown's twice a week'. Her usual work was in the dairy, but she sometimes assisted with 'extra cleanings, or preservings or picklings' as the need arose.[124] Gertie Mellor's mother also worked for the same employer as her husband – he was a gardener for Buxton Gardens and she did some laundry work for visitors to the gardens.[125]

For the most part, working women in rural districts participated in some form of agricultural or domestic work for the large estates, but there were a few exceptions. In districts with thriving cottage industries, married women typically earned extra income for their household by this means instead. Glovemaking,[126] hosiery,[127] netmaking,[128] lacemaking,[129] ribbon-weaving[130] and straw-plaiting[131] were all mentioned by the autobiographers. And some rural families earned a living through small businesses rather than agriculture, where once again the pattern of family members working alongside one another in certain age- and gender-specific roles is apparent. To give one example, Andrew Baxter's father was a fisherman and his wife assisted in his trade. As his son explained, his mother had 'had all the fisher work to do shelling mussels and baiting lines and selling the fish at the market'. As the children grew older, they too 'had to assist'.[132] A windmill,[133] a butcher's shop,[134] a basket-making business[135] and a bacon-curing business were all given as examples of small ventures in which husbands and wives worked alongside each other in mutually supporting roles.[136] Repeatedly, the rural writers described households that functioned thanks to the combined efforts of all family members. Rural homes were unmodernised and required a large amount of labour just to keep them going, especially if they had gardens or allotments attached. As Margaret Bondfield explained, 'Each of us made our contribution to the many jobs to be done about the place, suitable to our ages.'[137] Within these busy households, mothers took on a diverse range of roles, one part of which sometimes included working for money.

Yet for all that paid work was relatively common in rural families, the financial contribution these women made was in reality usually very small, and certainly less than that made by women in towns. Of course, part of the reason for this was simply because female pay here, as elsewhere, was much lower than male pay. Although we do not have much information in the autobiographies about the rate of women's pay in rural areas, what we have confirms what has been demonstrated in other studies: the day rate for a woman's work in agriculture was about half the male rate.[138] Alice Bond reported that the women in her village received much less than their male counterparts for the labour: precisely 'half as much as men, that is 1s 6d a day'.[139] More significant, however, is the number of hours that rural women worked. In the countryside, married women's paid work tended to be short term in nature – a few weeks scattered here and there throughout the year, sometimes even just a few days. Country estates offered work to women on a part-time basis. Edith Pratt's mother, for example, returned from work at four o'clock, presumably so that she could see to her children after school.[140] Mary King's mother worked two days a week at Farmer Brown's, as did Fred Kitchen's at Sandbeck Park in Maltby, Yorkshire.[141] These shortened working hours hint at a shared expectation within the rural community that women's paid work had to be slotted around their domestic responsibilities.

It was very unusual for rural women to embark upon a more substantial business enterprise. Just one example is contained in the autobiographies. In

6.4 In rural areas, women and children worked alongside men to bring in the harvest. This photograph from George Woods's collection illustrates a young mother's solution to childcare while she picks hops in Sussex.

North Yorkshire, Rosina Harrison's mother earned income for her family by doing the personal laundry of the Marquess of Ripon, despite the fact that her husband earned a respectable £1 a week as a stonemason as well as more through his position as sexton, caretaker and gravedigger for the parish church. As Rosina explained, her 'Mum didn't just "take in washing"; it was much more like a full-time job, and a skilled one too'. Nobody in the family knew how much she earned through her work, not even her husband, but it allowed her to buy a piano, to pay for music lessons, and ensured she always had 'what was needed in a crisis'.[142] But Mrs Harrison's cottage laundry was highly unusual. Indeed, our collection of rural autobiographers provides no other examples of rural wives who made a long-term and sizeable financial contribution to the household.

The fleeting nature of rural women's work may also help to explain why some of the authors wrote that their mothers had not gone out to work, whilst going on to indicate that they had, in fact, sometimes gone to work. We saw a moment ago, for example, that Dorothy Park's mother used to work at Sherborne Castle when they were busy. But the first page of Dorothy's autobiography contains the statement that her mother did not go to work: she 'looked after the home and us children'.[143] Mary Coe also indicated that her mother 'didn't go out to work', although she did, she elsewhere explained, work in the fields on a seasonal basis.[144] These writers were not seeking to deceive: they simply did not perceive their mothers to have been workers. They remembered them as housewives, which further suggests that such work that they did was of an occasional nature.

The autobiographies are filled with unique stories. Within our entire collection of more than six hundred autobiographies, there is, for example, nobody else quite like Mrs Wheeler, who regularly kept her girls from school so that they could help her with her ever-changing kaleidoscope of small businesses. Nor for that matter was there anybody like Mick Burke's mother. We met her in passing above – she kept a cookshop and provided hot dinners for her son's workmates. There was nothing particularly unusual in that, but, as her son continued, she also took a week off once a year: 'She'd say, "It's my week this week," and be on the booze all week.' She'd stack the house with food and her husband and two sons 'all had to help ourselves'.[145] Most mothers did not take a week's holiday a year, and the few that did most certainly did not spend it on a good old drunken knees-up.

But the autobiographies are not just good for colourful vignettes. If we analyse the material systematically, it soon becomes evident that there are some overarching structures that allow us to make sense of the diverse and often idiosyncratic stories they contain. Victorian and Edwardian culture had only one template for family life: a father who was the breadwinner; and a mother who was, primarily, the homemaker. Primarily, but not exclusively: it was widely understood that married women might do some paid work in certain circumstances. Almost half of the mothers amongst the rural autobiographers worked for pay, and there was clearly nothing exceptional in their doing so. In towns, some mothers embarked upon part-time work or a home-based enterprise that helped to generate extra income for the household. But everywhere the primacy of women's domestic work meant that paid work tended to be short-term, occasional, episodic – always secondary to their domestic labours. Women's pay was low, and their work was not supposed to equal or substitute a man's wage. They worked for the proverbial pin money – a small addition for personal expenditure, not a breadwinning wage designed to sustain a family.

The problem, as we have seen, is that some families did not have a breadwinner. This was not of course a phenomenon unique to the Victorian and Edwardian periods. Owing to the relatively high death rate, there had always been some households who lacked a male wage earner and which were consequently headed by working mothers instead. But over the nineteenth century, the rising male wage created a new set of problems to sit alongside that of mortality. A deterioration in the quality of male breadwinning and rise in family breakdown worked against the declining death rate to keep large numbers of women in the role of the family breadwinner – sometimes on a temporary basis, sometimes for the long term. Their challenge was not simply to supplement the male wage: it was to replace it. There was certainly work available for women, but the low and unequal pay coupled with the absence of childcare made the task of female substitution for the male breadwinner extremely difficult.

Let us close this chapter with one final story – that of Molly Morris, who lived with her family in Leyland, Lancashire, in the 1890s. In the beginning, there was nothing unusual about the Morris household. For the first ten years of Molly's life, her father was a factory overlooker. The family lived in a six-roomed house, enjoying the modest affluence afforded by his status as a skilled workman. But following a dispute at work, Mr Morris fell out with his employers and decided to trade his managerial position for one on the shop floor in solidarity with his workers. Unable to find decent work, his earnings dwindled, and Mrs Morris made a return to the labour market in order to make good the loss.

So far, so typical. At this point, however, the Morris family's story dramatically departs from the usual script. For in stark contrast to her peers, Mrs Morris managed to find work that paid more – significantly more – than Mr Morris had ever been able to earn. Her daughter can take up the story.

Molly was around ten years of age when her father threw in his work at the factory and her mother took up a post, with accommodation, as the 'lady manager' of a baking business.[146] From that point, 'instead of the family being dependent on my father's earnings, mother became the breadwinner'.[147] Of course, many women became 'breadwinners' for their families for one reason or another, but low pay ensured that their efforts on the labour market never rivalled that of their husbands. But Mrs Morris made a particular success of her business – a move which (Molly later realised) signalled 'the ascendancy of my mother in the home'. She later got involved in the local Mother's Institute, and from there trained to become a health officer. Her earnings steadily rose beyond the wage that her husband had once brought into the home.

Yet whilst Mrs Morris's skills and industry brought economic security for her family, it was bought at a high personal price, for this unusual turn of events was also accompanied by a marked deterioration in marital harmony. As Molly explained, although the bakery business was ostensibly a joint venture, in reality her father had to play 'second fiddle' and he 'was chafing under the new regime'.[148] With the upending of the usual gender roles, 'personal relations between my parents went from bad to worse'. The discord between them began to fester and the quarrel would 'soon boil up again'. In the end, Mr Morris left the family home and did not return.[149] The Murphys could simply not find a way of existing as a family in which the income was provided by the mother rather than the father.

Yet the most remarkable feature of Mrs Murphy's story is its exceptional nature. Of more than six hundred autobiographies, more than 250 mothers worked, yet Mrs Murphy appears to have been the only one to out-earn her husband – and it came ultimately at the cost of her marriage. It is really no exaggeration to say that there was just one model for family life, and it involved husbands earning more money than their wives. The drawbacks of this model as a form of social organisation are everywhere apparent in the autobiographies – almost half of all the writers had spent at least some part of their childhood in a household that lacked a reliable male breadwinner. This was not a rare or exceptional problem; it was extremely common. But the Morrises' story reminds us that money is not just about welfare; it is about power. Low female wages made it virtually impossible for the great majority of working-class women to live independently of their fathers and husbands. Financial inequality may not have been helpful for ensuring social welfare and well-being for all, but it served a greater purpose: it sustained inequality between the sexes.

PART THREE

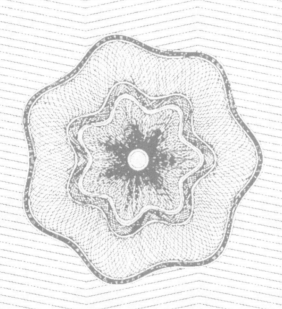

LIFE

ᐊ 7 ᐅ
'GOT A LOAF, DAD?'
FOOD[1]

James Nye was an agricultural labourer who spent his life within a few miles of his place of birth, East Chiltington – a small village in the Sussex Weald. It was an obscure existence and one that would have disappeared from view had Nye not decided to write a *Small Account* of his life in old age. Like many working-class autobiographies before the twentieth century, his account was stripped bare of personal detail. His childhood was described in a handful of pages, and he provided almost no detail of his family life or parents.

Yet there was one aspect of his childhood that Nye could not neglect to mention: the hunger. When young, he and his siblings used to 'go very short of food'. Despite his mother's good housekeeping, each meal brought 'not more than half a bellyful in general, and but a little more than bread'. He recalled what a 'little white weakly boy' he had seemed to the neighbours, and no wonder: 'so hungry I used to be nearly all day long'.[2] Nye's book was a spiritual autobiography. Its purpose was to recount his conversion to Christianity, his journey from the darkness to the light. As such, it was emphatically concerned with the soul, not the body. Yet the memory of that physical sensation gnawing at the pit of his stomach remained so acute that despite Nye's spiritual ambitions, he was unable to write his *Small Account* without some intrusion of the carnal dimension to life.

Food is a fundamental human requirement, but human societies have sourced and prepared their food in countless unique ways. By the nineteenth century, Britain had long since ceased to be a subsistence society. Few families produced their own food; they instead bought it from other, larger producers. But households purchased their food in raw and largely unprocessed form, so it required considerable additional labour before it was ready for consumption. Diet therefore catches the intersection between a host of forces, some economic, some not. Household income of course set a limit to the quantity and quality of foodstuff to enter the household, but unpaid labour was also required to turn that food into meals, and it was culture that determined who provided that labour, as well as how meals were shared between family members of unequal status. As such, diet provides a unique window into living standards. Mealtimes, food and the lack thereof were also themes to which the autobiographers frequently returned, and we thus possess a rich seam of material with which to explore them.

From the great mass of information concerning food contained in the autobiographies, let us start by disentangling one thread: hunger. Hunger was not eliminated at any point before 1914, and it therefore crops up with some regularity in the sources. We can open the analysis with a simple exercise: let us note all the instances in which autobiographers recalled having gone hungry. This indicates that only about 14 per cent of all writers indicated they had lacked food to the point of hunger, suggesting that James Nye's experiences of an empty belly were relatively unusual. Yet that global figure also conceals some very marked variations over the period. Amongst those born in the 1830s, the proportion of writers who had experienced hunger was much higher than the average of 14 per cent. For this particular decade, just over a third – 34 per cent – had gone hungry, so James's experience of a childhood that was haunted by hunger was in fact far from atypical for his generation. In the 1840s, however, this level dropped substantially, to 18 per cent; and after hovering around this level for the next three decades, it dropped once again. By the 1880s, the proportion of writers having experienced hunger had dipped to 12 per cent; but having reached this level, the problem of hunger stubbornly persisted, so that by the 1900s it remained at exactly the same level. Despite a definite decrease in the proportion of writers having experienced hunger, therefore, the overall picture is not one of steady and continuous decline. Although the rate of hunger dropped to a lower level, it then plateaued at that level rather than continuing to taper away.

The pattern of decline emerges yet more clearly if we include the collection of earlier autobiographies from the pre-1830 period. If we run the very same exercise and make a note of the number of writers who recalled having gone hungry in their life, it becomes readily apparent that the high level of hunger reported in the 1830s was not an aberration, but entirely of a piece with trends in pre-industrial Britain. Across the period from 1750 to 1830, the proportion of writers who had experienced hunger was almost identical to our figure of

34 per cent for the 1830s: 35 per cent of autobiographers reported having gone hungry. By decade, the proportion having gone hungry was never lower than 20 per cent, and rose in one decade to more than 50 per cent, but the dataset is relatively small so we should not attach too much importance to the ways in which the figures fluctuated from one decade to the next. In general terms, the earlier records suggest that something in the region of one third of all writers had experienced hunger throughout this eighty-year period – a very similar proportion to those who went hungry in the 1830s, and significantly higher than the proportion thereafter. For this reason, it is helpful to alter the chronology that has structured other chapters of this book. In this chapter we will use 1840, rather than 1830, as the cut-off date between the two periods under consideration.

There were, then, two distinct moments in the history of hunger in Britain: a period down to the 1830s in which hunger was common, affecting around one-third of all writers; and a second period between 1840 and the outbreak of the First World War, during which levels of hunger were lower – they dropped to less than half of the earlier level. Yet this second period was not one of simple decline, for having fallen from their previously high levels by more than half, improvement then levelled out and the rate of hunger remained broadly stable right down to 1914.

This summarises the broad contours of the history of hunger, yet the autobiographies allow us to go far deeper. Hunger was unpleasant and memorable, and it called for further discussion. As a consequence, those who went hungry often provided a host of ancillary information about the experience, such as who else in the family had gone hungry, when it had happened and what had caused it. This contextual detail allows us to do more than map the decline of hunger. It also permits us to unpack the constellation of forces that had caused it.

Most striking is the fact that hunger was not spread evenly across the population, but was closely linked to other demographic variables, in particular to age. In fact, it was very rare for the later cohort of autobiographers to indicate that they had gone hungry after they had reached adulthood. The last references to adult men experiencing hunger date from the 1840s: just a handful reported hunger during that decade and none after that date.[3] We have too few female writers for this period to comment reliably on female experiences. One woman implied that her household was short of food in the

1850s, but her account does not make clear exactly who in the family lacked food.[4] Adolescents continued to suffer from hunger for a little longer, though only modestly so. This age group mentioned hunger in the 1840s and 1850s,[5] but there were very few instances mentioned after that date – just two in the 1860s[6] and one in the 1870s.[7] According to the autobiographies, hunger had become quite rare for any adolescent or adult after around 1850.

But whilst the autobiographical writers had stopped reporting hunger during their adulthoods by the 1850s, they continued to describe having gone hungry as children for many more decades, right down to the 1900s and even the 1910s. Pat O'Mara recalled going 'very hungry' in Liverpool in the 1900s.[8] Another (along with his siblings) 'went b— hungry' in Grimsby in the same decade.[9] There are many other examples of hungry children contained in the autobiographies, both for that decade and the next. In the 1910s, Jane Walsh had 'a continual hole in my tummy' during her childhood.[10] Or in the genteel town of Bath, Louie Stride endured 'continual hunger' throughout her early years. As she explained:

> I was in a perpetual state of hunger and would do anything for food. At the school I would steal from the younger children, can you picture it me 4 years old or so, grabbing an infants piece of bread and running into the lavatory to eat it . . . so I grew up scavenging food where I could, in the gutter pretty often, surprising what one can find edible.[11]

By the Edwardian period, hunger had not disappeared, but it was an experience that belonged primarily to childhood.

Yet it had not always been like this. The earlier autobiographies reveal a very different pattern for the distribution of hunger across the generations. Prior to 1840, 122 writers reported having gone hungry and although hunger was concentrated amongst the younger age groups, a substantial number of writers in the older age groups were afflicted too. More than half of the writers who had experienced hunger – 65 per cent – had been children at the time. But adolescents in work were also at risk – 18 per cent of those writers who had experienced hunger had done so at this time of life. Most significantly of all, however, adults were also at risk: the remaining 17 per cent of instances of hunger had occurred during adulthood. Most of those adults who reported hunger were men, though this is because men wrote the great majority of autobiographies during this period rather than indicative of a greater risk of hunger amongst men.[12] Nonetheless, the fact that before 1840 adult men reported hunger is significant: men were the most likely to be in work and were likely to earn the highest wages, yet they were still at risk of going hungry, as also were male adolescents who were active in the labour market. This forms a very marked difference from the later period, when adults and workers, both male and female, were unlikely to lack food and it was non-wage-earning children who were at the greatest risk of going without.

Indeed, these differences in the distribution of hunger between the autobiographers born before and after the 1830s belong to a larger set of contrasts in access to food between the two time periods. When we look at why Jane Walsh had a hole in her tummy or Louie Stride scavenged food from the gutter in the Edwardian period, it becomes clear that the reasons behind their struggle to procure food were very different indeed to those that had faced James Nye a century earlier.

We can explore this development by looking more closely at the pre-1840 writers. If we examine the stories these autobiographers told about when and why they had suffered from hunger, one cause explains their hunger in the majority of instances: a lack of money. This shortage of money could stem from low wages, insufficient work or high food prices, though very often, of course, a combination of these factors all worked together. But the outcome was always the same: these families simply could not procure sufficient food on the income they had. This had been the problem in James Nye's household. James's mother was, he wrote, an excellent housekeeper and his father was a steady worker, but his wages were low and the family was large – eleven children in all, 'which caused us young ones to go very short of food'.[13] There was never enough to go around and the problem only eased as the children became old enough to work for their own food.

The problem faced by the Nye family was particularly acute in agricultural regions, where wages were very low and were not sufficient to cover the costs of food for a large number of non-wage-earning dependants, no matter how carefully they were stewarded. Another writer recalled that his father had earned between seven and nine shillings a week for a family of eight, and when none of the children could get work 'it was a hard matter to get enough to eat' on the father's sole wage.[14] For some rural children, the spectre of hunger had never really disappeared from their childhood. In Cambridgeshire, for example,

Robert Crane and his young siblings 'often went very hungry'.[15] As a child in rural Sussex, Eli Ashdown 'had a very small allowance of food, and often suffered hunger'.[16] What emerges time and again is that there was just too little income coming into these rural homes, and there was very little that the household could have done to procure adequate food for all the family on the level of income that it had.

Low income was also a problem for the handloom weavers, who were dependent upon an insecure industry that was subject to severe trade fluctuations.[17] By the 1830s, these families faced the additional problem of working in an industry that faced competition from the mechanisation of weaving in the new factory sector.[18] Thomas Wood's father was a handloom weaver, and he recalled that as a child he and his siblings 'knew what hunger was'. Their 'food was of the plainest' and 'the quantity seldom sufficient'.[19] But it was not just the farm labourers and the doomed handloom weavers who were at risk of going hungry. The families of a broader range of skilled workers were also at risk of food shortages, particularly if the breadwinner encountered a shortage of work or if the price of bread rose rapidly. The families of carpenters,[20] millers,[21] shoemakers,[22] printers[23] and small shopkeepers[24] all reported that they had sometimes lacked food to the point of hunger. As with the agricultural and weaving families, their situation was very often exacerbated by external factors outside their control, such as poor harvests or wars which led to a temporary rise in the price of bread.[25]

A shortage of money was the most immediate trigger for hunger in the pre-1840 households, but the reason short-term money crises had such serious consequences was because these households were already suffering from a shortage of food. Many of the early autobiographers indicated that their childhood diet had at all times been extremely restricted, and hunger was simply the most extreme manifestation of this chronic and ongoing problem. Some of those who did not describe having actually gone hungry revealed nevertheless that their rations had at all times been very meagre, and rarely included any meat. For example, 'Potatoes with a little bacon fat on them' were all that George Mockford ate as a small child.[26] As a farm-boy, Benjamin North ate 'bread-and-lard, sometimes a little cheese, and once a week a mite of meat – oh what a treat!'[27] It was not uncommon for children to recall having been raised on a largely vegetarian diet, owing to the expense of meat: bread, lard, skimmed milk and vegetables formed the basis of many of the children's diets.[28]

The difficulties of feeding families on a typical agricultural worker's wage were recalled with particular clarity by some of the female writers from this period. Emma Thompson, the wife of a Bedfordshire farm labourer, remembered: 'The chief of their living [the children] was bread soaked in water and a little salt in it, and vegetables. Meat we never thought of . . . My children have many a time cried over night to know if they should have a bit of bread in the morning.'[29] Another writer, described simply as 'A Norfolk labourer's wife', fed her family largely on carbohydrates – flour, barley meal, rice and potatoes were all mentioned. She purchased a small quantity of butter weekly (four ounces), but also indicated that the butter was not for the children, whilst 'meat we did not have [in the house] for weeks together'.[30] Elizabeth Oakley also had no meat of any kind 'in my house for the six months together' in some years. Bread and treacle formed the basis of most meals, served with cold water rather than tea.[31] Similar and equally restricted diets were also consumed by those who lived in the weaving districts. In Hebden Bridge, Joseph Greenwood and his family ate oatmeal porridge and skimmed milk 'with rarely a change during the week'.[32] As a child, William Farish had never seen a 'joint of meat of any kind at my father's table, oatmeal porridge and potatoes with the occasional taste of bacon being our principal food'.[33] 'Small in quantity and unnourishing in quality,' wrote another of his childhood diet. 'No wonder though I did not become a giant in stature.'[34]

With food so limited in the first place, even the smallest drop in income or rise in the price of bread was a serious matter; and in a finely balanced family budget, any disruption was likely to affect adults as well as children. Many working families consumed a very poor diet at the best of times and so had no line of security against any possible adversity that might be caused by a period of unemployment or high bread prices. The ripple effect can be seen in the family of John Lincoln, an unemployed ordinance worker living in Woolwich, following the harvest failures of 1816. It seems likely that his two children were already severely malnourished by the spring of that year: both contracted measles and died within a fortnight – their quick deaths may have owed something to prior malnourishment. But both John and his wife were also deprived of food before the winter's end following the calamitous harvest. Little by little, they 'sold and pawned all our furniture and all Sunday Clothes – for bread – some times we went the whole day with about two or three potatoes twice in that time'.[35] John and his wife finally sold their bed, at which point they 'had nothing to sell more to raise a single shilling' and passed three days without food 'even so much as a potato' before John found work and received a much-needed gift of five shillings to spend on food.[36]

Nor was it simply individual families that suffered from food shortages. These writers often indicated that it was not only their own household that lacked food, but those of their neighbours, too. During times of wars or bad harvests, there had been very little edible food available; their neighbours had been just as poor as themselves and faced just the same struggle to procure the wherewithal to eat. For 'several years' during his childhood, Joseph Barker's family had earned insufficient income from their weaving to feed the family adequately: 'We had no work, and when we had work, wages were very low, while provisions were very high.'[37] During this period, he had been unable 'to satisfy the cravings of hunger, except on rare occasions'.[38] But his family were not alone in their difficulties: 'The distress which we suffered was general in our neighbourhood.'[39] John Bennett and his family 'almost starved' during the harvest failures of 1799 and 1800, which had 'provisions rising to a great price'. Bread and potatoes rose in price and 'everything else as dear, except wages'. The family subsisted on barley cakes. As the crisis worsened, the local supply of potatoes ran out altogether – 'there were none at any price'.[40] Thomas Carter made similar observations of the same year. Bread rose to an 'enormous price . . . potatoes were also excessively dear, and moreover were of bad quality through the wetness of the preceding summer'.[41] This was a common refrain, with several of the writers indicating that it was not simply that food had become too expensive for their family's income, but also that there was in fact very little food available to buy. 'The times was very bad,' declared Tommy Mitchell of his childhood in Bristol in the 1840s. 'Bread was 1/1 a loaf, meat dear, [tea, sugar] and all other things dear.' Following the Irish potato famine, potatoes 'got dear' too, and the family's diet was reduced to 'oatmeal, once or twice a day, and we were very thankful to get that'.[42]

For the most part, these earlier autobiographers described a neat symmetry between a family's income and their diet. In the majority of households, diets were set by economic factors, in particular the relationship between the family's income and the price of bread. Yet there were other writers whose stories did not fit this template. Procuring adequate food was not simply a matter of wage rates and bread prices. At the level of the household, meals were put on the table thanks to the combined efforts of both parents: the father who earned the wages and the mother whose unpaid labour took those wages and turned them into meals. Any break in the two-parent household risked disrupting the pathways by which unprocessed foodstuffs were paid for and transformed into meals, and the autobiographers provide testimony to the nature and consequences of those breaks.

Given the father's role as the primary wage earner within the family, paternal loss could hardly fail to harm a child's access to food. Joseph Bell, for example, went hungry as a child because his father had died and his mother and sisters' lacemaking earnings were insufficient to keep themselves and Joseph in food.[43] The death of a male breadwinner caused the most problematic and long-term disruption to a family's income, but any serious incapacity could leave a family without. John Shinn's father had a mental breakdown and 'was quite unable to do any work' for three years. During that period, the whole family went 'terribly short of food and clothing'.[44]

Less obviously, the loss of mothers removed a vital link in the transformation of wages into nutrition and was also a trigger for childhood hunger. Lone fathers did not make effective housekeepers. Their long hours of work, coupled with cultural expectations about the gendered nature of domestic work, meant that bereaved fathers did not usually take on the day-to-day running of the house. They found other women to whom they delegated the housekeeping – typically elder daughters, or, if none were available, paid nurses or housekeepers.[45] But the substitute housekeepers they found usually failed to replicate the labour of mothers effectively, and many of the children who had lost their mother reported lacking food in the years after this event.[46] As with fathers, the most common reason for a child to become separated from his or her mother was death, but absence did occasionally take other forms and any kind of maternal absence put a child at risk of hunger. For example, when Joseph Terry was a small child, his mother had a mental breakdown and was unable to attend properly to the house. It was during this period that Joseph was 'often under the most pressing pangs of hunger'.[47] As Joseph explained, the problem was not simply that his father's wage was very low, but that 'poor mother could seldom settle her mind to home, and lay it out to the best advantage'. His mother would often wander from home, so 'we had often no fire and no food in the house' and Joseph was left to 'procure a little food of any kind where [he] could'.[48] William Heaton's family also suffered from hunger when his wife was burned in a housefire and never fully recovered.

Over the nine months of her decline, William sometimes 'had no bread, nor any prospect of any . . . At this time I have been a day or two and never tasted food.' For a brief period, this was because he stayed at home to care for his very sick wife and therefore had no income, but William continued to experience hunger even after he had he returned to work. Then he had the money to buy food but no one to prepare it.[49] The desperate struggles of these households remind us that pre-modern houses needed female labour simply in order to function on the most basic level. There was a large amount of work involved in fetching water, lighting fires and purchasing and preparing food.[50] Households were gendered, and men and women could not easily substitute for each other, so any household lacking two parents had an increased risk of going hungry.[51]

The death, or illness, of either parent was a serious risk to food security within families, yet the problems with the family as a mechanism for distributing food went further. Households were also at risk of hunger when one of either parents, though alive, was failing to fulfil its expected role within the family unit; indeed, among the autobiographers this was a greater risk than death or incapacity. Twelve cases of hunger mentioned by the autobiographers were triggered by the death or illness of a parent. However, a further twenty-one writers indicated that their family had gone hungry owing to the actions of a living parent. In these instances, hunger cannot be directly traced to mortality, illness or low earnings, but was instead rooted in a more complex breakdown in the way in which money was distributed inside the family unit. Most commonly the problem was one of the father either failing to earn a steady wage or to share it with his family, though occasionally the problems stemmed from the mother failing to do the domestic work necessary to turn money into meals. Eight fathers had deserted their family,[52] one was in prison for assault[53] and in another case a mother and stepfather were simply failing to provide meals for the children.[54] The single greatest cause of hunger, however, was drunkenness: eleven autobiographers reported that their own or their father's drinking had left them (or their families) without sufficient food to eat.[55]

All of these behaviours had a tangible impact on a family's access to food. Edward Rymer's father, for example, was working as ganger for the building of the North-Eastern Railway and doubtless able to earn a good wage in that capacity. But when Edward was six he left his wife, Edward and his three siblings 'to face the world and fight for existence' on their own. The whole family was plunged into destitution. Edward ruefully recalled that food had sometimes been so scarce in his home that he had had to forage in the fields for young nettles, crab apples and cat-haws to appease his hunger. Often he 'went hungry to bed and breakfasted on nothing'. As for items such as tea and sugar, they 'were luxuries hardly to be thought of'.[56] But even where fathers did not desert, there was no shortage of ways to separate a man's wages from his family. George Mitchell grew up on a diet of 'barley-cake, potatoes and salt, tea kettle broth, and barley "flippet" '. He never tasted meat and often went hungry. His father was a quarry worker and earned double the agricultural wage, but as George angrily observed, they lived 'on a par with the wretched ploughman's families in the village' owing to his father's love of strong cider.[57]

As men had greater independent access to money than women and a greater capacity to direct money away from the home, they inevitably appear more frequently as the source of family hardship. There were also, however, a small number of households (three) in which mothers were not making the gender-appropriate contribution. In one household an alcoholic mother was failing to prepare food for children with the result that they went without.[58] In another, the mother was absent from the family home for reasons that were unexplained – she was simply described as 'a very helpless woman'.[59] Another man's wife deserted both him and her children.[60] The consequence in all of these instances was that their children, and sometimes also husbands, went hungry, underscoring once more the importance of unpaid, female labour in the pre-Victorian household. The absence of processed foods and the primacy of home cooking elevated the value of women's labour within the household, but it also rendered the absence of a wife or mother a serious matter.

Superimposed upon these gendered patterns were regional and occupational characteristics. As we know, wages were highest in urban and industrial occupations and lowest in the agricultural sector. But (and as we also know) high male wages also went hand in hand with an elevated risk of family breakdown and unreliable breadwinning. It should occasion little surprise that these characteristics were etched into all facets of the experience of hunger.

In the countryside, low male wages kept family incomes low and the risk of hunger high. Despite their proximity to food production, rural households were at the greatest risk of experiencing hunger: 42 per cent of the rural writers indicated that they lacked food to the point of going hungry, whereas the figure for those living in urban or industrial areas was closer to 30 per cent. Yet rural households tended to be very stable, and low income or mortality were far more likely to be cited as the cause of hunger than the failures of living parents. There were just two instances where rural children went hungry owing to the absence or shortcomings of a parent – in both instances the father. William Milne's father had refused to marry his mother; and John Gibbs's father spent his earnings in the alehouse rather than at the market.[61] For both Milne and Gibbs, the father's actions left his children short of food. But it is also worth emphasising how rare such examples were. In the great majority of rural households, male earnings were passed from husband to wife who duly went about purchasing and preparing food for the family. It was the smallness of the earnings, rather than any deviation from this principle, that caused family members to go without.

For families living in towns and cities, by contrast, deviations from the expected pattern could not be described as rare. Of the twenty-four instances mentioned in the autobiographies, all but two (the just-mentioned cases of Gibbs and Milne) were located in industrial areas. Certainly low incomes, particularly during times of high food prices triggered by poor harvests, and particularly amongst families employed in the doomed weaving industry, played a role in causing families to lack food. But problems within the family were common here too. Taking the entire collection of writers who reported having experienced hunger in an urban context, the causes of their hunger were evenly split between forces external to the family and forces within it.

These sharply defined differences between urban and rural communities not only powerfully shaped experiences of hunger before 1840, they also controlled the pattern of change over the following seventy years. Indeed, there is no way to make sense of the population's changing relationship with food during the Victorian and Edwardian periods without disentangling the very different experiences of urban and rural communities.

The most striking development of the period after 1840 is the almost complete disappearance of hunger from the countryside. Rural privation, which had been such a chronic problem for those born before that date, was rapidly and almost entirely eliminated thereafter. The proportion of rural autobiographers who had experienced hunger fell from more than 40 per cent in the cohort before 1840 to little more than 5 per cent in the cohort after – there were just thirteen cases in all. Seven of these had occurred in the 1840s and 1850s,[62] and the remaining six were scattered across the following fifty years. Four occurred in the 1860s and 1870s,[63] but just one writer reported having gone hungry as a child in the 1880s,[64] and one in the 1890s.[65] In both of these later cases, the writer also indicated that the father was drinking and that there was domestic abuse in the home. In little more than a generation, hunger, which had once been endemic in childhood and far from uncommon for older age groups, had disappeared from the rural environment.

As we have just seen, for the pre-1840 families hunger in rural areas was primarily an economic problem caused by an imbalance between household incomes and the cost of food. It logically follows, therefore, that a rise in family incomes was the primary driver behind the elimination of hunger from rural areas after that date. Central to this was the well-documented improvement in the male wage in all sectors of the economy after around 1850.[66] As agricultural labourers shared in these wage improvements and as the fit between male wages and household incomes was very close in most rural households, rising wages had an immediate and tangible effect on rural living standards. At the same time, changes in the processes of production and distribution lowered the cost of food and helped to establish more stable prices which were less sensitive to the vagaries of the season and the harvest. A fall in the cost of imports following the abolition of the Corn Laws also helped to soften the devastating consequences of poor harvests. The mechanisation of some elements of farming and of bread-making had helped to reduce the cost of this staple and the development of the railways and a drop in the cost of transporting goods had also helped to make food cheaper and prices more stable and to improve the range of food on offer.[67]

Such forces were not directly captured by the autobiographers, but the writers do provide testimony to families who were less oppressed by the struggle to procure the wherewithal to eat. Rural wages were still lower in agriculture than elsewhere and many rural writers commented on how small their family's income had been. Yet they now indicated that low income meant a lack of luxuries, rather than a lack of basic nutrition. As Fred Gresswell explained: 'In our house money was scarcer than food.'[68] Doris Gold commented that during the early years of her childhood 'it must have been an awful struggle as father's wages were only 14 shillings a week', but again the family's low income did not translate to a lack of food. Instead she observed that 'there was no money for toys of any description' – she and her sister dressed up pegs for dolls instead.[69] Susan Silvester was raised in rural Bedfordshire in the first decade of the twentieth century and observed that 'in spite of my father's low wages [eighteen shillings a week] we were always well fed'. The effect of low income, she continued, 'was not felt in lack of food; it was felt in the lack of things which had to be bought for cash'.[70] To be sure, these rural writers were not enjoying a life of affluence – a point they repeatedly stressed. Yet poverty and low wages notwithstanding, their families had enough to feed their children well, which constituted a very real difference from the experiences of the earlier rural generation.

The autobiographical writers also provide evidence of rural communities with better access to cheaper and more varied food items for sale. In part this was owing to changes in transport and distribution, which lowered food transit costs and made it possible to consume fresh foods other than those that could be produced in the immediate vicinity. In Edward Ambrose's quiet Suffolk village there were regular visits from an egg man, a muffin man, a tea seller and 'someone selling chitterlings or hot rolls' for two a penny. Apples, pears, strawberries and watercress could be bought in season on the streets from itinerant sellers. In the summer, an ice-cream seller came to ply his trade. On Sundays, enterprising local men used the railways to bring boxes of fish from Lowestoft by the early train. Thanks to the railways, Ambrose noted, families living thirty-five miles from the sea could now eat 'fish dainties for Sunday tea'.[71] Mechanisation of food production, processing and transportation all helped to lower the price of food and allow male wages to spread further.

Equally, however, it is clear that food bought on the market was only one part of the reason for the better diets consumed by rural children by the end of the century. Several of the autobiographers reveal that unpaid work by both parents in growing and preparing food had also played a vital role in providing food for the household.[72] Gardens, allotments and the keeping of pigs, hens and chickens were common in rural areas. Over 40 per cent of the rural autobiographers indicated that their family had either tended an allotment or raised animals – many, of course, had done both – and these activities were capable of making a significant addition to a family's store of food. Susan Silvester put her good childhood diet down to the fact that her parents 'produced a lot of their own food'. Her father cultivated an allotment in addition to his large garden, 'several times a year a pig would be killed; eggs were always to be had from our own hens and the hens would finally end up in the pot'.[73] Rosina Harrison made much the same observation about her childhood: 'we fed well because we lived to a large extent off the land'.[74] A small minority of the rural families even kept a cow,[75] though this was unusual and the keeping of pigs and chickens was far more widespread. It is not entirely clear why access to home-grown produce had improved for the later autobiographers, though of course the widespread availability of well-paid male work in the urban and industrial areas may well have prompted rural landowners, who had a pressing need for some workers to remain on their estates, to make their living and working conditions more favourable.[76] At any rate, growing and cooking home produce required considerable labour, both male and female, and helped to reinforce the long-standing tradition of the rural household as a joint enterprise dependent upon work, both paid and unpaid, from all family members in order to thrive.

Victorian economic growth enriched rural families to the point that they were now unlikely to suffer from hunger. But what about those living in Britain's ever-expanding network of towns and cities? Did wage growth here have a similarly positive outcome on family living standards? Certainly, improvements to male wages had the power to raise family incomes here too and allowed some previously precarious families to consume more and better food. Indeed, just as low income had virtually disappeared as a cause of hunger in the countryside, so too was it disappearing from towns. Taking the entire collection of over four hundred urban autobiographers born after 1840, just fourteen were living in two-parent households and indicated that low income had caused their family to go hungry – in almost every one of these cases, it was caused by a temporary bout of paternal unemployment.[77] As a result, the overall rate of hunger fell. For the earlier cohort of writers, the rate of hunger had been 30 per cent; for the cohort born after 1840 this halved, to 15 per cent.

Yet 15 per cent is not negligible. In a reversal of the pre-1840 situation, the risk of going hungry was now significantly higher for urban children than it was for rural ones. This was because in urban areas the relationship between rising incomes and working-class diets was not linear. As we know, high male wages had the power to destabilise families rather than enrich them. This created a core of women and children cut out from the advantages of economic growth who remained at risk of hunger, despite increasing affluence. Indeed, problems within the family now easily outstripped low incomes as the cause of childhood hunger. Set against the fourteen writers who gestured towards low income as the cause of their hunger, forty gestured to either family disintegration or a more complex set of problems related to a breakdown in the way that their parents had procured and prepared food for their children.[78]

Overwhelmingly, the kinds of difficulties these writers described were a continuation of those that had affected urban families in the earlier period. Mostly these were problems with the male breadwinner – the death or absence of the father or the presence of a father who either worked irregularly or did not share his wages. More infrequently, there were problems with the mother – usually death,[79] but maternal neglect, separation and drunkenness also occasionally featured.[80] And of course a small number of children were doubly disadvantaged, with one parent dead or absent and the other also unable or failing to provide for them in some way. As a result, the Victorian period witnessed a fundamental transition in the causes and context of hunger. Over a span of little more than sixty years, hunger was transformed from a problem created by a lack of resources, to one caused by failures in the distribution of resources.

Our discussion has focused on hunger, but we have only been able to provide an account of how this changed over this period by making some assumptions about the stability of the experience that we label 'hunger'. It is now time to think more carefully about that assumption. Hunger is certainly rooted in a physical, bodily experience that is ahistorical in nature, but it also brings together a more complex constellation of social and cultural forces that are malleable and can change over time. Hunger in the 1830s and earlier was widespread, endemic and a risk for adult men as well as children. By the 1900s, it had shifted to the fringes of society: it was more uncommon and had been recast as something that happened to children rather than adults. It is necessary to ask whether these shifts were accompanied by a rewriting of the cultural significance and experience of hunger. When children in Edwardian Britain spoke of having gone hungry, were they really talking about the same thing as those who had used the word a century earlier?

There is no way of addressing this question directly, but it is possible to approach it indirectly by situating the experience of hunger within the broader context of household diets and access to food. The autobiographers provide a unique window to the wider history of food. In fact, the writers discussed food much more widely than hunger. Almost two-thirds of the writers born after 1840 provided some information about diet. For some, this discussion turned upon the sufficiency (or otherwise) of food in the home, but many others discussed a much wider range of topics, such as how food was procured and prepared, what was eaten at meals and how they were taken. All of this evidence helps us to stitch together a rich account of the changing relationship between hunger, food and want.

This evidence also makes clear that even in the absence of hunger, the majority of working-class children consumed diets that were restricted and often nutritionally poor. Bread made up a significant proportion of the Victorian child's diet and formed the basis of two of the three daily meals. It was usually served for breakfast, either sliced or served as a 'sop' – that is, the pieces of bread were crumbled into a basin with hot milk or water poured over and flavoured with small pieces of butter, lard or sugar.[81] In parts of Scotland and the north of England, bread was replaced with porridge or oatmeal instead.[82] Most children had a second meal of the day also composed largely of bread, either eaten at school or at home in the evening.[83] The remaining third meal was called 'dinner', and it was distinguished by its content rather than the time of day it was served: dinner was a meal of hot, cooked food. In many households, children returned from school at the end of the morning to take their hot dinner at home, but some children took bread to school and ate their dinner in the evening. The exact composition of the two bread-based meals and of the hot dinner were heavily dependent on income and varied both between regions and between one household and the next, but the general pattern of two bread-based meals and one hot dinner was remarkably widespread.

In rural areas, self-provisioning made a considerable difference to the exact composition of the two bread-based meals, at least amongst the 40 per cent of households who kept gardens and livestock. Breakfasts, for examples, could be enlivened through the addition of some bacon or home-made jam.[84] Where families kept hens, eggs might appear at breakfast,[85] though eggs were not a standard part of children's diets. Many writers recalled having got no more than an egg at Easter or the occasional top off their father's egg.[86] A few households produced their own butter, either through keeping a cow or from milk obtained through the father's employment, though again butter was an expensive treat and did not form a part of most children's daily diet.[87] Edward Brand's family kept cows, but even he ate 'very little butter', as the butter was 'mostly for sale'.[88] Margarine could not always be obtained in small villages, so lard, dripping or bacon fat took the place of butter in households that could not afford it.

For those living in the countryside, almost every element of every meal was prepared within the home. As George Gregory indicated, his mother bought no tinned foods and never shopped at the baker's shop: 'We depended completely on what mother made.'[89] Most of the bread that formed such a staple element of this diet was baked within the home, and many rural housewives in addition baked a range of cakes, mostly leavened with yeast rather than eggs and butter. As Joan Bellan noted, 'butter was so scarce and expensive you couldn't use it to put in a cake'.[90] Martha Heaton remembered enjoying her mother's 'plain bread, brown and white tea cakes, suet cakes, "Walk Cakes", buns, biscuits, parkins, pasties, fruit and rice tarts'.[91] For those living in the country but without much in the way of a smallholding, the children's regular diet was considerably more restricted, with bread and lard making up the majority of the bread-based meals and much less in the way of home-baking. 'Meals of the plainest character,' recalled Lewis Watson – bread and skimmed milk for breakfast and bread and seam (lard) for tea.[92] Richard Hillyer's evening meal consisted of nothing more than 'two slices of bread and dripping with a cup of cold water'.[93] Families without a garden had no means of providing anything better.

Allotments and gardens were much less widespread in the towns. Fewer than 10 per cent of the urban autobiographers mentioned self-provisioning – most were keeping pigs and chickens, though a handful were tending a garden as well. As a result, home-produced foodstuffs made a significantly smaller contribution to the children's diets. Urban families could, however, enhance their two bread-based meals with a wide range of items purchased from the market. Several different products were mentioned – kippers,[94] bloaters,[95] jam,[96] milk,[97] sugar,[98] butter,[99] bacon[100] and eggs.[101] Of course, in many families, these items were enjoyed in some combination, depending on the family's income and tastes. Nora Hampton, for instance, enjoyed 'plenty of milk . . . twice a day, plenty of butter, home-made jam, . . . plenty of oranges and apples'.[102] As in rural areas, a mother's weekly baking often helped to enliven the menu, with bread and other sweet breads and cakes being freshly baked in the home once or twice a week.[103] Once again, however, family diets were much more restricted in the poorer families. Eggs, bacon and other such luxuries were dispensed with and butter and jam were replaced with dripping, lard or the new processed substitutes – margarine and treacle.[104] Home-baking was also much rarer in impoverished, urban households: although bread was sometimes home-baked in these households, pastries and cakes were much less likely to be produced within the home.[105]

For children everywhere, the monotony of their bread-based diet was broken by the daily hot dinner. The content of this meal also varied widely according to the family budget, yet it is evident that for most Victorian and Edwardian children, dinner meant meat. In the countryside, dinners consisted largely of meat stews made from home-reared cured pork, or possibly butcher's meat, along with seasonal (and often home-grown) vegetables. Some combination of suet pudding, bread or potatoes accompanied the stews, and were very often served first, so as (as one writer recalled) 'to take the edge off our appetites before the meat, for there was precious little of that'.[106] Bernard Taylor thought that the meals he had consumed as a child in rural Nottinghamshire had been 'more starch than protein' and declared that his mother's stew was called 'fifty-to-one' because there were fifty pieces of potato to one piece of meat: 'To express our delight when we got a piece of meat, we would call "Snap".'[107] Meat stews served with large portions of the usual carbohydrates – suet puddings, dumplings, bread and potatoes – were also extremely widespread in urban areas, and formed the staple of many children's diets.[108] In addition, however, the urban autobiographers recalled dinners made from a wide variety of offal bought from the butchers. Black pudding, brawn, chittlerlings, cowheel, faggots, sheep's heads, pig's head, calf's head, liver, oxtail, sausages, saveloys and tripe were all mentioned.[109] Sometimes these were served as an alternative to the usual stews and soups, but often these cuts too were served up as a stew.

In both rural and urban areas, there was an expectation of a daily serving of meat, albeit in small quantities, even in the very poorest households. Jim Garnett, for example, was raised by a single mother on a 'poverty diet' following the death of his father when he was five, yet his dinners nonetheless included meat and potatoes as well as some butter and milk.[110] Vere Garratt lived in an equally impoverished household: he was one of nine children and his father was in the habit of gambling away his earnings. There was, he noted, 'no danger of over-feeding'. Yet the children ate offal stews most days.[111] These writers repeatedly underscored that their mother's meat stews had been made from the cheapest cuts of meat – bones with scrapings of meat attached, which could be bought for as little as twopence and rarely cost more than sixpence, and which went by a variety of different names: 'pieces', 'bones', 'stewing bits', 'cuttings', 'bitties', 'clippings' or 'block ornaments'.[112] One of Richard Heaton's chores was running over to 'a place called Markendales' first thing every morning 'where you could get two pounds of bits of meat for threepence'. Markendales were skin dealers, and the meat, he later learned 'was the ears and lips from the skins'.[113] These children were not eating substantial or nutritious servings of meat, but the popularity of meat-based stews is surely symptomatic of changing dietary expectations. The largely vegetarian diets eaten by many children in the pre-Victorian period had become a thing of the past. By the Edwardian period, even the poorest of households aspired to eat meat.

In addition to a widespread expectation of a small daily serving of meat, many of the autobiographers expected a more substantial meat-based meal on Sunday, though, as ever, the quality, and even the existence, of the Sunday dinner was closely linked to the family income. A joint of meat was a point of pride for working-class families, and the better-off amongst them always spent a few shillings on a joint for a shared meal. Frank Rayment was raised in a respectable home in Ulverston, Cumbria, and noted approvingly that his family always enjoyed a 'joint of meat' on Sundays.[114] Grace Foakes recalled that her mother used to spend nearly two shillings on half a leg of mutton for a Sunday joint for a family of seven.[115] The remains formed the basis of meals on the following Monday, Tuesday and Wednesday as well. Inevitably, however, the weekly budget did not stretch to a joint in poorer households, so the Sunday dinner was yet another meat stew of some description made from the very cheapest cuts of meat. In George Meek's childhood, the Sunday fare differed little from the diet of the rest of the week – bacon or smaller cuts of cheap meat that were cooked into a pudding. Roast or baked joints of meat on a Sunday were 'undreamed-of luxuries'.[116] For families like George Meek's, the Sunday dinner was a cultural reference point rather than a reality.

The Sunday dinner also had a significance that went beyond its calorific or nutritional content. Putting a joint of meat on the table required a well-ordered two-parent family conforming to social norms. The Sunday roast depended upon a father providing the funds to purchase the meal and a mother providing the labour to cook it. It was thus a mark of social respectability, as much as it was a meal. As Charlie Chaplin explained: 'Even the poorest of children sat down to a home-cooked Sunday dinner. A roast at home meant respectability, a ritual that distinguished one poor class from another.' It was not something that his own mother, lacking both a husband and cooking skills, was able to provide. Those who did not 'sit down to a Sunday dinner at home were of the mendicant class, and we,' Chaplin ruefully noted, 'were that'.[117] Every Sunday towards noon, Nellie Carbis's father opened the front door and sharpened the carving knife on the sandstone doorstep, regardless of whether or not there was a joint to carve (and there often was not).[118] In a similar vein, Edward Robinson's mother noisily rattled the plates at one o'clock on Sundays 'for other tenants to hear that we had a Sunday dinner, whether we had a dinner or not'.[119]

Although the actual diets that children consumed differed significantly across the social spectrum, there were some interesting points of continuity across almost all of our working-class writers. For instance, there was very little in the way of innovation in any of the writers' households. Mothers served up the same hot meals over and again, week in week out, year in and year out. Meals were supposed to satisfy, not to surprise. John Bayes was raised on the customary Victorian diet: boiled puddings, spotted dick, fifty pudding (meat, bacon, potatoes and onion) and he remembered it as 'all delicious food'. It may have been unvarying, but in John's eyes it served its purpose: 'to keep us fit for the hard work we had to do'.[120] Good cooking did not mean variation; it meant cooking the traditional meals well. Frank Rayment thought that his mother was a good cook, but also indicted that there 'there was never anything elaborate' on the menu – 'plenty of soups, Suet Puddings in winter and Peas Pudding'.[121] 'There was very little – if any – experimentation,' recalled Alice Markham. 'The same things were made year after year.'[122] Harry Burton remembered 'vividly the addition of "sausage and tomato pie" to the family repertory'. As he noted, the family proceeded to eat the new pie for 'years thereafter and the fact that its advent stands out so clearly in memory shows how rare was any innovation'.[123] Even the writers who wrote in flattering tones about their mothers' cooking nonetheless testified to a largely unchanging menu. Minnie Vandome, for example, described her mother as a 'good cook', but also indicated that she 'kept to the usual dishes, good stews, meat puddings and pies, joints, steamed puddings and so on'.[124]

Not only were many autobiographers fed the same meals throughout their childhood, some also indicated that the weekly menu had followed the same rotation from one week to the next. A common pattern amongst the better-off families was a Sunday meat dinner, with the leftovers served cold on the

Monday, and then reheated as shepherd's pie or 'hash' on the Tuesday.[125] Some mothers even managed to get a fourth meal from the Sunday meat on Wednesday.[126] Thursdays and Fridays brought various kinds of offal stews, or meals of liver and bacon, fish or pig's fry.[127] And for the most part, writers did not complain about the lack of variety. It was universally accepted as a necessity in a world in which food was valuable and scarce. There was simply no scope for experimenting with new meals that might be rejected. Looking back on the 'depressingly unvaried' diet he had consumed as a child, Harry Burton concluded that 'with our limited finances, it had to be'.[128]

Alongside this largely unchanging diet within households, there was very little sharing of food between households. The autobiographers provided virtually no evidence of their own families sitting down to dine with another, except in the most exceptional – usually desperate – circumstances. Children did not eat meals at their friends' or neighbours' houses, though they were sometimes fed at their grandparents' house,[129] or perhaps that of an aunt or uncle[130] – either when there was no food at home or as part of an established routine. On these occasions, they dined as lone visitors, and not in the company of their parents or other family members. A family's hot dinners were a strictly private affair. As Ernie Benson explained: 'If a neighbour came knocking and asking if they could come in [his father] would say "No, bugger off, we're having our tea", (or dinner, whichever meal it happened to be). He didn't care for neighbours to see what we were eating.'[131] Of course, not everybody took quite such a dim view of the neighbours popping in during mealtimes as Ernie's father, yet there is little evidence of hospitality and sharing of food and meals with anyone outside the nuclear household. It was not part of the culture. Food was a private, family concern, not the business of the wider community.

Even within the household, meals were not widely relished as convivial or sociable occasions. In many homes, there was no space for the family to sit together at a table, so standing at meals and shift-eating were common. In some families, the austere nature of mealtimes was extreme. 'Children were to be seen and not heard in those days. We all stood around the table for our meals and dare not speak, only for grace.'[132] In Daisy Noakes's home, a walking stick was hung over the back of one of the parents' chairs before the meal and the meal was eaten in silence.[133] Any whispering, reading, or looking at cigarette cards under the table and 'we'd get a stroke with the stick'.[134] Beatrice Stallan explained that in her home, a cane was laid on the table at every meal. It was never actually used, she hastened to add, it was 'just to let us know who was master in the house'.[135] But even in more relaxed households, meals were not the moment for communication. Fred Boughton was raised in a contented, rural household – 'home life was wonderful' – but the children still sat down to dinner 'as quiet as mice. Mother said it was rude to talk about nothing at meal times.'[136] 'Meal was no time for talk,' another writer confirmed. 'Our business at table was to eat, and while our parents talked, we listened.'[137] So far as eating was concerned, the motto of Fred Gresswell's mother was ' "every word hinders a champ" ', and he and his siblings 'were not encouraged to spend time dawdling over food'.[138] What emerges from the autobiographies time and again is the scarce and precious nature of food, and a shared appreciation that food was foremost a necessity, not a pleasure.

And in all homes, there was an obvious tension at family mealtimes, as food was not shared equally by all seated at the table. It was the custom in all working-class homes to feed the male breadwinner better than the rest of the family. The breadwinner's labour paid for the food that the whole family enjoyed, and this entitled him to a special place at the head of the family as well as to certain food privileges. The logic was summed up by Ethel Goulden's mother. She taught Ethel, ' "always look after the wage earners. Keep them warm and their bellies filled with good wholesome food; home grown if possible, to keep them healthy and strong. Where would we all be if there were no wages coming in?" In the workhouse.'[139] And so another memory from childhood was watching father eating foods that were unobtainable for everyone else.

This preferential feeding took a number of different forms. At shared family meals it was normal to serve fathers the greater portion of whatever was provided. As Gladys Ottespoor explained, at dinner 'we didn't get meat. My father had the meat.' The meat puddings her mother prepared were shared so that 'Father had the meat and we had the onions and the gravy'.[140] Christopher Bush likewise noted that his father 'always had special meals and whatever meat was available . . . If a rabbit was roasted for dinner, my father would have the leg and maybe part of the back.' The children got the 'head, with its brains, and the neck'. And (as in Gladys's household), there was sometimes no meat for the children at all, just 'enormous helpings of vegetables and gravy'.[141] Having assumed the role of housekeeper and cook following the death of her mother, Marjory Todd struggled to know how to feed a family of six on her small budget, when her father 'would take a pint of milk with his breakfast porridge and needed bacon and egg as well, took sandwiches to work and demanded meat for his dinner and plenty of vegetables'. She did her best to provide this diet for him so as to 'forestall [the] row' that would follow if he considered his rations to fall short of his due. As a consequence, though, the meals for everybody else 'were bound to be sketchy affairs'.[142]

By the same logic, fathers did not share the cold, bread-based meals that children were universally served in the evening. As Christopher Bush continued, whilst the children had their customary bread with butter or dripping for tea, 'my father might have a bloater or a kipper'. How the children's 'mouths would water at the smell of our father's bloater'.[143] Some fathers treated their children with scraps from their plates, though in practical terms this rarely amounted to a significant quantity of food. Nellie Carbis's father liked a kipper or bloater for his Friday tea, and if Nellie was a 'good girl and stood quietly by his side he would give me a piece of the skin to chew'.[144] Others recalled getting the top of father's egg from time to time.[145] And, needless to say, not all fathers were so indulgent. Robert Roberts remarked that although in some of his neighbour's homes the father would 'save a bit of their "relish" – the tail of a finnan haddock, the top of a boiled egg – and give it to each child in turn', his own father 'never indulged us in this fashion'.[146] To spare himself the inconvenience of the children's gaze, Agnes Cowper's father went and ate his meals in a separate room.[147]

Within this unequal division of resources between male breadwinners and their children, mothers occupied a complicated position. Certainly, if the family finances permitted, mothers shared in the superior meals that breadwinners enjoyed. Leonard Ellisdon, for example, recalled that in his home only the adults had a choice of 'savoury' at breakfast time (the children, he complained, were 'palmed off with bread and a scrape of butter').[148] Alice Chadwick described the cod steak as her father's privilege, but she also noted that 'adults only had the good part', so it is possible that her mother was eating some of the cod as well.[149] Christopher Bush described how when his mother baked a rabbit, his father would enjoy 'the best part'. He would have 'the leg and maybe part of the back', whilst 'she herself might have the other leg'.[150] In more impoverished families, however, the better diet stopped with the breadwinner. One of Vere Garratt's abiding memories of his desperately poor childhood was the 'eventful afternoon' when his mother sat down and ate a boiled egg for her tea: his 'astonished eyes . . . fixed on the luxury while I pondered the problem of how she came into possession of it'.[151] Eggs were clearly not a regular part of her diet any more than they were of his.

As the family housekeeper and cook, mothers were of course able to allow themselves small culinary treats. Yet it also clear that they did not enjoy food privileges that equalled those of their husbands. A father's better food was conspicuously displayed in front of the family: his dietary privileges were *supposed* to be seen, and their significance understood, by everybody else within the household. Elizabeth Twist, for example, recalled the daily theatre of watching enviously as her mother beat up an egg in a glass of milk which her father than proceeded to drink in front of his family.[152] In Francis Crittall's household, 'eggs were a delicacy enjoyed by father alone . . . At breakfast, ten pairs of eyes would watch father cracking his egg shell, removing the top, dipping his spoon or "fingers" of bread into the succulent white and yellow mass, and conveying [it] to his envied lips.'[153] Better rations for male breadwinners were ostensibly justified by the hard and heavy work that working men had to perform, but not all breadwinners did in fact undertake manual work: Elizabeth Twist's father was an elementary schoolteacher, whilst Francis Crittall's was a shopkeeper. As both writers later realised, their father's daily egg was a means of underscoring his special status as the male breadwinner rather than a calorific necessity. As Elizabeth wrote of her father's daily egg: 'Nobody else was so indulged. Consequently, from my earliest years I, too, got the impression that there was something very special about my father.'[154] In broadly similar vein, Francis concluded that his father's daily egg ritual involved something more than the egg itself: 'It was privileges of this kind,' he declared, 'that did more than anything else to foster in us an understanding of the sovereignty and unapproachable superiority of our parents in the family scale.'[155]

Mothers did not enjoy an equal status to that of the male breadwinner and they did not automatically qualify for better rations. As adults within the household, dietary privilege passed to mothers before it passed to children, yet some struggled to exert this privilege. Alice Foley reported that at teatime, her mother shared 'a savoury tit-bit' from one plate with her husband. But as Alice went on to point out, it was father who got 'the lion's share', whilst mother 'doled out tiny morsels from her portion to the younger children'.[156] Bert Edwards used to puzzle why he was asked to buy a small quantity of the grocer's most expensive butter as he never saw it on the family table. He later discovered that the butter was a small luxury for his mother – 'mother's special'.[157] Mothers' treats were more occasional and consumed far more discreetly. James Brady's mother's treat was the odd serving of 'two-pen'orth of potato pie, garnished with black pudding'.[158] A potato pie was not a luxury food and it is not hard to imagine that the real treat for Mrs Brady lay simply in eating a hot meal that she had not had to prepare herself.

The two-penny potato pie that Mrs Brady liked as an occasional treat hints at one other change: the emergence of pre-cooked food for sale outside the home. This era witnessed an explosion in the availability of high-calorie, cheap, pre-prepared meals that could be purchased rather than cooked at home. The autobiographers recall a wide range of fish shops selling ready-to-eat seafood such as cockles, mussels and jellied eels alongside those selling fried fish and chips; pork butchers selling cooked pies, sausages and faggots; bakers selling varieties of cakes and biscuits; and cook-shops selling cheap meals of meat, vegetables and pudding.[159] By the end of the century, cities teemed with a wide range of hot, cooked food as well as fatty, salty and sugary foods of a kind that would have been quite unknown to those born earlier in the century.

London was particularly well supplied with food outlets of this kind, and the majority of the metropolitan autobiographers had memories of some of the cooked foods of their childhood.[160] Shop-cooked food 'cost extremely little', recalled James Hawke. 'A halfpenny bought a scoop of fried potatoes, and for another halfpenny you received a large piece of fried skate.'[161] In Elizabeth Flint's household, the children's evening meal of bread and jam was occasionally swapped for fish and chips bought from 'Tom's Fish Emporium in the Commercial Road . . . a treat indeed, especially on a cold winter's night'.[162] V. S. Pritchett considered that his mother had not been a good cook, but the family's diet was enlivened by some of the purchases she made: pease pudding, a few slices of pickled pork or the occasional meal of fish and chips.[163] And cooked food did not simply add variety to otherwise drab diets: it also replaced the labour of cooking meals from scratch, a significant consideration for women who worked outside the home. Walter Southgate recalled that on the days his mother worked at the laundry, 'a meat faggot and a dollop of pease pudding' was the regular family dinner.[164]

Whilst nowhere boasted quite such a range of pre-cooked food options as London, cookshops and bakeries were mentioned in a wide range of other urban areas. All towns sold meals that did not need to be cooked and prepared at home.[165] In Manchester, for instance, Mary Bertenshaw recalled shops in the city centre where you could get 'the largest potato, or meat, or rabbit pies you've ever seen in your whole life'.[166] In Portsmouth, Frederick Wynne remembered the 'shop on the corner of Sultan Road that sold the best "chidlings" and peas pudding and faggots anywhere in the world'.[167] As in London, some writers recalled that cooked food was a treat to be bought when the family was in funds, whilst others indicated that cooked meals were bought to relieve the mother of the burden of cooking.[168]

This availability of ready-made food impacted life in other ways and subtly reshaped the meaning and experience of hunger. Those who had lacked food in the early part of the century had generally lived in communities that also lacked food. A few of the earlier writers recalled an experience of hunger that had been profoundly distressing, a desperate feeling of having no food compounded by the knowledge that there was also none to have. Following the poor harvests of 1799 and 1800, John Younger spent two or three years 'pinched of all matters in the consistence of human food'. The ongoing food shortage, he reflected, had produced 'a feeling none can thoroughly comprehend', causing him to dream of potatoes and chew on wood bark in an effort to allay his pangs of hunger.[169] Another writer suffering from the decline of the handloom industry observed that 'a scantiness of food for a length of time causes such an uneasiness, that there is not any thing can compensate for the want if it . . . hunger is always gnawing us, and disturbs our peace'.[170] For these writers, hunger had been an extreme and intense experience that lay beyond the bounds of what could reasonably be endured.

The experience of going hungry was very different for those living in the late Victorian city. The problem here was no longer one of whole communities lacking food, but of specific, foodless households situated within communities that did not lack food. This novel situation was captured by Arthur Harding's autobiography. Harding was raised in the East End of London in the 1890s and his account provided page after page of information about the fish and chip shops, cook-shops, pudding-shops, pie-shops and other outlets selling hot food in the neighbourhood. Yet the situation at Arthur's home was very different and typified many of the problems that stood in the way of children eating well. His father was initially failing to support the family and later absent, whilst his crippled mother was struggling by on the pittance she could earn from the sweated trade of matchbox making. Her steady descent into alcoholism did little to help. Arthur's mother only provided one meal for her family a day – the evening meal. Arthur's childhood was thus characterised by a home where food was scarce within a neighbourhood where it was abundant.[171] The situation for Kathleen Dayus in Hockley, inner Birmingham, was very similar. Her family was large and the household lacked sufficient food but the streets outside sold an enticing array of foodstuffs. Much later in life she could still remember the 'homemade cook shop' that she used to pass on her way to school every day, 'with all the nice things on show . . . pigs' pudding, hot meat pies, hock, tripe and cakes of every sort staring back at us'.[172] Food scarcity in communities where the food was actually there – as Kathleen wrote, 'staring back at' you – was very different from food scarcity in a community that had none.

It is also noticeable that writers who indicated that their homes had lacked adequate food still sometimes claimed that they had never really gone hungry. For example, Charlie Chaplin, aged about twelve and living without a legal guardian once his mother had been committed to the insane asylum, reported, 'I always managed to get food somewhere.'[173] Sid Causer, also living in a deprived

7.1 By the late nineteenth century, Britain's towns and cities boasted a wide range of shops selling partially processed and cooked food. This photo, taken in 1894, shows customers milling outside a Sheffield pork butchers.

inner London community (Bermondsey) thought that the 'kids of my time never used to be hungry', although there were certainly many households that lacked food. He put this down to what he described as the 'ways and means' that were available to get hold of food outside the home.[174] Or there is the account provided by Thomas Luby, whose childhood was amongst the most deprived of any of the autobiographers. Thomas Luby was interviewed by a television reporter for Granada TV in the 1960s, and told a story of desperate neglect. As a child in the 1880s, Thomas was living in Manchester with his mother, who had separated from his father – a man he described as 'an absolute drunkard'.[175] Food was scarce. On a good morning she gave him a round of bread, but if he returned later in the day, rather than getting fed he simply 'got into trouble . . . No food of course.' Thomas was at work by the age of nine or ten, and at around this age he was living apart from both his parents and with a sweet-maker he had befriended. Neither of his parents was providing either food or shelter. As he explained to his interviewer: 'When I went home I got in trouble, when I went to father's I got in trouble – all right, I went with him [the sweet-seller].'[176] Yet despite the desperate poverty of his home, Thomas was keen to explain to his interlocutor that he had not gone hungry as a child: 'I'll tell you this, I always got plenty to eat. I was never short of food. If I couldn't find it one way, I should get it another.'[177] And later again: 'I always looked after food. It was rather strange. All my life, you know, I've always seemed to have got it from somewhere.'[178] And at the conclusion of his interview, when a clearly shaken TV interviewer asked how he had survived these abysmal conditions, Thomas repeated once more: 'Well . . . I always had plenty to eat.'[179] These examples are not given in order to suggest that hunger had ceased to be a problem. There were clearly complex, multi-layered problems in the lives of these children that need to be acknowledged, and the worry of getting hold of sufficient food was definitely one of them. Furthermore, alongside these writers' rather ambiguous statements around food and hunger were others who made it plain that they *had* gone hungry owing to food shortages at home. Yet their comments do capture something of the change that occurred over the century. Hunger had become localised as a problem for specific households, rather than something that affected the entire community, and the local availability of food softened the severity of food scarcity for the individual.[180]

One of the strategies that the writers gave for warding off hunger was begging, scrounging or stealing food from others in the neighbourhood. As

Arthur explained, if you could not get any from your parents, 'you had to use your brains'. His first strategy was to visit his aunt and ask for a penny to spend at the fish shop. If that failed, he would just head down to the fish shop anyway: 'We would wait outside the shop and cadge – "Got a 'apenny governor, got a 'apenny for a bit of fish?" Outside all the eating shops you used to do that sort of thing. Outside the fish shop you'd say, "Give us a tater, give us a tater, missus".'[181] Jack Lanigan's home also lacked food. He begged bread off the workmen leaving a large engineering workshop at the end of the day and stood outside the fish and chip shops asking customers, ' "Can you spare any scrapings, Sir?" . . . These scrapings with some bread made a meal.'[182] The 'ways and means' of getting hold of food that Sid Causer and his friends had included walking by the food carts in the streets and 'knocking off big carrots to eat or apples, oranges, bananas'. They also used to 'pinch off' hot potatoes and sweets.[183] Again, these examples are not given with the intention of minimising the extent or significance of hunger. The point, rather, is that the meaning of hunger had changed. It had moved from the belly to the head – as Harding said, 'you had to use your brains'. These children were trying to get a share of food that was available, but not to them. This was a very different proposition to warding off hunger in a community where there was simply no food to be had, but one which nonetheless imposed a heavy mental load on children whose developing minds should have been elsewhere.

Pinching and scrounging was just one small part of poor children's strategies for obtaining food. More usually, those in need obtained meals through more formal, charitable efforts established to deal with hunger. The late nineteenth-century cities were home to the activities of an organised network of charities providing cooked food to children who were not getting fed sufficiently at home. By the Edwardian period, charitable efforts were supplemented by school dinners.[184] It is clear from the autobiographies that this growing network of charitable efforts to cook and distribute hot meals to needy children was making a substantial contribution to the diets of the poorest children.

Once again, Arthur Harding illustrates the trend. His mother only cooked one meal a day, but he got a regular free breakfast of bread and milk from the City Mission and a free lunch from Father Jay's – provided he could get there before they were all given away. It was only when that failed that he hung around the fish and chip shops trying to beg some chips off the customers as they left.[185] Arthur Harding certainly knew what hunger felt like, but soup kitchens and charity provided him with a layer of protection from the unwelcome sensation.

Of course, accepting food charity may have helped to dampen hunger but it also stoked up a host of negative emotions. Margaret Powell recalled the shame she used to feel when visiting the soup kitchen and walking back through the streets with her free soup. The poverty of Margaret's family was such that they lacked an enamel jug suitable for use in the kitchen so she had to take instead a bathroom vessel covered in pink roses: 'To walk through the streets, carrying a large washstand jug full of pea soup pretending you hadn't been up there and got it for nothing, that you've not been accepting charity, well, then you've got to be very clever indeed.'[186] As Margaret was acutely aware, outsiders distributed food on a very different set of terms to those that operate within the family. Perhaps the shame she had felt in collecting the soup also played some part in her verdict of how it had tasted – it was 'thin, watery' and tasted 'terrible'.[187]

It was common for the children who made only occasional use of soup kitchens to remember the food in negative terms. 'Very poor indeed,' declared

7.2 A soup kitchen run by the Salvation Army out of Keyworth's Yard, Sheffield, during a miner's strike in 1911.

Mrs Davis when a stint of unemployment forced her and her sister to take up the school's free school dinners.[188] When John Bennett ate the free soup that his school served up, he was left with 'a memory of some burnt pea soup as well as the hurt of feeling really poor'.[189] A child's distress about free food was easily transferred to the actual food itself. When Ernie Benson's father was out of work one winter and he and his sister qualified for free dinners, the stew 'revolted' him and left him 'with a feeling of sickness'. He much preferred to eat the 'meagre meals' that his mother prepared on the Sunday when no free dinners were served.[190]

But although some children felt an acute sense of shame about free food, we should not assume these feelings were universal. Alongside those who felt shame were many others who were too hungry to care, or for whom free food was a normal occurrence rather than an aberration during their childhood. Regular, as opposed to occasional, users of soup kitchens tended to regard the food in a more positive light. Albert Paul remembered with evident fondness the large white tickets that entitled him to a free breakfast of milk and scones before school and a free dinner of hot soup or stew and a large slice of currant roly-poly at midday – 'And this for 5 days a week.' In the evenings a soup kitchen served up a 'very tasty soup' made from vegetables, potatoes and large meaty bones, along with as many slices of bread as the child had brothers and sister – this was 'sold' for however many pennies the parents could afford.[191] Brighton was not a poor town, but as the ninth of ten children and with a father who suffered chronic unemployment, Albert Paul belonged to one of those families 'whose parents hadn't got a lot of food for the family'.[192] John Langley, who lived in nearby Hove, shared his view. The soup he got from Corporation Soup Kitchen was 'really delicious . . . they thought they were giving us all the old rubbish that was thrown away by the trades people . . . [but] it was really good and nutritious'.[193] The fact that his 'home was very miserable', lacking a mother, cooked food and even heating may, once again, have helped to shape his attitude.[194] 'Simple but delicious' was the verdict of Kay Pearson of the hot soup, 'thick slice of bread' and mug of cocoa that she got as a free dinner.[195] Louie Stride's recollection of her charity dinners brought back warm memories of 'such food I can't describe, the smell alone would make me faint with delight at the anticipation of the good things to come'.[196] For some of these children, free food prepared and eaten outside the home, rather than within it, was too normal a part of life to occasion feelings of shame. This was certainly the case for Esther Saggers. Her father earned two shillings a day laying out the stalls for Islington market, and her family was 'very, very poor'. But this did not mean she went hungry. As she continued, 'if you really knew those places, and you weren't proud to line up with the other children, you didn't do too bad, even if you were very poor'.[197]

Soup kitchens provided a solution to the problem of childhood hunger, but rather like their twenty-first century successor, the Food Bank, they are also a signal that something was wrong. Children were not supposed to eat their meals in institutions or church halls. They were supposed to eat with their families. Everybody knew that. This was why children who were normally fed at home found the charity food so distasteful. This was why Louie Stride, when remembering that two other children from her school had been picked out to eat at the free canteen meals, decided that 'perhaps I hadn't better mention names'.[198] Parents too understood that providing and preparing food was something that should done by the family. When Percy Brown went with some lads from school to the soup kitchen, his mother slapped him: 'I had shamed her, she said.'[199] Soup kitchens filled many a child's empty belly and were a powerful force in diminishing the extent and severity of hunger. But they are also testament to the failure of an increasingly wealthy society to feed its people.

Food availability improved dramatically between the 1830s and 1914. At the start of this period, Britain had not provided enough food for all, and no matter how carefully families laid out their meagre resources, there was little they could do to mitigate the risk of hunger when harvests or industries failed. An increase in food production, a lowering of food prices and a rise in male wages all helped to lower the cost of feeding a family. Yet the degree to which this improved food security for the most vulnerable was decidedly mixed. The country's expanding network of soup kitchens is evidence that, for all this progress, a great many families still struggled to feed themselves.

Britain was much richer in 1914 than at any time previously, but it was still a gendered society in which men earned the bread and women baked it. Not only this, but the very process of economic growth had made these gender divisions sharper. Higher male wages enhanced the power and status of men within their families and broke down the rough equivalence that had previously existed between paid male labour and unpaid female labour. Victorian prosperity was founded upon a sharpening of inequality between the sexes, which destabilised the traditional family and uncoupled the living standards of women and children from male incomes. At the heart of Victorian society was a gendered inequality, and it is only by grasping this simple truth that the true meaning of economic growth can be uncovered.

⋅←⋅ **8** ⋅→⋅

'WE WEREN'T HAPPY, BUT WE WERE A FAMILY'
EMOTIONS[1]

In the 1970s, Les Moss shared his life story through a series of interviews with members of the QueenSpark historical collective based in Brighton. It was subsequently edited and published by the collective as *Live and Learn: A Life and Struggle for Progress*. As the editors explained, Les provided the wool for the book, whilst they 'weaved it into the final cloth'.[2] Despite its somewhat unusual means of creation, the finished piece of cloth followed the usual conventions of the autobiographical genre. Life stories typically begin with childhood and schooling, and then move on to entry to the workforce and adult life, which tends to revolve around the themes of marriage and family for women, and work and (often) achievements for men. The format of Les Moss's *Live and Learn* was no exception.

The book began with the customary first chapter about childhood – 'A London childhood' – where Les provided a narrative account of his family. He described a father who had two jobs: a day job running an insurance book for the Prudential and an evening job as a band member playing in pubs and music halls; and a mother who, like many, did not work outside the home. She 'ran everything' in the house, and kept him fed, clothed and clean. The second chapter had him 'Starting Work', and captured his transition from family, school and childhood to the adult world of work, and established the theme for the remaining four chapters. Yet reminiscing about his parents with members of the collective clearly drew Les to reflect upon those early experiences of family in new ways. He talked not simply about the work his parents had done, but also about how life had felt in the home he and his sister had shared with them all those years ago. In so doing, he skated onto more unfamiliar territory, creating a decidedly less stable narrative.

Like many writers looking back at their parents, Les's impulse was to say something good. His father, he remembered, was 'passionately fond of music' and was a talented musician too. Whatever faults he may have had, he was 'never aggressive' – indeed, he 'would have done anything' for his son.[3] As for his mother, she, he declared, was 'a good mother'; in fact, he 'couldn't have had a better mother'. The good qualities of his parents required emphasis: he had 'two good parents, there's no shadow of a doubt about that'. Should there be any confusion, he felt the need to 'keep on impressing that' to the oral historians with whom he worked.[4]

But gnawing away at this account of an ordinary London childhood is another story. Les may have described his father as 'good', but this was not all he had to say about him. He was also (Les explained) an alcoholic whose drinking reduced the family to poverty and was the cause of serious marital conflict. He provided further information about his mother, as well. She was 'very strong willed . . . [and] a jawpot. She couldn't seem to be enjoying herself unless she was jawing at something.' All this had had serious implications for his childhood self. His mother's 'weakness', he admitted, had actually 'spoilt everything in the family'. When his parents began fighting late at night, he was 'frightened to death . . . and used to dread what was going to happen'.[5] The fights made him 'shrivel up . . . That's how my life was, and I used to hate it, hate it.'[6] Moss's autobiography provides his reader with two very different versions of his family: a home with two good parents doing their best in a difficult world; and another with two flawed individuals whose actions had shattered his well-being and left him feeling fearful and unsafe. His account illustrates both the promise of autobiographies for unpacking the history of emotions, and also the many obstacles that lie in our way.

At heart, the problem is that writers tended to be far more reticent about the emotional elements of life than the material. In many respects, the accounts of working-class autobiographers bore the hallmarks of the far less expressive culture in which they had been raised. Victorian parents were often not demonstratively affectionate. As one writer explained, although there had been 'affection' in his family, it had been kept 'mostly "on ice" '.[7] Another wrote that 'any feelings of affection – kissing and huggings and exaggerated expressions were taboo in our family'.[8] And another that her family had been 'shy of the word "love" '.[9] It is little surprise, then, that working-class writers did not automatically reach to the language of emotion in order to describe their upbringings or find it natural to dwell upon emotions or feelings.

And yet by the time that many autobiographers put pen to paper, things had started to change. Autobiographers were not writing about their childhood at the time that it occurred, but many decades later. For those born in the late Victorian or Edwardian eras, their life story might be created in the 1960s, 1970s or even the 1980s – a period of rising affluence and rapidly changing family values. In the second half of the twentieth century, love and nurture were established as a fundamental component of child-raising and this new climate encouraged many to reconsider their own, more austere, upbringing and provided a framework within which working-class autobiographers could re-evaluate their early years.[10] As a result, and as we can see in the case of Les Moss, the life story sometimes takes the form of a renegotiation, a reassessment – and not always an entirely coherent one – of a Victorian childhood through twentieth-century eyes, rather than a straightforward narration of earlier life events. Although Victorian families were not necessarily demonstrative and affectionate in ways that are recognisable to modern readers, these relationships mattered. Writers may not have consistently reflected upon how they felt about their parents, but many nonetheless wrote enough about their experiences of family life for us to attempt to explore the emotional fabric of family life.

Of familial relationships, it was those between parents and children that the autobiographers returned to most regularly, and of these, relationships with fathers are in many ways the most straightforward to comprehend. Across a wide selection of autobiographies, there were, inevitably, a great many different sentiments expressed. Some writers loved their fathers dearly, some evinced a visceral hatred and there was a kaleidoscope of every imaginable emotion between these two extremes. Families are messy, and so too are emotions.[11] As we have seen in the writing of Les Moss, there can be a variety of expression within one text: inevitably that variety is vastly amplified if we read across hundreds of texts as well.

Let us wade into this tangle of emotions by thinking about breadwinning. Breadwinning and love are not, of course, the same thing. Yet the stereotype of the breadwinning father loomed so large in Victorian and Edwardian culture that it is difficult to make sense of the emotional texture of father–child relationships without acknowledging the centrality of wage-earning.[12] Breadwinning provided the scaffolding upon which writers could construct their narratives. A father's employment fixed his child's position in the world and in the social order. Families lived where they did because of where their father worked. They lived how they did because of how well he worked and how he shared his earnings. A narrative of childhood was thus often arranged around a succession of facts about a father's line of work, his earnings, his place of work, job moves and so forth.[13] And it was from this perspective that emotional experiences were also described and explained.

The elision between breadwinning and emotion can be seen with particular force in the case of fathers who were failing in their role as providers, especially those whose failings stemmed from heavy drinking. A small core of fathers had combined drinking with violence and abuse. They had made their family's lives simply miserable and their children were resolutely unforgiving. William Miles, for instance, described his childhood home as 'most unhappy'. This he put down to the fact that his father 'was an incurable victim of alcoholism, which caused me to crouch under the table with fear when he was abusing my mother'.[14] Betty May's father was 'naturally cruel, and when drunk, which he usually was, he became a fiend'.[15] Lilian Westall, noted that her father's habitual drinking 'brought out a curious hate for his wife and children'. (It was to the whole family's 'great relief' that he joined the army in 1914 and 'went off to do battle with someone other than his wife and children'.[16]) In a handful of extreme cases, the autobiographers described childhoods that had been destroyed by alcoholism and domestic abuse.[17] At the age of eighteen, Jack Martin ran away from a home that had been irrevocably damaged by his father's drinking and continual attacks on his mother. On the day of his departure, Jack

> reviewed my life up to that time. I had been nothing but a drudge . . . I could hardly think of one redeeming feature connected with my home . . . [If] I went out on a Saturday night my mother would most certainly be waiting for me in the street. My father would have come in drunk and turned her and all the younger children out . . . He would nail up the front and back doors. I would then have to go and borrow a ladder from somewhere, get in the house through the back bedroom window, come down-stairs and pull the nails out of the door to let them back in.[18]

Like others in this situation, his relationship with his father had irretrievably broken down by late adolescence and was not maintained after he had escaped from the misery that was his home.

Of course, a father's heavy drinking was not always accompanied by extreme violence and abuse, yet it was almost always deleterious to the family in some way, and played a major role in shaping how children later assessed their fathers. Hostility towards fathers who had siphoned their earnings towards their own drinking rather than the family was expressed with remarkable consistency across a large number of writers, and the feelings were sometimes intense. Ernie Benson, for example, provided a detailed account of his father's neglect and mistreatment of his family over many years and confessed that at the time of his father's death, his feelings had been ones of 'resentment and hatred'.[19] Not all admitted to hatred, but complaints were certainly frequent. Len Wincott, for instance, dismissed his father as an 'illiterate, drunken bully of a man'.[20] Stanley Rice's father was 'fond of his beer' and 'bad tempered and quarrelsome'.[21] Alice Foley's father was given to 'bouts of heavy drinking' and was 'morose' with 'a murderous temper'.[22] A current of deeply negative emotions towards fathers runs through the autobiographers, and it is particularly concentrated among those whose childhoods had been affected by alcohol. And because drinking rates were so high amongst men, the problem was depressingly widespread. Almost 15 per cent of all the working-class autobiographers positively identified their father as drinking heavily and problematically. In almost every one of these cases this drinking was signalled as also having been to the detriment of the author's childhood and home life, and often of their relationship with their father as well.

Drinking drained vital and scarce resources away from the family, and was a cause of resentment. But drinking did not simply remove a man's money from the household; it also removed the man who earned it. The lives of fathers who were drinking heavily tended to be centred on the pub, rather than the home, and this created a physical absence between fathers and children which further weakened their relationships. As Emanuel Lovekin wrote of a father who 'spent most of his wages in drink', he was 'a man that did not seem to take very little interest in home Matters'.[23] It was a common observation. Albert Jasper considered that his father's 'main object in life was to be continually drunk'.[24] He thought 'it hardly mattered to [his father] where he lived, he was hardly ever in: so long as a pub was near he didn't care'.[25] Herbert Bennett similarly described his father as a heavy drinker and 'a frequenter of pubs'.[26] Some writers indicated that alcohol occasionally lured their fathers away from home for yet longer periods, as they absented themselves on drunken sprees that might last for weeks at a time.[27] Others drew attention to the role that alcohol had played in the ultimate breakdown of their family and their father's permanent departure.[28]

It is sometimes difficult to disentangle the cause from the effect in these accounts with authors describing a vicious cycle of worsening familial relationships: as the family's hostility to their father's drinking intensified, the father sought solace in the male companionship of the pub, pushing him yet further from the home and its inhabitants. Robert Roberts, for instance, observed that his father's drinking 'divided [his parents] like a wall'. Every time his father returned home the worse for wear, his mother would withdraw from him a little more. As the time passed, he resorted ever more to the easy companionship of the pub and became like 'a stranger in his own home'.[29] Or, as Lucy Miller explained, after six births in relatively quick succession, her parents' relationship was disintegrating: 'mother having developed into a nagger – a perpetual fault finder – and dad took refuge in the local pub'.[30] More unusually, in the writings of Deborah Smith we are presented with the deterioration of a marriage from a wife's perspective. Reflecting upon when her husband 'became a drunkard' and took to spending his evenings at the pub, she wrote:

> How often I had to sit alone till a late hour on a Saturday night. Sometimes a neighbour would come in for a little company. Sometimes I knitted or sewed, weary and tired of waiting. I was a neglected wife, and with the years I grew cold and silent . . . Like the flowers that die when the sun has ceased to shine and the cold wind blows, happiness fades away.[31]

Drinking soured family relationships, driving a wedge between fathers and their children. But drinking was not the only drain on family resources. There were also fathers who, though not great drinkers, nonetheless spent the family's money on themselves, who worked irregularly, or deserted the family. Any kind of lapses in a father's commitment to breadwinning played a powerful role in shaping how children felt towards their fathers, and rumblings of hostility were extended to any father who had, in their children's estimation, misappropriated the family funds. John Allaway, for example, confessed that whilst growing up he had often felt 'bitter against my father for spending so much of his time and money' at the pub.[32] He was not drinking himself, but

8.1 In the late nineteenth-century city, sociability and companionship for many men was centred upon male-only pubs and clubs rather than home. This postcard depicts a group of working men heading off on a charabanc for a day trip organised by the Plough Inn at Penwortham, just outside Preston.

treating his workmates to beer and cigarettes in a bid to purchase a popularity that was otherwise denied him. John felt no 'great warmth or affection' for the man.[33] Arthur Harding's father was 'too lazy to earn a living' for his family, and Arthur had 'no respect for [him] – no feeling at all'.[34] Christopher Bush's father ran up debts and left his wife to face the creditors who came calling for payment: 'I rarely recall feeling for him the faintest glow of affection.'[35] The failure to provide for one's family was too serious a dereliction of paternal duty, and its consequences too severe, to be overlooked, forgotten or forgiven.

In emphasising the strain of resentment and hostility that writers felt towards fathers who had failed in their breadwinning duties, it should not be imagined that the writers felt nothing but negativity. In reality, human emotions are complex, variable and often contradictory. Writers did not always hold fixed and stable judgements of their fathers: it was possible to judge a man quite harshly in one part of the narrative, and yet to take a more conciliatory tone somewhere else. We are dependent upon the words of individuals who were intimately bound up in these relationships and who brought a degree of ambivalence to their writing. What, for instance, did John Edwin really think of his father? He was, John wrote, an alcoholic, 'unreliable and erratic', frequently losing his jobs, and 'offtimes unfaithful thus causing emotional upsets at home'. Apart from that, though, 'he was a lovable character and we loved him'.[36]

The picture is further complicated by the fact that the autobiographers were looking back over childhoods that had long since ended. Very often a writer's father had passed away by the time he or she started writing, and those considering their fathers retrospectively sometimes found an understanding of their father's behaviour which had not, one imagines, been apparent when they were children. A child's resentment could thus sit together with an adult's pity. As an adolescent, Harry Young 'detested and despised' his father for mismanaging his bike shop, for reducing the family to penury and for mistreating his mother. Writing as a much older man, however, Harry also recognised that the abysmal poverty and neglect of his father's childhood had broken his health and left him ill equipped for a life of adult responsibility.[37] Lottie Barker condemned her father's heavy drinking and the 'self-administered holidays' he regularly indulged in and concluded that he had been 'a very irresponsible man, selfish and thoughtless'. With hindsight though, she also conceded that his work as a furnaceman was 'exceedingly hard'. It was 'no wonder he broke out at times'.[38]

Yet fascinating as the complexities surrounding these paternal assessments are, we should not allow them to distract us from some more fundamental truths. Stories of fathers and their provision for their families were told over and over by the autobiographers, and for the most part there is a consistency to these stories. Writers expressed a range of negative emotions towards their fathers, and they were repeatedly directed towards fathers who had failed to share their earnings with their family. A father's failure to provide for his family was simply too severe to be wiped over by some other attribute or to be forgotten with the passage of time. Herbert Bennett accepted that his father's drinking had slowed as he aged and that he had 'mellowed and [become] easier to live with', but from Herbert's perspective, it was all a little too late: 'I find it hard to forget those earlier [years].'[39]

The reverse side of this was that writers wrote more warmly about fathers who had exerted themselves to provide for their families. Fathers were supposed to be breadwinners, and so long as they had fulfilled this role their children tended to be satisfied. The assessment had little to do with how *much* a father had actually provided. Instead, it turned on a father's effort and commitment towards his family. Thus the autobiographers were rarely critical of fathers who had struggled to provide for their family through no fault of their own. Men who earned low wages, or who suffered from unemployment or ill health were praised and respected for their efforts as readily as those who did better in the labour market. It was the commitment to family that counted, not the size of the wage packet. Margaret Powell had an impoverished upbringing in Hove, Sussex, owing in large part to the seasonal unemployment from which her father suffered, but she did not condemn him. None of the family did: 'We knew he did his best.'[40]

Yet when we look more closely at the ways in which these authors wrote about their fathers, it becomes apparent that many of their descriptions were in fact rather thin. Provision and other qualities were often elided together, and the author's testimony did not amount to much more than indicating their father had worked hard and been a conscientious provider. So, for example, Richard Meads's father was 'a good sober man';[41] or James Brady's a 'proud, caring, responsible, family-man'.[42] Joseph Wilson's father was 'good to please: a steady, hard-working man'.[43] Frequently, the sheer fact of working hard and providing for the family elicited a positive judgement, a judgement which was not ultimately sustained by any other kind of evidence or information. Some writers indicated that they had admired or respected their father;[44] others described themselves as 'grateful' to them.[45] Many more liked to point out that their father had been greatly respected by their neighbours.[46] Otherwise the adjectives for fathers who worked hard for their families do not systematically imply affection: 'stern',[47] 'severe',[48] 'strict'[49] and 'hasty'.[50] As one man summarised: 'I admired my father, feared him a little, and understood him not at all.'[51]

Although the autobiographers wrote far more positively about fathers who had done their best for their families than they did about those who had not, it is striking that these 'good' fathers were often no more integrated in their children's lives. Certainly, these writers were deeply appreciative of the efforts their fathers had made for them, yet at the same time they indicated that their fathers had been largely detached from their childhood. In fact, the very process of providing for their families had played a role in driving fathers apart from their families. Long hours of work had kept fathers outside the home and made them a distant presence, a rather hazy figure far in the background of their children's consciousness. Margaret Bondfield, for example, admitted that she had simply never known the man who spent most of his waking hours in the lace factory in order to provide for her and the rest of the family. He had been a 'stranger' and 'very remote' when she was a child. The most memorable thing about him was his punishments, which he delivered with the help of a slipper.[52] Long working hours created a literal, physical absence between fathers and children which was particularly acute when children were small. Observations such as 'we had little contact with father';[53] 'we seldom saw him . . . he was a shadowy figure';[54] 'we often didn't see Father during the week'[55] and he 'did not enter much into our lives'[56] were made frequently by the autobiographers, not because their fathers were out drinking at the pub, but simply because they were at work. One writer had to confess that he had almost nothing to say about his father, who had died when he was eight years old. His work had kept him away from home for long periods, and he had 'almost no memory of him'.[57]

Yet although long working hours restricted the time that men had available to spend with their families, some writers indicated their separation from their father had been compounded by the fact that he had also opted to spend his non-working hours outside the home rather than within. Thomas Westwater, for example, noted that his father worked a twelve-hour day in a signal box, but he also observed that his father's free time was filled with various duties and responsibilities for the Sunday school and the Railwaymen's Union, so that in the end he 'spent little time at home except to eat and sleep'. Nor, Thomas indicated, was his father's absence from the home entirely accidental – after all his parents' 'tastes differed in almost every way' and there was not much 'felicity' between them.[58] Wilfred Pickles's father began to absent himself from the home following the death of Wilfred's younger brother, much to the regret of his remaining son who loved nothing more than the cosy evenings the sadly reduced family sometimes spent together. He had warm memories of the times his father would stop at home in the evenings: 'he would sit with my mother and me round the fire reading . . . I loved every minute of this intimate, peaceful family life.' But it never lasted long. His friends in the pub were like 'an ever present magnet, pulling stronger sometimes than others, but always likely to draw him away from [the] hearth'.[59]

Long hours spent outside the home placed restrictions on the time that fathers and families had together, yet some of the writers hinted that their detachment from their fathers went beyond the limited amount of time their father had spent in the home, and was rooted in a more fundamental difficulty that some fathers had in finding their place in a domestic sphere that was powerfully stamped as 'female'. Writers frequently described their mother as the manager of the home and indicated that even when fathers spent time at home they remained on the periphery of family life. Charles Doyle's father, for example, had liked to sit by the fire in his favourite chair in the evenings whilst the children played by his feet. It is a homely image, but Charles went on to stress that his father had not actually interacted with the family whilst sitting in his chair: 'I wondered sometimes if he realised I was his son or some urchin from the tenement.'[60] Charles had been fourteen when his father passed away, and 'had a memory of him speaking to me personally only once'. This was a rare occasion when sickness had kept Charles home from school: 'He came into the bedroom and said: "Hello Charles, how are you feeling?" I felt so important at such special attention I could only whisper, "I'm fine".'[61] Margaret Perry's father was similarly removed from family matters: he had 'his job, his hobbies, and his Sunday morning in the pub with his brothers'. When he was home, he scarcely engaged with his family: he 'didn't talk to either my mother or we children'.[62] Matters were very similar in Jack Jones's home. His father was a hard-working and sober miner, but, 'We didn't know our dad very well.' The only day he was in the house with the family was Sunday, but he was so tired that all he wanted to do was sleep; he 'seldom talked to us on Sundays – hardly looked at us'.[63] By the same token, those with a closer relationship with their father sometimes noted how this had been unusual for the times. Mick Burke, for instance, had a close and friendly relationship with his stepfather, but he also added that he 'used to talk to us kids more than most fathers did in those days'.[64]

Occasionally, writers were critical of fathers for the lack of interest they had taken in their family.[65] But for the most part, writers were not voicing a complaint, or pining for a relationship they believed they ought to have. There was a widespread resignation that this was just the way that things were in those days. Margaret Perry, for example, did not condemn her father for not speaking to her. She knew he 'loved us'; he just 'wasn't interested in us'.[66] Likewise, Jack Jones was not objecting when he recalled that his father had not so much as looked at the family on Sundays. They all knew he was tired after a week's work at the mine and that he made his contribution to the family in a different way – 'he worked hard and long' for them.[67] Lionel Fraser agreed that the problem with his father was not a 'lack of interest in us on his part', and acknowledged that he 'was perfectly content to spend his few leisure hours with his family'. Yet it still remained the case that his children hardly knew him: 'There was not that degree of paternal intimacy which characterizes most families.'[68] Looking back over her father's relationship with the family, Daisy Cowper concluded that there was none 'of the intimate love and friendliness which youngsters nowadays have for their Dads'.[69] Repeatedly, the autobiographers not only describe a lack of intimacy in their own relationships with their fathers, they also suggest it was usual for the times.

Of course, this pattern was not universal. The collection of autobiographies is large and there are always some writers whose narratives do not fit the general pattern – in this case, describing fathers who were more actively involved in the lives of their children. A few of the autobiographers remembered fathers who were fond of their children and played games with them,[70] who played the piano or sang for them,[71] brought them sweets[72] or took them out on walks.[73] Adeline Hodges' father liked telling stories to the children and stopped going out in the evenings so that he could spend time with them: making toffee was a favourite activity.[74] May Wasson's father 'liked having a daughter' and 'in my early years he took me about a lot, walking in the country around the village and often to London'.[75] Edward Brand also recalled his father with particular fondness. Unlike his mother, who 'never seemed to have time to play and read to us', his father liked to sit the children on his knee and 'sing all the old songs to us'.[76] And as children, boys especially, grew older, it was not unusual for a closer relationship to develop, particularly when sons started work. This was most evident in rural areas, where fathers were often involved in preparing their sons for agricultural labour some years before they left school,[77] though it also applied in mining communities where fathers and sons often worked together.[78] Some older sons, and occasionally daughters, found common interests with fathers through leisure or politics.[79] But the shared interests between fathers and (mostly) sons that sometimes developed during adolescence should not be overexaggerated. Family life was complex and varied, and of course there were men who found interest and pleasure in home and children. But when we survey the sources in their entirety, we are forced to recognise that this was not the dominant motif. Most working-class children in Victorian and Edwardian Britain were raised in sharply gender-divided households and a great many men struggled to occupy a place in the domestic sphere. Children could of course still love and respect their family figurehead, yet the overall impression is one of father–child relationships characterised by detachment, not intimacy.

Relationships with mothers were very different. Most obviously, mothers were not distant figures whom their children rarely saw or scarcely knew. In the great majority of working-class households, mothers provided all childcare from birth, so their children knew them well. Frederick Spencer's father went to work before he got up and came home shortly before he went to bed. Like many children, he was 'hardly conscious of him'.[80] His mother, by contrast was 'the institution' that enabled all elements his childhood existence. For most writers, their mother had played a vital role in sustaining their life and well-being throughout childhood, and the relationship between mother and child was substantial. But we should beware of thinking that physical proximity necessarily created emotional intimacy in a simple and straightforward way. Relationships between mothers and children were complex and mediated by a host of factors beyond the physical closeness that thrust mothers and their children together.

Furthermore, although writers clearly knew their mothers more intimately than their fathers this does not mean that they necessarily wrote about them in ways that were more forthcoming. In fact, many used a similar script for both parents, focusing on the external rituals of parenthood rather than the emotional substance of the relationship. The Victorian household was gendered, with specific and distinct expectations for mothers and for fathers. Fathers were supposed to be breadwinners: their primary task was to bring income to the home, and descriptive accounts of fathers turned largely upon how (and how well) they did this. A mother's duties involved the wise spending of a husband's meagre wage, along with the endless round of cleaning, cooking and sewing that was required to ensure the physical well-being of the household's inhabitants. And just as writers tended to describe and evaluate their father from the perspective of his breadwinning, so did their mother's domestic activities feature prominently in their writing about their mothers. Ben Turner, for instance, declared his mother was 'a good 'un, bless her', but to substantiate his judgement he referred to the fact that she was 'a good sewer' and she ran the house well: 'My mother always contrived to keep a roof over our heads and to have us neat and tidy.'[81] He was just one of several autobiographers who framed their discussion of their mother in terms of how well she had run the home: 'She counted and took care of the scanty wages. She planned out the week's need.'[82] She was 'up with the lark in the summer, and long before daylight in winter, preparing the meagre morning meal of oatmeal and skimmed milk'.[83] She 'baked her own bread and all those fancy bread-stuffs that the dales people know so well'.[84] She 'made everything that was worn by the family except boots and my father's hats . . . [and] did the washing for us all'.[85] A mother's role was not primarily to earn the wherewithal to keep the family – though circumstances sometimes dictated that she did this too. Instead it was to transform her husband's wages into a tolerably comfortable domestic existence for each and every member of the family, and writing about how she did this provided a safe and familiar structure for narratives of childhood.

At the same time, however, it is clear that in remembering their mothers some writers wanted to talk about something else. Autobiographers were by and large satisfied with fathers who had worked steadily and shared their wage; most had not expected anything more. But they were not always so easily satisfied by a mother who had dutifully cooked and cleaned. Children wanted to feel loved and cared for as well, and they looked to their mothers to provide this nurture.

As might be imagined, within a collection of more than six hundred autobiographies, there are plenty of examples of mothers who met their children's emotional needs. Some writers even employed a language of love to capture this. Joe Williamson, for example, declared that his mother had raised him with a 'natural mother's love and care'.[86] Rosie Hannan's mother had a 'passionate love for all children' and created a home of 'love, comfort and happiness' for them.[87] Looking back at his childhood, William Bell, concluded that his mother's 'love for her children was the main spring of her life'.[88] Daisy Cowper's mother had given 'all her children love in fullest measure . . . Just to be with her was to sense warmth and safety.'[89] The word 'love' was not a regular part of all writers' vocabulary, however, so some turned to a different language in order to describe their early home life. They referred to 'affection' rather than 'love', or drew attention to a wide range of specific maternal qualities, such as gentleness, warmth, kindness, good humour and sympathy in order to capture the essence of their relationship.[90] They recalled such things as the 'smile on her face;'[91] her 'large heart [and] warm temperament';[92] or specific acts of kindness and care that had sustained their young bodies in an otherwise rather harsh environment.[93] Len Wincott's mother, for example, stood as 'firm as a rock' in a 'poverty-stricken' household destabilised by a drunken father. She was 'as soft and comforting as the warm sand on a beautiful beach'.[94] Ernest Shotton's mother was 'calm and peaceful'.[95] The autobiographers used varied vocabularies for describing their relationships with their mothers, a result, no doubt, of the fact that they were writing about an era that did not readily employ a language of familial love in an era that did. Yet regardless of the exact words they employed, these writers all somehow managed to convey the sense of warmth, safety and contentment that had been created by their mothers.

But we must not let the scatter of such comments across the autobiographies wrongfoot us. Certainly, some of the writers wrote about maternal love and kindness. But a great many did not. Of course, some simply kept well clear of the emotional aspects of their childhood experiences. They focused their writing steadily upon the objective and away from feelings and sentiment, so we cannot know how matters stood inside their families. Yet others *did* address the emotional texture of their childhood but in so doing provided a different, and rather less comforting, account of family life. They wrote about mothers who had performed the housework, sometimes to a laudable degree of efficiency, but who had gone about these tasks without much joy, and certainly without much tenderness for the children in their charge. There is thus a narrative that runs counter to that of mothers and children bound together by strong ties of love and affection, a more uncomfortable narrative that signals the absence of ties of this kind.

Some of the writers suggested that their mothers had just been too busy to provide close supervision or to enter into the emotional worlds of their children. John Holt, for example, thought that his mother had her hands full running the house and helping her husband on the farm. She 'had not much time or inclination to coddle me'.[96] Wilfred Pickles's mother was 'preoccupied in the struggle to keep us going in food and clothes', and for this reason was not 'ever attentive to our antics'.[97] Robert Roberts recalled how his mother used to hurry through one room to another and ask him in passing: ' "What do you want? . . . Bun? Banana? Either, neither, both?" ' On her next passage, he would answer and she would promptly supply the requested goods. She met his physical needs, but 'she lacked a sensitivity of feeling'.[98] The word that some writers employed to describe their mother was 'reserved',[99] some also indicating that their mothers had not believed in talking to the children. In old age, Amy Langley recalled that she had 'never heard her [mother] give any of us an endearing word'.[100] Daisy Noakes described her mother as 'very strict . . . she never showed affection, or had time to listen to us . . . I can never remember having a conversation with her.'[101] Though the word 'strict' was most readily used to describe fathers, it was frequently used to describe mothers as well.[102]

The accounts that writers gave of their mothers inevitably sit on a continuum. Whilst some writers described mothers who were orderly and efficient if somewhat reserved, at some point the emphasis in these narratives shift, and we are left with writers recalling an unloving, albeit efficient, mother. Mrs Davies, for example, wrote that her 'mother was as hard as nails . . . She never, ever sympathised with you.'[103] It was the absence of affection that Amy

8.2 Daisy Noakes's mother with her younger brother: 'Mum was very strict ... I expect she loved us in her peculiar way, but she never showed affection, or had time to listen to us. She kept us clean and tidy and fed and that's about it. I can never remember having a conversation with her.'

8.3 Alice Mullen's mother 'was so often tried and her patience gave out. She was very quick tempered and there was the stick very quickly or anything else handy.'

Grace Rose also remembered the best. As a child, she 'always used to feel that nobody loved me'. Her mother was a 'severe kind of woman . . . not kind and gentle'; it was unthinkable to 'put [your] arms around her and kiss her'.[104] Some mothers were kind and gentle, but there again others were harsh and had a sharp tongue. Harry Burton, for example, cast his eye back over a childhood where 'gentleness and loving kindness' were 'completely absent'.[105] Annie Jaeger admitted that she was 'afraid' of her mother, 'who could by one little look or word make you smart'.[106]

And there was a darker side to domestic life. Where some writers wrote about an absence of affection, others described a more potent cocktail of anger, hostility and violence. Take, for instance, George Acorn, raised in desperate poverty in a one-roomed hovel with a hard-drinking and often unemployed father and a mother who was 'incapable' of affection. As a child he felt unloved and unsafe. The warring between his parents was continual, with regular night-time rows that had the children cowering in their beds and the neighbours racing upstairs to separate the combatants.[107] When she was not fighting with her husband, Mrs Acorn battled against her eldest son, using taunts and physical violence to extract compliance. As an adult, George could recognise that his mother, living with a precarious breadwinner and too many children (one of whom died before the age of two), faced multiple challenges. 'Her struggles to supply our physical needs, especially during my father's enforced absence, were quite, quite heroic.' Yet her heroic toil could not fill the void created by her years of harsh words and rough treatment. 'If only to her strength of purpose had been added some spiritual sympathy, some ray of tender love, I know I should have responded with generous affection – my mother would have been so much to me.'[108]

There were others who shared a similar story of mothers who were effective housewives, yet who were at best emotionally distant, at worst outright hostile. Kathleen Woodward mused that she had been bound to her mother by 'ties which existed without love or affection'. Her mother 'sweated and laboured for her children, equally without stint or thought, but was utterly oblivious to any need we might cherish for sympathy in our little sorrows, support in our strivings. She simply was not aware of anything beyond the needs of our bodies.'[109] Faith Osgerby's mother was a competent housewife, who worked hard for her husband and seven children, one of whom was unable to walk. But these competencies did not compensate, in Faith's eyes, for a childhood that 'was really ruled by FEAR' and was devoid of affection – 'I can never remember in all my life being cuddled or kissed or "loved" as we love our babies today'.[110] Hannah Mitchell also made a clear distinction between good housekeeping and good mothering. With respect to the former, her mother could not be faulted – she was a well-dressed housewife, 'everything in order', 'work and cleanliness were her gods'.[111] But her temper was 'so uncertain that we lived in constant fear of an outbreak'. Her 'violent passions', triggered by 'the merest trifles', could last for days and sometimes ended with the children spending the night without food in the outside barn.[112] Clean or not, it was not, Hannah concluded, 'a good atmosphere to grow up in'.[113]

Then there was the widespread practice of corporal punishment. It is widely acknowledged that corporal punishment was part and parcel of a nineteenth-century upbringing; yet historians have struggled to incorporate this knowledge into their understanding of motherhood. After all, it is one thing to accept that the stern Victorian paterfamilias sometimes beat his children in order to extract obedience; it is quite another to recognise that mothers, the primary caregivers, were also involved in the practice. Female aggression, particularly within the context of the family, sits so far outside our understanding of feminine behaviour that scholars have ultimately dismissed the evidence of maternal physical chastisement as a long-discarded and ultimately trivial element of family life.[114]

Some of the autobiographers did indeed dismiss their mother's fondness for physical force as trivial: a stick that was used to stir dirty clothes and 'our backs when we tried her patience beyond endurance';[115] the absurdity of going into the woods to find the 'jinni fetw', or birch, which would be used on one's own back.[116] Corporal punishment is everywhere in the autobiographies, and (as historians have suggested) some writers simply made light of it. But to suggest that such a sentiment was universal fails to do justice to the violence that ruled in too many of the autobiographers' homes. Dozens of the autobiographers indicate that their mothers had administered punishment through the use of fists, sticks and belts. It had the capacity both to shame and to inflict considerable pain. And rarely did the recipient dismiss it as trivial.

Perhaps unsurprisingly, there was a considerable overlap between writers who complained of emotionally distant mothers and those who reported high levels of violence. George Acorn, Kathleen Woodward and Faith Osgerby all had a large stock of such memories. Acorn remembered countless thrashings, a 'good hiding', 'savage punishment' and objects of various kinds being hurled in his direction – a fork, a loaf of bread, a knife, 'a fusillade of cups' that had been sitting on the table.[117] Woodward's mother's anger was 'frequent and violent' and 'she aimed her blows without feeling or restraint'. Once she split Kathleen's head open, and another time aimed a fork at her, 'which dangerously pierced my side'.[118] Faith Osgerby could never remember having been 'cuddled, or kissed or "loved" ' as a child, but could remember being hit only too clearly. The punishment, she grimly recalled, 'was always done by my mother, and truly she was very capable at the job'. Her bottom 'was smacked so very often sometimes for such small faults, such as a sulky look . . . if any of us cried for some reason she was not aware of we got a smacked bottom so that she *would* know what we were crying for'.[119] And many other writers had similar tales to tell. Jack Lawson described several incidents of physical violence at the hands of his mother, including one where she tore into the children's bedroom in a fury, ripped off their clothes and a 'leather strap swished and crackled against our bare bodies'.[120] Such was her loss of control that her husband ordered her to stop, fearful for his children's lives. One writer remembered a mother's 'solid, terrifying discipline',[121] and another living in fear of a 'cruel and spiteful' mother with a short temper and a long cane that was frequently taken down from its place on the wall.[122]

Some degree of physical violence within the home was normal in Victorian and Edwardian Britain, and within certain bounds it was tolerated. Yet as the level of violence intensified, so did the damage it wrought on relationships. Amongst Hannah Mitchell's complaints about her mother were her 'nagging, ravings and beatings'.[123] It was not the basis of a successful relationship, she concluded, but helped to create 'an antipathy . . . between us, which lasted all our lives'.[124] William Hocking recalled how often 'parts of my body [were] warmed by my mother's hand' and how 'very fond' she had been of this mode of punishment. The adult Hocking was not so fond of it. He considered that when mothers resorted to such physical punishment, it simply served to make 'their children hate them', and wished he were able to 'blot out the memory of the aches and pains of my boyhood caused by her hand'.[125] The reverse was also true. A few adult writers appreciated that their parents had not hit them when they were children,[126] though they often added that their parents' restraint had been somewhat unusual for the time.[127] Almost all of those who reported high levels of physical punishment did not do so in the context of loving or successful family relationships. Sticks, straps and belts may have been commonplace, but they still had the power to damage.

We have looked so far at mothers who managed to live up, in some measure at least, to the normal expectations of motherhood. They kept their children housed, fed and clothed, even if some were less successful at meeting the emotional needs of their children. But as we continue to read across the autobiographies we are soon forced to confront an uncomfortable truth. Not all mothers could manage this. In a small number of cases, mothers were unable to fulfil the most basic of duties, such as the provision of food, warmth and shelter. Let us take our analysis of working-class families further by looking at some of these.

A small minority of writers had never known their mothers. Almost all of these had been born illegitimate and had been permanently separated from their mothers shortly after birth. Edwin Purkiss, for example, was one of the few autobiographers who knew almost nothing about his parents. 'I find great difficulty in writing about my early days,' he wrote, 'as I am not able to obtain full particulars.' He knew simply that he had been born in the Marylebone workhouse and was transferred from there to St Cyprian's Orphanage a few years later. He had an elder brother – Leonard Purkiss – who had lived with him in the orphanage. He described his brother as an orphan, and appears to have believed that he was an orphan too.[128]

In reality, however, though Edwin and Leonard were motherless, they were not orphans. Their mother was Louisa Purkiss and the census reveals that she was alive and well. By the 1891 census she was married to a man called William Henry Herbert, and the couple went on to have at least two further children – George and Edith.[129] Although Louisa and her new family lived no more than a few miles away from her two illegitimate sons, Louisa never made further contact with the boys, and they both died believing they had no family besides each other. Outcomes such as these were depressingly common. Although some unmarried mothers managed to keep their newborn infants with them,[130] others did not.[131] As we well know, nineteenth-century Britain was not a supportive place for single mothers. Working mothers faced low pay and childcare that was virtually non-existent, so the material obstacles that stood in the way of establishing a home together were formidable. In the case of illegitimacy, they had social stigma to contend with as well. Bonar Thompson's unmarried mother was living in rural Ulster, and 'disappeared to

England' after the birth of her child because she was 'unable to bear the disgrace of having given me birth'.[132] It is hardly surprising, then, that so many became separated from their child soon after birth, having entrusted their infants either to the care of their own mother or to the workhouse or some other institution. Those left with grandparents were sometimes retrieved once their mother's situation in life improved, though not always with great success.[133] Zoe Fairhurst recalled being returned to her mother and 'the strange man called "Father" ' when she was three years old. The happy times she had spent with her grandmother were over and fear now pervaded her childhood: she 'lived in a world uncertain and often afraid . . . My mother's face, when I touched her, was always cold and I knew that all was not well.'[134] But most of the abandoned illegitimates were never faced with this kind of upheaval as they were not reunited with their mothers, or at least not permanently.[135]

Illegitimacy carried a high risk of maternal separation, but scattered throughout the autobiographies were others who had become separated from their mothers later in childhood. A small handful of children were moved out of the family home and dispersed to another household, most commonly one set of grandparents. Parents usually resorted to these kinds of separations in order to cope with large families and overcrowded homes or a short-term crisis, and most remained in contact with their children despite living apart from them.[136] But alongside these managed separations were a number of more complex family breakdowns in which either mothers fled, or children were cast away from, homes and relationships that were already crumbling. Thomas Luby, for example, left his mother's scarcely functioning household at the age of nine to live with a man he had befriended on the streets. When that arrangement broke down, he returned to his mother. Yet once again, she proved unable to provide a home for him: 'She'd got four of us, four she couldn't keep, so I had to start the best way I could.'[137] Reflecting on why he had been living on the streets rather than with his mother from the very young age of nine, Thomas made the following observation of the home he had shared with his mother: 'I hadn't been used to much all my life, much like a dog or any animal.'[138]

Luby did not explain why his mother was unable to keep him, but others gestured to addiction as a cause of relationship breakdown. Mrs Layton, for example, believed that her mother had done the best she could rearing a large family of fourteen children in Bethnal Green, but she also added that the 'continual grinding away at work for her own family' eventually broke her constitution and she took to gin-drinking.[139] Rebecca Jarrett was raised in appalling poverty in London in the 1850s by a mother who worked as a prostitute and who had put Rebecca to prostitution by the age of twelve. She accounted for her mother's actions by observing that she was 'drinking hard ... [she was] so under the influence of drink'.[140] Unlike many unmarried mothers, Kate McMullen remained in contact with her daughter, also called Kate, throughout her childhood. But the young Kate's childhood was shattered by two difficult pieces of information she had to digest at the age of seven. The first was the 'sickening revelation' that her big sister Kate, an occasional visitor to her home, was a drunk. The second was that Kate was not in fact her sister at all; she was her mother.[141] William Parrish's mother 'began to drink' whilst he was still a small child, and her neglect of her four children was serious enough that the local authorities stepped in and placed the youngest two in an orphanage.[142]

Alcoholism also played its part in the difficulties in Arthur Harding's East End household. In contrast to the fine and upright housekeepers depicted elsewhere in the autobiographies, Harding described his mother as a 'forager', whose special skill was telling the 'hard-luck story' to the do-gooders in the East End who dispensed charity. She did work hard for her family – she made matchboxes in their one-roomed home – but she also added to the family coffers by 'pinch[ing] a lot of clothes at the church sales' and selling them on for a profit.[143] Over the years, her working and foraging declined and her drinking increased, until his elder sister, rather than his mother, 'kept the house together'. His sister was 'more a mother than anybody else', he concluded.[144] These kinds of accounts of serious maternal neglect or addiction were not common. Drinking was quite easily incorporated into narratives about fathers; but alcoholic mothers were an object of shame. As Kay Garrett explained, 'In our street it was normal for a father to come home drunk on a Saturday night . . . but not your Mum.' Her mother's drinking made her want to 'hang my head in shame'.[145] It was not easy for authors to talk about maternal neglect and abuse, and we should not imagine that the inclusion of such themes was accidental or decorative.[146] It may have been comparatively infrequent, but it certainly did happen.

Alongside the mothers who were unable to provide a proper home for their children were a handful who abandoned their children altogether. For example,

James Hawke and his sister lost contact with their mother when he was around six years old.[147] She was raising the children alone following her husband's desertion, and relying heavily upon her own mother for support. One day, she left the children with their grandmother and they never saw her again.[148] Betty May's mother also gave up her attempt to raise her children single-handedly. After a particularly furious row between Betty and her brother, their mother unceremoniously dumped the pair of them with their father – an alcoholic running a brothel – from whom she had separated many years previously, where Betty's well-being became considerably more precarious.[149] Mothers who lived apart from their children were usually single,[150] but occasionally married women were also unable to provide a home for their children, and found surrogates or institutions to take them in – sometimes just one child, sometimes a whole brood.[151] George Severn's mother was married, but got on so badly with her husband that she eventually left both him and her two children to go and work as a domestic servant. George was left with an uncle and aunt who terrorised him with tales of goblins. He spent three unhappy years away from his mother, with 'a lump in my throat' all the while.[152]

We have seen that there was not one single template for motherhood. The autobiographers described kind and loving mothers; tireless, housekeeping mothers; mothers who (in their children's estimation) had failed to provide adequate warmth, love, affection; and even mothers who had been unable to provide any kind of home at all. The variety is so great it would be tempting to declare it 'complex' or 'nuanced', and to leave the matter there. But can we get behind this complexity and unpack why mothering came in so many different forms? Or even make connections between mothering styles and other elements of material and family life?

At the outset, it is important to recognise that we cannot provide complete answers to our questions as the evidence itself is not complete. More than one-third of all the autobiographers did not write about their mothers in any depth at all. They provided at best a few biographical details, such as her maiden name and occupation before marriage, possibly a brief comment on her housekeeping skills or any paid employment she had undertaken, perhaps some other incidental mention – a dream, an accident, the church she attended. Some did not even provide this. It is indeed notable that mothers, despite being so fundamental to a child's survival and well-being, were not fleshed out in any detail in so many of the autobiographies. In step with the Victorian values with which they had been raised, some writers kept the details of their family relationships private.

The problem is not simply that so many writers did not discuss their mothers, but also that those who did sometimes wrote in ways that can be difficult to decipher or open to more than one interpretation. As Kay Garrett indicated of her mother's drinking, some maternal behaviours were shameful. They could be unpleasant to remember and difficult to write about, and we cannot imagine that writers spoke about dysfunctional families as readily as they spoke about stable homes and loving mothers. Herbert Harris wrote about his separation from his mother and subsequent incarceration in an orphanage some seventy years after it had happened, yet confessed that 'even now I have pangs of anguish and depression when I give thought to the story'.[153] He, like many others, wanted to brush over negative experiences and offered no more than the sketchiest outline of this part of his life.[154] Indeed, his account is so elliptical that I am unable to establish exactly what had caused the break-up of his family when he was three years old. Whilst autobiographers could chatter away freely about their mothers' domestic virtues and the quality of their needlework, they found it much harder to commit to paper any criticism. The result was family stories that were sometimes incomplete, muddled or incoherent.

Writers deployed a number of different strategies for addressing difficult personal experiences. For example, when recalling her hard childhood and the many chores she had had to perform for her mother, Mrs Wrigley got around the problem of expressing any direct criticism by putting her thoughts in the mouth of her sister: 'I'm not saying what my other sister said, but she thought my mother was very cruel.'[155] Kathleen Hilton-Foord's childhood was rudely disrupted when she was shipped off to live with her grandmother, ostensibly because her elderly and ailing father was struggling to provide. She turned to poetry to address how she felt about this separation from her family. The original prose version of her autobiography provided a simple narrative account of her childhood with her grandmother; the subsequent verse version revealed the emotional pain caused by her exclusion from the home her parents shared with her four brothers – the heavy 'feeling of rejection' that she carried round for many years afterwards.[156] Others opted simply to omit any discussion of their early years at all. Frank Bullen wrote four volumes of autobiographical reminiscences, but it was only in the fourth that he referred to his early home life and the absence of his mother, and even then did so in the most coded of terms.[157] Earlier versions of his lengthy life story had begun when he was aged nine. Some writers deferred addressing certain aspects of their family life to later chapters or drafts of their autobiography. Arthur Goffin, for example, declared in an early chapter entitled 'My Parents' that 'no man had a better mother than mine'. But a later coda to his life history, ominously entitled the 'Skeleton in the Closet', told a very different story of an unhappy family, with a 'strong-willed mother' and frequent 'jangling' between family members. Whatever 'maternal love' his mother possessed, she 'could not let it blossom'. When he was small, she used violence to extract compliance and when he became too old for that, she used her tongue instead: she 'poured out the acid'.[158] It is also probably significant that some of the more unsatisfactory stories of family life were retold through interviews rather than freely committed to paper. Arthur Harding, Thomas Luby and Les Moss all told their stories to interviewers and much of the unflattering detail about their mothers unfolded in the course of these conversations. How much they would have divulged about these experiences if they had had greater control over their narrative is very much open to question.[159]

The tendency of writers to provide ambiguous accounts emerges particularly clearly in cases of neglect and abandonment. These authors were not writing proto-versions of the 'misery memoir', in which the author's goal was, precisely, to write about dysfunction and misery. Most simply did not want to analyse a childhood that had contained a prolonged period of neglect or separation. Rebecca Jarrett, for example, had plenty of misery to write about. Her mother was an alcoholic and a prostitute who had started selling Rebecca for sex at the age of twelve. But her memoir did not dwell on this; indeed it was positively upbeat, even insisting (despite overwhelming evidence to the contrary) that her mother was a 'good mother'.[160] Mrs Layton's mother took to drinking gin when her children were small, leading to years of poor health and an early death. But like Rebecca Jarrett, the adult Mrs Layton refused to countenance that the alcoholism may have ultimately diminished the quality of the care she had provided: she was 'a good kind mother . . . she could not have done much better for her children than she did'.[161]

A similar tension is evident in those who were abandoned by their mothers. James Hawke, for example, spoke in warm tones about the mother who had left him. He concluded that she 'must have had great courage', adding that he had 'always felt kindly towards my mother', and expressing regret that he had not been able to find her as an adult. But the truth was that James's mother had left him at such a young age that he could not really remember 'anything personal' about her. And those things that he could remember do not make easy reading. Before abandoning James, his mother 'did not show much affection for [me]'. His few recollections of their years together included an 'unmerciful hiding' and a 'sound beating with the buckle-end of a belt' that he received at her hands.[162] The only other things he could remember were the ache in his heart when he realised his mother preferred his sister to him, and the actual moment of her departure.[163] Betty May interpreted her abandonment in a similar way. She did not condemn her mother for sending her to live in a dirty and unsafe home with her drunken father; in fact she took much of the blame for the calamity upon herself. After all (she reasoned), she and her siblings had 'needed a great deal of looking after' and was it not her own misbehaviour – she had thrown her brother's boots into the canal – that had precipitated the separation?[164]

Repeatedly writers made brave attempts to reframe the circumstances of their abandonment, so that although this vital detail is shared with the reader, no complaint is made of the mother for her role in it. Others provided flat narrative accounts of their mother's departure without making any attempt to explore its meaning or significance. Jim Uglow, for instance, recalled how his father had returned from a two-year trip at sea to find 'a three months old baby in a pram, a pile of debts and three very neglected children'. After a few ugly scenes, his mother left with the new baby and its father. She 'just disappeared from our lives'. By the same token, she just disappeared from Jim's narrative.[165] Yet no matter how these writers chose to frame or interpret their early years, they also made plain that their maternal abandonment had been a hugely significant event, involving domestic upheaval, a move to a new (and rarely better) home, a defining moment that indelibly changed the course of their lives. In recounting these stories, the autobiographers produced unsteady narratives that sought to explain the separation from their mother but at the same time to confine and minimise its significance.

Yet for all that these are slippery narratives, and despite the pains that some writers went to avoid publicly criticising or condemning their mothers, they have bequeathed a body of evidence that allows us to probe both when motherhood worked and why and how it failed. It is simplest to start by separating the outward conventions of motherhood – the shopping, cooking and cleaning – from the emotions. These were the aspects of motherhood that authors returned to most readily. As was the case for breadwinning and fatherhood, housekeeping was safe territory, providing a subject matter around which childhood experiences could be organised and understood. And the autobiographies suggest that the majority of mothers succeeded in providing the necessary physical care. The proportion of mothers who were separated from their children or who were not, for one reason or another, providing them with food and lodging was low. Just 8 per cent of the autobiographers indicated that their mother had been either absent during their childhood or failing in a significant way to provide an adequate home for them. Of course, because so many writers were largely silent about their mothers we cannot be certain that the remaining 92 per cent were all present and providing a decent home for their children, though there are grounds for assuming that the majority were. After all, as we have seen, households simply broke down if mothers did not pay the rent, cook the meals and look after the children – and autobiographers could scarcely write about their childhood without mentioning that their home had been significantly fractured. It may be that a handful of authors did not want to air these kinds of details and found ways to conceal them, but such silences are unlikely to significantly alter the general picture, which suggests that the majority of mothers were present and performing their household duties.

Eight per cent is not insignificant, but it is worth contrasting with the proportion of fathers who were absent or failing in their primary role as family breadwinner. To recap the evidence presented in part two: ineffective breadwinning was a common problem amongst fathers. Amongst those providing a sufficiently detailed account of their father, over 40 per cent indicated he had not been a good provider – including 14 per cent whose father had been absent altogether. Clearly, it was much rarer for mothers to renege on their half of the breadwinning compact. Most mothers did not neglect the housekeeping or abandon their children. The autobiographers did not repeatedly describe mothers who pursued their own hobbies or interests to the neglect of the cooking or who spent the housekeeping money on themselves rather than the children in the way they did their fathers. Alcoholism and desertion, though not unheard of in mothers, were also less common.

Yet housework and emotions were tied together in complex ways and having a mother present did not guarantee a loving and nurturing relationship.

Getting at this, the emotional content of mother–child relationships, is a more difficult task, as the writers tended to be more hesitant to discuss their emotions but, as we have seen, some writers certainly did touch upon these themes. Amongst such writers, the greater proportion wrote in positive terms, yet once again the number of those who did not was negligible. Ten per cent described problems, ranging from a reserved indifference to children's emotional welfare to a more toxic blend of anger, hostility and violence. If we add this 10 per cent to the 8 per cent who described the more serious forms of neglect, addiction and abandonment, the proportion of writers describing domestic problems becomes substantial. And, of course, we know that autobiographers did not relish talking about maternal failings and that many did not talk about their mothers at all, so the true figure could be higher. Even at nearly 20 per cent, however, this amounts to a fairly sizeable subset indicating that they had not enjoyed a close and loving (or, sometimes, any) relationship with their mother. As such, it becomes necessary to think more critically about the traditional Victorian family and to question why it was creating such poor outcomes for a large minority of children.

Let us begin by looking at the 8 per cent of mothers who were either absent or not providing a safe home for their children. Whilst the precise dynamic of each story was unique, there is a thread that runs throughout all of these fractured mother–child relationships: some form of prior breakdown of the two-parent family. The Victorian family required a male breadwinner and a female housekeeper, and was very vulnerable in the absence of a breadwinner and his wage. This vulnerability was most acute in the case of unmarried mothers, who by definition had no male to support them and so deposited their children with other carers so that they could continue to work.[166] But the same dynamic was also sometimes at work amongst married mothers who became separated from their children. Marriages could break down and when they did so, married women were in just the same position as their unmarried counterparts in needing to earn their own living. Edward Brown, for example, was shipped off to an aunt (who in the event maltreated him) after his parents had separated. His father 'disappeared into the void, never to be heard of again' and his mother needed to find a new means of support for both herself and her son.[167] As Edward explained, his mother 'gave up her home, made arrangements in regard to me, and set to work to earn her own living again'.[168] Most single mothers initially sought to keep their households and children together, but some eventually found the strain of full-time work and housekeeping too much to bear. Betty May's description of the home she was eventually banished from reveals a household that was already struggling. Betty's father had deserted the family some years previously and her mother was working twelve hours a day at the chocolate factory in an attempt to keep the home running. Despite her efforts, Betty and her three siblings were living in 'squalor and misery'. 'It would have been excusable if she had neglected us,' she ruefully noted.[169]

Broken households were usually the context for mothers battling an alcohol addiction as well. William Parrish, for example, linked his mother's drinking to the 'grief and anguish' she had felt at the death of her husband.[170] Kate McMullen's mother was unmarried, and Kate considered that 'the hopelessness of her life . . . drove her to an antidote to enable her to go through with it'.[171] Rebecca Jarrett explained that her mother had started to drink after her father's final departure. He had previously left her mother several times and lived with other women before abandoning her permanently with eight children, including a baby in arms.[172] Arthur Harding's mother faced a range of problems that worked against her ability to provide for her children and contributed to her descent into alcoholism. Following an accident in the street in early adulthood, she was unable to walk properly and suffered chronic pain. Early in her marriage, she lost her first child, a boy, at the age of two years and nine months.[173] And her husband, though present, was hardly an effective family breadwinner. According to Arthur, he was 'too lazy to earn a living' and 'just an encumbrance really'.[174] In the absence of a regular male wage, Mrs Harding took up sweated labour, working long hours to make matchboxes for a pittance. It is little wonder that her children were neglected, and that her drinking eventually spiralled out of control. Wherever mothers were drinking, the autobiographers narrated similar tales of family dysfunction, absent or unsatisfactory husbands and chaotic and difficult homes.[175]

An inability to provide a home for children sat at the most extreme end of maternal failing. It was also possible, however, for mothers to be present and providing the rudiments of physical care, yet doing so in ways that felt harsh and austere to their children. This was an altogether more complex problem, in which fathers sometimes played a role, but which was also connected to a host of broader social forces largely unconnected with male actions. Certainly, any situation that forced women to take on a full-time wage-earning role risked undermining the emotional well-being of the whole family. The problem was not work in and of itself, but rather the very unfavourable terms upon which work was made available to women, and the fact that it added to, rather than replaced, their domestic work. Working hours were so long and the work often so arduous, that it was not usually compatible with a contented family life. Alfred Coppard, for example, thought that after his father's death his mother had 'became something of a martinet; she had no time to be kind'.[176] Backbreaking laundry work and the endless round of domestic chores turned her life into a battle to be endured rather than something to enjoy. It was only as an adult that Kay Pearson understood some of the reasons why, when she was growing up, 'no one in our house showed affection'.[177] Then she saw the 'heartache, poverty, hunger, and above all the loneliness which pervaded her [mother's] existence' following her husband's desertion.[178]

The double burden of paid work and housework was greatest for single mothers, but, as we well know, women married to an unreliable breadwinner sometimes found themselves in a broadly similar situation. The consequences for their (and their children's) well-being were also broadly the same. George Williams, for example, described the deterioration in his relationship with his mother once she agreed to her husband's plan to run a public house: she became 'a scolding and overworked figure in the background'.[179] Annie Jaeger's mother had five children and a hat-renovating business to look after. Annie found her harsh and critical, and as she grew older it only got worse: 'because of overwork and strain [she] became harder and harder'.[180] Kathleen Woodward's mother had escaped an abusive father to marry at the age of eighteen, but shortly after her wedding her new husband 'fell sick with an illness which left him half invalid for the rest of his life'. Her 'bright prospects for rest and a change were thus rudely and abruptly set aside'.[181] Kathleen believed that her mother had succeeded in the material work of motherhood – she did a valiant job of keeping the household running in difficult circumstances – but had failed in the emotional sphere. The absence of a capable or reliable male wage forced women to re-enter the labour market. Long hours away from home not only made it very difficult to provide adequate care to young children, it was also exhausting and left mothers without the resources to enjoy life.

It is not difficult to imagine that absent or errant fathers played a role in undermining the emotional well-being of a family. But one of the more unexpected findings to emerge from the autobiographies is the limitations of this as an explanatory force. Fathers were not to blame for every family's woe. Some of the writers outlined difficulties in their relationships with their mothers that were independent of their fathers' actions. They reported that their father had worked regularly and shared their wages. They also indicated that their mother had not worked for pay. Yet the effective operation of the breadwinning family had not created happiness. To understand what was going on within these families, we need to move away from the dynamics of individual family units and look instead at the broader societal forces that helped to structure women's lives.

In the first instance, we should recognise that the harsh and distant mothering that some of the autobiographers described was not regarded as problematic or abnormal. There was a widely shared cultural belief within many working-class families that mothers should not overindulge their children. Recall once more John Holt's observation that he had not been 'coddled' as a child because his mother lacked both time *and inclination* to do so.[182] His mother, like many others, did not show emotion, because she did not believe that it was necessary, or indeed desirable, to do so. Francis Crittall believed that his parents had had 'strong affections' for their eleven children, but also added that 'warm sentiments or expressed feelings were seldom allowed to obtrude' in family life.[183] The Victorian mother was supposed to be busy looking after the home, not pandering to the needs of small children.

This was a fundamentally different perception of what mothering involved, and one that was widely shared. It placed the focus upon the physical aspects of care, on the daily routine of putting meals on the table and clothes on bodies, of cleaning up and supervising the children. Norah Brain, for instance, declared that her mother 'kept me clean and fed and that was that'.[184] In very similar terms, Daisy Noakes observed that her mother had kept her ten children: 'clean and tidy and fed and that's about it'.[185] Lucy Miller also conceded that her 'mother did her best to look after us physically'. The problem, she continued, was that she did so in a joyless fashion:

there was not only no love around but even worse, there was always discouragement and frustration. Nothing was ever right for mother however much you tried and I cannot remember one single instance of being praised or pleasure shown for anything I did in my childhood.[186]

Some of the writers also suggest that this focus on the externalities of care was an active choice on the part of their mother, not an omission. Alfred Rowse initially explained his mother's inattention to him during his early years by pointing to the pressures of time: 'my mother's time and attention [was] occupied wholly by house-work, cooking, scrubbing, washing, cleaning, plus looking after the shop. She had no time to display much interest in me'. He also added, however, he didn't 'think she had' much interest in him either.[187] Elizabeth Twist paid lip service to the notion that mothering was a form of physical, not emotional, labour, and emphasised how her mother had busily and efficiently gone about that labour. She wrote that her 'mother had more than enough to do with cooking, cleaning, washing and serving in the shop, as well as two small children and a third one on the way'.[188] But elsewhere in her story she also indicated that parents in her day had had a more restricted conception of their role: 'our elders dismissed our physical aches as "growing pains". There were no psychologists to analyse our mental and emotional development.'[189] And this emotional restraint extended to expressions of physical intimacy as well. George Williams explained that his mother had never caressed her children: 'it simply wasn't in her nature'.[190] What these writers suggest is not that their mothers were failing to do something that most other mothers did, but rather that they were mothering to a different template. Jack Lawson recalled that his mother had been 'grim [and] dominating' to her first nine children, but she liked 'to cuddle and "make of" her last-born'. She took care to do so 'surreptitiously', however: 'If she considered she had been caught in the act, she would become very stern with us, evidently considering it a weakness.'[191]

Sitting alongside the general belief that mothers needed to feed and protect their children rather than cuddle them, was something yet more intangible. Certainly, some mothers did not show affection because this was how they themselves had been raised and they believed it to be the proper way to raise a child, but some of the writers hint at something else. There was a powerlessness to women's lives, and it is clear that some of the mothers described in the autobiographies were railing against a life that felt limited, unjust and wholly unsatisfactory. Having moved from his aunt's home in rural Ulster to live with his mother and stepfather in Manchester, Bonar Thompson considered his mother's household relatively well off, but he also noted his mother's unhappiness with her situation. She was prone to frequent outbursts, 'her way of releasing long-pent-up feelings'.[192] John Vose's father was also an adequate provider, yet his mother too was a deeply dissatisfied woman who (according to John) 'screeched and ranted and constantly rowed with my father'.[193] Thomas Westwater's father led an enjoyable life as a railway worker with varied interests in his church and the union, but his mother rarely left the home at all. She was also prone to 'frequent outbursts of temper', always 'flaring up about something'.[194] And one final example: Arthur Goffin's father earned enough to keep his family in relative comfort, but his mother was 'hard, calculating and bitter . . . she was never satisfied . . . an unhappy, discontented spirit'.[195] At the centre of many of these accounts were mothers who were deeply unhappy with the way their lives had turned out, an unhappiness that gave way to hostility, anger and frustration. With the options for an independent life outside the confines of marriage extremely limited, women remained trapped within the domestic sphere, and the children were simply collateral damage in a separate war.[196]

None of the working-class writers enjoyed lives of affluence, and those facing the greatest poverty also faced the greatest difficulty in maintaining strong ties with their children. At the same time, however, there were also women who struggled with motherhood whilst not suffering from the most acute forms of poverty. For them, the problem was not strictly material, but stemmed from frustration about a life that felt impoverished and restricted. Consider, for example, the family described by the novelist H. G. Wells. Compared to most of the working-class autobiographers, Herbert Wells was raised in relative comfort. The family had no servants, but they did enjoy the luxury of sufficient domestic space for the parents to sleep in separate bedrooms – 'their form of birth control', opined the adult Wells – which at least permitted his mother to limit the size of her family.[197] Yet it was still far from the comfort that the daughter of a respectable innkeeper might have hoped for. Mr Wells ran his china shop inattentively (he preferred to play cricket) and ineffectively, and he was insolvent before any of the couple's four children had reached adulthood. Mrs Wells's female status rendered her dependent upon the hopelessly irresponsible breadwinner her husband proved to be and left her unable to forge an alternative, more satisfactory life. Herbert's mother was not negligent, but she was 'a tired woman', 'overstrained by dingy toil' and she struggled to form an emotional connection with her son.[198] She was, quite simply, fed up. Marriage and motherhood had fallen far short of her hopes, and she was powerless to do anything about it.

These kinds of stories about unsatisfactory lives and relationships were retold in many different ways. Harry Burton, for instance, mused upon the fundamental mismatch between his parents: his father easy-going and none too hard-working; his mother 'a woman from a gentle home with memories and ambitions that were so different' from his.[199] The mismatch led to constant conflict throughout his childhood: the word to summarise his family life, he concluded, was 'quarrels'.[200] Richard Hillyer's father was a kind and hard-working agricultural labourer, but his pay was low and his family poor. Richard explained that this was not the life his mother had hoped for: she felt 'the bitter injustice of the life she led'. And, as others indicated, this general discontent seeped into her familial relationships: she was 'hard', 'withdrawn' and 'strange to me'. In conclusion: 'I do not know if it would be right to say that I loved her.'[201] Muriel Box described a similarly ill-sorted set of parents. Mr Box did not share his wife's ambitions for a genteel life. His earnings were lower than his potential, and he frittered away much of what he did earn on his own interests and gambling, keeping the family in a more economically precarious situation than his wife considered necessary. His behaviour inevitably created tension in the household. Mrs Box could not materially change this situation – she could only get irritated about it, and the whole family had to live with her periodic 'outbursts of temper'.[202] Underpinning all these stories is a reminder of the power imbalance between husbands and wives, and the consequence of this imbalance for family relations. The breadwinning model was founded upon an unequal power between marriage partners, and when male wages increased, that power imbalance intensified as well, creating the kinds of problems that we see here.

Matters were not helped, of course, by the fact that women were frequently unable to control their family size, so even those married to sober, wage-earning husbands risked adding new members to the family. As a result, mothers who were only barely coping were further taxed with the exhausting round of pregnancy and birth. Faith Osgerby's mother let all her children know that 'babies were not welcomed in the family' and even told Faith about her unsuccessful efforts to abort her.[203] Alfred Rowse's mother thought that she had successfully limited her family to just two children, but five years later Alfred made an appearance. From early childhood he was made to realise what a 'regrettable accident' his birth had been, and he grew up with a 'feeling of not being wanted'.[204] Hannah Mitchell noticed how matters at home had deteriorated after the birth of her mother's last two children. This, she opined, 'seemed to be more than she could endure and our home became more unhappy than ever'.[205] Herbert Wells found his mother's diary following her death, and it taught him that she had lived 'quite plainly, in perpetual dread of further motherhood. "Anxiety relieved", became her formula.'[206] Of course, at his own conception that anxiety had not been relieved, and Wells was not in much doubt about the heavy shadow this contraceptive failure had cast over their relationship.

Life writing provides wonderful and unparalleled detail about the interior workings of intimate relationships, but it also reveals the dark side to family life in Victorian Britain. Undoubtedly, some themes echo far more loudly throughout the records than others. If there was one thing that autobiographers liked to write about, it was their responsible fathers and hard-working mothers, but the ease with which the autobiographers wrote about such things should not be mistaken for their universality in their lives. Sitting beside the happy families described by some writers was an unmistakable strain of hostility to fathers who were perceived to have failed in their breadwinning duties, as well as accounts of mothers who were emotionally distant, hostile or neglectful of their children. The autobiographies are filled with discordant voices and subversive stories, and we need to make sense of their ambiguities, evasions and silences.

The point is not simply to condemn Victorian and Edwardian parents for their failings, but rather to open a space for reflecting upon the myriad difficulties they faced. All our working-class parents battled against circumstances that were extremely hard, with fathers working long hours in back-breaking work and mothers struggling to provide for their children in a world where they had very little control over the family income. Of course, some men and women struggled against these odds to provide a warm, safe and loving home for their families, but others did not. It was not a failing that deserves to be condemned. Instead, these stories of family life remind us of the economic context in which family relationships exist and of the power with which material circumstances shape our emotional lives.

⊰⊱ 9 ⊰⊱
'I LEARNED TO SPEAK'
MAKING CITIZENS[1]

In December 1920, John Murphy and Molly Morris got married. The pair were united by a commitment to socialist causes, and as both had turned thirty at the time of their wedding, they had already chalked up some experience as political activists. Having begun working as a lathe turner in a Sheffield engineering shop at the age of thirteen, Jack, by his late teens, was immersed in self-improvement and his local Sunday school. In his early twenties, he became a member of the engineers' union, joined its local committee and subsequently became its secretary. He organised strikes during the First World War and become a leading figure in the Shop Stewards' and Workers' Committee movement. He stood as a Socialist Labour Party parliamentary candidate in 1918, and following defeat continued his work for the Shop Stewards' Movement. In this capacity he had been elected to travel to Amsterdam and Moscow as a delegate at conferences of the Communist International. By the time of his marriage to Molly, he had travelled very widely for the times, both at home and abroad, and hobnobbed with Lenin, Trotsky, Stalin and other leaders of the Russian Revolution.[2]

As the eldest daughter in a family of seven children, Molly had enjoyed far less freedom of action. Her parents had separated whilst she was a child and her mother had become the family breadwinner. Inevitably, therefore, Molly spent most of her childhood and adolescence assisting her mother in running the home. As her younger siblings grew older, however, these 'household duties had lessened', and at the age of sixteen Molly became heavily involved in her local branch of the Women's Social and Political Union (WSPU) – a militant suffragette movement – first in Manchester and subsequently in Sheffield. Indeed, it was through her suffrage campaigning that Jack and Molly had first met. She had sold him a copy of the *Suffragette* at an open-air meeting in Sheffield, and he had been a frequent visitor to the WSPU's premises ever since. With the outbreak of war in 1914, her local WSPU branch closed, and Molly's involvement with the suffrage movement came to an end.[3] She left Sheffield to follow her dream of training as a nurse, moving a year later to London to take up a post at the West London Hospital in Hammersmith.[4] It was at this hospital that a breathless Jack turned up five years later and asked her (not for the first time) to marry him. Molly had held out because she 'wanted to be a nurse and not a housewife', but she knew she was not getting any younger. 'I was thirty years of age. If I was ever going to get married I should not delay much longer.' Jack made the arrangements, and within six weeks the deed was done.[5] Unusually, both Jack and Molly wrote an autobiography, which provides us with the possibility of comparing the different life courses of each half of the married couple.

Their writing makes clear that despite a deep similarity in their political outlook and values, the actual nature of their political experiences was very different. Jack's work for the union very quickly developed into a full-time, paid position and Jack remained continually active in the labour movement throughout his adult life. Molly's work for the WSPU, by contrast, was unpaid and her immersion in the suffrage movement proved to be an interlude of around eight years. When the First World War brought an end to her local committee's activities, she redirected her energies to getting her training as a nurse. That, followed by marriage to Jack and by motherhood, brought a hiatus to her political activism of more than ten years. Jack's biographer described him as 'one of the most important self-educated worker-intellectual figures of the early twentieth century British revolutionary socialist tradition', but no such claims could be made of Molly.[6] As Jack's star rose in the 1920s, Molly 'was a full-time housewife bringing up their son'.[7] It was only once their son had reached an age where Molly felt able to entrust him to other caregivers that she re-entered the political sphere, though always in a supportive, and unpaid, capacity and never in a way that rivalled that of her husband. Indeed, these differences are even manifest in the creation of their autobiographies. Jack's was written and published whilst he was in his early fifties, whereas Molly's was written many years later and no publisher was found for it during her lifetime.[8]

The divergence between Jack and Molly's adult lives was not of course unique to this particular couple. They belonged to a much wider set of differences in the life opportunities of men and women that are writ large across the autobiographies. Even the most cursory glance at the records reveals the far wider and more varied lives led by male writers. For working-class men, the dominant motif of their autobiographical writing was achievement. The journey that male authors took away from their working-class roots to positions of leadership and authority is apparent in the jaunty titles of some their works: *From Workhouse to Lord Mayor*; *From Workshop to War Cabinet*; *Pitman & Privy Councillor*; *From a Stonemason's Bench to the Treasury Bench*. Such dramatic upward social mobility was not, of course, the lot of all men. Amongst the autobiographers were many others who spent their adult lives as builders, labourers, farm workers, shopkeepers, transport workers, miners and factory workers. Yet the overall balance was weighted towards those who left these kinds of occupations rather than towards those who stayed in them. Indeed, we can put some numbers to this statement: from our collection of almost 450 male-authored autobiographies, two-thirds had entered middle-class or professional occupations by the time of writing their autobiography, as against the one-third who continued in manual labour.

These crude figures concerning the adult occupations of the autobiographical writers are not offered in order to sustain claims of a more general nature about patterns of social mobility during this period. The fact of being socially mobile prompted autobiographical writing for both genders to some degree, so we would expect to see far more social movement within these kinds of records than in the population as a whole. But they do allow for a meaningful comparison between male and female writers. If we track the adult destinations of the female autobiographers, more than two hundred in all, the difference in their trajectories is immediately apparent. Female writers were far more likely to remain in the furrow they had been allotted at birth. In fact, for women the numbers were reversed: around two-thirds of the female writers had spent their adult lives either engaged in manual work or, more commonly, as unpaid housewives, whilst one third narrated a story of movement away from modest origins and into the professional sphere. Social mobility for women, where it did occur, tended to follow their husband's employment trajectory, rather than their own.

In fact, this simple headcount of destinations obscures the true extent of the division between the adult lives of men and women. It may be that one-third of women autobiographers entered the professions, but they did so in a very limited number of ways – in fact, just two: almost all the female writers who entered middle-class professions did so as teachers or secretaries. A handful more women became professional writers, but there were no female academics, artists, entrepreneurs, inventors, civil servants, managers, ministers or missionaries amongst the autobiographers. Male writers, by contrast, were not only more likely to enter the professions, but they did so in a much wider variety of ways. Working-class men entered every facet of the worlds of the arts, education, science, business and management and at every level. To be sure, they faced numerous barriers compared to their more affluent peers, yet those barriers were simply insurmountable for women of their class.

Most commonly of all, the male writers became involved in politics. This umbrella terms refers to a very wide range of activities, some paid, some not, across a yet wider array of organisations. Indeed, politics was the single largest preoccupation of the male autobiographers: more than one-quarter of the male writers reported having been involved in some form of political movement or organisation, as MPs, councillors, organisers, officials, writers, agents and active members. The movements they joined were almost exclusively on the left of the political spectrum and as such they promoted not only social mobility for the specific individuals who joined them but also the collective interests of working people as a whole.[9] They were thus part of a larger transition that occurred between the 1860s and 1930s, which saw the wrangling of political power out of the hands of the social elites who had traditionally claimed it as their special prerogative. This marked a permanent break from the old regime with working men both claiming and starting to exercise a right to participate in the nation's political machinery.[10]

This development involved a shift in the balance of power between social classes, yet like all elements of Britain's cultural and economic life during this period, this transition was gendered in nature. Power was tilting towards working-class men, but working-class women remained firmly on the fringes. The overall proportion of female autobiographers who became involved in politics reveals the problem. Whereas around one-quarter of the male writers described some form of political activism, only around half that proportion of female writers did (13 per cent). Furthermore, beneath these headcounts for political involvement lay a further set of differences in the timing and nature of men and women's engagement in the political sphere.[11]

Men's engagement in politics was continuous throughout the period: it was certainly more sustained from the 1880s onwards, but it was not new to that decade. In fact, there is a strand of working-class political activism that can be traced in autobiographical writing all the way back to the eighteenth century.[12] No less significantly, there were differences in the capacities within which men and women operated. Men described becoming leaders and organisers of the organisations they joined, whereas women, for the most part, were foot soldiers. From our collection of almost 450 male autobiographers, fifty-seven became MPs, and a further forty, whilst never serving as MPs, nonetheless played significant roles in national, as opposed to local, organisations. This group of forty includes men such as Joseph Burgess, a founding member of the Labour Party; Tom Mann, leader of the London Dock Strike of 1889 and secretary of the Independent Labour Party; and Harry Pollitt, leader of the Communist Party of Great Britain. Most of these men held paid positions in the organisations they were involved in; and a majority have entries in the *Dictionary of National Biography*. This forty, along with the fifty-seven MPs, produces a total of almost one hundred male autobiographers who held formal positions of political power, whether inside or outside the Houses of Parliament. Alongside these men were a further forty male autobiographers who testified to engagement on a more local level. For these writers, an active membership of local political organisations and unions sat alongside their working lives rather than replacing it.

The global picture of political engagement for women is dissimilar in several respects. Whereas nearly 140 of the male autobiographers mentioned political activism, fifty-seven of them as MPs, just thirty-four of the female writers mentioned any kind of involvement with a political organisation at all. Furthermore, these women tended to assume different kinds of positions in the movements and organisations they joined. Just four of the thirty-four became MPs: Margaret Bondfield, Bessie Braddock, Jennie Lee and Ellen Wilkinson – all of them representing the Labour Party.[13] A further twelve, whilst never serving as MPs nonetheless made a sustained contribution to political life on the national stage. These twelve include women like Helen Crawfurd: suffragette, pacifist and prominent figure in the Communist Party; Elizabeth Andrews: suffragist, and leading figure in the women's branch of the Labour Party; and Jessie Stephen: militant suffragette, union organiser for domestic workers, and political agent for the Labour Party. All received national recognition for their work and are also honoured with an entry in the

Dictionary of National Biography. The remaining cohort of politically active women had agitated on a smaller, more local scale, and in ways that did not earn them either an income or national recognition.

Female engagement in the political sphere was also sharply bounded chronologically. Although we know that women were involved in anti-Poor Law, factory and Chartist movements in the first half of the nineteenth century, there is little evidence that these earlier activists turned to autobiographical writing in order to retell their experiences – a sharp distinction from male political activists.[14] Instead, virtually all the female political activity described in the autobiographies took place in the 1890s or in the twentieth century. Female suffrage was the most common point of entry into politics for the autobiographers, but it was precisely that – a point of entry, and the politically active women tended, like men, to move across a wide range of allied left-wing causes. Yet the autobiographies suggest an unequal opportunity for men and women to engage in the political sphere, and the task of this chapter is to consider why. It is my goal to bring together the usually separate histories of working-class politics (male) and the suffrage movement (female), and explore the role of gender in shaping who had the opportunity to influence the nation's political life.

The point is perhaps obvious, but individuals did not find themselves working in the factory one day and sitting as an MP the next. Instead they travelled this journey through a unique series of intermediate, and sometimes lengthy, steps. It was not for nothing that the left-leaning *Pearson's Weekly* series containing short autobiographical summaries of twenty-four Labour MPs was entitled 'How I Got On'.[15] It was widely recognised that the elementary schooling available to the children of the working poor was woefully deficient and unfit to equip anyone for a life of public service. Thus a recurring theme in these autobiographical vignettes, as in the autobiographies of a great many other politicians and agitators, was an explanation of how the writer had overcome his (or, more occasionally, her) disadvantages and acquired the requisite skills for political leadership. The regularity with which the writers returned to the question of their political training makes it possible to explore both the routes by which men penetrated the nation's political life, as well as the constraints that made it so difficult for women to do so.

Our starting point must be the nature of work, and its split into paid/male and unpaid/female forms. Working-class jobs were arduous and the hours were nearly always long. But despite these drawbacks, for any given individual work could also be empowering and, perhaps counter-intuitively, offered the opportunity to do something other than wage earning. The most straightforward link between work and politics was the trade union movement, with several of the male writers reporting how they had developed an interest in the union once they had started work.

Some, particularly those whose fathers worked in heavily unionised industries, were already well versed in the purpose and process of collective action. The father of Thomas Williams, for example, was a committee member of the local branch of his mining union and Thomas had grown up with 'strikes and lockouts'. It was somewhat inevitable, therefore, that when he started working in the mines himself, he took an interest in union affairs and 'began to take a more prominent part in my own right'.[16] But union meetings were open to all male employees and were also accessible to workers without any prior experience or knowledge of labour organisations. Meetings introduced workers to other, like-minded, men, as well as to the order and conduct of committees. George Hardy knew nothing about unions when he first started work in a shipyard, but he immediately joined up and 'became a silent but regular attender at branch meetings'.[17] The flat hierarchical structures of unions made it easy for members to progress from silent attendance to a more active participation in union affairs. When Walter Citrine started work as an electrician at a new firm he found his fellow electricians 'were all strong trade unionists', and he quickly fell in with them and joined the union too. From the outset, he took 'an active interest in its work'. He attended the branch meetings on Monday evenings and 'it wasn't long before [he] became responsible' for submitting reports of their meetings to the union's national journal. Such was his enthusiasm that he also embarked upon a reading programme so as to learn more about 'the theory and practice of trade unionism'.[18] For those not already drawn towards the union and all it stood for, workplace disputes often formed a trigger that drew the previously uninterested into the realm of workplace politics.[19]

There were a number of other, less direct, ways that work facilitated political activism. Starting work introduced adolescent boys to older men and their ideas. Sometimes these new acquaintances shared the beliefs and political leanings of the writer's parents; but at other times they held new political opinions and opened the writer's mind to ideas that they had not previously encountered.[20] Frank Hodges, for example, recalled the lengthy conversations he had enjoyed with one of his older workmates, 'a geologist, a mining student, and a keen mathematician', as well as the owner of a copy of Darwin's *Origin of Species*. Through their long conversations, Frank found himself 'undergoing a mental revolution'.[21] Following the breakdown of relations with his mother and stepfather, Bonar Thompson moved in with a workmate who was a supporter of the Labour Party, and who 'aroused my interest' in labour questions.[22] Will Crooks worked with a man who was 'a thinker and reformer, far ahead of his times' and who 'encouraged [him] to read by lending [him] books and newspapers'.[23] The sheer fact of going to work gave young men access to a novel world of people and ideas. William Steadman turned his hand to the usual wide range of jobs between starting work at the age of eight and taking up an apprenticeship at age fifteen, including a position behind the bar in a public house. Looking back on the experience, Steadman declared that it 'widened my mental horizon and gave me an interest in the social and political matters which I heard the customers discuss'.[24] Stephen Walsh's political education began at the age of thirteen when he started work in the mine. As he explained, 'there is no place like a mine for promoting discussion. There is something . . . in being shut away underground, that draws men to each other, and makes them anxious to break the darkness and sense of loneliness by talk on subjects many and various . . .'[25]

There was also something less concrete about wage-earning status that fed into men's ability to engage in the political sphere. As we have seen elsewhere in this book, wage-earners were, from a very early age, taught that earning a wage brought certain privileges in the form of a small amount of spending money and a matching quantity of leisure time in which to spend it. Initially boys spent their spare pennies on sweet foods, theatre trips and boys' magazines. Edgar Wallace, for example, confessed to spending his boyhood earnings from his newspaper-selling 'in dissipation – ginger-beer, theatres, and a succulent toffee called "Devona" '.[26] As boys entered adolescence, their spending money grew and their interests widened. Looking back over the years when he had started working on the North Eastern Railway, Thomas Westwater declared that his life at that time had been 'free and happy'. He and his workmates had amused themselves with sing-songs, football games, cricket matches and courting.[27] As a grocer's assistant in Edwardian

Manchester, Jack Lanigan's teenage interests were wide and varied. He joined 'Hugh Oldhams Lads Club' (an athletics club – 'What a Club!'), bought a bike and took an annual camping holiday with his club mates. He read the 'Health & Strength Magazine' and took a few lessons in jujitsu when it was introduced to Manchester. He enjoyed regular visits to the local music halls and theatres, sang at a few concerts in local pubs and 'also found time to play football' with a team he had formed with his 'pals'.[28] There was nothing deeply significant about the activities that either Thomas Westwater or Jack Lanigan pursued; the point simply is that wage-earning provided them with both the income and the autonomy to follow their own interests. This indeed explains no small part of the enthusiasm that most young boys expressed for starting work. John Clynes was one of the many male writers who did not particularly regret the passing of his schooldays. He was content to follow the path of the older lads he knew, who had already left school to start work, who got paid 'real money' with which 'they could buy things really for themselves'.[29] Or, as William Collison cheerfully recalled of starting work, 'The work was hard, but the money was sweet, and the freedom sweeter still.'[30]

Many young men were content to work hard all week and to fill their free time with sports and pubs, but, of course, there were others who wanted something else from life. For some of the autobiographers, their encounter with the new world of work brought the realisation that their meagre elementary schooling had not adequately fitted them up for all that life had to offer and awakened a desire for further learning. These men used their free time to embark upon a programme of reading and self-improvement rather than on trips to the theatre and football.[31] When Tom Honeyford started work, for example, he joined the 'Co-op library'. It was just enough to 'keep alive [his] thirst for knowledge'.[32] Others haunted the second-hand booksellers in search of suitable reading material. Herbert Morrison, for example, liked to spend his Saturday afternoons combing second-hand bookshops for 'cheap copies of works on ethics, history, economics, and sociology'.[33] Thomas Jackson similarly made it part of his 'normal routine' to visit Bookseller's Row with his wages after finishing work on Saturdays.[34] In South Shields, Emanuel Shinwell spent his spare pennies 'searching in second-hand bookshops and looking over junk barrows'.[35] He ended up with a collection of some 250 books. These, along with his use of the public library, introduced him not only to the world of literature and poetry, but also to 'scores of scientific and philosophical works'.[36]

These self-directed attempts to expand one's knowledge brought men to a range of new ideas, but many also struggled to comprehend their books and soon realised that they needed additional help. Bonar Thompson's interest in Socialism had been whetted by a workmate, but his patchy years of schooling in rural Ireland left him poorly equipped to access and understand the issues at stake. He attended a speech by the newly elected Labour MP John Clynes, 'but could not grasp the full meaning of much that was said'. He picked up books but found everything inside them was 'outside the scope of my experience and beyond my intellectual development . . . famous books . . . were impossible for me to understand'.[37] He was certainly not alone. Indeed, a few years earlier, the MP John Clynes whose speech so baffled Bonar Thompson had been on his own journey of self-improvement. He had been 'drawn to the bookshops', but he too had found that 'my education had been too slender for me to go forward alone on the road of literature'.[38] What both men had needed was a teacher to help them navigate the new material.[39]

Some of the autobiographers indicated that they had paid for a private teacher, and a great many more recalled attending night classes. Indeed, it would be hard to exaggerate the significance of night schools, which were mentioned over and again by the male autobiographers.[40] Arthur Henderson, for example, described how, in his late teens, he was filled with a wish to learn more about the world around him: 'I set to work resolutely and systematically to educate myself, attending night schools and evening classes, and reading everything I could lay my hands on.'[41] For the lone student, the lessons on offer at night school were (in the opinion of one writer) 'tremendously helpful'. They 'arranged one's books on a better plan'.[42] It might have been either a desire to make progress at work or a nascent political interest that brought a young man to the doors of a night school, but it is perhaps inherent in the nature of education that the process of learning can ignite a desire for more learning in new, unanticipated directions. This, at any rate, was what many of the writers described, entering the night school for one reason, and whilst there becoming drawn to the burning political issues of the day. As William Johnson explained, he initially took classes in geology, agriculture, chemistry, French and German, but later learned about co-operation and political economy. His studying 'broadened my mind and gave me that capacity for looking at both sides of a question, which is invaluable to a man in public life'.[43]

Most of the male autobiographers who became involved in politics described having made some attempt to further their meagre education. At some point, however, they progressed from self-improvement to discussion groups, where the focus was not on the acquisition of further knowledge but rather on the sharing and debating of ideas. Effective political engagement required the ability to articulate arguments in public, and several of the writers credited informal discussion groups for developing their public speaking skills. As Herbert Morrison explained, 'My first steps towards a practical participation in the problems of my age came when I joined the Brixton Discussion Forum.' The group met on Saturday mornings 'to talk, argue, and plan'. It brought him to a deeper understanding of ideas that had hitherto 'merely been printed words on a page', as well as encouraging him to 'stand up and say something' himself.[44] Cities were the centres of a vast array of political groups, and there was something for every taste. William Gallacher fell out with his local Temperance movement and found that his local branch of the Independent Labour Party 'smacked too much of the Sunday School'. So he and his friend 'searched around for something more suited to our temperaments, and discovered a small group of Marxists who met in a cobbler's shop'.[45] George Lansbury became 'great pals' with the railway men he worked with, and they set up their own guild to 'meet once a week in our lobby and talk things over'.[46] George Hodgkinson described at some length the Adult School Movement with which he had become involved and which 'provided a forum for a wide variety of interests'. He attended talks on religion, literature, sociology and local government, as well as hobbies such as pigeon racing and pig breeding. At the Adult School, his 'horizons grew wider' and he also became 'involved in the administrative work' of the Schools. Hodgkinson directly traced his career as a political agent for the Labour Party and a Labour councillor to his formative experience at the School.[47]

So far as hobbies went, self-improvement was not the most expensive. But it was not free either. There was a cost to both book buying and night classes, and participation in these kinds of activities rested upon having a small income to spend as one wished. Nor was self-improvement simply dependent upon an income. These activities required a significant investment of time, and the self-improvers needed non-working hours that were free of commitments to the household. Wage-earning bought that freedom. Michael Conway noted that for 'the males' in his Lancashire neighbourhood, 'the rest of the weekend [after the midday meal on Saturday] was left free'. They 'would clear off . . . to their football, fishing, pigeons, gambling, whippet-racing, or any other hobby'.[48] Jack Lawson indicated that evenings during the week were free as well: 'Now that I was a wage-earner I could go out at night for as long as I liked and where I liked.'[49] Tom Honeyford's father did not approve of his son's book-reading – he thought it was 'filling [his son's] head with nonsense'. But he did not have the power to prevent it. As Tom explained, 'As I was working now, I was not expected to do any housework, so I was able to devote my evenings to practice and reading.'[50]

The autobiographies powerfully underscore the complex nature of the relationship between schooling, work and education for working-class boys. For most of the autobiographers, the lessons taught at school were dull and irrelevant, and few regretted the passing of their schooldays. In their eyes, the end of school meant the start of work, and the true beginning of a man's education. Of course, quitting school also closed down the possibility of following the conventional route to knowledge mapped out for middle-class boys of secondary school and (possibly) university. Yet paid work gave men the money and space to pursue their own intellectual agenda outside the formal frameworks of school and served as a point of entry to a different kind of education. Certainly, this was not for the faint-hearted, and several of the self-improvers recalled the great challenge of getting to (and indeed focusing on) an evening class after a hard day's work. But if self-improvement was not easy, it was possible, owing to the structures that working men had established for enhancing their education and speaking skills after their schooldays had ended.

The connection between male labour and political engagement was close and can be demonstrated by looking at the pathways by which men who had enjoyed at best a few years of basic schooling nonetheless managed to become agile and effective politicians. It might be imagined that the handful of working men who made it all the way to the Houses of Parliament had enjoyed certain advantages through childhood and adolescence that had extended their schooling and eased their path to power. Yet if we look closely at the social backgrounds of the twenty-four Labour MPs who submitted a brief autobiography in *Pearson's Weekly*'s 'How I Got On' series, published in 1906, it is clear that this was not the case.[51] Certainly, some of these men had enjoyed relatively comfortable childhoods. For example, George Henry Roberts, the MP for Norwich, wrote that though his family were poor, 'I cannot say that I endured any of the early privations or hardships that have fallen to the lot of so many of my fellow Labour members.'[52] Meanwhile, John Jenkins, the MP for Chatham, declared that as a child he had enjoyed a 'comfortable home' and the 'best of parents'.[53] Yet comfort was very far from being the hallmark of the men's families. Of these twenty-four MPs, almost half (eleven) had spent some part of their childhood in fatherless households, with all the poverty and hardship that went hand in hand with fatherlessness. William Steadman, for example, spent his early years living with an aunt, before returning to a home in London that comprised just his mother and one sibling. 'She toiled late and early, but, despite her exertions, we suffered much, and were often hungry.'[54] Thomas Richards was one of at least nine children of a travelling salesman. In his life story, Thomas wrote that his father had died when he was eleven, and whilst he does disappear from both the family home and the census around that time, it has not proved possible to locate his death in the death registers, so it may be that he had left his family rather than this world. Whatever the truth of the matter, the consequences of his absence for the family can be easily foretold: the family were 'totally unprovided for'; things were 'desperately bad'; and Thomas was dragged from school and put to work at the earliest opportunity.[55] One of the MPs had started life without any family at all. Stephen Walsh's earliest memory was of being picked off the streets of Liverpool by a friendly policeman. He was placed into the care of the state and spent his childhood in an industrial school in Kirkdale.[56]

This pattern is also discernible among the thirty-seven MPs who wrote an autobiography outside the *Pearson's Weekly* series. None had gone to university, and just three had enjoyed a childhood sufficiently prosperous to permit a stint of secondary education.[57] Of the rest, although a few had been raised in relative comfort, none had progressed beyond elementary school. Furthermore, there were many who could not be considered prosperous at all. This group included men from very large families, illegitimate children raised by single mothers or grandparents and children whose fathers had either died, fallen ill, drunk to excess or abandoned the family.[58] More than one-third of these men had spent their childhoods in fatherless households, most having been seriously impoverished as a consequence.

Taken as a whole, the evidence from the life stories of the fifty-seven men who became MPs is clear. This first generation of Labour MPs included many

EARLY LEADERS OF THE LABOUR PARTY—1906: MESSRS. ARTHUR HENDERSON, G. N. BARNES, J. RAMSAY MACDONALD, PHILIP SNOWDEN, THE LATE WILL CROOKS, THE LATE KEIR HARDIE, MR. JOHN HODGE, CAPTAIN J. O'GRADY, AND SIR DAVID SHACKLETON (LEFT TO RIGHT).

Representatives of the Labour Party first appeared in the House of Commons in 1892, when there were 15 Labour Members. In 1895 there were 12; in 1900, 11; in 1906, 52; in January, 1910, 40; in December, 1910, 42; in 1918, 62; in 1922, 139. At the end of the recent General Election there were 191 Labour Members.—[*Photograph by Barratt.*]

9.1 Labour MPs photographed after the 1924 general election. Henderson, Barnes, Crooks and Shackleton contributed to *Pearson Weekly*'s 'How I Got On' series following the 1906 election, and Barnes, Hodge and Snowden published fuller autobiographies of their own in the 1920s and 1930s.

who came from deprived – sometimes extremely deprived – backgrounds. Yet their very humble origins had not proved to be an insurmountable obstacle to citizenship. In explaining how they had (to paraphrase *Pearson's Weekly*) 'got on', these men did not trace their stories back to their families and schools. Instead, the unifying theme was work. They repeatedly described an arc in which starting work was the beginning of a political journey. The workplace provided access to new people and ideas, the wages to spend on books and night school and the status that permitted a man to follow his own path. These forces combined to enable men to enter the political sphere.

Indeed, it is perhaps for this reason that work figured so prominently in the titles of the male autobiographies. The constant elision between honest labour and public service was surely not accidental. It served to underscore a more fundamental point: that the writer's experience of work had helped to qualify him for public service. Indeed, it was for the same reason that the political party that developed from this tradition took 'Labour' as its name – a choice that stemmed from the close association between these labouring men and their politics.

Work played a pivotal role in facilitating men's access to politics, yet women, as we know, did not experience work in the same way as men. It is therefore inevitable that their political trajectories were also distinct. Men's lives were focused on the outside world: primarily work and to a lesser extent leisure. By contrast, women's lives were focused on the home. These material differences in the context of men and women's lives shaped dramatically different patterns of political engagement.

As we have seen, women's responsibility for domestic work did not entirely preclude them from working outside the home. And when young women went to work, they sometimes encountered new acquaintances with new ideas in just the same way as men and boys. One of the things that Nellie Scott liked best about working in the hat industry was the conversations that took place in the workrooms. In one place, she worked with 'a Conservative, an Irish girl, and some Radicals and Socialists and we used to have full dress debates. When we began someone would call "Parliament is now sitting" . . . and we would discuss everything.'[59] When Alice Foley's older sister started working at the local factory she promptly joined 'her particular section of the textile trade union' and became an 'active and reforming' influence there. She found a group of like-minded friends and on Sundays they would take over the family's living room – 'all sedulously imbibing socialistic ethics and culture'. At the time, Alice, along with the rest of the family, looked on her older sister's 'newfound assumption of independence and aloofness' with some derision.[60] But when Alice herself started at the mill a few years later, she quickly became drawn into much the same pattern of behaviour.[61] She too was now 'enthusiastically imbibing socialistic doctrines' and getting involved in the factory's workplace politics. Indeed, it was 'almost inevitable . . . that I should become a critical spokeswoman for other fellow workers'.[62]

And Alice was not alone in finding that taking part in a strike with one's fellows could act as the spur for a deeper relationship with the union.[63] At seventeen years of age, Alice Collis had become involved in a strike over pay at the printing firm where she worked. The immediate outcome of their strike was a 50 per cent pay rise for Alice and her co-workers, but there was also a second, unanticipated outcome: the strike proved to be a catalyst for further activism. As Alice explained, 'When we had fully recovered from the surprise of our success, we formed a branch of the National Federation of Women Workers.' Alice herself was elected to represent her fellow workers for the branch.[64]

The women who gained an introduction to politics through their workplace often encountered the same kinds of obstacles as men. Elementary schooling was designed to provide a basic grounding in reading, writing and arithmetic, not to create an understanding of abstract ideas, and women who had left school at a young age struggled to make sense of complex debates they encountered, and still more to intervene in them. Annie Kenney, for instance, had left school when she was ten years old to start at the mill – she was still a mere child at the time who spent her free time playing with dolls and reading girls magazines. Around the age of sixteen, she agreed to accompany a friend to a suffrage meeting, although at that point she had 'never heard about Votes for Women'. One of the speakers referred to 'Limited Suffrage'. It was all 'Greek to me. I did not know to what they were referring.'[65] Deborah Smith felt similarly out of her depth when she found herself on the committee of her town's newly formed Women's Co-operative Guild. 'I had no education in my youth; my life had been filled up with work, and there was no time to learn . . . What mistakes I made! What sheets of paper I tore up before I could write and spell and put my sentences together.'[66] Many politically inclined working-class women realised, like their male peers, that they needed to improve their education if they were to engage in any meaningful way. Unlike their male counterparts, however, they frequently encountered obstacles that were difficult to overcome

On the face of it, women had access to the same kinds of post-school educational organisations – night schools, Clarion Clubs and (Socialist) Sunday schools – that proved so valuable to men seeking to further their education.[67] Certainly, some of these institutions opened their doors to women and some women found them to be an effective route to enlightenment. Isabel Templeton, for example, spent a portion of her wages as a typist on 'evening studies' at the Whitehill School in Glasgow. There, 'as one might expect, [the teachers] were often of strong political feelings'. Thanks to encouragement from some particular teachers, Isabel 'first became aware of the injustices that abound in life. It is no surprise really that I should later attempt to speak up for my fellow typists.'[68]

Yet positive experiences such as these were far from universal. Night schools did admit women, but not usually to the same classes as men. For many women, night school meant classes in sewing and cookery. They were designed to improve their housewifery skills, not to open their minds or to prepare them for public service. As a young adult, Alice Foley decided to sign up for classes in economics, logic and elocution at the evening school held in Great Moor Street, but her 'odd choice . . . landed me before the Director and Chairman' of the local education committee. The two men wanted to know why 'a nice, quiet girl wanted to study economics and logic'. Her answer obviously failed to convince them of her suitability, because the chairman retorted 'that I would be allocated to a millinery class at the Women's Institute as more suitable to my aptitude and ability'.[69] She dutifully attended the prescribed sewing class, but when she realised that it met at the same time as her preferred classes in economics and logic she quietly switched herself back to the classes of her choice. The fact that her preference drew the attention of the director and chairman of the local education committee speaks volumes about the choices that mill girls in Bolton were expected to make. And inevitably, not all teenage girls had the confidence to disobey the men in charge. Maggie Newbery's experience contains less to celebrate. Maggie was fed up with working in the mill and had agreed with a friend to enrol at night school. She dreamed of being a teacher, but she knew her parents could not support her on that path, so she 'settled for office work'. In the event, however, not even that was possible. At her night school interview, she was told she 'couldn't possibly take short hand and typing and was advised to go in for dressmaking, needlework and cookery'.[70] This she duly did.

Indeed, throughout the period down to the outbreak of the First World War, the political world was powerfully coded as masculine in ways that hindered the integration of women. The spaces that working men described moving into with relative ease and with such positive results appear decidedly less welcoming in the narratives of women. This was particularly so in the case of the unions, which were, for men at least, perhaps the most accessible form of political action. Alice Foley, for example, noted that there was a strong tradition of industrial organisation in her Bolton factory, but she also indicated that it was dominated by 'a body of male weavers'. When the female weavers were merged into the existing labour association, 'these men controlled a virile "shop committee" ' that was far quicker to promote the men's interests than the women's.[71] Over in Blackburn, Elizabeth Blackburn also found that the union was a very male affair. She joined up when she first started at the mill but admitted to not being very regular in attendance, as 'the meetings were so dull'. In her autobiography, Elizabeth, who became an active unionist later in life, was apologetic for her earlier apathy, but she also placed some of the blame on the culture of the union: 'It must be said that young women were not given much encouragement to take part in the Trade Union affairs.'[72] When Elizabeth Andrews started attending the local meetings of the newly formed Independent Labour Party, she 'often found I was the only woman present'.[73]

It was all part and parcel of a more widespread pattern in which women were not encouraged to speak in public. When Emma Sproson turned up to a public meeting in the 1880s and asked a question of the speaker, it was, she thought, 'to the great astonishment of all present'. Her voice was both unexpected and, in the event, ignored: he 'declined to answer it because I was a woman and had no vote'.[74] In the same decade, Elizabeth Layton found that her gender precluded her from taking a seat on the management committee of her local co-operative society. 'There was such a storm at the idea of a woman on a Management Committee' that she stepped down from the election: 'The members put my husband on instead.'[75] In the 1890s, Hannah Mitchell attended a local debating society with a friend to hear a debate on the subject of 'women and politics'. At that time, she explained, 'the idea of women in politics was very unpopular' and she was 'both surprised and indignant at the sex prejudice displayed by most of the debaters'.[76] When Nellie Scott got involved with her local co-operative society in the early 1900s there were no women in any formal positions, and if a 'woman stood for any position in those days the abuse they met with was awful'.[77] Indeed, Annie Barnes was drawn into the suffragette movement by the curious sight of seeing 'four women on a cart speaking' when she was on her way home from shopping. For

9.2 An undated
photograph of the
working-class
suffragette Ada Chew,
rejecting the
expectation that women
had no place speaking
in public and standing
on a cart to address a
crowd.

the period (it was around 1905), she thought, 'that was unusual, to see women talking'.[78]

Although the men who credited their discussion groups for their political education did not generally dwell upon their gender composition, their writing reveals that they had, in fact, very often been male-only spaces. For example, the 'local debating society' that Frank Hodges had attended was composed of 'schoolmasters and teachers, preachers, journalists, business men, students and working men'. He thought this kind of make-up was 'common to nearly all the local debating societies' in the area.[79] In explaining to his reader how, as a working man, he had 'learned to speak', George Lansbury credited his church's Young Men's Association, which encouraged debates amongst its

9.3 The members of the 'Men's Bible Class' of St Andrew's Church, Wigan.

members over the political controversies of the day.[80] The members were mostly 'old men' until he and 'one or two other boys joined'.[81] The Beeston Adult School that had been the incubator for George Hodgkinson's widening horizons was also, in fact, a male-only space comprised largely of skilled workmen. It was, he accurately noted, 'a fraternity'.[82]

There were, of course, some groups and clubs that did open their doors to women as well as men, yet if we investigate more closely how these organisations worked it becomes clear that women were not necessarily included in ways that enabled them to acquire the skills required for political action. As a young man, John Paton had been invited by a like-minded customer in his barber's shop to accompany him to the local Clarion Club and was delighted to do so. 'The members,' he recalled, 'were mostly young men but there was a sprinkling of girls.' In the early part of the evening, 'both men and women would be found' talking socialist politics together. But it was much later in the evening, with 'the main body', including the women, gone, that those remaining would 'begin the real talk'. This, he considered, was the 'best time'. It was the time for serious discussion, and this, of course, was for the men only – the time when Paton could soak up the opinions of 'men [who] had all read widely and well'.[83]

Kathleen Woodward's perspective on the depth and significance of male conversation was somewhat different. She and a friend from work became members of 'a little company of persons who met in a back room in Camberwell' to discuss the issues of the day. Unfortunately, though, the meetings were somewhat spoiled by the 'dominating spirit of . . . the black beady-eyed Jasper' – an overzealous crusader and 'wind-bag', who repeated his platitudes about feeding the hungry and clothing the naked 'with tedious frequency'.[84] Both Paton and Woodward's progressive groups accepted women members alongside the men, yet struggled to treat them equally, hinting at a deep-rooted ambivalence within the radical tradition regarding how women should fit within the movement.

Night schools, unions and political discussion groups were intrinsically male institutions, and although some women managed to pass through their doors, they were less likely to find their experiences there sufficient to propel them into the public sphere. Nor was this the only difficulty that women faced. In addition, there was a host of structural forces that made it difficult for women to access such organisations in the first place. Young male workers took it for granted that they were able to spend their non-work hours in the company of like-minded individuals in the pursuit of self-improvement or the greater social good. Young women, even those in work, simply did not enjoy the same degree of autonomy The largest single employer of women was domestic service, so many female workers were dispersed amongst an atomised workforce that was notoriously difficult to organise.[85] But even women who were less tightly under their employers' grip than domestic servants were often controlled by their families instead. As we have already seen, some women remained at the beck and call of their family well into their twenties, entering and exiting the labour market according to their family's need for domestic labour rather than their own wishes. It is hardly surprising, then, to find that these familial responsibilities also hindered their political activism.

In theory, wage-earning freed the earner from domestic chores, and some of the female autobiographers noted, with some satisfaction, that starting work had indeed liberated them from the tiresome round of domestic chores. But for women, and in very sharp contrast to men, this was not universal. In practice, a women's dispensation from chores was always tempered by the needs of the family. The discrepancy was noted by Michael Conway. He recalled (as we saw a moment ago) that the 'males would clear off' after lunch on

Saturday to pursue their hobbies. Yet he continued: 'Though the males had the weekend free, the womenfolk were more industrious than ever, with washing, mending, patching, baking, cooking and knitting . . . the daughters would be busy about the house.'[86] Lily Purvis lived with her grandmother, who made very full use of her granddaughter's domestic labour, even after she had begun at the factory:

> You would think that now I was working full time my grandmother would have done most of the housework . . . Not on your life! She certainly arranged a regular routine for me . . . [which] I had to do after coming home from the mill at 6. P. M. and having tea. Naturally I had to clear the dishes before I started . . .[87]

Nellie Scott loved discussing politics with her friends in the workroom, but she found it difficult to translate their discussions into action, because the women were not always free to attend meetings. In the evenings after work, 'there was housework to be done, baking at night and cleaning'.[88] Alice Foley noted a similar problem with the union meetings at her Bolton factory. 'If talks dragged on,' she noted, the 'married women grew restless about possible irate husbands awaiting their delayed evening meal.'[89]

Much of the reason that women's paid work was secondary to their domestic work was connected to the fact that their wages were so low. It thus comes as no surprise to find that most of the female autobiographers involved in political work were concentrated in a small number of relatively well-paid sectors. Most – thirteen – were working in factories, usually in the Lancashire cotton industry. A further nine were employed in roles that were unusually well paid for women – office workers,[90] highly skilled dressmakers,[91] shopwork,[92] a health visitor.[93] In order for women to exercise their right to spend time and money pursuing interests outside the domestic sphere, their paid work needed to have value within their own domestic setting: the higher a woman's wages the greater her bargaining power within the family unit.[94]

Women's different relationship to paid labour, added to their low status and the low regard in which their voices were held, made it far more difficult for young women to take up political work than their male counterparts. Furthermore, as young women became adults these difficulties increased, rather than lessened. Whereas ageing brought ever-greater money, freedom and independence for young men, the reverse was true for women. Their usual milestones of adulthood – marriage and motherhood – added to their domestic responsibilities and were often sufficient to bring a permanent end to their campaigning activities. Working-class women never really escaped the burden of domestic responsibility, and this exerted a lifelong drag on their political interests and involvement.

It is indeed striking that the very small number of working-class women who had managed to forge a political career for themselves had avoided the path of marriage and motherhood altogether. Of the four female MPs, for example, two never married and none had children. The reasons for this were something they chose not to address. In fact, Jennie Lee's biographer suggests that the topic of children was out of bounds even between Lee and her closest friends.[95] Margaret Bondfield wrote simply that as a young woman in her late teens she had 'just lived for the Trade Union Movement . . . undisturbed by love affairs . . . [with] no vocation for wifehood or motherhood'.[96] Not only were these women childless, the whole topic of their childlessness or how motherhood and politics might be combined was largely closed for discussion.

Much the same pattern is also evident among the twelve women who, whilst not serving as MPs, nonetheless played a prominent role in national organisations. Well over half of these twelve women (eight) had no children. Of the remaining four, three had just one child,[97] and just one had more – Emma Sproson, who gave birth to four, of whom three survived. In all, then, three-quarters of the female autobiographers who had participated in politics on a national level had never had children; and among the few who did, very small families were the norm.

Indeed, if we expand our frame to consider all of the female autobiographers who mentioned any kind of political involvement, no matter how small scale, we find the very same pattern. This group contains a further eighteen writers, and an unusually high proportion of them – half, nine in total – had no children.[98] Of the other nine, most had unusually small families of just one or two children,[99] and just three had families of four or more children.[100] Only one had what might be described as a large family. This was Mrs Smith, a miner's wife living in the Rhondda Valley, who had given birth to no fewer than nine children in the years before getting involved with her local Women's Guild. At the time of writing her short autobiographical account her youngest child was five, and it is not clear whether her involvement went beyond attending the Guild's lectures. At any rate, she was an outlier, for overwhelmingly the female autobiographers found it difficult to combine outside interests with large families. Admittedly, the autobiographers who became involved in politics were describing the period after 1890 when the birth rate was falling, so we might expect somewhat smaller families amongst these women anyway.[101] Yet even within the context of this general decline, the small size of the families of the women who were politically active is remarkable. In all, thirty-four of the two hundred female autobiographers had played some political role. Between them, these thirty-four women had thirty-five children, giving an average family size of one child per woman. More than half (twenty-one) bore no children at all. These rates of fertility and childlessness clearly bore no relationship to those of the general population.

The autobiographers occasionally indicated that the sheer fact of marriage had been detrimental to their ambition to lead a life outside the home. Hannah Mitchell, for instance, had had a difficult childhood and escaped from her family in her early teens. A decade on, she was growing 'tired of living in lodgings'. Her strong desire for 'a home of my own' played a central role in her decision to marry in her early twenties. Yet no sooner had she married than she realised 'that the price of a home of one's own was going to be pretty high for me'.[102] Despite all the talk of 'marriage as a comradeship, rather than a state where the woman was subservient to, and dependent on, the man', her own husband had very traditional views about the division of resources and labour within the home. With hindsight she thought that perhaps she should not have married, as it had closed off her chance of 'solitude, time for study, and the opportunity for a wider life'.[103]

But for most women, it was not marriage per se that was detrimental to a public life. Most unmarried women were either working in service or still living with their parents, so their scope for outside interests was already controlled to some degree, and marriage, particularly if it was to a man with similar political beliefs, promised to make things better rather than worse. Rather, the problem with marriage was that motherhood usually followed, and the heavy labour involved in the care of infants and small children introduced restrictions of a more immovable kind. New mothers needed to be at home and the impossibility of working-class mothers contracting out their childcare to other women made motherhood a serious impediment to political engagement. It is little wonder, then, that the onset of pregnancy a few short months into marriage filled Hannah Mitchell with further gloom about her situation: 'I foresaw that the coming of a baby would mean giving up my own work . . . I felt desperate, and wept many bitter tears.'[104] A very small family offered Hannah the only prospect of returning to any of the outside interests that had sustained her before marriage. Hannah deliberately limited her fertility so that she could pursue a life outside the domestic sphere, and although most of the female autobiographers were not forthcoming about their family-planning choices, their lowered fertility suggests she was not the only one to do so.[105]

It was not simply the labour involved in raising a family that militated against a public life. There was also something about the status of motherhood that kept women out of politics. In addition to deeply held cultural assumptions that mothers ought to be occupied with their homes and families, motherhood did not provide women with either the income or the status to take up interests of their own. Several of the autobiographers commented that their mother had not really enjoyed leisure of any kind.[106] Nellie Carbis's mother, for example, liked to settle down with a good book, but her 'household jobs didn't leave her much time for reading'.[107] Henry Turner noted that his mother never went to the pictures; indeed he considered that his mother had no leisure at all.[108] Arthur Goffin's mother was bad tempered and irritable, but he also observed that she did not have much to lighten her mood: 'Not many pleasures came her way – an occasional concert, tea with a friend.'[109] 'Never a holiday, never any leisure or amusement,' wrote Tom Barclay of his mother; and 'she was not permitted . . . to indulge in beer and dominoes of an evening like my father'.[110] It was not unusual for writers to notice that church on a Sunday evening was their mother's only weekly outing. 'Sunday evening was my mother's one evening out,' noted John Murphy. But a Sunday evening at the church was very far from what passed for leisure for men. After all, as Murphy continued, she took the children with her.[111]

Some of the writers commented that it had actually been quite rare for their mothers to venture beyond their immediate neighbourhood. Thomas Westwater contrasted the busyness of his father's life – he was heavily involved in the local church and his union – with that of his mother's – she 'went out very little'.[112] Mrs Roberts worked as hard as any keeping a household of seven and running a small grocery shop at the same time: she just 'went on working, scrubbing bare bedroom floors, kitchen, shop; washing, baking, and caring for children in between looking after business'. But none of this labour brought her the kind of leisure that her husband enjoyed. He 'had his regular weekends in the pub', but his wife's trips to the theatre at the end of the street were 'occasional'. Apart from that, she only went out to do the shopping.[113] James Brady captured the crampedness of his mother's world, which was rooted in the fact that she rarely left the neighbourhood at all: 'The cobble-stoned cul-de-sac, with its squalid row of shared privies in the middle, was her world from Monday to Sunday, a grey world of hard times and hard work, bringing up a family of five on a purse forever running empty.'[114]

By the same token, those few mothers who did become involved in local women's movements or organisations at any point before the First World War often stressed how much the experience had done to broaden and add interest to their otherwise very restricted lives. One of the most frequently recurring themes in the collection of letters about the Women's Guild collected by Margaret Llewelyn Davies in the 1930s was the sheer joy of having something beyond the family to consider. Mrs Smith was a mother of nine children and thought that the women in her village 'feel sometimes that we are not living but just existing somehow'. She continued that the 'beautiful lectures' organised by her local Women's Co-operative Guild helped to change that: 'It seems to uplift us and help us to carry on.'[115] For Mrs Layton, the delight of her involvement with the Guild was that 'my life was brightened to such an extent that everything seemed changed'.[116] One anonymous contributor wrote of the 'latent sparks which [the Guild] has kindled and caused to burn brightly'.[117] These views were widely repeated. Another guild member reflected upon the transformative experience of joining the newly formed Women's Guild in her town in very similar terms: 'Sometimes I went weary and discouraged, and returned wonderfully strengthened . . . It opened up a new life to me.'[118]

Underpinning the general inability of mothers to pursue any kind of interest outside the family was the fact that married women lacked an income of their own, and thus did not enjoy the pocket money that wage earners had. Several of the autobiographers observed that any windfalls or extras that came their mothers' way were invested in the family, rather than spent on themselves as individuals. William Brown, for example, recalled that 'whatever came into the house she spent on my father, and on us children. For her it was always, with food and everything else, what was "left over".' As a result, she was 'very shabby': she wore 'cracked, worn and shabby boots . . . laced up boots which a tramp

9.4 The Mothers' Union of Wigan met regularly on Thursday afternoons. Its members were photographed by William Wickham, the vicar at St Andrew's parish, in the 1890s.

would have looked at twice before accepting as a gift', and her dress was 'old and stained and equally shabby'.[119] With the endless housework and repeated cycle of pregnancy and childbearing his mother had 'slowly faded into a grey domestic drudge'.[120] When writers retold stories of their mothers managing to prise money out of the hands of unco-operative husbands, they always stressed that their mothers spent the loot on the children rather than themselves.[121] One writer thought that her father's attitude to treats was typical of the 'Lancashire working man's'. He 'never found any extra money [for treats] over and above the weekly sum he handed over' for housekeeping. That was his wife's reponsibility.[122]

What is evident from such accounts of outlay within the household is the fact that marriage and motherhood did not confer the same rights to personal spending money that wage-earning conferred. As the family housekeeper, mothers did have access to money; what they lacked was the right to spend it on themselves. Percy Wall noted that his mother 'loved a play' but he added in the same breath that 'only very occasionally could [she] afford to take a seat'. As he explained, within the household economy, his mother's evening at the theatre meant 'a meal less' for the family.[123] This drawing of a direct connection between mother's leisure and the family's meals is in stark contrast to the way the autobiographers wrote about their father's leisure. As we have seen, some writers certainly did regard their father's attendance at the theatre, the pub, the club or wherever it might be as a drain on the family's resources, yet male spending was never directly equated with the loss of a meal for other family members. This responsibility of mothers to feed the family was also given by some as one of the reasons that it was so hard to organise women. Kathleen Woodward was frustrated that the women she worked with in the factory were so reluctant to join the union, but she also understood the root of their reluctance. The two-penny weekly fee 'represented a loaf of bread that, for a time at least, would quiet a family of hungry children'.[124]

A mother's access to time – that other precursor to political action – was rather similar to her access to money. It was not that she lacked it entirely, but rather that she lacked the right to use it as she wished. When Elizabeth Layton's local Co-operative Guild decided to set up a Women's Guild she only had one child, yet she still declared that she was 'far too busy' to attend meetings in the middle of the week: 'It was quite impossible.' Her friend encouraged her, suggesting that it might do her good to get out once a week, and 'leave [her] worries behind [her] for a few hours'. Elizabeth decided to give it a try and found she that she could spare the time. Furthermore, the long walk there and back, something 'fresh' to listen to and something to think about all week did indeed bring the kind of benefit her friend had predicted.[125] Her experience suggests that it was not simply a question of time, for once the decision had been taken she did find the time to participate in the weekly meeting. What she had lacked was not time itself, but the belief that those hours were hers for the taking.

For all women, and for mothers in particular, the barriers to participating in political movements were high and it all took very careful planning. Some details about the challenges inherent in combining campaigning activity with motherhood are contained in the account that Doris Nield Chew gave of her mother, the suffragist and trade union organiser Ada Nield Chew. Ada was the eldest daughter in a family of nine children, most of them boys, so her life had been filled with domestic responsibilities from a very young age. By her early twenties, with economic need in the family pressing and with a younger sister of an age to take over the domestic work, Ada started working outside the home in a clothing factory and soon became involved in agitating for an improvement in the pay and conditions of the women. When this caused her to lose her job, she became an active member of the newly created Independent Labour Party, writing for various left-leaning publications, and touring as a public speaker. By her late twenties, she was still living at home, combining her work for the Labour Party with her family's housework, and clearly viewed marriage as the chance to escape a life of unpaid service to her family. She had no intention of following in the footsteps of her mother. By the time she left home, she 'had had enough, particularly of boys' and told her mother she intended to have only one child – something she accomplished by dint of a supportive husband and separate bedrooms.[126] Yet even with only one child, Ada's political travelling was brought 'perforce to an end for the time being' after her child's birth. Ada stayed at home for the first two years of her daughter's life and then took up a position with the Women's Trade Union League. In order to square her responsibility for her daughter with the travelling required of a union organiser, she took the unusual decision to travel with her daughter in tow. The union sympathisers who offered hospitality to the travelling speaker were given to understand that their hospitality 'must include [the] organiser's child'. It was a solution that, as her daughter recognised, 'was only possible because my mother had no more than one child'.[127]

There were many barriers in the way of women effectively voicing political thoughts, and these barriers lay at the root of one final difference in the ways that men and women accessed power. For men, as we have seen, work provided the gateway to the public sphere. It was a force far more powerful than family background. Although a handful of the male politicians had enjoyed relatively affluent childhoods, this was far from universally the case, and a substantial minority of men from the most poverty-stricken backgrounds had managed to overcome their disadvantage and forge a successful political career. Women's lives, by contrast, were far more squarely centred on home and family. It follows, therefore, that they found it much more difficult to enter politics without the active support and encouragement of their families.

None of the four female MPs, for example, had experienced serious poverty during their childhoods; they were all raised in loving and supportive homes. It was a point that they all took care to stress in their writing.[128] Ellen Wilkinson's father was a cotton worker and ambitious for his family – three of his four children ended up attending college. Owing to his support, Ellen progressed to secondary school, attended open lectures at the Free Trade Hall, took up a bursary as a pupil teacher, and then won a scholarship to Manchester University.[129] Jennie Lee's parents agreed to her spending a year at the secondary school with the expectation that that would mark the end of her education. But at the end of that year, she took first place in the examinations and 'Mother was determined that I should go on'. She too went to university.[130] Braddock and Bondfield both remained at school until the relatively late age of fourteen, and although they did not attend university they were both raised in stable, moderately prosperous homes with fathers who were present, in work and doing their best for their families.[131]

These general characteristics were shared by almost all of the women who became involved in some form of national political work. Only two, Alice Foley and Emma Sproson, had been raised in difficult circumstances with a father who was drinking heavily and failing to provide properly.[132] A further two had also been raised in poverty, but had experienced a greater degree of family stability.[133] Most of the rest, however, had enjoyed childhoods in comfortable working-class homes. In contrast to the great majority of working-class girls whose education had ended with elementary school, several of these women had progressed to secondary school,[134] although their stays were sometimes brief.[135] And those whose schooling had ended early did not usually explain this with reference to an acute economic need within the family, but rather to its need for additional female labour.[136]

Nor was this the only characteristic that defined the backgrounds of the female politicians. Not only had most been raised in comparative comfort; they also had fathers, and more occasionally mothers, who were already involved in some branch of the labour movement. Admittedly, the tendency of children to follow in the footsteps of their fathers was also apparent among some of the male autobiographers, particularly where both father and son worked in a heavily unionised industry. But overall the connection between the political values of fathers and sons was not particularly strong. Male adulthood meant economic and residential independence from one's parents, and intellectual independence was a natural extension of this pattern. The female writers, by contrast, frequently underscored the affinity between their own beliefs and those with which they had been raised. Mary Brooksbank's father was a founding member of the Aberdeen Dockers' Union, and had met some of the leading lights in the union movement – Tom Mann, Jim Larkin and Jim Sexton.[137] Mary Gawthorpe's father was a political agent and Mary's first foray into politics was a newspaper round delivering his political material to like-minded workmates.[138] Rose Kerrigan's father was 'a radical, a Trade Unionist and very outspoken'.[139] Rose and her brothers were 'up to our eyes in the political scene at a very early age'.[140] Jessie Stephen's father was not able to keep her at secondary school long enough that she could apply to the university, but he did manage to keep her there until the age of fifteen. He was also a member of the Independent Labour Party and had a 'passion for knowledge'.[141] Bessie Braddock indicated that not only her father, but also her mother, had been 'mixed up in the struggle to win better conditions' for the working class throughout her childhood. The class struggle was part of her life from 'as early as I can remember', and as an adult she 'tried to carry on where [her mother] left off'.[142]

These two characteristics – families that enjoyed relatively favourable economic circumstances and shared political values between parents and daughters – are surely significant, as they reveal something fundamentally different between the route to activism taken by men and women. For men, work provided access to politics. The opportunities provided by the workplace were a powerful force that could override a family's political persuasions and overcome even the most acute familial disadvantage. The extent to which work could facilitate women's entry into the political sphere was much more limited. It was certainly a spur to engagement for women working in the factory districts who had access not only to waged work but also to relatively good wages, but elsewhere its effect was far more muted and was only occasionally sufficient to free women from the grip of their families and enable them to pursue their own independent interests and activities. It is surely also for this reason that the connections between women and their parents were so much more significant. The support, economic, emotional and intellectual, that families provided for their daughters was a key driver behind their ability to access the political sphere.

Indeed, it is remarkable that many female writers commented on the support (or otherwise) that they received from the men in their lives. Doris Chew, for example, explained that her father's attitude to her mother's campaigning work 'was simple . . . It must be remembered that he had been brought up in the home of Lancashire weavers who took it for granted that the wife should go out to work.' By the same token, she added, he did not object to her political campaigning.[143] Mrs Layton wrote that her husband 'sometimes . . . rather resented' the teachings of her Women's Guild.[144] Mrs Yearn was more fortunate: 'I have the best husband in the world.' Though she also realised how lucky she was to have a husband who 'allowed me to leave my home many times without a grumble'.[145] Isabel Templeton had to think hard about marriage. Her suitor was 'all for fair play for women. What he objected to was women working. And, if they did work, he did not think they should do the agitating.' Both work and politics 'was man's business'. Nor was he particularly regressive in this respect: 'even [her] own brothers held such views'.[146] For the suffragette Annie Barnes, the role played by her father was different again. Her parents did not approve of the suffragettes and they 'would have died if they'd known I was involved'. But fortunately, her father was so indifferent to what Annie got up to – as she repeated twice in her autobiography, 'he didn't care about us kids' – that it was relatively easy to pull the wool over his eyes and slip out to deliver leaflets and attend to campaigning business. 'The old man didn't know where I was. Not that he took any interest anyway in anything we did. He used to think I was upstairs.'[147] All these women were adults in their twenties or older, yet they nonetheless thought the attitude of the men in their lives was relevant to their political activities outside the home.

There is clearly something to celebrate in the enormous achievements of the working-class men and women who, despite being born to a class that was neither expected nor encouraged to contribute to the nation's political life, overcame the odds and managed to do precisely that. Their stories reveal something of the social changes that had helped to create a space for their activism: new opportunities for paid work, small families and support from male relatives – all played a role in allowing working-class women to take up a role outside the home.

At the same time, however, we need to grasp the gendered nature of politics, the wide range of impediments that stood in the way of women and the inequality between working men and women. The political sphere was not entirely closed to women, but a range of subtle barriers existed that made it far harder for women to access. Low female wages coupled with the widespread need for domestic labour within families left women without the time, money or right to pursue their own interests and activities. This, compounded with deeply held cultural assumptions about the inferiority of women and their innate inability to handle abstract ideas, helped to ensure that all women struggled to articulate themselves effectively. Above all, the evidence about political engagement points once more to the broader significance of the cultural forces that kept most women confined to the home and consigned those who did work to very low pay. The economic inferiority of women disempowered them not only as individuals with respect to their families, but also as citizens with a place in society. Low wages and the absence of economic opportunity were thus not simply a reflection of women's low status in Victorian and Edwardian Britain. Their impact was far more invidious. Women's economic inferiority also played an active role in ensuring that that low status was maintained.

CONCLUSION

This book opened with the enigma – or at least the contradiction – articulated by Henry George in the 1870s, that material progress did not seem to be reducing poverty so much as creating it. It is now time to return to that puzzle. Does our study of six hundred-odd autobiographies help us to understand why decades of robust economic growth failed to lift all out of poverty?

Of course, it is always possible for growth and poverty to co-exist. All economies have their poorest quartile, and so by definition have a subset who are poorer than everyone else. At the same time, the absolute level of wealth held by that poorest quartile can shift upwards over time, so that poverty, whilst never disappearing, nevertheless changes significantly in substance and form. If this is the case, George's enigma might be chimerical – a true statement, yet one that fails to capture the secular improvements that even those at the bottom enjoyed.

To some extent, this was the case for nineteenth-century Britain. In 1830, the poorest families faced a very real and continuous struggle to feed themselves, a struggle that was shared by many neighbours, and which could rarely be alleviated through the better stewarding of the meagre resources they had to hand. By the end of the century, food was both cheaper relative to incomes and more plentiful, so children who were not being fed in their homes now had a reasonably good chance of finding food by some other means. Recall Louie Stride picking edible food out of the gutters and snatching it off other children at school, or Sid Causer pinching fruit from barrels in the street piled high with tempting produce, or Arthur Harding making a satisfactory dinner from the chips he cadged off customers at the fish and chip shop. It is objectively true that these children of late Victorian and Edwardian Britain consumed a better diet than those a century earlier living in homes and communities that had no food to pinch or share. And yet to dwell upon this alleviation of hunger would surely be to place the emphasis in the wrong place. This was not a linear march towards progress. Edwardian Britain had sufficient food for all, but that Louie Stride got it by picking it from the gutter is also a signal that something was deeply wrong.

In seeking to understand the survival of poverty in an increasingly prosperous society, *Bread Winner* picks up themes that historians have long wrestled with. But if the problem is old, the method I have pursued here is not. As a historical source, working-class autobiographies are well known and widely used – just not to understand 'big' problems like the extent and meaning of economic growth. The colourful personal stories contained in life histories are presumed to belong to the realm of social and cultural history, whilst economic historians for the most part turn to statistical records collected by social elites and modern economic theory in order to explain how and when the economy grew, and who really benefited. What happens if we link these two traditions? I have tried to show here that we can use autobiographical accounts to bridge the social and the economic. We can mine these sources not simply for lively descriptions of the period. Working-class voices can shed light on large economic questions as well.

Louie Stride, the illegitimate child of a petty thief and sex-worker born and raised in the affluent city of Bath, was the epitome of poverty amidst plenty. She received a schooling that was even more scanty than that typical of a working-class child and spent her adult life as a domestic, cleaner, chambermaid, cook and tea-lady. No one turns to the tea-lady for economic wisdom, but Louie Stride *did* have insight into why as a child she picked food out of the gutter rather than ate it from a plate. She did not gesture to impersonal, economic forces but to matters much closer to home: an absent father, later a drunken stepfather and a mother suffering from mental illness and wholly unable either to earn the family bread or to bake it. Nor was this all. As Louie correctly observed, her problems were compounded by the individualistic political ethos of the times. There were no 'Welfare State bounties', no 'public body to do something in such cases as mine'; 'no one cared' about vulnerable children who slipped through the net. Louie Stride understood the political and economic realities of her situation. Now it is time for us to listen.

All families are unique and Louie Stride's was particularly so. But the advantage of surveying several hundred autobiographies is that it permits us to distinguish between the superficial peculiarities unique to particular families (a mother who paid the rent and other debts with sex rather than money, edible food picked out of the gutter) and the underlying forces that unified diverse experiences (gendered pay, fatherlessness, alcoholism, the absence of welfare). And if the specifics of Louie's household were unusual, the general contours that shaped her experiences were far less so. Men took the lion's share of the nation's wage bill: women provided the lion's share of the domestic work that kept families fed, clothed, housed. All working-class men faced a struggle to procure sufficient income for decent living, but many households faced an additional challenge in getting money from male earners into the hands of wives and mothers, either through the absence of a breadwinner or the tight hold he kept on his own earnings. If we can grasp this and position it at the centre of our understanding of economic change, the enigmas and contradictions about late Victorian and Edwardian Britain largely disappear.

Economic growth in the eighty years after 1830 was real and substantial and it was accompanied by steady increases in the real wage as well. But the benefits of wage growth were not shared equally between the sexes owing to the custom of paying women much lower wages than men and their exclusion from most sectors of the new, high-wage economy. Historians (so far as they have troubled about the history of gendered pay) have generally made sense of the large gender pay gap by pointing to the different productivity of male and female workers, or simply by reading low pay as a reflection of that society's lower regard for women. But from the perspective of the autobiographies, the context and consequence of low female pay appear in a very different light. Women's low wages were not simply a reflection of their low status; they were a vital prop that served to maintain that reality. After all, nothing kept women subordinate to men so effectively as depriving them of money of their own. Low female wages ensured that all households had access to the unpaid female labour necessary for the maintenance of a home, and they forced women into a position of dependency with respect to the men in their lives. This unequal access to wages – to money – is foundational to understanding the developments we have studied here.

Wage growth diverted a greater share of the nation's wealth directly to men's hands, and for this reason, wage growth and living standards were locked in a troubled embrace. A good male wage could enrich the family fund, but it could also destabilise it, leaving families no richer than before. The male wage is thus the key to understanding both rising levels of prosperity and also deepening inequality and the very substantial segment of the population who were left behind.

So long as men conformed to social expectations, working hard and sharing their wages with their wives, the fit between real wages and living standards was good. Around 30 per cent of the autobiographers had a father present throughout their childhood who behaved in this way, and whilst this was rarely sufficient to ensure luxurious living, it certainly ensured some degree of comfort and created an equivalence between male earnings and family living conditions. But over and again, high male wages did not have this outcome. Indeed, one of the most extraordinary and unexpected discoveries from the autobiographies is that a good male wage was not always the unmitigated blessing that we might expect.

The low wages of pre-industrial Britain had kept families poor, but they had also established an equality within the household between the value of money income and the value of the unpaid labour that transformed that money into meals and comfort. So long as a male worker could not afford to purchase cooked meals, he could only fulfil his subsistence needs by handing his full wage to his wife. He may have been the notional head of household, but in reality he was every bit as dependent upon his wife's efforts to provide habitable lodging, cooked meals and adequate clothing as she was dependent upon his wage. The high male earnings created by industrialisation snapped apart this equality between wage-earning husbands and their non-wage-earning wives and children. A man could now maintain a reasonable standard of living by depositing a part of his wage with his wife and keeping a part back for his own personal consumption. This alternative form of family life was not merely hypothetical. It was the lived experience of a large minority – nearly 20 per cent – of all families.

Nor was this the only force creating a breach between male wages and family living standards. Fully one-quarter of the autobiographers had, at some point during their childhood, lived in a household without a breadwinner at all. Fatherlessness had two distinct causes. The mortality rate was relatively high: paternal death deprived just over 10 per cent of all writers of their father, and consequently their household of a male wage. Of even greater significance, however, was the large number of fathers who were living but absent – nearly 15 per cent of the total. And as with unreliable breadwinning, paternal desertion was closely related to the high-wage economy, as men were only empowered to live away from their wives when they earned enough to buy the services she provided – cooked meals and clean clothes – on the open market. When put together with the families who had lost their breadwinner through death, the outcome was a very large subset of families – almost half of all the autobiographers – who were not carried along on the tide of economic growth, whose experiences were largely divorced from trends in the real wage.

Of course, the family had never been entirely reliable as a means of ensuring all citizens received a share of resources adequate for a decent living. In the eighteenth century and before, the death rate was high, so some families had lacked a male breadwinner; and there had also, inevitably, been some men who had successfully managed to evade their family responsibilities. Yet the face-to-face nature of pre-industrial society had done a reasonably good job of mitigating these problems and forcing families to look after their own – fathers after their families and (when fathers died) extended male kin to step into their place. We must not idealise this pattern of behaviour or imbue it with a cultural significance it does not deserve. There is no evidence in the earlier autobiographies that strong family units could overcome the disadvantages posed by low incomes, or that they created especial happiness and well-being for those involved. The pooling of all available money and labour was not rooted in particular emotional values: it was nothing more than a strategy for survival.

As male wages started to rise, new choices opened to the men who earned them, but they were just that: a choice – and not one that every man made. In rural areas in particular most men conformed to social expectations about male provision. Even as agricultural wages began to increase in the late nineteenth century, prising open a gap between the value of male wages and female labour, farm workers overwhelmingly continued to share their earnings with their wives, though, of course, the absence of conveniences like hot, running water and cooked food in their communities may have played some role in encouraging them to do so. Many men in urban areas also made this choice, sharing their higher wages with their wives to the benefit of both themselves and all the others in the household. However, good wages offered men a new kind of autonomous decision-making power – a power that some grasped for their families and some grasped for themselves alone. Money enabled, rather than mandated, irregular working patterns, the non-sharing of wages, heavy drinking and paternal desertion. Indeed, the back-breaking labour that some men needed to perform in order to earn a wage may have contributed to excessive drinking and all the problems that flowed from it. At any rate, the outcome was that new strains were imposed upon the family model, turning a system that functioned crudely into one that struggled in some areas to function at all.

At the same time, these developments established a more complex hierarchy of working-class families. There was, of course, considerable variation in male wages across and within different trades. Superimposed upon this variation in wage rates, however, was great variety in the degree to which men funnelled their wages into the common family fund. The failure of some fathers to disperse their earnings to their families created further divisions and inequalities between men and women, between fathers and children, and amongst all those we conveniently label 'the working class' as well. With little doubt, rising male wages and deepening social inequality were interconnected, rather than distinct, aspects of the period.

In drawing attention to the negatives carried along by economic progress – widening gender inequality, deepening social inequality and the widespread misuse of alcohol – it should not be imagined that I am singing an elegy for the simpler, purer world of pre-industrial Britain. Regret for historical change is pointless. The Industrial Revolution did happen, Britain did urbanise, male wages did rise. In any case, as I have argued elsewhere, there is little to envy about the pre-industrial world of low wages, under-employment, crushing poverty and widespread hunger. Our challenge is to understand historical change without slipping into an unwarranted nostalgia for the poverty and hardship endured by earlier generations.

There can be no denying that Victorian economic growth had vastly increased the wealth of the nation by the outbreak of war in 1914. Yet whilst industrial capitalism could create wealth, it was itself unable to distribute it in such a way that a child such as Louie Stride had enough food to eat. At the time this book closes, we are still some way away from those 'Welfare bounties' that an older Louie identified as a useful response to 'cases' such as hers. As such, her problems were rooted not simply in failings within her own family, but also in a wider political failing to provide welfare to those in serious want. In the second half of the twentieth century, state-sponsored initiatives introduced a layer of defence for families lacking income and successfully swept away the worst excesses of inequality and deprivation. As our forensic analysis of the family makes clear, government-funded welfare provision offered the promise of a far more robust form of social protection for the poor and vulnerable than wages had ever been able to achieve.

Above all, *Bread Winner* has sought to show how much we can learn by looking at those little historical details that do not usually make the cut. Our starting point has been a scattered collection of life-writing by ordinary men and women, produced in different forms and formats, and of vastly differing levels of quality, lucidity and insight. Some (as the early champions of this material suggested) might even be considered 'anecdotal', 'desultory' and 'personal' in nature. But the 'personal' is not separate from those other big categories with which historians work – the 'political' and the 'economic'. Left to their own devices, people will talk about their families, not because they cannot see the big picture, but because this is precisely the way that individuals can make sense of the big picture. And if we want to address large historical questions, we can do no better than heed their account.

ENDNOTES

ABBREVIATIONS

ALS	Archives and Local Studies
AS	Archives Service
ARS	Archives and Records Service
CL	Central Library
CRO	County Record Office
HC	Heritage Centre
LHC	Local History Centre
LHLA	Local History Library and Archives
LSAC	Local Studies and Archives Centre
LSL	Local Studies Library
MRC	Modern Records Centre
RL	Reference Library
RO	Record Office
WCML	Working Class Movement Library

NOTE ON THE TEXT AND ACKNOWLEDGEMENTS

1. Woodward, *Jipping Street*, p. vii.

INTRODUCTION: 'THE GREAT ENIGMA OF OUR TIMES'

1. O'Mara, *The Autobigraphy of a Liverpool Slummy*, pp. 30–1, 36. Mary Ann Molloy and her family are present in the 1871 and 1891 censuses. Her marriage to James O'Meara was registered in March 1894 and their fifth child, Timothy O'Meara, was born in 1901. The O'Meara family appears in the 1901 census, though not in the 1911 census. By the time of writing his autobiography in the 1930s, Timothy O'Meara had emigrated to the United States and was using the name Patrick O'Mara.
2. O'Mara, *Liverpool Slummy*, p. 28.
3. For some introductory works on the period, see: David Cannadine, *Victorious Century: The United Kingdom, 1800–1906* (London, 2017); Susie L. Steinbach, *Understanding the Victorians: Politics, Culture and Society in Nineteenth-Century Britain* (Abingdon, 2012); Martin Daunton, ed., *Cambridge Urban History of Britain, 1840–1950* (Cambridge, 2000); K. Theodore Hoppen, *The Mid-Victorian Generation: 1846–1886* (Oxford, 1998); Roderick Floud, *The People and the British Economy, 1830–1914: Land of Hope and Glory* (Oxford, 1997). See also: James Vernon, *Distant Strangers: How Britain became Modern* (Berkeley, 2014).

4. C. H. Feinstein, *National Income, Expenditure and Output of the United Kingdom, 1855–1965* (Cambridge, 1972); R. C. O. Matthews, C. H. Feinstein and J. C. Odling-Smee, *British Economic Growth, 1856–1973* (Oxford, 1982); N. F. R. Crafts and Terence Mills, 'Trends in real wages in Britain, 1750–1913', *Explorations in Economic History*, 31/2 (1994), pp. 176–94; Gregory Clark, 'The condition of the working class in England 1209–2004', *Journal of Economic History*, lviii (2005), pp. 1307–40; Stephen Broadberry, 'Relative per capita income levels in the United Kingdom and the United States since 1870: Reconciling time-series projections and direct benchmark estimates', *Journal of Economic History*, 63 (2003), pp. 852–63; Stephen Broadberry and Alexander Klein, 'Aggregate and per capita GDP in Europe, 1870–2000: Continental, regional and national data with changing boundaries', *Scandinavian Economic History Review*, 60/1 (2012), pp. 79–107, table 3; Nicholas Crafts and Terence C. Mills, 'Six centuries of British economic growth: A time-series perspective', *European Review of Economic History*, 21/2 (2017), pp. 141–58.

5. John Archer and Jo Jones, 'Headlines from history: Violence in the press, 1850–1914', in Elizabeth A. Stanko, ed., *The Meanings of Violence* (London, 2003); Robin J. Barrow, 'Rape on the railway: Women, safety, and moral panic in Victorian newspapers', *Journal of Victorian Culture*, 20/3 (2015), pp. 341–56.

6. For more on the dark side of Victorian life, see: L. Perry Curtis, Jr, *Jack the Ripper and the London Press* (New Haven, 2001); Alexandra Warwick and Martin Willis, eds, *Jack the Ripper: Media, Culture, History* (Manchester, 2007); Sarah Wise, *The Blackest Streets: The Life and Death of a Victorian Slum* (London, 2009); Drew D. Gray, *London's Shadows: The Dark Side of Victorian London* (London, 2010).

7. Charles Booth, *Life and Labour in London* (London, 1889–91). For discussion of his work, see: Jose Harris, *Private Lives, Public Spirit: A Social History of Britain, 1870–1914* (Oxford, 1993); David Englander and Rosemary O'Day, eds, *Retrieved Riches: Social Investigation in Britain, 1840–1914* (Aldershot, 1995); Thomas R. C. Gibson-Brydon, *The Moral Mapping of Victorian and Edwardian London: Charles Booth, Christian Charity, and the Poor-but-Respectable* (Montreal, 2016).

8. Bernard Harris, 'Seebohm Rowntree and the measurement of poverty, 1899–1951', in Roy Sainsbury and Jonathan Bradshaw, eds, *Getting the Measure of Poverty: The Early Legacy of Seebohm Rowntree* (Aldershot, 2000), pp. 60–84; George R. Boyer, 'Living standards, 1860–1939', in Roderick Floud and Paul Johnson, eds, *The Cambridge Economic History of Modern Britain Volume 2: Economic Maturity, 1860–1939* (Cambridge, 2004); Ian Gazeley, 'Income and living standards, 1870–2010', in Roderick Floud, Jane Humphries and Paul Johnson, eds, *The Cambridge Economic History of Modern Britain Volume 2: 1870–the Present* (Cambridge, 2014), pp. 151–80, esp. pp. 164–8.

9. Henry George, *Progress and Poverty: An Inquiry into the Causes of Industrial Depressions and of Increase of Want with Increase of Wealth: The Remedy* (New York, 1879), p. 9.

10. Thomas Piketty, *Capital in the Twenty-First Century* (Cambridge, MA, 2014), reference to Kuznets p. 11.

11. Roderick Floud and Bernard Harris, 'Health, height and welfare: Britain, 1700–1980', in Roderick Floud and Richard Hall Steckel, eds, *Health and Welfare During Industrialization* (Chicago, 1997), pp. 91–126; Roderick Floud et al., *The Changing Body: Health, Nutrition, and Human Development in the Western World since 1700* (Cambridge, 2011).

12. David Meredith and Deborah Oxley, 'Blood and bone: Body mass, gender and health inequality in nineteenth-century British families', *History of the Family*, 20/2 (2015), pp. 204–30; Sara Horrell, David Meredith and Deborah Oxley, 'Measuring misery: Body mass, ageing and gender inequality in Victorian London', *Explorations in Economic History*, 46/1 (2009), pp. 93–119; Roderick Floud, 'The dimensions of inequality: Height and weight variation in Britain, 1700–2000', *Contemporary British History*, 16/3 (2002).

13. Robert Woods, *The Demography of Victorian England and Wales* (Cambridge, 2000); Eilidh Garrett et al., *Changing Family Size in England and Wales: Place, Class and Demography, 1891–1911* (Cambridge, 2001); Eilidh Garrett et al., 'Infant Mortality: a social problem?', in Robert Woods et al., eds, *Infant Mortality: A Continuing Social Problem* (Aldershot,

2007), pp. 3–16. For nutrition, see: Ian Gazeley and Sara Horrell, 'Nutrition in the English agricultural labourer's household over the course of the long nineteenth century', *Economic History Review*, lxvi (2013).

14. Boyer, 'Living standards, 1860–1939'; Gazeley, 'Income and living standards'.

15. For the enduring hold of the prosperity thesis, see: Christopher Harvie and Colin Matthew, *Nineteenth-Century Britain: A Very Short Introduction* (Oxford, 2000); Jeremy Black and Donald MacRaild, *Nineteenth-Century Britain* (Basingstoke, 2003); Chris Cook, *The Routledge Companion to Britain in the Nineteenth Century, 1815–1914* (London, 2005); Eric J. Evans, *The Shaping of Modern Britain: Identity, Industry and Empire, 1780–1914* (Harlow, 2011); Carol Leonard and Jonas Ljungberg, 'Population and living standards, 1870–1914', in Stephen Broadberry and Kevin H. O'Rourke, eds, *The Cambridge Economic History of Modern Europe, Volume 2, 1870–the Present* (Cambridge, 2012), pp. 108–30. For the contradiction, see: Ian Gazeley and Andrew Newell, 'Urban working-class food consumption and nutrition in Britain in 1904', *Economic History Review*, 68/1 (2015), pp. 101–22.

16. O'Mara, *Liverpool Slummy*, pp. 19–21, quote p. 21.

17. *Ibid.*, pp. 30–4, 43, 29. Besides Patrick (registered and christened as Timothy), Mary O'Meara had two stillbirths and Mary (1894–99); James (1895–6); Catherine (1897–1900); and Alice (b. 1898).

18. For the politics of the breadwinner wage, see: Barbara Taylor, ' "The men are as bad as their masters": Socialism, feminism, and sexual antagonism in the London tailoring trade in the early 1830s', *Feminist Studies*, 5/1 (1979), pp. 7–40; S. O. Rose, 'Gender antagonism and class conflict: Exclusionary strategies of male trade unionists in nineteenth century Britain', *Social History*, 13/2 (1988), pp. 191–208; H. Benenson, 'The "family wage" and working women's consciousness in Britain, 1880–1914', *Politics and Society*, 19/1 (1991), pp. 71–108; Sonya O. Rose, *Limited Livelihoods: Gender and Class in Nineteenth Century England* (Berkeley, 1992); Anna Clark, *The Struggle for the Breeches: Gender and the Making of the British Working Class* (Berkeley, 1995).

19. Important contributions to the extent and significance of the breadwinning family model include: Wally Seccombe, 'Patriarchy stabilized: The construction of the male breadwinner wage norm in nineteenth-century Britain', *Social History*, 11/1 (1986); Ellen Ross, *Love and Toil: Motherhood in Outcast London, 1870–1914* (New York, 1993), esp. pp. 69–78; Joanna Bourke, 'Housewifery in working-class England 1860–1914', *Past and Present*, 143/1 (1994), pp. 167–97, esp. pp. 171–2; Sara Horrell and Jane Humphries, 'Women's labour force participation and the transition to the male-breadwinner family, 1790–1865', *Economic History Review*, 48/1 (1995); Colin Creighton, 'The rise of the male breadwinner family: A reappraisal', *Comparative Studies in Society and History*, 38/2 (1996), pp. 310–37; Angelique Janssens, 'The rise and decline of the male breadwinner family? An overview of the debate', *International Review of Social History*, 42/55 (1997); Maria Mies, *Patriarchy and Accumulation on a World Scale: Women in the International Division of Labour* (London, 1998).

20. Jane Whittle very helpfully problematises the meaning of 'work' and its division into paid and unpaid forms in 'A critique of approaches to "domestic work": Women, work and the preindustrial economy', *Past and Present*, 243 (2019), pp. 35–70.

21. For the significance of family economics see also: Richard Wall, 'Economic collaboration of family members within and beyond households in English society, 1600–2000', *Continuity and Change*, 25/1 (2010), pp. 83–108; Peter Scott, 'The household economy since 1870', in Roderick Floud, Jane Humphries and Paul A. Johnson, eds, *The Cambridge Economic History of Modern Britain Volume 2: Growth and Decline, 1870 to the Present*, 2nd edn (Cambridge, 2014), pp. 362–86.

22. Anna Clark, *Women's Silence, Men's Violence: Sexual Assault in England, 1770–1845* (London, 1987); Jane Lewis, *Women in England, 1870–1950: Sexual Divisions and Social Change* (Brighton, 1984), pp. 8–14; *idem*, ed., *Labour and Love: Women's Experience of Home and Family, 1850–1940* (Oxford, 1986); Elizabeth Roberts, *A Woman's Place: An Oral History of Working-class Women, 1890–1940* (Oxford, 1984); Ross, *Love and Toil*; Melanie Tebbutt,

Making Ends Meet: Pawnbroking and Working-Class Credit (London, 1983); Pat Thane, 'Women and the Poor Law in Victorian and Edwardian England', *History Workshop Journal*, 6 (1978). See also the useful summary text: Kathryn Gleadle, *British Women in the Nineteenth Century* (London, 2001).

23. Margaret Williamson, ' "He was good with the bairns": Fatherhood in an ironstone mining community, 1918–1960', *North East History*, 32 (1998), pp. 87–108; Lynn Abrams, ' "There was nobody like my daddy": Fathers, the family and the marginalisation of men in modern Scotland', *Scottish Historical Review*, 78/206 (1999), pp. 219–42; Julie-Marie Strange, *Fatherhood and the British Working Class, 1865–1914* (Cambridge, 2015); Trev Lynn Broughton and Helen Rogers, eds, *Gender and Fatherhood in the Nineteenth Century* (Basingstoke, 2007).
24. See also: Whittle, 'A critique of approaches', esp. pp. 67–70.
25. Bourke, 'Housewifery', pp. 171–2; Roberts, *Woman's Place*, pp. 110–21; Ross, *Love and Toil*, pp. 56–90, 128–65; Nancy Tomes, 'A "torrent of abuse": Crimes of violence between working-class men and women in London, 1840–1875', *Journal of Social History*, 11 (1978), pp. 328–45.
26. Burnett Archive: Harrison, née Twist, 'Poor and Proud', p. 10.
27. *Ibid.*, p. 14.
28. Figures from Angus Maddison, 'A comparison of levels of GDP per capita in developed and developing countries, 1700–1980', *Journal of Economic History*, 43/1 (1983), pp. 27–41, table 2, p. 3.
29. E. A. Wrigley, *The Path to Sustained Growth: England's Transition from an Organic Economy to an Industrial Revolution* (Cambridge, 2016); Garrett et al., *Changing Family Size*, esp. pp. 412–21.
30. Samantha Shave, *Pauper Policies: Poor Law Practice in England 1780–1850* (Manchester, 2017); Steven King, 'Thinking and rethinking the New Poor Law', *Local Population Studies*, 99 (2017), pp. 5–19; Nadja Durbach, 'Roast beef, the new Poor Law, and the British nation, 1834–63', *Journal of British Studies*, 52/4 (2013), pp. 963–98.
31. John Cooper, *The British Welfare Revolution, 1906–14* (London, 2017); Pat Thane, 'The Liberals and family welfare, 1906–1922', *Cercles*, 21 (2011), pp. 1–10; Chris Renwick, *Bread for All: The Origins of the Welfare State* (London, 2017); Marjorie Levine-Clark, *Unemployment, Welfare, and Masculine Citizenship: So Much Honest Poverty in Britain, 1870–1930* (Basingstoke, 2015), esp. pp. 216–76.
32. John Burnett, David Vincent and David Mayall, *The Autobiography of the Working Class: An Annotated, Critical Bibliography, 1790–1900*, i–ii (New York, 1984–7).
33. The literature on autobiographies as historical source is extensive. See: Helen Rogers and Emily Cuming, 'Revealing fragments: Close and distant reading of working-class autobiography', *Family & Community History*, 21/3 (2018), pp. 180–201; Penny Summerfield, *Histories of the Self: Personal Narratives and Historical Practice* (London, 2018), pp. 300–402; Strange, *Fatherhood*; idem, 'Fathers at home: Life writing and late-Victorian and Edwardian plebeian domestic masculinities', *Gender & History*, 27/3 (2015), pp. 703–17; Megan Doolittle, 'Fatherhood and family shame: Masculinity, welfare and the workhouse in late nineteenth century England', in Lucy Delap, Ben Griffin and Abigail Wills, eds, *The Politics of Domestic Authority in Britain from 1800* (Basingstoke, 2009), pp. 84–110; Carolyn Steedman, 'History and autobiography: Different pasts', in idem, ed., *Past Tenses: Essays on Writing, Autobiography and History* (London, 1992), pp. 41–50; Regenia Gagnier, *Subjectivities: A History of Self-Representation in Britain, 1832–1920* (Oxford, 1991); J. Pennef, 'Myths in life stories', in R. Samuel and P. Thompson, eds, *The Myths We Live By* (London, 1990).
34. The census of 1851 indicated that 54 per cent of the population lived in towns of more than 2,500 souls. Amongst the autobiographies, 51 per cent of the cohort from 1830 to 1870 lived in towns of over 2,500. By 1891, the census recorded 74 per cent of the population living in towns, as did 66 per cent of the cohort from 1871 to 1903. In 1911, the census-recorded urban population had risen to 79 per cent and that of the autobiographers born

1904–6 to 73 per cent. Urbanisation figures taken from C. M. Law, 'The growth of urban population in England and Wales, 1801–1911', *Transactions, Institute of British Geographers*, 41 (1967), pp. 125–43, table III.

35. The wide range stems from the fact that family breakdown in all its forms is difficult to detect historically. See the discussion in Jane Humphries, *Childhood and Child Labour in the British Industrial Revolution* (Cambridge, 2010), pp. 64–5; Michael Anderson, *Family Structure in Nineteenth-Century Lancashire* (Cambridge, 1971); Barry Reay, *Microhistories: Demography, Society and Culture in Rural England, 1800–1930* (Cambridge, 1996). The evidence for the autobiographical sample suggests 24 per cent of female writers and 27 per cent of male writers had lost one parent by the age of sixteen.

36. Norfolk RO: Hemmingway, 'Character', unpaginated introduction.

37. Webb, 'Reminiscences', p. 66. More generally, see also: Emma Griffin, *Liberty's Dawn: A People's History of the Industrial Revolution* (London, 2013).

38. The largest such project was that led by Paul Thompson, 'Family life and work experience before 1918', which formed the basis of Paul Thompson, *The Edwardians: The Remaking of British Society* (London, 1975).

39. For example, Mellor, *Gertie's Story*; Rogers, *Funny Old Quist*.

40. *Like it Was Yesterday*, foreword, no pag.

41. Burnett Archive: Hansford, 'Memoirs of a Bricklayer', no pag.

42. Burnett Archive: Harris, 'Autobiographical letters', letter dated 18 April 1978.

43. Oxfordshire HC: Joel, 'Autobiography', letter dated 28 April 1985.

44. *Ibid.*, letter dated 11 November 1985.

45. Surrey HC: Wallis, née Fowler, 'Down Memory Lane', p. 1. On this, see also: Florence Boos, *Memoirs of Victorian Working-Class Women: The Hard Way Up* (Basingstoke, 2017).

46. Oxfordshire HC: Joel, 'Autobiography', letters dated 28 May 1985 and 11 November 1985.

47. *Ibid.*, letter dated 11 November 1985.

48. Margaret Spufford, 'Introduction', in Lorna Delanoy, ed., *Women's Work is Never Done* (Mepal, 2007), p. 7.

49. S. Barbara Kanner, *Women in English Social History 1800–1914: A Guide to Research*, vol. 3, Autobiographical Writers (London, 1987); Jane Rendall, ' "Short account of my unprofitable life": Autobiographies of working class women in Britain *c.* 1775–1845', in Trev Broughton and Linda Anderson, eds, *Women's Lives/Women's Times* (Albany, 1997); Tess Cosslett, Celia Lury and Penny Summerfield, eds, *Feminism and Autobiography: Texts, Theories, Methods* (London, 2000); Helen Rogers, 'In the name of the father: Political biographies by radical daughters', in David Amigoni, ed., *Life Writing and Victorian Culture* (Aldershot, 2006); Jane McDermid, 'The making of a "domestic" life: Memories of a working woman', *Labour History Review*, 73/3 (2008), pp. 253–68; Kelly J. Mays, 'Domestic spaces, readerly acts: Reading(,) gender, and class in working-class Autobiography', *Nineteenth-Century Contexts*, 30/4 (2008), pp. 343–68; Seth Koven, *The Match Girl and the Heiress* (Princeton, NJ, 2014); Boos, *Memoirs of Working-Class Women*.

50. John, *Tabitha*.

51. Burnett et al., *Autobiography of the Working Class*, vol. 1, p. 174.

52. Cookson, *Our Kate*.

53. Robert Colls, 'Cookson, Chaplin and Common: Three northern writers in 1951', in K. D. M. Snell, ed., *The Regional Novel in Britain and Ireland, 1800–1990* (Cambridge, 2009), pp. 164–201, quote p. 106; Dominic Sandbrook, *The Great British Dream Factory: The Strange History of our National Imagination* (London, 2015), p. 313.

54. Brady, 'Long trail', p. 318.

55. Aird, *Autobiography*, p. 8.

56. Catton, *Short Sketch*, p. 1.

57. Hanson, *Life of Hanson*, p. 3.

58. Barr, *Climbing the Ladder*, p. 16.

59. Sanderson, 'Life and adventures', p. 6.

60. Harley, *Short Account*, p. 3.

61. Templeton, *Old Lady*, p. 99.
62. Jasper, *Hoxton Childhood*, p. 83.
63. Dayus, *Her People*, p. 81.
64. Stride, *Memoirs*, p. 12; Crosby Library: Fairhurst, 'Our Zoe', pp. 2–3.
65. WCML: Honeyford, 'Tom Honeyford', p. 5; Miller, 'Wasted life', pp. 4–5; Campion, *Sunlight*, p. 12.
66. Bondfield, *Life's Work*, p. 26; Wheway, *Edna's Story*, pp. 14–15. Oxfordshire HC: Davies, 'Autobiography', pp. 3–4.
67. Chaplin, *My Autobiography*, pp. 66–70.
68. Oxfordshire HC: Crawford, 'Autobiography', p. 12.
69. For a consideration of some of these issues in non-British different contexts, see: James R. Barrett, 'Was the personal political? Reading the autobiography of American communism', *International Review of Social History*, 53 (2008), pp. 395–423; Ryan Hanley, 'Calvinism, proslavery and James Albert Ukawsaw Gronniosaw', *Slavery & Abolition: A Journal of Slave and Post-Slave Studies*, 35/1 (2015), pp. 1–22; Annie Devenish, 'Performing the political self: A study of identity making and self representation in the autobiographies of India's first generation of parliamentary women', *Women's History Review*, 22/2 (2013), pp. 280–94; Igal Halfin, *Terror in my Soul: Communist Autobiographies on Trial* (Cambridge, MA, 2003).
70. Burnett Archive: Balne, 'Autobiography', pp. 1–3.
71. Wakefield Prison Records, Nominal Registers: August–September 1889; September–February 1891.
72. Rawtenstall LSL: Luty, 'My Life has Sparkled', p. 1. Contrast with Luty, *Penniless Globetrotter*.
73. Thompson, *Lark Rise*, pp. 262–3.
74. Thompson, *Country Calendar*, pp. 83, 6. See also: Barbara English, ' "Lark Rise" and Juniper Hill: A Victorian community in literature and in history', *Victorian Studies*, 29/1 (1985), pp. 7–34.
75. Burnett Archive: Downer, 'A Bygone Age'. Rose May's marriage was registered in the period April–June 1909 and her son's birth date was registered in the following three-month period. He was baptised on 15 July 1909 and his birth date was recorded as 6 July 1909 in the 1939 England and Wales Register.
76. The marriage of his mother, Emily Beckett, to William James was registered in the period April–June 1898 and his birth date was recorded as 6 November 1897 in the 1939 England and Wales Register.
77. Bishopsgate Institute Library: Harding 'My Apprenticeship'.
78. *Ibid.*, pp. 48–9.
79. *Ibid.*, p. 49.
80. *Ibid.*, pp. 8, 42.
81. *Ibid.*, p. 49.
82. Harding, *East End Underworld*, pp. 24, 28–9, 69, 65.
83. Martin, *Ups and Downs*. Other stories of serious abuse and neglect are retold in: Bowyer, *Brought Out in Evidence*; Drawbell, *Sun Within Us*; Kate Edwards, *Fenland Chronicle*; May, *Tiger-Woman*; O'Mara, *Liverpool Slummy*; O'Reilly, *Tiger of the Legion*; Stride, *Memoirs*. Burnett Archive: Cain, 'Memories'; Westall, 'Good Old Days'. Salvation Army HC: Jarrett, 'Rebecca Jarrett'.

1. 'I WORKED ALRIGHT, BUT I NEVER GOT PAID FOR MY LABOUR': WOMEN AND WORK

1. Burnett Archive: Chase, 'Memoirs', p. 30.
2. Burnett Archive: Morris, Untitled, p. 4. She is described in the 1911 census, aged fifteen, as a 'house servant'.
3. For this, see also: Jane Whittle, 'A critique of approaches to "domestic work": Women, work and the preindustrial economy', *Past and Present*, 243 (2019), pp. 35–70.
4. Burnett Archive: Purvis, 'Reminiscences', p. 1.

5. Burnett Archive: Hunt, Untitled, p. 1.
6. Burnett Archive: Langley, Untitled, no pag. See also: Chew, *Life and Writings*, pp. 8–9. Burnett Archive: Gold, 'My Life', pp. 12–13; Williams, Untitled, p. 4.
7. Cooke, *Hired Lass*, p. 3.
8. Templeton, *Old Lady*, p. 13.
9. *Ibid.*, p. 14.
10. *Ibid.*, pp. 13–14. See also: Ellen Ross, *Love and Toil: Motherhood in Outcast London, 1870–1914* (New York, 1993), pp. 148–55.
11. Burnett Archive: Chase, 'Memoirs', p. 30.
12. Templeton, *Old Lady*, p. 13.
13. Burnett Archive: Gomm, 'Water under the bridge', p. 59.
14. Cambridgeshire RO: Rose, née Andrews, Untitled, p. 5. See also: Lynn Jamieson, 'Limited resources and limiting conventions: Working-class mothers and daughters in urban Scotland *c.* 1890–1925', in Jane Lewis, ed., *Labour and Love: Women's Experience of Home and Family, 1850–1940* (Oxford, 1986), pp. 49–69.
15. See also: Elizabeth Roberts, *A Woman's Place: An Oral History of Working-Class Women, 1890–1940* (Oxford, 1984), pp. 39–40.
16. Andrews, *Woman's Work*, pp. 9–10; Barnes, *Tough Annie*, pp. 7–8; Payne, 'Derbyshire schooling', p. 170; Pratt, *As If It Were*, p. 25; Walker, *Heart to Heart*, p. 9. Burnett Archive: Barker, 'My life', [pp. 38–9]; Collis, 'From paper blankets', [p. 7]; Cutts, Untitled, p. 22; Frisby, 'Memories', p. 16; Holborow, 'My Village', no pag.; Hughes, Untitled, p. 4; Hunt, Untitled, pp. 5–6, 8; May Jones, Untitled, p. 26; Lea, 'Reflections', p. 7;' Squires, Untitled, pp. 4–5. Bexley LSL: Wasson, 'Memories', p. 16. Also the references in note 17 below.
17. Bellan, *Them Days*, pp. 94–5. Couldn't take up (or keep) scholarships: Heaton, *Tale that is Told*, pp. 24–5; Southwark LHL: Meader, Untitled, [p. 3]. Todd, *Snakes and Ladders*, pp. 89–91. Burnett Archive: Bell, 'Rosa Bell Remembers', pp. 106–7; Wallis, 'Yesterday', p. 16; Williams, Untitled, p. 7; Hannan, 'Happy Highways', p. 36. Manchester CL: Snowden, Untitled, p. 13. Oxfordshire HC: Landymore, 'Autobiography', p. 8.
18. Burnett Archive: May Jones, Untitled, p. 26.
19. Burnett Archive: Collis, 'From paper blankets', [p. 7].
20. Pratt, *As If It Were*, p. 25. See also: Andrews, *Woman's Work*, p. 10; Walker, *Heart to Heart*, p. 9.
21. Heaton, *Tale that is Told*, pp. 24–5. See also: Burnett Archive: Williams, Untitled, p. 7. More generally, see also: Jonathan Rose, *The Intellectual Life of the British Working Classes* (New Haven, 2001), pp. 172–86; Kelly J. Mays, 'Domestic spaces, readerly acts: Reading(,) gender, and class in working-class autobiography', *Nineteenth-Century Contexts*, 30/4 (2008), pp. 343–68; Florence Boos, *Memoirs of Victorian Working-Class Women: The Hard Way Up* (Basingstoke, 2017), pp. 33–61.
22. Burnett Archive: Chase, 'Memoirs', p. 30.
23. Cowper, *Backward Glance*, p. 40.
24. Pearson, *Life in Hull*, p. 65. See also: Templeton, *Old Lady*, p. 14.
25. Burnett Archive: Gomm, 'Water under the bridge', p. 109.
26. *Ibid.*, p. 107.
27. Hoare, née Barter, *Winton Story*, pp. 33–4.
28. Foakes, *Between High Walls*, pp. 72–4. See also: Burnett Archive: Lea, 'Reflections', p. 9.
29. Burnett Archive: Wallis, 'Yesterday', p. 21.
30. Osman, *Love of Ada*, pp. 9–10.
31. Starn, née Clark, *When I was*, pp. 19–20. See also: Burnett Archive: Squires, Untitled, pp. 6–7.
32. Cambridgeshire RO: Rose, née Andrews, Untitled, p. 9.
33. Penn, née Stringer, *Manchester Fourteen Miles*, pp. 42–4.
34. Mitchell, *Hard Way Up*, pp. 57–8.
35. Mellor, née Slack, *Gertie's Story*, pp. 31, 35. See also: Guildford Museum: Chadwick, 'Maude's Memoirs', p. 12. Bristol RL: Dark, Untitled, no pag.

36. For these debates, see: Joyce Burnette, 'Married with children: The family status of female day-labourers at two south-western farms', *Agricultural History Review*, 55 (2007), pp. 75–94; Michael Anderson, 'What can the mid-Victorian censuses tell us about variations in married women's employment?', *Local Population Studies*, 62 (1999), pp. 9–30; John Mckay, 'Married women and work in nineteenth-century Lancashire: The evidence of the 1851 and 1861 census reports', *Local Population Studies*, 61 (1998), pp. 25–37. See also: Jamieson, 'Limited resources', pp. 49–69.
37. Burnett Archive: Gomm, 'Water under the bridge', pp. 92–6.
38. Wright, *As I Remember*, p. 22.
39. Edwards, née Curtis, *Our City*, pp. 50–4.
40. Hoare, née Barter, *Winton Story*, p. 28. See also: Foakes, *Between High Walls*, p. 72. Bexley LSL: Wasson, 'Memories', p. 28.
41. Barnes, *Tough Annie*, p. 9; Farningham, *Working Woman's Life*, pp. 43–4; Rushmer, 'Alice Rushmer', p. 78. Burnett Archive: Barker, 'My life', [p. 39]; McLouglin, Untitled, [pp. 7–9]. Southwark LHL: Meader, Untitled, [p. 3].
42. Barnard, *Life in Charing*, p. 5.
43. Burnett Archive: Bell, 'Rosa Bell Remembers', pp. 145–6.
44. Oxfordshire HC: Landymore, née Churchman, 'Autobiography', p. 6. Also: Burnett Archive: Triggle, Untitled, no pag., letter dated 3 July 1974.
45. Burnett Archive: Gill, née Calvert, 'Ellen Gill's Diary', p. 3.
46. Burnett Archive: Marrin, Untitled, p. 2.
47. Guildford Museum: Chadwick, 'Maude's Memoirs', p. 12.
48. Coleman, née Holder, *Tangled Garden*, pp. 13–15.
49. The laundry workers were: Minnie Ferris; Nellie Hoare; Amy Gomm (Burnett Archive); Lilian Westall (Burnett Archive).
50. Grace Foakes; Kay Garrett (Burnett Archive).
51. Mildred Edwards. A handful of others moved into nursing in their late teens, for example: Molly Keen (Burnett Archive); Molly Murphy; Alice Mullen; Maggie Newbery. Nursemaid: Alice Pidgeon; Dorothy Squires; Vera Ward.
52. Beatrice Stallan.
53. Christian Watt; Mrs Burrows; Lizzie Holborrow (Burnett Archive); Lucy Linnett (Northamptonshire RO). For more on the employment of women in agriculture, see: Nicola Verdon, *Rural Women Workers in Nineteenth-Century England: Gender, Work and Wages* (Woodbridge, 2002); *idem*, 'A diminishing force? Reassessing the employment of female day labourers in English agriculture, *c*. 1790–1850', in Penelope Lane, Neil Raven and K. D. M. Snell, eds, *Women, Work and Wages in England, 1600–1850* (Woodbridge, 2004); Joyce Burnette, 'Labourers at the Oakes: Changes in the demand for female day-laborers at a farm near Sheffield during the agricultural revolution', *Journal of Economic History*, 59 (1999), pp. 41–67.
54. See also: Andrew August, *Poor Women's Lives: Gender, Work, and Poverty in Late-Victorian London* (Madison, 1999); Kathryn Gleadle, *British Women in the Nineteenth Century* (Basingstoke, 2001); Verdon, *Rural Women Workers*; Louise Jackson and Krista Cowman, 'Introduction: Women's work a cultural history', in *idem*, eds, *Women and Work Culture: Britain* c. *1850–1950* (Aldershot, 2005), pp. 1–26; Lydia Murdoch, *Daily Life of Victorian Women* (Westport, 2013), pp. 171–204.
55. Domestic service or allied: [Margaret Jane] (Burnett Archive); Mary Barnet (Norfolk RO); Rosa Bell (Burnett Archive); Joan Bellan; Norah Brain (Burnett Archive); Alice Chadwick (Guildford Museum); Elizabeth Coleman; Isabella Cooke; Catherine Cookson; Gertrude Cottrell; Hannah Cullwick; Mrs Dark (Bristol RL); Kate Edwards; Elizabeth Flint; Minnie Frisby (Burnett Archive); Dorothy Fudge; Rose Gibbs; Daisy Hills; Mrs Hills (Huntingdonshire Archives); Ada Jefferis (Burnett Archive); Margery Johnstone (Bedfordshire LSL); Mrs Nora Jones (Burnett Archive); Mrs Layton; Rosa Lewis; Ethel Ley (Burnett Archive); Annie Lord (Burnett Archive); Grace Martin (Burnett Archive); Ivy Meader (Southwark LHL); Gertie Mellor; Hannah Mitchell; Bronwen Morris (Burnett

Archive); Daisy Noakes; Elizabeth Oakley; Elsie Osman; Annie Passiful (Burnett Archive); Maria Payne; Kay Pearson; Alice Pidgeon (Burnett Archive); Margaret Powell; Edith Pratt; Amy Rose (Cambridgeshire RO); Susan Silvester (Burnett Archive); Emma Smith; Emma Sproson (Wolverhampton Archives); Dorothy Squires (Burnett Archive); Kate Taylor; Laura Walker; Bessie Wallis (Burnett Archive); Pearl Wallis (Surrey HC); May Wasson (Bexley LSL); Edna Wheway; Mrs Wrigley.

56. Hoare, née Barter, *Winton Story*, p. 25.
57. Cullwick, *Diaries*, p. 36. See also: Diane Atkinson, *Love and Dirt: The Marriage of Arthur Munby & Hannah Cullwick* (London, 2003).
58. Norfolk RO: King, 'Barnet's Autobiography', p. 10.
59. Wrigley, 'Plate-Layer's wife', pp. 57–8; Wolverhampton Archives: Sproson, 'My Child Life', p. 4. For domestic service in this period more generally, see: Carolyn Steedman, *Master and Servant: Love and Labour in the English Industrial Age* (Cambridge, 2007).
60. See however, Harvey, 'Youthful memories', pp. 75–6. For more on the changing nature of service, see: Michael Drake, 'Aspects of domestic service in Great Britain and Ireland, 1841–1911', *Family & Community History*, 2 (1999), pp. 119–28; John Benson, 'One man and his woman: Domestic service in Edwardian England', *Labour History Review*, 72 (2007), pp. 203–14; Siân Pooley, 'Domestic servants and their urban employers: A case study of Lancaster, 1880–1914', *Economic History Review*, 62 (2009), pp. 405–29; Lucy Delap, *Knowing Their Place: Domestic Service in Twentieth Century Britain* (Oxford, 2011); Sheila McIsaac Cooper, 'From family member to employee: Aspects of continuity and discontinuity in English domestic service, 1600–2000', in Antoinette Fauve-Chamoux, ed., *Domestic Service and the Formation of European Identity: Understanding the Globalization of Domestic Work* (New York, 2004).
61. Burnett Archive: Passiful, Untitled, no pag.
62. Coleman, née Holder, *Tangled Garden*, pp. 7, 135–6.
63. Burnett Archive: Bell, 'Rosa Bell Remembers', pp. 145–6.
64. Burnett Archive: Westall, née Mara, 'Good Old Days', p. 6.
65. Pratt, *As If It Were*, p. 26.
66. *Ibid.* See also: Wrigley, 'Plate-Layer's wife', p. 58.
67. Harvey, 'Youthful memories', p. 76.
68. See also: Cottrell, *My Life*, p. 23; Coleman, *Tangled Garden*, pp. 8–10. Burnett Archive: Westall, 'Good Old Days', p. 5. More generally, see also: Roberts, *Woman's Place*, pp. 54–9.
69. Burnett Archive: Frisby, née Jones, 'Memories', pp. 17–18.
70. *Ibid.*, p. 7. See also: Burnett Archive, Martin, 'From 1906', pp. 9–10; Squires, Untitled, p. 8.
71. Gibbs, *In Service*, pp. 5–14.
72. Guildford Museum: Chadwick, 'Maude's Memoirs', p. 11.
73. *Ibid.*, p. 16. See also: Wrigley, 'Plate-Layer's wife', pp. 58–60.
74. Burnett Archive: Silvester, 'World that has Gone', p. 13.
75. Coleman, *Tangled Garden*, pp. 9–10. See also: Lucy Delap, ' "Campaigns of Curiosity": Class crossing and role reversal in British domestic service, 1890–1950', *Left History: An Interdisciplinary Journal of Historical Inquiry and Debate*, 12/2 (2007), pp. 33–63, esp. pp. 35–7.
76. Layton, 'Memories', pp. 22–3.
77. Cottrell, *My Life*, p. 26.
78. Wrigley, 'Plate-Layer's wife', pp. 59–60.
79. See also: Kristina Straub, *Domestic Affairs: Intimacy, Eroticism, and Violence between Servants and Masters in Eighteenth-Century Britain* (Baltimore, 2009).
80. Burnett Archive: Westall, née Mara, 'Good Old Days', p. 7.
81. Bellan, *Them Days*, p. 100.
82. Wolverhampton Archives: Sproson, 'My Child Life', p. 5.
83. Lewis, *Queen of Cooks*, p. 6.
84. Watt, *Christian Watt*, pp. 33–4.

85. Gibbs, *In Service*, p. 15.
86. Burnett Archive: Frisby, née Jones, 'Memories', pp. 17–18.
87. See in particular: Maxine Berg, 'What difference did women's work make to the Industrial Revolution?', *History Workshop Journal*, 35 (1993), pp. 22–44; Carol E. Morgan, *Women Workers and Gender Identities, 1835–1913: The Cotton and Metal Industries in England* (London, 2002); Robert Gray, 'Factory legislation and the gendering of jobs in the north of England, 1830–1860', *Gender & History*, 5 (1993), pp. 56–80.
88. Factories and mills: Mary Bertenshaw; Elizabeth Blackburn; Mary Brooksbank; Phyliss Buss (Burnett Archive); Anne Chapman (Manchester CL); Doris Cookson (Burnley LHC); Ruth Cox (Burnett Archive); Kathleen Dayus; Miss Grimshaw (Burnley LHC); Martha Heaton; Anita Hughes (Burnett Archive); Doris Hunt (Burnett Archive); Tabitha John; Ellen Johnston; Annie Kenney; Mary Luty (Rawtenstall LSL); Catherine McLouglin (Burnett Archive); Lucy Marshall; Maggie Newbery; Elsie Oman; Ellen O'Neill; Lily Purvis (Burnett Archive); Jean Rennie; Deborah Smith; Mrs Snowden (Manchester CL); Hilda Snowman (Bolton ALS); Jane Walsh; Vera Ward; Margaret Watson (Burnett Archive); Mrs Yates (Burnett Archive).
89. The topic of historic gender pay gaps has been little studied, but see: Tricia Dawson, 'Out of sight, out of pocket: Women's invisibility in the British printing industry and its effect on the gender pay gap', *Historical Studies in Industrial Relations*, 29/30 (2010), pp. 61–98; Jacob F. Field, 'Domestic service, gender, and wages in rural England, *c.* 1700–1860', *Economic History Review*, 66 (2013), pp. 249–72; Janet Greenlees, 'Equal pay for equal work?: A new look at gender and wages in the Lancashire cotton industry, 1790–1855', in Margaret Walsh, ed., *Working out Gender: Perspectives from Labour History* (Aldershot, 1999), pp. 167–90; Jane Lewis, *Women in England, 1870–1950: Sexual Divisions and Social Change* (Brighton, 1984), pp. 162–73.
90. See, for example: Brooksbank, *No Sae Lang Syne*, pp. 6–7; Heaton, *Tale that is Told*, p. 26; Johnston, 'Autobiography', p. 7; Kenney, *Memories*, p. 14; Luty, *Penniless Globe Trotter*, p. 37; Newbery, *Picking Up Threads*, p. 45; [O'Neill], *Extraordinary Confessions*, p. 4; Smith, *My Revelation*, pp. 16–17; Walsh, *Not Like This*, pp. 20–3. Burnett Archive: Hughes, Untitled, p. 5; Hunt, Untitled, p. 9; Purvis, 'Reminiscences', p. 3; Yates, 'Before My Time', pp. 8–21. Bolton ALS: Snowman, Untitled, p. 22. Burnley LHC: Cookson, 'Autumn leaves', p. 6; Grimshaw, 'Memories', p. 1.
91. Peter Kirby, *Child Labour in Britain, 1750–1870* (Basingstoke, 2003); Per Bolin-Hort, *Work, Family, and the State: Child Labour and the Organization of Production in the British Cotton Industry, 1780–1920* (Lund, 1989); Hilary Challand and Michael Walker, ' "No school, no mill; No mill, no money": The half-time textile worker', in Michael J. Winstanley, ed., *Working Children in Nineteenth-Century Lancashire* (Preston, 1995), pp. 48–71; Michael Lavalette, *A Thing of the Past?: Child Labour in Britain in the Nineteenth and Twentieth Centuries* (Liverpool, 1999); Carolyn Tuttle and Simone A. Wegge, 'Regulating child labor: The European experience', in Avner Greif et al., eds, *Institutions, Innovation, and Industrialization : Essays in Economic History and Development* (Princeton, NJ, 2015), pp. 337–78.
92. Bertenshaw, *Sunrise to Sunset*, p. 109; Blackburn, *In and Out*, p. 31. Burnett Archive: Cox, 'White Knob Row', p. 5; Gill, 'Ellen Gill's Diary', pp. 2–3; Watson, Untitled, pp. 11ff. See also: Rennie, *Every Other Sunday*, pp. 15–17.
93. Burnett Archive: Gill, née Calvert, 'Ellen Gill's Diary', p. 3.
94. Oman, née Dutton, *Salford Stepping Stones*, p. 29.
95. Burnett Archive: Triggle, née Sutton, Untitled, letter dated 26 July 1974.
96. Heaton, *Tale that is Told*, pp. 43, 36. See also: John, *Tabitha*, p. 25; Emma Robertson, ' "It was just a real camaraderie thing": Socialising, socialisation, and shopfloor culture at the Rowntree Factory, York', in Louise Jackson and Krista Cowman, eds, *Women and Work Culture: Britain c. 1850–1950* (Aldershot, 2005), pp. 107–22.
97. Luty, *Penniless Globe Trotter*, p. 39.
98. Burnett Archive: Hughes, Untitled, p. 4.

99. Burnett Archive: Gill, née Calvert, 'Ellen Gill's Diary', p. 3. See also: Luty, *Penniless Globe Trotter*, p. 39. Burnett Archive: Hunt, Untitled, p. 9; Yates, 'Before My Time', pp. 11–21.
100. Brooksbank, *No Sae Lang Syne*, p. 9; Luty, *Penniless Globetrotter*, pp. 39–43; Newbery, *Picking up Threads*, pp. 73–97. Burnett Archive, Hunt, Untitled, pp. 10–11.
101. Bolton ALS: Snowman, née Snape, Untitled, pp. 22–7.
102. *Ibid.*, pp. 27–8.
103. *Ibid.*, p. 28.
104. Burnett Archive: Hughes, Untitled, p. 4; Hunt, Untitled, p. 9.
105. Burnett Archive: Hughes, Untitled, p. 5.
106. Burnett Archive: Hunt, Untitled, pp. 9, 11. Also Burnett Archive: Triggle, Untitled, letter dated 26 July 1974; and Buss, 'Driver became Buss', p. 8.
107. Kenney, *Memories*, p. 16.
108. Heaton, *Tale that is Told*, p. 36.
109. Blackburn, *In and Out*, p. 32.
110. Newbery, *Picking Up Threads*, p. 50. See also: Carol Morgan, 'Women, work and consciousness in the mid-nineteenth-century English cotton industry', *Social History*, 17/1 (1992), pp. 23–41; Selina Todd, *Young Women, Work and Family in England, 1918–1950* (Oxford, 2005); Roberts, *Woman's Place*, pp. 59–62.
111. Smith, *My Revelation*, pp. 18–19.
112. Burnett Archive: Yates, 'Before My Time', pp. 6–7.
113. Burnett Archive: Cox, 'White Knob Row', p. 5.
114. Foley, *Bolton Childhood*, pp. 44–6.
115. On this see also: Southwark LHL: Roberts, 'Ups and Downs', p. 5.
116. Walsh, *Not Like This*, p. 20.
117. Burnett Archive: Hunt, Untitled, pp. 9, 11.
118. Taylor, 'Kate Taylor', p. 308.
119. Workshops and packing: Lottie Barker (Burnett Archive); Bessie Braddock; Leily Broomhill; Ada Chew; Alice Collis (Burnett Archive); Margaret Fish (Southwark LHL); Winifred Griffiths; Annie Howell (Southwark LHL); Sarah Landymore (Oxfordshire HC); Charlotte Meadowcroft (Burnett Archive); Lily Mullins (Southwark LHL); Florrie Roberts (Southwark LHL); Nellie Scott; Ruth Slate; Bertha Thornton (Southwark LHL); Laura Tomlin (Southwark LHL); Mary Triggle (Burnett Archive); Vera Ward; Jane Warren (Southwark LHL); Kathleen Woodward. The dividing line between factories and workshops can be quite fine. I allocated workers to one or other according to information they provided about pay, location and skill.
120. Southwark LHL: Mullins, née Astell, 'Life', no pag.
121. Dressmaking: Elizabeth Andrews; Hilda Barnard; Alice Chase (Burnett Archive); Isabella Davis (Southwark LHL); Mrs R. Downer (Burnett Archive); Eliza Freeston (Northamptonshire RO); Ellen Gill (Burnett Archive); Olive Gold (Burnett Archive); Ethel Goulden (Warrington LSL); Rosina Harrison; Louise Jermy; Charlotte Jordan (Burnett Archive); Amy Langley (Burnett Archive); Mrs P. Marrin (Burnett Archive); Margaret Penn; Edith Williams (Burnett Archive)
122. Shopworkers: Madge Barnetson; Margaret Bondfield; Ada Chew; Agnes Cowper; Mrs G. Davies (Oxfordshire HC); Mrs A. Davis (Southwark LHL); Alice Foley; Beatrice Hamm; Dora Hannan (Burnett Archive); Bessie Harvey; May Jones (Burnett Archive); Rose Kerrigan; Emily Lea (Burnett Archive); Ada Matthews; Dot Starn; Jessie Stephen; Flora Thompson; Margery Todd.
123. Mullen, née Green, *Alice from Tooting*, p. 38.
124. Jermy, née Withers, *Memories*, p. 42. See also: Andrews, *Woman's Work*, p. 15.
125. Burnett Archive: Chase, 'Memoirs', p. 32. See also: Burnett Archive: Langley, Untitled, no pag.
126. Southwark LHL: Davis, née Piper, 'Life and Memories', no pag.

127. Penn, *Manchester Fourteen Miles*, p. 214. See also: Harrison, *Rose*, p. 16 (unpaid for two years). Burnett Archive: Gold, 'My Life', p. 12 (no wages for the first year); Jordan, 'Memories', p. 3 (unpaid for six months).
128. Southwark LHL: Davis, 'Ermine and Persian Lamb', p. 1.
129. Burnett Archive: Chase, 'Memoirs', p. 32.
130. Burnett Archive: Lea, 'Reflections', p. 8.
131. Southwark LHL: Mullins, née Astell, 'Life', no pag.
132. Oxfordshire HC: Landymore, née Churchman, 'Autobiography', p. 8.
133. Burnett Archive: Collis, 'My first strike', [p. 3].
134. Southwark LHL: Howell, Untitled, no pag. (9s rising to 10s week); and Tomlin, Untitled, no pag. (11s). Burnett Archive: Meadowcroft, 'Bygones', p. 9. Braddock, *Braddocks*, p. 13 (5s); Griffiths, *One Woman's Story*, p. 37.
135. Southwark LHL: Davis, née Piper, 'Life and Memories', no pag.
136. Griffiths, *One Woman's Story*, p. 42. See also: Roberts, *Woman's Place*, pp. 64–8.
137. John, *Tabitha*, p. 34.
138. Burnett Archive: Downer, née Hackett, 'A Bygone Age', pp. 2, 31.
139. Andrews, *Woman's Work*, p. 15.
140. Mitchell, *Hard Way Up*, pp. 67–75.
141. Burnett Archive: Chase, 'Memoirs', p. 32.
142. Mullen, née Green, *Alice from Tooting*, p. 101.
143. Burnett Archive: Lea, 'Reflections', p. 13.
144. Jermy, née Withers, *Memories*, pp. 63–4.
145. *Ibid.*, p. 83.
146. Cowper, *Backward Glance*, pp. 71–2.
147. Teachers were: Janet Bathgate; Mary Bentley; Edna Bold; Alice Bond; Nellie Carbis; Maud Clark (Burnett Archive); Daisy Cowper (Burnett Archive); Alice Drummond; Norah Elliot (Burnett Archive); Nora Hampton (Burnett Archive); Adeline Hodges (Burnett Archive); Mary Howitt (Burnett Archive); Faith Osgerby; May Owen (Burnett Archive); Elizabeth Rignall (Burnett Archive); Jessie Sharman (Burnett Archive). (In addition, Kay Pearson became a music teacher and Maggie Newbery a swimming teacher.) The secretaries were: Minnie Bowles; Henrietta Burkin (Burnett Archive); Clare Cameron; Zoe Fairhurst (Crosby Library); Kay Garrett (Burnett Archive); Florence Gibbs (Manchester CL); Amy Gomm (Burnett Archive); Kathleen Hilton-Foord (Burnett Archive); Molly Keen (Burnett Archive); Lucy Miller (WCML); Mrs L. Parker (Burnett Archive); Margaret Penn; Isabel Templeton; Minnie Vandome (Warwick MRC); Bessie Wallis (Burnett Archive); Bertha Wood (Oxfordshire HC).
148. Burnett Archive: Hunt, Untitled, p. 11; and Wallis, 'Yesterday', p. 31.
149. Templeton, *Old Lady*, pp. 14–16. See also: Burnett Archive: Keen, 'Childhood', p. 30 (started on 7/6); WCML: Miller, 'Wasted talent', p. 13.
150. Todd, *Snakes and Ladders*, p. 110. Marjory reasoned her only solution was domestic service: 'I would get food and lodging and a small wage as well.' For girls without homes, this really was their only option.
151. Burnett Archive: Clarke, Untitled, no pag., section entitled 'Another chapter'.
152. Bond, *Life of a Yorkshire Girl*, p. 59.
153. Of the small handful that made it to secondary school, just four progressed to university: Wilkinson, 'Ellen Wilkinson'; Lee, *To-Morrow*; Bryson, *Look Back*; Tibble, *Greenhorn*.
154. Political activism is considered in more detail in chapter nine below. A few managed to make a living in entertainment (*Confessions of a Dancing Girl*; Gracie Fields; Marjorie Graham; Betty May); and a few by writing (Muriel Box; Catherine Cookson, Kathleen Dayus; Kay Garratt; Ethel Mannin; Margaret Powell; Flora Thompson; Anne Tibble; Marjorie Todd; Kathleen Woodward).
155. Barnetson, Untitled in *To Make Ends Meet*, p. 83.
156. Lewis, *Queen of Cooks*, pp. 16ff.
157. O'Mara, *Liverpool Slummy*, p. 30.

2. 'A MAN'S WORK WAS A MAN'S LIFE': MEN AT WORK

1. Stamper, *So Long Ago*, p. 20.
2. Northamptonshire RO: Alexander, 'Village Memories', no pag.
3. Lawson, *Man's Life*, pp. 7, 10–12.
4. *Ibid.*, pp. 46–7.
5. *Confessions of a Dancing Girl*; Gibbs, *In Service*; Lewis, *Queen of Cooks*; Newbery, *Picking Up Threads*; Walker, *Heart to Heart*.
6. The legislation is described in: J. T. Ward, *The Factory Movement, 1830–1855* (London, 1962). See also: Carolyn Tuttle and Simone Wegge, 'Regulating child labor: The European experience', in Avner Greif, Lynne Kiesling and John V. C. Nye, eds, *Publication Details: Institutions, Innovation, and Industrialization; Essays in Economic History and Development* (Princeton, NJ, 2015), pp. 337–78; Robert Gray, *The Factory Question and Industrial England, 1830–1860* (Cambridge, 1996).
7. Benjamin Brierley; George Mitchell; Joseph Sharpe.
8. William Arnold; Richard Cook (Lincoln LSL); Noah Cooke; Edward Davis; George Edwards; *Life of Chimney Boy*; George Marsh (Barnsley ALS); Edward Rymer; Will Thorne; Benjamin Tillett; Joseph H. Wilson; Joseph Wright.
9. Isaac Anderson; James Bent; [Bill H.]; Edward Hughes (Flintshire CRO); Tom Mullins; Charles Shaw; Richard Weaver.
10. Thomas Barclay; Joseph Burgess; Henry Coward; James Dunn; Samuel Fielden; James Hawker; George Mockford; Thomas Oliver; J. Milliot Severn; Sam Shaw; Jesse Shervington (Worcestershire AS); James Turner; William Wright.
11. N. J. Smelser, *Social Paralysis and Social Change: British Working-Class Education in the Nineteenth Century* (Berkeley, CA, 1991).
12. Gosling, *Up and Down Stream*, pp. 14–15. See also: Lipton, *Lipton Logs*, pp. 52–3.
13. Coppard, *It's Me, O Lord!*, pp. 28–9.
14. Shaw, *Guttersnipe*, pp. 26–35.
15. Fletcher, *Life on the Humber*, pp. 19–38, 91, 64.
16. Kelly, *Prodigal of the Seas*, pp. 1–9.
17. Farm work: Isaac Anderson; Charles Bacon (David Wandilson Library); George Baldry; Walter Barrett; Joseph Bell (Bedfordshire ARS); Edward Brand; Percy Brown; Belding Colman (Rotherham LSL); Robert Crane (Cambridgeshire RO Archives); Mr Easter (Huntingdonshire Archives); Samuel Fielden; C. V. Horner (Burnett Archive); Thomas Irving (Carlisle Library); Henry Jones; Harry Lauder; Alexander Murison; John Patterson; Arthur Randall; Henry Smith (Hampshire ALS); Henry Snell; John Taylor; Bonar Thompson; Tom Tremewan; Frank Wensley (Burnett Archive); Frank West; James Whittaker.
18. More than a dozen milk-sellers: William Bell; Ben Bright; John Bull (Burnett Archive); Arthur Collinson (Burnett Archive); Charles Davis (Battersea LSL); Leslie Evans (Rotherham LSL); W. H. Frame; William Gallacher; John Griffin; Jack Hilton; George Hodgkinson; Edward Humphries (Burnett Archive); Septimus O'Reilly; Stanley Rice (Burnett Archive); George Rowles (Burnett Archive); Arthur Seymour (Burnett Archive); Walter Southgate.
19. Newspaper boys: Fred Bower; Al Burnett; Sidney Campion; Walter Chinn (Birmingham Archives); Walter Citrine; Arthur Collinson (Burnett Archive); Michael Conway; Aubrey Darby; James Drawbell; William Elliott (Burnett Archive); Albert Ellis (Blackburn LSL); James Hawke; Richard Heaton; Thomas Jordan; Henry Kelly; Rowland Kenney; Jack Killian (Walsall LHC); Herbert Morrison; Howard Spring; Allan Taylor; Joseph Toole; Henry Turner; Percy Wall (Burnett Archive); Thomas Williams; Joseph H. Wilson; Len Wincott.
20. Errand and shop boys: William Bell; Harry Bellamy (Burnett Archive); Herbert Bennett; John Blake; Fred Boughton; Edward Brown (Burnett Archive); Harold Brown; John Bull (Burnett Archive); Mick Burke; Charlie Chaplin; Walter Citrine; James Clunie; James

Crawford (Oxfordshire HC); David Davies; James Dellow; Jim Garnett (Warwick MRC); Len Fagg (Warwich MRC); Allen Hammond (Burnett Archive); Wal Hannington; Herbert Hodge; John Hodge; William Holt; Arthur Horner; Clayton Joel (Oxfordshire HC); Jack Lanigan (Burnett Archive); Thomas Lipton; Jack Martin; Bob Moody; T. Morgan-Hinwood; J. T. Murphy; Albert Paul; Harry Pollitt; Edwin Purkiss (British Library); George Ratcliffe; John Smith; J. Bernard Taylor; James Thomas; Percy Wall (Burnett Archive); Lewis Watson (Tameside LS). Other part-time workers. W. J. Brown; Huw Edwards; Philip Inman; Albert Jasper; Harry Ward; William Watson.

21. Bennett, *Walworth Boy*, p. 36.
22. Warwick MRC: Garnett, 'My Autobiography', p. 2.
23. Taylor, *Glasgow Slum*, pp. 1–6.
24. Edwin, *I'm Going*, pp. 36–7, 15, 8.
25. Bell, *Pioneering Days*, p. 21; Hodge, *It's Draughty*, pp. 30–1. Compare with: Starn, *When I Was*, pp. 19–20. Burnett Archive: Chase, 'Memoirs', pp. 32, 19–20; Langley, Untitled, no pag.; Lea, 'Reflections', p. 8.
26. Clunie, *Voice of Labour*, p. 18. See also: Griffin, *This is My Life*, p. 4; Horner, *Incorrigible Rebel*, p. 12. Compare with: Coleman, *Tangled Garden*, p. 135; Hoare, *Winton Story*, p. 25. Burnett Archive: Squires, Untitled, p. 8; Westall, 'Good Old Days', p. 4. Southwark LHL: Davis, 'Ermine and Persian Lamb', pp. 1–2; Davis, 'Life and Memories', no pag. WCML: Stephen, 'Submission', p. 14.
27. Warwick MRC: Garnett, 'My Autobiography', p. 2.
28. Citrine, *Men and Work*, p. 26.
29. Campion, *Sunlight*, p. 18.
30. Taylor, *Uphill all the Way*, p. 11.
31. Brady, 'Long trail', p. 321.
32. Burnett Archive: Dorrell, 'Falling Cadence', p. 30. See also: Ash, *Memories*, p. 28; Griffiths, *Pages from Memory*, p. 8; Murray, *Call to Arms*, p. 13; Southgate, *That's the Way it Was*, p. 90. Burnett Archive: Goffin, 'Story of a grey life', chapter six.
33. Burnett Archive: Lanigan, 'Thy Kingdom', p. 9.
34. Tiffy, *Pillar to Post*, pp. 13–16. Burnett Archive: Bellamy, 'Early Memories', pp. 2–3.
35. Brown, *Most Splendid*, p. 21; Gape, *Half a Million Tramps*, p. 1; Mann, *Memoirs*, p. 4; Wardle, 'Mr Wardle'. See also: Jonathan Rose, 'Willingly to school: The working-class response to elementary education in Britain, 1875–1918', *Journal of British Studies*, 32 (1993), pp. 114–38; and *idem*, *The Intellectual Life of the British Working Classes* (New Haven, 2001), pp. 172–86.
36. Burnett Archive: Smith, 'Bosley Cloud', p. 20.
37. Griffiths, *Pages from Memory*, p. 8.
38. Paton, *Proletarian Pilgrimage*, p. 49.
39. Beswick, *Industrialist's Journey*, pp. 20–1.
40. Pugh, 'I helped', p. 78. A few other examples of people who didn't want to stay on at school though their parents did: Hodge, *It's Draughty*, p. 36; Lipton, *Lipton Logs*, p. 53; Ratcliffe, *Sixty Years*, p. 5. Burnett Archive: Dorrell, 'Falling Cadence', pp. 9–10. And others pleased to leave: Brown, *Round the Corner*, pp. 30–1; Clynes, *Memoirs*, p. 32; Howlett, *The Guv'nor*, p. 28; Jones, *Unfinished Journey*, p. 67; Moss, *Live and Learn*, p. 19; *Narrow Waters*, pp. 34–5; Rogers, *Labour, Life and Literature*, p. 32. Burnett Archive: Prevett, 'Memoirs', p. 3.
41. Toole, *Fighting Through Life*, p. 23.
42. Stonelake, *Autobiography*, no pag.
43. *Narrow Waters*, pp. 34, 40. See also: Bowerman, 'Mr Bowerman'. Burnett Archive: Humphries, 'Childhood', p. 22.
44. Humphris, *Garden Glory*, pp. 28–9.
45. Thompson, *Lancashire for Me*, p. 21.
46. Pollitt, *Serving My Time*, pp. 27–8. These sentiments were particularly common amongst mill workers. See also: Clynes, *Memoirs*, pp. 29–30; Hilton, *Caliban Shrieks*, p. 6; Wrigley, *Rakings Up*, p. 30.

47. Burnett Archive: Humphries, 'Childhood', p. 26.
48. Humphris, *Garden Glory*, p. 29.
49. Oxfordshire HC: Crawford, 'Autobiography', pp. 5–6.
50. Hodge, *It's Draughty*, p. 32.
51. Burnett Archive: Lanigan, 'Thy Kingdom', p. 9. For pride at being a wage earner, see also: Murray, *Call to Arms*, p. 15; Steadman, 'Mr Steadman'. Rotherham LSL: James, 'We tread but one path', p. 3.
52. Hannington, *Never On Our Knees*, p. 26.
53. Burnett Archive: Harwood, 'Down Memory Lane', p. 14.
54. Oxfordshire HC: Edwards, 'Autobiography', p. 20.
55. Moss, *Live and Learn*, p. 19.
56. David Wandilson Library: Bacon, 'Life Story', p. 14. See also: Murphy, *New Horizons*, p. 23. Walsall LHC: Brockhurst, Oral History, pp. 7–8.
57. Adsetts, *Ernest Adsetts Story*, p. 24.
58. Kenney, *Westering*, pp. 33–4.
59. Thompson, *Hyde Park Orator*, pp. 64–5. See also: Holt, *Looking Backwards*, p. 16.
60. Burnett Archive: Bellamy, 'Early Memories', p. 3.
61. Coombes, *These Poor Hands*, p. 8.
62. Westwater, *Early Life*, p. 9.
63. Burnett Archive: Ellisdon, 'Starting from Victoria', p. 37.
64. Cardus, *Autobiography*, p. 23.
65. Burnett Archive: Rice, 'Memories', p. 3.
66. Watson, *Machines and Men*, p. 10.
67. Pollitt, *Serving My Time*, p. 32.
68. Brady, 'Long trail', p. 316. See also: Ley, *Story of my Life*, p. 23 (agriculture); Howlett, *The Guv'nor*, pp. 30–1, 34–5 (engineering).
69. Bell, *Pioneering Days*, pp. 21–5, 61–2.
70. Burnett Archive: Roberts, 'Before my Time', pp. 12–13.
71. Collison, *Apostle of Free Labour*, p. 10.
72. *Ibid.*, p. 14. For docks, see also: Jones, *Lively Life*, p. 17; Hunt, *Life Story*, p. 25 (paper mill).
73. Burnett, *Knave of Clubs*, p. 13.
74. Compare with: Burnett Archive: Buss, 'Driver became Buss', p. 8; Griffiths, *One Woman's Story*, p. 37.
75. Barber, *Workhouse to Lord Mayor*, pp. 4–5.
76. Burnett Archive: Evett, 'My Life', p. 3.
77. Oxfordshire HC: Edwards, 'Autobiography', pp. 30, 32. See also: Hawke, *From Private*, p. 32.
78. Wells, *Fenland Boyhood*, pp. 20–4.
79. Southgate, *That's the Way it Was*, p. 91. See also: Horrocks, *Reminiscences*, p. 15.
80. Stewart, *Breaking the Fetters*, pp. 18–21.
81. *Ibid.*, pp. 18–20.
82. Watson, *Machines and Men*, pp. 9–11.
83. Healey, *Life*, pp. 1–45.
84. Pugh, 'I helped', pp. 78–82. See also: Prevett's journey through the ranks of railway work; Burnett Archive: Prevett, 'Memoirs', pp. 3–6.
85. Smillie, *My Life*, pp. 13–23.
86. Northamptonshire RO: Mallard, 'Memories', pp. 3–12. See also: Anderson, *Life History*, p. 8.
87. Hodgkinson, *Sent to Coventry*, p. 15.
88. Burnett Archive: Lanigan, 'Thy Kingdom', pp. 19–30. See also: Howlett, *The Guv'nor*, pp. 30–1, 51.
89. Hunt, *Life Story*, p. 18.
90. Shinwell, *Conflict without Malice*, pp. 31–2.
91. Hemmens, *Such Has Been My Life*, p. 8.
92. Grossek, *First Movement*, p. 17.
93. King, *Green Baize Door*, p. 10.

94. Armstrong, *Pilgrimage*, pp. 23–6.
95. Fraser, *Sixty Years*, pp. 36–7.
96. Norfolk RO: Hemmingway, 'Character', pp. 379–402.
97. Mayett, *Autobiography*, p. 85.
98. Burnett Archive: Wallis, 'Yesterday', p. 16.
99. Bell, *Road to Jericho*, p. 3.
100. Sexton, *James Sexton*, p. 28.
101. Pickles, *Between You and Me*, p. 31.
102. Davies, *In Search of Myself*, p. 24.
103. Patterson, *My Vagabondage*, p. 64.
104. Conway, *Half Timer*, p. 49.
105. Brown, *Most Splendid*, p. 24.
106. Lawson, *Man's Life*, pp. 56–7.
107. Turner, *About Myself*, p. 34.
108. Arnold, *Recollections*, pp. 101–4.
109. *Ibid.*, p. 105.
110. Anna Clark, *The Struggle for the Breeches: Gender and the Making of the British Working Class* (Berkeley, 1995).
111. Emma Griffin, *Liberty's Dawn: A People's History of the Industrial Revolution* (London, 2013).

3. 'REAL DRUDGERY': HOUSE WORK

1. Bedfordshire LSL: Card, 'Working-class lad', p. 1.
2. Burnett Archive: Fowler, 'Look after', p. 18.
3. Burnett Archive: Clarke, Untitled, no pag., section entitled 'Another chapter'. Nehemiah Clarke and Maud Mills married in West Bromwich in the three-month period July–September 1913. In the 1911 census Nehemiah Clarke was living with his parents and working as a plater.
4. 1939 England and Wales Register.
5. See also: Ellen Ross, *Love and Toil: Motherhood in Outcast London, 1870–1914* (New York, 1993), pp. 65–84; Jane Lewis, *Women in England, 1870–1950: Sexual Divisions and Social Change* (Brighton, 1984), pp. 8–14; Elizabeth Roberts, *A Woman's Place: An Oral History of Working-Class Women, 1890–1940* (Oxford, 1984), pp. 125–68.
6. Templeton, *Old Lady*, p. 28.
7. Blake, *Memories*, p. 8. See also: Templeton, *Old Lady*, p. 28.
8. As such, this chapter taps into an older literature on housework that grew out of second-wave feminism in the 1970s and 1980s. See: Ann Oakley, *Women's Work: The Housewife, Past and Present* (New York, 1974); Terry Fee, 'Domestic labor: An analysis of housework and its relation to the production process', *Review of Radical Political Economics*, viii (1976), pp. 1–8; Wally Seccombe, 'The housewife and her labour under capitalism', *New Left Review*, 83 (1974), pp. 3–24; Stevi Jackson, 'Towards a historical sociology of housework: A materialist feminist analysis', *Women's Studies International Forum*, xv (1992). See also: Joanna Bourke, 'Housewifery in working-class England 1860–1914', *Past and Present*, 143/1 (1994), pp. 167–97; Judy Giles, 'Good housekeeping: Professionalising the housewife, 1920–50', in Louise Jackson and Krista Cowman, eds, *Women and Work Culture: Britain c. 1850–1950* (Aldershot, 2005), pp. 70–88; Lynn Abrams and Linda Fleming, 'From scullery to conservatory: Everyday life in the Scottish home', in Lynn Abrams and Callum Brown, eds, *A History of Everyday Life in Twentieth-Century Scotland* (Edinburgh, 2009), pp. 48–75, esp. pp. 59–66; Victoria Kelley, ' "The virtues of a drop of cleansing water": Domestic work and cleanliness in the British working classes, 1880–1914', *Women's History Review*, 18/5 (November 2009), pp. 719–35; Jane Whittle, 'A critique of approaches to "domestic work": Women, work and the preindustrial economy', *Past and Present*, 243 (2019), pp. 35–70.

9. Burnett Archive: Till, 'Early Years', p. 4.
10. Tameside LS: Watson, 'Autobiography', p. 1.
11. Murdie, 'Robert Kerr Murdie', p. 41. See also: Northamptonshire RO: Linnett, 'Village Memories', no pag.
12. Howard, *Winding Lanes*, p. 33.
13. Citrine, *Men and Work*, p. 18; *Narrow Waters*, p. 37. See also: Burnett Archive: Hammond, 'Tomorrow', p. 2. Interior cold-water taps were also sometimes found in Scottish tenements, though not universally. Compare: McGeown, *Heat the Furnace*, pp. 15, 18, with Bell, *Pioneering Days*, p. 18.
14. Broomhill, 'In memory of my mum', no pag. See also: Martin, E., *The Best Street in Rochdale*, p. 11; Paton, *Proletarian Pilgrimage*, p. 1. Burnett Archive: Barker, 'My life', [p. 13]. More generally, see: M. J. Daunton, *House and Home in the Victorian City: Working-Class Housing 1850–1914* (London, 1983), pp. 246–62.
15. Oman, née Dutton, *Salford Stepping Stones*, p. 5.
16. Manchester CL: Mrs Snowden's elder sister, Untitled, p. 14. See also: Blackburn LSL: Ellis, 'As it was', [p. 1] (his family had an outdoor flush toilet in Blackburn in 1904); Walsall LHC: Brockhurst, Oral History, p. 1 (gas laid on and an outdoor flush toilet).
17. Cowen, *Mining Life*, p. 1.
18. Penn, *Manchester Fourteen Miles*, p. 134. See also: Wright, *As I Remember*, p. 9. David Wandilson Library: Bacon, 'Life Story', p. 1. Huntingdonshire Archives: Easter, 'Memories', p. 8.
19. Paul, *Poverty*, p. 20.
20. Bullard, *Camels Must Go*, p. 20. See also: Sturgess, *Northamptonshire Lad*, p. 5 (the first family in the village to install electric lighting). Burnett Archive: Hannan, 'Happy Highways', p. 1 (a cold-water tap and a gas cooker). More generally, see: Daunton, *House and Home*, pp. 237–42.
21. Burnett Archive: Clarke, Untitled, no pag., section entitled 'A new house'.
22. Cottrell, *My Life*, p. 10; Carbis, *Nellie Carbis*, p. 45.
23. Tameside LS: Watson, 'Autobiography' p. 9.
24. Wright, *As I Remember*, p. 3.
25. Martin, *Scotsman's Wanderings*, p. 6. See also: Burnett Archive: Clarke, Untitled, no pag., section entitled 'A new house'.
26. Rotherham LSL: Evans, 'From the glow of the lamp', p. 2. Burnett Archive: Betts, Untitled, p. 4; Powell, 'Forest memories', p. 1.
27. North, *Autobiography*, pp. 1, 21–2.
28. Sexton, *James Sexton*, p. 24. See also: Bellan, *Them Days*, pp. 34–8; Carbis, *Nellie Carbis*, pp. 43–7; Cottrell, *My Life*, pp. 10–11; [Kate Edwards], *Fenland Chronicle*, pp. 214–20; Flint, *Hot Bread*, pp. 17–25; Inman, *No Going Back*, pp. 18–19; Ireson, 'Reminiscences,' p. 72; Steel, *Ditcher's Row*, pp. 8, 55; Whittaker, *Life's Battles*, pp. 5, 14. Bedfordshire LSL: Card, 'Working-class lad', p. 3. Burnett Archive: Seymour, 'Childhood', p. 10.
29. For some examples, see: Horrocks, *Reminiscences*, p. 6; Martin, *Best Street*, pp. 11–12. Burnett Archive: Heslop, 'Tyne to Tone', pp. 16–17; Shotton, 'Personal history', no pag., section entitled 'Childhood'; Tobias, 'Childhood Memories', pp. 5–7. Oxfordshire HC: Edwards, 'Autobiography', p. 14. Walsall LHC: Brockhurst, Oral history transcript, p. 2. For laundry, see also: Victoria Kelley, *Soap and Water: Cleanliness, Dirt and the Working Classes in Victorian and Edwardian Britain* (London, 2010), pp. 79–84; Abrams and Fleming, 'Scullery to conservatory', pp. 61–4.
30. Burnett Archive: Clarke, Untitled, no pag., section entitled 'Another chapter'. Guildford Museum: Chadwick, 'Maude's Memoirs', pp. 3–4.
31. Oxfordshire HC: Rayment, 'Autobiography', p. 5. Burnett Archive: Clarke, Untitled, no pag., section entitled 'Wash day'.
32. Turner, 'Henry Turner', p. 17.
33. Bell, *Pioneering Days*, p. 18; Fraser, *Sixty Years*, p. 18; Jackson, *Solo Trumpet*, p. 39; Pollitt, *Serving My Time*, pp. 18–19; Spring, *Heaven Lies about Us*, pp. 52–6.

34. Armstrong, *Pilgrimage*, p. 32; Carbis, *Nellie Carbis*, p. 23; King, *Green Baize Door*, p. 9.
35. Ratcliffe, *Sixty Years of It*, pp. 5–6.
36. Crittall, *Fifty Years of Work*, p. 10.
37. Burnett Archive: Gregory, Untitled, p. 32. See also: Okey, *Basketful*, p. 15; Turner, *About Myself*, p. 42. See also: Vivienne Richmond, *Clothing the Poor in Nineteenth-Century England* (Cambridge, 2013).
38. Andrews, *Woman's Work*, p. 11.
39. Bond, *Life of a Yorkshire Girl*, p. 14.
40. Bolton ALS: Snowman, Untitled, p. 20.
41. *Ibid.*, p. 17.
42. Carbis, *Nellie Carbis*, p. 28.
43. Walsall LHC: Brockhurst, Oral history transcript, p. 2.
44. Mullen, *Alice from Tooting*, p. 58.
45. Conway, *Half Timer*, p. 32. See also: Burnett Archive: Fowler, 'Look after', p. 18.
46. Ambrose, *Melford Memories*, p. 28.
47. Hemmens, *Such Has Been My Life*, p. 11. See also: Bullock, *Them and Us*, p. 14; [Kate Edwards], *Fenland Chronicle*, p. 216; Okey, *Basketful*, pp. 15–16. Burnett Archive: Morris, 'Autobiography', p. 2.
48. Mullen, née Green, *Alice from Tooting*, p. 60.
49. Carbis, *Nellie Carbis*, p. 21.
50. Oman, née Dutton, *Salford Stepping Stones*, p. 5.
51. Hillyer, *Country Boy*, p. 72. See also: Newbery, *Picking Up Threads*, p. 30; Jaeger, *Annie Jaeger*, p. 17. On domestic pride, see also: Bourke, 'Housewifery'; Kelley, *Soap and Water*, pp. 25–52; Abrams and Fleming, 'Scullery to conservatory', pp. 59–66.
52. Walsh, *Not Like This*, pp. 14–15, 24, 6.
53. Pollitt, *Serving My Time*, pp. 19, 18. The photo of Pollitt and his siblings on p. 112 below exhibits the very high standard of cleanliness that the author describes.
54. Foley, *Bolton Childhood*, p. 94. See also: Jackson, *Solo Trumpet*, p. 39; Spring, *Heaven Lies about Us*, pp. 52–6; Wallis, *Autobiography*, p. 10. Burnett Archive: Meadowcraft, 'Bygones', p. 6; Yates, 'Before My Time', p. 22.
55. See also: Bourke, 'Housewifery', pp. 181–8; Kelley, *Soap and Water*, pp. 103–12, 119–20; Giles, 'Good housekeeping', pp. 70–88.
56. Wrigley, née Jones, 'Plate-Layer's wife', p. 60.
57. *Ibid.*
58. Burnett Archive: Lanigan, 'Thy Kingdom', p. 26.
59. Wrigley, née Jones, 'Plate-Layer's wife', pp. 60–1.
60. Mitchell, *Hard Way Up*, p. 96.
61. Eilidh Garrett et al., *Changing Family Size in England and Wales: Place, Class and Demography, 1891–1911* (Cambridge, 2001); B. Reay, *Microhistories: Demography, Society and Culture in Rural England, 1800–1930* (Cambridge, 1996); Jean Robin, 'Illegitimacy in Colyton, 1851–1881', *Continuity and Change*, II/2 (1987); Peter Laslett, Karla Oosterveen and Richard Smith, eds, *Bastardy and Its Comparative History* (London, 1980), pp. 12–19. See also: Florence Boos, *Memoirs of Victorian Working-Class Women: The Hard Way Up* (Basingstoke, 2017), p. 15.
62. Walsall LHC: Taylor, Oral history transcript, pp. 6–7.
63. Wheway, *Edna's Story*, pp. 14–15. See also: Oxfordshire HC: Davies, 'Autobiography', p. 4.
64. Bondfield, *Life's Work*, pp. 25–6. See also: Bond, *Life of a Yorkshire Girl*, pp. 58–9.
65. McGeown, *Heat the Furnace*, p. 21. See also: John, *Tabitha*, p. 12. Burnett Archive: Marrin, Untitled, p. 1. WCML: Miller, 'Wasted talent', p. 12.
66. David, *Autobiography*, p. 28.
67. Kerr, *Eager Years*, pp. 6–7.
68. Sparkes, *Life and Times*, p. 9.
69. Hodge, *It's Draughty*, p. 34.

70. Bellan, *Them Days*, p. 20; Bertenshaw, *Sunrise to Sunset*, p. 85; Foakes, *Between High Walls*, pp. 15–17; Starn, *When I Was*, p. 3. Burnett Archive: Hampton, 'Memories', p. 29. Walsall LHC: Taylor, Oral history transcript, p. 6.

71. Drawbell, *Sun Within Us*, p. 11.

72. Lee, *To-Morrow*, p. 4. See also: Pearson, *Life in Hull*, p. 83.

73. Bondfield, *Life's Work*, p. 26.

74. Pearson, née O'Loughlin, *Life in Hull*, p. 64.

75. Burnett Archive: Clarke, Untitled, no pag. See also: Box, *Odd Woman Out*, p. 20; Pollitt, *Serving Time*, pp. 18–19. Burnett Archive: Hannan, 'Happy Highways', p. 32.

76. Bertenshaw, née Flood, *Sunrise to Sunset*, pp. 10–12.

77. *Ibid.*, p. 12.

78. Burnett Archive: Harrison, 'Poor and Proud', p. 10.

79. Pearson, *Life in Hull*, p.64.

80. Oxfordshire HC: Gear, 'Autobiography', p. 19.

81. Graham, *Love, Dears!*, p. 13.

82. Fryett, 'Maggy Fryett', p. 73.

83. Ward, *Memories*, p. 16.

84. Walsh, *Not Like This*, pp. 46–7. See also: Ward, *Memories*, pp. 20–1.

85. Cambridgeshire RO: Rose, Untitled, pp. 24–5. See also: Coleman, *Tangled Garden*, p. 156.

86. Oxfordshire HC: Davies, 'Autobiography', p. 3.

87. Fryett, 'Maggy Fryett', p. 73. See also: Lydia Murdoch, *Daily Life of Victorian Women* (Westport, 2013), p. 152; Roberts, *Woman's Place*, pp. 16–19, 93–100; Ross, *Love and Toil*, pp. 97–106 and *idem*, ' "Fierce questions and taunts": Married life in working-class London, 1870–1914', *Feminist Studies*, 8/3 (1982), pp. 575–602, esp. pp. 593–5.

88. Wally Seccombe, 'Starting to stop: Working-class fertility decline in Britain', *Past and Present*, 126 (1990), pp. 1, 4; J. W. Innes, *Class Fertility Trends in England and Wales, 1876–1934* (Princeton, NJ, 1938); J. A. Banks, *Victorian Values: Secularism and the Size of Families* (London, 1981); Garrett et al., *Changing Family Size*, pp. 210–336, 376–400.

89. Bullock, *Them and Us*, p. 16.

90. Oxfordshire HC: Edwards, 'Autobiography', p. 14.

91. Southwark LHL: Howell, Untitled, no pag. See also: Lansbury, *My Life*, p. 19.

92. Fryett, 'Maggy Fryett', p. 74.

93. For a much fuller picture of demographic change over the period, see: Simon Szreter, *Fertility, Class, and Gender in Britain, 1860–1940* (Cambridge, 1996); Garrett et al., *Changing Family Size*; Barry Reay, *Microhistories: Demography, Society and Culture in Rural England, 1800–1930* (Cambridge, 1996).

94. Hayhoe, 'Aida Hayhoe', p. 77.

95. John, *Tabitha*, p. 51.

96. See, for example: Box, *Odd Woman Out*, p. 14; Rowse, *Cornish Childhood*, p. 80; Wells, *Experiment*, p. 40.

97. Osgerby, 'My memoirs', p. 79.

98. Langley, *Always a Layman*, p. 14. See also: WCML: Miller, 'Wasted talent', p. 8.

99. Southgate, *That's the Way it Was*, pp. 21–2. See also: Bowles, 'Minnie Bowles', p. 7 (the strong base on which all else depended); Blake, *Memories*, p. 8; Hillyer, *Country Boy*, p. 71; Jobson, *Creeping Hours*, p. 15 ('pivot around which our family life revolved'); Martin, *Best Street*, p. 12.

100. Cookson, *Our Kate*, p. 37.

101. Wells, *Experiment*, p. 40.

102. Kirkwood, *Life of Revolt*, p. 25. See also: Campion, *Sunlight*, p. 12; *Narrow Waters*, p. 22.

103. Toole, *Fighting Through Life*, p. 7.

104. Kitchen, *Brother to the Ox*, p. 9.

105. Scott, 'Felt hat worker', p. 91.

106. Templeton, *Old Lady*, p.12.

107. Wincott, *Invergordon Mutineer*, p. 3.

108. Mitchell, *Hard Way Up*, p. 100.
109. Layton, 'Memories', pp. 7, 1.
110. Newton, *Years of Change*, p. 12.
111. Oxfordshire HC: Wood, née Whittle, 'Autobiography', pp. 1–3. Also Burnett Archive: Lanigan, 'Thy Kingdom', pp. 26–70.

4. 'THE MEAL-TICKET': FATHERS AND BREADWINNING

1. Burnett Archive: Cowper, 'De Nobis', no pag.
2. *Ibid.*
3. For the elision between fatherhood and providing, see also: Julie-Marie Strange, *Fatherhood and the British Working Class, 1865–1914* (Cambridge, 2015), pp. 21–48; Joanna Bourke, 'Housewifery in working-class England 1860–1914', *Past and Present*, 143/1 (1994), pp. 167–97; Ellen Ross, *Love and Toil: Motherhood in Outcast London, 1870–1914* (New York, 1993).
4. Cotton, *Did it My Way*, p. 16. See also: Macadam, *Macadam Road*, p. 12.
5. Burnett Archive: Robinson, 'I Remember', p. 7.
6. Gosling, *Up and Down Stream*, p. 7.
7. Taylor, *Uphill all the Way*, p. 4.
8. Horner, *Incorrigible Rebel*, p. 12.
9. Clynes, *Memoirs*, pp. 27–8.
10. Armstrong, *Pilgrimage*, p. 26.
11. Harrison, *Rose*, p. 1.
12. Brady, 'Long trail', pp. 316–22.
13. Burnett Archive: Buss, 'Driver became Buss', pp. 2–3. Others with second jobs or working overtime: Dorothy Fudge; Olive Gold (Burnett Archive); Arthur Goodwin (Burnett Archive); Elizabeth Layton; Richard Meads; Gertie Mellor; Wilfrid Middlebrook (Burnett Archive); Bob Moody; Minnie Vandome (Warwick MRC). Others described as working hard: Wilfred Beswick; Mrs Dark (Bristol RL); James Hawker; William Hocking; Anita Hughes (Burnett Archive); May Jones (Burnett Archive); Ivy Meader (Southwark LHL); Susan Silvester (Burnett Archive); Joseph Wilson. Others described as sharing their wages: Mary Coe; Elizabeth Flint; Richard Hillyer; Polly King (Norfolk RO); Isaac Mead; Bernard Taylor; George Tomlinson; Christina Watt.
14. Shepherd, *Memoirs*, pp. 6–7. Others tending allotments: Elizabeth Andrews; Charles Bacon (David Wandilson Library); John Bayes (Northamptonshire RO); Elizabeth Bondfield; Fred Boughton; Edward Brand; Albert Card (Bedfordshire LSL); Arthur Gair; Olive Gold (Burnett Archive); Ethel Goulden (Warrington LSL); Richard Hillyer; Mary Howitt (Burnett Archive); Lucy Linnett (Northamptonshire RO); Edith Pratt; Vera Wright.
15. Turner, 'Henry Turner', pp. 19–20.
16. Bower, *Rolling Stonemason*, p. 23. Others with few hobbies or abstaining from alcohol: Chester Armstrong; 'Autobiography' (British Library); Fred Bower; Alfred Cox; Mr Easter (Huntingdonshire Archives); Lionel Fraser; Ellen Gill (Burnett Archive); Arthur Goffin (Burnett Archive); Fred Greswell; Adeline Hodges (Burnett Archive); Abe Moffat; Ernest Shotton (Burnett Archive); William Sutton (Burnett Archive); Wilfred Wellock.
17. Burnett Archive: Howitt, Untitled, p. 2.
18. Sturgess, *Northamptonshire Lad*, p. 5.
19. Fudge, *Sands of Time*, p. 2. Other fathers investing wages in home, children or holidays: Reader Bullard; Jim Bullock; Maud Clarke (Burnett Archive); G. Henton Davies; Harry Dorrell (Burnett Archive); Ronald Gould; Mark Grossek; Tom Honeyford (WCML); Alfred Ireson; Jennie Lee; Taffy Lewis; Wilfred Pickles; Albert Pugh; George Reakes; Edward Sladen; Beatrice Stallan; Bessie Wallis (Burnett Archive); Charles Welch; Bertha Wood (Oxfordshire HC). See also: Strange, *Fatherhood*, pp. 21–48.

20. Powell, *Below Stairs*, p. 5.

21. Powell, *Mother and I*, p. 113.

22. Powell, *Below Stairs*, p. 3.

23. Powell, *Mother and I*, p. 112. The twenty-four suffering from serious unemployment were: Harry Benjamin; Mary Brooksbank; Thomas Burt; Andrew Carnegie; Alice Collis; Noah Cooke; Kathleen Dayus; Bert Edwards; Minnie Ferris; Frank Goss (Burnett Archive); Joseph Greenwood; Wal Hannington; Richard Heaton; William Holt; Tom Honeyford (WCML); Ada Matthews; Albert Paul; Margaret Powell; Arthur Seymour; Charles Shaw; Deborah Smith; Joseph Stamper; Bertha Thornton (Southwark LHL); James Whittaker. Short-term or occasional unemployment affected many more. Other fathers who suffered from unemployment but who died before the end of the writer's childhood are considered in chapter six.

24. Burnett Archive: Collinson, 'One way only', p. 4. The fourteen fathers suffering from long-term ill health were: Nora Adnams; Mrs Burrows; Anne Chapman (Manchester CL); Arthur Collinson (Burnett Archive); Idris Cox; David Davies; Rose Gibbs; Allan Jobson; Wil Paynter; Amy Rose (Cambridgeshire RO); James Shinn; Tom Tremewen; Mary Triggle; Kathleen Woodward. Short-term health problems afflicted many more. Again, other fathers who were sick but also died before the end of the writer's childhood are considered in chapter six.

25. George R. Boyer, 'Living standards, 1860–1939', in Roderick Floud and Paul Johnson, eds, *The Cambridge Economic History of Modern Britain Volume 2: Economic Maturity, 1860–1939* (Cambridge, 2004), pp. 305–8. See also: Strange, *Fatherhood*, pp. 49–81.

26. Wright, *Life of Joseph Wright*, p. 26.

27. Rennie, *Every Other Sunday*, p. 12.

28. Coward, *Reminiscences*, p. 8.

29. Harding, *East End Underworld*, pp. 24, 28–9, 69, 65. For some other examples of fathers who were irregular workers, see also: Acorn, *One of the Multitude*, p. 5; Bryson, *Look Back*, pp. 20, 36, 43; Cast, *Harry's Story*, pp. 8, 43–4; John, *Tabitha*, p. 31; Murphy, *Molly Murphy*, pp. 5–6; Murphy, *New Horizons*, pp. 17–18; O'Mara, *Liverpool Slummy*, pp. 36–7; *Spike*, pp. 1–2; Severn, *Life Story*, p. 10; Sparkes, *Life and Times*, p. 3.

30. Cast, *Harry's Story*, p. 44.

31. This issue has been largely neglected since Laura Oren, 'Welfare of women in laboring families: England, 1860–1950', *Feminist Studies*, 1 (1973), pp. 107–25, though see also: Ross, *Love and Toil*, pp. 31–6, 76–8; *idem*, ' "Fierce questions and taunts": Married life in working-class London, 1870–1914', *Feminist Studies*, 8/3 (1982), pp. 575–602; Bourke, 'Housewifery', pp. 181–2; Sebastien Rioux, 'Capitalism and the production of uneven bodies: Women, motherhood and food distribution in Britain *c.* 1850–1914', *Transactions of The Institute of British Geographers*, 40/1 (2015), pp. 1–13.

32. Box, *Odd Woman Out*, p. 16.

33. *Ibid.*, p. 16.

34. See, for example: Acorn, *One of the Multitude*, pp. 5–7; Hodge, *It's Draughty*, p. 27; Pritchett, *Cab at the Door*, p. 105; Sparkes, *Life and Times*, p. 3; Thompson, *Country Calendar*, pp. 83, 6; Wincott, *Invergordon Mutineer*, p. 2. Burnett Archive: Goring, Untitled, p. 12. Burnley LHC: Bates, 'Joe's Your Uncle', p. 30. Oxfordshire HC: Davies, 'Autobiography', pp. 2–3. This was also a particular complaint of fathers who worked away from home. See: Benson, *To Struggle*, p. 28; Mullen, *Alice From Tooting*, p. 49. Warwick MRC: Fagg, 'Man of Kent', pp. 4–5, 7.

35. Williams, *George*, p. 16. See also: Ross, *Love and Toil*, pp. 76–8.

36. Broomhill, 'In memory of my mum', no pag.

37. Jasper, *Hoxton Childhood*, pp. 40, 51.

38. Oakley, 'Autobiography', p. 143.

39. Allaway, 'Untitled', pp. 5–6.

40. Taylor, 'Kate Taylor', p. 305. See also: MacKenzie, *Been Places*, p. 12.

41. Foakes, *Between High Walls*, p. 76.
42. Paton, *Proletarian Pilgrimage*, pp. 12–13, quote p. 13. See also: Gould, *Life-Story of a Humanist*, p. 1.
43. Garratt, *Man in the Street*, pp. 4–6.
44. Gawthorpe, *Up Hill to Holloway*, pp. 21–2, 26, 36.
45. Sharpe, *Dark at Seven*, p. 1.
46. Lewis, *Queen of Cooks*, p. 4.
47. Benson, *To Struggle*, pp. 151–2.
48. O'Reilly, *Tiger of the Legion*, p. 26.
49. Pritchett, *Cab at the Door*, p. 67.
50. Bowyer, *Brought Out in Evidence*, pp. 70–1.
51. Gawthorpe, *Up Hill to Holloway*, pp. 21–2. Also: Box, *Odd Woman Out*, p. 22; Edwin, *I'm Going*, p. 37; Paton, *Proletarian Pilgrimage*, pp. 13, 14; Burnett Archive: Jack Jones, Untitled, p. 2.
52. Hoare, *Winton Story*, p. 3. See also: Paton, *Proletarian Pilgrimage*, pp. 19–20.
53. Coppard, *It's Me, O Lord!*, p. 14.
54. Jasper, *Hoxton Childhood*, p. 9.
55. Walsh, *Not Like This*, p. 8.
56. Foley, *Bolton Childhood*, pp. 8–10, 43.
57. Fathers drinking: George Acorn; Thomas Barclay; Lottie Barker (Burnett Archive); William Bell; Herbert Bennett; Ernie Benson; Harry Brearley; Leily Broomhill; J. Barlow Brooks; Mick Burke; Harry Burton; Edward Cain (Burnett Archive); S. T. Causer (Southwark LHL); Alice Chadwick (Guildford Museum); Charlie Chaplin; Walter Citrine; [Andie Clerk]; Alfred Coppard; Henry Coward; Daisy Cowper (Burnett Archive); Idris Cox; Robert Dollar; James Drawbell; James Dunn; Kate Mary Edwards; John Edwin; John Eldred; Len Fagg (Warwick MRC); Alice Foley; William Gallacher; Kay Garrett (Burnett Archive); Marjorie Graham; Walter Greenwood; Leslie Halward; Allen Hammond; Charles Lewis Hansford (Burnett Archive); Arthur Harding; Herbert Hodge; Annie Jaeger; Rebecca Jarrett (Salvation Army HC); A. S. Jasper; Margery Johnstone (Bedfordshire LSL); Jack Jones (Burnett Archive); Jack Lanigan (Burnett Archive); Annie Lord (Burnett Archive); William Luby; Mary Luty; John McGovern; Lucy Marshall; Jack Martin; Betty May; William Miles; Les Moss; J. T. Murphy; *Narrow Waters*; Pat O'Mara; Septimus O'Reilly; May Owen (Burnett Archive); John Paton; Harry Pollitt; J. H. Powell; Raymond Preston; John Edward Reilly; James Rennie; Jean Rennie; Stanley Rice (Burnett Archive); Robert Roberts; Alec Robson; J. Milliot Severn; Joseph Sharpe; Henry Smith (Hampshire ALS); Sam Smith (Burnett Archive); Mrs Snowden; J. H. Sparkes; Emma Sproson (Wolverhampton Archives); Flora Thompson; Wil Thorne; Benjamin Tillett; Margery Todd; James Turner; Jim Uglow; Edgar Wallace; Jane Walsh; Robert Watchorn; Robert Wearmouth; Lilian Westall (Burnett Archive); George Williams; Len Wincott. This note contains all instances of paternal drinking, including some who died or deserted their families. Fathers who died or deserted are considered in chapter five and are not included in any of the calculations in this chapter. Ellen Ross made a similar observation about the impact of male drinking on family budgets in, *Love and Toil*, pp. 42–4, but the topic has been neglected in the more recent literature on fatherhood.
58. For failures of breadwinning see also: Ginger Frost, ' "I am master here": Illegitimacy, masculinity and violence in Victorian England', in Lucy Delap, Ben Griffin and Abigail Wills, eds, *The Politics of Domestic Authority in Britain from 1800* (Basingstoke, 2009), pp. 27–42; Megan Doolittle, 'Fatherhood and family shame: Masculinity, welfare and the workhouse in late nineteenth century England', in *ibid.*, pp. 84–110.
59. Cambridgeshire RO: Rose, Untitled, pp. 1–2.
60. Burnett Archive: Goodwin, Untitled, pp. 2–3, 12.
61. O'Reilly, *Tiger of the Legion*, pp. 26–30.
62. Bertenshaw, *Sunrise to Sunset*, pp. 13, 17, 45, 117–19; Martin, *Ups and Downs*, pp. 45–6, 47, 91–3.

63. This figure has been calculated from the twenty-four fathers suffering chronic unemployment, the fourteen suffering from ill health, seventy-nine who were either working irregularly or not sharing their wages and the eight authors who did not provide detailed information about the causes of their family's poverty.
64. Walsh, *Not Like This*, pp. 19–20.
65. Bennett, *Walworth Boy*, pp. 11–12.
66. Burnett Archive: Cowper, 'De Nobis', no pag.
67. Rogers, *Funny Old Quist*, p. 17. See also: Burnett Archive: Barker, 'My life', no pag. [pp. 4, 15].
68. The potential of autobiography to 'hurt' its reader is discussed in: Carolyn Steedman, 'History and autobiography: Different pasts', in *idem*, ed., *Past Tenses. Essays on Writing, Autobiography and History* (London, 1992), pp. 42–3.
69. Martin, *Ups and Downs*, p. 92. See also: Walsh, *Not Like This*, pp. 8–9. Burnett Archive: Cain, 'Memories', pp. 2–5.
70. Burrows, 'Childhood', p. 113; Tremewan, *Cornish Youth*; pp. 14–15. Cambridgeshire RO: Rose, Untitled, pp. 1, 4.
71. Anderson, *Life History*, pp. 6–7; Edwards, *Crow-Scaring*, pp. 13–15. Cambridgeshire RO: Crane, 'Old Man's Memories'.
72. Bellan, *Them Days*, pp. 60–2; Bedfordshire LSL: Johnstone, 'A real good life', p. 7. Hampshire ALS: Smith, 'Autobiography', p. 7. Oakley, 'Autobiography', pp. 130–1.
73. Thompson, *Lark Rise*, pp. 262–3.
74. [Kate Edwards], *Fenland Chronicle*, pp. 169, 254, 260, 263–4.
75. Bexley LSL: Wasson, 'Memories', pp. 1–3.
76. Miles, *Autobiography*, pp. 1–2.
77. 'A Norfolk labourer's wife', pp. 24–9, 28.
78. [Bill H.], 'Autobiography of a navvy'; Nye, *Small Account*, pp. 11–12.
79. Buckley, *Village Politician*, pp. 2–14; Gibbs, *Life and Experience*, pp. 27–30; Gifford, *Memoir*, p. viii; Jewell, 'Autobiographical memoir', pp. 126–7; Mitchell, 'Autobiography', p. 96. It is also interesting to note that four of these households were not a conventional two-parent family, as in each case the mother had passed away.
80. Burnett Archive: Lovekin, 'Some Notes of my Life', p. 290.
81. McCurrey, *Life of McCurrey*, p. 12.
82. Mitchell, 'Autobiography,' p. 96.
83. Love, *Life of David Love*, pp. 2–3.
84. Lackington, *Memoirs*, pp. 59–60. See also: Bent, *Autobiography*, pp. 5–11; Bezer, 'Autobiography', pp. 159–61; 'Colin', pseud., *Wanderer Brought Home*, pp. 10–12; Davis, *Some Passages*, p. 6; *An Exposition*, pp. 4–6; Gibbs, *Life and Experience*, p. 27; Gifford, *Memoir*, p. viii; Henderson, *Incidents*, pp. 1–37; 'Life of a journeyman baker', 13 & 20 December 1856; 'Life of a journeyman baker', 2 May 1857; McCurrey, *Life of McCurrey*, pp. 11–17; Place, *Autobiography*, pp. 33–40, 92–3, 97–8; Watkins, *Sketch of the Life*, pp. 34–70; Weaver, *Richard Weaver*, p. 30.
85. British Library: 'Autobiography of an Ordinary Man', p. 6.
86. Arnold, *Recollections*, p. 107.
87. Harrison, *Rose*, p. 13.
88. Rowse, *Cornish Childhood*, pp. 12, 21.
89. Coombes, *These Poor Hands*, p. 13.
90. Bond, *Life of a Yorkshire Girl*, p. 21.
91. Northamptonshire RO: Linnett, 'Village Memories', no pag.
92. Mellor, *Gertie's Story*, p. 23. For shoes, see also: Cannell, *Memories*, no pag.
93. Boughton, 'The forest', pp. 310, 314.
94. Snell, *Men, Movements and Myself*, p. 6.
95. Jones, *Old Memories*, p. 24.
96. O'Mara, *Liverpool Slummy*, p. 52.
97. *Ibid.*, p. 36.

98. *Ibid.*, pp. 36–7.
99. Fathers who worked irregularly included: George Acorn (London labourer); Lottie Barker (Nottingham head furnaceman); Elizabeth Bryson (bookkeeper); Harry Cast (Nottingham miner); Henry Coward (London shopkeeper and clerk); Alice Foley (Bolton mill worker); Arthur Harding (London labourer); J. T. Murphy (Sheffield blacksmith striker); Molly Murphy (Nelson factory overlooker); Pat O'Mara (Liverpool docker); Jean Rennie (Greenock ship-worker); Alec Robson (miner); J. Milliot Severn (middle-man for silk firm); Sam Shaw (Birmingham electro-plate polisher); Joseph Wright (quarryman). Some later died or deserted their families and so have not been included in any of the calculations in this chapter.
100. Burnett Archive: Wallis, 'Yesterday', h. Several of the writers noted that money their fathers earned through music brought little benefit to the family. Jack Goring, for instance, observed that his father's music hall singing was 'probably not altogether an advantage to his family'. Burnett Archive: Goring, Untitled, pp. 19–20. See also: Moss, *Live and Learn*, pp. 6–9; Chaplin, *My Autobiography*, pp. 15–16; Coward, *Reminiscences*, p. 6.
101. Jasper, *Hoxton Childhood*, pp. 51–2. See also the discussion in Ross, *Love and Toil*, pp. 75–6.
102. Burnett Archive: Garrett, Untitled, pp. 1–2.
103. Murphy, *New Horizons*, pp. 18–19. See also: Citrine, *Men and Work*, p. 15; Cookson, *Our Kate*, p. 50; Acorn, *One of the Multitude*, p. 5.
104. Benson, *To Struggle*, p. 76; Walsh, *Not Like This*, pp. 19–20; Burnett Archive: Westall, 'Good Old Days', p. 3; Battersea LSL: Davis, 'Reminiscences', no pag.
105. Phillips, *Reminiscences*, pp. 11–15.
106. Arnold, *Recollections*, p. 107. A very similar connection between income and drinking was also described by some of the autobiographers born before 1830. See: [Bill H.], 'Autobiography', pp. 143, 149; 'Colin', pseud., *Wanderer*, p. 12; *An Exposition*, pp. 4–6; [Holkinson], 'Life', chapter vi; 'Life of a journeyman baker', *Commonwealth*, 13 December 1856; 'Life of a journeyman baker', *Commonwealth*, 2 May 1857; McCurrey, *Life of McCurrey*, p. 20; Weaver, *Richard Weaver*', pp. 34–41.
107. Turner, *Hard Up Husband*, p. 2.
108. Harding, *East End Underworld*, pp. 5–8, 10, 26–9.
109. See, more generally: James Nicholls, *The Politics of Alcohol: A History of the Drink Question in England* (Manchester, 2009); John Burnett, *Liquid Pleasures: A Social History of Drinks in Modern Britain* (London, 1999).
110. The full list of references is given in note 57 above. Heavy drinking was also mentioned with reference to mothers, step-parents and other carers, and the autobiographical writers themselves, bringing the total percentage of writers mentioning harmful drinking to nearly 20 per cent.
111. The rural autobiographers with fathers drinking were: Kate Edwards; Marjorie Johnstone (Bedfordshire LSL); William Miles; Henry Smith (Hampshire ALS); Flora Thompson. Also suspected in the case of Charles Hansforth (Burnett Archive). All the remaining writers listed in note 57 were living in urban/industrial areas.
112. Mothers: Frank Bullen; Catherine Cookson; Mrs Layton; William Parrish (Treorchy LSL). Step-parents: Guy Aldred; Mary Bertenshaw; Mrs Davies (Oxfordshire HC); William Freer; John Gray; Henry Holloway; Doris Hunt (Burnett Archive); John Kemp; Louie Stride; Margaret Watson (Burnett Archive). Husbands: Rosa Lewis; Deborah Smith. Self: William Arnold; John Phillips.
113. Jasper, *Hoxton Childhood*, p. 83.
114. Stamper, *So Long Ago*, pp. 42, 106–7.
115. Allaway, 'Untitled, pp. 5–6.
116. Bent, *Autobiography*, p. 9.
117. Southgate, *That's the Way it Was*, p. 49. Oxfordshire HC: Davies, 'Autobiography', p. 2; Citrine, *Men and Work*, p. 15.
118. *An Exposition*, p. 6.
119. Blow, *Autobiography*, p. 9.

120. McCurrey, *Life of McCurrey*, p. 20. See also: 'Jacques', 'Glimpses', 8 November 1856, who took to 'dram-drinking' when his wife died, leaving him with eight dependent children.
121. Miller, *Schools*, pp. 158–9. See also: Horner, *Incorrigible Rebel*, p. 11.

5. 'FATHER DISAPPEARED AND LEFT MOTHER TO BRAVE THE STORM': FAMILY BREAKDOWN

1. Turner, *Hard Up Husband*, p. 1.
2. Chaplin, *My Autobiography*, p. 88.
3. *Ibid.*, pp. 26–40.
4. *Ibid.*, p. 20.
5. *Ibid.*, p. 15.
6. *Ibid.*, pp. 20, 23, 50.
7. On the consequences of fatherlessness, see also: Lydia Murdoch, *Imagined Orphans: Poor Families, Child Welfare, and Contested Citizenship in London* (New Brunswick, NJ, 2006), pp. 67–91.
8. R. Woods, *The Demography of Victorian England and Wales* (Cambridge, 2000), figure 1.1, p. 6; Jane Humphries, *Childhood and Child Labour in the British Industrial Revolution* (Cambridge, 2010), pp. 64–6. For the period post 1891, see: Eilidh Garrett et al., *Changing Family Size in England and Wales: Place, Class and Demography, 1891–1911* (Cambridge, 2001), table 5.3.1, p. 240
9. Compare Jane Humphries's suggestion that for the period 1627–1878, 'well over a third of children appear to have grown up in families that were without the steady support of a male head'. *Idem, Childhood*, pp. 66–7, 101–2. See also: Lynn Jamieson, 'Limited resources and limiting conventions: Working-class mothers and daughters in urban Scotland *c.* 1890–1925', in Jane Lewis, ed., *Labour and Love: Women's Experience of Home and Family, 1850–1940* (Oxford, 1986), pp. 49–69.
10. Burnett Archive: Pidgeon, 'Looking over', p. 4. See also: Barker, 'Life', [p. 20].
11. Burnett Archive: Ley, Untitled, pp. 13–14.
12. Burke, *Ancoats Lad*, p. 3.
13. Foley, *Bolton Childhood*, p. 67.
14. Wincott, *Invergordon Mutineer*, p. 6. See also: Benson, *To Struggle*, pp. 158–62; Bowyer, *Brought Out in Evidence*, p. 122; Burnett Archive: Cowper, 'De Nobis', no pag. A similar sense of relief was shared by Pat O'Mara and Jack Martin when their fathers went to prison (see: Martin, *Ups and Downs*, p. 47; O'Mara, *Liverpool Slummy*, pp. 124–7); and by Jane Walsh and Lilian Westall when their fathers went off to fight in the First World War (see: Walsh, *Not Like This*, pp. 19–20; Burnett Archive: Westall, 'Good Old Days', p. 3).
15. Oxfordshire HC: Relph, 'Autobiography', p. 1.
16. Oxfordshire HC: Joel, 'Autobiography', p. 4.
17. Cowper, *Backward Glance*, p. 67.
18. Williamson, *Dangerous Scot*, p. 17. See also: Fagan, 'Hymie Fagan', p. 24.
19. Edwards, *From the Valley*, p. XX.
20. Royce, *I Stand Nude*, p. 10. Also: Burnett Archive: Bellamy, 'Early Memories', p. 4.
21. They had discovered he had been 'going about with other women', including one 'as his wife, and she has two children by him'.
22. [Slate], *Dear Girl*, pp. 21, 30. Also Ewart Johnson and family in 1891 and 1901 census.
23. Rawtenstall LSL: Luty, 'My Life has Sparkled', pp. 1–2.
24. Aldred, *No Traitor's Gait!*, pp. 10, 23–4, 31.
25. Ley, *Story of my Life*, pp. 14–15.
26. The difficulties faced by men is beyond the scope of this chapter, but for more detail see: Emma Griffin, 'The value of motherhood: Understanding motherhood from maternal absence', *Past and Present* (2020).

27. Burke, *Ancoats Lad*, p. 3.
28. Burnett Archive: Chase, 'Memoirs', p. 11.
29. Burnett Archive: Burkin, 'Memoirs', p. 7.
30. See, however: Essex RO: Castle, 'Diary of John Castle', p. 4.
31. Burnett Archive: Burkin, 'Memoirs', p. 7.
32. Holloway, *Voice from Convict Cell*, pp. 3–4.
33. Burnett Archive: Hunt, Untitled, p. 6.
34. *Ibid.*
35. Thorne, *My Life's Battles*, p. 30. See also: Aldred, *No Traitor's Gait!*, pp. 37–9; Bertenshaw, *Sunrise to Sunset*, pp. 120–7; Coward, *Reminiscences*, p. 8; Murphy, *New Horizons*, pp. 17–19; Paton, *Proletarian Pilgrimage*, pp. 60–6. Oxfordshire HC: Davies, 'Autobiography', p. 2.
36. For changes in the illegitimacy rate, see: A. Hinde, *England's Population: A History since the Domesday Survey* (London, 2003), pp. 219–43; R. Woods, *The Demography of Victorian England and Wales* (Cambridge, 2000), pp. 110–69; Garrett et al., *Changing Family Size*, pp. 210–13; B. Reay, *Microhistories: Demography, Society and Culture in Rural England, 1800–1930* (Cambridge, 1996); J. Schellekens, 'Illegitimate fertility decline in England, 1851–1911', *Journal of Family History*, xx (1995); Jean Robin, 'Illegitimacy in Colyton, 1851–1881', *Continuity and Change*, II/2 (1987).
37. Grandparents: Doris Perry (Walsall LHC); Emma Smith; Henry Stanley; James Henry Thomas; Pearl Wallis (Surrey HC). Aunt: Bonar Thompson. Foster parents: William Milne; Margaret Penn; Edgar Wallace. Institutions: H. J. Harris (Burnett Archive); Edwin Purkiss (British Library). Those who later reunited with their mothers were: Zoe Fairhurst (Crosby Library); Percy Brown.
38. Joseph Ashby; Neville Cardus; Catherine Cookson; Henry Snell; Louie Stride; Allan Taylor.
39. Cardus, *Autobiography*, pp. 15–16.
40. Bowyer, *Brought Out in Evidence*, p. 68.
41. Gawthorpe, *Up Hill to Holloway*, pp. 21–3.
42. Penn, *Manchester Fourteen Miles*, p. 43.
43. *Ibid.*, p. 44.
44. Cookson, *Our Kate*, pp. 41–2, 68–9. For the changing culture of illegitimacy, see also: Emma Griffin, 'Sex, illegitimacy and social change in industrialising Britain', *Social History*, 38/2 (2013), pp. 139–61; Alysa Levene, Samantha Williams and Thomas Nutt, eds, *Illegitimacy in Britain, 1700–1920* (Basingstoke, 2005); Ginger Frost, *Illegitimacy in English Law and Society, 1860–1930* (Manchester, 2016).
45. This was the case with Henry Snell and John Henry Thomas, neither of whom revealed their illegitimacy in their writing.
46. See also: Humphries, *Childhood*, pp. 65–7.
47. Chaplin, *My Autobiography*, pp. 15–16.
48. *Ibid.*, pp. 19, 33.
49. Paternal departures: [Andie Clerk], W. E. Adams; Guy Aldred; Ernie Benson; John Barlow Brooks; John Bull (Burnett Archive); Edward Brown (Burnett Archive); S. T. Causer (Southwark LHL); Charles Chaplin; *Confessions of Dancing Girl*; Aubrey Darby; William Davies; James Drawbell; William Eacott (WCML); Len Fagg (Warwick MRC); John D. Fox; Charles Hansford; Arthur Harding; James Hawke; Herbert Hodge; Rebecca Jarrett; Ellen Johnston; Jack Jones (Burnett Archive); George Lloyd; William Luby; Lucy Luck; Mary Luty; E. Martin; Jack Martin; Betty May; Molly Murphy; *Narrow Waters*; Pat O'Mara; Septimus O'Reilly; John Paton; Kay Pearson; John Reilly; James Rennie; Jean Rennie; James Royce; Alice Rushmer; Edward Allen Rymer; Edmund Stonelake; Allan Taylor; T. Thompson; James Turner; George Wood; Joseph Wright.
50. Aldred, *No Traitor's Gait!*, pp. 9–10. For other early departures, see also: Darby, *View from the Alley*, p. 9; WCML: Eacott, 'Grandad tapes', p. 4; Hawke, *From Private*, p. 13; *Narrow Waters*, pp. 5–6.
51. Burnett Archive: Brown, Untitled, pp. 3–4.
52. James Royce, *I Stand Nude*, pp. 9, 41–7.

53. Norfolk RO: Hemmingway, 'Character', pp. 47–50.
54. Pearson, *Life in Hull*, p. 72.
55. Warwick MRC: Fagg, 'Man of Kent', p. 5. See also: Murphy, *Molly Murphy*, pp. 5–6; Rennie, *Converted Shepherd Boy*, pp. 3–4; Turner, *Hard Up Husband*, p. 1; Wright, *Life of Joseph Wright*, pp. 26–7.
56. Luby, 'William Luby', pp. 89–90.
57. Luck, née Marshall, 'Lucy Luck', p. 354.
58. Drawbell, *Sun Within Us*, pp. 26, 68.
59. Harding, *East End Underworld*, pp. 24, 28–9, 69, 65. See also: O'Mara, *Liverpool Slummy*, pp. 42ff.
60. Mothers who tried to leave but returned, or who could not leave at all: [Kate Edwards], *Fenland Chronicle*, pp. 264–5; Murphy, *Molly Murphy*, p. 6; Pollitt, *Serving My Time*, p. 20. Burnett Archive: Rice, 'Memories', p. 6; Westall, 'Good Old Days', p. 2; Young, 'Harry's Biography', section entitled 'My Mother', p. 1.
61. Drawbell, *Sun Within Us*, p. 72.
62. Bowyer, *Brought Out in Evidence*, p. 93.
63. *Ibid.*, p. 100.
64. Broomhill, 'In memory of my mum', no pag.; Kerr, *Eager Years*, pp. 8–9; Brooks, *Lancashire Bred*, pp. 14, 20–5.
65. Kerr, *Eager Years*, pp. 8–9.
66. Both parents absent: Francis Anthony; Edward Balne (Burnett Archive); Thomas Burke; Joe Davis; John Fox; Albert Hammond; Kathleen Hilton-Foord (Burnett Archive); Edward Humphries (Burnett Archive); Thomas James; Henry Kelly; George Meek; Samuel Nuttall (Flintshire CRO); Lily Purvis (Burnett Archive); Harry Reffold. A small number left their family whilst still young: William Gape; Emma Sproson.
67. Separations from single fathers: Margaret Abbley; 'Autobiography of Scotch convict'; George Barber; Frank Bullen; Walter Freer; John Gibbons; Alfred Lay; Ethel Ley (Burnett Archive); George Lloyd (Burnett Archive); Elsie Oman; John Patterson; J. Milliot Severn; Benjamin Tillett; Jim Uglow.
68. Burnett Archive: Jack Jones, Untitled, p. 3.
69. Warwick MRC: Fagg, 'Man of Kent', p. 14.
70. Paton, *Proletarian Pilgrimage*, pp. 13–16.
71. Rennie, *Converted Shepherd Boy*, pp. 3–4. See also: Martin, *Ups and Downs*, p. 47; Humphries, *Childhood*, pp. 101–2, 136.
72. Paton, *Proletarian Pilgrimage*, pp. 13–16, 60–6, 257–62.
73. Burnett Archive: Hansford, 'Memoirs of a Bricklayer', no pag.
74. Adams, *Memoirs*, p. 36; Rymer, 'Martyrdom of the mine', p. 3.
75. There is, in fact, considerable overlap between the fathers who were bad providers and those who were absent. Poor breadwinning was often a prelude to death or desertion, but for the purposes of this analysis, and to avoid double counting, any father who disappeared from his child's life before they reached the age of sixteen has been classed as dead or absent rather than as a poor provider, even though they may have been both.
76. Jaeger, *Annie Jaeger*, pp. 10–12.
77. Those residing in the country were: Joseph Ashby; Percy Brown; William Milne; Margaret Penn; Henry Snell; Henry Morton Stanley, Bonar Thompson, Pearl Wallis (Surrey HC).
78. Adsetts, *Ernest Adsetts Story*, p. 7; Burke, *Ancoats Lad*, p. 3; Chaplin, *My Autobiography*, p. 16; Coppard, *It's Me, O Lord!*, p. 14; Coward, *Reminiscences*, p. 6; Dunn, *Coal Mine Upwards*, p. 3; Foley, *Bolton Childhood*, p. 67; Greenwood, *There was a Time*; Thorne, *My Life's Battles*, p. 14; Turner, *Hard Up Husband*, pp. 4–5. Burnett Archive: Cowper, 'De Nobis', no pag.; Lanigan, 'Thy Kingdom', pp. 2–3, 10.
79. Bright, *Reminiscences*, p. 3; Edwards, *From the Valley*, p. 7. Oxfordshire HC: Rawlings, 'Autobiography', p. 25. Walsall LHC: Wood, 'Untitled'. Burnett Archive: Holborow, 'My Village', no pag. (cause of death not given). See also: Paynter, *My Generation*, p. 12 (his father had lost the sight in one eye through a mining accident).

80. Burnett Archive: Cowper, 'De Nobis', no pag.; Treorchy LSL: Parrish, 'This is my story', p. 1.
81. Williamson, *Dangerous Scot*, p. 16.
82. Williamson, *Father Joe*, p. 20.
83. Oxfordshire HC: Davies, 'Autobiography', p. 1.
84. Thorne, *My Life's Battles*, p. 30.
85. Wilson, *Memories*, pp. 59–67.
86. Burnett Archive: Fowler, 'Look after', unpaginated introduction. Also: Sparkes, *Life and Times*, p. 11 (flour mill); Burnett Archive: Jordan, née Marr, 'Memories', p. 3 (foundry). Walsall LHC: Killian, 'Autobiography', p. 1 (army). Hull HC: Ammon, 'A Long Road', p. 1 (cutler cause not given).
87. Burnett Archive: Brain, Untitled, pp. 4–5; Hansford, 'Memoirs of a Bricklayer', no pag. Flintshire CRO: Nuttall, 'My recollections'. Patterson, *My Vagabondage*, pp. 29–38; Rushmer, 'Alice Rushmer', p. 78.
88. Rushmer, 'Alice Rushmer', p. 78.
89. Burnett Archive: Brain, Untitled, pp. 31ff. Flintshire CRO: Nuttall, 'My recollections', p. 3.
90. Patterson, *My Vagabondage*, pp. 29–38.
91. For example: Burnett Archive: Balne, 'Autobiography', pp. 1–3; Hilton-Foord, 'Survivor', p. 1; Humphries, 'Childhood', pp. 10–11, 25; Purvis, 'Reminiscences', pp. 1–3. Meek, *George Meek*, pp. 7–8; Reffold, *Pie for Breakfast*, pp. 8–10; Davis, *Breaks Came*, pp. 4–5.
92. For example: Barber, *Workhouse to Lord Mayor*, pp. 2–3; Oman, *Salford Stepping Stones*, pp. 4ff.; *Confessions of a Dancing Girl*, pp. 7–9.
93. Turner, *Hard up Husband*, p. 1.
94. For the pre-1850 period, see: Shipp, *Path of Glory*, p. 1; Keighley Library: Kitson, 'Diary', no pag. Post 1850 see: Pearson, *Life in Hull*, pp. 33, 72–3. Burnett Archive: Lloyd, 'Autobiography', p. 8.
95. Rymer, 'Martyrdom of the mine', p. 3. Warwick MRC: Fagg, 'A Man of Kent'. Stonelake from census.
96. O'Mara, *Liverpool Slummy*, pp. 30ff.
97. Adams, *Memoirs*, p. 35.
98. Drawbell, *Sun Within Us*, p. 24.
99. Rawtenstall LSL: Luty, 'My Life has Sparkled'. His occupation has been derived from the census.
100. Murphy, *Molly Murphy*, pp. 1–6.
101. Wright, *Life of Joseph Wright*, p. 17.
102. Rennie, *Every Other Sunday*, p. 8.
103. *Narrow Waters*, p. 4; John Paton (baker); James Rennie (maltster); James Turner (shopkeeper); Jack Jones (Burnett Archive – dairyman); Sid Causer (Southwark LHL – publican); Lucy Marshall (bricklayer); Charles Chaplin (music hall singer).
104. Illegitimate: James Davis; James Dawson; William Marcroft; William Milne; James Murdoch; Henry Price (Finsbury Library); John Stradley (Greenwich HC).
105. 'Autobiography of a Scotch convict'; James Houston; Joseph Terry (Burnett Archive).
106. Thomas Dunning; John Hemmingway (Norfolk RO); John Kitson (Keighley Library); David Love; John Shipp.
107. Shipp, *Path of Glory*, p. 1.
108. Love, *Life of David Love*, pp. 2–3.
109. 'Autobiography of a Scotch convict'; Thomas Dunning; John Hemmingway (Norfolk RO).
110. Holloway, *Authentic History*, pp. 38–9. For community pressures, both before and during the Industrial Revolution, see: Emma Griffin, *Liberty's Dawn: A People's History of the Industrial Revolution* (London, 2013), pp. 107–63.

6. 'TOIL IN THE FACTORY, TOIL IN THE HOME': WORKING MOTHERS

1. Outlines are given in her son's autobiography (Murphy, *New Horizons*, pp. 17–18) with additional detail obtained from the censuses of 1861, 1881 and 1891.
2. Murphy, *New Horizons*, pp. 17–18.
3. *Ibid.*, pp. 18–20.
4. Turner, 'Henry Turner', p. 17.
5. Interestingly, however, the proportion of male and female writers who indicated that their mother had worked was roughly equal. This is striking as female writers tended to write about their mothers more often and usually provided much more detail about every aspect of their lives, so we might reasonably expect that they would be more likely to mention their mother's employment. Yet despite the generally richer detail that women provided about their mother's life, the rate of maternal employment is the same between both sexes, which suggests that all autobiographers tended to regard their mother's employment as significant and worthy of record. For working mothers, see also: Ellen Ross, *Love and Toil: Motherhood in Outcast London, 1870–1914* (New York, 1993), pp. 45–6; Lara Marks, *Working Wives, Working Mothers: A Comparative Study of Irish and East European Jewish Married Women's Work and Motherhood in East London, 1870–1914* (London, 1990); Joyce Burnette, 'Married with children: The family status of female day-labourers at two south-western farms', *Agricultural History Review*, 55/1 (2007), pp. 75–94.
6. For women's working patterns, see also: Elizabeth Roberts, *A Woman's Place: An Oral History of Working-Class Women, 1890–1940* (Oxford, 1984), p. 206; *idem*, 'Women's strategies, 1890–1941', in Jane Lewis, ed., *Labour and Love: Women's Experience of Home and Family, 1850–1940* (Oxford, 1986), pp. 223–47, esp. table 9.1, p. 227; Lynn Jamieson, 'Limited resources and limiting conventions: Working-class mothers and daughters in urban Scotland *c.* 1890–1925', in Lewis, ed., *Labour and Love*, pp. 49–69; Andrew August, 'How separate a sphere? Poor women and paid work in late-Victorian London', *Journal of Family History*, 19/3 (1994), pp. 285–309; Jane Humphries, 'Women and paid work', in June Purvis, ed., *Women's History: Britain, 1850–1945: An Introduction* (London, 1995), pp. 90–8; Sara Horrell and Jane Humphries, 'Women's labour force participation and the transition to the male-breadwinner family, 1790–1865', *Economic History Review*, 48/1 (1995), pp. 94–5; Michael Anderson, 'What can the mid-Victorian censuses tell us about variations in married women's employment?', in Nigel Goose, ed., *Women's Work in Industrial England: Regional and Local Perspectives* (Hatfield, 2007), pp. 182–208; Edward Higgs and Amanda Wilkinson, 'Women, occupations and work in the Victorian censuses revisited of England and Wales: 1851–1901', *History Workshop Journal*, 81 (2016); Jane Humphries, *Childhood and Child Labour in the British Industrial Revolution* (Cambridge, 2010), pp. 102–16.
7. R. C. O. Matthews, C. H. Feinstein and J. C. Odling-Smee, *British Economic Growth, 1856–1973* (Oxford, 1982); N. F. R. Crafts and Terence Mills, 'Trends in real wages in Britain, 1750–1913', *Explorations in Economic History*, 31/2 (1994), pp. 176–94.
8. Anna Clark, *The Struggle for the Breeches: Gender and the Making of the British Working Class* (Berkeley, 1995). See also: Barbara Taylor, ' "The men are as bad as their masters": Socialism, feminism, and sexual antagonism in the London tailoring trade in the early 1830s', *Feminist Studies*, 5/1 (1979), pp. 7–40; S. O. Rose, 'Gender antagonism and class conflict: Exclusionary strategies of male trade unionists in nineteenth century Britain', *Social History*, 13/2 (1988), pp. 191–208.
9. Griffin, *This is My Life*, p. 6.
10. Southwark LHL: Bustin, 'My two square miles', pp. 59–72. See also: Blatchford, *My Eighty Years*, pp. 2–16, whose widowed mother worked as a singer until his adolescence.
11. Llewelyn, *Sand in the Glass*, pp. 1–20, 106.
12. Burnett Archive: Yates, 'Before My Time', pp. 1–2, 22. See also: Martin, *Best Street*, p. 6; Welch, *Autobiography*, p. 16.

13. Snowden, *Autobiography*, p. 20. See also: Burgess, *A Potential Poet?*, pp. 16, 26; Wilson, *Joseph Wilson*, p. 7.
14. Wrigley, *Rakings Up*, p. 32. See also: Conway, *Half Timer*, p. 6, whose mother worked a three-day week.
15. Burnett Archive: Yates, 'Before My Time', p. 21.
16. Gawthorpe, *Up Hill to Holloway*, pp. 8, 54–5. Compare with: John McKay, 'Married women and work in nineteenth-century Lancashire: The evidence of the 1851 and 1861 census reports', in Goose, ed., *Women's Work in Industrial England*, pp. 164–81.
17. Smith, *My Revelation*, p. 27. See also: Burnett Archive: Smith, 'Bosley Cloud', pp. 3, 22.
18. Brooks, *Lancashire Bred*, p. 13.
19. Burnett Archive: Smith, 'Bosley Cloud', p. 3.
20. Taylor, *Glasgow Slum*, pp. 1–2.
21. Burgess, *A Potential Poet?*, p. 26.
22. *Ibid.*, pp. 26–9.
23. For more on this see: Emma Griffin, 'The value of motherhood: Understanding motherhood from maternal absence', *Past and Present* (2020).
24. Gosling, *Up and Down Stream*, p. 7.
25. Lipton, *Lipton Logs*, pp. 39–41; Haddow, *My Seventy Years*, p. 9; Turner, *Hard Up Husband*, p. 1; Hodge, *Workman's Cottage*, pp. 17–21. For other shops, see also: Wells, *Experiment*, pp. 22ff.; Thomas, *Shop Boy*, pp. 5–9; Davis, *Breaks Came*, pp. 3–4. For other pubs: Williams, *George*, pp. 20–7. Southwark LHL: Causer, Autobiographical Letter, pp. 8, 12.
26. Haddow, *My Seventy Years*, p. 9.
27. Southwark LHL: Mullins, née Astell, 'Life', no pag.
28. Barnes, *Tough Annie*, pp. 7–8.
29. Burnett Archive: Nicholls, née Kerby, 'My Story', no pag., section entitled 'Chapter one'.
30. Burnett Archive: Shotton, 'Personal history', no pag., section entitled 'Childhood'.
31. Hemmens, *Such Has Been My Life*, p. 11.
32. Lee, *To-Morrow*, pp. 5–15; Grundy, *Fifty Years*, p. 5.
33. Grossek, *First Movement*, p. 14 (tailors); Hawker, *Poacher*, p. 1 (tailors); Jaeger, *Annie Jaeger*, pp. 10–15 (hat-repair; the business was subsequently taken over by Annie's mother and aunt whilst her father found work in a hat factory). See also: Fletcher, *A Life on the Humber*, pp. 3, 55–66 (barge).
34. Horner, *Incorrigible Rebel*, p. 11 (grocers); Burnett Archive: Harrison, 'Poor and Proud', pp. 13–15 (tobacco shop). Southwark LHL: Davis, 'Life and Memories', no pag. (sweet shop).
35. Southwark LHL: Fish, née Wheeler, 'Memoirs', pp. 27–34.
36. Coward, *Reminiscences*, p. 8; Grossek, *First Movement*, pp. 16–17. Burnett Archive: Goffin, 'Story of a grey life', no pag., section entitled 'My parents'. Guildford Museum: Chadwick, 'Maude's Memoirs', p. 4.
37. Burnett Archive: Downer, 'A Bygone Age', pp. 16–24.
38. Martin, *Scotsman's Wanderings*, p. 7. Burnett Archive: Chase, 'Memoirs', p. 17.
39. Burke, *Ancoats Lad*, p. 4. See also: Martin, *Best Street*, pp. 5–6. Burnett Archive, Middlebrook, 'Trumpet Voluntary', pp. 50–4.
40. Noakes, *Town Beehive*, p. 14; Ratcliffe, *Sixty Years*, p. 4; Wright, *As I Remember*. Burnett Archive: Yates, 'Before My Time', p. 22.
41. Burnett Archive: Gomm, 'Water under the bridge', p. 89. See also: Jermy, *Memories*, pp. 28–9; Oman, *Salford Stepping Stones*, pp. 14–16.
42. Southwark LHL: Davis, née Piper, 'Life and Memories', no pag.
43. Burnett Archive: Chase, née Moody, 'Memoirs', p. 17.
44. Burnett Archive: Gomm, 'Water under the bridge', p. 95.
45. Southwark LHL: Fish, née Wheeler, 'Memoirs', pp. 27–34. See also: Burke, *Ancoats Lad*, pp. 3–5.
46. Horner, *Incorrigible Rebel*, p. 11.
47. Southwark LHL: Mullins, née Astell, 'Life', no pag.
48. Burnett Archive: Middlebrook, 'Trumpet Voluntary', p. 55 (quote is correct).

49. Burnett Archive: Nicholls, née Kerby, 'My Story', no pag., section entitled 'Chapter one'.
50. Barnes, *Tough Annie*, p. 7; Davis, *Breaks Came*, p. 5; Williams, *George*, p. 27. Burnett Archive: Downer, 'A Bygone Age', pp. 23–4; Goffin, 'Story of a grey life', no pag., section entitled 'My parents'; Pidgeon, 'Looking over', p. 1.
51. Burnett Archive: Gomm, 'Water under the bridge', p. 92.
52. Martin, *Scotsman's Wanderings*, p. 8.
53. Burnett Archive: Middlebrook, 'Trumpet Voluntary', p. 47.
54. Burnett Archive: Chase, née Moody, 'Memoirs', p. 17.
55. Burnett Archive: Harrison, 'Poor and Proud', p. 10.
56. *Ibid.*, p. 13. See also: Wilson, *Joseph Wilson*, pp. 4–5, 7.
57. Southwark LHL: Howell, Untitled, no pag.
58. Burnett Archive: Wallis, 'Yesterday', k. See also: Wilson, *Joseph Wilson*, pp. 4–5, 7.
59. Southwark LHL: Fish, née Wheeler, 'Memoirs', p. 27. See also: Josephine Maltby, ' "The wife's administration of the earnings?" Working-class women and savings in the mid-nineteenth century', *Continuity & Change*, 26/2 (2011), pp. 187–217.
60. On this point, see also: Joanna Bourke, 'Housewifery in working-class England 1860–1914', *Past and Present*, 143/1 (1994), pp. 176–81; Paul Johnson, 'Credit and thrift and the British working class, 1870–1939', in Jay Winter, ed., *The Working Class in Modern British History: Essays in Honour of Henry Pelling* (Cambridge, 1983), p. 148; Humphries, *Childhood*, pp. 116–18; Victoria Kelley, 'Home and work: Housework and paid work in British homes', in Jane Hamlett, ed., *A Cultural History of the Home in the Age of Empire (1800–1920)* (London, forthcoming); Jane Whittle, 'A critique of approaches to "domestic work": Women, work and the preindustrial economy', *Past and Present*, 243 (2019), pp. 35–70.
61. Forty-eight working widows: John Allaway; Charles Ammon (Hull HC); Dorothy Ash; Joseph Bell (Bedfordshire ARS); Robert Blatchford; Mick Burke; Henrietta Burkin (Burnett Archive); Al Burnett; James Clunie; A. E. Coppard; Henry Coward; Mrs Davies (Oxfordshire HC); James Dunn; Wil Jon Edwards; Edward Ezard; Hymie Fagan; Hilda Fowler (Burnett Archive); William Gallacher; Walter Greenwood; Leslie Halward; [Lilian Hind]; Lizzie Holborrow (Burnett Archive); Henry Holloway; Doris Hunt (Burnett Archive); Philip Inman; C. E. Joel (Oxfordshire HC); Jack Jones (Burnett Archive); John Joseph Jones; John Kemp; Jack Killian (Walsall LHC); Ernest King; Fred Kitchen; Jack Lanigan (Burnett Archive); Harry Lauder; John Carter Ley; George Meek; William Parrish (Treorchy LSL); Jacob Primmer; Father Smith; Hilda Snowman (Bolton ALS); Howard Spring; Rose Stokes; John Sykes; Wil Thorne; H. M. Tomlinson; Joe Williamson; John Williamson; Joseph Wilson. The fourteen writers who did not indicate their widowed mother had worked were: Ernest Adsetts; Ben Bright; James Henry Cliff; Daisy Cowper (Burnett Archive); Nora Elliot (Burnett Archive); Jim Garnet (Warwick MRC); Bill Horrocks; James McKenzie; George Marsh (Barnsley ALS); Tom Mullins; Raymond Preston; Joe Rawlings (Oxfordshire HC); John Taylor; Bert Wood (Walsall LHC). I have used fourteen rather than sixteen years as a cut-off age, as by this age most boys were able to earn more than their mothers and thus replace them in the labour market.
62. Stamper, *So Long Ago*, pp. 26–7.
63. Humphreys, *Life of Humphreys*, p. 16. See also: Reffold, *Pie for Breakfast*, p. 8.
64. Gibbs, *In Service*, p. 1.
65. Bertenshaw, *Sunrise to Sunset*, pp. 7, 17, 118. For others in this situation, see: Askham, *Sketches*, p. vi; Cottrell, *My Life*, p. 31; Cox, 'Idris Cox', p. 13; Davies, *In Search of Myself*, pp. 20–2; Jobson, *Creeping Hours*, p. 16; Paynter, *My Generation*, pp. 11–12; Smith, 'Does some one say?', p. 145; Williamson, *Dangerous Scot*, pp. 15–17; Woodward, *Jipping Street*, pp. 10–12. Bolton ALS: Snowman, Untitled, pp. 2–5. Burnett Archive: Collinson, 'One way only', p. 4. Walsall LHC: Killian, 'Autobiography', p. 1.
66. Unreliable breadwinners: George Acorn; Thomas Barclay; Lottie Barker (Burnett Archive); Joan Bellan; Harry Brearley; Mary Brooksbank; Leily Broomhill; Elizabeth Bryson; Harry Cast; J. T. Causer (Southwark LHL); Kate Edwards; John Edwin; Alice Foley; Jack

Goring; F. J. Gould; Marjorie Graham; Walter Greenwood; Allen Hammond (Burnett Archive); Annie Jaeger; Rebecca Jarrett (Salvation Army HC); A. S. Jasper; Tabitha John; Jack Jones; Lucy Miller (WCML); Alice Mullen; J. T. Murphy; Molly Murphy; Harry Pollitt; Robert Roberts; J. Milliot Severn; Sam Shaw; John Henry Smith (Hampshire ALS); Sam Smith (Burnett Archive); Mrs Snowden (Manchester CL); Walter Southgate; J. H. Sparkes; John Birch Thomas; T. Thompson; May Wasson (Bexley LSL); Herbert Wells; George Williams; Len Wincott; Harry Young (Burnett Archive).

67. Thirty-three deserted, working wives: W. E. Adams; Guy Aldred; J. Barlow Brooks; Leily Broomhill; Edward Brown (Burnett Archive); John Bull (Burnett Archive); Charlie Chaplin; Aubrey Darby; William Davies; James Drawbell; Bill Eacott (WCML); Len Fagg (Warwick MRC); Arthur Harding; James Hawke; Herbert Hodge; Rebecca Jarrett (Burnett Archive); Ellen Johnston; Jack Jones; James Kerr; William Luby; Mary Luty; E. Martin; Jack Martin; Betty May; Molly Murphy; Pat O'Mara; John Paton; Kay Pearson; Edward Rymer; Allan Taylor; James Henry Thomas; T. Thompson; James Turner. Of the seven whose mother did not work, one was too ill to work and had to take refuge in the workhouse following her husband's desertion (Lucy Marshall), and the others do not indicate their mother did not work – they provided very little information about their mothers at all (*Narrow Waters*; Septimus O'Reilly; James Rennie; James Royce; Edmund Stonelake; George Wood). Although the mortality rate and rate of paternal absence were roughly equivalent, the number of single mothers with a living husband is lower than the number of widows as the group of those with absent fathers includes those separated from both parents, as explained at pp. 150–1 above. Unmarried mothers were also usually at work.

68. Burnett Archive: Lanigan, 'Thy Kingdom', p. 9. Gallacher, *Revolt*, pp. 1–2, 5.

69. Walker, *Heart to Heart*, p. 10. See also: Clunie, *Voice of Labour*, p. 16; Coward, *Reminiscences*, p. 6; Halward, *Let me Tell You*, pp. 24–7; Primmer, *Life of Primmer*, p. 2; Wilson, *Stormy Voyage*, p. 7.

70. Bolton ALS: Snowman, Untitled, p. 1.

71. See also: Pearson, *Life in Hull*, pp. 56–8.

72. Tomlinson, *Mingled Yarn*, pp. 9–10.

73. Needlework: Coward, *Reminiscences*, p. 8; Gould, *Life-Story*, pp. 2–3; Graham, *Love, Dears!*, p. 17; Jasper, *Hoxton Childhood*, pp. 9, 105. Oxfordshire HC: Joel, 'Autobiography', p. 2. Johnston, 'Autobiography', p. 5; King, *Green Baize Door*, p. 8; Kitchen, *Brother to the Ox*, p. 36; Smith, *Water Under the Bridge*, p. 2; Turner, *Hard Up Husband*, p. 1. Finsbury Library: Price, 'My diary', pp. 4–5. Burnett Archive: Brain, Untitled, pp. 4–5; Goss, 'My Boyhood', [p. 35]; Hunt, Untitled, p. 5; Young, 'Harry's Biography', section entitled 'My Mother', p. 1. Hull HC: Ammon, 'A Long Road', p. 2. See also: Cast, *Harry's Story*, pp. 23, 33 (domestic lace-making).

74. Lodgers: Burgess, *Potential Poet?*, p. 29; Davies, *In Search of Myself*, p. 22; Hawke, *From Private*, pp. 14–15; Hodge, *It's Draughty*, p. 15; Williamson, *Dangerous Scot*, p. 17. Oxfordshire HC: Edwards, 'Autobiography'. Warwick MRC: Fagg, 'Man of Kent'. WCML: Miller, 'Wasted talent', p. 8. Taking in washing: Brearley, *Knotted String*, p. 11; Cookson, *Our Kate*, pp. 108–10; Foley, *Bolton Childhood*, pp. 7, 9; Hannington, *Never On Our Knees*, p. 17; Holloway, *Voice from Convict Cell*, p. 3; Martin, *Ups and Downs*, p. 47; Paynter, *My Generation*, p. 12; Whittaker, *I James*, p. 117; Wincott, *Invergordon Mutineer*, p. 3; Woodard, *Jipping Street*, pp. 10–12. Burnett Archive: Brain, Untitled, pp. 4–5; Lanigan, 'Thy Kingdom', p. 4. Southwark LHL: Thornton, 'Memories', p. 9. Manchester CL: Snowden, Untitled, p. 13.

75. Whittaker, *I James*, p. 117.

76. Martin, *Ups and Downs*, p. 47.

77. Edwards, *From the Valley*, pp. 28–9. See also: Spring, *Heaven Lies about Us*, p. 55; Brearley, *Knotted String*, p. 17.

78. Bolton ALS: Snowman, Untitled, p. 1.

79. Wells, *Experiment*, p. 44. See also: Blatchford, *My Eighty Years*, pp. 2–4; Halward, *Let Me Tell You*, pp. 24–7; Roberts, *Ragged Schooling*, pp. 12, 36–7; Williams, *George*, p. 27. Burnett Archive: Lanigan, 'Thy Kingdom', pp. 4, 9.

80. Married women's pay. See also: Kelley, 'Home and work'.
81. Factories: Brooks, *Lancashire Bred*, p. 13; Brooksbank, *No Sae Lang Syne*, p. 6; Burgess, *Potential Poet?*, pp. 26–9; Luty, *Penniless Globetrotter*, pp. 32–4; Pollitt, *Serving My Time*, p. 17; Taylor, *Glasgow Slum*, p. 1; Wright, *Life of Joseph Wright*, p. 28.
82. Laundries or laundry work outside the home: Coppard, *It's Me, O Lord!*, p. 30; Mullen, *Alice from Tooting*, p. 27; Southgate, *That's the Way it Was*, pp. 50, 65; Sparkes, *Life and Times*, p. 4. Burnett Archive: Hammond, 'Tomorrow', p. 3. Other factories and workshops: Aldred, *No Traitor's Gait!*, pp. 10, 23; Broomhill, 'In memory of my mum', no pag.; Darby, *View from the Alley*, p. 9; May, *Tiger-Woman*, p. 14. Burnett Archive: Jack Jones, Untitled, p. 9.
83. Charring: Benson, *To Struggle*, p. 162; Fagan, 'Hymie Fagan', p. 24; Hodge, *It's Draughty*, p. 30; Jobson, *Creeping Hours*, p. 16; Powell, *Below Stairs*, p. 5; Stride, *Memoirs*, p. 6; Wright, *Life of Joseph Wright*, pp. 27–8. Burnett Archive: Collinson, 'One way only', p. 4. Oxfordshire HC: Davies, 'Autobiography', pp. 2–3; Joel, 'Autobiography', p. 4.
84. Cooking: Cottrell, *My Life*, p. 31. Warwick MRC: Fagg, 'A Man of Kent', pp. 8–9.
85. Inman, *No Going Back*, pp. 14–16.
86. Osman, *Love of Ada*, pp. 20–1.
87. O'Mara, *Liverpool Slummy*, pp. 35–127 *passim*; Oxfordshire HC: Davies, 'Autobiography', pp. 2–3.
88. Martin, *Ups and Downs*, p. 47. See also: Gallacher, *Revolt*, p. 1.
89. Sexton, *James Sexton*, pp. 19–20.
90. [William Edwards], *Fenland Chronicle*, p. 35.
91. Noakes, *Farmer's Boy*, pp. 5 and 9.
92. Oman, *Salford Stepping Stones*, p. 1.
93. Darby, *View from the Alley*, p. 9. See also: Foley, *Bolton Childhood*, p. 9. Oxfordshire HC: Davies, 'Autobiography', p. 3.
94. Left with neighbours: Ash, *Memories*, p. 10; Hawke, *From Private*, p. 1; Humphreys, *Life of Humphreys*, p. 12; Campion, *Sunlight*, pp. 8–9; Finsbury Library: Price, 'My diary', p. 1. See also: Williamson, *Father Joe*, p. 22. Burnett Archive: Yates, 'Before My Time', p. 1 (mothers took in neighbours' children). For childcare, see also: Ross, *Love and Toil*, pp. 133–7; Burnette, 'Married with children', pp. 92–4; Marks, *Working Wives*.
95. Luty, *Penniless Globetrotter*, pp. 32–4. See also: Conway, *Half Timer*, p. 41.
96. Ash, *Memories*, p. 10; Drawbell, *Sun Within Us*, pp. 77–8.
97. Greenwood, *There was a Time*, pp. 54, 59, 79.
98. Ash, *Memories*, p. 10.
99. Hannington, *Never On Our Knees*, p. 17.
100. See for example: Spring, *Heaven Lies about Us*, pp. 54–5. Walsall LHC: Killian, 'Autobiography', pp. 1–2.
101. Coppard, *It's Me, O Lord!*, p. 30.
102. May, *Tiger-Woman*, p. 14.
103. Jasper, *Hoxton Childhood*, p. 59.
104. Mullen, *Alice of Tooting*, p. 18.
105. Burnett Archive: Lanigan, 'Thy Kingdom', p. 9.
106. Humphreys, *Life of Humphreys*, p. 16.
107. Paton, *Proletarian Pilgrimage*, p. 1.
108. Powell, *Below Stairs*, p. 5; Sparkes, *Life and Times*, p. 4.
109. Southwark LHL: Thornton, 'Memories', pp. 8, 9.
110. Davies, *In Search of Myself*, pp. 20–2. See also: Oxfordshire HC: Relph, 'Autobiography', p. 1.
111. Gresswell, *Bright Boots*, p. 20; Mitchell, *Hard Way Up*, p. 39; West, *Struggles*, p. 7; Thompson, *Hyde Park Orator*, pp. 19–20.
112. Heaton, *Tale that is Told*, pp. 13–16; Bondfield, *A Life's Work*, p. 23; Pratt, *As if it Were*, p. 18.

113. Mellor, *Gertie's Story*, pp. 19–21; Rogers, *Funny Old Quist*, pp. 21–2.
114. Brown, *Round the Corner*, p. 20. Burnett Archive: Frisby, 'Memories', p. 16.
115. Markham *Back of Beyond*, pp. 25–9; Rawtenstall LSL: Luty, 'My Life has Sparkled', p. 5.
116. Bond, *Life of a Yorkshire Girl*, pp. 24, 26, 27; Coombes, *These Poor Hands*, p. 12; Holt, *Looking Backwards*, pp. 1–16; Jones, *Old Memories*, p. 24; Lewis, *Life's History*, p. 21; Ley, *Story of my Life*, p. 15; Mellor, *Gertie's Story*, p. 23. Burnett Archive: Frisby, 'Memories', pp. 7, 16. Northamptonshire RO: Bayes, Linnett and Rigby, 'Village Memories', no pag.
117. Bond, *Life of a Yorkshire Girl*, p. 16.
118. Snell, *Men, Movements and Myself*, pp. 3–4.
119. Arnold, *Recollections*, p. 99.
120. Coe, 'Mary Coe', pp. 28–9. See also: Nicola Verdon, *Rural Women Workers in Nineteenth-Century England: Gender, Work and Wages* (Woodbridge, 2002), p. 128; Joyce Burnett, 'Married with children: The family status of female day-labourers at two south-western farms', *Agricultural History Review*, 55/1 (2007), pp. 75–94.
121. Burnett Archive: Silvester, 'World that has Gone', p. 4; *I Walked by Night*, p. 4.
122. Fudge, née Park, *Sands of Time*, p. 12.
123. Bristol RL: Dark, Untitled, no pag.
124. Norfolk RO: Barnet, née King, 'Barnet's autobiography', pp. 2–3.
125. Mellor, *Gertie's Story*, p. 4. See also: Noakes, *Farmer's Boy*, p. 14; Wright, *As I Remember*, p. 2.
126. Stallan, 'Childhood recollection', pp. 146–7.
127. Leicester LSL: Bacon, 'Life Story', p. 3.
128. Ireson, 'Reminiscences', pp. 75–6.
129. Thompson, 'Good old times', pp. 126–8.
130. Barr, *Climbing the Ladder*, p. 16.
131. Humphreys, *Life of Humphreys*, p. 12.
132. Aberdeen LSL: Baxter, 'Memoirs', p. 1. See also: Watt, *Christian Watt*, pp. 11, 22–4.
133. Willson, *Recollections*, p. 19.
134. Morgan-Hinwood, *Memories*, p. 1.
135. Bexley LSL: Wasson, 'Memories', pp. 1–3.
136. Carlisle Library: Irving, 'Farming and Country Life', p. 12.
137. Bondfield, *Family Tapestry*, p. 23. It was an observation often repeated by rural autobiographers. See, for example: Bond, *Life of a Yorkshire Girl*, p. 24; Boughton, 'The forest', pp. 309–10; Moffitt, *Autobiography*, p. 25; Cannell, *Memories*, no pag., section entitled 'Sundays'.
138. Verdon, *Rural Women Workers*; *idem*, 'A diminishing force? Reassessing the employment of female day labourers in English agriculture, *c.* 1790–1850', in P. Lane, N. Raven and K. D. M. Snell, eds, *Women, Work and Wages in England, 1600–1850* (Woodbridge, 2004), pp. 190–211.
139. Bond, *Life of a Yorkshire Girl*, p. 16. Also: Ley, *Story of my Life*, pp. 22–3. See also: Nicola Verdon, 'Hay, hops and harvest: Women's employment in agriculture in nineteenth-century Sussex', in Goose, ed., *Women's Work in Industrial England*; Joyce Burnette, *Gender, Work and Wages in Industrial Revolution Britain* (Cambridge, 2008), pp. 72–135.
140. Pratt, *As if it Were*, p. 23.
141. Norfolk RO: Barnet, 'Tale for Mothers', p. 3; Kitchen, *Brother to Ox*, pp. 19–20.
142. Harrison, *Rose*, pp. 1–2, I.
143. Fudge, née Park, *Sands of Time*, p. 1.
144. Coe, *Mary Coe*, pp. 28–9.
145. Burke, *Ancoats Lad*, p. 5.
146. Murphy, née Morris, *Molly Murphy*, pp. 4–5.
147. *Ibid.*, p. 5.
148. *Ibid.*, p. 5.
149. *Ibid.*, pp. 5–6.

7. 'GOT A LOAF, DAD?': FOOD

1. Shaw, *Guttersnipe*, p. 8.
2. Nye, *Small Account*, p. 11.
3. The last male writers to recall hunger in adulthood are: Bowd, 'The life', p. 298; Gutteridge, 'Autobiography', p. 120; Hammond, *Recollections*, pp. 24–5; Mockford, *Wilderness Journeyings*, pp. 16–20; Spurr, 'Autobiography', pp. 285–6. It is not always clear whether they are referring to the 1830s or 1840s.
4. Oakley, 'Autobiography', pp. 142–3.
5. 1830s: Hillocks, *Life Story*, pp. 22–3; Holkinson, 'Life'. 1840s: Anderson, *Life History*, p. 7; Greenwood, 'Reminiscences', p. 131; Mitchell, 'Autobiography', pp. 105–7; Milne, *Reminiscences*, pp. 112–22. 1850s: Worcestershire AS: Shervington, 'Autobiography', pp. xv–xvi, xix.
6. Luck, 'Lucy Luck', p. 362; Moffitt, *Autobiography*, p. 29.
7. Mullins, 'Tom Mullins', p. 64.
8. O'Mara, *Liverpool Slummy*, p. 43.
9. Sparkes, *Life and Times*, p. 3.
10. Walsh, *Not Like This*, p. 8.
11. Stride, *Memoirs*, pp. 8, 11, 13. See also: Dayus, *Her People*, pp. 16–20; Luby, 'William Luby', p. 93. Burnett Archive: Hilton-Foord, 'Survivor', p. 5.
12. Hunger in childhood and adolescence is discussed below. Those who described hunger in adulthood are: Bathgate, *Aunt Janet's Legacy*, p. 178; Bowd, 'The life', p. 298; Burrows, 'Childhood', p. 113; Gutteridge, *Autobiography*, p. 120; Hammond, *Recollections*, pp. 24–5; Mayett, *Autobiography*, pp. 65–6; Mockford, *Wilderness Journeyings*, pp. 16–18; Oakley, 'Autobiography', pp. 142–3; Jacques, 'Glimpses'; Spurr, 'Autobiography', pp. 285–6; Thom, *Rhymes and Recollections*, pp. 22–3; Thomson, *Autobiography*, p. 201. Bradford CL: Harland, 'Diary', extract no. 8. Cumbria RO: Sankoffsky, 'Diary', p. 2. Essex RO: Castle, 'Diary of John Castle', p. 21. Norfolk RO: Lincoln, 'Memoirs', pp. 37–44. Writers also sometimes indicated that their parents had lacked food, see: Harris, *My Autobiography*, p. 6; Horne, *What the Butler*, p. 12; Langdon, *Life of Langdon*, p. 18. See also: Emma Griffin, 'Diets, hunger and living standards during the British Industrial Revolution', *Past and Present*, 239 (2018), pp. 71–111.
13. Nye, *Small Account*, p. 11.
14. [Bill H.], 'Autobiography', p. 140.
15. Cambridgeshire RO: Crane, 'Old Man's Memories'.
16. Ashdown, *Gleanings*, p. 5. See also: Anderson, *Life History*, p. 6; [Bill H.], 'Autobiography', p. 140; Johnston, *Life and Times*, p. 10; Mayett, *Autobiography*, pp. 65–6; North, *Autobiography*, pp. 23, 31; Watt, *Christian Watt*, p. 25. Cambridgeshire RO: Crane, 'Old Man's Memories'. Norfolk RO: Lincoln, 'Memoirs', pp. 37–44.
17. Barker, *Life*, pp. 30–6; [Butler], *Narrative*, p. 12; Gutteridge, 'Autobiography', pp. 115–26; Hillocks, *Life Story*, pp. 22–3; Jacques, 'Glimpses'; *A Short Account of Weaver*, p. 5. Cumbria RO: Sankoffsky, 'Diary', p. 2. Norfolk RO: Hemmingway, 'Character', pp. 2–9. Norwich Castle Museum: Short, 'Recollections', no pag. For other domestic manufacturers, see also: Deacon, *Memoir*, p. 2. Bradford CL: Harland, 'Diary', extract no. 8. Nottinghamshire Archives, Burdett, 'Memoirs', p. 16.
18. Essex RO: Castle, 'Diary of John Castle', p. 21. Farish, *Autobiography*, pp. 6–7, 34; Greenwood, 'Reminiscences', p. 131; Gutteridge, 'Autobiography', pp. 115–26; Hammond, *Recollections*, pp. 24–5; Thom, *Rhymes and Recollections*, pp. 21–38. Bradford CL: Wood, 'Autobiography', p. 8. Rawtenstall LSL: Heap, 'Life and times', p. 4.
19. Bradford CL: Wood, 'Autobiography', pp. 8–10.
20. George Smith, *Autobiography*, pp. 6–7. Bristol Archives: Bennett, 'Manuscript autobiography', p. 2.
21. Maybee, *Sixty-Eight Years'*, pp. 3, 10–12.

22. Spurr, 'Autobiography', pp. 285–6.
23. Horne, *What the Butler*, p. 12.
24. Cooper, *George Cooper*, [p. 14].
25. For this, see: Oliver, *Autobiography*, p. 12; Bristol Archives: Mitchell, 'Tommy's Book', p. 2.
26. Mockford, *Wilderness Journeyings*, pp. 2–3.
27. North, *Autobiography*, p. 37.
28. For examples of restricted diets, see also: Lipton, *Lipton Logs*, p. 37; Oliver, *Autobiography*, p. 12; Rushton, *Farmer's Boy*, pp. 81–2. Lincoln LSL: Cook, 'Memoirs', p. 5. See also: Griffin, 'Diets, hunger'.
29. Thompson, 'Good old times', p. 126.
30. 'A Norfolk labourer's wife', p. 26.
31. Oakley, 'Autobiography', pp. 142–3.
32. Greenwood, 'Reminiscences', p. 131.
33. Farish, *Autobiography*, p. 9.
34. Hillocks, *Life Story*, p. 13. Also Hammond, *Recollections*, pp. 24–5 (vegetarian).
35. Norfolk RO: Lincoln, 'Memoirs', p. 37.
36. *Ibid.*, pp. 37–44.
37. Barker, *Life*, pp. 61–2.
38. *Ibid.*, p. 62.
39. *Ibid.*, p. 77. For general distress shared also by neighbours, see also: Edwards, *Crow-Scaring*, pp. 13–15; Mayett, *Autobiography*, pp. 65–6. Bedfordshire ARS: Bell, 'The Story', pp. 5–6.
40. Bristol Archives: Bennett, 'Manuscript autobiography', p. 2.
41. Carter, *Memoirs*, pp. 42–3. See also: Roger Wells, *Wretched Faces: Famine in Wartime England, 1798–1801* (Gloucester, 1988); Carolyn Steedman, *Labour's Lost: Domestic Service and the Making of Modern Britain* (Cambridge, 2009), pp. 255–75.
42. Bristol Archives: Mitchell, 'Tommy's Book', p. 2. See also: North, *Autobiography*, p. 23. Worcestershire AS: Shervington, 'Autobiography', p. xvii.
43. Bedfordshire ARS: Bell, 'The Story', pp. 4, 9–10. Dead fathers: Bathgate, *Aunt Janet's Legacy*, p. 178; [Sti(r)rup], 'Autobiography', 22 November 1856. Barnsley ALS: Marsh, 'A Sketch', pp. 1–2. Essex RO: Castle, 'Diary of John Castle', p. 4. Norfolk RO: Lincoln, 'Memoirs', p. 1.
44. Shinn, 'A Sketch', p. 188.
45. Emma Griffin, 'The value of motherhood: Understanding motherhood from maternal absence', *Past and Present* (2020). On single parents, see also: Lydia Murdoch, *Imagined Orphans: Poor Families, Child Welfare, and Contested Citizenship in London* (New Brunswick, NJ, 2006), pp. 77–8. For the divided nature of the working-class home, see: Ellen Ross, *Love and Toil: Motherhood in Outcast London, 1870–1914* (New York, 1993), pp. 69–81; *idem*, ' "Fierce questions and taunts": Married life in working-class London, 1870–1914', *Feminist Studies*, 8/3 (1982), pp. 575–602.
46. See: Buckley, *Village Politician*, p. 11; Hillocks, *Life Story*, pp. 11–12; Jewell, 'Autobiographical memoir', p. 128.
47. Burnett Archive: Terry, 'Recollections', pp. 7–12, quote p. 12.
48. *Ibid.*, p. 9.
49. Heaton, *Sketch*, p. xx.
50. Two dead parents: Munday, 'Early Victorian recollections', pp. 111–14.
51. See also the parallels with institutionalisation in Murdoch, *Imagined Orphans*, pp. 67–91.
52. Absent fathers: Love, *Life of David Love*, pp. 2–3; Rymer, 'Martyrdom of the mine', p. 3; Sanderson, 'Life and Adventures', pp. 7–9; Shipp, *Path of Glory*, p. 1. Norfolk RO: Hemmingway, 'Character', pp. 47–50. Also three with fathers absent since birth: J. Davis, *Passages*, p. 5; Milne, *Reminiscences*, pp. 46–7. Greenwich HC: Stradley, 'Memoirs', [p. 1].
53. Whittaker, *Life's Battles*, p. 15.
54. Hodgson, *Memoir*, p. 7.

55. Allen, *Machine Breaker*, pp. 15–19; Bent, *Autobiography*, pp. 13–14; Bezer, 'Autobiography', pp. 159–63; 'Colin', pseud., *Wanderer Brought Home*, p. 38; E. Davis, *Some Passages*, pp. 5–7; Dunn, *Coal Mine Upwards*, pp. 3–4; *An Exposition*, pp. 4–7; Gibbs, *Life and Experience*, p. 27; Love, *Life of David Love*, pp. 2–4; Mitchell, 'Autobiography', pp. 96–7; Powell, *Life Incidents*, p. 1.

56. Rymer, 'Martyrdom of the mine', p. 3.

57. Mitchell, 'Autobiography', pp. 96–7.

58. *An Exposition*, pp. 7, 19, 21.

59. Turner, *Life of a Chimney Boy*, pp. 13–14, 19.

60. Preston, *Life and Opinions*, p. 18.

61. Gibbs, *Life and Experience*, pp. 25–7; Milne, *Reminiscences*, pp. 46–7.

62. 'A Norfolk labourer's wife', p. 26; Burrows, 'Childhood'; Edwards, *Crow-Scaring*, pp. 13–15; Humphreys, *Life of Humphreys*, p. 15; Luck, 'Lucy Luck', pp. 354–68 *passim*. Bedfordshire ARS: Bell, 'The Story', pp. 6–7. Worcestershire AS: Shervington, 'Autobiography', pp. xvi–xxi.

63. Arnold, *Recollections*, pp. 95–7; Baldry, *Rabbitskin Cap*, pp. 44–7; Harvey, 'Youthful memories', p. 75; Howard, *Winding Lanes*, p. 20.

64. Miles, *Autobiography*, pp. 1, 6.

65. Hampshire ALS: Smith, 'Autobiography', p. 19.

66. R. C. O. Matthews, C. H. Feinstein and J. C. Odling-Smee, *British Economic Growth, 1856–1973* (Oxford, 1982); N. F. R. Crafts and Terence Mills, 'Trends in real wages in Britain, 1750–1913', *Explorations in Economic History*, 31/2 (1994), pp. 176–94; C. H. Feinstein, 'Pessimism perpetuated: Real wages and the standard of living in Britain during and after the Industrial Revolution', *Journal of Economic History*, lviii (1998); Gregory Clark, 'Farm wages and living standards in the industrial revolution: England, 1670–1869', *Economic History Review*, liv (2001), table 9, 496; Gregory Clark, 'The condition of the working class in England 1209–2004', *Journal of Economic History*, lviii (2005), pp. 1307–40, esp. p. 1308, see also table A2, 1325.

67. John Burnett, *Plenty and Want: A Social History of Food in England from 1815 to the Present Day* (London, 1989).

68. Gresswell, *Bright Boots*, p. 48.

69. Burnett Archive: Gold, 'My Life', pp. 10–11.

70. Burnett Archive: Silvester, 'World that has Gone', p. 3.

71. Ambrose, *Melford Memories*, pp. 13–15.

72. Tangible difference to diet: Gair, *Copt Hill*, p. 20; Griffiths, *Pages from Memory*, p. 2; Moffit, *Autobiography*, p. 28; Pugh, 'I helped', pp. 75–7; Sturgess, *Northamptonshire Lad*, p. 5. David Wandilson Library: Bacon, 'Life Story', pp. 1–2. Northamptonshire RO: Bayes, 'A few memories', pp. 2, 7. Surrey HC: Wallis, 'Down Memory Lane', p. 4. See also the references for those who kept cows in note 75 below.

73. Burnett Archive: Silvester, 'World that has Gone', p. 3.

74. Harrison, *Rose*, p. 9.

75. Cows: Boughton, 'The forest', p. 310; Bowen, 'Recollections', p. 35; Brand, *Fenman Remembers*, p. 14; Heaton, *Tale that is Told*, p. 12; Holt, *Looking Backwards*, pp. 2–3, 12; Moffit, *Autobiography*, p. 28; Osgerby, 'My memoirs', p. 78; Phillips, *Reminiscences*, p. 5; Tremewan, *Cornish Youth*, p. 23; Thomas, *Looking Back*, p. 11; Turnbull, *Reminiscences*, p. 14; Wells, *Fenland Boyhood*, p. 5. Burnett Archive: Frisby, 'Memories', pp. 15–16. Flintshire CRO: Hughes, Untitled, p. 14.

76. See, more generally: Nicola Verdon, 'Adaptable and sustainable? Male farm service and the agricultural labour force in midland and southern England, c. 1850–1925', *Economic History Review*, 61/2 (2008), pp. 467–95, esp. pp. 480, 484.

77. Alice Collis (Burnett Archive); Rose Gibbs; George Gregory (Burnett Archive); Richard Heaton; William Holt; Ada Matthews; Margaret Powell; Esther Saggers; Emanuel Shinwell; John Henry Smith; Joseph Stamper; Ben Turner; Percy Wall (Burnett Archive); James Whittaker.

78. George Acorn; Nora Adnams (Burnett Archive); Ernie Benson; William Bowyer; Al Burnett; Charles Chaplin; Henry Coward; *Confessions of a Dancing Girl*; James Drawbell; Vere Garratt; Allen Hammond (Burnett Archive); Arthur Harding; Ted Harrison; Kathleen Hilton-Foord (Burnett Archive); Henry Kelly; Frank Kitz; Amy Langley (Burnett Archive); John Langley; Jack Lanigan (Burnett Archive); George Lloyd (Burnett Archive); William Luby; Jack Martin; Betty May; [A Miner]; Pat O'Mara; Joseph Sharpe; Sam Shaw; Emma Smith; J. H. Sparkes; Frank Steel; Rose Stokes; Edmund Stonelake; Louie Stride; John Birch Thomas; Will Thorne; Benjamin Tillett; Jane Walsh; Margaret Watson (Burnett Archive); Robert Wearmouth; Lilian Westall (Burnett Archive); Joe Williamson; Bert Wood (Walsall LHC).

79. For example: *Confessions of a Dancing Girl*; John Langley; George Lloyd (Burnett Archive); Benjamin Tillett; Margaret Watson (Burnett Archive); Robert Wearmouth.

80. For example: Nora Adnams (Burnett Archive); Arthur Harding; Henry Kelly; Emma Smith; Louie Stride.

81. Sop: Baldry, *Rabbitskin Cap*, p. 34; Meek, *George Meek*, pp. 32–3; Noakes, *Town Beehive*, p. 6. Warwick MRC: Garnett, 'My Autobiography', p. 3. Tameside LS: Watson, 'Autobiography', p. 2.

82. Wrigley, *Rakings Up*, p. 31.

83. Tomlinson, *Coal-miner*, from Library, p. 35; Turner, *About Myself*, p. 21. Burnett Archive: Elliott, 'Octogenarian', p. 4.

84. Rural bacon: Brand, *Fenman Remembers*, pp. 14–15 (eggs, jam and ham); Markham, *Back of Beyond*, p. 30; Thomas, *Shop Boy*, p. 22. Burnett Archive: Gregory, Untitled, p. 32 (jam, bacon and eggs); Howitt, Untitled, p. 1.

85. Rural eggs: Murdie, 'Robert Kerr Murdie', p. 44 (egg for breakfast); Pratt, *As if it Were*, p. 18; Thomas, *Looking Back*, pp. 11, 18; Tibble, *Greenhorn*, p. 43. Burnett Archive: Hodges, 'I Remember', pp. 45–6; Howitt, Untitled, p. 1. Huntingdonshire Archives: Hills, 'Reminiscences', no pag. (one egg a week).

86. Rural no eggs: Burnett Archive: Hughes, Untitled, p. 3; Jones, Autobiographical Letters, p. 5. Huntingdonshire Archives: Easter, 'Memories', p. 4.

87. Rural butter: Gresswell, *Bright Boots*, p. 21 (bacon); Mellor, *Gertie's Story*, pp. 18–19; Thomas, *Looking Back*, p. 14. Burnett Archive: Anderson, 'Vapourings', p. 8; Hampton, 'Memories', p. 29. Flintshire CRO: Hughes, Untitled, p. 14.

88. Brand, *Fenman Remembers*, pp. 14–15. Others who do not eat much butter: Barrett, *Fenman's Story*, p. 2.

89. Burnett archive: Gregory, Untitled, p. 32. See also: Thomas, *Looking Back*, pp. 11, 14, 18.

90. Bellan, *Them Days*, p. 37.

91. Heaton, *Tale that is Told*, p. 15. Rural baking: Armstrong, *Pilgrimage*, p. 32; Boughton, 'The forest', p. 310; Cooke, *Hired Lass*, p. 8; Griffiths, *Pages from Memory*, p. 10; Mellor, *Gertie's Story*, pp. 17–18; Thomas, *Shop Boy*, pp. 22–3. Burnett Archive: Frisby, 'Memories', p. 8.

92. Tameside LS: Watson, 'Autobiography', p. 2.

93. Hillyer, *Country Boy*, p. 25. See also: Arnold, *Recollections*, p. 95; Baldry, *Rabbitskin Cap*, pp. 44–5; Barrett, *Fenman's Story*, p. 2; [Kate Edwards], *Fenland Chronicle*, p. 219; Harvey, 'Youthful memories', p. 75. Bedfordshire LSL: Johnstone, 'A real good life', p. 14.

94. Burton, *Young Man*, p. 45 (kippers, bloaters, bacon).

95. Cameron, *Rustle of Spring*, p. 12. Burnett Archive: Robinson, 'I Remember', p. 7.

96. Gray, *Gin and Bitters*, p. 20 (jam and milk).

97. Burnett Archive: Hannan, 'Happy Highways', p. 6.

98. Burnett Archive: Clarke, Untitled, no pag.

99. Templeton, *Old Lady*, p. 11 (milk, butter, jam). Bedfordshire LSL: Card, 'Working-class lad's view', p. 3 (butter or jam).

100. Burnett Archive: Buss, 'Driver became Buss', p. 3 (bacon).

101. Hoare, *Winton Story*, p. 4 (eggs); Burnett Archive: Lea, 'Reflections', p. 1.

102. Burnett Archive: Hampton, 'Memories', p. 33.

103. Urban cake baking: Bentley, *Born 1896*, p. 5; Burton, *Young Man*, p. 44; Edwards, *Our City*, p. 54; Hoare, *Winton Story*, p. 6; Tomlinson *Coal-miner*, pp. 20–1. Oxfordshire HC: Rayment, 'Autobiography', p. 15, Sladen, 'Autobiography', p. 13. Bedfordshire LSL: Card, 'Working-class lad', p. 3. Southwark LHL: Davis, 'Caraway Seeds', p. 2. Burnett Archive: Shotton, 'Personal history', no pag.

104. Bennett, *Walworth Boy*, p. 22; Foley, *Bolton Childhood*, p. 8; Gibbs, *In Service*, p. 2; Garratt, *Man in the Street*, p. 12; Hodge, *It's Draughty*, p. 14; Pearson, *Life in Hull*, p. 28; Powell, *Below Stairs*, p. 9; Taylor, *Glasgow Slum*, p. 3; Wearmouth, *Pages*, pp. 7–8; Williamson, *Father Joe*, p. 39. Battersea LSL: Davis, 'Reminiscences', no pag. Burnett Archive: Elliott, 'Octogenarian', p. 4; Westall, 'Good Old Days', p. 3.

105. Urban bread baking: Burnett Archive: Hughes, Untitled, p. 3; Wallis, 'Yesterday', c.

106. Bond, *Life of a Yorkshire Girl*, p. 23. See also: Brand, *Fenman Remembers*, p. 14; Crittall, *Fifty Years of Work*, p. 10.

107. Taylor, *Uphill all the Way*, pp. 3–4. For the rural diet, see also: Northamptonshire RO: Bayes, 'A few memories', pp. 2, 7.

108. Urban meat stews: Blake, *Memories*, p. 10; Humphreys, *Life of Humphreys*, p. 15. Battersea LSL: Davis, 'Reminiscences', no pag. Burnett Archive: Seymour, 'Childhood', p. 10; Westall, 'Good Old Days', p. 3. Wright, *Life of Joseph Wright*, pp. 21–2.

109. Urban meat: Harding, *East End Underworld*, pp. 27–8 (sheep's head and tripe); Newbery, *Picking up Threads*, p. 34 (sheep's head); Pearson, *Life in Hull*, p. 28 (cowheel and tripe); Foakes, *Between High Walls*, p. 14; Bennett, *Walworth Boy*, p. 12 (tripe). Rotherham LSL: Evans, 'From the glow of the lamp', p. 2 (oxtail and rabbit coat).

110. Warwick MRC: Garnett, 'My Autobiography', pp. 2–3; Fagg, 'Man of Kent', p. 9.

111. Garratt, *Man in Street*, pp. 12–13.

112. Southgate, *That's the Way it Was*, pp. 48–9. See also: *Narrow Waters*, p. 22; Cast, *Harry's Story*, pp. 24–5; Hoare, *Winton Story*, p. 5; Hodge, *It's Draughty*, pp. 13–14; Noakes, *Farmer's Boy*, p. 16; Pearson, *Life in Hull*, p. 28; Powell, *Below Stairs*, pp. 8–9; Rennie, *Every Other Sunday*, p. 8; Taylor, *Glasgow Slum*, p. 3.

113. Heaton, *Salford*, p. 1.

114. Oxfordshire HC: Rayment, 'Autobiography', p. 15. See also: Bellan, *Them Days*, p. 34; Ezard, *Battersea Boy*, pp. 24–7; Mellor, *Gertie's Story*, p. 17; Murdie, 'Robert Kerr Murdie', p. 44. Burnett Archive: Harwood, 'Down Memory Lane', p. 4.

115. Foakes, *Between High Walls*, p. 15.

116. Meek, *George Meek*, pp. 32–3. See also: Hawke, *From Private*, pp. 15–16; Sexton, *James Sexton*, p. 20; Steel, *Ditcher's Row*, pp. 55–6.

117. Chaplin, *My Autobiography*, p. 50.

118. Carbis, *Nellie Carbis*, p. 45.

119. Burnett Archive: Robinson, 'I Remember', p. 9.

120. Northamptonshire RO: Bayes, 'A few memories', p. 11.

121. Oxfordshire HC: Rayment, 'Autobiography', p. 15.

122. Markham, *Back of Beyond*, p. 30.

123. Burton, *Young Man*, p. 44. See also: Cast, *Harry's Story*, p. 23.

124. Warwick MRC: Minnie Vandome, Untitled, p. 11.

125. Oman, *Salford Stepping Stones*, p. 11; Templeton, *Old Lady*, p. 11. Burnett Archive: Hannan, 'Happy Highways', p. 6. Walsall LHC: Brockhurst, Oral History, p. 2.

126. Edwards, *Our City*, pp. 52–3.

127. *Ibid.*, p. 53. See also: Starn, *When I Was*, p. 1. Burnett Archive: Wallis, 'Yesterday', c; Yates, 'Before My Time', p. 5.

128. Burton, *Young Man*, p. 44.

129. Noakes, *Farmer's Boy*, p. 16; Heaton, *Salford*, p. 3.

130. Pearson, *Life in Hull*, pp. 30–1; Bertenshaw, *Sunrise to Sunset*, p. 36.

131. Benson, *To Struggle*, p. 37. See also: Dayus, *Her People*, p. 10; Burton, *Young Man*, p. 45. Burnley LHC: Bates, 'Joe's Your Uncle', p. 71.

132. Burnett Archive: Hughes, Untitled, p. 3. See also: Hoare, *Winton Story*, p. 5; Foley, *Bolton Childhood*, p. 8.
133. Noakes, *Town Beehive* p. 9.
134. *Ibid.*, p. 9. Also Starn, *When I Was*, p. 6; Martin, *Best Street*, p. 10.
135. Stallan, 'Childhood recollection', p. 149.
136. Boughton, 'The forest', p. 310.
137. Home, pseud. of Bush, *Autumn Fields*, p. 8.
138. Gresswell, *Bright Boots*, p. 29. See also: Bond, *Life of a Yorkshire Girl*, p. 41.
139. Warrington LSL: Goulden, 'When we were young', p. 6. See also: Harrison, *Rose*, p. 12. Burnett Archive: Clarke, Untitled, no pag.
140. Ottespoor, 'Gladys Ottespoor', p. 36.
141. Home, pseud. of Bush, *Winter Harvest*, p. 50.
142. Todd, *Snakes and Ladders*, p. 102.
143. Home, pseud. of Bush, *Winter Harvest*, p. 50.
144. Carbis, *Nellie Carbis*, p. 39. See, also: Bennett, *Walworth Boy*, p. 22. Burnett Archive: Westall, 'Good Old Days', p. 3. Guildford Museum: Chadwick, 'Maude's Memoirs', pp. 7–8. Walsall LHC: Brockhurst, Oral History, p. 2.
145. Burnett Archive: Hughes, Untitled, p. 3; Middlebrook, 'Trumpet Voluntary', pp. 51–2. See also: Cookson, *Our Kate*, p. 62.
146. Roberts, *Classic Slum*, p. 117.
147. Cowper, *Backward Glance*, p. 16.
148. Burnett Archive: Ellisdon, 'Starting from Victoria', p. 3.
149. Guildford Museum: Chadwick, Maude's Memoirs', p. 8.
150. Home, pseud. of Bush, *Autumn Fields*, p. 143; *idem*, *Winter Harvest*, p. 50.
151. Garratt, *Man in the Street*, p. 13. Mothers eating the children's meal: Hillyer, *Country Boy*, pp. 47–8.
152. Burnett Archive: Harrison, née Twist, 'Poor and Proud', p. 14.
153. Crittall, *Fifty Years of Work*, p. 10.
154. Burnett Archive: Harrison, née Twist, 'Poor and Proud', p. 14.
155. Crittall, *Fifty Years of Work*, p. 10. See also: Ross, *Love and Toil*, pp. 585–6.
156. Foley, *Bolton Childhood*, p. 8.
157. Oxfordshire HC: Edwards, 'Autobiography', p. 5.
158. Brady, 'Long trail', p. 319 (Dad's chop was also 2p, p. 318).
159. Harding, *East End Underworld*, pp. 5–8, 10, 26–9.
160. See, for example, Ash, *Memories*, esp. p. 22; Blake, *Memories*, p. 10; Chaplin, *Autobiography*, pp. 50, 63; Cotton, *Did it My Way*, p. 21; Jasper, *Hoxton Childhood*, pp. 17, 42–3; Matthews, *Recollections*, p. 6; Okey, *Basketful*, p. 34; Shinwell, *Conflict without Malice*, p. 19. Burnett Archive: Owen, Autobiographical Letter, p. 2; Young, 'Harry's Biography', pp. 3–4. Southwark LHL: Causer, Autobiographical Letter, pp. 3–6; Fish, 'Memoirs', pp. 17–18.
161. Hawke, *From Private*, p. 18.
162. Flint, *Hot Bread*, pp. 20, 24. See also: Royce, *I Stand Nude*, p. 19.
163. Pritchett, *Cab at the Door*, p. 61.
164. Southgate, *That's the Way it Was*, p. 50. See also: Burke, *Wind and Rain*, p. 32.
165. Martin, *Scotsman's Wanderings*, p. 5; Oman, *Salford Stepping Stones*, p. 11; Stamper, *So Long Ago*, pp. 72–3. Burnett Archive: Averil Thomas; Wallis, 'Yesterday', c.
166. Bertenshaw, *Sunrise to Sunset*, p. 40.
167. Burnett Archive: Wynne, 'Old Pompey', p. 22. See also: Walsall LHC: Brockhurst, Oral History Collection, p. 6.
168. Oman, *Salford Stepping Stones*, p. 11; Southgate, *That's the Way it Was*, p. 50; Cast, *Harry's Story*, p. 25.
169. Younger, *Autobiography*, pp. 128–31.
170. *A Short Account of Weaver*, p. 6.

171. Harding, *East End Underworld*, pp. 21–31.
172. Dayus, *Her People*, pp. 16–17.
173. Chaplin, *My Autobiography*, p. 71.
174. Southwark LHL: Causer, Autobiographical Letter, p. 6.
175. Luby, 'William Luby', pp. 89–90.
176. *Ibid.*, p. 95.
177. *Ibid.*, p. 90.
178. *Ibid.*, p. 93.
179. *Ibid.*, p. 99.
180. Compare also with the evidence from the 1904 Board of Trade enquiry into consumption and cost of food: Ian Gazeley and Andrew Newell, 'Urban working-class food consumption and nutrition in Britain in 1904', *Economic History Review*, 68/1 (2015), pp. 101–22; Ian Gazeley, Andrew Newell and Mintewab Bezabih, 'The transformation of hunger revisited: Estimating available calories from the budgets of late nineteenth-century British households', *Journal of Economic History*, 75/2 (2015), pp. 512–25.
181. Harding, *East End Underworld*, p. 27.
182. Burnett Archive: Lanigan, 'Thy Kingdom', p. 1.
183. Southwark LHL: Causer, Autobiographical Letter, pp. 6–7. See also: Luby, 'William Luby', p. 96.
184. For these developments, see: James Vernon, *Hunger: A Modern History* (Cambridge, MA, 2007), pp. 161–80; H. Hendrick, *Child Welfare: England 1872–1989* (London, 1994); John Stewart, 'The campaign for school meals in Edwardian Scotland', in Jon Lawrence and Pat Starkey, eds, *Child Welfare and Social Action in the Nineteenth and Twentieth Centuries: International Perspectives* (Liverpool, 2000); E. Ross, 'Hungry children: Housewives and London charity, 1870–1918', in Peter Mandler, ed., *The Uses of Charity: The Poor on Relief in the Nineteenth-Century Metropolis* (Philadelphia, 1990), pp. 161–96; Kate Bradley, 'Saving the children of Shoreditch: Lady Cynthia Colville and needy families in East London, *c.* 1900–1960', *Law, Crime & History*, 7/1 (2017), pp. 145–63.
185. Harding, *East End Underworld*, pp. 25–31.
186. Powell, *Below Stairs*, p. 24.
187. *Ibid.*
188. Southwark LHL: Davis, 'Ermine and Persian Lamb', p. 1.
189. Bennett, *Walworth Boy*, p. 4.
190. Benson, *To Struggle*, p. 41.
191. Paul, *Poverty*, p. 19.
192. *Ibid.*, p. 18.
193. Langley, *Always a Layman*, p. 4.
194. *Ibid.*, pp. 5–6.
195. Pearson, *Life in Hull*, p. 30.
196. Stride, *Memoirs*, p. 20.
197. Saggers, 'Esther Saggers', pp. 24–5. See also: Blake, *Memories*, p. 10; Harrison, 'Childhood', pp. 11–12; Heaton, *Salford* p. 1. Burnett Archive: Lanigan, 'Thy Kingdom', p. 4; Gregory, Untitled pp. 15–16; Westall, 'Good Old Days', p. 3.
198. Stride, *Memoirs*, p. 21.
199. Brown, *Round the Corner*, p. 33. See also: Stonelake, *Autobiography*, no pag. Burnett Archive: Collis, 'From paper blankets', [p. 6].

8. 'WE WEREN'T HAPPY, BUT WE WERE A FAMILY': EMOTIONS

1. Manchester CL: May Snowden's eldest sister, Untitled, p. 15.
2. Moss, *Live and Learn*, unpaginated introduction.
3. *Ibid.*, pp. 3, 7.
4. *Ibid.* p. 7.

5. *Ibid.*, pp. 6–7.
6. *Ibid.*, pp. 8, 10.
7. Cast, *Harry's Story*, p. 15. See also: Martin, *Best Street*, p. 12.
8. Burnett Archive: Hampton, 'Memories', p. 8.
9. Bryson, *Look Back*, p. 30. For shifts in the meaning of romantic 'love', see: Claire Langhamer, 'Love and courtship in mid-twentieth-century England', *Historical Journal*, 50/1 (2007), pp. 173–96; Claire Langhamer, *The English in Love: The Intimate Story of an Emotional Revolution* (Oxford, 2013)
10. For these shifts, in addition to *ibid.*, see: Deborah Cohen, *Family Secrets: Living with Shame from the Victorians to the Present Day* (London, 2013); Deborah Thom, ' "Beating children is wrong": Domestic life, psychological thinking and the permissive turn', in Lucy Delap, Ben Griffin and Abigail Wills, eds, *The Politics of Domestic Authority in Britain from 1800* (Basingstoke, 2009), pp. 261–83: Cathy Urwin and Elaine Sharland, 'From bodies to minds in childcare literature: Advice to parents in inter-war Britain', in Roger Cooter, ed., *In the Name of the Child: Health and Welfare, 1880–1940* (London, 1992), pp. 174–99; Denise Riley, 'War in the nursery', *Feminist Review*, 2 (1979), pp. 82–108.
11. Langhamer, *English in Love*, pp. xv–xxi, 4.
12. For fathers and the importance of providing, see: Julie-Marie Strange, 'Fatherhood, providing, and attachment in late Victorian and Edwardian working-class families', *Historical Journal*, 55/4 (2012), pp. 1007–27.
13. Clynes, *Memoirs*, pp. 27–8; Hardy, *Stormy Years*, pp. 1–2; Jones, *I Was*, p. 6; Moody, *I Remember*, p. 7; Morrison, *Autobiography*, pp. 11–12. Burnett Archive: Cox, 'White Knob Row', p. 1; Gill, 'Ellen Gill's Diary', p. 1; Hughes, Untitled, pp. 1–5. See also: Carolyn Steedman, *Landscape for a Good Woman* (London, 1986), pp. 18–19.
14. Miles, *Autobiography*, p. 1.
15. May, *Tiger-Woman*, p. 22.
16. Burnett Archive: Westall, 'Good Old Days', pp. 2–3.
17. Drawbell, *Sun Within Us*, p. 59; [Kate Edwards], *Fenland Chronicle*, pp. 152–3, 254, 263–5; Jasper, *Hoxton Childhood*, pp. 7–126 *passim*; Luby, 'William Luby', pp. 89–99; Martin, *Ups and Downs*, pp. 42–60; O'Mara, *Liverpool Slummy*, pp. 30–127; Sharpe, *Dark at Seven*, p. 1; Shaw, *Guttersnipe*, pp. 2–13; O'Reilly, *Tiger of the Legion*, p. 26.
18. Martin, *Ups and Downs*, pp. 91–2.
19. Benson, *To Struggle*, p. 159.
20. Wincott, *Invergordon Mutineer*, p. 2.
21. Burnett Archive: Rice, 'Memories', p. 6.
22. Foley, *Bolton Childhood*, pp. 8, 43. For male violence, see also: Florence Boos, *Memoirs of Victorian Working-Class Women: The Hard Way Up* (Basingstoke, 2017), pp. 16–20.
23. Burnett Archive: Lovekin, 'Some Notes of my Life', p. 1.
24. Jasper, *Hoxton Childhood*, p. 9.
25. *Ibid.*, pp. 15–16.
26. Often at the pub: Bennett, *Walworth Boy*, p. 11; Brearley, *Knotted String*, p. 10; Acorn, *One of the Multitude*, p. 2; Pickles, *Between You and Me*, pp. 27–8; Williams, *George*, pp. 19–20. Southwark LHL: Causer, Autobiographical Letter, pp. 8, 12.
27. Sparks, *Life and Times*, p. 3; Murphy, *New Horizons*, pp. 17–18; Foley, *Bolton Childhood*, pp. 8, 43.
28. Brooks, *Lancashire Bred*, p. 14; Broomhill, 'In memory of my mum', no pag.; Chaplin, *My Autobiography*, pp. 15, 34–9, 58–60; Luck, 'Lucy Luck', p. 354; Reilly, *I Walk*, p. 9; Turner, *Hard Up Husband*, p. 1. Burnett Archive: Cain, 'Memories', p. 2; Lanigan, 'Thy Kingdom', pp. 23. Salvation Army HC: Jarrett, 'Rebecca Jarrett', [pp. 3–4]. Wolverhampton Archives: Sproson, 'My Child Life', p. 1.
29. Roberts, *Ragged Schooling*, p. 8.
30. WCML: Miller, 'Wasted talent', p. 3. See also: Eldred, *I Love the Brooks*, pp. 19–25; Moss, *Live and Learn*, pp. 3–7; Smith, *My Revelation*, pp. 25–9.

31. Smith, *My Revelation*, pp. 25–9, quote p. 29. The gendered nature of the pub is problematised in: D. W. Gutzke, 'Gender, class and public drinking in Britain during the First World War', *Social History* (1994), pp. 367–91, Claire Langhamer, ' "A public house is for all classes, men and women alike": Women, leisure and drink in Second World War England', *Women's History Review*, 12/3 (2003), pp. 423–44.
32. Allaway, Untitled, pp. 5–6.
33. *Ibid.*, p. 5.
34. Harding, *East End Underworld*, pp. 29–30.
35. Home, pseud. of Bush, *Autumn Fields*, pp. 10–11; *idem*, *Winter Harvest*, pp. 44–5. Lack of respect: see: Burnett Archive: Humphries, 'Childhood', pp. 17–18.
36. Edwin, *I'm Going*, pp. 36–7. Compare with Moss, *Live and Learn*, pp. 3–10, as discussed above.
37. Burnett Archive: Young, 'Harry's Biography', section entitled 'My father', pp. 1–5.
38. Burnett Archive: Barker, 'My life', no pag. [p. 15]. See also: McGovern, *Neither Fear*, p. 24.
39. Bennett, *Walworth Lad*, pp. 11–12. See also: Citrine, *Men and Work*, p. 15 (more forgiving); Brearley, *Knotted String*, p. 10 (not forgiving).
40. Powell, *Below Stairs*, p. 113.
41. Meads, *Growing-up*, p. 2.
42. Brady, 'Long trail', p. 316.
43. Wilson, *Joseph Wilson*, p. 4.
44. Allaway, Untitled, p. 5; Lewis, *Seventy Years*, p. 4; Moffit, *Autobiography*, p. 25.
45. Horner, *Incorrigible Rebel*, p. 12; Armstrong, *Pilgrimage*, pp. 30–1; Richards, *Honest to Self*, p. 24.
46. Brown, *Memories*, p. 1; Finch, *Memoirs*, p. 10; Fraser, *Sixty Years*, p. 17; Haddow, *My Seventy Years*, p. 9; Howlett, *The Guv'nor*, p. 16; Westwater, *Early Life*, p. 1. WCLM: Anon., 'Autobiography', p. 4.
47. [David], *Autobiography*, pp. 30, 31; Home, pseud. of Bush, *Autumn Fields*, pp. 8–11; Mullen, *Alice from Tooting*, p. 32. WCML: Honeyford, 'Tom Honeyford', p. 5. Tameside LS: Watson, 'Autobiography', p. 5.
48. Fielden, 'Autobiography', no pag. See also: Cottrell, *My Life*, p. 9; Powell, *Below Stairs*, p. 7. Burnley LHC: Bates, 'Joe's your Uncle', pp. 21, 30.
49. Cowper, *Backward Glance*, p. 16; Ferris, 'Minnie Ferris', p. 30; Fudge, *Sands of Time*, p. 10 (though also jolly and kind); Kitchen, *Brother to Ox*, p. 5; Markham, *Back of Beyond*, p. 27; Taylor, 'Kate Taylor', p. 305; Turner, 'Henry Turner', p. 17. Bolton Archives: Snowman, Untitled, p. 2.
50. Arnold, *Recollections*, p. 103. See also: Burnett Archive: Heslop, 'Tyne to Tone', p. 22. Northamptonshire RO: Rigby, 'Village Memories', p. 1. See also more generally: Hodges, *My Adventures*, p. 2; *I Walked by Night*, p. 4; Rogers, *Funny Old Quist*, pp. 16–17. Burnett Archive: Hannan, 'Happy Highways', p. 33.
51. [David], *Autobiography*, p. 30. See also: Ellen Ross, *Love and Toil: Motherhood in Outcast London, 1870–1914* (New York, 1993), pp. 72–6; Jane Humphries, *Childhood and Child Labour in the British Industrial Revolution* (Cambridge, 2010), pp. 136–7. Compare with the more favourable accounts of working-class fathers contained in: Margaret Williamson, ' "He was good with the bairns": Fatherhood in an ironstone mining community, 1918–1960', *North East History*, 32 (1998), pp. 87–108; Lynn Abrams, ' "There was nobody like my daddy": Fathers, the family and the marginalisation of men in modern Scotland,' *Scottish Historical Review*, 78/206 (1999), pp. 219–42; Julie-Marie Strange, *Fatherhood and the British Working Class, 1865–1914* (Cambridge, 2015); Helen Rogers, ' "First in the house": Daughters on working-class fathers and fatherhood', in Trev Lynn Broughton and Helen Rogers, eds, *Gender and Fatherhood in the Nineteenth Century* (Basingstoke, 2007), pp. 126–67
52. Bondfield, *Life's Work*, p. 23.
53. Ash, *Memories*, p. 7.
54. Burnett Archive: Gomm, 'Water under the bridge', p. 11.

55. Burnett Archive: Fowler, 'Look after', p. 8.
56. Burnett Archive: Goffin, 'Story of a grey life', no pag., section entitled 'Early childhood'. See also: Lax, *His Book*, p. 24; Richards, *Honest to Self*, pp. 23–4. Burnley LHC: Bates, 'Joe's your Uncle', p. 72. Welch, *Autobiography*, p. 32.
57. Oxfordshire HC: Joel, 'Autobiography', letter dated 11 November 1985. Also Jasper, *Hoxton Childhood*, p. 38.
58. Westwater, *Early Life*, pp. 1–2. See also: Healey, *Life*, p. 1.
59. Pickles, *Between You and Me*, pp. 27–9. See also: Burnett Archive: Wallis, 'Yesterday', k. For more on working men's leisure, see: Melanie Tebbutt, 'Rambling and manly identity in Derbyshire's Dark Peak, 1880s–1920s', *Historical Journal*, 49/4 (2006), pp. 1125–53, esp. pp. 1136–8.
60. WCML: Doyle, 'Hammer and Thistle', p. 6. Compare with: Julie-Marie Strange, 'Fatherhood, furniture and the inter-personal dynamics of working-class homes, *c.* 1870–1914', *Urban History*, 40/2 (2013), pp. 271–86.
61. WCML: Doyle, 'Hammer and thistle', p. 37.
62. Perry, 'Unpublished autobiography', p. 338.
63. Jones, *Unfinished Journey*, p. 44; Clynes, *Memoirs*, p. 27.
64. Burke, *Ancoats Lad*, p. 6.
65. Barnes, *Tough Annie*, p. 18. Burnley LHC: Bates, 'Joe's your Uncle', pp. 18–32, 71.
66. Perry, 'Unpublished autobiography', p. 338.
67. Jones, *Unfinished Journey*, p. 44.
68. Fraser, *All to the Good*, p. 6.
69. Burnett Archive: Cowper, 'De Nobis', no pag.
70. Edwards, *Paper Sir?*, p. 14; David Wandilson Library: Bacon, 'Life Story', p. 3.
71. Burnett Archive: Hampton, 'Memories', p. 12; Frisby, 'Memories', p. 1. Gair, *Copt Hill*, p. 23.
72. Oxfordshire HC: Landymore, 'Autobiography', p. 6.
73. Gander, *After These*, p. 17 (to museums); Templeton, *Old Lady*, p. 12 (Sunday trip to park).
74. Burnett Archive: Hodges, 'I Remember', p. 57.
75. Bexley LSL: Wasson, 'Memories', p. 2.
76. Brand, *Fenman Remembers*, p. 13.
77. Wells, *Fenland Boyhood*, pp. 18–20.
78. Jordan, 'Thomas Jordan', pp. 102–4.
79. See for examples: David Wandilson Library: Bacon, 'Life Story', p. 3. Oxfordshire HC: Rayment, 'Autobiography', pp. 5, 15 (fishing). Burnett Archive: Till, 'Early Years', pp. 24–6 (walks and outings); Gold, 'My Life', p. 11 (walks and star-gazing). Layton, 'Memories', p. 30 (walks); Wellock, *Off the Beaten Track*, p. 9 (walks); Bowles, 'Minnie Bowles', pp. 6–7 (reading and London walks); Harris, *Under Oars*, pp. 11–14 (work); Jones, *Unfinished Journey*, pp. 69–72 (work). Southwark LHL: Thornton, 'Memories', p. 5 (walks). See also: Strange: 'Fatherhood, providing, and attachment'; and *idem*, *Fatherhood*, pp. 111–76.
80. Spencer, *Inspector's Testament*, p. 46. See also: Lydia Murdoch, *Daily Life of Victorian Women* (Westport, 2013); Ross, *Love and Toil*, pp. 129–44. Sarah Knott, *Mother: An Unconventional History* (London, 2019).
81. Turner, *About Myself*, p. 42; Eldred, *I Love the Brooks*, p. 20. See also: Jordan, 'Thomas Jordan', p. 100.
82. Kirkwood, *Life of Revolt*, p. 25; Fraser, *Sixty Years*, p. 18.
83. Sexton, *James Sexton*, p. 24.
84. Armstrong, *Pilgrimage*, p. 32.
85. Ratcliffe, *Sixty Years*, p. 6.
86. Williamson, *Father Joe*, p. 20.
87. Burnett Archive: Hannan, 'Happy Highways', pp. 2, 5.
88. Bell, *Road to Jericho*, p. 17.
89. Burnett Archive: Cowper, 'De Nobis', no pag.
90. Ireson, 'Reminiscences,' pp. 71–2.
91. Lipton, *Lipton Logs*, p. 37. See also: Fraser, *Sixty Years*, p. 18.

92. Whittaker, *Life's Battles*, pp. 14, 5.
93. Oakley, 'Autobiography', pp. 113–50.
94. Wincott, *Invergordon Mutineer*, pp. 1–2.
95. Burnett Archive: Shotton, 'Personal history', no pag.
96. Holt, *Looking Backwards*, p. 2.
97. Pickles, *Between You and Me*, pp. 11–12.
98. Roberts, *Ragged Schooling*, pp. 12, 36–7.
99. Brand, *Fenman Remembers*, pp. 13–14; Hillyer, *Country Boy*, pp. 71–2; Pickles, *Between You and Me*, p. 15. Burnett Archive: Hampton, 'Memories', p. 4. Cambridgeshire RO: Rose, Untitled, p. 2.
100. Burnett Archive: Langley, Untitled, no pag.
101. Noakes, *Town Beehive*, p. 9.
102. 'Strict' mothers: Brand, *Fenman Remembers*, pp. 13–14; Coleman, *Tangled Garden*, p. 16; Crittall, *Fifty Years of Work*, p. 7; [William Edwards], *Fenland Chronicle*, p. 21; Mellor, *Gertie's Story*, p. 5; Roberts, *Fred Roberts*, p. 7; Rowse, *Cornish Childhood*, pp. 80, 86. Burnett Archive: Abbley, 'Soul Adrift', pp. 20–3; Goodwin, Untitled, pp. 2–3; Hampton, 'Memories', p. 8; May Jones, Untitled, p. 4; Lea, 'Reflections', p. 1; Wallis, 'Yesterday', p. 20. Hampshire ALS: Smith, 'Autobiography', pp. 3–4. More generally, see also: Melanie Tebbutt, *Women's Talk: A Social History of Gossip in Working-class Neighbourhoods, 1880–1960* (Aldershot, 1995), pp. 102–14, esp. pp. 112–14.
103. Oxfordshire HC: Davies, 'Autobiography', p. 4.
104. Cambridgeshire RO: Rose, Untitled, pp. 1–2.
105. Burton, *Young Man*, p. 46.
106. Jaeger, *Annie Jaeger*, p. 17.
107. Acorn, *One of the Multitude*, pp. 2–4.
108. *Ibid.*, p. 281. See also: Meek, *George Meek*, pp. 21, 40, 42, 45–6.
109. Woodward, *Jipping Street*, pp. 18–19. See also Steedman's insightful interpretation of Woodward's complex text in Woodward, *Jipping Street*, pp. xi–xv, esp. p. xiv, and Steedman, *Landscape for a Good Woman*, pp. 91–2.
110. Osgerby, 'My memoirs', pp. 82, 79. Aggression also noted in: Dayus, *Her People*, p. 6; O'Reilly, *Tiger of the Legion*, p. 26; Vose, *Diary of a Tramp*, p. 9.
111. Mitchell, *Hard Way Up*, pp. 39, 57.
112. *Ibid.*, pp. 39–40.
113. *Ibid.*, p. 62. For female violence, see also: Nancy Tomes, 'A "torrent of abuse": Crimes of violence between working-class men and women in London, 1840–1875', *Journal of Social History*, 11 (1978), pp. 328–45.
114. Humphries, *Childhood*, p. 143. See also: Ross, *Love and Toil*, pp. 149–51.
115. Sexton, *James Sexton*, pp. 24–5.
116. Edwards, *From the Valley*, pp. 13, 26, 27–8.
117. Acorn, *One of the Multitude*, pp. 62, 42, 14, 12, 63.
118. Woodward, *Jipping Street*, p. 19.
119. Osgerby, 'My memoirs', p. 79.
120. Lawson, *Man's Life*, p. 23.
121. Burnett Archive: Garrett, Untitled, p. 1.
122. Dayus, *Her People*, p. 6. Corporal punishment, see also: [William Edwards], *Fenland Chronicle*, p. 21; Mullen, *Alice of Tooting*, p. 18; Reakes, *Man of the Mersey*, p. 10. Burnett Archive: Gregory, Untitled, pp. 7–8; Jones, Untitled, p. 4.
123. Mitchell, *Hard Way Up*, pp. 55, 62.
124. *Ibid.*, p. 57.
125. Hocking, *Bench and Mitre*, p. 35.
126. Bryson, *Look Back*, pp. 15–16.
127. Page, 'No green pastures, p. 36; Warwick MRC: Minnie Vandome, Untitled, p. 14. Burnett Archive: Goss, 'My Boyhood', [p. 105]. For more on violence in homes, see also: Tomes, ' "Torrent of abuse" ', pp. 328–45; Elizabeth Foyster, *Marital Violence: An English*

Family History, 1660–1857 (Cambridge, 2005); Ben Griffin, *The Politics of Gender in Victorian Britain: Masculinity, Political Culture and the Struggle for Women's Rights* (Cambridge, 2012), pp. 65–110.

128. British Library: Purkiss, 'Memories', pp. 1–2.

129. 1891 Census and 1901 Census. Married, December 1882. For orphans and institutions, see, more generally: Lydia Murdoch, *Imagined Orphans: Poor Families, Child Welfare, and Contested Citizenship in London* (New Brunswick, NJ, 2006), pp. 67–91, esp. tables 3.1 and 3.2 pp. 73–5.

130. Ashby, *Joseph Ashby*, pp. 1–3; Cardus, *Autobiography*, pp. 15–16; Cookson, *Our Kate*, pp. 4–42; Marcroft, *Marcroft Family*, pp. 18–22; Stride, *Memoirs*, p. 6. See also: Snell, *Men, Movements and Myself*; Taylor, *Glasgow Slum*, neither of whom mentioned their illegitimacy in their autobiographies.

131. Illegitimates separated at birth: Brown, *Round the Corner*, pp. 11–23; J. Davis, *Passages*, p. 5; Milne, *Reminiscences*, p. 18; Smith, *Cornish Waif*, pp. 15–28; Stanley, *Autobiography*, pp. 6–10; Thompson, *Hyde Park Orator*, p. 19; Wallace, *Autobiography*, p. 7. Crosby Library: Fairhurst, 'Our Zoe', pp. 2–3. Finsbury Library: Price, 'My diary', pp. 3–5. Surrey HC: Wallis, 'Down Memory Lane', pp. 1–2. Walsall LHC: Perry, Oral History Collection, pp. 1–2.

132. Thompson, *Hyde Park Orator*, p. 19.

133. Edward Brown; Zoe Fairhurst.

134. Crosby Library: Fairhurst, 'Our Zoe', pp. 2–3.

135. Smith, *Cornish Waif*, pp. 1–30, 69–73, 203, 209. See also: Brown, *Round the Corner*, pp. 23–4; Milne, *Reminiscences*, p. 18. Finsbury Library: Price, 'My diary', pp. 3–5. Surrey HC: Wallis, 'Down Memory Lane', p. 2. See also: Murdoch, *Imagined Orphans*, pp. 67–91

136. Bryson, *Look Back*, pp. 20–31; Davis, *Breaks Came*, pp. 3–4; Meek, *George Meek*, pp. 7–8; Reffold, *Pie for Breakfast*, pp. 8–10. Burnett Archive: Hilton-Foord, 'Survivor', p. 1; Humphries, 'Childhood', pp. 10–22; Purvis, 'Reminiscences', pp. 1–3. WCML: Honeyford, 'Tom Honeyford', p. 3.

137. Luby, 'William Luby', p. 96.

138. *Ibid.* Other separations, see also: Burke, *Wind and Rain*, pp. 17–20; Davies, *Autobiography*, pp. 18–41 *passim*. Burnett Archive: Adnams, 'My memoirs', p. 1; Balne, 'Autobiography', pp. 1–3. See also: Gape, *Half a Million Tramps*, pp. 1–7. Wolverhampton Archives: Sproson, 'My Child Life', p. 4.

139. Layton, 'Memories', p. 8.

140. Salvation Army HC: Jarrett, 'Rebecca Jarrett', [p. 1].

141. Cookson, née McMullen, *Our Kate*, pp. 40–2, 64.

142. Treorchy LSL: Parrish, 'This is my story', p. 1.

143. Harding, *East End Underworld*, pp. 24–5.

144. *Ibid.*, p. 24. For mothers who drank, see also: Bullen, *Recollections*, p. 29; G. J., *Prisoner Set Free*, p. 8; O'Mara, *Liverpool Slummy*, pp. 103–4, 112; Shaw, *Guttersnipe*, pp. 2, 6. Burnett Archive: Garratt, Untitled, p. 1; Lord, 'My Life', p. 1. As well as stepmothers: Chaplin; Gray; Freer; Watson.

145. Burnett Archive: Garrett, Untitled, p. 1. See also: Thomas R. C. Gibson-Brydon, *The Moral Mapping of Victorian and Edwardian London: Charles Booth, Christian Charity, and the Poor-but-Respectable* (Montreal, 2016), pp. 156–62.

146. See also Carolyn Steedman's comment upon the inclusion of material designed to 'hurt' the reader in *idem*, 'History and autobiography: Different pasts', in *idem*, ed., *Past Tenses: Essays on Writing, Autobiography and History* (London, 1992).

147. Hawke, *From Private*, pp. 13–14.

148. *Ibid.*, p. 14. When the Board of Guardians later threatened to stop his grandmother's relief unless James was put into an institution, James left his grandmother to enter a 'Home'. He considered himself 'extremely lucky' for those four years, so good was his treatment in the Home, pp. 16–18.

149. May, *Tiger-Woman*, pp. 10–14.

150. Single mothers: Brooks, *Lancashire Bred*, pp. 18–19, 33–5; Kerr, *Eager Years*, pp. 8–9; Wheway, *Edna's Story*, p. 1. Burnett Archive: Brown, Untitled, pp. 3–4. Treorchy LSL: Parrish, 'This is my story', p. 1.

151. Married: separated from children: Hammond, *This Was My Life*, p. 7; Uglow, *Sailorman*, p. 16. Burnett Archive: Adnams, 'My memoirs', pp. 1, 23–6; Harris, 'Autobiographical letters', letter dated 4 May 1978. Both parents' whereabouts unknown: Anthony, *Man's a Man*, p. 7; Kelly, *Prodigal of the Seas*, pp. 1–9; Reilly, *I Walk*, p. 9. Three writers also became separated through their mother's mental illness. See: Chaplin, *My Autobiography*, pp. 33–72 *passim*; Gray, *Gin and Bitters*, pp. 11–12. Burnett Archive: Terry, 'Recollections', pp. 7–10.

152. Severn, *Life Story*, pp. 5–9.

153. Burnett Archive: Harris, 'Autobiographical letters', letter dated 4 May 1978.

154. *Ibid.*, letter dated 3 May 1978, pp. 2–3.

155. Wrigley, 'Plate-Layer's wife', p. 57.

156. Burnett Archive: Hilton-Foord, 'Survivor', pp. 1–7; and 'Grannie's Girl', no pag.

157. Bullen, *Recollections*, p. 29.

158. Burnett Archive: Goffin, 'Story of a grey life', no pag.

159. See also the discussion of Harding on p. 131 above.

160. Salvation Army HC: Jarrett, 'Rebecca Jarrett', [pp. 1–3].

161. Layton, 'Memories', p. 8. The idea of the 'good mother' is also problematised in Steedman, *Landscape for a Good Woman*, pp. 1, 16–7. See also: Victoria Kelley, *Soap and Water: Cleanliness, Dirt and the Working Classes in Victorian and Edwardian Britain* (London, 2014), pp. 91–8.

162. Hawke, *From Private*, pp. 13–14.

163. *Ibid.*, p. 14.

164. May, *Tiger-Woman*, pp. 14, 17–18. See also: Finsbury Library: Price, 'My diary', p. 5.

165. Uglow, *Sailorman*, p. 16. See also: Burnett Archive: Balne, 'Autobiography', pp. 1–3.

166. This appears to be the case with all of the following: Brown, *Round the Corner*, pp. 11–22; J. Davis, *Passages*, p. 5; Milne, *Reminiscences*, p. 18; Smith, *Cornish Waif*, pp. 15–28; Stanley, *Autobiography*, pp. 6–10; Thomas, *My Story* (not discussed in the autobiography); Thompson, *Hyde Park Orator*, p. 19; Wallace, *Autobiography*, p. 7. Crosby Library: Fairhurst, 'Our Zoe', pp. 2–3. Finsbury Library: Price, 'My diary', pp. 3–5; British Library: Purkiss, 'Memories', pp. 1–2. Surrey HC: Wallis, 'Down Memory Lane', p. 1. Walsall LHC: Perry, Oral History, pp. 1–2.

167. Burnett Archive: Brown, Untitled, p. 3.

168. *Ibid.*, p. 4.

169. May, *Tiger-Woman*, p. 14. See also: Hawke, *From Private*, p. 14; Luby, 'William Luby', pp. 89–95.

170. Treorchy LSL: Parrish, 'This is my story', p. 1.

171. Cookson, née McMullen, *Our Kate*, p. 38.

172. Salvation Army HC: Jarrett, 'Rebecca Jarrett', p. 3.

173. Harding, *East End Underworld*, pp. 22, 24–5, 28–9, 65.

174. *Ibid.*, pp. 69, 65.

175. See also: Burnett Archive: Garrett, Untitled, pp. 1–2. Shaw, *Guttersnipe*, pp. 1–27.

176. Coppard, *It's Me, O Lord!*, p. 30.

177. Pearson, *Life in Hull*, p. 68.

178. *Ibid.*, p. 72.

179. Williams, *George*, p. 27.

180. Jaeger, *Annie Jaeger*, pp. 10, 12–13.

181. Woodward, *Jipping Street*, p. 10. Stressed single mothers, see also: Blatchford, *My Eighty Years*, pp. 2–4; Cookson, *Our Kate*, pp. 109–10; Halward, *Let Me Tell You*, pp. 24–7; Williamson, *Father Joe*, pp. 18–19. Burnett Archive: Lanigan, 'Thy Kingdom', pp. 4, 9. Oxfordshire HC: Joel, 'Autobiography', letter dated 11 November 1985.

182. Holt, *Looking Backwards*. Cambridgeshire RO: Rose, Untitled, p. 2.

183. Crittall, *Fifty Years of Work*, pp. 7, 32. See also: Ross, *Love and Toil*, pp. 128–58, 185–94.
184. Burnett Archive: Brain, Untitled, p. 3.
185. Noakes, *Town Beehive*, p. 9.
186. WCML: Miller, 'Wasted talent', p. 3.
187. Rowse, *Cornish Childhood*, p. 86.
188. Burnett Archive: Harrison, née Twist, 'Poor and Proud', pp. 24–5.
189. *Ibid.*, p. 29. See also: Barnes, *Workshop to War Cabinet*, pp. 7–8. Burnett Archive: Marrin, Untitled, p. 1.
190. Williams, *George*, p. 27. Also: Reakes, *Man of the Mersey*, p. 10.
191. Lawson, *Man's Life*, p. 31.
192. Thompson, *Hyde Park Orator*, p. 61.
193. Vose, *Diary of a Tramp*, p. 9.
194. Westwater, *Early Life*, p. 2.
195. Burnett Archive: Goffin, 'Story of a grey life', no pag., section entitled 'Skeleton'. Short-tempered, see also: Acorn, *One of the Multitude*, pp. 2–4; Blatchford, *My Eighty Years*, p. 3; John, *Tabitha*, p. 40; Mitchell, *Hard Way Up*, pp. 39–41, 54–7; Mullen, *Alice from Tooting*, p. 18; O'Reilly, *Tiger of the Legion*, p. 26; Osgerby, 'My memoirs', pp. 79–82; Reffold, *Pie for Breakfast*, p. 7; Roberts, *Ragged Schooling*, pp. 12, 36–7. Burnett Archive: Gill, 'I remember!', p. 8.
196. See also: Acorn, *One of the Multitude*, pp. 2–4; Burton, *Young Man*, pp. 36–46; Eldred, *I Love the Brooks*, pp. 19–25; Moss, *Live and Learn*, pp. 3–10; O'Reilly, *Tiger of the Legion*, p. 26; Osgerby, 'My memoirs', p. 82; Pritchett, *Cab at the Door*, pp. 25–121 *passim*; Roberts, *Ragged Schooling*, pp. 1–37; Severn, *Life Story*, pp. 5–6, 10–11. Crosby Library: Fairhurst, 'Our Zoe', p. 3. WCML: Miller, 'Wasted talent', pp. 3–4. See also: Steedman, *Landscape for a Good Woman*; Ross, *Love and Toil*, pp. 56–90, 128–65.
197. Wells, *Experiment*, p. 24.
198. *Ibid.*, pp. 42, 32.
199. Burton, *Young Man*, p. 36.
200. *Ibid.*, p. 39.
201. Hillyer, *Country Boy*, pp. 103, 71–2.
202. Box, *Odd Woman Out*, pp. 15–6. There were several discordant marriages described by the autobiographers, including by: George Acorn; Joe Bates (Burnley LHC); Herbert Bennett; Ernie Benson; Joseph Barlow Brooks; Harry Burton; John Eldred; Len Fagg (Warwick MRC); Arthur Goffin (Burnett Archive); Herbert Hodge; Annie Jaeger; Lucy Miller (WCML); Hannah Mitchell; Les Moss; Alice Mullen; Molly Murphy; Faith Osgerby; Elsie Osman; V. S. Pritchett; Jean Rennie; J. Milliot Severn; Jane Walsh; Thomas Westwater; Harry Young (Burnett Archive). Also some cases of serious domestic abuse: William Bowyer; Edward Cain (Burnett Archive); Kate Edwards; Jack Martin; Pat O'Mara; Septimus O'Reilly; Stanley Rice (Burnett Archive); Lilian Westall (Burnett Archive). See also: Tebbutt, *Women's Talk*, pp. 113–14.
203. Osgerby, 'My memoirs', p. 79. See also: Langley, *Always a Layman*, p. 14.
204. Rowse, *Cornish Childhood*, pp. 80, 86.
205. Mitchell, *Hard Way Up*, p. 40.
206. Wells, *Experiment*, p. 40; Box, *Odd Woman Out*, p. 14; Brand, *Fenman Remembers*, p. 13.

9. 'I LEARNED TO SPEAK': MAKING CITIZENS

1. Lansbury, *My Life*, p. 38.
2. Murphy, *New Horizons*, pp. 23, 29–177.
3. Murphy, *Molly Murphy*, pp. 5–31.
4. *Ibid.*, pp. 32–63.
5. *Ibid.*, pp. 64–7.

6. See Ralph Darlington's editorial introduction to: Murphy, *Molly Murphy*, p. ii. See also his biography: Ralph Darlington, *The Political Trajectory of J. T. Murphy* (Liverpool, 1998).

7. Murphy, *Molly Murphy*, p. iii.

8. Compare also with the experiences of Philip and Ethel Snowden; though both were politically active, only Philip wrote an autobiography (Snowden, *Autobiography*).

9. In fact, we do know that there was considerable working-class support for conservatism, so the absence of working-class conservatism from the autobiographical record suggests an additional set of connections between men, self-improvement, life-writing and socialism broadly defined. For working-class politics more broadly, see: Marc Brodie, *The Politics of the Poor: The East End of London, 1885–1914* (Oxford, 2004).

10. David Amigoni, 'Victorian life writing: Genres, print, constituencies', in *idem*, ed., *Life Writing and Victorian Culture* (Aldershot, 2006), pp. 6–7; Eugenio F. Biagini and Alastair J. Reid, eds, *Currents of Radicalism: Popular Radicalism, Organised Labour and Party Politics in Britain, 1850–1914* (Cambridge, 1991); James Vernon, *Politics and the People: A Study in English Political Culture, 1815–1867* (Cambridge, 1993); Rohan McWilliam, *Popular Politics in Nineteenth-Century England* (London, 1998); Jon Lawrence, *Speaking for the People: Party, Language and Popular Politics in England, 1867–1914* (Cambridge, 1998); *idem*, 'The transformation of British public politics after the First World War', *Past and Present*, 190 (2006), pp. 185–216.

11. Of course, women of all classes struggled to operate in the political sphere. For some examples, see: Jon Lawrence, 'Contesting the male polity: The suffragettes and the politics of disruption in Edwardian Britain', in Amanda Vickery, ed., *Women, Privilege and Power: British Politics, 1750 to the Present* (Stanford, 2001), pp. 201–26, 368–80; Kathryn Gleadle, *Borderline Citizens: Women, Gender and Political Culture in Britain, 1815–1867* (Oxford, 2009); Megan Smitley, *The Feminine Public Sphere: Middle-Class Women and Civic Life in Scotland, 1870–1914* (Manchester, 2009); Sarah Richardson, *The Political Worlds of Women: Gender and Politics in Nineteenth-Century Britain* (London, 2013); Jennifer Davey, *Mary, Countess of Derby, and the Politics of Victorian Britain* (Oxford, 2019). See also: Simon Morgan, *A Victorian Woman's Place: Public Culture in the Nineteenth Century* (London, 2007), pp. 62, 9, 72, 106, 136.

12. Emma Griffin, *Liberty's Dawn: A People's History of the Industrial Revolution* (London, 2013).

13. Patricia Hollis, *Jennie Lee: A Life* (London, 2014); Laura Beers, *Red Ellen: The Life of Ellen Wilkinson, Socialist, Feminist, Internationalist* (Boston, MA, 2016).

14. For this earlier working-class, female political activism, see: Helen Rogers, ' "What right have women to interfere with politics?": The address of the Female Political Union of Birmingham to the women of England (1838)', in T. G. Ashplant and Gerry Smyth, eds, *Explorations in Cultural History* (London, 2001), pp. 65–100; *idem*, 'From "monster meetings" to "fire-side virtues"? Radical women and "the people" in the 1840s', *Journal of Victorian Culture*, 4/1 (1999), pp. 52–75; *idem*, ' "The good are not always powerful, nor the powerful always good": The politics of women's needlework in mid-Victorian London', *Victorian Studies*, 40 (1997), pp. 589–623. Compare also with Griffin, *Liberty's Dawn*, pp. 212–40.

15. In addition to these sketches, see also the profiles provided by: W. T. Stead, 'The Labour Party and the books that helped to make it', *Review of Reviews*, 33 (June 1906), pp. 568–82.

16. Williams, *Digging for Britain*, p. 20.

17. Hardy, *Stormy Years*, p. 15.

18. Citrine, *Men and Work*, pp. 36–7.

19. Barnes, 'Pushed into Fame'; Bell, *Pioneering Days*, p. 26; Cowen, *Mining Life*, p. 11; Horner, *Incorrigible Rebel*, p. 21; Jones, *Lively Life*, pp. 19–20; MacPherson, 'How I got on'; Richards, 'Mr Richards'; Taylor, 'Mr Taylor'; Watson, *Machines and Men*, pp. 13–15; Wilkie, 'Alexander Wilkie'. Warwick MRC: Garnett, 'My Autobiography', p. 3.

20. Bell, 'Richard Bell'.

21. Hodges, *My Adventures*, p. 16.

22. Thompson, *Hyde Park Orator*, pp. 68–9.

23. Crooks, 'Mr Crooks'. See also: Taylor, 'Mr Taylor'.
24. Steadman, 'Mr Steadman'.
25. Walsh, 'A Policeman gave him his first lift'. See also: Shinwell, *Conflict without Malice*, pp. 22, 25.
26. Wallace, *Autobiography*, p. 31. For boyhood spending, see also: Cast, *Harry's Story*, p. 49; Morrison, *Autobiography*, p. 22; Tillett, *Memories*, p. 35; Toole, *Fighting Through Life*, pp. 35–41.
27. Westwater, *Early Life*, p. 13.
28. Burnett Archive: Lanigan, 'Thy Kingdom', pp. 12–16.
29. Clynes, *Memoirs*, p. 28.
30. Collison, *Apostle of Free Labour*, p. 10.
31. See also: Jonathan Rose, *The Intellectual Life of the British Working Classes* (New Haven, 2001); Kelly J. Mays, 'Domestic spaces, readerly acts: Reading(,) gender, and class in working-class autobiography', *Nineteenth-Century Contexts*, 30/4 (2008), pp. 343–68.
32. WCML: Honeyford, 'Tom Honeyford', p. 6.
33. Morrison, *Autobiography*, p. 27.
34. Jackson, *Solo Trumpet*, p. 18.
35. Shinwell, *Conflict*, p. 24.
36. *Ibid.* See also: Citrine, *Men and Work*, p. 37; Ward, 'Rise of a ploughboy'.
37. Thompson, *Hyde Park Orator*, pp. 69–71.
38. Clynes, *Memoirs*, p. 33.
39. *Ibid.*, p. 35; Thompson, *Hyde Park Orator*, pp. 70–1.
40. Barnes, 'Pushed into Fame'; Gill, 'Mr Gill'; Hodgkinson, *Sent to Coventry*, p. 15; Johnson, 'William Johnson'; Pollitt, *Serving My Time*, p. 31; Shackleton, 'Unemployment bought success'; Smillie, *My Life*, p. 28; Steadman, 'Mr Steadman'; Murphy, *New Horizons*, p. 24; Wellock, *Off the Beaten Track*, p. 11. See also: Griffin, *Liberty's Dawn*, pp. 165–85.
41. Henderson, 'From errand boy'.
42. Hodges, *My Adventures*, p. 15.
43. Johnson, 'William Johnson'.
44. Morrison, *Autobiography*, p. 30. See also: Hodge, *Workman's Cottage*, p. 21.
45. Gallacher, *Revolt*, p. 6.
46. Lansbury, *My Life*, p. 36.
47. Hodgkinson, *Sent to Coventry*, pp. 25–6.
48. Conway, *Half-Timer*, pp. 19–20.
49. Lawson, *Man's Life*, p. 47.
50. WCML: Honeyford, 'Tom Honeyford', p. 6.
51. The authors of these pieces were: George N Barnes; Richard Bell; Charles William Bowerman; William Brace; Will Crooks; Charles Duncan; A. H. Gill; Arthur Henderson; J. H. Jenkins; John Johnson; William Johnson; John T. MacPherson; T. Frederick Richards; G. H. Roberts; D. J. Shackleton; William Charles Steadman; T. Summerbell; J. W. Taylor; Stephen Walsh; John Ward; G. J. Wardle; Alexander Wilkie; J. Havelock Wilson; John Wilson.
52. Roberts, 'Mr Roberts'.
53. Jenkins, 'Shipwright who wasn't content'.
54. Steadman, 'Mr Steadman'.
55. Richards, 'Mr Richards'.
56. Walsh, 'A policeman gave him his first lift'.
57. For secondary schooling: Brown, *So Far*, pp. 20–37; Reakes, *Man of the Mersey*, pp. 12–13; Snowden, *Autobiography*, pp. 37–40.
58. For example: Jack Jones (Burnett Archive); John Paton; Robert Smillie; James Henry Thomas; Will Thorne; Benjamin Tillett; Thomas Williams; John Wilson.
59. Scott, 'Mrs Scott', pp. 88–9.
60. Foley, *Bolton Childhood*, pp. 43–7.
61. *Ibid.*, pp. 57, 59–60.

62. *Ibid.*, pp. 62–3.
63. See, for example, Chew, *Life and Writings*, pp. 13–14; Kerrigan, 'Rose Kerrigan', p. 35; Yearn, 'Public-spirited rebel', p. 103.
64. Burnett Archive: Collis, 'My first strike', [pp. 4–5]. See also: Yearn, 'Public-spirited rebel', p. 103. See also: Selina Todd, *Young Women, Work and Family in England, 1918–1950* (Oxford, 2005)
65. Kenney, *Memories*, pp. 27–8.
66. Smith, *My Revelation*, p. 48.
67. Rose, *Intellectual Life*; June Purvis, *Hard Lessons: Lives and Education of Working-Class Women in Nineteenth-Century England* (Oxford, 1989). See also: Mays, 'Domestic spaces'.
68. Templeton, *Old Lady*, pp. 16–17. See also: Luty, *Penniless Globe Trotter*, pp. 39, 42. WCML: Stephen, 'Submission', pp. 8, 10–11.
69. Foley, *Bolton Childhood*, pp. 55–6.
70. Newbery, *Picking up Threads*, p. 73.
71. Foley, *Bolton Childhood*, p. 64.
72. Blackburn, *In and Out*, p. 36. See also: Todd, *Young Women*.
73. Andrews, *Woman's Work*, p. 15. For more on the history of female political activism, see: Rogers, 'What right?', pp. 65–100; *idem*, 'Monster meetings', pp. 52–75; *idem*, 'The good are not always powerful', pp. 589–623; Carol Morgan, 'Women, work and consciousness in the mid-nineteenth-century English cotton industry', *Social History*, 17/1 (1992), pp. 23–41.
74. Wolverhampton Archives: Sproson, 'My Child Life', p .6.
75. Layton, 'Memories', p. 41.
76. Mitchell, *Hard Way Up*, p. 89.
77. Scott, 'Felt hat worker', pp. 95–6.
78. Barnes, *Tough Annie*, p. 12. Also noted by: Gillian Scott, 'The Women's Co-Operative Guild and suffrage', in Myriam Boussahba-Bravard, ed., *Suffrage outside Suffragism: Women's Vote in Britain, 1880–1914* (New York, 2007), esp. pp. 133–4. See also: Helen Rogers, 'Any questions? The gendered dimensions of the political platform in nineteenth-century England', *Nineteenth-Century Prose*, 29/1 (2002), pp. 18–132.
79. Hodges, *My Adventures*, p. 17.
80. Lansbury, *My Life*, pp. 38–9.
81. *Ibid.*, p. 39.
82. Hodgkinson, *Sent to Coventry*, pp. 25, 27. See also: Stonelake, *Autobiography*, no pag.
83. Paton, *Proletarian Pilgrimage*, pp. 109–10.
84. Woodward, *Jipping Street*, pp. 113–14.
85. See: Laura Schwartz, ' "What we feel is needed is a union for domestics such as the miners have": The Domestic Workers' Union of Great Britain and Ireland, 1908–1914', *Twentieth-Century British History*, 25/2 (2014), pp. 173–92.
86. Conway, *Half Timer*, pp. 19–20.
87. Burnett Archive: Purvis, 'Reminiscences', p. 4. See also: Jaeger, *Annie Jaeger*, pp. 17, 19; John, *Tabitha*, p. 38.
88. Scott, 'Felt hat worker', p. 92.
89. Foley, *Bolton Childhood*, p. 64.
90. Bowles, 'Minnie Bowles', pp. 9–10; Slate, *Dear Girl*, pp. 25–6; Templeton, *Old Lady*, pp. 15–29. Warwick MRC: Minnie Vandome, Untitled, pp. 50–7.
91. Andrews, *Woman's Work*, p. 15; Mitchell, *Hard Way Up*, pp. 72–87.
92. Bondfield, *Life's Work*, pp. 27–37; Griffiths, *One Woman's Story*, pp. 59–65; Wolverhampton Archives: Sproson, 'My Child Life', p. 6.
93. Clara Morris, in Murphy, *Molly Murphy*, p. 7.
94. For a similar interpretation for a later period, see: Helen McCarthy, 'Women, marriage and paid work in post-war Britain', *Women's History Review*, 26/1, 2017, pp. 46–61; R. E. Pahl, *Divisions of Labour* (Oxford, 1984).
95. Patricia Hollis, *Jennie Lee: A Life* (London, 2014).
96. Bondfield, *Life's Work*, p. 36.

97. Ada Chew; Annie Kenney; Hannah Mitchell.

98. Minnie Blackburn; Minnie Bowles; Alice Collis; Mary Luty; Nellie Scott; Ruth Slate; Minnie Vandome; Edith Williams; Kathleen Woodward.

99. Winifred Griffiths; Elizabeth Layton (her one son died); Molly Murphy; Maggie Newbery; Isabel Templeton; Fanny Yearn.

100. Sarah Wrigley; Mrs Smith; Deborah Smith.

101. Eilidh Garrett et al., *Changing Family Size in England and Wales: Place, Class and Demography, 1891–1911* (Cambridge, 2001), table 5.5.3, p. 241.

102. Mitchell, *Hard Way Up*, p. 97.

103. *Ibid.*, p. 88.

104. Mitchell, *Hard Way Up*, p. 100.

105. Sex and contraception were largely off limits for the autobiographers. See the discussion on pp. 97–102 above.

106. For working-class women and leisure, see also: Elizabeth Roberts, *A Woman's Place: An Oral History of Working-Class Women, 1890–1940* (Oxford, 1984); Ellen Ross, *Love and Toil: Motherhood in Outcast London, 1870–1914* (New York, 1993).

107. Carbis, *Nellie Carbis*, p. 3.

108. Turner, 'Henry Turner', p. 19.

109. Burnett Archive: Goffin, 'Story of a grey life', chapter four.

110. Barclay, *Memoirs*, pp. 9–10.

111. Murphy, *New Horizons*, pp. 21–2.

112. Westwater, *Early Life*, pp. 1–2.

113. Roberts, *Ragged Schooling*, pp. 12, 16.

114. Brady, 'Long trail', p. 318. See also: Oman, *Salford Stepping Stones*, p. 16. Northamptonshire RO: Freeston, 'Village Memories', no pag.

115. Smith, 'In a mining village', p. 72.

116. Layton, 'Memories', p. 39.

117. Anon., 'London Guildswoman', pp. 140–1.

118. Smith, *My Revelation*, p. 48. See also: Martin, *Best Street*, p. 13. Middle- and upper-class women sometimes reported a similar experience. See: Lyndsey Jenkins, *Lady Constance Lytton: Aristocrat, Suffragette, Martyr* (London, 2015); Julia Bush, 'The National Union of Women Workers and women's suffrage', in Boussahba-Bravard, ed., *Suffrage outside Suffragism*, pp. 105–31, esp. pp. 109–12.

119. Brown, *So Far*, p. 18.

120. Ibid., p. 19. See also: Drummond, *Some Memories*, p. 3.

121. Burnett Archive: Wallis, 'Yesterday', h; Jasper, *Hoxton Childhood*, pp. 51–2.

122. Chew, *Life and Writings*, p. 30. See also: Roberts, *Woman's Place*; Ross, *Love and Toil*.

123. Burnett Archive: Wall, 'Hour at Eve', p. 5.

124. Woodward, *Jipping Street*, p. 121.

125. Layton, 'Memories', pp. 39–40. See also: Llewelyn Davies, *Women's Guild*, p. 21.

126. Chew, *Life and Writings*, pp. 8–10, 29–30.

127. *Ibid.*, pp. 27–8.

128. Bondfield, *Life's Work*, pp. 19–24; Braddock, *Braddocks*, p. 6; Lee, *To-Morrow*, p. 33; Wilkinson, 'Ellen Wilkinson', p. 401.

129. Wilkinson, 'Ellen Wilkinson', pp. 405–16.

130. Lee, *To-Morrow*, pp. 55–6.

131. Bondfield, *Life's Work*, p. 13; Braddock, *Braddocks*, p. 6; Lee, *To-Morrow*, pp. 38–54; Wilkinson, 'Ellen Wilkinson', pp. 400–1, 404–5.

132. Wolverhampton Archives: Sproson, 'My Child Life', pp. 1–4; Foley, *Bolton Childhood*, pp. 8, 43.

133. Brooksbank, *No Sae Lang Syne*, pp. 5–7; Mitchell, *Hard Way Up*, pp. 37–53.

134. Marx Memorial Library: Crawfurd, Untitled, pp. 15–17, 26. Gawthorpe, *Up Hill to Holloway*, pp. 38, 41–50; Barnes, *Tough Annie*, pp. 7–8; Bowles, 'Minnie Bowles', p. 9. Warwick MRC: Minnie Vandome, Untitled.

135. WCML: Stephen, 'Submission', pp. 13–14.
136. Chew, *Life and Writings*, pp. 8–9; Barnes, *Tough Annie*, p. 8; Andrews, *Woman's Work*, pp. 9–10; Murphy, *Molly Murphy*, p. 5.
137. Brooksbank, *No Sae Lang Syne*, p. 3.
138. Gawthorpe, *Up Hill to Holloway*, pp. 28–9.
139. Kerrigan, Untitled, p. 34; Andrews, *Woman's Work*, p. 14.
140. Kerrigan, 'Rose Kerrigan', p. 77.
141. WCML: Stephen, 'Submission', pp. 13–14, 2–3.
142. Braddock, *Braddocks*, p. 6.
143. Chew, *Life and Writings*, pp. 28–9.
144. Layton, 'Memories', p. 48.
145. Yearn, 'Public-spirited rebel', p. 105.
146. Templeton, *Old Lady*, p. 29.
147. Barnes, *Tough Annie*, pp. 12, 16, 21, 18.

BIBLIOGRAPHY OF AUTOBIOGRAPHIES

ARCHIVES

Aberdeen Local Studies Library, Central Library, Aberdeen
Baxter, Andrew, 'Memoirs by Andrew Baxter of Footdee', 17/3/62

Barnsley Archives and Local Studies, Barnsley
Marsh, George, 'A Sketch of the life of George Marsh, a Yorkshire collier, 1834–1921', B920 MAR

Battersea Local Studies Library, London
Davis, Charles, 'Reminiscences'

Bedfordshire Archives and Records Service, Bedford
Bell, Joseph, 'The Story of 12 Years in the Life of an Orphan 1846–1858 told by himself: Chapters from the autobiography of a village lad', 2 volumes, Z1288/1/1–2

Bedfordshire Local Studies Library, Central Library, Bedford
Card, Albert, 'A working-class lad's view of life in Bedford in the early part of the century narrated by Albert Edwin Card', LS BED/CAR
Johnstone, Margery, 'A real good life growing up in the south east midlands. The life of Margery "Mum" Johnstone in her own words', B/JOH

Bexley Local Studies and Archives Centre, Central Library, Bexleyheath
Wasson, May, 'Memories of Ninety Years', 920

Birmingham Archives and Heritage, Birmingham
Chinn, Walter, 'From Victoria's Image: A Reminiscence in Reflection'

Bishopsgate Institute Library, London
Harding, Arthur 'My Apprenticeship to Crime: an Autobiography'

Blackburn Local Studies Library, Central Library, Blackburn
Ellis, Albert, 'As it was and Twenty One Today', G3 ELL

Bolton Archives and Local Studies, Bolton
Snowman, Hilda, née Snape, Untitled MS, ZZ/199

Bradford Central Library (Local Studies Collection), Bradford
Harland, John, 'Diary', 1810–1815, 1831, 920 Har.
Wood, Thomas, 'Autobiography by Thomas Wood, 1822–1880', 920 Woo

Bristol Archives, Bristol
Bennett, John, 'Manuscript autobiography of John Bennett of Bristol', 36907
Mitchell, Tommy, 'Tommy's Book', TS, B29411 – Pr.2 pb Biog. M–P

Bristol Reference Library, Bristol
Mrs M. M. Dark, Untitled, B29503

British Library, London
'Autobiography of an Ordinary Man, with odds and ends to match', TS
Purkiss, Edwin, 'Memories of a London Orphan Boy, etc' (Bexley, 1957)

Broadstairs Library, Kent
Pointer, Thomas, 'Extracts from the memoirs of Thomas James Pointer of St Peters', 52 POI

Burnett Archive of Working-Class Autobiography, Brunel University
Abbley, M., 'Soul Adrift – being the memoirs of a queer child', Uncatalogued
Adnams, Nora Isabel, 'My memoirs of Dr Barnardo's Home', 2:859
Anderson, J. R., 'Vapourings of an Old Ploughman: Memoirs of 1892–1914', 1:1016
Ashley, James, Untitled TS, 1:24
Balne, Edward, 'Autobiography of an ex-Workhouse and Poor Law School boy', 1:37
Barker, Lottie, 'My life as I remember it', 2:37
Bell, Rosa, 'Rosa Bell Remembers', 2:59
Bellamy, Harry, 'Early Memories', 3:9
Betts, Frank, Untitled, 1:857
Bold, Edna, 'The Long and Short of It Being the Recollections of Edna Bold', 2:85
Brain, Norah, Untitled, 2:872
Brown, Edward, Untitled, 1:93
Bull, John, 'Early childhood', 2:114
Burkin, Henrietta, 'Memoirs of Henrietta Burkin', 2:118
Buss, Phyllis L., 'A. Driver became A. Buss', 2:124
Cain, Edward, 'Memories', 1:119
Chase, Alice Maud, 'The Memoirs of Alice Maud Chase', 1:141
Clarke, Maud, Untitled, 1:156
Collinson, Arthur T., 'One way only: an autobiography of an old-time trade unionist', 3:30
Collis, Alice, 'My first strike' and 'From paper blankets to central heating', 3:230
Cowper, Daisy, 'De Nobis', 1:182
Cox, Ruth, 'White Knob Row', 1:184
Cutts, Mabel, Untitled, 1:196
Dorrell, Harry, 'Falling Cadence: An autobiography of failure', 2:231
Downer, Mrs R., 'A Bygone Age', 1:211
Elliott, Norah, Untitled drafts of autobiography, 2:242
Elliott, Walter John Eugene, Untitled, 1:227
Elliott, William George, 'An Octogenarian's Personal Life Story', 1:228
Ellisdon, Leonard, 'Starting from Victoria', 1:229
Evett, Paul, 'My Life in and out of Print', 1:233
Farndon, Reg, Untitled, 2:269
Fowler, Hilda Rose, 'Look after the little ones', 1:243
Frisby, Minnie, 'Memories', 1:250
Garrett, Kay, Untitled, 2:305
Gill, Arthur, 'I remember! Reminiscences of a Cobbler's son'
Gill, Ellen, 'Ellen Gill's Diary', 1:269
Goffin, Arthur Frederick, 'The Story of a grey life, being the autobiography of Arthur Frederick
    Goffin', 1:271

Gold, Olive Doris, 'My Life', 2:321

Gomm, Amy Frances, 'Water under the bridge', 2:324

Goodwin, Albert, Untitled, 1:273

Goring, Jack, Untitled, 1:274

Goss, Frank, 'My Boyhood at the Turn of the Century', 2:331

Gregory, George, Untitled, 1:283

Hammond, Allen, 'Tomorrow couldn't be worse', Uncatalogued

Hampton, Nora, 'Memories of Baptist End, Netherington, Dudley, 1895–1918', 3:68

Hannan, Dora R., 'Those Happy Highways: an Autobiography', 2:357

Hansford, Charles Lewis, 'Memoirs of a Bricklayer: the Life of Charles Lewis Hansford', Uncatalogued

Harris, H. J., Autobiographical letters, 1978–1984, 2:363

Harrison, E., 'Poor and Proud in Preston', Uncatalogued

Harwood, Cecil George, 'Down Memory Lane', 1:309

Heslop, Harold, 'From Tyne to Tone: a Journey', 3:75

Hilton-Ford, Kathleen, 'Grannie's Girl', 2:398

Hilton-Ford, Kathleen, 'The Survivor: the memoirs of a little Dover girl', 2:398

Hodges, Adeline, 'I Remember', 2:411

Holborow, Lizzie, 'My Village at Waunarlwydd', 1:868

Horner, C. V., 'Ups and Downs: A Lifetime spent in the Yorkshire Dales', 2:422

Howitt, Mary, Untitled, 1:355

Hughes, Anita Elizabeth, Untitled, 1:357

Humphries, Edward S., 'Childhood. An Autobiography of a Boy from 1889–1906', 1:361

Hunt, Doris, Untitled, 2:428

Jefferis, Ada M., 'The Memories of A. M. Jefferies. Written by her Daughter', 1:379

Jones, Jack, Untitled, 2:443

Jones, May, Untitled, 1:401

Jones, Mrs Nora, Autobiographical Letters, 2:444

Jordan, Charlotte, 'My memories of early life', 3:101

Jordan, Thomas, Untitled, 1:405

Keen, Molly, 'Childhood memories', 2:449

Langley, Amy, Untitled (in two parts), 2:466

Lanigan, Jack, 'Thy Kingdom DID come', 1:421

Lay, Alfred George Henry, 'Adventure', 3:211

Lea, Emily Gertrude, 'Reflections in the setting sun, or "I remember" after fifty years commencing 1902', 2:469

Ley, Ethel Mary Ellen, Untitled, 1:872

Lloyd, George, 'The Autobiography of George Brawd', 3:108

Lord, Annie, 'My Life' 2:486

Lovekin, Emmanuel, 'Some Notes of my Life', 1:452

[Margaret Jane], Untitled, Uncatalogued

Marrin, Mrs P., Untitled, 1:493

Martin, Grace, 'From 1906', 2:515

McKenzie, James H., 'Strange Truth: The Autobiography of a Circus, Showman, Stage & Exhibition Man', 1:473

McLouglin, Catherine, Untitled, 1:477

Meadowcroft, Charlotte Dorothy, 'Bygones', 2:523

Middlebrook, Wilfred, 'Trumpet Voluntary', 2:527

Morris, Bronwen, Untitled, 2:541

Morris, R. W., 'Autobiography of R. W. Morris', 1:520

Nicholls, Dora Adeline, 'My Story', 1:532

Oulton, Marjorie, 'Memories', Uncatalogued

Owen, May, Autobiographical Letter, 2:574

Parker, Mrs L., Untitled, 2:583
Passiful, Annie Elizabeth, Untitled, 3:132
Philips, Irene, Untitled, 2:612
Pidgeon, Alice, 'Looking over my shoulder to childhood days and after', 2:619
Powell, Eric F., 'Forest memories: the autobiography of a Dean Forester', 2:630
Prevett, Frank, 'Memoirs of a railway man', 2:638
Purvis, Lily, 'Reminiscences of my childhood days in Lancashire', 2:643
Raymont, Thomas, 'Memories of an Octogenarian, 1864–1949', 1:571
Rice, Stanley, 'The Memories of a Rolling Stone: Times and incidents remembered', 2:661
Rignall, Elizabeth, 'All so long ago'
Roberts, Mr, 'Before my Time', Uncatalogued
Robinson, E., 'I Remember', 1:593
Rowles, George, 'Chaps among the Caps', 1:600
Seymour, Arthur, 'Childhood Memories', 1:616
Sharman, Jessie Ravenna, 'Recollections of Jessie Ravenna Sharman', 1:618
Shotton, Ernest Richard, 'Personal history and memoirs of Ernest Richard Shotton', 1:627
Silvester, Susan, 'In a World that has Gone', 1:628
Skargon, Charles, 'From boy to man the hard way', 2:712
Smith, Sam, 'Bosley Cloud: a North Country Childhood', 3:168
Squires, Dorothy, Untitled, 2:735
Sutton, William Harry, Untitled, 1:678
Terry, Joseph, 'Recollections of my Life', 1:693
Thomas, Averill, Untitled, 1:892
Till, Winifred, 'The Early Years of a Victorian Grandmother', 2:763
Tobias, Wilhelmina, 'Childhood Memories', 2:766
Triggle, Mary Laura, Untitled, 1:719
Wall, Percy, 'Hour at Eve', 3:186
Wallis, Bessie, 'Yesterday', 2:794
Watson, Margaret, Untitled, 2:802
Wensley, Frank, 'My Memories, 1890–1914', 1:1022
Westall, Lilian, 'The Good Old Days', 1:746
Williams, Edith A., Untitled, 2:832
Wynne, Frederick, 'Old Pompey and Other Places', 2:854
Yates, Mrs, 'Before My Time', Uncatalogued
Young, Harry, 'Harry's Biography', 2:858

Burnley Local History Collection, Burnley Library
Bates, Joe, 'Joe's Your Uncle', LG3 Bates
Cookson, Doris, 'Autumn leaves', LG3 Cookson
Grimshaw, Miss M., 'Memories of Burnley', LG3 Grimshaw

Cambridgeshire Record Office, Cambridge
Crane, Robert, 'An Old Man's Memories', 231/Z65
Rose, Amy Grace, Untitled volume of reminiscences, MS (1945), P137/28/3

Carlisle Library (Local Studies Department), Carlisle
Irving, Thomas, 'Farming and Country Life in Cumberland 100 Years ago', B600

Crosby Library, Liverpool
Fairhurst, Zoe, 'Our Zoe of Gilling West: Her Life Story', 920.7 FAI

Cumbria Record Office
Sankoffsky, Johan, 'Diary', ex-DX 644/1–2

David Wandilson Library, University of Leicester
Bacon, Charles, 'The Life Story of Charles Bacon (as told by himself)', MS88

Derbyshire Record Office, Matlock
Storey, John, 'The Way we Lived', D2222/F1

Doncaster Local Studies Library, Doncaster
Fowlstone, W. R., 'Life of W. R. Fowlstone', L920 FOW

East Riding Archives and Local Studies, Beverley
Taylor, Hasslewood, 'Untitled MS', DDX1077/11

Essex Record Office, Chelmsford, Essex
Castle, John, 'The Diary of John Castle', B/CAS

Finsbury Library (Islington Local History Centre), London
Price, Henry Edward, 'My diary', 1032 S/HEP

Fleetwood Local Studies Collection, Fleetwood Library
Porter, Ralph, 'Personal recollections of Fleetwood, by a Native', LG3 PORTER

Flintshire County Record Office, Hawarden
Hughes, Edward, Untitled MS, D/NM/852
Nuttall, Samuel, 'My recollections and life', D/DM/742/1

Greenwich Heritage Centre, Woolwich, London
Stradley, John, 'Memoirs of John Stradley, 1757–1825', 920 Strad

Guildford Museum, Guildford
Chadwick, Alice Maude, 'Maude's Memoirs'

Halifax Central Library (Local Studies), Halifax
Dodgson, Joshua, 'Diary of Joshua Dodgson', *Halifax Weekly Courier and Guardian*, 19 and 25 May 1956

Hampshire Archives and Local Studies, Winchester
Smith, H. F. 'Autobiography or memoir "The Life Story of Henry Frederick Smith" ', 134M96/A2

Huddersfield Local History Library, Huddersfield
Blackburn, Minnie, 'Memories of the Dearne Valley some Seventy Years ago: conversations with Miss M. W. Blackburn of Scissett'

Hull History Centre, Hull
Ammon, Charles George, 'A Long Road: an Autobiography', U DMN/9/6

Huntingdonshire Archives
Easter, Mr E., 'Memories', Early reminiscences of members of Eynesbury Darby and Joan Club, 5379
Hills, Mrs, 'Reminiscences of Mrs. Hills', HP53/29/5

Imperial War Museum
Kibblewhite, F. H., Private Papers of F. H. Kibblewhite, Document 4766

BIBLIOGRAPHY OF AUTOBIOGRAPHIES

Keighley Local Library, Keighley
Kitson, John, 'Diary of John Kitson of Haworth', 920 HAW KIT

Leicester Local Studies Library, Leicester
Bacon, Charles, 'The Life Story of Charles Bacon (as told by himself)', MS88

Leicestershire Record Office, Wigston Magna, Leicester
Goodliffe, Arnold, 'Memoirs of Arnold Goodliffe', DE7196

Lincoln Local Studies Library, Lincoln
Cook, Richard, 'The Memoirs of Richard Cook', LOC L.921.COO

Manchester Central Library
Mary Turner, ed., 'Collyhurst Then', GB127.Broadsides/F1990.56 (recollections by: Anne Chapman née Griffiths; Florence Gibbs née Mitchell; May Snowden née Dickinson; Mrs Snowden's elder sister)

Marx Memorial Library, London
Crawfurd, Helen, Untitled, HC/1/3

Mitchell Library, Glasgow
Morton, Alfred, 'Biography of Alfred Morton, by Himself, From Memory and Diaries', 596897

Newport Central Library (Local Studies Collection) Newport
Hughes, Henry, 'Autobiography', qM380.920.HUG

Norfolk Record Office, Norwich
Barnet, Mrs [King, Mary (Polly)], 'A Tale for Mother's Meetings Mrs Barnet's Autobiography' by J. Augusta Fry, FX 319
Hemmingway, John, 'The Character or Worldly experience of the writer from 1791 to 1865', MC 766/1, 795X5
Jex, Frederick, Untitled, in Norwich Labour Party, Miscellaneous papers including transcripts of oral history interviews, SO 198/5/52, 940x1
Lincoln, John, 'Memoirs of John Lincoln', MC 2669/29, 991X9

Northamptonshire Record Office, Northampton
Bayes, John, 'A few memories of my life', ZB1648
Mallard, George, 'Memories', ZA9908/3, X9908/4–15
'Village Memories', X2959 (Recollections by Mrs A. E. Chapman, Eliza Freeston, W. Alexander, Mrs Lucy Linnett, F. R. Rigby, John Whitlock)

Norwich Castle Museum, Norwich
Short, Obadiah, 'Recollections, 1861', NWHCM: 1964.590.2

Nottinghamshire Archives
Joseph Burdett, 'Memoirs of Joseph Burdett, Stockinger and sometime apprentice to Mr Kirk of Lambley, Nottinghamshire, 1813–1917', DD1177/1

Oxfordshire History Centre, Oxford
Crawford, James, 'Autobiography', O45/26/18/MSI/1
Davies, Mrs G., Interview Transcript, 'Autobiography', O45/26/9/A1/2
Edwards, R. H. (Bert), 'Autobiography', vol. 1, O45/26/15/MS1
Gear, Jessie, 'Autobiography', O45/26/13/MS1
Joel [Clayton Edward], 'Autobiography', O45/26/12/MS1

Landymore, Sarah, 'Autobiography', O45/26/8/MS1
Rawlings, Joe, 'Autobiography', O45/26/2/MS1
Rayment, Frank, 'Autobiography', O45/26/7/MS1
Relph, Winifred, Autobiography, O45/26/6/MS1
Sladen, Edward, 'Autobiography', O45/26/25/MS1
Wood, Bertha, 'Autobiography', O45/26/24/MS1

Rawtenstall Local Studies Library, Rawtenstall
Heap, Moses, 'My life and times', TS ed. J. Elliott. LG3 HEAP
Luty, Mary, 'My Life has Sparkled', LG3 LUTY, Mary/LUT

Rotherham Local Studies Library, Rotherham
Colman, Belding, 'Autobiography 1900–1951', 942.741.920 COL
Evans, Leslie, 'From the glow of the lamp', 942.741.920 EVA
James, T. H., 'We tread but one path', 942.741.920 JAM

Salvation Army International Heritage Centre, William Booth College
Jarrett, Rebecca, 'Rebecca Jarrett: written by her own self', RJ/2/2

Southwark Local History Library and Archive
Bustin, Percy, 'My two square miles of London: Reminiscences of a Bermondsey Boy'
Causer, S. T., Autobiographical Letter
Davis, Mrs A. C., 'Hearthstone and Vinegar', 'Caraway Seeds' and 'Ermine and Persian Lamb'
Davis, Isabella, 'My Life and Memories'
Fish, Margaret, 'Memoirs'
Howell, Annie, Untitled, in Sidney Fagan, ed., 'Bermondsey Born, Stories of Old Bermondsey and Rotherhithe'
Meader, Ivy Violet, Untitled
Mullins, Lily, 'Life in my Younger Days'
Roberts, Florrie, 'The Ups and Downs of Florrie Roberts'
Thornton, Bertha, 'Memories of Childhood'
Tomlin, Laura, Untitled in Sidney Fagan, ed., 'Bermondsey Born, Stories of Old Bermondsey and Rotherhithe'
Warren, Jane, Untitled in Sidney Fagan, ed., 'Bermondsey Born, Stories of Old Bermondsey and Rotherhithe'

Surrey History Centre, Woking
Wallis, Pearl R., 'Down Memory Lane by Margaret Fowler', 1674/10

Tameside Local Studies and Archives Centre, Central Library, Ashton-under-Lyne
Holland, John, 'Life with Grandfather', L614.6HOL
Watson, Lewis, 'Autobiography of A . . .', L329.3WAT

Treorchy Local Studies Library, Treorchy
Parrish, William, 'This is my story', R9 (922)

Walsall Local History Centre, Walsall
Jones, Gwen, 'Sunshine After Dawn: The Autobiography of Gwen Jones', 920 JAM
Killian, Jack, 'Autobiography and Testimonial of Mr. J. T. Killian, Walsall', 1216
Wood, Bert, Untitled, 920 WOO

Oral History Collection:
Brockhurst, Alan, 263/3
Farmer, Percy, 426/28

Haddock, Jack, 162/1/120
Killian, Jack, 162/1/61
Perry, Doris, 162/1/206
Price, Edith, 426/49
Taylor, Amy, 426/52
Wilkes, Madge, 426/48

Warrington Local Studies Library, Warrington
Goulden, Ethel, 'When we were young. A "living history" of a village girl', MS 2168

Warwick Modern Records Centre
Fagg, Len, 'A Man of Kent: the Autobiography of Len Fagg', MSS.120/45
Garnett, Jim, 'My Autobiography', MSS.21/1633/1
Plastow, William, 'William Plastow's story', MSS.172/LP/A/115
Vandome, Albert, Untitled Autobiography, MSS.158/2/1
Vandome, Minnie, Untitled Autobiography, MSS.158/2/2

Wolverhampton Archives, Wolverhampton
Sproson, Emma, 'My Child Life', DX 686/1

Worcestershire Archive Service, Worcester
Shervington, Jesse, 'Autobiography of an agricultural labourer', BA 5518 Ref: 970.5: 645
   Parcel 1

Working Class Movement Library, Salford
Doyle, Charles, 'The hammer and thistle: the making of a rebel, by Charles A. Doyle',
   PP/BIOG/19
Eacott, Bill, 'The Grandad tapes: Memories of William "Bill" Eacott', PP/BIOG/14
Holden, Mrs P., 'True Story of a Lancashire Pit Brow Lass by Mrs P Holden', PP/BIOG/1
Honeyford, Tom, 'Tom Honeyford's autobiography: poverty, exploitation and war 1891–1937',
   PP/BIOG/13
[James], 'Autobiography', PP/BIOG/10
Miller, Lucy, 'A wasted talent, autobiography by Lucy Miller', PP/BIOG/15
Stephen, Jessie, 'Submission is for slaves by Jessie Stephen', PP/BIOG/16
Warmsley, Arthur, 'Autobiography of Arthur Warmsley', PP/BIOG/2

PRINTED AUTOBIOGRAPHIES

'A Coal miner's defence', *Potters' Examiner and Emigrants' Advocate*, no. 29, vol. x, 11 (January
   1851)
[Acorn, George, pseud.], *One of the Multitude*, with an introduction by Arthur C. Benson
   (London, 1911)
Adams, W. E., *Memoirs of a Social Atom*, 2 vols (London, 1903)
Adsetts, Ernest, *The Ernest Adsetts Story: 'For Children Up To 90'*, as told to Keith Farnsworth
   (n.p., [1987])
Aird, Andrew, *Autobiography* (Glasgow, 1899)
Aitken, William, 'Remembrances and struggles of a working man for bread and liberty', in
   Robert G. Hall and Stephen Roberts, eds, *William Aitken, the Writings of a Nineteenth Century
   Working Man* (Tameside, 1998)
Aldred, Guy, *No Traitor's Gait! The Autobiography of Guy A. Aldred* (Glasgow, 1955–63)
'A light in the gloom; or the politics of the past. An old man's tale', *People's Paper*, 8 May–14
   August 1852 (10 articles in all)

Allaway, John, Untitled, in Ronald Goldman, ed., *Breakthrough: Autobiographical Accounts of the Education of some Socially Disadvantaged Children* (London, 1968), pp. 1–18

Allen, George, *The Machine Breaker; Or, the Heart-rending Confession of George Allen . . . Written by Himself* (London, [1831?])

Ambrose, Ernest, *Melford Memories: Recollections of 94 Years* (Lavenham, Suffolk, 1972)

[A Miner], 'A trade union solitary: memoir of a mid-nineteenth century miner', *History Workshop Journal*, 25/1 (1988), pp. 148–65

Anderson, Isaac, *The Life History of Isaac Anderson. A Member of the Peculiar People* (n.p., 1896)

Andrew, Jane, *Recorded Mercies: Being the Autobiography of Jane Andrew, living at St Ive, Liskeard, Cornwall* (London, [1890])

Andrews, Elizabeth, *A Woman's Work is Never Done*, ed. Ursula Masson (Dinas Powys, 2006)

An Exposition of the Nefarious System of Making and Passing Spurious Coin . . . Being the Confessions of a Coiner (Preston, n.d.)

'A Norfolk labourer's wife', *Eastern Counties Magazine*, 1901–1902, vol. 1–2; repr. E. A. Goodwyn and J. C. Baxter, eds, *East Anglian Reminiscences* (Ipswich, 1976), pp. 24–9

Anthony, Francis, *A Man's a Man* (London, 1932)

Arch, Joseph, *Joseph Arch: The Story of his Life, Told by Himself*, ed. with a preface by the Countess of Warwick (London, 1898)

Armstrong, Chester, *Pilgrimage from Nenthead: An Autobiography* (London, 1938)

Arnold, William, *The Recollections of William Arnold*, ed. with an introduction by Keith Brooker (Northampton, 2014)

Ash, Dorothy L., *Memories of a London Childhood, recalled by Dorothy L. Ash* (London, 1984)

Ashby, Joseph, *Joseph Ashby of Tysoe, A Study of English Village Life*, ed. Mabel Kathleen Ashby (London, 1974)

Ashdown, Eli, *Gleanings by a Watchman on a Dark Corner of Zion's Walls . . . Being the Autobiography of Eli Ashdown* (London, 1904)

A Short Account of the Life and Hardships of a Glasgow Weaver . . . Written by Himself (Glasgow, 1834)

Askham, John, *Sketches in Prose and Verse* (Wellingborough, 1893)

Autobiography of a Private Soldier, Showing the Danger of Rashly Enlisting (Sunderland, 1838)

'Autobiography of a Scotch convict', *Daily News*, 5 June 1849

Autobiography of a Scotch Lad: Being Reminiscences of Threescore Years and Ten (Glasgow, 1887)

Bain, Alexander, *Autobiography*, ed. William L. Davidson (London, 1904)

Baldry, George, *The Rabbitskin Cap: A Tale of a Norfolk Countryman's Youth, written in his Old Age*, ed. Lilias Rider Haggard (Woodbridge, 1979)

Ball, F. C., *A Breath of Fresh Air: Memories of a Country Childhood before the First World War* (London, 1961)

Barber, George H., *From Workhouse to Lord Mayor: An Autobiography*, with a foreword by Rev. Geo H. Marshall (Tunstall, 1937)

Barclay, Thomas Patrick, *Memoirs and Medleys: The Autobiography of a Bottle-Washer*, ed. James K. Kelly, with a foreword by Sydney A. Gimson (Leicester, 1934)

Barker, Joseph, *Life of Joseph Barker, Written by Himself*, ed. John Thomas Barker (London, 1880)

Barlow, Richard Gorton, *Forty Seasons of First-class Cricket* (Manchester, [1908])

Barnard, Hilda, *A Life in Charing* (Charing and District Local History Society, 1986)

Barnes, Annie, *Tough Annie: From Suffragette to Stepney Councillor* (London, 1980)

Barnes, George Nicoll, *From Workshop to War Cabinet*, with an introduction by the Rt Hon D. Lloyd George, MP (London, [1923])

—, 'How I got on: Pushed into fame', *Pearson's Weekly*, 8 March 1906

Barnetson, Madge, Untitled, in *To Make Ends Meet, Women Over 60 Write about their Working Lives: Memories Collected by the Older Women's Project*, ed. Jo Stanley (London, [1989?]), pp. 83–5

Barr, David, *Climbing the Ladder: The Struggles and Successes of a Village Lad* (London, 1910)

Barrett, Walter Henry, *A Fenman's Story*, with a foreword by Enid Porter (London, 1965)

Basset, Josiah, *Life of a Vagrant: Or the Testimony of an Outcast to the Value and Truth of the Gospel* (New York, 1852)

Bates, Herbert Ernest, *The Vanished World: An Autobiography of Childhood and Youth* (London, 1969)

Bates, John, *John Bates, the Veteran Reformer: A Sketch of his Life* (Queensbury, 1895; facs. repr. London, 1986)

Bathgate, Janet, *Aunt Janet's Legacy to Her Nieces: Recollections of Humble Life in Yarrow in the Beginning of the Century* (Selkirk, 1894)

Bayley, Stanley James, 'Village life in Llanfi hangel Crucorney', *Gwent Local History*, 48 (1980), pp. 14–17

Behan, Kathleen, *Mother of All the Behans: The story of Kathleen Behan as told to Brian Behan* (London, 1984)

Belcher, Richard Boswell, *Autobiography of Richard Boswell Belcher of Banbury and Blockley*, eds A. W. Exell and Norah M. Marshall (Blockley Antiquarian Society, 1976)

Bell, Thomas, *Pioneering Days* (London, 1941)

Bell, William, *The Road to Jericho*, with an introduction by Sid Chaplin and paintings by the Ashington Group (North Shields, 1980)

Bellan, Joan, *Them Days; Devon Life of the 1890s–1920s; From the Memories of Joan Bellan*, ed. Joy Lakeman (Padstow, 1982)

Benjamin, Harry, *Adventure in Living: Autobiography of a Myope* (London, 1950)

Bennett, Herbert John, *I Was a Walworth Boy* (London, 1980)

Benson, Ernie, *To Struggle is to Live: A Working Class Autobiography*, i (Newcastle, 1979)

Bent, Charles, *Autobiography of Charles Bent, a Reclaimed Drunkard* (Sheffield, 1866)

Bent, James, 'Introduction', *Criminal Life: Reminiscences of 42 Years as a Police Officer* (Manchester, [1891]), pp. iii–vi

Bentley, Mary, *Born 1896: Childhood in Clayton and Working in Manchester and Cheshire* (Manchester, 1985)

Bertenshaw, Mary, *Sunrise to Sunset: An Autobiography by Mary Bertenshaw. A Vivid Personal Account of her Life in Manchester*, adapted by Alan Yardley (Bury, 1991)

Bertram, James Glass, *Some Memories of Books, Authors and Events* (London, 1893)

Beswick, Wilfred, *Industrialist's Journey (Memoirs of a Northern Business Man)* ([Harrogate], [n.d.])

Bethune, John, *Poems by the Late John Bethune with a Sketch of the Author's Life, By His Brother* (London, 1841)

Bezer, John James, 'The autobiography of one of the Chartist rebels of 1848', in David Vincent, ed., *Testaments of Radicalism: Memoirs of Working-class Politicians, 1790–1885* (London, 1977)

Bickerton, Fred, *Fred of Oxford, Being the Memoirs of Fred Bickerton, Until Recently Head Porter of University College*, with a preface by G. D. H. Cole (London, 1953)

Black, James, 'Local autobiography: Glasgow in the past century', *Glasgow Herald*, 5 May 1851

Blackburn, Elizabeth K., *In and Out the Windows: A Story of the Changes in Working Class Life 1902–77 in a Small East Lancashire Community* (Burnley, 1980)

Blake, John, *Memories of Old Poplar* (London, 1977)

Blatchford, Robert, *My Eighty Years*, with a preface by Alexander M. Thompson (London, 1931)

Blow, John, *Autobiography of John Blow* (Leeds, 1870)

Bodell, James, *A Soldier's View of Empire: The Reminiscences of James Bodell, 1831–92*, ed. Keith Sinclair (London, 1982)

Bond, Alice, *Life of a Yorkshire Girl* (Hull, 1981)

Bondfield, Margaret Grace, *A Life's Work* (London, [1948])

Boughton, Fred, 'The forest in my younger days', in John Burnett, ed., *Destiny Obscure: Autobiographies of Childhood, Education and Family from the 1820s to the 1920s* (London, 1982), pp. 309–15

Bowd, James, 'The life of a farm worker', *The Countryman*, 51/2 (1955), pp. 293–300

Bowen, Jack, 'Recollections of a farm worker', *Journal of the North Yorkshire County Record Office*, 1 (1975), pp. 35–9

Bower, Fred, *Rolling Stonemason: An Autobiography*, ed. with a foreword by John Brophy (London, 1936)

Bowes, John, *The Autobiography, or History of the Life of John Bowes* (Glasgow, 1872)

Bowles, Minnie, 'Minnie Bowles', in *Childhood Memories, recorded by some Socialist Men and Women in their Later Years*, ed. with an introduction by Margaret Cohen, Marion and Hymie Fagan (n.p., [1983?]), pp. 4–10

Bowyer, William, *Brought Out in Evidence: An Autobiographical Summing-Up* (London, [1941])

Box, Muriel, *Odd Woman Out: An Autobiography* (London, 1974)

Braddock, Jack and Bessie, *The Braddocks* (London, 1963)

Brady, James, 'A long, long trail a-winding', in John Burnett, ed., *Destiny Obscure: Autobiographies of Childhood, Education and Family from the 1820s to the 1920s* (London, 1982), pp. 316–22

Brand, E. P., *A Fenman Remembers* (Huntingdon, 1977)

Brearley, Harry, *Knotted String: Autobiography of a Steel-Maker* (London, 1941)

Brierley, Benjamin, *Home Memories: The Autobiography of a Handloom Weaver* (Manchester, 1886; repr. Bramhall, 2002)

Bright, Ben, *Shellback: Reminiscences of Ben Bright, Mariner*, recorded, edited and with a foreword by Ewan MacColl and Peggy Seeger (Oxford, [1979])

Britten, Barnabas, *Woodyard to Palace: Reminiscences* (Bradford, 1958)

Broadhurst, Henry, *Henry Broadhurst M.P.: The Story of his Life from a Stonemason's Bench to the Treasury Bench* (London, 1901)

Brooks, J. Barlow, *Lancashire Bred* (Stalybridge, 1929)

Brooksbank, Mary, *No Sae Lang Syne: A Tale of this City* (Dundee, [1971])

Broomhill, Leily, 'In memory of my mum', in *'Like it Was Yesterday': Childhood Memories, Islington Council Libraries Department* (London, 1989), no pag.

Brown, Sir Edward, *Memories at Eventide* (Burnley, 1934)

Brown, Harold, *Most Splendid of Men: Life in a Mining Community*, with a foreword by the Rt Hon. Lord Robens (Poole, 1981)

Brown, John, 'A memoir of Robert Blincoe, an orphan boy (1832)', in James R. Simmons and Janice Carlisle, eds, *Factory Lives: Four Nineteenth-Century Working-Class Autobiographies* (Ontario, 2007)

Brown, John, *Sixty Years' Gleanings from Life's Harvest: A Genuine Autobiography* (Cambridge, 1858)

Brown, Percy, *Round the Corner* (London, 1934)

Brown, W. J., *So Far . . .* with a preface by John Buchan (London, 1943)

Brown, William, *A Narrative of the Life and Adventures of William Brown* (York, 1829)

Bryson, Elizabeth, *Look Back in Wonder*, with an introduction by K. L. Brooker (Dundee, 1967)

Buckley, John, *A Village Politician: The Life-Story of John Buckley*, ed. J. C. Buckmaster (London, 1897)

Bullard, Sir Reader, *The Camels Must Go: An Autobiography* (London, 1961)

Bullen, Frank Thomas, *Confessions of a Tradesman* (London, 1908)

—, *Recollections: The Reminiscences of the Busy Life of One Who has Played the varied Parts of Sailor, Author & Lecturer* (London, 1915)

Bullock, Jim, *Them and Us, With a Last Word by Lord Robens* (London, 1972)

Burchett, George, *Memoirs of a Tattooist, From the Notes and Diaries and Letters of the late 'King of Tattooists'*, compiled and edited with a foreword by Peter Leighton (London, 1958)

Burgess, Joseph, *A Potential Poet? His Autobiography and Verse* (Ilford, 1927)

Burke, Mick, *Ancoats Lad: The Recollections of Mick Burke* (Manchester, 1985)

Burke, Thomas, *The Wind and the Rain: A Book of Confessions* (New York, 1924)

Burland, John, *John Hugh Burland by Himself* (Barnsley, [1902?])

Burn, James Dawson, *The Autobiography of a Beggar Boy, 1855*, ed. with introduction by David Vincent (London, 1978)

Burnett, Al, *Knave of Clubs: The Memoirs of Al Burnett, Leading Impressario and Entertainer* (London, 1963)

Burrows, Mrs, 'A childhood in the fens about 1850–1860', in Margaret Llewelyn Davies, ed., *Life as we have Known It, by Co-Operative Working Women* (London, 1931)

Burt, Thomas, *Thomas Burt: Pitman & Privy Councillor: An Autobiography* (London, 1924)

Burton, H. M., *There Was A Young Man* (London, 1958)

[Butler, Robert], *Narrative of the Life and Travels of Sergeant B—. Written by Himself* (Edinburgh, 1823)

Buxton, Richard, 'A brief memoir of the author', in his *A Botanical Guide to the Flowers and Plants . . . within Sixteen Miles of Manchester* (London, 1849)

Bywater, James, *The Trio's Pilgrimage: An Autobiography of James Bywater, including Brief Life Sketches of his Wives Maria Thomas, Hanna Maria Jenson*, ed. Hyrum W. Valentine ([Salt Lake City], [1947])

Cameron, Clare, *Rustle of Spring: An Edwardian Childhood in London's East End* (London, 1979)

[Cameron, William], *Hawkie: The Autobiography of a Gangrel*, ed. John Strathesk (Glasgow, 1888)

Campbell, Duncan, *Reminiscences and Reflections of an Octogenarian Highlander* (Inverness, 1910)

Campion, Sidney R., *Sunlight on the Foothills* (London, [1941])

Cannell, Nora, *Memories of a Haslingfield Childhood* (Haslingfield, [1983])

Carbis, Nellie, *Nellie Carbis Looks Back: Recollections of a Childhood Spent in Newton-le-Willows* (Kendal, n.d.)

Cardus, Neville, *Autobiography* (London, 1947)

Carley, Gauis, *The Memoirs of Gauis Carley, A Sussex Blacksmith. Written by Himself*, ed. with notes by Francis W. Steer and with a foreword by the Earl of Cottenham (Chichester, 1964)

Carnegie, Andrew, *Autobiography of Andrew Carnegie* (Cambridge, MA, and London, 1920)

Carter, Thomas, *Memoirs of a Working Man*, ed. Charles Knight (London, 1845)

Cassiel [Richard Gooch], *Memoirs, Remarkable Vicissitudes, Military Career and Wanderings* (Norwich, 1852)

Cast, Harry, *Harry's Story: The Memoirs of Harry Cast. Memories of a Nottingham Childhood, of life as a Young Miner, and of the Privations and Horrors of the Great War* (Nottingham, 2015)

Castle, John, 'Memoirs', in A. F. J. Brown, ed., *Essex People 1750–1900, from their Diaries Memoirs and Letters* (Chelmsford, 1972)

Catling, Thomas Thurgood, *My Life's Pilgrimage* (London, 1911)

Catton, Samuel, *A Short Sketch of a Long Life of Samuel Catton once a Suffolk Ploughboy* (Ipswich, 1863)

Chadwick, William, *Reminiscences of a Chief Constable* (Manchester, 1900; facs. repr. Longdendale, 1974)

Chaplin, Charles Spencer (Charlie), *My Autobiography* (London, 1964)

Chatterton, Daniel, *Biography of Dan Chatterton, Atheist and Communist* (London, 1891)

Chew, Ada Nield, *The Life and Writings of a Working Woman*, ed. Doris Nield Chew with a foreword by Anna Davin (London, 1982)

Choyce, James, *The Log of a Jack Tar; or The Life of James Choyce, Master Mariner* (London, 1891; facs. repr. 1973)

Christie, A. V., *Brass Tacks and a Fiddle* (Kilmarnock, 1943)

Church, Richard, *Over the Bridge: An Essay in Autobiography* (London, 1955)

Citrine, Walter, *Men and Work: An Autobiography* (London, 1964)

Clark, Elspeth, 'New Elgin's grand old lady: Reminiscences of past century', *Elgin Courant*, 19 September 1941

[Clerk, Andie], *Arab: A Liverpool Street Kid Remembers* (Liverpool, 1969)

Cliff, James Henry Treloar, *Down to the Sea in Ships: The Memoirs of James Henry Treloar Cliff, as told to P. W. Birkbeck*, ed. Rita Tregallas Pope (Redruth, 1983)

Clifford, John, *Dr John Clifford, C. H. Life, Letters and Reminiscences* (London, 1924)

Clift, William, *Reminiscences of William Clift* (Basingstoke, 1908)

Clunie, James, *Voice of Labour: The Autobiography of a House Painter* (Dunfermline, 1958)

Clynes, J. R., *Memoirs, 1869–1924* (London, 1937)

Cocking, George, *From the Mines to the Pulpit; or Success Hammered Out of the Rock*, with an introduction by A. L. T. Ewert (Cincinnati, 1901)

[Coe, Mary], 'Mary Coe', in Mary Chamberlain, *Fenwomen: A Portrait of Women in an English Village* (London, 1975)

Coleman, Elizabeth, *The Tangled Garden: Memories of my Girlhood* (London, 1988)

[Colin, pseud.], *The Wanderer Brought Home: The Life and Adventures of Colin. An Autobiography*, ed. with reflections by the Rev. B. Richings (London, 1864)

Collier, Mrs, *A Bible-woman's Story: Being the Autobiography of Mrs Collier of Birmingham*, ed. with an introduction by Eliza Nightingale (London, 2nd edn, 1885)

Collison, William, *The Apostle of Free Labour: The Life Story of William Collison, Founder and General Secretary of the National Free Labour Association, Told by Himself* (London, 1913)

Collyer, Robert, *Some Memories* (Boston, 1908)

Confessions of a Dancing Girl. By Herself (London, [1913])

Constantine, Joseph, *Fifty Years of the Water Cure. With Autobiographical Notes*, 2nd edn (London, 1893)

Conway, Michael, *Half Timer: A Stockport Mill Boy Remembers* (Stockport, 1983)

Cooke, Isabella, *A Hired Lass in Westmoreland: The Story of a Country Girl at the Turn of the Century* (Penrith, 1981)

Cooke, Noah, 'Autobiography', in introduction to his *Wild Warblings* (Kidderminster, 1876)

Cookson, Catherine, *Our Kate: An Autobiographical Memoir* (London, 1969)

Coombes, Bert Lewis, *These Poor Hands: The Autobiography of a Miner Working in South Wales* (London, 1939)

Cooper, Francis, *The Life of Francis Cooper, Written by Himself* (Nottingham, 1856)

Cooper, George, *George Cooper, Stockport's Last Town Crier, 1824–1895, Presented by Anne Swift* (Stockport, [1974])

Cooper, Thomas, *The Life of Thomas Cooper, Written by Himself* (London, 1872; facs. repr. Leicester, 1971)

Coppard, A. E., *It's Me, O Lord! An Abstract and Brief Chronicle of Some of the Life with Some of the Opinions of A. E. Coppard, Written by Himself* (London, 1957)

Corben, James, *A Langton Quarryman's Apprentice 1826–1837: James Corben's Autobiography*, ed. R. J. Saville (Langton Matravers Local History and Preservation Society, 1996)

Cotton, Billy, *I Did it My Way: The Life Story of Billy Cotton* (London, 1970)

Cottrell, Gertrude Mary, *My Life* (Groombridge, 1968)

Cowan, Gibson, *Loud Report* (London, [1938])

Coward, Sir Henry, *Reminiscences of Henry Coward* (London, 1919)

Cowen, Ned, *Of Mining Life and Aal its Ways* (n.p., 1973)

Cowper, Agnes, *A Backward Glance on Merseyside* (Birkenhead, 1948)

Cox, Alfred, *Among the Doctors* (London, [1950])

Cox, Idris, 'Idris Cox', in *Childhood Memories, recorded by some Socialist Men and Women in their Later Years*, ed. with an introduction by Margaret Cohen, Marion and Hymie Fagan (n.p., [1983?]), pp. 11–17

Crittall, Francis Henry, *Fifty Years of Work and Play by Mr. and Mrs. Crittall* (London, 1934)

Croll, James, *Autobiographical Sketch of James Croll, with Memoir of his Life and Work* (London, 1896)

Crooks, Will, 'How I got on', *Pearson's Weekly*, 22 February 1906

Crowe, Robert, 'Reminiscences of Robert Crowe, the octogenarian tailor', in Dorothy Thompson, ed., *Chartists Biographies and Autobiographies* (London, 1986)

Cullwick, Hannah, *The Diaries of Hannah Cullwick*, ed. Liz Stanley (London, 1984)

Cummins, Jack, *The Landlord Cometh* (Brighton, 1981)

Dale, Nathaniel, *The Eventful Life of Nathaniel Dale, with Recollections and Anecdotes containing a great variety of Business Matters &c.* (Kimbolton, [*c.* 1871])

Darby, Aubrey S., *A View from the Alley*, ed. with notes by J. G. Dony (Luton, 1974)

[David], *The Autobiography of David ---*, ed. with an introduction by Ernest Raymond (London, 1946)

Davies, David Richard, *In Search of Myself: The Autobiography of D. R. Davies* (London, 1961)

Davies, Elizabeth, *An Autobiography of Elizabeth Davies. Betsy Cadwaladyr: A Balaclava Nurse*, ed. Jane Williams with an introduction by Deirdre Beddoe (Cardiff, 1987)

Davies, G. Henton, Untitled, in Ronald Goldman, ed., *Breakthrough: Autobiographical Accounts of the Education of some Socially Disadvantaged Children* (London, 1968), pp. 40–56

Davies, Thomas, *Short Sketches from the Life of Thomas Davies* (Haverfordwest, [1887?])

Davies, William Henry, *The Autobiography of a Super-tramp*, with a preface by G. Bernard Shaw (New York, 1917)

Davis, Edward G., *Some Passages from My Life* (Birmingham, 1898)

Davis, James, *Passages in the Life of James Davis, Wandering Musician, Twenty Years on the Road* (Bristol, 1865)

Davis, Joe, *The Breaks Came my Way* (London, 1976)

Dayus, Kathleen, *Her People*, with an introduction by John Rudd (London, 1982)

Deacon, Abraham, *Memoir of Abraham Deacon* (London, 1912)

Dellow, James, *Memoirs of an Old Stager* (Newcastle-upon-Tyne, 1928)

Dodd, William, 'A narrative of the experiences and sufferings of William Dodd, a factory cripple, written by himself (1851)', in James R. Simmons and Janice Carlisle, eds, *Factory Lives: Four Nineteenth-Century Working-Class Autobiographies* (Ontario, 2007)

Dollar, Robert, *Memoirs of Robert Dollar* (San Francisco, 1917)

Drawbell, James Wedgwood, *The Sun Within Us* (London, 1963)

Drummond, Alice, *Some Memories* (Edinburgh?, 1970)

Duke, Robert Rippon, *An Autobiography, 1817–1902* (Buxton, 1902)

Duncan, Charles, 'How I got on: Mr. Charles Duncan, M.P.', *Pearson's Weekly*, 5 February 1906

Dunn, James, *From Coal Mine Upwards, or Seventy Years of an Eventful Life* (London, [1910])

Dunning, Thomas, 'Reminiscences of Thomas Dunning', in David Vincent, ed., *Testaments of Radicalism: Memoirs of Working-class Politicians, 1790–1885* (London, 1977)

Edwards, Fred, *Paper Sir? The Autobiography of an Old News Boy* (London, [1912])

Edwards, George, *From Crow-Scaring to Westminster: An Autobiography*, with a foreword by the Rt Hon. Lord Ailwyn of Honingham, intro. W. R. Smith (London, 1922; repr. Dereham, 2008)

Edwards, Huw T., *Hewn From the Rock: An Autobiography of Huw T. Edwards* (Cardiff, 1967)

Edwards, John Passmore, *A Few Footprints* (London, 1905)

Edwards, Kate, *Fenland Chronicle: Recollections of William Henry and Kate Mary Edwards*, ed. Sybil Marshall (Cambridge, 1967)

Edwards, Mildred, *Our City, Our People 1889–1978: Memories* (Carlisle, 1978)

Edwards, Wil Jon, *From the Valley I Came* (London, 1956)

Edwards, William Henry, *Fenland Chronicle: Recollections of William Henry and Kate Mary Edwards*, ed. Sybil Marshall (Cambridge, 1967)

Edwin, John, *I'm Going – What Then?* (Bognor Regis, [1978])

Eldred, John, *I Love the Brooks* (London, 1955)

Elson, George, *The Last of the Climbing Boys: An Autobiography*, with a preface by the Dean of Hereford (London, 1900)

Emsley, J. W., Autobiographical Introduction to *Social Questions and National Problems their Evils and Remedies* (Bradford, 1901), pp. 9–28

Evans, Edmund, *The Reminiscences of Edmund Evans*, ed. and introduced by Ruari McLean (Oxford, 1967)

Ezard, Edward, *Battersea Boy* (London, 1979)

Fagan, Hymie, 'Hymie Fagan', in *Childhood Memories, recorded by some Socialist Men and Women in their Later Years*, ed. with an introduction by Margaret Cohen, Marion and Hymie Fagan (n.p., [1983?]), pp. 18–43

Fairbairn, William, *The Life of Sir William Fairburn* (London, 1877; facs. repr. 1970)

Farish, William, *The Autobiography of William Farish: The Struggles of a Handloom Weaver. With Some of his Writings* (London, 1996)

Farningham, Marianne, *A Working Woman's Life: An Autobiography* (London, 1907)

[Farquhar, Barbara H.], 'Sketch of the author's life', in *The Pearl of Days, by a Labourer's Daughter* (London, 1848), pp. 1–20

Featherstone, Peter, *Reminiscences of a Long Life* (London, 1905)

Ferris, Minnie, 'Minnie Ferris', in *The Island: The Life and Death of an East London Community, 1870–1970* (London, 1979)

Fielden, Samuel, 'Autobiography of Samuel Fielden', in Philip S. Foner, ed., *The Autobiographies of the Haymarket Martyrs* (New York, 1969)

Fields, Gracie, *Sing as We Go: Autobiography* (London, 1960)

Finch, Harold, *Memoirs of a Bedwellty M.P.* (Newport, 1972)

Finney, John, *Sixty Years' Recollections of an Etruscan* (Stoke-on-Trent, n.d.)

Fletcher, Cheetham William, *A Bradwell Man: Inspired by the Writing of Cheetham W. Fletcher, a Peak District Village Joiner (1894–1943)*, eds Cheetham W. Fletcher, Bill Fletcher and Barry Fletcher (Hathersage, 1998)

Fletcher, Harry, *A Life on the Humber: Keeling to Shipbuilding*, with an introduction by L. T. C. Rolt (London, 1975)

Flint, Elizabeth, *Hot Bread and Chips* (London, 1963)

Flockhart, Robert, *The Street Preacher, Being the Autobiography of Robert Flockhart*, ed. Thomas Guthrie (Edinburgh, 1858)

Foakes, Grace, *Between High Walls: A London Childhood* (London, 1972)

Foley, Alice, *A Bolton Childhood* (Manchester, 1973)

Foster, Ethel, *Childhood Memories of Earl Shilton* (Earl Shilton, 1992)

Fox, John D., 'My life', in *Life and Poems of John D. Fox, 'Throstle Nest', Bingley, Yorks.* (Bingley, 1914), pp. 17–42

Frame, W. F., *W. F. Frame Tells His Own Story* (Glasgow, n.d.)

Fraser, John, *Sixty Years in Uniform* (London, 1939)

Fraser, Lionel, *All to the Good* (London, 1963)

Freer, Walter, *My Life and Memories*, with a foreword by E. Rosslyn Mitchell (Glasgow, 1929)

Frost, Thomas, *Forty Years' Recollections: Literary and Political* (London, 1880)

[Fryett, Maggy], 'Maggy Fryett', in Mary Chamberlain, *Fenwomen: A Portrait of Women in an English Village* (London, 1975)

Fudge, Dorothy, *Sands of Time: The Autobiography of a Dorset Woman*, ed. Frank Alcock (Wimborne, 1981)

G. J., *Prisoner Set Free: The Narrative of a Convict in the Preston House of Correction with a Few Remarks by the Rev. John Clay* (Preston, 1846)

Gabbitass, Peter, 'The poet's autobiography', in his *Heart Melodies: For Storm and Sunshine. From Cliftonia the Beautiful* (Bristol, 1885)

Gair, Arthur, *Copt Hill to Ryhope: A Colliery Engineer's Life* (Chester-le-Street, 1982)

Gallacher, William, *Revolt on the Clyde: An Autobiography* (London, 1949)

Gallagher, Patrick, *My Story by Paddy the Cope* (London, 1939; Tralee, Ireland, 2006)

Gander, Marsland, *After These Many Quests* (London, 1949)

Gape, William A., *Half a Million Tramps* (London, 1936)

Garratt, Vere W., *A Man in the Street* (London, 1939)

Gawthorpe, Mary, *Up Hill to Holloway* (Penobscot, ME, 1962)

Gibbons, John, 'John Gibbons', in *Childhood Memories, recorded by some Socialist Men and Women in their Later Years*, ed. with an introduction by Margaret Cohen, Marion and Hymie Fagan (n.p., [1983?]), pp. 44–54

Gibbs, John, *The Life and Experience of the Author and some Traces of the Lord's Gracious Dealings towards the Author* (Lewes, 1827)

Gibbs, Rose, *In Service: Rose Gibbs Remembers* (Orwell, 1981)

Gifford, William, *Memoir of William Gifford, Written by Himself* (London, 1827)

Gilchrist, Alfred, *Naethin' at A': Stories and Reminiscences*, with a foreword by Norman Bruce (Glasgow, [1940])

Gill, A. H., 'How I got on: Made by self help', *Pearson's Weekly*, 22 March 1906

Gompers, Samuel, *Seventy Years of Life and Labour, an Autobiography*, ed. Nick Salvatore (Ithaca, NY, 1984)

Goodwin, Albert, 'Life of a potter', in John Burnett, ed., *Destiny Obscure: Autobiographies of Childhood, Education and Family from the 1820s to the 1920s* (London, 1982), pp. 293–301

Gosling, Harry, *Up and Down Stream* (London, 1927)

Gough, John Bartholomew, *The Autobiography of John B. Gough with a Continuation of his Life up to the Present Time* (Glasgow, 1872)

Gould, F. J., *The Life-Story of a Humanist* (London, 1923)

Gould, Ronald, Sir, *Chalk up the Memory: An Autobiography of Sir Ronald Gould* (Birmingham, 1976)

Graham, Marjorie, *Love, Dears!*, ed. Clive Murphy (London, 1980)

Gray, John, *Gin and Bitters*, with an introduction by Ethel Mannin (London, [1938])

Greenwood, Joseph, 'Reminiscences of sixty years ago', *Co-Partnership*, n.s. 15/177 (1909)

Greenwood, Walter, *There was a Time* (London, 1967)

Gresswell, Fred, *Bright Boots* (London, 1956)

Griffin, John Barrett, *This is My Life* (Bognor Regis, 1979)

Griffiths, James, *Pages from Memory* (London, 1969)

Griffiths, Mrs James, *One Woman's Story* (Ferndale, 1979)

[Grossek, Mark], *First Movement* (London, 1937)

Grundy, Anthony George, *My Fifty Years in Transport* (Chetwode, 1997)

[Guest, Francis Harold], *Limey Breaks In, by James Spenser [pseud.]* (London, 1934)

Gutteridge, Joseph, 'Autobiography of Joseph Gutteridge', in V. E. Chancellor, ed., *Master and Artisan in Victorian England; The Diary of William Andrews and the Autobiography of Joseph Gutteridge* (London, 1969)

Gwyer, Joseph, 'Life and poems of Joseph Gwyer', in his *Sketches of the Life of Joseph Gwyer, Potato Salesman, with his Poems* (Penge, [1877]), pp. 5–42

[H., Bill] 'Autobiography of a navvy', *Macmillan's Magazine*, v, 1861–2. Extracts repr. in John Burnett, ed., *Useful Toil: Autobiographies of Working People from the 1820s to the 1920s* (London, 1974), pp. 55–64

Haddow, William Martin, *My Seventy Years*, with a foreword by John S. Clarke (Glasgow, 1943)

Halward, Leslie, *Let Me Tell You* (London, 1938)

Hamm, Beatrice, 'Beatrice Hamm', in Jane Tordy, ed., *Looking Back: A Selection of Northumbrian Childhood Memories, 1891–1945* (Morpeth, 1983)

Hammond, Albert, *This Was My Life . . . !* (n.p., 1979)

Hammond, William, *Recollections of William Hammond, a Glasgow Hand-loom Weaver*, with a preface by William Winthrope (Glasgow, [1904])

Hannington, Wal, *Never On Our Knees* (London, 1967)

Hanson, William, *The Life of William Hanson, Written by Himself*, 2nd edn (Halifax, 1883)

[Harding, Arthur], *East End Underworld: Chapters in the Life of Arthur Harding*, ed. Raphael Samuel (London, 1981)

Hardy, George, *Those Stormy Years: Memories of the Fight for Freedom on Five Continents* (London, 1956)

Harley, Sukey, *A Short Account of the Life and Conversion of Sukey Harley of the Parish of Pulverbatch Near Shrewsbury. Taken from her lips by the late Rector's Daughter* (London, 1849)

Harold Brown, *Most Splendid of Men: Life in a Mining Community 1917–25* (Poole, 1981)

Harris, Harry, *Under Oars: Reminiscences of a Thames Lighterman, 1894–1909* (London, 1978)

Harris, John, *My Autobiography* (London, 1882)

Harrison, Rosina, *Rose: My Life in Service* (London, 1975)

Harrison, Ted, 'My childhood in Hoxton from 1902–1918', in Louise Cook et al., eds, *When We Were Kids on the Corner of the Street* (London, 1983), pp. 2–22

Hart, William, 'The autobiography of William Hart, Cooper', eds Pat Hudson and Lynette Hunter, *London Journal*, 7/2, 1981, and 8/1, 1982

Harvey, Bessie, 'Youthful memories of my life in a Suffolk village', in A. M. Hassall, ed., *Suffolk Review*, 2/3 (1960), pp. 73–7

Hawke, James (Major), *From Private to Major* (London, 1938)

Hawker, Henry Edward, *Notes of My Life* (Stonehouse, 1919)

Hawker, James, 'The life of a poacher', in Garth Christian, ed., *A Victorian Poacher: James Hawker's Journal* (Oxford, 1978)

Hayes, Thomas, *Recollections of Sixty-three Years of Methodist Life* (London, 1902)

[Hayhoe, Aida], 'Aida Hayhoe', in Mary Chamberlain, *Fenwomen: A Portrait of Women in an English Village* (London, 1975)

Healey, George, *Life and Remarkable Career of George Healey* (Birmingham, n.d.)

Heard, P. A., *An Octogenarian's Memoirs* (Ilfracombe, 1974)

Heaton, Martha, *A Tale that is Told* (Bradford, 1983)

Heaton, Richard, *Salford: My Home Town* (Manchester, 1982)

Heaton, William, 'A sketch of the author's life', in *The Old Solider; the Wandering Lover and other Poems* (London, 1857), pp. xv–xxiv

Hemmens, Harry Lathey, *Such Has Been My Life: An Autobiography*, with an introduction by Hugh Martin (London, 1953)

Henderson, Arthur, 'How I got on: From errand boy to MP', *Pearson's Weekly*, 8 March 1906

Henderson, Robert, *Incidents in the Life of Robt. Henderson; or, Extracts from the Autobiography of 'Newcassel Bob'*, ed. Rev. J. Martin (Carlisle, 1869)

Herbert, George, 'Autobiography', in C. S. Cheney and B. S. Trinder, eds, *Shoemaker's Window: Recollections of Banbury in Oxfordshire before the Railway Age* (Chichester, 1971), pp. 1–38

Hesling, Bernard, *Little and Orphan* (London, 1954)

Hillocks, James I., *Life Story: A Prize Autobiography* (London, [1860?]))

Hills, Miss Daisy, *Old Frimley* (Faringdon, 1978)

Hillyer Richard, *Country Boy: The Autobiography* (London, 1966)

Hilton, Jack, *Caliban Shrieks* (London, 1935)

Hoare, Nellie, *A Winton Story* (Bournemouth, 1982)

Hocking, W. J., *Bench and Mitre: A Cornish Autobiography* (London, 1903)

Hodge, Herbert, *It's Draughty in Front: The Autobiography of a London Taxidriver* (London, 1938)

Hodge, John, *Workman's Cottage to Windsor Castle* (London, [1931])

Hodges, Frank, *My Adventures as a Labour Leader* (London, [1924])

Hodgkinson, George, *Sent to Coventry*, with an introduction by R. H. S. Crossman ([London], 1970)

Hodgson, Joseph, *Memoir of Joseph Hodgson, Glazier, a Native of Whitehaven, Cumberland* (Whitehaven, 1850)

Hogg, James, *Memoir of the Author's Life; and, Familiar Anecdotes of Sir Walter Scott*, ed. Douglas S. Mack (Edinburgh, 1972)

[Holkinson, Jacob], 'The life of Jacob Holkinson, tailor and poet, written by himself', *The Commonwealth*, 24 & 31 January 1857

Hollingsworth, William, *An Autobiographical Sketch of the Life of Mr Wm. Hollingsworth* (London, n.d.)

Holloway, Henry, *A Voice from the Convict Cell; or, Life and Conversion of H. Holloway, etc. with an Account of his Trials and Sufferings as an Evil-Doer* (Manchester, [1877])

Holloway, John William, *An Authentic and Faithful History of the Atrocious Murder of Celia Holloway including the Extraordinary Confessions of John William Holloway* (Brighton, 1832)

Holt, J. A., *Looking Backwards* (Bolton, 1949)

Holt, William, *I haven't Unpacked: An Autobiography* (London, 1939; repr. 1966)

Holyoake, George Jacob, *Sixty Years of an Agitator's Life*, 6th edn (London, 1906)

Home, Michael [pseud. of Christopher Bush], *Autumn Fields* (London, 1944; repr. 1945)

—, *Winter Harvest: A Norfolk Boyhood* (London, 1967)

Hopkinson, James, 'Memoirs', in Jocelyne Baty Goodman, ed., *Victorian Cabinet Maker, the Memoirs of James Hopkinson, 1819–1894* (London, 1968)

Horler, Moses, *The Early Recollections of Moses Horler*, eds M. F. Coombs and H. Coombs (Radstock, 1900)

Horne, Catherine, 'Ramsbottom's oldest lady, lived in six reigns', *Bury Times*, 18 November 1911

Horne, Eric, *What the Butler Winked At: Being the Life and Adventures of Eric Horne* (London, 1923)

Horner, Arthur, *Incorrigible Rebel* (London, 1960)

Horrocks, Bill, *Reminiscences of Bolton* (Manchester, 1984)

Houston, James, *Autobiography of James Houston* (Glasgow, 1889)

Howard, Rev. J. H., *Winding Lanes: A Book of Impressions and Recollections* (Caernarvon, [1938])

Howlett, John, *The Guv'nor: The Autobiography of John Howlett O.B.E., as told to Iris Woodford*, with a foreword by Sir Aubrey Burke (London, 1973)

Huffer, Tansley, *The Autobiography of Tansley Huffer of Swineshead, 1828–1901*, ed. with an introduction by Pamela A. Southworth (Boston, 1998)

Hull, Maria, 'A Derbyshire schooling: 1884–1893', *History Workshop Journal*, 25 (1988), pp. 166–70

Humphreys, Charles, *The Life of Charles Humphreys, bookseller, of Paternoster Row, Streatham and Peckham Rye* (London, [1928?])

Humphris Ted, *Garden Glory: From Garden Boy to Head Gardener at Aynhoe Park* (London, 1969)

Hunt, T. J., *Life Story T. J. Hunt*, 3rd edn (London, 1937)

Hurcomb, William Edward, *Life and Diary of W. E. Hurcomb* (London, 1928)

Hutton, William, *The life of William Hutton, F.A.S.S., Including a Particular Account of the Riots at Birmingham in 1791* (London, 1817).

Iles, Percy, *Experiences of a Happy Life*, with a foreword by F. W. Long (Bristol, n.d.)

Inman, Philip, *No Going Back: An Autobiography* (London, 1952)

Innes, William, 'Autobiography of William Innes', in *Memorials of a Faithful Servant, William Innes* (Edinburgh, 1876)

Ireson, Alfred, 'Reminiscences', in John Burnett, ed., *Destiny Obscure: Autobiographies of Childhood, Education and Family from the 1820s to the 1920s* (London, 1982), pp. 70–7

I Walked by Night, Being the Life and History of the King of the Norfolk Poachers. Written by Himself, ed. Lilias Rider Haggard (London, 1935)

Jackson, Thomas, *Recollections of My Own Life and Times*, ed. Rev. B. Frankland and with an introduction and postscript by G. Osborn (London, 1873)

Jackson, Thomas Alfred, *Solo Trumpet: Some Memories of Socialist Agitation and Propaganda* (London, 1953)

'Jacques', 'Glimpses of a chequered life', *The Commonwealth*, 1, 8 & 15 November 1856

Jaeger, Annie, *Annie Jaeger Tells her Own Story*, ed. Clara Jaeger (Pinner, 1968)

Jasper, A. S., *A Hoxton Childhood* (London, 1969)

Jenkins, J. H., ' How I got on: The shipwright who wasn't content', *Pearson's Weekly*, 12 April 1906

Jermy, Louise, *Memories of a Working Woman* (Norwich, 1934)

Jewell, Joseph, 'Autobiographical memoir of Joseph Jewell, 1763–1846', ed. Arthur Walter Slater, *Camden Miscellany*, xxii (1964)

Jobson, Allan, *The Creeping Hours of Time* (London, 1977)

John, Tabitha, *Tabitha: The Story of a Llanelli Character* (Llanelli, 1979)

Johnson, John, 'How I got on: Mr. John Johnson, M.P.', *Pearson's Weekly*, 10 May 1906

Johnson, William, 'How I got on: Mr. William Johnson, M.P.', *Pearson's Weekly*, 1 March 1906

Johnston, David, *Autobiographical Reminiscences of David Johnston, an Octogenarian Scotchman* (Chicago, 1885)

Johnston, Ellen, 'Autobiography', in *Autobiography, Poems and Songs of Ellen Johnston, the 'Factory Girl'* (Glasgow, 1867), pp. 3–15

Johnston, William, *The Life and Times of William Johnston* (Peterhead, 1859)

Jones, Abel L., *I Was Privileged* (Cardiff, [1942])

Jones, Sir Henry, *Old Memories: Autobiography by Sir Henry Jones*, ed. Thomas Jones (London, 1923

Jones, Jack, *Unfinished Journey* (London, 1937)

Jones, John, Autobiographical extract in Samuel Smiles, *Men of Invention and Industry* (London, 1884), pp. 364–8

Jones, John, 'John Jones, an old servant: An account of his life written by himself', in Robert Southey, *Lives of the Uneducated Poets*, ed. J. S. Childers (London, 1925)

Jones, John Joseph (Jack), *My Lively Life* (London, 1928)

Jones, Thomas, *Rhymney Memories* (Newtown, 1938)

Jordan, Mary, *Hulme Memories* (n.p., 1989)

Jordan, Thomas, 'Thomas Jordan, coal-miner', in John Burnett, ed., *Useful Toil: Autobiographies of Working People from the 1820s to the 1920s* (London, 1974), pp. 99–107

Jowett, Frederick William, 'Bradford seventy years ago', in F. Brockway, ed., *Socialism Over Sixty Years Ago: The Life of Jowett of Bradford (1864–1944)*, with a preface by J. B. Priestley (London, 1946), pp. 13–24

Keating, Joseph, *My Struggle for Life* (London, 1916)

Kelly, Henry Warren, *Prodigal of the Seven Seas*, ed. with a preface by Rita F. Snowden (London, 1947)

Kemp, John, 'Autobiography', in *Memoir of John Kemp, First Pastor of 'Ebenezer' Strict Baptist Chapel, Bounds Cross, Biddenden, Kent. Including Autobiography, with a foreword by his son, Mr J. Kemp* (London, 1933)

Kenney, Annie, *Memories of a Militant* (London, 1924)

Kenney, Rowland, *Westering: An Autobiography by Rowland Kenney* (London, 1939)

Kerr, James Lennox, *The Eager Years: An Autobiography* (London, 1940)

Kerrigan, Rose, 'Rose Kerrigan', in *Childhood Memories, Recorded by some Socialist Men and Women in their Later Years*, ed. with an introduction by Margaret Cohen, Marion and Hymie Fagan (n.p., [1983?]), pp. 69–80

—, Untitled, in *To Make Ends Meet, Women Over 60 Write about their Working Lives. Memories Collected by the Older Women's Project*, ed. Jo Stanley (London, [1989?]), pp. 33–7

King, Ernest, *The Green Baize Door* (London, 1963)

Kirkwood, David, *My Life of Revolt*, with forewords by the Rt Hon. Winston S. Churchill and the Rt Hon. George Lansbury (London, 1935)

Kitchen, Fred, *Brother to the Ox: The Autobiography of a Farm Labourer* (London, 1940)

Kitz, Frank [Francis Platt], 'Recollections and reflections', *Freedom,* January 1912: www.katesharpleylibrary.net/3r2368

Lackington, James, *Memoirs of the Forty-Five First Years of the Life of James Lackington* (London, 1795)

[Langdon, Ellen], autobiographical fragment in Roger Langdon, *The Life of Roger Langdon, Told by Himself* (London, 1909)

Langdon, Roger, *The Life of Roger Langdon, Told by Himself* (London, 1909)

Langley, John, *Always a Layman* (Brighton, 1976)

Lanigan, Jack, 'Incidents in the life of a citizen', extracts in John Burnett, ed., *Destiny Obscure: Autobiographies of Childhood, Education and Family from the 1820s to the 1920s* (London, 1982), pp. 85–90

Lansbury, George, *My Life*, with an introduction by Harold Laski (London, 1928)

Lauder, Harry, *Sir Harry, Roamin' in the Gloamin'* (London, [1928])

Lawrence, William, *The Autobiography of Sergeant William Lawrence* (London, 1886)

Lawson, Jack (John James), *A Man's Life* (London, 1932)

Lax, W. M., *His Book: The Autobiography of Lax of Poplar* (London, 1937)

Layton, Mrs, 'Memories of seventy years', in Margaret Llewelyn Davies, ed., *Life as We Have Known It by Co-Operative Working Women*, intro. Anna Davin (London, 1990), pp. 1–55

[Leask, W.], *Struggles for Life; or the Autobiography of a Dissenting Minister* (London, 1854)

Leatherland, J. A., *Essays and Poems with a Brief Autobiographical Memoir* (London, 1862)

Lee, Jennie, *To-Morrow is a New Day* (London, 1939)

Leno, John Bedford, *The Aftermath: With Autobiography of the Author* (London, 1892; facs. repr. London, 1986)

Lewis, Rev. Thomas, *My Life's History: The Autobiography of Rev. Thomas Lewis, Baptist Minister, Newport*, ed. W. Edwards (Bristol, 1902)

Lewis, Rosa, *Queen of Cooks – and Some Kings (the Story of Rosa Lewis)*, ed. Mary Lawton (New York, 1925)

Lewis, Taffy, *'Any Road': Pictures of Small Heath, Sparkbrook and Further Afield, 1902–39* (Birmingham, 1979)

Lewis, Thomas, *These Seventy Years (1883–1923): An Autobiography* (London, [1930])

Ley, John Carter, *The Story of my Life* (Ilfracombe, 1978)

Lidgett, Thomas Laming, *The Life of Thomas L. Lidgett, one of Lincolnshire's Best Known Men, as Written by Himself* (Lincoln, [1908])

'Life of a cotton spinner, written by himself', *The Commonwealth*, 27 December 1856

'Life of a handloom weaver, written by himself', *The Commonwealth*, 25 April 1857

'Life of a journeyman baker, written by himself', *The Commonwealth*, 13 & 20 December 1856

'Life of a journeyman baker, written by himself', *The Commonwealth*, 2 May 1857

'Life of a letterpress printer, written by himself', *The Commonwealth*, 7 February 1857

'Life of an Irish tailor, written by himself', *The Commonwealth*, 18 April 1857

Like it Was Yesterday: Childhood Memories, Islington Council Libraries Department (London, 1989)

Linton, William James, *Memories* (London, 1895)

Lipton, Sir Thomas J., *Leaves from the Lipton Logs*, with a foreword by W. Blackwood (London, n.d.)

Livesey, Joseph, 'The author's autobiography', 12 articles in *The Staunch Teetotaler*, 1868

Llewelyn, Michael Gareth, *Sand in the Glass* (London, 1943)

Lockley, R. M., *Myself when Young: The Making of a Naturalist* (London, 1979)

'London guildswoman', in Margaret Llewelyn Davies, ed., *Life as We Have Known It by Co-Operative Working Women*, intro. Anna Davin (London, 1990), pp. 140–1.

Love, David, *The Life, Adventures, and Experience, of David Love, Written by Himself*, 4th edn (Nottingham, 1824)

Lovekin, Emanuel, 'Mining butty', in John Burnett, ed., *Useful Toil: Autobiographies of Working People from the 1820s to the 1920s* (London, 1974), pp. 289–96 (full manuscript in Burnett Archive)

Lovett, W., *Life and Struggles of William Lovett, in his Pursuit of Bread, Knowledge and Freedom with some Short Account of the Different Associations he Belonged to and of the Opinions he Entertained* (London, 1876; repr. London, 1967)

Lowery, Robert, 'Passages in the life of a temperance lecturer', in Brian Harrison and Patricia Hollis, eds, *Robert Lowery: Radical and Chartist* (London, 1979)

Luby, William, 'William Luby, sweet-boiler', in John Burnett, ed., *Useful Toil: Autobiographies of Working People from the 1820s to the 1920s* (London, 1974), pp. 89–99

Luck, Lucy, 'Lucy Luck, A little of my life', *London Mercury*, viii/76 (November–April 1926). Extracts reprinted in John Burnett, ed., *Useful Toil: Autobiographies of Working People from the 1820s to the 1920s* (London, 1974), pp. 67–77

Luty, Mary, *A Penniless Globe Trotter* (Accrington, 1937)

Macadam, John, *Macadam Road* (London, 1955)

McAdam, John, *Autobiography of John McAdam (1806–1883): With Selected Letters*, ed. with an introduction by Janet Fyfe (Edinburgh, 1980)

McCurrey, James, *The Life of James McCurrey (from 1801–1876), Containing Thirty-Nine Years' Experience as a Temperance Advocate and Missionary, Collated from his Personal Narrative, Journals* (London, [1876])

McGeown, Patrick, *Heat the Furnace Seven Times More: An Autobiography*, with an introduction by Asa Briggs (London, 1967)

MacGill, Patrick, *Children of the Dead End: The Autobiography of a Navvy* (London, 1914)

McGovern, John, *Neither Fear nor Favour* (London, 1960)

McGuigan, John, *A Trainer's Memories: Being Sixty Years' Turf Reminiscences and Experiences at*

Home and Abroad, ed. J Fairfax-Blackborough with an introduction by Lord Hamilton of Dalzell (London, 1946)

MacKenzie, Kenneth, *Been Places and Seen Things*, with an introduction by George Blake (London, 1935)

MacLellan, Angus, *The Furrow Behind Me: The Autobiography of a Hebridean Crofter*, trans. from the Gaelic, with an introduction by John Lorne Campbell (Edinburgh, 1997)

MacPherson, John T., 'How I got on: Mr. John T. MacPherson, M.P.', *Pearson's Weekly*, 1 March 1906

Mann, Tom, *Tom Mann's Memoirs* (London, 1923)

Mannin, Ethel, *Confessions and Impressions* (London, 1936)

Mansbridge, Albert, *The Trodden Road: Experience, Inspiration and Belief* (London, 1940)

Marcroft, William, *The Marcroft Family* (Manchester, 1886)

Markham, Alice M., *Back of Beyond: Life in Holderness before the First World War*, with an introduction by John Markham (Beverley, 1979)

Martin, David R., *A Scotsman's Wanderings: A 'Keelie' Looks Back Seventy-Odd Years* (Dumfries, 1976)

Martin, E., *The Best Street in Rochdale* (Rochdale, 1985)

Martin, Jack, *Ups and Downs: The Life Story of a Working Man* (Bolton, 1973)

Mason, Francis D. D., *The Story of a Working Man's Life: With Sketches of Travel in Europe, Asia, Africa, and America, as Related by Himself* (New York, 1870)

Massey, Bill, *Shepherds Bush Memories* (London, [1984])

Matthews, Ada, *Recollections of Life in Shepherds Bush* (London, *c.* 1989)

May, Betty, *Tiger-Woman: My Story* (London, 1929)

Maybee, Robert, *Sixty-Eight Years' Experience on the Scilly Islands* (Penzance, 1884)

Mayett, Joseph, *The Autobiography of Joseph Mayett of Quainton, 1783–1839*, ed. Ann Kussmaul (Aylesbury, 1986)

Mead, Isaac, *The Life Story of an Essex Lad, Written by Himself* (Chelmsford, 1923)

Meads, Richard James, *Growing-up With Southall from 1904: Memories of R. J. MEADS* (London, 1979)

Meek, George, *George Meek, Bath Chair-Man. By Himself*, with an introduction by H. G. Wells (London, 1910)

Mellor, Gertie, *Gertie's Story: Memories of a Moorland Octogenarian*, ed. Betty Gouldstone (Hollinsclough, 1994)

M'Gonagall, William, *The Authentic Autobiography of the Poet M'Gonagall* (Dundee, n.d.)

Miles, William, *An Autobiography. From Pit Bank to Balliol College. A Mineworker became a Labour Election Agent for 20 Years*, with a foreword by Christopher Hill (n.p., 1972)

Miller, Hugh, *My Schools and Schoolmasters: or, the Story of my Education*, 5th edn (Edinburgh, 1856)

Milne, Christian Ross, *Simple Poems on Simple Subjects by Christian Milne, Wife of a Journeyman Ship-Carpenter in Footdee, Aberdeen* (Aberdeen, 1805)

Milne, William J., *Reminiscences of an Old Boy: Being Autobiographic Sketches of Scottish Rural Life from 1832 to 1856* (Forfar, 1901)

Mitchell, George, 'Autobiography and reminiscences of George Mitchell, "One from the plough" ', in Stephen Price, ed., *The Skeleton at the Plough, or the Poor Farm Labourers of the West: With the Autobiography and Reminiscences of George Mitchell* (London, [1874])

Mitchell, Hannah, *The Hard Way Up: The Autobiography of Hannah Mitchell, Suffragette and Rebel*, with a preface by George Ewart Evans and ed. with intro by Geoffrey Mitchell (London, 1968)

Mockford, George, *Wilderness Journeyings and Gracious Deliverances: The Autobiography of George Mockford* (Oxford, 1901)

Moffat, Abe, *My Life with the Miners* (London, 1965)

[Moffitt, William], *The Autobiography of the 'Sark' MP* (London, [1910])

Moody, Bob, *I Remember, I Remember* (n.p., 1995)

Morgan-Hinwood, T. G., *Memories of Morgan* (n.p., 1976)

Morrison, Herbert, *Herbert Morrison: An Autobiography by Lord Morrison of Lambeth* (London, 1960)

Moss, Les, *Live and Learn: A Life and Struggle for Progress* (Brighton, 1979)

Mountjoy, Timothy, *The Life, Labours and Deliverances of a Forest of Dean Collier* (n.p., 1887). Extract in *Hard Times in the Forest, Extracts from '62 years in the Life of a Forest of Dean Collier'*, by Timothy Mountjoy (Coleford, 1971)

Muckle, William, *No Regrets*, with a foreword by William Muckle (Newcastle upon Tyne, 1981)

Muir, Edwin, *The Story and the Fable: An Autobiography* (London, 1940)

Mullen, Alice, *Alice from Tooting (1879–1977)*, ed. Anne Bott (Warwick, 1997)

Mullins, Tom, 'Tom Mullins, farm labourer', in John Burnett, ed., *Useful Toil: Autobiographies of Working People from the 1820s to the 1920s* (London, 1974), pp. 64–7

Munday, John, 'Early Victorian recollections: John Munday's memories', in Reginald Blunt, ed., *Red Anchor Pieces* (London, 1928), pp. 99–121

Murdie, Robert Kerr, 'Robert Kerr Murdie', in *Looking Back: A Selection of Northumbrian Childhood Memories, 1891–1945*, ed. Jane Torday (Morpeth, 1983)

Murdoch, James, 'Autobiography', in his *The Autobiography and Poems of James Murdoch* (Elgin, 1863), pp. 1–17

Murison, Alexander, 'Recollections', in A. F. Murison, *Memoirs of 88 years (1847–1934), Being the Autobiography of Alexander Falconer Murison* (Aberdeen, 1935), pp. 209–18

Murphy, J. T., *New Horizons* (London, 1941)

Murphy, Molly, *Molly Murphy: Suffragette and Socialist*, with an introduction by Ralph Darlington (Salford, 1998)

Murray, Joseph, *Call to Arms: From Gallipoli to the Western Front* (London, 1980)

'Narrative of a miner', *The Commonwealth*, 25 October 1856

Narrow Waters: The First Volume of the Life and Thoughts of a Common Man (London, 1935)

Newbery, Maggie, *Picking Up Threads: The Complete Reminiscences of a Bradford Mill Girl*, ed. James Ogden (Bradford, 1992)

Newnham, Charles, 'Memoirs of Charles Newnham', in John Burnett, ed., *Useful Toil: Autobiographies of Working People from the 1820s to the 1920s* (London, 1974), pp. 283–9

Newton, Arthur, *Years of Change: Autobiography of a Hackney Shoemaker* (London, 1974)

Nicholson, Hamlet, *An Autobiographical and Full Historical Account of Hamlet Nicholson in his Opposition to Ritualism at the Rochdale Parish Church* (Manchester, 1892)

Noakes, Daisy, *The Town Beehive: A Young Girl's Lot, Brighton, 1910–1934* (Brighton, 1980)

Noakes, George, *To Be a Farmer's Boy* (Brighton, 1977)

North, Benjamin, *Autobiography of Benjamin North* (Aylesbury, 1882)

Nye, James, *A Small Account of my Travels Through the Wilderness*, ed. Vic Gammon (Brighton, [1981?])

Oakley, Elizabeth, 'The autobiography of Elizabeth Oakley, 1831–1900', *Norfolk Record Society*, 56 (1993), pp. 113–50

Okey, Thomas, *A Basketful of Memories: An Autobiographical Sketch* (London, 1930)

Oliver, Thomas, *Autobiography of a Cornish Miner* (Camborne, 1914)

Oman, Elsie, *Salford Stepping Stones* (Manchester, 1983)

O'Mara, Pat, *The Autobiography of a Liverpool Slummy* (London, 1934; Liverpool, 2009)

[O'Neill, Ellen], *Extraordinary Confessions of a Female Pickpocket* (Preston, 1850)

O'Reilly, Septimus, *The Tiger of the Legion. Being the Life Story of 'Tiger' O'Reilly as told to William J. Elliott* (London, [1936])

Osgerby, Faith Dorothy, 'My memoirs', in John Burnett, ed., *Destiny Obscure: Autobiographies of Childhood, Education and Family from the 1820s to the 1920s* (London, 1982), pp. 77–85

Osman, Elsie, *For the Love of Ada – and Salford* (Manchester, 1984)

[Ottespoor, Gladys], 'Gladys Ottespoor', in Mary Chamberlain, *Fenwomen: A Portrait of Women in an English Village* (London, 1975)

Page, Ethel, 'No green pastures', *East London Papers*, 9/1 (1966), pp. 27–40, and 9/2 (1966), pp. 84–100

Palmer, Lilian, 'Long, long ago', in *Like it Was Yesterday': Childhood Memories, Islington Council Libraries Department* (London, 1989)

Palmer, Margaret, *Childhood Memories of Rye & Winchelsea, 1910–1918* (St-Leonards-on-Sea, 1987)

Parkinson, George, *True Stories of Durham Pit-Life* (London, 1912)

Paterson, James, *Autobiographical Reminiscences: Including Recollections of the Radical Years, 1819–20 in Kilmarnock* (Glasgow, 1871)

Paton, John, *Proletarian Pilgrimage: An Autobiography* (London, 1935)

Patterson, John Edward, *My Vagabondage: Being the Intimate Autobiography of a Nature's Nomad* (London, 1911)

Paul, Albert, *Poverty – Hardship but Happiness: Those were the Days, 1903–1917* (Brighton, 1981)

Payne, Maria, 'A Derbyshire schooling: 1884–1893', ed. Maria Hull in *History Workshop Journal*, 25 (1988), pp. 166–70

Paynter, Will, *My Generation* (London, 1972)

Pearson, Kay, *Life in Hull From Then Till Now* (Hull, 1979)

Penn, Margaret, *Manchester Fourteen Miles* (Cambridge, 1947)

Perry, Margaret, 'Unpublished autobiography', in John Burnett, ed., *Destiny Obscure: Autobiographies of Childhood, Education and Family from the 1820s to the 1920s* (London, 1982), pp. 336–42

Phillips, John, *Reminiscences of my Life* (Wrexham, 1902)

Pickles, Wilfred, *Between You and Me: The Autobiography of Wilfred Pickles* (London, 1949)

Pinches, Beatrice M., *Memories of an Octogenarian Lady* (Bolton, 1980)

Place, Francis, *The Autobiography of Francis Place*, ed. Mary Thale (Cambridge, 1972)

Plummer, John, *Songs of Labour, Northamptonshire Rambles and other Poems (with an Autobiographical Sketch of the Author's Life)* (London, 1860)

Pollitt, Harry, *Serving My Time: An Apprenticeship in Politics* (London, 1940)

Porteus, Mary, *The Power of Faith and Prayer Exemplified in the Life and Labours of Mary Porteus* (London, 1862)

Powell, J. H., *Life Incidents and Poetic Pictures* (London, 1865)

Powell, Margaret, *Below Stairs* (London, 1968)

—, *My Mother and I* (London, 1972)

Pratt, Edith, *As If It Were Yesterday* (Huntingdon, 1978)

Preston, Raymond, *British and Australian Evangelist: Life Story and Personal Reminiscences*, ed. W. K. Greenland (London, 1930)

Preston, Thomas, *The Life and Opinions of Thomas Preston, Patriot and Shoemaker* (London, 1817)

Primmer, Jacob, *Life of Jacob Primmer, Minister of the Church of Scotland*, ed. and compiled by J. Boyd Primmer (Edinburgh, 1916)

Pritchett, V. S., *A Cab at the Door. An Autobiography: Early Years* (London, 1968)

Pugh, Albert, 'I helped to build railroads', ed. Charles Madge, *Pilot Papers, Social Essays and Documents,* 1/4 (November 1946), pp. 75–98

Pyke, Richard, *Men and Memories* (London, 1948)

Randall, Arthur R., *Sixty Years a Fenman*, ed. Enid Porter (London, 1966)

Ratcliffe, George, *Sixty Years of It: Being the Story of my Life and Public Career* (London, [1935])

Reader, Ralph, *Ralph Reader Remembers* (Folkestone, 1974)

Reakes, George L., *Man of the Mersey* (London, 1956)

Redfern, Percy, *Journey to Understanding*, foreword by Albert Mansbridge (London, 1946)

Reffold, Harry, *Pie for Breakfast: Reminiscences of a Farmhand* (Beverley, 1984)

Reilly, John Edward, autobiographical chapter in Sarah A. Reilly, *I Walk with the King: The Life Story of John Edward Reilly* (London, 1931), pp. 9–25

Reminiscences of a Stonemason, By a Working Man (London, 1908)

Rennie, James, *The Converted Shepherd Boy: The Life of James Rennie, Colporteur* (London, [1878])

Rennie, Jean, *Every Other Sunday* (Bath, 1975)

Richards, Daniel, *Honest to Self* (Swansea, 1971)

Richards, T. Frederick, 'How I got on: Mr. T. F. Richards, M.P.', *Pearson's Weekly*, 26 April 1906

Ricketts, Joseph, 'Notes on the life of Joseph Ricketts, written by himself *c.* 1858', *Wiltshire Archaeological and Natural History Magazine*, 60 (1965), pp. 120–6

Roberts, Fred, *Fred Roberts, 1884–1982, Recollections: Memories of a Victorian Childhood and Working Life in Miles Platting, Manchester* (Manchester, 1983)

Roberts, G. H., 'How I got on: Mr. G. H. Roberts, M.P.', *Pearson's Weekly*, 17 May 1906

Roberts, Robert, *The Classic Slum: Salford Life in the First Quarter of the Century* (London, 1971)

Roberts, Robert, *The Life and Opinions of Robert Roberts, a Wandering Scholar as Told by Himself*, ed. J. H. Davies (Cardiff, 1923)

—, *A Ragged Schooling: Growing up in the Classic Slum* (Manchester, 1976; repr. 1984)

Robson, Alec 'Spike', *Spike. . . Alec 'Spike' Robson, 1895–1979: Class Fighter* (North Tyneside, 1987)

Rogers, Evan, *A Funny Old Quist: The Memoirs of a Gamekeeper*, ed. Clive Murphy (London, 1986)

Rogers, Frederick, *Labour, Life and Literature: Some Memories of Sixty Years* (London, 1913)

Rolph, Cecil Hewitt, *Living Twice: An Autobiography* (London, 1974)

Rooney, Ralph, *The Story of my Life*, with a preface by J. H. (Bury, 1947; 4th edn 2011)

Rowley, Charles, *Fifty Years of Work without Wages (Laborare est Orare)* (London, 1912)

Rowse, A. L., *A Cornish Childhood: Autobiography of a Cornishman*, 6th edn (London, 1956)

Royce, James, *I Stand Nude* (London, 1937)

[Rushmer, Alice], 'Alice Rushmer', in Mary Chamberlain, *Fenwomen: A Portrait of Women in an English Village* (London, 1975)

Rushton, Adam, *My Life as Farmer's Boy, Factory Lad, Teacher, and Preacher* (Manchester, 1909)

Rymer, Edward Allen, 'The martyrdom of the mine, or 60 years' struggle for life', ed. with an introduction by Robert G. Neville, *History Workshop Journal* (1976), pp. 220–44

Saggers, Esther, 'Esther Saggers', in Nicci Crowther, ed., *I Can Remember* (London, 1976)

Sanderson, Thomas, 'The life and adventures of Thomas Sanderson, As written by himself, in 1861, in the 53rd year of his age', in *idem*, *Chips and Shavings of an Old Shipwright; or, the Life, Poems, & Adventures of Thomas Sanderson* (Darlington, 1873), pp. 5–41

Saville, Jonathan, 'Autobiography', in Francis A. West, *Memoirs of Jonathan Saville*, 3rd edn (London, 1848)

Scott, J. P. Mrs [Nellie], 'A felt hat worker', in Margaret Llewelyn Davies, ed., *Life as We Have Known It by Co-Operative Working Women*, intro. Anna Davin (London, 1990), pp. 81–101

Severn, J. Milliot, *The Life Story and Experiences of a Phrenologist* (Brighton, 1929)

Sexton, Sir James, *Sir James Sexton, Agitator: The Life of the Dockers' MP. An Autobiography*, with a preface by the Rt Hon. David Lloyd George, MP (London, 1936)

Shackleton, D. J., 'How I got on: Unemployment brought success', *Pearson's Weekly*, 15 March 1906

Sharpe, Joseph, *Dark at Seven: The Life of a Derbyshire Miner, Being an Account of his Life as told by Joseph Sharpe of Coal Aston, 1859–1936*, eds Nellie Connole, Geoffrey Senior and Barbara Whitehead (York, 1988)

Shaw, Benjamin, *The Family Records of Benjamin Shaw, Mechanic of Dent, Dolphinholme and Preston, 1772–1841*, ed. Alan G. Crosby (Record Society of Lancashire and Cheshire, vol. 13, 1991)

Shaw, Charles, *When I was a Child, by 'an Old Potter'* (London, 1903; facs. repr. Wakefield, 1969)

Shaw, Sam, *Guttersnipe*, with a foreword by Bertrand Watson (London, [1946])

Shepherd, A. E., *Memoirs of a Loughborough Man*, ed. Joy Cross and Margaret Staple with a preface by Christopher Wrigley (Nottingham, 1994)

Shinn, John, 'A Sketch of my life and times', in John Burnett, ed., *Destiny Obscure: Autobiographies of Childhood, Education and Family from the 1820s to the 1920s* (London, 1982), pp. 186–92

Shinwell, Emanuel, *Conflict without Malice* (London, 1955)

Shipp, John, *The Path of Glory: Being the Memoirs of the Extraordinary Military Career of John Shipp, Written by Himself*, ed. C. J. Stranks (London, 1969)

Skeen, Robert, *Autobiography of Mr. Robert Skeen, Printer* (London, 1876)

[Slate, Ruth], *Dear Girl: The Diaries and Letters of two Working Women, 1897–1917*, ed. Tierl Thompson (London, 1987)

Smillie, Robert, *My Life for Labour*, with a foreword by J. Ramsay MacDonald (London, 1924)

Smith, Deborah, *My Revelation: An Autobiography. How a Working Woman finds God* (London, 1933)

Smith, Emma, *A Cornish Waif's Story: An Autobiography with a Foreword by A. L. Rowse* (London, 1956)

Smith, [Father], 'Does some one say "What about the writer's olden times?": A short autobiography by Father Smith', in *Nelson District Illustrated History, From Roman Times till 1922* (Nelson, [1922]), pp. 145–6

Smith, Mrs. F. H. 'In a mining village', in Margaret Llewelyn Davies, ed., *Life as We Have Known It by Co-Operative Working Women*, intro. Anna Davin (London, 1990), pp. 67–72.

Smith, George, *The Autobiography of George Smith, 1800–1868: An Autobiography of One of the People* (London, 1923)

Smith, John Henry, *Water Under the Bridge* (Bristol, 1979)

Smith, Mary, *The Autobiography of Mary Smith, Schoolmistress and Nonconformist* (London, 1892)

Smith, Thomas W., *A Narrative of the Life, Travels, and Sufferings of Thomas W. Smith* (Boston, MA, 1844)

Snell, Henry (Baron), *Men, Movements and Myself* (London, 1936)

Snowden, Philip Viscount, *An Autobiography*, 2 vols (London, 1934)

Southgate, Walter, *That's the Way it Was: A Working Class Autobiography, 1890–1950*, with a foreword by Stan Newens, M.P. and ed., with an afterword by Terry Philpot (Oxted, 1982)

Soutter, Francis William, *Recollections of a Labour Pioneer*, with an introduction by T. P. Connor (London, 1923)

Sparkes, J. H., *The Life and Times of a Grimsby Street Urchin* (Ilfracombe, 1981)

Spencer, F. H., *An Inspector's Testament* (London, 1938)

Spring, Howard, *Heaven Lies about Us* (London, 1956)

Spurr, R., 'The autobiography of Robert Spurr', ed. R. J. Owen, *Baptist Quarterly*, xxvi (1976), pp. 282–8

Stallan, Beatrice, 'Childhood recollection of Beatrice Stallan', ed. Christopher Ellis, *Saffron Walden History*, 5/39 (Spring 1991), pp. 144–51 and 5/40 (Autumn 1991), pp. 175–80

Stamper, Joseph, *So Long Ago* (London, 1960)

Stanley, Sir Henry Morton, *The Autobiography of Sir Henry Morton Stanley*, ed. with a preface by Dorothy Stanley (London, 1909)

Starn, Dot, *When I Was a Child . . .* (London, 1973)

Steadman, William Charles, 'How I got on: Mr. W. C. Steadman, M.P.', *Pearson's Weekly*, 8 February 1906

Steel, Frank, *Ditcher's Row: A Tale of the Older Charity* (London, 1939)

Stevens, W. H., *A Likely Victorian Lad: An Autobiography* (Leicestershire, [1985])

Stewart, Robert, *Breaking the Fetters: The Memoirs of Bob Stewart* (London, 1967)

Stibbons, Fred, *Norfolk's Caddie Poet: His Autobiography, Impressions and some of his Verse* (Holt, 1923)

[Stir(r)up], 'The autobiography of a journeyman shoemaker', *The Commonwealth*, 22 and 29 November 1856

Stokes, Rose Pastor, *I Belong to the Working Class: The Unfinished Autobiography of Rose Pastor Stokes*, ed. Herbert Shapiro and David Sterling (Athens, GA, 1992)

Stonelake, Edmund, *The Autobiography of Edmund Stonelake* (Bridgend, 1981)

Stride, Louie, *Memoirs of a Street Urchin*, ed. Graham Davis (Bath, 1984)

Sturgess, Arthur, *A Northamptonshire Lad* (Northampton, 1982)

Summerbell, T., 'How I got on: From barber's shop to Parliament', *Pearson's Weekly*, 22 March 1906

Swan, William, 'The journal of William Swan, born 1813', in *The Journals of Two Poor Dissenters, 1786–1880*, ed. with preface by Guida Swan and introduction by John Holloway (London, 1970), pp. 42–102

Swan, William Thomas, 'The journal of William Thomas Swan, born 1786', in *The Journals of Two Poor Dissenters, 1786–1880*, ed. with preface by Guida Swan and introduction by John Holloway (London, 1970), pp. 1–41

Sykes, John, *Slawit in the Sixties: Reminiscences of the Moral, Social and Industrial Life of Slaithwaite and District in and about the Year 1860* (Huddersfield and London, 1926)

Tayler, William, *Diary of William Tayler, Footman, 1837*, ed. Dorothy Wise (London, 1998)

Taylor, Allan K., *From a Glasgow Slum to Fleet Street* (London, [1949])

Taylor, Bernard, *Uphill all the Way: A Miner's Struggle by Lord Taylor of Mansfield* (London, 1972)

Taylor, J. W., 'How I got on: Mr J. W. Taylor, M.P.', *Pearson's Weekly*, 3 May 1906

Taylor, John, 'Autobiographical sketch', in *Poems; Chiefly on Themes of Scottish Interest* (Edinburgh, 1875), pp. 1–48

Taylor, Kate, 'Kate Taylor', in John Burnett, ed., *Destiny Obscure: Autobiographies of Childhood, Education and Family from the 1820s to the 1920s* (London, 1982), pp. 301–9

Taylor, Peter, *Autobiography of Peter Taylor* (Paisley, 1903)

Teasdale, Harvey, *The Life and Adventures of Harvey Teasdale, The Converted Clown and Man Monkey*, 7th edn (Sheffield, [1870?])

Teer, John, *Silent Musings* (Manchester, 1869)

Templeton, Isabel Molison, *The Old Lady in Room Two* (Maidstone, [1976])

Thom, William, *Rhymes and Recollections of a Hand-Loom Weaver* (London, 1844)

Thomas, Albert, *Wait and See* (London, 1944)

Thomas, James Henry, *My Story* (London, 1937)

Thomas, John Birch, *Shop Boy: An Autobiography*, with an introduction by Jean Sutherland Moore (London, 1983)

Thomas, John Miles, *Looking Back: A Childhood in Saint Davids a Century Ago* (Carmarthen, 1979)

Thompson, Bonar, *Hyde Park Orator*, with a preface by Sean O'Casey (London, 1934)

Thompson, Emma, 'The good old times', in *The Bedfordshire Farm Worker in the Nineteenth Century*, Bedfordshire History Record Society, 60 (1981), pp. 126–8

Thompson, Flora, *A Country Calendar and other Writing*, selected and ed. Margaret Lane (Oxford, 1984)

—, *Lark Rise to Candleford*, with an introduction by H. J. Massingham (Oxford, 1939; repr. London, 1973)

Thompson, T., *Lancashire for Me: A Little Autobiography* (London, 1940)

Thomson, Christopher, *Autobiography of an Artisan* (London, 1847)

Thorne, Will, *My Life's Battles*, with a foreword by the Rt Hon. J. R. Clynes, M.P. (London [1925])

Tibble, Anne, *Greenhorn: A Twentieth-Century Childhood* (London, 1973)

Tiffy, R. A., *From Pillar to Post* (Ilfracombe, 1974)

Tillett, Ben, *Memories and Reflections*, with a foreword by the T. Hon. Philip Snowden, M.P. (London, 1931)

Todd, Marjory, *Snakes and Ladders: An Autobiography* (London, 1960)

Todd, Thomas, *My Life as I have Lived it: Autobiography of Thomas Todd of Middleton-in-Teasdale*, compiled by George Reginald Parkin (Leeds, 1935)

Tomlinson, G. A. W., *Coal-miner*, with a preface by Arthur Bryant (London, [1937])

Tomlinson, H. M., *A Mingled Yarn: Autobiographical Sketches* (London, 1953)

Toole, Joseph, *Fighting Through Life* (London, 1935)

Tough, John, *A Short Narrative of the Life . . . of an Aberdonian* (Aberdeen, 1848)

Townend, Rev. Joseph, *Autobiography of the Rev. Joseph Townend*, 2nd edn (London, 1869)

Tremewan, Tom, *Cornish Youth: Memories of a Perran Boy (1895–1910)* (Truro, 1968)

[Turnbull, James B.], *Reminiscences of a Stonemason, by a Working Man* (London, 1908)

BIBLIOGRAPHY OF AUTOBIOGRAPHIES

Turner, Ben, *About Myself, 1863–1930*, with a foreword by the Rt Hon. J. Ramsay Macdonald P.C. (London, 1930)

Turner, Henry, 'Henry Turner', in *The Island: The Life and Death of an East London Community, 1870–1970* (London, 1979)

Turner, James, *Hard Up Husband: James Turner's Diary, Halifax, 1881/2* (Orwell, 1981)

Turner, John Arthur, *The Life of a Chimney Boy, written by himself*, ed. and concluded by J. A. Turner (London, 1901)

Uglow, Jim, *Sailorman: A Barge-master's Story* (London, 1975)

Vose, John D., *Diary of a Tramp* (St Ives, 1981)

Walker, Laura Maple, *Heart to Heart, Being the True Life Story of a Retired Nurse and Midwife* (Nottingham, 1971)

Wallace, Edgar, *People: A Short Autobiography* (London, [1926])

Wallis, Thomas Wilkinson, *Autobiography of Thomas Wilkinson Wallis, Sculptor in Wood, and Extracts from his Sixty Years' Journal* (Louth, 1899)

Walsh, Jane, *Not Like This* (London, 1953)

Walsh, Stephen, 'How I got on: A policeman gave him his first lift', *Pearson's Weekly*, 29 March 1906

Ward, Harry, *My Early Recollections of Charing since 1868* (Charing and District Local History Society, 2002)

Ward, John, 'How I got on: The rise of a ploughboy', *Pearson's Weekly*, 15 March 1906.

Ward, Vera, *Memories* (Bognor Regis, 1984)

Wardle, G. J., 'How I got on: Mr. G. J. Wardle, M.P.', *Pearson's Weekly*, 22 February 1906

Warr, Thomas, *Fogs Lifted: A Slum Child's Story* (London, 1909)

Watchorn, Robert, *The Autobiography of Robert Watchorn*, ed. with an introduction by Herbert Faulkner West (Oklahoma City, 1958)

Watkins, Miles, *A Sketch of the Life of Miles Watkins of Cheltenham: wherein is Related the Particular Incidents Related with his History . . . Written by Himself* (Cheltenham, 1841)

Watson, James, 'Reminiscences of James Watson', in David Vincent, ed., *Testaments of Radicalism: Memoirs of Working-class Politicians, 1790–1885* (London, 1977), pp. 103–14

Watson, William Foster, *Machines and Men: An Autobiography of an Itinerant Mechanic* (London, 1935)

Watt, Christian, *The Christian Watt Papers*, ed. with an introduction by David Fraser (Edinburgh, 2004)

Wearmouth, Robert F., *Pages from a Padre's Diary: A Story of Struggle and Triumph, of Sorrow and Sympathy* (North Shields, n.d.)

Weaver, Richard, *Richard Weaver's Life Story*, ed. James Paterson (London, [1913])

Webb, William, 'Reminiscences of an ordinary life', in John Burnett, ed., *Destiny Obscure: Autobiographies of Childhood, Education and Family from the 1820s to the 1920s* (London, 1982), pp. 65–70

Welch, Charles Henry, *An Autobiography*, with a preface by Ruth Baker (Banstead, 1960)

Wellock, Wilfred, *Off the Beaten Track: Adventures in the Art of Living*, with a foreword by Jayaprakash Narayan (Tanjore, India, 1961)

Wells, Elijah, *Fenland Boyhood* (Mildenhall, 1983)

Wells, Herbert George, *Experiment in Autobiography: Discoveries and Conclusions of a Very Ordinary Brain (since 1866)* (London, 1934)

Welsh, James C., 'Introduction', in his *Songs of a Miner* (London, 1917), pp. 7–13

West, Frank, *Frank West, or the Struggles of a Village Lad* (London, 1880)

Westall, Lilian, 'Lilian Westall, house-maid', in John Burnett, ed., *Useful Toil: Autobiographies of Working People from the 1820s to the 1920s* (London, 1974), pp. 213–20 (full manuscript in Burnett Archive)

Weston, Mary, *The Story of Our Sunday Trip to Hastings, as related by One of the Party* (London, 1879)

Westwater, Thomas Arthur, *The Early Life of T. A. Westwater: Railway Signalman, Trade Unionist and Town Councillor in County Durham* (Oxford, 1979)

Whetstone, Charles, *Truths, No. 1, or the Memoirs of Charles Whetstone* (n.p., 1807)

Wheway, Edna, *Edna's Story: Memories of Life in a Children's Home and in Service, in Dorset and London* (Dorset, 1984)

White, Robert, *Autobiographical Notes* (Newcastle upon Tyne, 1966)

Whittaker, James, *I James Whittaker*, with a foreword by Gilbert Frankau (London, 1934)

Whittaker, Thomas, *Life's Battles in Temperance Armour* (London, 1884)

Wilkie, Alexander, 'How I got on: Councillor Alexander Wilkie, M.P.', *Pearson's Weekly*, 4 May 1906

Wilkinson, Dyke, *Rough Roads: Reminiscences of a Wasted Life* (London, [1912])

Wilkinson, Ellen, 'Ellen Wilkinson', in Margot Asquith, Countess of Oxford, ed., *Myself When Young by Famous Women of Today* (London, 1938), pp. 399–416

Williams, Emlyn, *George: An Early Autobiography* (London, 1961)

Williams, Thomas (Baron Williams of Barnburgh), *Digging for Britain*, with a foreword by Earl Atlee (London, 1965)

Williamson, Joe, *Father Joe: The Autobiography of Joseph Williamson of Poplar and Stepney* (London, 1963)

Williamson, John, *Dangerous Scot: The Life and Work of an American 'Undesirable'* (New York, 1969)

Willson, Robert, *Recollections of a Lincolnshire Miller: Robert Willson (1838–1912) of Huttoft*, ed. Gordon Wills (Louth, 1994)

Wilson, J. Havelock, 'How I got on: The seaman's champion', *Pearson's Weekly*, 29 March 1906

Wilson, John, 'How I got on: An act that changed a life', *Pearson's Weekly*, 12 April 1906

Wilson, John, *Memories of a Labour Leader: The Autobiography of John Wilson, J.P., M.P.*, ed., with introduction, John Burnett (Firle, 1980)

Wilson, Joseph, *Joseph Wilson, His Life and Work, with a foreword by the Rev. H. J. Taylor* (London, n.d.)

Wilson, Joseph Havelock, *My Stormy Voyage Through Life*, with a foreword by Sir Walter Runciman (London, 1925)

Wincott, Len, *Invergordon Mutineer* (London, 1974)

Wolfit, Donald, *First Interval: The Autobiography of Donald Wolfit* (London, 1954)

Wood, George, *I Had to be 'Wee'*, with foreword by Naomi Jacob (London, [1948])

Wood, John, *Autobiography of John Wood, an Old and Well Known Bradfordian* (Bradford, 1877)

Woodward, Kathleen, *Jipping Street*, with introduction by Carolyn Steedman (London, 1983)

[Wright, Joseph], *The Life of Joseph Wright*, by Elizabeth Mary Wright (Oxford, 1932)

Wright, Vera, *As I Remember Them* (Frisby-on-the-Wreake, 1977)

[Wright, William], 'Adventures and recollections of Bill o'th' Hoylus End. Told by himself', *Keighley Herald*, 2 June–8 December 1893

Wrigley, Ammon, *Rakings Up: An Autobiography*, with a preface by S. Seville (Rochdale, 1949)

Wrigley, Mrs, 'A plate-layer's wife', in Margaret Llewelyn Davies, ed., *Life as We Have Known It by Co-Operative Working Women*, intro. Anna Davin (London, 1990), pp. 56–72

Yearn, Mrs, 'A public-spirited rebel', in Margaret Llewelyn Davies, ed., *Life as We Have Known It by Co-Operative Working Women*, intro. Anna Davin (London, 1990), pp. 102–8.

Younger, John, *Autobiography of John Younger by John Younger* (Kelso, 1881)

INDEX

Page numbers in italics refer to content in images and accompanying captions.